Praise for *Web Protocols and Practice*

"This is the most comprehensive, well-researched coverage of the basic Web protocols that I have seen. The authors have done especially well at uncovering the history and rationale of the protocol design process."
    —*Jeffrey Mogul, coauthor of the HTTP/1.1 standard*

"This book will help demystify how the Internet and the Web work. Despite the current Web's size and importance, it can be broken down into a small number of components that can be understood and controlled. This encyclopedic tome can be read straight through or used as a reference by those trying to understand or build sophisticated Internet applications."
    —*Brewster Kahle, President, Alexa Internet; Inventor of WAIS*

"*Web Protocols and Practice* covers the most important Internet application— the Web—with unprecedented breadth, depth, and motivation. An important reference book for anyone who wants to understand the Web architecture inside and out."
    —*Steve McCanne, Chief Technology Officer, Inktomi*

"The authors have gathered and explained a great deal of material not found elsewhere and created an encyclopedia of the how and why of the Web."
    —*Larry Masinter, Principal Scientist, Adobe Systems Inc.;*
    past chair of HTTP and URI IETF working groups

"I learned a lot about the reasons for Web performance—from microscopic detail about specific interactions of layers to macroscopic traffic related issues. Everyone will want this book."
    —*Jon Crowcroft, Professor, Networks Systems, University College London*

"This book is likely to be an invaluable resource for anyone interested in understanding the protocols and infrastructure behind the Web. I especially like the attention to the evolution and historical development of the Web protocols and to the sometimes unanticipated interactions between the various protocols."
    —*Sally Floyd, Senior Scientist, AT&T Center for Internet Research*
    at the International Computer Science Institute

"This is a book that could very well have been entitled Everything You Ever Wanted to Know About the Web But Did Not Know Who to Ask."
  —*Roch Guerin, Alfred Fitler Moore Professor of Telecommunication Networks, University of Pennsylvania*

"The book is especially useful for Web site developers who can improve the user experience at their sites through a better understanding of the protocol performance issues discussed throughout the book. The material on the evolution from HTTP 1.0 to 1.1 is difficult to find outside of scattered research papers and standards documents. Overall, this book is a valuable resource for Web professionals and anyone interested in learning what makes the Web tick."
  —*Ramón Cáceres, Chief Scientist, Vindigo*

"The authors have done a superb job in explaining the complex interactions of the Web protocols. The book is a unique resource for anyone who wants to learn how the Web really works."
  —*Jörg Liebeherr, Professor, University of Virginia*

"It's a great book for anyone interested in deep knowledge of Web-based techniques and is a must for Web architects and administrators."
  —*Eduardo Krell, Chief Technology Officer and Web Architect, Adexus, Santiago, Chile*

"Good book! Describes things I have not seen before in print. Perfect for people who have a need to understand how HTTP works."
  —*Patrik Fältsröm, Applications Area Director, IETF*

Web Protocols and Practice

Web Protocols and Practice

HTTP/1.1, Networking Protocols, Caching, and Traffic Measurement

Balachander Krishnamurthy

Jennifer Rexford

Addison-Wesley

Boston • San Francisco • New York • Toronto • Montreal
London • Munich • Paris • Madrid
Capetown • Sydney • Tokyo • Singapore • Mexico City

Many of the designations used by manufacturers and sellers to distinguish their products are claimed as trademarks. Where those designations appear in this book, and Addison-Wesley, Inc. was aware of a trademark claim, the designations have been printed with initial capital letters or in all capitals.

The authors and publisher have taken care in the preparation of this book, but make no expressed or implied warranty of any kind and assume no responsibility for errors or omissions. No liability is assumed for incidental or consequential damages in connection with or arising out of the use of the information or programs contained herein.

The publisher offers discounts on this book when ordered in quantity for special sales. For more information, please contact:

Pearson Education Corporate Sales Division
201 W. 103rd Street
Indianapolis, IN 46290
(800) 428-5331
corpsales@pearsoned.com

Visit AW on the Web: www.awl.com/cseng/

Library of Congress Cataloging-in-Publication Data:
Krishnamurthy, Balachander, 1961–
    Web protocols and practice: HTTP/1.1, networking protocols, caching, and traffic measurement / Balachander Krishnamurthy, Jennifer Rexford.
        p. cm.
    Includes bibliographical references and index.
    ISBN 0-201-71088-9
    1. Web servers–Computer programs. 2. Computer network protocols. 3. Web site development. I. Rexford, Jennifer. II. Title.
    TK5105.888 .K75 2001
    004.6'2–dc21   2001022729
                                                          CIP

Text printed on recycled and acid-free paper.

ISBN 0201710889

2 3 4 5 6 7   MA   04 03 02 01

2nd Printing   July 2001

Dedicated with affection to

ராஜம் பஞ்ஜாபகேசன்

விஜயம் சந்திரமௌலி
—Balachander Krishnamurthy

To my parents, John and Susan Rexford, for their love and support.
—Jennifer Rexford

Contents

V Web Applications   405

List of Tables

List of Figures

Preface

Introduction

This book describes the technical underpinnings of the World Wide Web. We discuss the technology for transferring, caching, and measuring the messages that carry the content between Web sites and end users. The messages are exchanged between clients, proxies, and servers—the three main software components of the Web. The format and transfer of these messages are dictated by communication protocols codified in standards documents over a period of years. Evaluating and improving Web performance relies on having effective techniques for collecting and analyzing measurements of the message traffic. By moving Web content closer to the end users, caching reduces user-perceived latency, as well as load on the Web servers and the underlying network. Web traffic is moving from delivery of text and image content to include audio and video streaming. Multimedia streaming has its own suite of communication protocols. These topics, constituting the technical core of the Web, are discussed in detail in this book.

This book provides a comprehensive treatment of the systems and protocols responsible for the transfer of Web content. The audience for this book includes Web technologists, Web site administrators, developers who rely on the Web infrastructure, students in networking and the Web, and the Web research community. The book focuses on the mature and stable aspects of the Web. In contrast to the rapidly changing techniques for creating and displaying Web content, the standardized communication protocols discussed in the book change relatively slowly. A variety of examples, state-of-the-art reports, and case studies are used to illustrate the operation of the Web and the interplay among the various components. The book includes detailed examples of the HTTP protocol, a state-of-the-art overview of Web caching and multimedia streaming, and case studies of the Apache Web server, the Squid proxy, and traffic measurement techniques. The book is a valuable resource for understanding the technology and current practices of the Web.

Organization of the Book

The first section of the book consists of an opening chapter that provides a broad overview of the evolution of the World Wide Web and discusses the Web's naming infrastructure, document language, and message exchange protocol. The remainder of the book is divided into five sections consisting of 14 chapters:

- **Software components:** These three chapters present the inner workings of clients, proxies, and servers, including a discussion of related topics such as scripts, handlers, search engines, cookies, and authentication.
- **Web protocols:** The core of the book, these four chapters present the networking protocols underlying the Web (Internet Protocol, Transmission Control Protocol, and the Domain Name System), the design of HTTP/1.0, a comprehensive overview of HTTP/1.1, and the interaction between HTTP and TCP.
- **Traffic measurement and workload characterization:** These two chapters describe the various techniques for measuring and analyzing Web traffic, as well as an overview of the key parameters of Web workload models used in evaluating Web performance.
- **Web caching and multimedia streaming:** These two chapters provide a state-of-the-art overview of key Web applications. Web caching involves moving content closer to the user to reduce user-perceived latency and the load on the server and the network. Multimedia streaming involves overlapping the transfer of audio and video data with the playback at the receiver.
- **Research perspectives:** These three chapters present research perspectives on caching, measurement, and protocols to provide a glimpse of the evolving technology in these areas and reinforce the material presented in the earlier parts of the book.

Intended Audience

The book is self-contained and does not assume any prior knowledge of Web or networking technology. An extensive bibliography points readers to additional information on specific topics. The book has several audience segments, including:

- **Students:** Undergraduate students in advanced courses and graduate students can use the book as an introduction to the protocol, network, and measurement aspects of the Web. The book is self-contained and does not assume the student is familiar with network protocols. We do assume a basic familiarity with computer science concepts. The book includes case studies and research perspectives to guide students in applying the ideas they have learned. The book's focus on core concepts and protocol evolution ensures that the student acquires knowledge that has broad applications beyond any particular realization of Web technology.

- **Web technologists:** The book provides developers with an in-depth treatment of the various protocols and software components in the Web. A developer can learn about HTTP and the related networking protocols, such as IP, TCP, and DNS, and their relationship to Web clients, proxies, and servers. In addition, the book includes an extensive treatment of Web traffic measurement and workload characterization that can aid developers in evaluating and improving the performance of their software in realistic settings.
- **Web and networking researchers:** Academic and industrial researchers can use the book as a primary source of information about the technical underpinnings of the Web and its relationship to the Internet. The core portions of the book highlight the mature technologies underlying the Web, to provide the necessary context for research work in this area. The advanced material on research perspectives provides a timely view of ongoing work that may influence the evolution of the Web, and the extensive bibliography points the reader to research publications and standards documents with additional details.
- **Web administrators:** Administrators of Web proxies and servers can develop a deeper understanding of the operation of these software components. The book can serve as a reference for key concepts and protocol features. The emphasis on performance issues can aid administrators in tuning the configuration of a proxy or server, complementing other texts that present detailed guidelines of how to configure a particular hardware or software platform. The material on Web measurement and the interaction between HTTP and networking protocols can help administrators in diagnosing performance problems.

The book can be used as a reference, a self-study guide, or part of a one- or two-semester course on Web technology or networking. Readers may follow a variety of paths through the book, depending on their backgrounds and interests. Some readers may skip the elementary chapters, whereas other readers may skip the research perspectives material.

Acknowledgments

An endeavor such as this book does not come about solely because of the labors of the authors. In acknowledging the contribution of others we do two things: first we thank them for their time, effort, interest, diligence, and willingness to help us. Next, we reflect that this particular book describes technology in which dozens, if not hundreds, of people were involved. Several people who were responsible for some of the ideas discussed are not explicitly acknowledged.

The people involved with the creation, modification, and explication of the versions of the HTTP protocol deserve our thanks. We acknowledge the following people who took considerable interest in our efforts: Roy Fielding, Jeff Mogul, David Kristol, Koen Holtman, Henrik Frystyk-Nielsen, and Jim Gettys.

The comments of Adam Bradley (Chapters 6 and 7), Anja Feldmann (Chapters 9 and 10), Sally Floyd (Chapters 5 and 8), Patrick McManus (Chapters 5-8), Mikhail Mikhailov (Chapters 11 and 13), Erich Nahum (Chapter 8), Mark Nottingham (Chapter 11), and Robert Thau (Chapter 4) were very helpful. We thank them for taking the extra time needed to provide pointers to additional material and for their help in clarifying the text.

Many reviewers patiently read our drafts and offered constructive criticism. They include Patrick McManus, Craig Wills, Anees Shaikh, David Kristol, Koen Holtman, Karin Högstedt, Chris Malley, Ian Cooper, Polly Huang, Joe Parrish, Henrik Frystyk-Nielsen, and Duane Wessels.

Several individual chapters were read by colleagues and friends including Martin Arlitt, Vinay Badami, Steven Bellovin, Ed Blackmond, S. Byers, Eric Cheung, Chuck Cranor, Lorrie Cranor, Christof Fetzer, R. Gopalakrishnan, Joel Gottlieb, Tim Griffin, Tim Korb, Jeff Korn, Jim Kurose, Rob Lanphier, Brian F. Lavoie, Carlos Maltzahn, Jitendra Padhye, Venkat Padmanabhan, Reza Rejaie, Sue Rexford, Yuriy Reznik, Luigi Rizzo, Jens-S. Voeckler, and Jacobus Van der Merwe. We would also like to thank the reviewers selected by Addison-Wesley.

Several people answered specific questions often in surprising detail. They include Steven Bellovin, Tim Berners-Lee, Dan Connolly, Sally Floyd, Koen

Holtman, Brewster Kahle, Rohit Khare, David Kristol, Thomas Narten, Henrik Frystyk-Nielsen, Vern Paxson, and Jim Whitehead.

Walter Tichy and Michael Philippsen provided working and living space in Karlsruhe during the creation of the book proposal. We thank them for their warm hospitality and the University of Karlsruhe Informatik's facilities.

The support and encouragement of Hamid Ahmadi, David Belanger, Albert Greenberg, and Kiem-Phong Vo, our management at AT&T Labs–Research, is much appreciated. Several of our colleagues contributed to the quality of life needed for such an endeavor to succeed.

Several tutorials were presented before and during the preparation of the manuscript. The questions asked during the various tutorials helped us to improve the presentation of the concepts in the book. Notably, we thank the organizers of ACM SIGCOMM conference and the World Wide Web conference for giving us an opportunity to present tutorials.

We would like to thank the editorial, production, and publicity staff at Addison-Wesley for all their help in bringing the book to fruition. We thank Lorinda Cherry at AT&T for her help with the indexing program and Deborah Swayne for her help with S-Plus in the production of some of the plots in Chapter 10.

Balachander wrote virtually all of his part of the book on an IBM Thinkpad 770ED booted *only* with Linux. The book was written in many places around the world including Rio de Janeiro, Foz de Iguaçu, Santiago, Langensteinbach, Karlsruhe, Munich, Potsdam, Paris, and Amsterdam. Within the United States: Dean and Deluca (Greenwich Village, New York City), Ithaca, Boston, Boulder, various places in New Jersey, various parts of Silicon Valley, and Washington D.C. The hosts in various places deserve thanks: Eduardo Krell and Veronica Rodriguez Munoz, Chris and Mary Malley, Rob Mason, V. Srikant.

The book was written using Emacs under the X Windows System and typeset using LaTeX. The camera ready copy was sent to the publishers as a single compressed PostScript file.

Part I

Getting Started

1

Introduction

In its first decade of existence, the World Wide Web has altered the way information is created and exchanged and how business is conducted globally. Vannevar Bush, in his seminal 1945 article, "As We May Think," proposed a way to extend human memory via mechanical means [Bus45]. The Web can be seen as the logical realization of Bush's vision a half a century later, with the key intermediate steps being the development of hypertext and the Internet. This book focuses on the technical underpinnings of the Web as opposed to its history, uses, or social impact. The technology underlying the Web involved scores of researchers and developers in different institutions who came together to construct a system that is used by hundreds of millions of people in nearly every country in the world.

This chapter presents the key technical concepts underlying the Web, as well as an introduction to the rest of the book. We begin with a look at the evolution of the Web and examine the Web's relationship to other systems designed in the late 1980s and early 1990s to provide seamless access to information. We then briefly describe the three main semantic components of the Web: a naming infrastructure, a document language, and a message exchange protocol. These components are known by their acronyms—URI, HTML, and HTTP, respectively. We then describe the scope of the book in terms of key concepts related to requesting and delivering Web content. We conclude with a tour through the book that groups the remaining chapters into five parts: software components, protocols, measurement and workload characterization, applications, and research perspectives.

1.1 Origin and Growth of the World Wide Web

First proposed by Tim Berners-Lee in 1989, the World Wide Web, or simply the Web, is the universe of information accessible via networked computers. An intuitive graphical interface allows users to browse through a collection of Web pages by clicking on links, without worrying about the format or the

location of the content. In addition to viewing Web pages, users can search
for information, send and receive e-mail, and initiate business transactions.
The Web, in effect, is a networked application that links users and services
distributed across computers around the world. In this section, we describe how
the Web evolved into its current form and compare the Web with competing
systems developed in the late 1980s and early 1990s.

1.1.1 Historical evolution of the Web

The history of the Web begins, in some sense, with Vannevar Bush's proposal
for Memex, a way to harness mechanical means to "extend human memory."
The essence of Bush's 1945 proposal, written as an exhortation to scientists at
the end of the Second World War, was that scientists should make the existing
store of knowledge more accessible to mankind. He distinguished between the
speed with which knowledge was being created through publications and the
speed with which humankind was able to navigate the maze of information. In
Bush's own words:

> A memex is a device in which an individual stores all his books,
> records, and communications, and which is mechanized so that it may
> be consulted with exceeding speed and flexibility. It is an enlarged
> intimate supplement to his memory.

Bush anticipated association of ideas and ways to link them:

> Wholly new forms of encyclopedias will appear, ready made with a
> mesh of associative trails running through them, ready to be dropped
> into the memex and there amplified.

Bush's seminal article predicted large-scale indexing of text and multimedia resources that could be searched quickly. The article influenced researchers
over the course of the next 50 years. The next major step in the road to the
Web was the creation of hypertext. The term *hypertext* [Nel67] was coined by
Ted Nelson in 1965 to describe *nonsequential writing* that presents information
as a collection of linked nodes. Readers peruse the information in a variety
of ways by navigating from one node to another. Hypertext was independently
proposed by Doug Engelbart [EE68], the inventor of the mouse tracking device.
Hypertext postulated multiple authors reading, writing, and revising the same
document.

In the mid-1960s, the ARPANET was conceived as a communication infrastructure for sharing access to supercomputers among researchers in the
United States. The United States Department of Defense was interested in
studying techniques to provide vendor-independent data communication. The
mid-to-late 1960s saw the beginning of the effort to standardize the underlying network communication protocols. During the 1970s, the ARPANET was

used largely by the scientific community for connecting to remote machines, exchanging electronic mail, and copying files between machines. By the end of the 1970s, many universities and research organizations around the world could communicate via the ARPANET. The TCP/IP protocol suite was formalized in 1980. The deployment of the TCP/IP protocols on a variety of platforms facilitated the rapid growth in the size and scope of the ARPANET during the 1980s.

Influenced by hypertext, Tim Berners-Lee proposed linking information present on various machines at CERN, the European Laboratory for Particle Physics near Geneva. The initial proposal that Berners-Lee wrote in 1989 [BL90] postulated linking of documents in many different ways and was based on a system called Enquire Within, written a decade earlier. At the time of Berners-Lee's proposal, several other systems had been created to search and access documents over the Internet. Examples of such systems include FTP, Gopher, Archie, and WAIS (Wide Area Information Servers). Standardized in 1971, the File Transfer Protocol (FTP) allowed users to copy files to and from FTP server machines [PR85]. The FTP client allowed the user to establish an authenticated connection to the server by supplying a user identifier and a password. A special "anonymous" account permitted arbitrary users to connect to an FTP server without a password. In the 1970s and 1980s, FTP was the primary means for distributing software and large documents on the Internet. By the early 1990s, FTP was responsible for over half of the traffic on the Internet.

Retrieving files via FTP required the user to know in advance which server machine to contact. Gopher [AAL$^+$92, AML$^+$93] provided a way for users to search for information on a network of computers. A Gopher client would search databases around the world based on keywords or subjects. To be globally accessible, a Gopher server had to be registered with the top-level server. WAIS [KM91, Adi94] allowed users to send queries to databases on remote servers and obtain tailored responses. A WAIS search returned a list of files, ranked by their relevance to the query. In addition to flexible searching, WAIS also provided access to image files. Large companies created indices of their network-accessible material. The WAIS project was started in 1989, and by 1992 WAIS Inc., had become a successful company. At that time it was the only such company to commercialize technology related to accessing content on the Internet. In 1990, Archie was introduced as a tool for locating files at FTP servers throughout the Internet [ED92]. Archie built a global index of FTP servers and allowed users to search for file names matching particular patterns. Likewise, a tool called Veronica was created to search and access resources accessible on Gopher servers.

Each of these systems competed with the Web, and for a time the various systems coexisted before being subsumed by the Web. Although these systems are still used occasionally, most users access these systems via their Web browsers. The Web has several advantages over these systems. FTP is similar to the Web in that clients issue requests for diverse kinds of resources. However, most early FTP clients had relatively complex command-line interfaces, whereas a Web browser offers a simple graphical interface. Whereas FTP is limited to transferring files, the Web provides access to programs and services, such as scripts that query databases. Although Gopher was used for retrieving documents, the Web allows users to retrieve, modify, and store data and invoke programs on the remote machines. The Web allows access to resources independent of their type or format.

Archie, Gopher, and WAIS focused mainly on textual documents. The Web's use of hypertext is superior to the more straightforward menus found in Gopher. The task of linking documents is distributed across all of the users of the system. Although the Web can be used to access Gopher and WAIS servers, the reverse was not true because of the more primitive nature of the protocols in these other systems. Developed in 1991, the first official release of a Web browser took place in January 1992 [BL92c] and included support for FTP, Gopher, and WAIS. In effect, the Web succeeded largely by subsuming the capabilities of the competing systems. Users could access Archie, Gopher, and WAIS servers via their Web browsers, and Web search engines enabled users to search for Web pages on particular topics. The Web has now become the realization of the Memex. A detailed history of the Web can be found on the Web [Webc].

1.1.2 State of the Web

From the viewpoint of the millions of end users, the Web is simply a convenient way to access information and transact business using an intuitive graphical interface. In this section, we describe how the Web evolved during the 1990s into a global system with diverse content and a wide range of users. Then we discuss how Web traffic evolved during the same period.

WEB TRENDS

The Web has continued to grow at a remarkable pace since the introduction of the first Web browser and server in 1991. By the beginning of 1993, the Web consisted of approximately 50 servers. Marc Andreesen and Eric Bina wrote the Mosaic browser in December 1992 and released the first version of Mosaic for the X-Windows system in the spring of 1993. The introduction of a graphical user interface that could display text and images was directly responsible for the explosive growth of the Web. By the end of 1993, the number of Web servers had increased by a factor of 10, and the Web accounted for 1% of the traffic on the Internet. By the late 1990s, the Web was responsible for about 75% of Internet traffic [CMT98], the number of Web users had risen to a few hundred million, and the number of Web sites had reached into the millions. The distributed nature of the Web and the growth of the Web inside large organizations makes it difficult to obtain a precise estimate of its size. Conservative estimates suggest that more than a billion Uniform Resource Locators (URLs) are available to the public, with countless other URLs accessible within private institutions.

The graphical user interface and the relative ease of publishing new content spurred dramatic changes in how users and companies access information. The Web made it easier for businesses to reach a large segment of the market, allowing customers to browse product information and purchase via their computers. Hypertext offered a flexible way for customers to explore and compare products, and electronic commerce (e-commerce) removed the need for intermediaries by connecting the customer directly with the seller. In response, even more companies made their product literature available on the Web. Many new companies used the Web as their primary way of interfacing with customers. Companies also began to use the Web to conduct business with each other, bypassing traditional modes of interaction. In addition, the Web became an open market for direct interaction between users in the form of auctions, chatrooms, and games.

Although initially developed to provide public access to information, the Web is increasingly used within institutions to connect users with private or proprietary data. For example, many companies have internal Web sites that provide employees with access to databases with information about salaries and benefits. The number of internal Web sites has grown considerably in the past few years, possibly surpassing the number of pages that are available to the general public. The growing presence of internal Web sites highlights the difference between the Web and the Internet. A company may connect its computers on a private network without providing access to or from the rest of the Internet. Likewise, computers communicating via the Internet do not necessarily act as Web clients or Web servers. Still, the Internet is closely tied with the Web. The Internet provides a global communication infrastructure, allowing Web clients to access a wide variety of Web servers throughout the world.

WEB TRAFFIC

Although the Web continues to grow in both size and diversity, a relatively small number of Web sites and Web pages account for the vast majority of user requests. Certain popular sites attract an extremely large number of users. These sites include portal sites that connect users with a wide range of content, search engines that allow users to locate Web pages, and popular online businesses that enable users to buy products. In addition, special events, such as the Olympics or national elections, have transient Web sites that attract a large number of users over a short period. Bearing such a heavy load may require replicating the content on several computers, each handling a portion of the requests. In contrast, most Web sites receive relatively few requests, and many Web pages are rarely accessed. A single computer can easily handle the requests directed to a less popular Web site and may, in fact, service requests for multiple Web sites.

Initially, most of the data available on the Web consisted of small text files. Then Web pages began to include images such as GIF and JPEG files. As this book goes to press, text and images account for roughly one quarter and one half of Web requests, respectively. Because of the small size of most text and image files, the average size of a Web resource is about 8 KB. Despite the small average size, many resources are quite large. The Web does not impose any limit on the size of a resource. A text file could consist of a few bytes of data or the contents of an entire book. Images vary from small icons to large, detailed pictures. Other resources, such as computer animations or video files, may be very large. The size of resources has implications for the amount of storage space required at the Web server, the time required for the browser to download the content, and the load imparted on the network to transfer the data from one machine to another.

As the Web continues to evolve, a larger number of Web sites provides dynamically generated content. For example, a search engine generates a list of pointers to Web pages based on the keywords entered by the user. The content in this case is the result of the output of the query. More and more Web transactions involve accessing or transferring private data, such as credit card numbers. Consequently there is a growing interest in security and authentication issues associated with Web transactions. The Web is increasingly used as a way for users to create and transmit data, such as e-mail messages or jointly authored documents. In addition, Web browsers allow users to initiate requests for streaming audio and video. The browser invokes a separate application to play the audio and video data for the user; the multimedia player may also bypass the browser to communicate directly with a multimedia server. Initiating these requests from the Web browser provides the user with a seamless experience, independent of how the data are transmitted and displayed.

1.2 Semantic Components of the Web

The Web has three main semantic components: Uniform Resource Identifiers (URIs), Hypertext Markup Language (HTML), and Hypertext Transfer Protocol (HTTP). URIs are a universal naming mechanism for identifying resources on the Web. HTML is a standard language for creating hypertext documents. HTTP is the language for communication between Web clients and servers.

1.2.1 Uniform Resource Identifier (URI)

Accessing and manipulating resources distributed throughout the Web requires a way to identify them. A Web resource is identified by a Uniform Resource

Identifier (URI) [BLFM98]. Rather than representing something physical, a URI can be thought of as a pointer to a black box to which request *methods* can be applied to generate potentially different responses at different times. A request method is a simple operation such as fetching, changing, or deleting a resource. A URI denotes a resource independent of its current location or value. At a high level, a URI is simply a formatted string, such as `http://www.foo.com/coolpic.gif`. Informally, a URI usually consists of three parts: the protocol for communicating with the server (e.g., `http`), the name of the server (e.g., `www.foo.com`), and the name of the resource at that server (e.g., `coolpic.gif`). The most popular form of a URI is a Uniform Resource Locator (URL) [BLMM94, Fie95]. The common misconception that a URL and a URI are one and the same does not affect a layperson's understanding of the Web. The differences between them are discussed in Chapter 6 (Section 6.1.1). Throughout this book, we use the popular term URL instead of the more general term URI, except when the distinction between URI and URL is important.

1.2.2 Hypertext Markup Language (HTML)

The Hypertext Markup Language (HTML) provides a standard representation for hypertext documents in ASCII format. HTML is derived from the more general Standard Generalized Markup Language (SGML). HTML allows authors to format text, reference images, and embed hypertext links to other documents. The HTML syntax is relatively straightforward and easy to learn. The simplest HTML document is little more than a plain ASCII file with no special formatting of the text or references to other resources. Over the years, software tools have been developed for generating HTML files, obviating the need for most people to learn HTML. Software packages translate documents written in other formats into HTML. As a result, few large HTML documents are constructed by hand. HTML files are meant to be parsed by computer programs, such as Web browsers, rather than read by users.

1.2.3 Hypertext Transfer Protocol (HTTP)

The operation of the Web depends on having a standard, well-defined way for Web components to communicate. The Hypertext Transfer Protocol (HTTP) is the most common way of transferring resources on the Web. HTTP defines the format and meaning of messages exchanged between Web components, such as clients and servers. A protocol is simply a language, similar to natural languages used by humans, except that it is used by machines or software components. Like any other language, a protocol has specific syntax and semantics associated with the use of the language elements. HTTP defines the syntax of the messages and how the fields in each line of the message should be interpreted. HTTP is a *request-response* protocol—the client sends a request message and then the

Table 1.1. Common Web terms

Term	Definition
WWW/Web	World Wide Web, the universe of information accessible via networked computers
Hypertext	Nonlinear writing or linking related documents for navigation
Internet	Worldwide collection of interconnected networks using the Internet Protocol (IP)
Web page	Document accessible on the Web via a URI
Web site	Collection of related Web pages
Browser	Application for requesting and displaying Web resources

server replies with a response message. Client requests are typically triggered by user actions, such as clicking on a hypertext link or typing a URI in the browser window. HTTP is a *stateless* protocol—clients and servers treat each message exchange independently and are not required to maintain any state across requests and responses.

1.3 Terms and Concepts

This section introduces the key terms and concepts covered in the book. Table 1.1 lists familiar terms that appear in both the popular press and technical publications. The book focuses on core concepts and formal standards rather than transient applications built on top of the Web:

- **Content on the Web:** The Web provides users with access to resources through the exchange of HTTP messages.
- **Software components:** Web transfers involve the interaction between clients, intermediaries, and servers.
- **Underlying network:** The Internet provides a communication substrate for transporting messages between Web components.
- **Standardization:** The standardization of protocols helps ensure that Web software components can interoperate with each other.
- **Web traffic and performance:** The efficiency of the software components and the underlying network has a major impact on the user's perception of a Web transfer. Web traffic analysis yields valuable insight necessary to improve the communication efficiency.
- **Web applications:** Web caching and multimedia streaming are two major applications that have implications for Web performance and the user experience.

Table 1.2. Terminology related to Web resources and HTTP messages

Term	Definition
Resource	Network data object or service identified by a URI
Message	Basic unit of communication in HTTP
Sender/receiver	Component responsible for sending/receiving a message
Header	Control portion of a message
Entity	Information transferred in the body of a message
Upstream/ downstream	Directionality of message flow (from upstream sender to downstream receiver)

The key terms associated with these concepts are summarized in tables and examined in separate subsections.

1.3.1 Content on the Web

Table 1.2 presents a list of terms related to Web content and the HTTP protocol. The Web consists of a collection of *resources* or objects distributed throughout the Internet. Each resource is a network-accessible document or service, which may be available in different formats (such as HTML and PostScript). A resource may be a static file on a machine or generated dynamically at the time of the request. Each HTTP transfer concerns a single resource as identified by the URI in the request message. A Web page consists of a container resource, such as an HTML file, which may include links to one or more embedded resources, such as images or animations. Downloading a Web page involves separate HTTP transfers for the container and each of the embedded resources.

Each HTTP transfer consists of two *messages*: the request message first sent by the client and the corresponding response message from the server. The client is the *sender* of the request message and the *receiver* of the response message; similarly, the server is the *receiver* of the request message and the *sender* of the response message. The sender of the message is *upstream* of the receiver, and the receiver is *downstream* of the sender. A message is a sequence of bytes that starts with an optional *header* that contains control information. HTTP headers are in ASCII format; for example, the `Date` header present in request and response messages has the following format:

```
Date: Sat Oct 28 2000 11:29:32 GMT
```

In addition, a request or response message has an *entity body*—a representation of a resource. For example, the response to a request for `http://www.foo.com/coolpic.gif` could contain a GIF image as the entity body.

Table 1.3. Terminology related to the software components of the Web

Term	Definition
User agent	Client program that initiates a request (e.g., a browser)
Web client	Program that sends an HTTP request to a Web server
Web server	Program that receives an HTTP request from a Web client and transmits a response
Origin server	Server where the requested resource resides or is created
Intermediary	Web component in the path between the user agent and an origin server (e.g., a proxy or gateway)
Proxy	Intermediary program that functions as a server to a client and as a client to a server
Cookie	State information passed between the user agent and the origin server

1.3.2 Software components

Table 1.3 lists the main software components of the Web and some widely used terms in the software context. A *user agent* initiates an HTTP request and handles the response. The most common example of a user agent is a Web browser that generates requests on behalf of a user and performs a variety of other tasks, such as displaying Web pages and storing the user's bookmarks. A *client* is a program that sends an HTTP request and receives the response. The *origin server* is the program that provides or generates a Web resource. A *server* is a program that receives an HTTP request and sends a response. In practice, the client may send its HTTP request to an *intermediary*—another Web component en route to the origin server. For example, employees at a company could configure their browsers to direct requests through a shared proxy. A *proxy* plays the role of both a client and a server. Proxies can perform a variety of functions, such as filtering of requests to undesirable Web sites, providing a degree of anonymity to clients, and caching popular resources. HTTP is a stateless protocol; therefore the server does not have to maintain any information about the request once the response has been sent. The server may instruct the user agent to retain state across a series of requests and responses by storing a *cookie*.

1.3.3 Underlying network

Table 1.4 lists the main terms related to the network protocols underlying the Web. The client and server programs usually run on separate computers or *hosts*. Typically, the client and server reside at different locations in the Internet, although the use of the Web within individual organizations has been growing rapidly. Sending and receiving HTTP messages requires a way for the

Table 1.4. Terminology related to the Internet and its protocols

Term	Definition
Host	Computer or machine connected to the network
Packet	Basic unit of communication in the Internet
IP	Internet Protocol, a protocol that coordinates the delivery of individual packets between hosts
IP address	32-bit numerical address identifying an Internet host
Hostname	Case-insensitive string identifying an Internet host
DNS	Domain Name System, a distributed infrastructure for translating between hostnames and IP addresses
TCP	Transmission Control Protocol, a protocol that provides the abstraction of a reliable, bidirectional connection
Connection	Logical communication channel between two hosts

two hosts to identify each other and exchange information. The development of the Internet led to the definition of standard protocols that support a variety of networked services, such as FTP, e-mail, and the Web. At the lowest level, the Internet provides a very basic communication service—delivery of a *packet* of data from one host to another. The *Internet Protocol* (IP) coordinates the delivery of individual packets, where the sending and receiving hosts are identified by 32-bit *IP addresses*. These addresses are typically represented in dotted decimal notation, with a separate decimal number for each of the four octets (e.g., 10.243.74.5 or 10.4.170.124).

The simple packet-delivery service does not satisfy the needs of most networked applications, such as the Web. A Web client identifies the Web server by a *hostname* (e.g., `www.att.com` or `users.berkeley.edu`), rather than an IP address, and the two applications exchange HTTP messages rather than IP packets. The *Domain Name System* (DNS) and the *Transmission Control Protocol* (TCP) bridge the gap. Before contacting the Web server, the Web client first translates the hostname `www.att.com` into an IP address. The Web client invokes a system call to contact a DNS server that returns the IP address of `www.att.com`. Using this IP address, the Web client initiates communication with the Web server. The client and the server establish a TCP *connection,* a logical communication channel that provides bidirectional communication between the two applications. Implemented in the operating system of the two hosts, TCP hides the details of sending and receiving data via the Internet. Once the connection has been established, the client can use the TCP connection to send an HTTP request message to the server, and the server can reply with an HTTP response message.

Table 1.5. Terminology related to Internet protocol standards

Term	Definition
IETF	Internet Engineering Task Force, an open community contributing to the evolution of the Internet
Working Group	IETF group chartered to work on a particular standards specification
Internet Draft	Informal version of a standards document reflecting work in progress
RFC	Request For Comments, an official document related to Internet standards
MUST, SHOULD, and MAY	Requirement levels of compliance with a protocol specification

1.3.4 Standardization

Table 1.5 lists the main terms related to protocol standardization. Browsers, proxies, and servers cooperate to provide users with access to Web resources. Although each Web site may have a different collection of resources with a different mix of content types, access to these resources should be independent of their attributes. Protocol standards are vital to ensure that the components interact seamlessly. A client should be able to send a request with a clear expectation of the range of responses it might receive, and a server should be able to interpret the request unambiguously. Although Web software may be written by a variety of companies or research institutions, the interaction between the components should be predictable. The writing of Web software components and the construction of Web sites must be done with clearly defined interfaces. A protocol standard helps ensure that the components can interoperate, and the standardization process permits implementations to evolve to meet the standard.

The Internet does not have a governing body; the various hosts and networks adhere to protocol standards voluntarily. The *Internet Engineering Task Force* (IETF) [Bra96b] is an open community of network designers, product vendors, and researchers who contribute to the evolution and operation of the Internet. The description of standards in published documents provides the various implementors with a common basis of understanding. The IETF steers standards through a series of official publications called *Request for Comments* (RFCs). The first document in the RFC series was published in 1969.

IETF documents start as *Internet Drafts,* which are informal documents that undergo revisions based on comments from the community. Not all Internet Drafts become RFCs. RFCs are divided into different tracks: standards, historic, informational, and experimental. A standards document typically evolves

Table 1.6. Terminology related to Web traffic and performance

Term	Definition
Latency	Time between the initiation of an action and the first indication of a response
User-perceived latency	Time between a user action and the initial display of the content
Bandwidth	Amount of traffic that can be carried per unit time
Workload	Inputs received by a Web component over time
Log	Record of transactions performed by a Web component

as part of an IETF *Working Group,* a group created to work on a standard specification. Standards documents have compliance requirements of different levels: *MUST, SHOULD,* and *MAY.* Any compliant implementation has to meet all the MUST-level requirements, and an implementation can be considered conditionally compliant if it meets all the SHOULD-level requirements. The MAY-level requirements are optional for an implementation to meet. These requirement levels help ensure interoperability between different implementations. A standards document proceeds through three stages: Proposed Standard, Draft Standard, and Internet Standard, maturing progressively from a well-designed specification to one of high technical maturity based on operational experience. Some RFCs reflect the best current practices (BCP) and are known as a BCP document. Standards do not last forever; they can be retired and replaced by a superior specification.

In order to nurture and foster the growth of the Web, the World Wide Web Consortium (W3C) was founded in 1994. The W3C has developed a variety of standards, called Recommendations, related to the Web. The W3C tends to focus on the representation of Web content, such as the HTML language, rather than the networking aspects. The W3C works on architectural issues, user-interface issues dealing with formats and languages, social issues relating to legal and public policy matters, and accessibility issues to ensure that people with disabilities are able to have access to the technology.

1.3.5 Web traffic and performance

Table 1.6 catalogs the terms related to Web traffic and performance. The widespread popularity of the Web has led to a rapid increase in the number of users and Web sites. However, the capacity of the network and servers is limited. User expectations for quick responses have focused attention on performance issues. *Latency* is the time between the initiation of an action, such as the sending of a request message, and the first indication of a response. *User-perceived latency* is the delay between the time the user selects a hypertext

Table 1.7. Terminology related to Web caching and multimedia streaming

Term	Definition
Cache	Store of messages used to reduce user-perceived latency and load on the network and server
Cache coherency	Mechanism to lower the possibility of returning out-of-date messages from the cache
Replication	Duplication of resources on multiple origin servers
Content distribution	Delivery of resources on behalf of an origin server
Audio/video stream	Sequence of audio samples or video frames
Streaming	Overlap of the server transmission and client playback of audio/video data
Media player	Helper application for playing multimedia streams

link and the requested content starts to appear in the browser window. Each
software component and protocol contribute a varying amount to the user-
perceived latency. For example, the browser must construct the HTTP request,
determine the server's IP address, establish a TCP connection to the server,
transmit the request, wait for the response, and finally render the response for
the user. High user-perceived latency could stem from a variety of factors, such
as DNS overhead, network congestion, or load on the server.

In addition, the browser may have an Internet connection with relatively
low *bandwidth,* such as a 28.8 Kb/sec modem. Transferring a large resource
over the modem introduces noticeable delay, even if the Web server and the
rest of the Internet are lightly loaded. Analyzing the performance of a complex
and diverse system such as the Web is difficult in practice. Yet, understanding
the system is critical to identifying performance problems and improving the
technology. Measurement and analysis of Web traffic is necessary to characterize
the access patterns of users and the properties of the resources accessed on the
Web. Most analysis of Web traffic has drawn on *logs* that provide a record of
the HTTP transfers performed by Web software components. Analysis of logs
is useful for understanding the characteristics of the *workload* handled by Web
software components. A workload consists of the set of all inputs (e.g., HTTP
requests) received by a component over time. The workload characteristics,
such as the time between requests and the size and popularity of the various
resources, have important implications for the performance of Web protocols,
software components, and the underlying network.

1.3.6 Web applications

Table 1.7 enumerates terms related to Web applications. With the increasing
popularity of the Web, Web caching and multimedia streaming have become

important applications. The growth of the Web led to a heavy load on Web servers and the Internet and consequently to an increase in user-perceived latency in accessing Web content. Caching moves content closer to the user. This is a relatively simple idea that has existed since the early days of computing. A *cache* is a local store of messages. A cache can be located at a user's browser, an origin server, or a machine in the path between the user and the origin server. Although caching improves performance, a cached response might differ from the version available at the origin server. *Cache coherency* mechanisms are used to ensure that a cached message is up-to-date with the origin server. An alternative to caching, *replication* involves explicit duplication of Web content on multiple servers. A client request is directed to one of the replicas. Load balancing can be performed to manage the load on the origin server. An alternative to replicating the full contents of a Web site is to deliver content selectively from replicas on behalf of the origin server. This technique is called *content distribution*.

The Web provides access to diverse resources without regard to their format or location. In the past few years, audio and video content on the Web have become increasingly popular. Unlike traditional Web content, *audio* or *video streams* consist of a sequence of sounds (samples) or images (frames) spanning a period of time. In multimedia *streaming* applications, such as music jukeboxes or video-on-demand, the client plays the samples or frames as they arrive from the server, rather than downloading the content in its entirety before beginning playout. These applications typically consume a large amount of bandwidth and are sensitive to delay in receiving the audio samples and video frames. Although HTTP can be used to deliver multimedia content, most multimedia transfers are simply initiated via HTTP. Then a separate helper application, or *media player*, contacts a multimedia server using a different set of protocols that are better suited to streaming audio and video.

1.4 Topics Not Covered

Presenting the technical underpinnings of the Web is an ambitious venture. The rapid growth of the Web has led to unprecedented technological developments, including ideas adopted from earlier protocols, languages, and applications. The focusing of this book is on the protocols and software components involved in transferring Web content; therefore the book does not discuss other topics in depth, including the following:

- Languages such as the Hypertext Markup Language (HTML) and XML (eXtensible Markup Language)
- Perl and other scripting languages used in conjunction with Web servers
- Security issues surrounding the Web
- Social and policy issues relating to privacy, security, and accessibility

- Guidelines for administering and configuring Web proxies and servers
- Specific vendor products, such as particular proxy or server implementations

Detailed treatments of these topics is beyond the scope and intention of this book. These topics are covered in depth in other books. For example, many existing books provide a detailed overview of HTML and Web server configuration. Finally, certain topics, such as the details of vendor products, may not have sufficient longevity to warrant inclusion. Instead, we focus on specific concepts and technologies.

1.5 Tour Through the Book

We now provide a tour through the book. Readers might choose to skip certain parts or read each part in sequence. This chapter has provided a basic overview of the Web and the scope of the book. The remainder of the book is divided into five main parts, as follows:

- **Web software components:** The first part of the book discusses the three key software components in the Web: clients, proxies, and servers. The large-scale penetration of the Mosaic browser enabled the Web to succeed. Proxies were created subsequently to enable scalability. Web servers have grown from their initial simple designs to handle tens of millions of requests daily. This section of the book provides both a history of the evolution of the components and a functional overview of their key aspects. Although each of the components is discussed separately in its own chapter, they are linked via a canonical example of a typical Web transaction. The three chapters provide the necessary prerequisite to appreciate the details of the Web infrastructure presented later in the book. We present clients first, then proxies, and finally Web servers, following the path typically followed by Web messages. Apart from the most popular form of a Web client—the browser, we also examine special clients such as spiders, which have enabled popular search applications on the Web. Similarly, issues related to cookies, which are used to maintain state beyond the normal stateless exchange of Web messages, are examined from both a client and a server point of view. Because this part of the book precedes the protocol chapters, we defer discussion of issues related to the Web protocols. A case study of the Apache Web server is used to examine the architecture and functioning of a popular Web server.
- **Web protocols:** The delivery of Web content depends on a collection of standard protocols—IP, TCP, and, DNS, which provide the basic communication services, and HTTP, the application-level protocol. These protocols have evolved through many years of standardization in the IETF,

and together they form a stable substrate for requesting and transferring Web resources. The in-depth discussion of these protocols forms the core of the book and serves as important background material for the remainder of the chapters. The presentation follows a bottom-up approach, starting with a chapter on networking protocols—IP, DNS, TCP, and various application-level protocols that predated HTTP. The next two chapters provide a thorough examination of the HTTP protocol—both HTTP/1.0 and the more recent standard HTTP/1.1. The material is separated into two chapters to highlight the evolution of the protocol over time to cope with the rapid growth of the Web. The discussion demystifies the protocol evolution process, including the uncovering of problems in earlier versions of the protocol. The chapters present the syntax and semantics of HTTP with detailed examples. The two HTTP-related chapters complement the description of the protocol as specified in RFC 1945 and RFC 2616. This part of the book closes with a chapter on the interaction between HTTP and TCP, which has important performance implications for the delivery of Web traffic over the Internet.

- **Measuring and characterizing Web traffic:** In this part of the book, we provide a detailed overview of mature techniques for collecting and analyzing Web traffic measurements. Web proxies and servers create logs as a routine part of performing HTTP transactions. Measurements can also be collected by passively monitoring links in the network or actively generating requests to targeted servers. Since the early days of the Web, researchers and protocol designers have analyzed measurement data to characterize Web traffic and evaluate techniques for improving Web performance. Web performance depends on how user access patterns interact with the underlying protocols and software components. Measurement and analysis of Web traffic have also played a crucial role in the creation of benchmarks for comparing different proxy and server implementations. The first chapter discusses the three main steps in measuring Web traffic: monitoring the Web transfers, generating the measurement records, and preprocessing the data in preparation for analysis. We discuss client, proxy, and server logging, as well as packet monitoring and active measurement. Then we discuss how to address the inherent limitations of each of these measurement techniques, with case studies demonstrating how they have been applied in practice. The second chapter focuses on constructing workload models that capture the salient features of Web traffic. The detailed overview of Web traffic characteristics emphasizes the use of HTTP, the key attributes of Web resources, and the impact of user behavior on Web traffic. We also highlight how the workload characteristics may change with the continuing evolution of the Web.

- **Web applications:** The fourth part of the book focuses on two key applications—caching and multimedia streaming—that have considerable influence on the delivery of Web content. The rapid growth of the Web led to a remarkable increase in Internet traffic. No other technology has risen so swiftly to account for nearly three out of four packets on the Internet. This "success disaster" makes caching a necessity. In the chapter on caching, we present an overview of the key concepts and the mechanics of caching. The current state-of-the-art in caching in terms of inter-cache protocols, caching hardware, software, and recent move toward content distribution are all covered. The next chapter presents a detailed treatment of the delivery of audio and video content, a rapidly growing segment of Web traffic. As more users have access to high-bandwidth connections to the Internet, multimedia streaming has become more common. The chapter discusses the unique requirements of audio and video data, compared with traditional text and image content. We then describe the evolving suite of protocols for transferring multimedia streams, including an in depth look at the Real Time Streaming Protocol (RTSP) that borrows several key concepts from HTTP/1.1.

- **Research perspectives:** The final part of the book presents research perspectives on three important and timely topics: caching, measurement, and protocols. Rather than surveys of mature ideas, these chapters provide a glimpse of the evolving state of the art in these areas. These chapters motivate and explain individual strands of research and describe how the research ideas were evaluated. The ideas have been vetted by peer review but have not been widely deployed as this book goes to press. For each topic, we discuss the factors affecting the possible deployment of the ideas or the key conclusions of the studies. Even if the idea is never used in practice, the process of identifying and evaluating a solution has longer-term value in stimulating the next set of research ideas. Each section of the three chapters focuses on a different subtopic or research study. The chapters do not provide a complete overview of ongoing research on each topic. Instead, the focus reflects our bias and our expectations of the continuing importance of the topics. In addition, the selection of topics emphasizes research ideas that connect with the key concepts and standard protocols discussed in the earlier parts of the book.

Together, the following five parts of the book provide a description of the technology underlying the Web.

Part II

Web Software Components

2

Web Clients

In the previous chapter we introduced three major software components of the Web: client, proxy, and server. Most users of the Web come in direct contact with Web clients and almost never with proxies or Web servers. Web servers are a necessary component, proxies play a crucial role, and the network is crucial to transporting the bits. Yet, the *browser*—the best-known form of a Web client—is what is actually *seen* by end users as the interface to the Web.

It can be argued that the introduction of the Web browser Mosaic [Mos] is the primary reason the World Wide Web is a part of everyday life for millions of people. Barely three years passed between the creation of Mosaic, the first widely used browser, and the number of users on the Web reaching tens of millions. No other piece of software has brought so many new users to a new or existing technology in such a short interval of time. As a consequence, the number of documents accessible via the Internet grew. Even though the Web itself existed a few years before the popularization of Mosaic, the browser significantly reduced the barrier of entry for new users.

Although from an end user's perspective, the browser may be viewed as the central (or even only) part of their Web experience, other clients play an equally important but hidden role. This chapter examines three different Web clients: a browser as the most popular form of a Web client, a *spider* in its role as the key behind the most popular Web application—searching, and the less well known *agent* software.

This chapter begins with a discussion of the origin of Web client, a program that sends Web requests and receives responses. The popularity of bit-mapped displays and ease of navigation played a key role in the evolution of the browser. A canonical example is used to take a detailed look at the browser's role in Web interactions. A look at browser configuration involving the setting of physical attributes or the parameters that are specific to the HTTP protocol follows. A browser performs several functions that are unrelated to the HTTP protocol, such as invoking programs to interpret and display responses. The configurability of such actions is also examined.

The browser is the closest to the user of the three major Web software components. Security issues related to accessing resources and downloading scripts or other executable programs are an integral aspect of a browser's interaction with the Web. After examining browser security issues, we discuss the part played by cookies in managing state across Web transactions. The crucial, if largely hidden, role of the browser in dealing with cookies is explored.

A spider is an example of a client program that is not directly triggered by end users. Spiders are necessary for fetching and indexing resources. After some background on searching, we present the key niche that spiders fill on the Web.

Beyond browsers and spiders, the role played by agents—programs run on behalf of users for specific applications such as auctions and collaborative filtering—is less well-known. We examine some popular versions of such agents and miscellaneous clients such as offline browsers and co-browsers. We conclude by revisiting the principles shared by the different manifestations of the client and how they are used in practice.

2.1 Client as a Program

A Web client is a piece of software. The typical task of a Web client is to send a Web request on behalf of a user and receive the response. A client is also used for a variety of other purposes. The Web was developed after the advent of traditional client-server software, whereby a client connects to a server and sends it a request and obtains a response. At the time of the creation of the Web, other client-server systems (as discussed in Chapter 1) offered services similar to that of the Web. It was possible to send queries to search for resources by consulting searchable indexes. Each of the querying entities was a client. The Web evolved alongside these other systems (Archie, Gopher, Network News, etc.), and thus the initial Web client was similar to others in the traditional client-server genre.

In a typical client-server system, clients are relatively simple. A client formats a request, sends it to the server, and reads, parses, and displays the response. Typical client-server systems embed the intelligence in the servers. In the Web context, this is not the case. Servers still have a considerable amount of functionality to provide. However, in practice, Web clients are quite complex. The complexity does not stem from the bare-bones tasks that a Web client has to perform: constructing a properly formatted Web request, establishing a connection, and communicating with a Web server over a reliable transport-level connection. Many of the complexities of a client program spring from the environmental factors surrounding the basic request-response exchange— customizing request creation, interpreting the response, and tailoring its display.

2.2 Evolution of the Browser

Initially the browser was a simple program that permitted users to obtain resources from anywhere on the Web; that is, it was just an implementation of a Web client. Within a very short time, it became *the* front end to virtually all interactions with a computer for many users. Users utilize a browser to send and receive e-mail, read electronic news groups, enter chat sessions, and access the Web. A browser is often considered to be a *user agent* rather than simply a client because it *initiates* a Web request.

Most browser users do not know the difference between the Web and the Internet. Nor do they know that most of the applications that they are using—e-mail, news, and so on—existed long before the Web. In this chapter, we will concentrate on the role a browser plays in a user's interaction with the Web. In addition, we will discuss issues dealing with physical attributes of the browser that can be customized by the user.

Bit-mapped displays were common by the mid-1980s. A graphical interface was mandatory for any application intended to be be popular with a large number of users. The advantages of a graphical interface over a textual interface were already widely known. However, many computer users did not yet have access to bit-mapped displays and often used a textual interface to access their files. This was reflected in the late 1980s by the interfaces of the various wide area information access tools such as Archie, Gopher, and Wide Area Information Server (WAIS), discussed in Chapter 1. Users were moving from accessing local files to arbitrary resources all across the Internet. The manner of access was also changing from accessing a resource from a previously known location to accessing resources simply by searching across the Internet.

Users benefit by knowing the set of resources accessible at a given time and the history of recent accesses, as they navigate the collection of resources. While accessing resources from a vast collection on the Internet, the ability to move between collections quickly became crucial. The notion of navigation across sets of resources and between resources requires a clear and intuitive interface. A collection of resources at a given location might be arranged in a manner different from those of other locations. Although users now had access to a very large number of resources from all over the world, their cognitive ability to maintain context had not correspondingly increased. A tool that would let users to move across collections had to meet the following several requirements:

- A notion of current context (where a user is and what is accessible there)
- An idea of where else a user could go next and where a user has been recently
- An ability to customize the navigation and the display of the resources accessed
- An ability to search across a collection

The first browser was built at the CERN laboratory using the NeXTStep user interface tools [BLCGP92] and demonstrated the power of using hypertext links to traverse a collection of documents. It was called `WorldWideWeb` and was written by the inventor of the Web, Tim Berners-Lee. However, a text-based client program was also written that could operate in character-mode terminals. From the Web server's point of view, the client was just a program, regardless of the interface provided to the end user. Work on the first textual browser, called *linemode* [Pel91], began in late 1990 and became available in March 1991. Linemode was a basic browser that let users move across a collection of linked resources and served as a generic information retrieval tool. Linemode ensured that all users could access the Web, regardless of the terminal they used. Users could navigate around the Web document collection by using only a keyboard and only two control sequences: a carriage return and a line feed. A notion of a link, for example, was a number displayed between brackets. The user would enter the number via the keyboard to access the document referred to by the link. The client program had exactly seven commands [Pel91], such as `List` (to list all the links in the document), `K` to execute a keyword search, and `Recall` to list the documents seen thus far in the session (an early history mechanism).

The first browser was more than a proof of concept: It set the parameters around which modern browsers developed. Stripped of all the externalities, the key advance in modern browsers is the ability to seamlessly navigate across links around the Internet—a feature that was implemented in the very early days of the Web. In other words, the browser was a realization of the design goal to be able to permit users to move around collections of documents quickly and intuitively.

After LineMode, several other browsers were introduced, ranging from a cursor-addressable Curses browser to a range of browsers operating under various popular window manager software of the X11 Window System (Viola, tk-WWW, MidasWWW), a browser written for the Macintosh machines, and even ones written in scripting languages such as Perl. After the introduction of Mosaic, there was a significant movement toward using it as the primary browser. A text-based browser—Lynx—was introduced in 1992 and is still in limited use. Some of the developers of Mosaic then created the Netscape browser, and some years later the Internet Explorer browser was created. As this book goes to press, no significant new features have been added to browsers within the last year or so. In other words, the browser has reached a level of maturity. Meanwhile, Web servers are continually being updated to improve their performance and provide different levels of service to different clients.

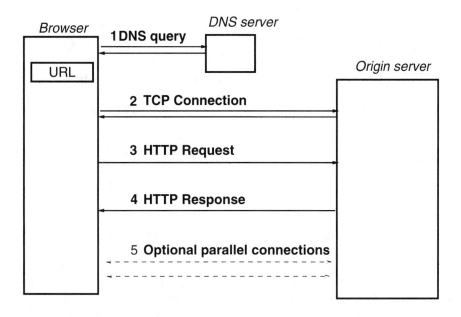

Figure 2.1. Steps in a browser process

2.3 Web-related Browser Functions

A browser primarily implements a Web client—constructs and sends an HTTP request, then receives, parses, and displays the response. A browser session is thus a series of requests sent by the user, possibly based on the responses received at each stage. A browser session may last for a few minutes or for a very long time. Figure 2.1 shows the various steps in the process involved in a Web request as processed by a typical browser. At a very high level, the selected URL is parsed to determine the Web server that must be contacted, a connection is set up with the server, and an HTTP request is sent with the URL to obtain the response. Note that some of the steps may not be necessary for each request because of reasons such as *caching*—a browser may have a copy of a response received earlier, eliminating the need for sending a request for it again. Caching is explained in more depth in Section 2.3.3.

The URL may be supplied in several ways; the most common way is clicking on an existing link in a page. It could also be typed into a window or selected from a *bookmark* file (a file created by the user of frequently visited sites) or a history list in the browser. Browsers may prepend `http` as the default protocol if none is specified and help complete the string the user is typing by offering

Table 2.1. User actions leading to request generation

Input choice	Request constructed from
Forward/Backward button	Browser's history mechanism
Selecting a link	Corresponding URL string in HTML text
Bookmarks	User's collection of interesting links
Click on Submit/Press Return	URL corresponding to button/form
URL Window	User input
Various menus	Menu item selected
Images	User click, automatically generated request
Reload	Current URL

past URLs accessed by the user for selection. Table 2.1 shows some of the various user actions that can trigger a Web request.

We begin this section with a canonical example to illustrate the functions of a Web browser. Next we examine a common occurrence in the construction of requests—form filling. Then we will look at the role played by caching at the browser level. We then consider the role of a proxy if present in the path between the client and the server. The browser's function in the construction of HTTP message request headers is then examined. Finally, the browser's handling of an HTTP response is discussed.

2.3.1 Canonical Web transfer example

We use the following example throughout the book. A document consisting of a few embedded images must be downloaded by a client from an origin server. For this example, we assume that the client communicates directly with the origin server and does not go through an intermediary, such as a proxy. Also, we assume no caching of resources is involved.

Typically a link to an object is presented, while the URL is hidden from the browser user. The "active text" displayed to the user is typically explanatory of the link that would be followed by selecting it, although many links simply use the phrase "click here." A link to the resource referred to by the URL is displayed in the browser, often in some highlighted fashion—in a different color or underlined—instead of the actual URL. The user selects the link by clicking on it via a mouse or types the URL in a specific location in the browser. Suppose the user selects the link `http://www.bar.com/foo.html`. The browser parses the URL `http://www.bar.com/foo.html`. The first part preceding the ':' character is the protocol that the browser should use to fetch the resource `www.bar.com/foo.html`. In this case it is `http`, though as we will see later, other protocols such as File Transfer Protocol (FTP) or Telnet can be used. The

Table 2.2. Resources referred to in the canonical example and their content type

Resource	Description	Content type
`/foo.html`	HTML container document	HTML
`/foo1.gif`	Embedded image	GIF
`/foo2.gif`	Embedded image	GIF
`/foo3.jpg`	Embedded image	JPEG
`/book.cgi`	Executable script	CGI
`/mp.tv`	Multimedia document	Special format

resource `www.bar.com/foo.html` itself has two parts: the initial part consisting of the machine (`www.bar.com`) on which the Web server is running and the name of the resource (`/foo.html`) accessible from the server `www.bar.com`. The browser has to access a Domain Name System (DNS) server to "look up" the Internet Protocol (IP) address of the origin server corresponding to the string `www.bar.com` (step 1 in Figure 2.1). After obtaining the IP address of the machine `www.bar.com`, the browser sets up a transport-level connection with the origin server using the Transmission Control Protocol (TCP) (step 2). After a successful connection, the browser sends the formatted HTTP request asking for the resource `/foo.html` (step 3). The origin server `www.bar.com` responds with the current contents of the resource `/foo.html` (step 4).

The browser parses the response and may make additional connections to fetch any embedded resources. For this example, we assume that there are three embedded images referenced in `/foo.html`. The page also has a reference to a Common Gateway Interface script resource (discussed in Chapter 4, Section 4.2.3) and a reference to a multimedia object. Table 2.2 shows the various resources in the example. The browser may already start displaying the partially fetched contents of `/foo.html`, even as it makes additional connections to request the embedded images. The additional connections needed to fetch the images may be established in parallel. The connections may not all be with the same origin server because some of the embedded resources in `/foo.html` may be resident on other origin servers. The browser may also begin to render each image as it arrives. The browser's task is complete after it has received all the embedded images and displayed them. Figure 2.2 shows what the container document `foo.html` might look like with its three embedded images, a form, and a reference to a multimedia document.

2.3.2 Issuing a request from a browser

Most users issue a request by clicking on a link on a Web page or typing the URL. However, there are many instances in which the construction of the request is a bit more complex. Consider the example of ordering a book on the

Figure 2.2. Container document `foo.html`

Web by filling out a form consisting of many fields whose values must be selected from menus or typed in. E-commerce and search applications are examples in which requests are generated as a result of a user filling out a form. One reason to consider the construction of requests via forms as a distinct case is that search sites on the Web receive a considerable fraction of all requests. A user typically executes a search by filling out a search form and clicking on submit or hitting return. The triggering of search execution or selecting a URL link both result in the same action—construction of a properly formatted HTTP request.

Consider our earlier example, which includes a reference to an executable script `/book.cgi`. The book ordering page includes a form that the user fills out with the information necessary to purchase the book. The set of fields to be filled out by the user typically includes name, address, credit card number, and the title of the book. The completed form can be sent to the origin server in at least two ways. One way is to treat each of the values filled out and the corresponding fields as (name, value) pairs. The collection of (name, value) pairs is encoded into the arguments of a HTTP `GET` request. For example, if one of the fields in a form is the name and the user types in Noam Chomsky, the pair could be included in the URL as `http://www.foo.com/book.cgi?name=Noam+Chomsky`. Another way is to include the form as a body of an HTTP message with a different request method (`POST`).

2.3.3 Browser caching

In this section, we present a brief introduction to the topic of Web caching as it affects the browser. A cache is a local store of messages that can be used to lower the delay perceived by users in obtaining a response from a server. There are two kinds of caching that are common in browsers: a portion of memory of the running process and a portion of the filesystem's disk space that are dedicated to caching. If the network is congested or the Web server is busy, receiving resources from the site might take a long time. Because most users visit the same Web sites often, it is beneficial for a browser to cache the most recent set of pages downloaded. If the user tries to go back to a recently visited Web page, it could be displayed from the browser's cache. The user's tendency to go back to a page recently seen is so common that most browsers have a Back button to enable users to go back through their most recently requested collection of pages.

Suppose one of the embedded images in the resource `/foo.html`, say `/foo1.gif`, was stored in the browser's cache. To redisplay the image, the browser would not have to make a separate request for it. Because a separate HTTP request is not needed, the DNS lookup of the origin server, the HTTP and corresponding TCP connection to send the request, and the transmission of the bytes corresponding to `/foo1.gif` on the network are no longer necessary. All of this translates to considerable reduction in user-perceived latency—the duration between the time the user clicks on a link and actual contents begin to appear in the browser window.

However, it is possible that the cached resource may have been modified since the time it was cached. The browser may have to verify that the cached response is still *fresh* by checking the cached copy against the current copy on the origin server. Such checking is called *cache revalidation*. If the version on the origin server is newer, then the cached copy is *stale*. For example, the resource `/foo1.gif` may have changed since it was last downloaded.

A cache is said to maintain *consistency* of cached resources if the cache ensures that cached resources are still fresh at the origin server. A cache that revalidates the cached version against the origin server each time a request for the cached resource is made is said to maintain *strong* cache consistency. If the cache uses a heuristic to decide whether the cached response is still fresh, then it is said to maintain *weak* cache consistency. It is possible for such a cache to return responses without validating with the origin server. Several heuristics are used to maintain cache consistency. A cache could revalidate periodically at fixed intervals or vary the revalidation interval depending on attributes of the resource (size, the last time it was modified, content type, etc.). The decision to return a cached value depends on the consistency policy currently in effect in the browser. The browser might decide that image resources change less often than textual ones and use the cached value without checking with the origin server. Although the browser might not assume that `/foo.html` is still fresh on the origin server, it might assume that `/foo1.gif` has not changed recently. Thus it is possible for a stale cached resource to be returned as a response if the browser is maintaining weak cache consistency.

A user can bypass the browser cache revalidation heuristic and force the browser to send the request directly to the origin server. For example, on the Netscape browser this is done by the key-button combination `Shift-Reload`.

The response returned from the origin server that was cached includes a "last modification time" value indicating the time at which the resource was last modified at the origin server. The cache would store this value and include it in a request header as part of its revalidation request. If the original response from the server did not include a last modification time, a cache assigns a value based on a heuristic. For example, a cache could assign the time at which the response was received as the last modification value. The origin server would compare the current last modification time of the resource against the value included in the request from the cache to let the cache know if the resource has changed.

If the requested resource is not in the browser cache, the request is forwarded to the downstream server, which may or may not be the origin server.

We will discuss caching in depth in Chapter 11.

2.3.4 Request message headers

Thus far we have seen how a URL can be selected, how form input can be converted into a request, and how a browser decides to forward a request after checking its cache. Now we examine how a user's action in a browser translates into an actual HTTP request message. The HTTP request message is the unit of communication between a client and a server. A request message consists of a request header and an optional request body. Typical request headers include identification information about the user agent, acceptable encoding formats of the response, and the credentials to indicate that the user has access rights to the resource being requested. Request headers may be gleaned from the environment. For example, information about the user agent, such as the version of the browser or the operating system of the machine on which the browser is running, is included in a header. The e-mail address of the user obtained from configuration options specified in the browser is another example. The full request is constructed in adherence to the particular version of HTTP implemented by the browser. In Chapters 6 and 7, we will discuss various request message headers in detail.

2.3.5 Response handling

As the final step in the browser's functions, the browser has to handle the response sent by the server. The browser accepts the response and parses it to see what, if anything, must be displayed. The response may be displayed in the same browser window where the request originated or in a different window. The choice of a different window may be made by the user or by the selected link, or it may be made as a result of the response. For example, some browsers by default attempt to show the response in the same window if the left mouse button was used and open a new window if the middle button was used. Some links automatically cause the response to be displayed in a separate window. The response could contain a script (e.g., Javascript) that might cause the actual output to be displayed in a different window. In some cases, showing the response in a different window may shift the focus of attention of the user.

The display of the response is tailored to the user's preferences, such as the choice of fonts or colors (discussed in more detail in Section 2.4). The server's response may already be tailored based on the choices expressed as part of the request header—for example, choice of languages in response or encoding format. The control over the content and display of content is divided among the following:

- The user in terms of the actual input event (e.g., choice of button)
- The user's preference for content format expressed through request headers generated and sent by the browser
- The response of the link being selected
- The possible adaptation done by the origin server to serve the content in the user-desired format
- The content creator's desire to display the content in a separate window

The final result thus depends on different software components and the configurability and level of control at each stage.

The details of the various activities a browser has to perform to render a page are beyond the scope of this book. Readers interested in details are referred to books on popular browsers such as Netscape Navigator or Internet Explorer.

2.4 Browser Configuration

A browser, like most pieces of interactive software, can be customized by the user. Customizability has been a stable feature of interactive systems long before the Web. Users tailor systems to their needs in order to ensure an intuitive interface. With the advent of customizable window managers in user interfaces, various kinds of configuration became possible. Users try to make their interaction with a new interactive system similar to that with other systems they have used. The degree of customizability often dictates how quickly users adapt themselves to a new system. Two kinds of customization have been broadly recognized. The first is externally visible physical attributes such as size and color. The second is internal semantic attributes such as choice of languages or control over caching of responses. The range of customizable attributes is quite large. This is due to browsers becoming the primary portal to a very wide range of applications for a large number of users. Browsers are used as the starting point for virtually all the interactions of users with the Internet.

The browser takes into account the user's preferences at all stages of interaction. For example, the user could specify if the request should be routed via a proxy or some other intermediary or sent directly to the origin server. Similarly, the request could encode the user's desire to receive a response different from the default by stating choices of preferred languages or encoding formats.

A user should know about the configuration of a browser in order to interpret the response properly. For example, if the browser uses a cached response because the remote server is currently unavailable, the user may want to know that the response might be stale. If the response uses a specific set of fonts or a particular character set, then it must be rendered using the appropriate attributes available locally. Users' experiences are affected by the range of choices available to configure their interaction. We should note that in practice it is common for users *not* to customize any of the attributes of a browser. The decision is often done by system administrators at a client site, and few users change the default settings. System administrators themselves often use the default settings in the software.

In this section, we will examine how browsers are configured according to the user's choice with respect to both physical appearance and semantic options of interacting with the Web. This is followed by an examination of configurability of browser functions unrelated to the HTTP protocol.

2.4.1 Physical appearance

The browser has several configuration options for altering the appearance of its layout, the set of buttons visible, and so on. The responses displayed on a screen have several attributes, and the user's customization is taken into account while displaying them. For example, the size of the browser window varies with the user's machine, and the amount of information that can be displayed is dictated by the screen real estate and the size of the fonts. Different users pick different physical attributes for their browser. With its increasing popularity, browsers became the front end for a very large set of applications. Apart from browsing the Web, many users utilize the browser for sending and receiving e-mail, as a calendar manager or address book, for printing files, and so on. Each of these applications has its own collection of attributes, and many of them are configurable.

The following is a list of user-settable attributes that have a bearing on how Web pages are displayed.

- **External appearance:** This includes size of a browser window, presence of several palettes of buttons, and scrollbars. These are generic attributes available with most graphical interfaces. Many of the items related to external appearance are a function of the capabilities provided by the window manager that governs the user's display. The only attributes that affect the display of Web pages have to do with areas of the browser window where URLs can be typed and bookmarks can be selected.

- **Display of embedded images in a page:** Web pages have both text and images; therefore browsers by default will fetch and display all of the resources. However, images may take longer to download because they are on average larger than textual resources and Web pages may have several embedded images in them. Many users have low-speed connections to the Internet and may not want to wait a long time for downloading the full contents of a page—text and images. Other users may not be interested in seeing images whose information content may be considered to be less critical. The browser thus lets users specify if they want the images to be automatically downloaded or not. Most browsers also provide a button to let users request images for a specific page that was initially downloaded without the images. In addition to the delay in downloading the images, the browser has to *render* the images, which adds additional latency. However, the latency resulting from low connection speed is often the primary bottleneck.

- **Font:** Textual material is often displayed using multiple fonts. Users who were used to seeing different fonts in print naturally expected similar structure in displayed material. In the Web context, the browser must select between fonts available on the local machine and apply them to the information in the downloaded page. Choices include size and selection of fonts, encoding of fonts, fixed- versus variable-width fonts, and language-specific fonts. The downloaded Web page may indicate the choice of fonts, but users can override that specification. For example, some users might prefer fixed-width fonts for aesthetic reasons.

- **Color:** Simple options include selecting the foreground and background colors of the browser window while displaying a page or for selectable links on a page. Browsers often give users control over whether they want their selection of colors to override any colors specified in the pages they download. One way to permit this is for users to choose from a collection of colors (a palette). Another way is to let users directly mix arbitrary combinations of primary colors (red, green, and blue) and select a color according to their own sense of aesthetics. Many users' displays vary in resolution and sharpness. Browsers can attempt to find the best setting for colors, although automatic selection is rarely done because it requires changing the default setting, with which the user may be more comfortable.

Another way to set attributes is through the use of Cascading Style Sheets (CSSs) [CSSa]. CSSs were introduced in 1994 by the World Wide Web Consortium (W3C) as a generic way to describe how documents should be presented. CSSs obviate the need for the content creator to add new HTML language tags for altering the appearance of a document. The presentation may be on a user's display or in a printed form. A brief tutorial on CSSs can be found in [CSSb].

2.4.2 Semantic choices

Apart from the various physical attributes in a browser, there are several semantic attributes, such as choice of intermediaries and content language, that can also be set by the user. Some of the semantic attributes deal with protocol-specific issues that require an understanding of the details of the HTTP protocol (discussed in Chapters 6 and 7). A simple example of a customizable attribute is the language in which the requested resource should be obtained if it is available in more than one language. The choice of languages, once specified in the browser, is translated into appropriate syntax of HTTP and included in request headers. For example, if the user specified Swiss-Deutsch (`German/Switzerland[de-CH]`) as a preferred language, the HTTP request header

```
Accept-Language: de-CH
```

would be added to the list of headers sent with each request. The server receiving the request may take the `Accept-Language` header into account in generating the response. Such headers are an expression of user preference, and servers are not obligated to alter their responses.

Five categories of semantic choices can be configured via a browser. They are

- Connection related (proxies)
- Content or choice of resource related (acceptable languages)
- Caching (discussed earlier in Section 2.3.3)
- Handling of responses (discussed later in Section 2.4.3)
- Cookies (discussed later in Section 2.6)

The first two categories are discussed next; the others are described later in other sections. The browser permits the user to specify if a proxy should be used as an intermediary between the user and the Internet. If a proxy is to be used, the browser's configuration options are used to specify the proxy's name or IP address. The proxy configuration information can be specified for HTTP communication, as well as interaction with other servers, such as FTP or Gopher. The configuration is flexible enough to let users specify if there are specific domains (partitions of the Internet naming hierarchy) for which a proxy should or should not be used. For example, the browser can be configured so that only requests to pages within the domain `cnn.com` (typically, any URLs with the suffix `cnn.com`) will be sent to the proxy. Requests to all other domains would bypass the proxy, thus permitting the users to browse these sites avoiding proxy privacy issues.

Users can prevent certain automatic events from occurring when a page is downloaded. For example, downloading a page might trigger a Java language application to be loaded into the browser and executed. A user can disable this by setting a preference in the browser. One problem with this approach is that it might leave certain application capabilities out of the reach of such users because some popular applications on the Web depend on this facility. Browsers can enable script executions for specific applications only, such as reading electronic newsgroups or e-mail. Section 2.5 examines the security implications of downloading resources that can trigger actions automatically.

Some newer versions of popular browsers have an autoconfiguration mechanism that automatically sets the defaults for various semantic choices. For example, a proxy can be automatically chosen based on the client's IP address by downloading a script from a Web server and setting the default values.

2.4.3 Configuring browser for non-protocol functions

A browser may use several helper programs to handle responses, and choice and handling of such programs are configurable. If the response to a request is a text document or an image, the browser often knows how to render the response. However, some of the responses require *helper* applications for interpreting the response. For example, suppose a user wants to download a document in either the Portable Document Format (PDF) or PostScript (PS) formats. One possibility is for a browser to download the contents, save the document in a local file, and let the user invoke a separate program to display the contents. However, a browser could trigger the invocation of a helper program that transparently combines the steps of saving the downloaded resource and displaying the contents. For example, the browser could invoke *acroread,* a popular program that is able to display PDF files. Likewise, the browser could invoke *ghostview* to display PostScript files. The decision to invoke particular helper applications is made either by examining the suffix of the resource (`.pdf` or `.ps` for PDF and PostScript files, respectively) or by examining information about the content type present in the response header. A separate configuration often specifies the binding between the resource type and the helper application.

Table 2.3. Helper applications launched based on file/content types

Content type	MIME type	Helper application
Zip compressed data	application/x-zip-compressed	*gunzip*/WINZIP32
PostScript document	application/postscript	*ghostview*/GSVIEW32
Word document	application/msword	*catdoc*/WINWORD
PDF document	application/pdf	*acroread*/ACRORD32
audio/video	video/x-mpeg-2	*raplayer*/MPLAYER2

Table 2.3 lists a few common file content types recognized by the browser and the helper application triggered in response. The second column is the "media type" of the document, a standard way to represent document encodings. Media types were formerly known as MIME (Multipurpose Internet Mail Extensions) types. The third column gives examples of well-known programs in Unix and Microsoft that serve as the helper application.

Table 2.3 shows that if a resource's MIME type is `application/postscript`, the *ghostview* program is invoked to preview the PostScript content downloaded. The *ghostview* command opens a window separate from the browser application and has its own interface for changing magnification or printing the contents. The help application has thus been able to extend the basic functionality of the Web browser. As new MIME types are created, new helper applications that let the user interact with such content will be created. The browsers can continue to be the front end to fetch content and trigger appropriate helper functions.

Consider another popular application on the Web: downloading multimedia (e.g., audio and video) data. Rather than build all the capabilities of a multimedia reader and interpreter into a browser, the browser simply invokes the appropriate media player. Figure 2.3 shows how this process works.

The user selects a resource `http://www.bar.com/foo.ra`, and the browser sends an HTTP request to the origin server `www.bar.com` for the resource `/foo.ra` (step 1). The origin server sends back an HTTP response (step 2), but the content of the response is simply a pointer to the information. The response is meaningful only to an audio client rather than a Web browser. Typically, the response is a URL such as `pnm://ra-ms.com/foo.ra`, where `pnm` stands for "Progressive Networks Media" and `ra-ms.com` is the media server on which the resource `/foo.ra` resides.

Because the browser has been configured to invoke the helper program based on the file type, it would invoke the `real-audio` client program, which would contact the media server `ra-ms.com` (step 3) and start downloading the audio content. The real-audio client on the user's machine may pop up other windows to adjust the volume level or other audio attributes. As soon as

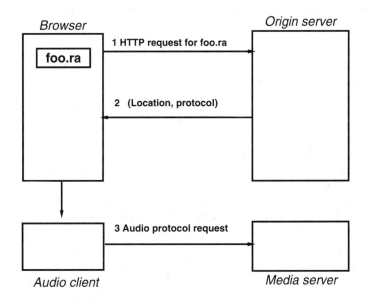

Figure 2.3. Listening to audio data

the HTTP response consisting simply of the `pnm://ra-ms.com/foo` has been downloaded, the Web portion of the original request for `http://www.bar.com/foo.ra` is complete. The browser separately invokes the real-audio client, which carries out a separate transaction with the media server. The audio client will have its own interface (volume control, pause, rewind, etc.) and will be able to interpret the bits it gets from the media server. In fact, the audio-client may use a different protocol (other than HTTP) to obtain the bits. The browser thus acts as a front end to the Web resource `http://www.bar.com/foo.ra`, and the audio-client takes control from the browser to complete the actual task of downloading audio content.

Plug-ins are small pieces of code that are supplied to interpret certain kinds of data within the context of a browser. Unlike some executable scripts interpreted at the browser, plug-ins are generally benign. Some plug-ins have had viruses associated with them, although in practice very few viruses are spread via plug-ins because they must be installed with the user's concurrence. An example of a popular plug-in is *Shockwave,* which is needed by a browser to display a specific kind of animation.

Not all responses can be handled by handlers at the browser. Some applications require the browser to speak protocols other than HTTP. The ability of a browser to speak other protocols enables it to be a uniform front end to a very wide range of applications.

2.5 Browser Security Issues

As the interface between the user and the Web, the browser is the program closest to the user and sends information about the user when needed. As the primary portal of sensitive information about the user, the browser provides maximum flexibility to the user in controlling privacy. At the same time, the browser ensures that remote programs are not given uncontrolled access to the user's machine.

A security risk is present when a piece of software is invoked without a clear idea of its capabilities. Initially, a Web browser was a relatively simple piece of software. Now, a browser is several tens of thousands of lines of code with the corresponding increased potential for security risks. Years of research into security issues have shown that it is generally harder to guarantee security when a complex piece of software is used. A browser is used *primarily* to access a large number of sites on the Web, with each site running another piece of complex software (server), and therefore the overall security risk is higher.

Security issues in a browser primarily arise in the context of access to the disk and computing resources of a machine. Although many of the documents downloaded onto a user's machine are static documents consisting of text and images, increasingly, several executable documents in Java, Javascript, ActiveX, Visual Basic Scripts, Perl, or other languages are downloaded. Several problems related to the security of executable documents have been discussed widely in the literature and in the popular press. Some of the flaws were quite serious, and new ones have been reported over the last several years. Security violations range from inappropriate access to users' files to even more serious problems such as taking over the computing resources of a user's computer. Multiple releases of the Netscape and Internet Explorer browsers have been updated as a result of security flaws that were found. Although users do not have to enable any automatically executable code to run on their machine, several browsers come with some or all of the code execution features enabled. It is possible for a user to change the default behavior. For a more comprehensive look at security issues related to the Web in general, the reader should consult several books written on this topic [Ste98a, RGR97].

If the user is on a personal computer that is not connected via a local area network to other machines, only the computing and file resources on the personal computer are vulnerable when a program is downloaded onto the user's machine. If the user's machine is connected to a local area network or has files and other resources accessible as a result of shared filesystems, then additional resources may be vulnerable. The very ability to use a machine may be at risk as a result of rogue programs mounting a *denial of service* attack. A denial of service attack implies that the machine under attack is forced to expend all its CPU, disk, and other resources on the attacking program, which effectively prevents the machine from servicing any other user. The CPU resources could be commandeered or files on the user's machine could be transferred to remote locations via e-mail originated from the user's machine.

Here we provide a brief look at security risks associated with some of the executable languages popular in the Web.

Java   Java was among the early languages enabling actions to be triggered on a user's machine as a result of being downloaded. Java is relatively resilient to security violations because of its *sandbox* approach of limiting access to resources on the user's machine. A Java *applet* is a small application created for performing a limited task in a secure way with limited access to a user's resources. Java applets downloaded to a user's machine are typically not permitted to read or write local files. Java's intermediate byte code approach reduces the possibility of access to the native machine layer. Even with the restricted access of Java applets, researchers have shown that inappropriate use of Internet protocols can lead to security holes. Even if an applet does not actually remove files on the user's machine, it can mount a denial of service attack simply by consuming all of the computing resources on the user's machine.

Javascript   Javascript, unlike Java, is easier to write and typically is used as an extension of HTML. Browsers that understand HTML have been extended to understand Javascript while keeping the Javascript language distinct from HTML. Javascript functions are parsed by browsers and the specified functions are triggered. Security problems abound because of the ability of Javascript to execute commands without the user's knowledge. For example, a downloaded Javascript program could send e-mail. Users' files are accessible to the scripts, and, unless the user can trust that the functions are safe, arbitrary execution of Javascript code is risky. Browsers can be customized to permit Javascript to be enabled only for specific applications.

ActiveX   ActiveX controls are similar to Java applets, and Visual Basic Script is similar to Javascript. ActiveX controls do not use the sandbox approach but instead rely on the *certificate* mechanism. Certificates are stamps of approvals by "trusted" third parties who can vouch for the ownership of a particular piece of software. If a certified control is shown to be a security risk, then the certificate can be revoked and the company that created that control might be prevented from ever getting a new certificate. The certificate model relies on third party approvals and corresponding lowering of the probability of inadvertent security holes. A well-intentioned software vendor may still accidentally release software that has security holes. The certificate approach can be used by Java and Javascript programs as well.

2.6 Cookies

HTTP is a stateless protocol—a Web server does not have to retain any information about past or future requests. However, a server may have a legitimate reason for wanting to keep information (i.e., state) across a series of requests within a Web browsing session or even across sessions. For example, a server may want to provide access to a set of pages only to a certain subset of users. If some identification information is necessary each time the user accesses any of the pages in this set, there is considerable overhead both to the user to include such information and to the server to process it. Potentially unnecessary transactions add to wasted bandwidth on the network as well. Maintaining some state across requests reduces the overhead on the user, network, and server. A browser plays a crucial role in supplying the required state with a user's request.

Cookies are a way to manage state in HTTP [MF00]. A cookie [Netd, KM00] is a small amount of state that is sent by the server at a Web site to the browser and stored on the user's machine on behalf of the server. The HTTP state management mechanism permits clients and servers to maintain context beyond a single request and response transaction. Cookies were first introduced by Netscape in 1994 [Netd]. Subsequently, standardization attempts began via the Internet Engineering Task Force (IETF) standardization process. The HTTP state management mechanism formalizing the use of cookies is detailed in the Request for Comments (RFC) 2965 [KM00], which was issued in October 2000 as an IETF Proposed Standard. RFC 2965 reflects the experience of various implementations.

In this section, we begin with a look at the motivations for cookies. The mechanics of how cookies are used with browsers is explored. We then examine the control users have over cookies. Cookies are a controversial topic because of their impact on user's privacy. There are differences of opinion within the scientific community on this topic. This section ends with a look at the various privacy issues associated with cookies. The role of an application on the server's side in generating, transmitting, and using cookies is discussed in Chapter 4 (Section 4.2.4).

2.6.1 Motivations for cookies

A server sends a cookie to a browser with its response, requesting that the browser include the cookie in subsequent requests to the server. The next time the user visits the Web site, the browser will include the cookie information in a request header. This way, the Web server at the site is able to keep track of the user within a session and across different sessions. The information sent in the cookie can be unique across all visitors to the Web site, and thus it is possible to track the user individually. Alternatively, the cookie information could be tailored so that the server is able to track a set of users at the granularity of an organization.

Many Web sites (e.g., The New York Times, `http://www.nytimes.com`) require that cookies be used for a browser to be able to download pages. Sites may require that users identify themselves with a userid and password. If this is required for downloading every one of the pages within the site, the user is not likely to spend much time on the site. Instead, the necessary identification information can be sent automatically via a cookie.

A common example of a use of cookies is that of a "shopping cart," where a user is gathering items to be purchased. There are several Web sites where users can selectively "pick up" items they are interested in purchasing, such as books and compact discs. As the user selects items for purchase, a virtual shopping cart shows the set of items currently selected.

In the absence of cookies, a Web server would have to maintain partial state for all its (potentially thousands of) customers on its machine for a long period. Information about what has already been put into the shopping cart or what was purchased last time are examples of state. Other examples include more detailed information, such as what else the user purchased or what pages the user has visited in the current session. The actual state is not fully encoded into cookies; cookies are often used as an index into a database maintained by the origin server to identify the user's state. The ability to encode the necessary information about a user enables an application to share it with other applications, possibly on other servers. Such sharing, often without the user's consent, leads to loss of a user's privacy.

2.6.2 Use of cookies in a browser

Figure 2.4 shows a client sending a request to an origin server A (step 1). The origin server in its response includes a header (`Set-Cookie`) with the cookie value (`XYZ`) (step 2). In all future requests to the origin server A, the client includes the cookie (step 3, sent with the request via the header `Cookie`).

Note that the client does not interpret the cookie string (XYZ) while storing it and including it in subsequent requests. The server is free to construct the string tailored to the client generating the request and to change the mechanism for constructing the cookie string. The figure also shows that the cookie is exchanged essentially without the knowledge of the user unless the user has requested to be notified each time cookies are sent. Such a notification is disruptive to users' Web experience, and thus only a small fraction of the users who even know about this possibility avail themselves of this feature.

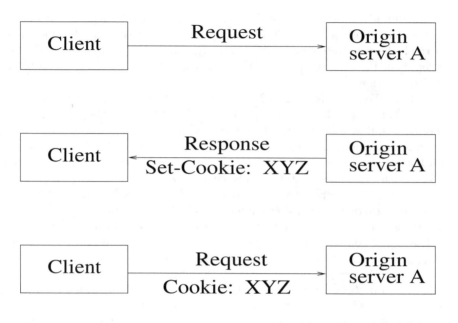

Figure 2.4. Client-server exchange of cookie information

Cookies are kept in browser memory initially and written to stable storage in disk files when the browser process exits. As per the implementation guidelines outlined in [KM00], while user agents are encouraged to store as many frequently used cookies as possible, some minimum capabilities have been outlined. A cookie can be up to 4KB long. Individual browsers provide a maximum of 20 cookies per server (or domain) and an overall total of 300 cookies, so that the site is not overloaded.

2.6.3 Users' control over cookies

Like other semantic attributes that can be controlled via the browser (as discussed earlier, in Section 2.4.2), users have a considerable degree of control over cookies. Users can

- **Decide if they accept any cookies at all:** Such a decision may make it impossible for users to download pages from some sites.
- **Set a limit on the size and number of cookies they accept:** This controls the amount of space they would have to allocate on their machine and reduces the risk of arbitrarily large cookies.

- **Decide whether they accept cookies from all sites or from specific sites/domains only:** Such control permits users to accept cookies from desired sites and eliminates the possibility of accepting cookies from others.
- **Narrow acceptance of cookies for the duration of a specific session:** A finer degree of control at a session level enables users to turn on acceptance of cookies for achieving a particular task. At the end of the session, they revert back to the default of not accepting cookies in future sessions.
- **Require that cookies must originate from the same server as the current page being viewed:** This control ensures that the user is aware of where cookies come from and prevents other sites that may be automatically contacted by the browser from sending cookies. For example, when a browser downloads a container document, embedded images may be fetched automatically. The embedded images may reside on a different server than the one that served the container document.

2.6.4 Privacy problems with cookies

Few topics have caused as much widespread consternation in technology related to the Web as cookies. Cookies are widely used and suspected to aid in the violation of user privacy. To begin with, if the use of cookies is permitted by default in a browser, many users may not even know that they are sending cookies. Cookies are transmitted as *cleartext*—in other words without any encryption applied to them. An eavesdropper program that is capable of intercepting the network traffic can learn the contents of the cookies. It might be possible for the cookie information to be modified as the packet traverses the network. Personal information thus should not be sent in cleartext as part of a cookie unless secure communication can be guaranteed between the client and the processes. Beyond the user's privacy, modification of the cookie value can result in changes on the origin server's side as well. An origin server might use portions of the cookie as an index into a back-end database, and alteration of the cookie can result in inadvertent modification of parts of the database unrelated to the user. Many users are not aware of who has access to their cookie information or what is done with the information. For example, cookie information may be shared between companies, and user profiles may be generated and sold.

The problem is worse when the cookie information is passed by a server different from the origin server to which the request was sent in the first place. Third party gathering of information is a subtle and serious loss of privacy. For example, a user agent, U, downloads a page with embedded images from a server, S. If the embedded images are on a different server, E, then the browser sends requests to server E, which may send cookies. Now, the browser has cookies from both S and E, even though the user never consciously visited server E. The HTTP state management mechanism requires user agents to stop accepting and sending cookies when an *unverifiable* transaction is made; that is, the user is not given an opportunity to review the URL being requested on its behalf. In other words, a request is made for a URL without the user being aware of it, and cookies are received from a site that is not directly visited by the user.

Consider the example of the information-gathering company DoubleClick. Suppose a user submits a search query to a popular search engine and receives ten possible matches for the search string. The URLs for the matches would not be of the form `http://www.foo1.com/foo.html`, `http://www.foo2.com/bar.html`, etc. Instead, they will be of the form:

```
http://ad.doubleclick.net/x26362d2/www.foo1.com/foo.html
```

Now, when the user selects one of the possible matches to the search, the request is sent to the `ad.doubleclick.net` server. The `ad.doubleclick.net` server logs the user's cookie information. The cookie information links two facts: the user who sent the request and the site visited: `www.foo1.com`. The request is then redirected to the `www.foo1.com` server. The redirection is in the form of an HTTP response that instructs the browser to send another request to a different URL. Request redirection happens *transparently* to most users. If different servers that use the services of DoubleClick cooperate and share the cookie information for the same user obtained from DoubleClick, they could construct a broader profile of the user.

The user cannot control how information gleaned from cookies is going to be used. A useful contribution by user agents and origin servers would be to assist the user in providing informed consent before using information about the user. This is known as the *opt-in* model; that is, users explicitly agree to give information about themselves. The alternative *opt-out* scheme, which requires content providers to offer ways for users to exclude themselves from sharing information, generally benefits information-gathering agencies. Such agencies count on the fact that, even when provided with the option of not automatically providing information, most users would not opt out. Reasons for this include inertia and lack of technical savvy in following the necessary instructions.

The basic problem with cookies is that many users are simply unaware of what is being done on their behalf. Even when they know what cookies are, they may not know how to disable cookies or use them selectively. Several sites provide information in detail about the problems with cookies and potential misuse of cookie information. Readers can obtain more information from sources such as [Jun, Muf, Coo].

2.7 Spiders

A spider is a program used to obtain some or all of the resources on a large number of Web sites. One early use of a spider [Fie94] was to help in the maintenance of Web sites. Currently, the resources are gathered and used later in a search application. Thus far we have seen the role browsers play on the Web as the most widely known form of a Web client. Searching on the Web remains one of the most popular applications and was the primary motivation for the creation of the spider tool. We will examine the spider client in detail and discuss how it is used in search engines.

In Chapter 1, we examined the role played by systems preceding and contemporaneous to the Web in aiding users to locate documents of interest on the Internet. These systems had catalogs or virtual directories that served as an index of a collection of documents. Gopher and WAIS additionally had the ability to index documents, though each site had to register its contents with central servers.

2.7.1 Searching on the Web

Systems related to the Web, such as Gopher, were also oriented around searching. The centralized nature of Gopher with its requirements of a global registry enabled comprehensive searching, but maintenance of a central registry hindered its success. From its inception, searching has been a widely used application on the Web. Along with the rapid increase in number of Web sites, users, and pages, there was no scalable technique to force individual users or site owners to link the rapidly growing collection of documents. The decentralized nature of the Web makes it necessary to seek out sites and pages. When a user looks for the occurrence of a string in a small file, it is possible to execute the search on demand. Performing the search on a collection of a few thousand files will require some time. Now, if tens of thousands of files have to be searched and the files are distributed across thousands of machines, the delay to the user is even higher. Finally, if hundreds of thousands of users are searching for strings in tens of millions of documents distributed over millions of machines, the problem is significantly harder. This is the current problem that search engines have to solve.

One way to speed up searching significantly is to have a collection of pointers to positions in documents of occurrences of search strings. Such a collection of pointers is called an *inverted index*. For example, the index at the back of this book is a subset of an inverted index; it points back to the pages where the indexed term appears. The authors have chosen not to list all the words that appear in the book in the index: This would make the index too long and would not be very useful. The index in the book points only to important occurrences of the indexed words, whereas an inverted index typically includes all occurrences of each of the indexed terms. The words that are excluded from indexing are called *stop words*. Examples include frequently occurring words such as "the" and "and." These words are not likely to be used in search strings and occur too frequently in documents. They are thus part of the *stop word* list.

Initially, when the collection of documents on remote sites was small, it was feasible to create a local inverted index on each of the remote sites. However, with the explosive growth of the Web and the inability to require creation of local indices, a few central indices that could be used by millions of users had to be created. The two components needed to aid searching on a large scale are *spiders* and *search engines*. In this section, we examine a spider and see how it is used in conjunction with a search engine.

2.7.2 Spider client

A spider is a key tool for a very popular Web activity: searching. As mentioned earlier, a spider is a program that obtains some or all of the resources on a large number of sites primarily for the purpose of generating an inverted index to be used later in a search application. Like other Web clients, a spider constructs HTTP requests to access resources at a Web site and parses the responses. The primary differences between a spider and a browser are the dramatically higher number of sites contacted and requests sent, the absence of any display of the responses, and the largely singular use of the response.

In practice, however, depending on the application the spider is used for, only a portion of the resources might be obtained. Many spiders, for example, do not fetch image or multimedia resources if the spider is going to be used to construct a searchable index of textual resources only.

Suppose a site `www.kandrse.com` wishes to provide a search engine service similar to the popular search engines `Excite` and `AltaVista`. The site `www.kandrse.com` uses a spider to fetch pages that need to be indexed. A spider typically starts with a base list of popular sites—known as the *start-list*—and follows all of the URLs within the site. One example of a start-list is the list of categories present in popular sites such as Yahoo. The construction of the base list of popular sites and the distribution of the tasks are an interesting technical challenge for spiders.

The spider obtains the starting page of a site (e.g., `http://www.cnn.com/`) and examines all the embedded hypertext references in it. For each of the references, it could fetch the corresponding page–this is a *breadth-wise* traversal. Each of the hypertext links *within* the site (i.e., URLs whose server name components have `cnn.com/` as suffix, such as `http://www.cnn.com/nebraska.html` or `http://www.cnn.com/weatherpage.html`) would be followed and then the links within them and so on. Alternatively, the spider could fetch the first embedded reference and, assuming that the reference is also to an HTML document, parse the document and fetch the first embedded reference (if any).

This is a *depth-wise* traversal. Care is taken to ensure cycles do not result by avoiding traversing a link that has already been fetched. Multiple pages can have embedded reference to the same page, or a page deep in the site hierarchy may have a reference to the top-level page. For example, `http://www.cnn.com/foreign/latvia/riga/opera/2000/schedule.html` may have a reference to `www.cnn.com` in it. A spider may also have other criteria to use in skipping an unwanted page or site; for example, contents of the site are considered unsuitable. Many spiders also decide not to index beyond a certain depth in a site. By a combination of breadth-first and depth-first sweep, the resources in a site are all harvested. The time at which a site was last visited is recorded to be used to decide when to visit it again.

A spider may attempt to fetch all of the resources on a site in one stretch or, in an attempt to be fair, might split its task over a period of time. Otherwise, the origin server on the site might become too loaded with requests from the spider and be unable to handle any of the normal user requests. Several of the prominent spiders on the Web try not to go back to the same site more than once or twice in the same minute. Some spiders may omit copying certain resources back to the search engine site `www.kandrse.com`. For example, if the search engine site intended only to construct an index for textual resources, there would be no need to copy image resources.

Once a site has been indexed, the spider has to revisit the site occasionally because the contents of the site may change. However, the contents of some sites do not change as often as the contents of some other sites. The spider should be intelligent enough to maintain some information on the rate of change of a site in order to reduce the amount of work it must do and to avoid contacting a site needlessly. Also, some parts of a site may change more often than others. A spider would thus have to maintain some intrasite information and examine the changing parts more often.

Whereas static resources may be easily fetched by a spider, dynamic resources typically are not indexed. Several of the resources on a site could be dynamically generated via Common Gateway Interface scripts (or CGI scripts, described in Chapter 4, Section 4.2.3). Scripts often take arguments, and the spider client has no way of knowing what arguments should be used in invoking them. One of the primary uses of indexing a site is to be able to return pages that exist in response to a query. Thus, even if it were possible, there may not be much point in indexing dynamic resources. If a spider labels an entire site to consist mostly of dynamic resources, it may not fetch any of the static pages in the site, including dynamically generated resources that don't change across requests. Occasionally, there are resources at a site that are not reachable by following links from outside. Spiders do not know about the existence of such resources, and they would not be fetched.

A site may not be able to prevent a spider from indexing it. Although many sites have Web pages that would benefit from indexing (many Web page creators want more people to see their pages), some sites may prefer not to be bothered. There are some conventions to help in this regard. There is no foolproof way to ensure that a resource is accessible to other clients but not spiders, because it may be impossible to distinguish between clients visiting a site. Every request that comes from a client is viewed as an independent request, and servers would have to maintain a significant amount of state to keep track of the rate of arrival of requests from specific clients in the hope of detecting a spider. Such mechanisms can still be defeated by spiders that do not send all of their requests from a single IP address or alter the frequency with which they send requests to a particular site. Even when an origin server knows that the client is a spider, it may be hard to provide selective access because the server would have to check each incoming request to see if it is coming from a known spider. Such an action would slow down access to all clients.

There are two conventions that are typically followed by sites in order to have some control over spiders visiting them. Spiders have an incentive to behave well; otherwise, adverse publicity might result for the search engine. The first way is at a site level: The Web site administrator maintains a file called `robots.txt`. Robot is just another word for an automated client (such as a spider), and the `robots.txt` has the access rules to be followed by robots. Web sites administer this file according to the so-called Robot Exclusion Standard [RES]. The file contains a list of directories that spiders should not follow and a specification of user agents to which these restrictions apply.

For example, consider the following `robots.txt` file:

```
User-agent: *
Disallow: /stats
Disallow: /cgi-bin/
Disallow: /Excite/
```

The example indicates that all user agents are permitted to fetch resources from the site for purposes of indexing. If one or more strings (instead of "*") appear in the `User-agent` field, such as:

```
User-agent: ArachnoPhobia, BlackWidow
```

then the two user agents listed would have to recognize that they may not visit the site for purposes of indexing. The Web server does not do any explicit checks or enforcement to deny access.

The `Disallow` lines are used to list directories (`/stats`, `/cgi-bin`, `/Excite`) that should not be traversed by robot programs such as spiders. Again, a server cannot enforce such restrictions. The Robot Exclusion Standard [RES] is a convention for a well-behaved robot to follow. The incentive for robots to adhere to the robot exclusion standard is that sites often know about sets of resources that do not make sense to index. In the above example, the `cgi-bin` direc-

Table 2.4. A small collection of search engines

Search engine	Agent name	Spider host name
AltaVista (normal spider)	Scooter/2.0 G.R.A.B. X2.0 Scooter/1.0 scooter@pa.dec.com	scooter.pa-x.dec.com scooter*.av.pa-x.dec.com
Euroseek	Arachnoidea (arachnoidea@euroseek.com)	*.euroseek.net (infra.euroseek.net)
Excite	ArchitextSpider	crawl*.atext.com
Google	BackRub/2.1	google.com
Inktomi	Slurp/2.0	*.inktomi.com
Infoseek	InfoSeek Sidewinder/0.9	*.infoseek.com
Lycos	Lycos_Spider (T-Rex)	lycosidae.lycos.com
Northern Light	Gulliver/1.2	taz.northernlight.com

tory is likely to consist of a set of resources that, when invoked with different arguments, is likely to return different results.

The second way robots can be told about resources that should not be indexed is via the `Robots` META tag, a feature in HTML. For example, a tag such as

```
<META NAME="ROBOTS" CONTENT="NOINDEX, NOFOLLOW">
```

informs the robot that the current resource should not be indexed *and* none of the links in the resource should be followed. In parsing the HTML document, spiders would notice the META tag and examine the CONTENT field to recognize that they are not supposed to index this document or to follow the links in it.

Table 2.4 shows a list of known spiders [Spi] used by some of the popular search engines. The first column is the name of the search engine, the second column is the name assigned to the spider tool, and the third column is the machine from which the spider originates. The information is provided in the form of identification that a Web site can use to ensure that a spider is not accessing the site too frequently. Most of the recognized spiders obey the Robot Exclusion Standard. Key differentiators between spiders include the total number of sites visited, total number of resources fetched, and frequency with which they span the Web. Several spiders are now capable of fetching over a billion Web pages and making them available for purposes of searching. A comparison of the effectiveness of the various search engines has been reported in [LG99]. Most companies do not reveal much information about their spiders because there is intense competition across search engines. A scalable Web crawler along with the design tradeoffs is discussed in [HN99].

2.7.3 Use of spiders in search engines

Spiders aid search engines gather pages from many Web sites. Depending on the sophistication of the spider, the size of the start-list, and the amount of storage space available, an inverted index can be created of all or some of the pages. Sophisticated algorithms for constructing indices of large sets of documents have been created in the last 20 years [WMB99].

Search engine sites are among the most popular destinations on the Web. *Portal* sites, such as yahoo.com, excite.com, and altavista.com are entry points to a variety of applications and have pointers to several information sources. Portal sites are discussed in more depth in Chapter 4, Section 4.1. Almost all portal sites have a search interface. A search engine provides a simple interface to the user to input one or more keywords (known as *search terms*). The keywords are looked up in the index, and the pointers to the documents (if any) containing them are returned. The searching can be local to a single database (e.g., electronic newsgroups and stock market reports) or the indexed contents of the Web. Many users spend a considerable amount of time searching. Part of the reason is the lack of a good index on the Web. Among the most popular sites is Yahoo!, which indexes sites but not contents of all the pages. In other words, only base pages of sites (the first page visited at a site) are gathered for purposes of indexing. Search sites such as AltaVista and Google index individual pages inside Web sites. Thus sites such as Yahoo! can be used to find general information about a topic at a coarser level of granularity, whereas AltaVista and Google give more results as a result of the indexing of all strings in documents.

The list of returned documents (or pointers to the documents) is known as the result set. Search engines vary in sophistication. Most search engines provide the simple search feature in which one or more terms are looked up in the index and pointers to documents that match *any* of the keywords are returned. The presence of multiple keywords is interpreted as a request for executing the Boolean *or* operation. The Google [Goo] search engine provides a single interface to users: The search terms are combined using the Boolean operator *and*, with the semantics that only documents containing *all* the terms are returned as a match. The advanced search version of the AltaVista [Alt] search engine and its variant Raging [Rag] has a more sophisticated interface: Users can use any combination of *and*, *or*, *not*, or *near* operators. The *not* is simply a unary negation, and documents containing the search term are eliminated from the result set. The *near* Boolean operator is used to see if the keywords occur within a few (often a few hundred) words of each other within a document. By sophisticated combination of the various operators, it is possible to obtain a result set with fewer and more tailored matches.

The two basic ideas in search engines that have directly descended from decades of research in the Information Retrieval community are *recall* and *pre-*

cision. Recall is a measure of the breadth of the search set: How large is the result set as a function of the total list of documents where the search terms have appeared. If the recall is high, users can be confident that they have received a more complete answer. Unfortunately, given the inherent ambiguity of natural languages, most of the "answers" in the result set are not relevant to the user.

For example, suppose a user is interested in determining the name of the architect of the Parthenon temple in Greece. The search string "architect parthenon" might result in a lot of pages having to do with the Parthenon book publishing company, Greek diners whose name is Parthenon, and software and hardware architects. A measure of the quality of answer is *precision*—the relevance of the documents in the search set. Often recall and precision are mutually exclusive: Returning fewer documents may increase precision, but recall may be lowered. Likewise, a broader set of results lowers the overall precision. The tension between precision and recall remains largely unsolved, and many search engines have spent a lot of effort trying to increase relevance while still returning a large set of matches. The complexity of natural language queries and lack of sophisticated queries lead to poor query results. A vast majority of queries—currently, around 90%—to the popular search engines such as AltaVista or Google consists of a single term.

After performing the search and locating all the documents where the search string appeared and filtering for recall and precision to decide the size of the result set, the search engine has to *rank* the results. Ranking is the order in which search results are returned. If the size of the result set for the search string "architect parthenon" was 823, some search engines may just return the "top" 200 matches. However, deciding the top 200 requires ranking of the entries in the result set. Ranking by frequency of occurrences of the search string in the matched document is not necessarily a good metric. Depending on the frequency of occurrences of search strings is a risk because some document creators deliberately fill their documents with terms known as "query traps." For example, because there is a considerable number of searches for pornographic material (not a widely discussed topic in scientific literature), creators of such Web pages add likely search terms multiple times to the pages. It is relatively straightforward to make these terms invisible in the rendered HTML document simply by setting their font size to be zero or the foreground and background colors of the terms to be black. In other words, these terms exist solely for the consumption of search engine's ranking software. The smarter search engines have been reducing the value of frequency of occurrence of terms as a ranking metric. Although ranking is a well-understood concept in the information retrieval field, studies have shown that most users examine only a few of the items in the result set. In fact, most of the popular search engines return 10 results at a time, and, even though hundreds of matches are available for examination, most users typically don't get past the second page of results; that is, at most

20 choices are examined. The popular search engine Google permits users to go directly to the first ranked result, bypassing the intermediate search results page.

Recently, some new research ideas have been incorporated into search engines. For example, search engines such as Google and Clever [Cle] use the notion of *authoritative* Web pages in conjunction with page ranking to improve relevancy of results. Many users believe that the New York Times newspaper Web site is a useful site and add links to that site from their own pages. The number of links to a page is an indicator of both its popularity and to some degree the trust that users had about the usefulness of the page. If the set of pages could be ranked on the basis of the number of links pointing to it, then highly ranked pages could be returned in the first set of matches to a search query. Such relevancy and authoritative ranking basically takes advantage of the implicitly expressed notion of reliability of a page by other users. The individual rankings of many users are collected by the spiders and used to rank search results. This has the potential to significantly increase the relevancy of a search result because most people do not create links to utterly useless sites. Site-categorization programs use specific characteristics of sites, such as a large number of small images and presence of certain keywords. Search engines can distinguish between the sites and return higher-quality search results. The actual search terms used in searches can be used to examine what is sought by users. For example, the user's name is the most often issued search keyword while searching for a user's home page. Thus when a search term that seems like a user's name is entered, a suitable ranking of pages that matched it might have the user's home page (if it exists) at the top.

The time interval between a spider fetching a document and a search engine indexing and returning it as a match for a search term can vary across search engines. Typically it can be anywhere from one to two weeks. If the document changes meanwhile, the search term may no longer be present in the document when the user initiates the search. Worse yet, the document may be removed from the site. The Web site may not be accessible at the time of the search. In fact, recognizing this to be a commonly occurring phenomenon, some search engines have begun to cache copies of the search results at the time of indexing. The dissatisfied user could at least see the version of the document that existed at the time of indexing. Often only the HTML text is cached, and the embedded images are ignored. A search engine may have to be concerned about potential copyright violations.

The spider is a busy client in terms of frequency and number of requests. It plays an important role in one of the most popular applications on the Web—searching. Improving the behavior and efficiency of a spider can have a significant impact on the Web.

2.8 Intelligent Agents and Special-purpose Browsers

Once search engines became widely available, the natural evolution was to have programs initiate searches on behalf of users. Users could express their preferences of search engines and rank ordering in a profile. Such programs, called *agents,* would execute searches, collate results, and present them in a manner tailored to fit a user's profile. The interface between the user and search agents is distinct from the interface between a user and a browser.

In this section, we examine

- **Intelligent agents:** These agents have been created for specific client tasks, such as searching, participating in auctions, and so on.
- **Special-purpose browsers:** These browsers are created to enable cooperating users to learn from or to permit joint browsing.

2.8.1 Intelligent agents

An intelligent agent works on behalf of users and attempts to provide an efficient service for different groups of users. We examine two kinds of intelligent agents:

- A meta-search engine, which trigger searches on multiple search engines
- An auction agent, which performs bidding function on behalf of a user

META-SEARCH ENGINE

A meta-search engine sends a user-specified search string to several popular search engines. The results are either concatenated together or grouped based on the search engine. A meta-search engine lets the user decide between the various ranking algorithms of the individual search engines, as well as their capabilities. The agent could filter out inaccessible sites returned in search results or unavailable pages on accessible sites. At a glance a user can see the common results across the search engines. A user might select a search result if it was ranked highly on more than one search engine. By its nature, a meta-search engine has to wait for responses from several search engines, adding to the overall delay. Additionally, extra load is placed on the network in sending requests to multiple search engines. Meta-search engines have not attained the popularity levels of ordinary search engines. Users tend to stick to search engines they are used to rather than sorting through the different search engine results, each with its own ranking criteria.

The agent could proactively fetch the pages and present the result not in terms of pointers to information but actual contents. Agents could continue searching offline and locate new pages that are created after the original search terms were specified. The information gathered could be made available to the user later via e-mail or be gathered for the next interactive session.

Meta-search engines and other search agents send normal HTTP requests like any other client except that the requests are focused queries, on behalf of one or more users, and to a specific collection of origin servers. Such agents can specialize their connection to these origin servers and learn to parse the responses. The agent software is narrower than that of a browser but must still implement the basic capabilities of a Web client.

AUCTION AGENTS

A search agent performs actions on behalf of a user in a very directed and narrow way. A search agent executes queries, gathers results and possibly filters them. However, some applications require additional intelligence and alternative actions—agents could actually *act* on behalf of the users, for example, by bidding at electronic auction sites. Auction sites permit users to make bids and wait to see if the bid is accepted at the time the auction closes. In between, others may submit bids, and this might require the user to make a higher bid if still interested in the item being auctioned. Because the user could not be expected to be available to react on a continuous basis and remember when the bidding time expires, it would be useful to have an *auction agent* performing the task on the user's behalf. An auction agent does not blindly execute canned commands but *reacts* to responses and takes additional actions. The user could specify thresholds of how high the agent should bid. It should be noted that such tools are not widely deployed.

Like a search agent, an auction agent sends tailored HTTP client requests to the auction sites and parses the response. The agent can quickly react based on the response and the user's constraints on making additional bids. The Web-client portion of an auction agent software is simple, whereas the back-end work of parsing the response and deciding on how to react is more complex.

2.8.2 Special-purpose browsers

A special-purpose browser is a version of a browser modified for a specific application. We examine three kinds of special-purpose browsers:

- **Co-browser:** A browser that helps a user by proactively requesting relevant resources in advance
- **Collaborative browser:** An extension of co-browser that lets a group of users browse in a collaborative fashion
- **Offline browser:** A browser that enables a user to browse offline a collection of pages that were downloaded earlier

CO-BROWSER

A co-browser is a helper program that selectively requests other related resources when a particular resource is requested. This is done under the assumption that a user who requested a particular resource might also be interested in the other resources. The program is responsible for knowing what resources might be related and creating links between related resources. A static form of creating this is a collection of links listed together with a specific resource. A dynamic form is for the co-browser to aggressively download the related resources and present them to the user. An example of a co-browser is the Letizia system [Lie95], which proactively downloads the resources identified by the links on a page under the assumption that the user is likely to select one of them next. In Chapter 13 (Section 13.3), we will examine prefetching at a broader level.

COLLABORATIVE BROWSER

An agent can work on behalf of multiple users. In a collaborative context, where several users are working on a single task, an agent can be employed to aid in the collaboration. A collaborative agent can watch multiple users and attempt to match users with similar interests. For example, if a user reads a particular electronic bulletin board and expresses interest in a small group of musical artists, then the agent can put the user in touch with others who have similar tastes. Such collaborative filtering has become common on the Web. Some popular Web sites inform customers who purchased a product about related products, based on the purchasing patterns of other users. An agent is watching the purchase patterns of users, and, when a pattern is detected (i.e., matched), the user is notified of other books purchased by similar users.

A collaborative browser agent lets multiple users browse together. The Let's Browse system [LDV99] is an extension to the co-browser Letizia mentioned earlier. A group of people can browse jointly, learning from each other's accesses. The system can recommend information about one user's access to the others in the group. Once a set of links in a document are prefetched, the links can be selectively filtered on the basis of what links others in the group are following.

OFFLINE BROWSER

The offline browser is a program that is capable of downloading the complete contents of one or more sites either on demand or on a periodic basis. Offline browsers have the advantage of bundling several targeted requests into a single series of requests and copying responses to a user's laptop for browsing the site later, when the user is disconnected from the network. Offline browsers typically work by starting from the given site's URL and acting like a spider, except that all the links followed are inside the site. For example, if the site `www.site.com` has to be gathered to browse later, the limited spider will follow all the embedded references in `www.site.com` but ensure that all the URLs have the prefix `www.site.com`. If a link leads to `www.offsite.com`, then that link would be ignored. By following in a depth-first and breadth-first manner, all the linked contents of `www.site.com` can be captured. The site can be reconstructed on the client's side with all the URLs renamed to ensure that the client can browse the site locally. Because the entire contents of the site have been copied to the client's disk, all the Web links can be renamed into static file links. Now, when the user browses the site offline, the files can serve as the cached copy of the resources without the need for any revalidation of resources against an origin server.

2.9 Summary

A client is a general-purpose piece of software, and the browser is the most popular version of it in practice. The various manifestations of a client differ in the principles that govern them and how they are used in practice. Being close to the user, a client has to meet all the security needs of the user and reduce the risk of any potential loss of privacy.

A browser fetches and renders resources on behalf of users. A browser is a graphical user interface for the entire Web, and this aspect alone was responsible for making it an extremely popular piece of software. Currently, only two versions of a Web browser are used widely: Netscape's Navigator and Microsoft's Internet Explorer.

The Web is decentralized and changing constantly, with no central database of URLs or the associated contents. Spiders help in gathering the pages and assist in searching. The principle behind the most popular operation on the Web is one of periodic crawling for resources, leading to selective fetching, followed by generation of a reverse index. Spiders provide resource access to users with one level of separation. Because there is a time lag between the time search engines trigger a spider and a user searches for those resources, a spider can succeed only in providing a pointer to the resource at the time it was fetched by the spider. Semantic accuracy of the current version of the resource cannot be guaranteed—the user's search string may no longer be present in the current version of the resource. All the popular search engines such as `www.altavista.com` and `www.google.com` use spiders to keep their index current.

Agents operate on the basis of prespecified constraints and send fewer requests than spiders. The more focused nature of an agent's behavior differs from that of a spider, which uses a more scattershot approach. There are several popular agents in daily use on the Web, for example, auction agents and purchasing agents.

3

Web Proxies

A traditional client/server communication model involves transferring requests from clients to servers and responses back to clients. There are no intermediaries in the path between the client and server. In the case of the Web, users, via user agents, would send requests to origin servers, and the responses would be returned directly to the browsers. The presence of an intermediary could help either side by reducing unwanted communication. For example, the intermediary might have a cache associated with it and deliver the response to the client without involving the origin server. The latency perceived by the client is lowered if the intermediary is closer to the client. The load on the network is reduced because the message has to travel a shorter distance. At the same time, the intermediary lowers the load on the server, which now has to deal with fewer messages. An intermediary could be a program on the same machine or on a machine different from where the request originates.

The notion of an intermediary exists in other protocols that were popular around the time of creation of the Web. For example, the File Transfer Protocol (FTP) and Network News Transfer Protocol (NNTP) have *proxies*—programs that act on behalf of a set of clients in communicating with servers. These proxies help offload work that must be done by servers.

In this chapter, we examine the role played by Web proxies, beginning from their humble origins to the important role they play now as a result of the explosion in Web traffic. A proxy acts as a server to clients and as a client to other proxies or origin servers. A primary role played by a proxy is that of a front end to many clients in their interaction with origin servers. As a front end, proxies enable sharing of access and provide a degree of anonymity to the clients. Proxies can be present at various places along the path of the message between clients and origin servers. They can be close to the client, close to the origin server, or somewhere in between. The presence of proxies has implications in terms of the number of Web components the messages have to travel through. Being in the path of requests and responses, proxies can act as filters and decide which requests should actually be forwarded and the responses that should be returned to clients. Proxies may modify the requests and responses that flow through them. For example, proxies can convert a client's Web request and forward it to an FTP server and return the response to the client via a regular HTTP response.

We begin by examining the history and evolution of intermediaries. The set of intermediaries examined is proxies, gateways, and tunnels. Proxies are the primary intermediary considered in this book; therefore we restrict our attention to proxies in the rest of this chapter. Next a high-level classification of the proxies used in practice is examined. The range of applications that proxies are used for includes enabling of sharing of resource access, caching of responses, and transformations and filtering of requests and responses. After this broad look at proxy application, we narrow our examination to a proxy's role as it relates to the HTTP protocol. These roles include handling HTTP requests and responses and the specific tasks of a proxy when it acts as a server and as a client. Multiple proxies can be present in the path between a client and an origin server, so next we examine how proxies are linked. The linking can be linear—a series of proxies each chained to the next. A group of proxies can also be jointly linked to a single higher-level proxy, which can be linked further to other proxies. We then discuss how clients can configure their access to proxies. The important role of a proxy in handling security and privacy issues is examined. More recently, nontraditional proxies, such as interception and reverse proxies, have become popular on the Web. We examine such proxies to distinguish them from traditional Web proxies. We conclude with a look at the principles behind proxies and their use in practice.

3.1 History and Evolution of Intermediaries

Although Web messages were initially transmitted directly between user agents and origin servers, intermediaries quickly became part of the picture. Three of the most common intermediaries are proxies, gateways, and tunnels. We examine the evolution of these intermediaries in this section.

Proxies began to play an increasingly important role as early as 1994. The growing popularity of the Web necessitated their role. The first draft document that described the syntax for Uniform Resource Identifiers (URI) [BL94] mentioned the role of a proxy as a *gateway,* that is, an HTTP server, through which request messages pass and may be translated into another protocol. Many organizations were not permitted to access the Internet directly for security reasons. Instead all their communication was routed through a *firewall* [BC95], a machine that performed the role of a security gatekeeper. Traffic to and from destinations that are considered insecure is filtered by the firewall. Because all traffic to and from the Internet went through a firewall, the firewall became a natural place for performing proxy functions. The original purpose of a Web proxy was to provide access to the Web for clients who are behind an organizational firewall [LA94]. The first stated design goal for a proxy was to ensure that clients did not lose any functionality by having their requests and responses routed through a firewall. The original Web proxy was actually a version of a gateway server [LA94] at the CERN laboratory, the site where the world's first Web server was created. A proxy's role in information hiding and encapsulation is described in detail in [Sha86].

The first draft document [BLFN95] outlining the HTTP/1.0 version of the protocol discussed the role of proxies as a communication intermediary to various other protocols, such as the Simple Mail Transfer Protocol (SMTP) [Pos82], NNTP [KL86], FTP [PR85], Gopher [AML+93], and WAIS [PFG+94]. These other protocols are the basis of popular systems such as e-mail, news, file transfer, and so on. The HTTP/1.0 draft document [BLFN95] also provided the first formal definition of a proxy:

> An intermediary program which acts as both a server and a client for the purpose of forwarding requests. Proxies are often used to act as a portal through a network firewall. A proxy server accepts requests from other clients and services them either internally or by passing them (with possible translation) on to other servers.

This definition largely remains as the definition in the latest HTTP Draft Standard specification. We use the same definition in this book.

Thus proxies began as gateway servers and have now become an integral part of a user's experience on the Web. A request from a client may terminate at a proxy if the proxy has a cache associated with it and the response is in the cache. Otherwise the request will be forwarded to another server, which may or may not be the final server that actually responds to the client's request. Figure 3.1 demonstrates a proxy playing the role of client and server. The figure shows client 1's request for resource B being forwarded by the proxy to server 1 and the response returned to the client. This response is not cached. The request from client 2 for resource A is forwarded to server 2, but the response is cached in the proxy and returned to the client. Now, when client 3 requests resource A, the request is not forwarded by the proxy; instead a cached copy of resource A is returned to client 3.

A proxy is not the only intermediary between a sender and a receiver of an HTTP message. A gateway is a server that typically acts as an intermediary for a non-HTTP server such as a mail or FTP server. In forwarding a message to a non-HTTP server, a gateway translates the HTTP request into the protocol of the other service. The response is returned to the gateway, which then forwards the response to the original sender after suitable translation. However, a difference exists between a proxy and a gateway. In the case of a proxy, the sender may be aware that the proxy could either respond to the request itself or forward the request. A gateway presents a different facade to the sender. As far as the sender is concerned, the gateway acts as the origin server. The

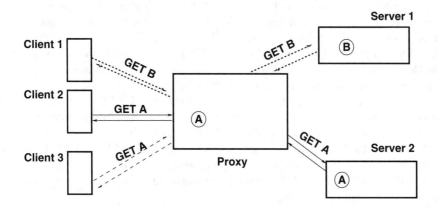

Figure 3.1. Proxy as an intermediary between a client and an origin server

requesting client is not necessarily aware that a gateway has interposed itself in the middle of the path. A gateway to another service such as mail or news must take the incoming request and encode it in the format necessary for the service to which the request is being forwarded.

A *tunnel* is an intermediary that relays bits between two connections. A tunnel acts at the syntactic level, unlike a proxy or a gateway; it does not parse or interpret the HTTP message flowing through it beyond the request line (the first line of an HTTP message) to locate the host to be contacted. A tunnel becomes active at the beginning of the communication, and, once it is active, it is no longer viewed as part of the HTTP communication. It functions as a relay between the connections. Once active, it is not considered part of the communication because it does not examine, create, or alter the content being transmitted. Tunnels do not cache responses, whereas gateways and proxies are capable of doing so. More important, unlike a proxy or a gateway, the lifetime of a tunnel is equal to the lifetime of the communication between the ends of the connection. If the two ends of the connection are closed, then the tunnel no longer exists.

Chapter 7 (Section 7.5) discusses the concept of persistent connections, whereby an HTTP connection lasts beyond a single request-response transaction. Proxies, gateways, and tunnels all play a role in maintaining a persistent connection between a client and a server if they are present in the middle of the transaction. All intermediaries must follow rules about forwarding headers of HTTP messages. Proxies and gateways also are required not to pass certain identification information (e.g., host names) when they are used as a conduit to transmit a message through a network firewall. Similarly, the most recent version of the HTTP protocol, HTTP/1.1, requires that gateways and proxies identify themselves when they are part of an HTTP transaction. Intermediaries must be careful about altering the body of the message. For example, the message might include an end-to-end integrity check, such as a checksum, that may be affected if the message body is altered.

Although there are three broad categories of intermediaries, we confine our discussion to proxies both in this chapter and in the rest of the book. A proxy is the primary intermediary on the Web with widespread deployment. Gateways and tunnels are relatively minor Web components.

3.2 High-level Classification of Proxies

There are two key operational axes on which proxies can be divided. First, some proxies have caches associated with them, whereas others do not. Second, independent of caching, some proxies modify messages as they flow through them, whereas others do not.

3.2.1 Caching proxy

The distinction between a regular proxy and a caching proxy is an important one. A regular proxy simply forwards requests and responses. A caching proxy, on the other hand, is capable of maintaining a private store of responses received in the past. When the proxy receives a request that can be satisfied by a cached response, the request message is not forwarded and the response is returned directly by the proxy. Certain conditions must be met before a cached response can be returned, as we will see later in this chapter. We use the term *caching proxy* to identify a proxy that normally has a cache associated with it.

3.2.2 Transparent proxy

In terms of forwarding messages, there are two kinds of proxies: transparent and non-transparent. The difference between them has to do with modification of the messages that flow through a proxy. A *transparent* proxy does not modify the request or response in anything more than a superficial manner. An example of a superficial change to a message by a transparent proxy is the addition of identification information about itself or the server from which the message was received. Such identification might even be required by the HTTP protocol. In Section 3.8 we discuss the improper use of the term transparent proxy in some sectors of the Web industry to refer to the more appropriately named interception proxies.

A *non-transparent* proxy, on the other hand, can modify the request and/or response. An example of a typical change to a request is anonymization, by which information about a proxy's client is obscured. An example of a change to a response is a media type transformation—an image is converted from one format to another to reduce the response size. Another example of a nontransparent proxy is one that translates a document from one natural language to another. There are rules that are common to both kinds of proxies, although some specific rules are associated with each kind of proxy. For example, a transparent proxy must ensure that the length of an entity in the message does not change as the message moves through the proxy. Note that transparent and non-transparent proxies are distinct from gateways and tunnels. Both kinds of proxies can have a cache associated with them, unlike tunnels. Both kinds of proxies act as intermediaries between a Web client and a Web server; that is, messages exchanged are in HTTP.

3.3 Proxy Applications

We now examine the various uses of a proxy apart from letting clients access resources on the Web. These include sharing of various resources, caching, anonymization, transformation of requests and/or responses, and, finally, filtering requests/responses.

3.3.1 Sharing access to the Web

A proxy acts as a front end to a group of clients and enables them to share access to the Web. Clients share connectivity through the proxy to the Internet and may also share resources. If many clients request the same resource from an origin server, a single connection could be established between the proxy and the origin server. The alternative would require establishing separate connections between the various clients and the origin server, adding to the load on the origin server. However, if requests to *different* resources are made, a proxy could serialize them. If there is a delay in obtaining a response for the first request, the second request would be delayed. Each of the connections between a client and the proxy is in some sense a *local* connection (short network distance), and the longer path between the proxy and the origin server is shared by all the clients. The requests and responses that are distinct across clients thus travel a short distance, whereas the common requests/responses across clients share the longer path between the proxy and the origin server.

Many Internet Service Providers (ISP) and corporations mandate users to go through proxies to access the Web. Although some users may learn ways of bypassing proxies and may be permitted to do so, most of the users of popular ISPs and content providers (such as America Online) often go through proxies. Several of these proxies are caching proxies.

3.3.2 Caching responses

One of the primary purposes of many proxies is caching. Caching is the storing of a response obtained earlier for later use, when clients request the same resource. The cache returns the response if it believes the response is still *fresh* (i.e., the origin server would have approved the response to be returned). Caching is explained in significant detail in Chapter 11. The caching function of a proxy is optional; that is, a proxy performs the role of a cache in addition to its role as a server to the clients behind it and as client to the origin servers. Many proxies on the Internet play the role of a noncaching proxy. Not all clients will benefit from a caching proxy in their path. For example, if a client is a spider, it might not make sense to route the requests through the proxy cache. The spider's access patterns are not likely to resemble those of ordinary clients. Many of the responses are not likely to be accessed again by a proxy's clients. Given that most proxies have a limited amount of disk space for caching responses, they can avoid caching the responses of requests made by spiders.

3.3.3 Anonymizing clients

A proxy plays an important role in anonymizing the various clients behind it. When a Web request is relayed through a proxy to the origin server, the origin server thinks that the proxy is the requesting client. When the origin server tries to identify the name of the machine from which it received a request, it finds the proxy instead of the client behind the proxy. Given that there could be hundreds of client machines behind a proxy, an origin server would not be able to distinguish the access patterns of any particular client. Anonymizing accesses might be very important to certain clients. Some users may be accessing sites that contain sensitive information (e.g., related to health matters) and may not want to reveal their identities. Of course, the proxy knows which client is accessing the resource, but no one else would know this unless the proxy released the information. Typically, the organization associated with the client machines has control over the proxy. An ISP may provide privacy guarantees against revealing information about individual clients' access patterns.

Some proxies can be configured explicitly not to provide anonymity and add a header indicating the client on behalf of whom the message was forwarded. In general, although proxies provide a level of anonymity, at least two potential pieces of information present in a request can reduce the user's anonymity:

- The first piece of information is the `User-Agent` header present in requests, which identifies the user's browser version and possibly the operating system version of the user's machine as well.

- The second piece of information is the state maintained across requests by
  the same client. The state is often stored in cookies (discussed in Chapter 2,
  Section 2.6) or in other session identifier fields explicitly set by the origin
  server. A proxy funnels requests of many users and thus introduces a degree
  of anonymity for them. The origin servers do not know the client machine's
  IP address because the request came via the proxy. Although cookies do
  not necessarily reveal the identity of the user, they remove the aggregate
  anonymity provided by the proxy.

With such information, an origin server can easily keep track of individual
users, even when they are behind proxies. If other information about the user
is also available to the origin server, the origin server can easily link that with
the cookie information to identify the user uniquely.

3.3.4 Transforming requests and responses

A proxy may just modify the request or the response and in several cases both
the request and the response. Clients can inform the proxy of their preferences
and the capabilities of their individual machines or connectivity. A proxy could
attempt to tailor the response to the capabilities of the particular client. For
example, a user behind a low-bandwidth connection might want to obtain responses that are compressed to speed up the transfer. The proxy's modification
is selective; often on a per-request and per-response basis.

A proxy might also transform a request independent of a client's capability. A proxy could include information in the request indicating its different
capability. For example, a proxy and an origin server might have the ability to
handle a particular compression algorithm that significantly reduces the size of
the request or response body. The client is not involved in this part of the message exchange, and the client's lack of support for the compression algorithm
does not deter the proxy and the server from using the bandwidth more efficiently. Likewise, a proxy and the origin server might be running a more recent
version of HTTP with additional capabilities. Thus a proxy might be able to
encode the request or handle a response in a better format. The transformation
should not affect the semantics of the request or response.

3.3.5 Gateway to non-HTTP systems

A proxy can also play the role of an intermediary to other systems that do not
communicate using HTTP. The Web was designed with the goal of providing
seamless access to resources across the Internet. It is important that a proxy,
as a Web component, participate in facilitating such access. For example, a
proxy can act as an intermediary between a Web client and an FTP server. A
proxy can act as it does in the case of a Web intermediary; the client's request
is forwarded to the server and the response is sent back to the client. However,

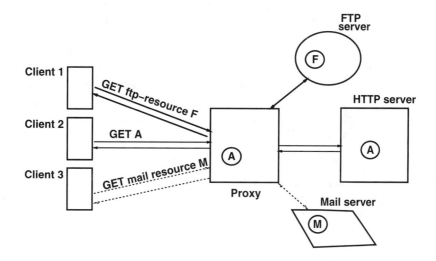

Figure 3.2. Proxy acting as a gateway to FTP, HTTP, and mail servers

because the Web client and the FTP server do not speak the same protocol, the proxy must translate the client's HTTP request into an FTP request and reformat the FTP server's response as an HTTP response. Thus the proxy is playing the role of a gateway. The absence of information on content type in responses from other protocols (such as FTP) may make such tasks difficult.

For example, suppose a Web client sends a request to an FTP server by requesting `ftp://ftp.research.att.com/F` via a proxy. The request to the proxy is a regular HTTP request. The proxy first converts the Web client's request into an FTP request, which might translate into issuing a series of FTP commands. For some protocols, request conversion could simply involve wrapping the HTTP request inside other headers. However, in the case of FTP, the proxy would first have to establish an FTP connection by acting as an FTP client. Unlike HTTP, FTP uses a separate data and control channel to communicate between the client and the server, as explained in more detail in Chapter 5 (Section 5.4.2). Thus the proxy would have to open a control channel to authorize itself and then use the data channel to transfer the contents of the file F requested by the Web client. Similarly, a proxy can act as a gateway to a mail server and obtain a mail resource M. Figure 3.2 shows how a proxy acts as a gateway to an FTP and mail server while also playing the role of an HTTP proxy.

From the Web client's viewpoint, a Web request was issued for `ftp://ftp.research.att.com/F`, and the resource (`/F`) is returned. The steps of an

FTP request process—setting up a connection, authorizing oneself, sending the sequence of commands, and closing the connection—are all performed by the proxy. The proxy would return the file to the Web client in the form of an HTTP response with appropriate response code and HTTP response headers.

At times, a proxy may have to play the role of a passive intermediary. For example, in handling secure communication on top of the Secure Socket Layer (SSL), a proxy simply acts as a tunnel. SSL performs end-to-end encryption of the contents of the message. A proxy ferries the bits in both directions. An application-level program such as a proxy might violate the expectation of privacy promised by SSL. Even if the proxy were able to see just the URL, enough information may be encoded in it to reduce the privacy of the communication. In fact, about all a proxy on top of SSL would be able to see is the target server and port number. The ability to function as a tunnel makes a proxy applicable to a broader set of circumstances. Details on SSL are provided in Chapter 6 (Section 6.4).

3.3.6 Filtering requests and responses

A proxy performs the role of a gatekeeper by filtering improper requests and responses. A proxy can assist in filtering certain requests based on destination sites and filter responses based on characteristics such as response size. An organization may have rules against users visiting a set of sites considered to be unsuitable, such as diversion sites (e.g., comics, games, puzzles, or pornographic sites), auction sites, and job search sites. A proxy could compare each request against a list of sites that an organization has deemed unsuitable and refuse to service those requests, instead sending back an error message. The comparison may not be done against the complete URL (e.g., `http://www.unitedmedia.com/dilbert`), but just against the server-name part of the URL (`www.unitedmedia.com`). There are obvious risks in filtering aggressively. There actually may be genuine reasons for someone in the organization to visit such sites. Either such clients could bypass a proxy or the proxy could permit access based on the IP addresses of certain special clients. The proxy is specialized software, and therefore it can be configured in a flexible way. Many of the well-known products (e.g., Netnanny, SurfWatch, etc.) that filter requests to sites deemed unsuitable to minors match the requested URL against a set of patterns. Another reason for a proxy to filter requests to a site may be that the responses from that site typically consume more resources. By limiting the set of sites that clients can access, a proxy might actually improve the performance for other clients.

Request filtering based on the URL is just one example of filtering. Another example is filtering requests to search engines when certain keywords appear in the search string. This requires the proxy to check first if the site being contacted is a search engine and then to match the search argument against a set of search strings deemed to be inappropriate. Other examples of request filtering include removing certain headers in the Web request that would reveal the identity of the client, such as the user's e-mail address. As we will see later, in Chapter 7, the HTTP protocol standard specifies the rules for proxies to remove or alter headers in a request message.

In filtering responses, a proxy typically removes certain responses containing data in questionable media formats. If some viruses are typically transmitted using certain media types, then the proxy can pay more attention to responses in such formats. The proxy could check such responses for viruses before returning the response to the client. Apart from the typical text and image resources, programs are often returned as responses on the Web. Examples are Java applets or JavaScript. A sophisticated proxy could perform extensive checks on such programs to ensure that they are not likely to cause security risks. Another criterion might be the size of the response. Suppose that a proxy is aware that the client is behind a low-bandwidth connection and the response exceeds a certain length threshold. The proxy might want to alter the format (e.g., compress the response) before forwarding it to the client.

3.4 HTTP-related Proxy Roles

In this section, we examine the roles played by a proxy in handling HTTP requests and responses. We begin by seeing the various steps involved when a proxy is present in the path of a request from a browser to an origin server. Then we see how a proxy handles HTTP requests and responses. Third, we explore the specific tasks of a proxy as a Web server. Fourth, we examine a proxy's role as a Web client distinct from that of sending requests to an origin server on behalf of clients. Finally, we look at an example use of a proxy.

3.4.1 Steps in request-response exchange with a proxy

Figure 3.3 shows the steps involved when a proxy is present in the path between the client and origin server. This is a modified version of the example shown in Figure 2.1 (Chapter 2, Section 2.3).

Upon a user's selection of a URL, the browser does the Domain Name System (DNS) lookup of the proxy that it has been configured with and then sets up a TCP connection to the proxy (steps 1 and 2). The HTTP request from the browser (step 3) triggers the proxy to do the DNS lookup of the origin server (step 4). Technically, the browser and proxy may use different DNS servers for their respective lookups. The proxy sets up a TCP connection to the origin server and then sends the HTTP request to the origin server (steps 5 and 6). The response from the origin server is sent back to the proxy, which forwards it to the browser (steps 7 and 8). At this stage, the browser might set up optional

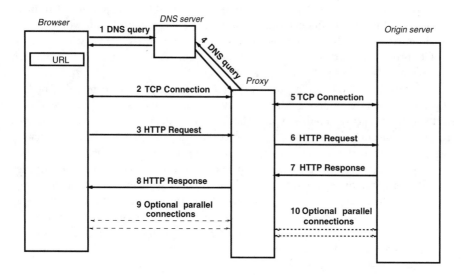

Figure 3.3. Steps in a browser process with proxy in the path

parallel connections to the proxy, and the proxy may set up its own optional parallel connections to the origin server (steps 9 and 10).

3.4.2 Handling HTTP requests and responses

Because a proxy is a key component in Web transactions, the rules of the HTTP protocol govern proxies. In Chapter 7 (Section 7.11), we discuss the specific rules governing the behavior of a proxy. Broadly speaking, a proxy must be able to abide by several syntactic and semantic requirements. The syntactic requirements typically concern headers that a proxy adds to messages and modifications of existing headers. The semantic requirements include proper handling of requests and responses and obeying the constraints on returning cached responses.

A proxy will forward any HTTP message headers that it does not understand, unless some protocol mechanisms are used to prevent it. A proxy may also add or modify headers in the request or response. The various requirements fall into the following categories:

Identification A proxy can identify itself in a header field so that other components in the request-response chain know that the message went through the proxy. In the later version of the protocol (HTTP/1.1), all proxies are obligated to identify themselves. One of the motivations for this is to be able to identify potential loops in the path.

Version number change   A proxy can change the request line (the first line of an HTTP request message), which includes the request method, URI, and version number. For example,

```
GET /foo/bar.html HTTP/1.0
```

sent by a client might be changed by an HTTP/1.1 proxy to

```
GET /foo/bar.html HTTP/1.1
```

before the message is forwarded. A proxy can apply the improvements in HTTP/1.1 (discussed in Chapter 7) to the message path between the proxy and the origin server even though the client is running an older version of the protocol. If a message is received at a proxy from a sender running a newer version of the protocol, then the proxy would "downgrade" the message before forwarding it. A proxy is not permitted to lie about its version number because this can cause problems with the semantics of interpretation of the HTTP message. If a proxy changes the version number, some header fields may have to be changed and some must remain unchanged. Additional requirements of HTTP/1.1 must be met before forwarding the request. Chapter 6 (Section 6.5) discusses details of the proper interpretation of HTTP version numbers,

Adding obligatory information about the resource   In returning a response from its cache, a proxy might be obligated to add some information about the resource. One example is the duration of time since the resource was known to have been validated at the origin server.

Semantic neutrality   One of the difficult tasks of a proxy is to react to problems in requests and responses. A proxy is not permitted to make semantic decisions such as declaring a request to be illegal. There is a delicate balance between the semantic expectations on a proxy and what it can actually do when faced with an illegal request or response. The duties of a proxy can be semantically ordered: See if the request can be handled locally (if the proxy is a caching proxy and the response can be returned from the cache) and, if not, forward the request. A proxy could behave like a tunnel and forward the request blindly upon receiving a message that it cannot understand. The tunneling behavior of a proxy is more in line with the expectation of a client and an origin server—the two principal parties in the message exchange.

Handling delays and buffering   As an intermediary, the proxy is responsible for maintaining a connection with the origin server while the response is being generated. The response could be dynamically generated. In this case, the proxy would have to maintain the connections, buffer portions of the response as they arrive from the sender, forward buffered parts to the receiver, and wait for the response to complete before closing the connections. The buffering requirements apply in the forward direction between the client and the origin server as well. However, requests are generally smaller than responses and do not consume a lot of resources on the proxy. The risk of a proxy having to buffer an indefinite amount of data led to careful specification of parts of the HTTP protocol relating to message transfers. Chapter 7 (Section 7.6) discusses this issue in more detail.

State maintenance and policy issues Acting as a front end to many clients, a proxy must maintain a considerable amount of state across the numerous ongoing requests and responses. The proxy cannot close a connection until the entire exchange is complete. If a user clicks on the Stop button on the browser and aborts the client request in progress, the proxy must close the connection to the server. The same request might be made by the same (or some other) client later. If the response from the origin server had been fully downloaded into the proxy cache, then the subsequent request could be handled locally at the proxy instead of transferring the bytes across the network. Policy decisions on deciding to cache downloaded responses even when the client aborted the connection are outside the scope of the protocol. They must be made by a caching proxy with an eye toward optimizing user-perceived latency and network bandwidth.

To function effectively as an intermediary, a proxy must balance the sometimes conflicting roles as a server and a client. The proxy has a different set of efficiency criteria than those of clients and origin servers. Whereas origin servers accept and respond to many thousands of requests, a proxy may have to maintain bidirectional connections and state associated with many clients and servers. As we will see later, a single transport-level connection can be used to transfer multiple requests and responses. An origin server, faced with thousands of requests per second, may decide to close an inactive connection sooner than others. A proxy on the other hand, may have a different criterion for deciding on the length of idle time before closing the connection with a client because the client is more likely to reuse its connection to the proxy.

Practical implementation issues A proxy must be able to accept and hold connections with hundreds of clients over varying periods of time. At the same time, it must maintain connections with hundreds of origin servers (or proxies). As a server accepting connections from thousands of clients, the proxy faces all the problems of a Web server. A proxy must accept connections, allocate a thread or a process to handle the request, and keep connection state until the request has been handled. Later, it may have to log the request and perform any necessary cleanups related to process state or allocated buffers. Such operations must be done while buffering responses from other servers for other requests. The number of connections available at the transport layer for a proxy is limited, and so new connections cannot be accepted unless some of the older ones are closed. Similarly, because a proxy is buffering responses and possibly caching them, it must balance space issues as well. Details of issues that a server faces in handling multiple simultaneous requests can be found in Chapter 4 (Section 4.4).

Handling cookies   In Chapter 2 (Section 2.6) we saw how a client treats cookies. In Chapter 4 (Section 4.4) we will see how cookies are handled by servers. Because a proxy acts like a client and a server, it sees cookies in the response message and returns the cookies in messages it forwards to the origin server, if they are present in the requests. For example, a client sends a request for a resource at origin server S via proxy P. The origin server S sends a cookie via the `Set-Cookie` as usual. From the origin server's point of view, the proxy P is the client where the cookie would be set. The proxy passes on the `Set-Cookie` header as required [KM00] to the client for storage. The next time the client contacts the origin server, the client uses the URL to decide which cookie to include in its `Cookie` header. The proxy passes this header on unchanged. In fact, a proxy is prohibited from adding its own cookie-related headers in either direction. Thus the mere presence of a proxy in the path does not alter the semantics of a cookie for the client or the server. However, a server can instruct the proxy not to cache certain headers. For example, it is possible to instruct that the `Set-Cookie` header not be cached (see Chapter 7, Section 7.3.3 for a variety of such mechanisms to control caching).

3.4.3 Proxy as Web server

A proxy, in its role as a Web server, is a target for requests from clients. A caching proxy acting as a Web server to a client's request might check to see if the request can be satisfied from its cache. It is also possible that the proxy may be the target server of a request. A client may want to obtain the response without potential delays in forwarding the request. There are specific HTTP protocol mechanisms that permit a client to request that the message *not* be forwarded past the proxy. In such cases, the proxy must respond by itself. The proxy would check to see if the response is in its cache. If the proxy is unable to find the response in its cache, it would have to respond with an error.

   If there are no requirements to respond locally, the proxy would check to see if the response is in its cache and if the response is fresh. Otherwise, the proxy would forward the request toward the origin server and wait for the response. The response may be returned from the origin server or an intermediate proxy before the origin server. When the response arrives at the proxy, it is returned to the client. The response may be cached at the proxy, depending on the proxy's caching policies.

Consider Figure 3.3, in which the client has been configured to go through a proxy that is capable of sending requests directly to the origin server. The proxy may have a cached copy of one of the embedded resources in `foo.html`, say, `foo2.gif`. Upon receiving the request for `foo2.gif`, the proxy looks up the resource to see if it is in the cache. If the resource is found in the cache, the proxy would have to ensure that the cached response is the same as what would have been obtained by contacting the origin server. The caching proxy could use a simple heuristic to treat any responses cached within the last several minutes as what it would receive by contacting the origin server. The proxy could then return the response from its cache instead of forwarding the request to the origin server. However, the choice of the duration of treating a resource as fresh depends heavily on the nature of the resource—a stock quote could not be assumed to be fresh for more than few seconds, for example.

From the client's point of view, the proxy behaves like an origin server. The obvious difference is the reduction in latency when a cached response is returned, because the proxy is typically much closer (fewer hops away) to the client than the origin server. Fewer bytes are transferred on the network between the caching proxy and the origin server, which helps to reduce the overall congestion in the network.

3.4.4 Proxy as Web client

A proxy plays the role of a client when it forwards the request to the origin server. There are two reasons for the proxy to forward the request:

- The proxy is a caching proxy but is unable to satisfy the request from its cache.
- The proxy is not a caching proxy or was explicitly instructed by the client to forward the request.

As a client, a proxy must perform all the tasks of a client. It has to determine the origin server's IP address by contacting the DNS server, open a connection to the origin server, write the request, and read the response returned by the origin server. The response is returned to the client that sent the request to the proxy. If the response references embedded resources, the client might send requests for these resources as well to the proxy. The proxy would treat each of these requests similarly to how it handled the first request, obtain responses from the server, and forward the responses to the client.

The proxy may have different capabilities compared with the client. For example, a proxy may have better connectivity to the Internet than a client. It is common for a proxy to be running an older version of the protocol compared with the clients. This is mainly because newer versions of browsers are often distributed faster and freely. Software upgrades of the intermediaries take longer. In fact, on the Web today, there are many more user agents and servers than proxies that run HTTP/1.1. If the proxy's protocol version is older than that of the client, the proxy would not be able to handle some of the newer features of the protocol. Any request using a later version would be downgraded by the proxy before the proxy forwarded it.

A proxy must not alter the semantics of the request. Otherwise the client that made the request might receive a response that was not expected or in a format that it cannot handle. For example, the server and the proxy might be able to understand a particular encoding of the response (say, a novel compression algorithm). However, the proxy may have to alter the response to ensure that the client would understand it. The version number of the client gives the proxy an indication of its capability. Thus a proxy may have to decompress the compressed message before forwarding the message to the client.

Compared with a client, a proxy contacts many more servers, and, because of the aggregate nature of its activity, it is likely to refer to the same Web site many times. Multiple DNS lookups of the same site can be avoided if one has been recently performed on behalf of a different client. Note that such DNS lookups are performed by a proxy only if it is last in the chain of proxies from the user agent to the server; otherwise it can simply forward the request to the next server in the chain.

As a Web client, the proxy makes decisions about opening and maintaining connections to many servers. A typical client acting on behalf of a single user may have only a few simultaneous connections operating in parallel. In acting on behalf of several clients, the proxy must be able to open and maintain many connections simultaneously. A proxy has to allocate significant resources to maintain state on behalf of these connections, download resources from a variety of servers, and buffer the data. If the response is dynamically generated, the proxy must buffer the response for a potentially longer duration before it can complete the forwarding of the response.

3.4.5 Example use of a proxy

We examine the use of a proxy via an example first discussed in Chapter 2 (Section 2.3). A client downloaded a container document with several embedded images. Now suppose that the browser was configured to go through a proxy.

Suppose `foo1.gif` was found in the browser's cache and `foo2.gif` was in the proxy's cache. The proxy could use its cache freshness policy to decide if the cached copy of `foo2.gif` could be returned to the client without revalidating with the origin server. If the proxy believes that the response is no longer fresh, it could revalidate the cached response by sending a modified request to the origin server. The modified request to the origin server requires that the

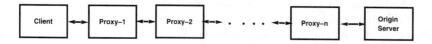

Figure 3.4. Proxy chain on the Web

contents of the resource be sent back only if the resource has changed since the time it was cached by the proxy. If the proxy does send a request and receive a new copy of the resource, it would cache the response and forward the response to the client. As far as the client is concerned, it received the resource foo2.gif from the proxy. The client has no knowledge of the steps undertaken by the proxy to return the resource. Thus, for the request for foo2.gif, the proxy acted as a Web server.

Now let us suppose that the resource foo3.jpg is not in the proxy's cache. The proxy now acts as a Web client and sends requests to the origin server on which this resource resides. If the user triggers the amex.cgi resource by filling out a form or selects the mp.tv resource, these requests are forwarded through the proxy as well. The proxy would open a separate connection to the respective origin servers in each of these cases. The amex.cgi might take a considerable amount of time to be processed, which would require the proxy to keep its connection to the origin server and the client open meanwhile.

3.5 Proxy Chaining and Hierarchies

When proxies entered the picture in the communication between user agents and servers, initially just a single proxy was in the path. Soon multiple proxies began to appear on the path between the user agent and the origin server. The structure of organizations where the Web was used was responsible for multiple proxies. For example, a university may have a single proxy for all its Web interaction, but some departments within the university may have their own proxies. The university might have its connectivity provided by an ISP who might have a proxy. Finally, an origin server might have a proxy in front of it. Thus the user's request and an origin server's response travel through several proxies chained together. On the Web today, it is quite common for a request to travel through a set of proxies that are chained together. The user agent may be directly configured to communicate with the proxy for all its Web interactions. Figure 3.4 demonstrates a simple configuration of such a setup.

Figure 3.4 illustrates that a message from a user agent may traverse through multiple servers before it reaches the origin server. Often, rather than the simple linear pipeline shown in Figure 3.4, the intermediate servers have other servers connected to them as well on both sides. It is common for a set of proxies within an organization to be connected in a hierarchy. For example, a regional proxy may be connected to other regional proxies, which in turn may be connected to a national proxy. Note that, in this case, many proxies could be behind a regional or a national proxy, compared with Figure 3.4, where there is a single linear chain. Such hierarchical proxy collections are fairly common and very useful in countries where communication costs for Internet access are high. By restricting a reasonable portion of the communication to stay within a regional or national boundary, an organization can significantly reduce its communication latency and costs. A group of proxies can maintain a larger cache of responses in its collection. However, with multiple proxies, a collection of caches may have to be searched for cache hits when a request is made.

3.6 Proxy Configuration

In Chapter 2 (Section 2.4), we saw how a user can configure a browser to set various physical and semantic attributes. In the case of proxies, however, end users typically do not have any influence in changing configuration information associated with a proxy. For example, a user typically cannot alter proxy-specific parameters such as its cache size or frequency of revalidation. Browsers may be used to specify if a proxy is to be used as an intermediary. A client can bypass a proxy and choose to have all requests go directly to the origin server, although the presence of firewalls may prevent this from occurring. Many browsers may be preconfigured with the proxy settings. In sites where users can override the default configuration, they may have nuanced control over the settings. Users can choose among no proxies, a specific proxy for all requests, or a proxy for all requests except ones destined for Web servers in certain domains. The last of these options gives maximal control for a user. The user may permit the use of a proxy for sites that do not violate the user's privacy or popular sites whose resources may be in the proxy's cache. For other domains, users can bypass the proxy. Most users do not change the default setting, and many users may not even be aware that they may be able to change the default setting. In some sites, attempts to configure a proxy setting manually may be impossible. Site administrators could impose a policy that ensures that all user requests go through a proxy.

Among the problems with configuring proxies are dealing with mobile clients and locating the appropriate proxy when more than one exists. This has led to some recent work on automatically locating the correct proxy. Rather than simply locating a single proxy, it might be more appropriate to have a dynamic mechanism that provides a way to locate configuration information that would, in turn, provide a pointer to the best proxy at the time of need. The work is still in experimental stage [CGC+00] and uses the Dynamic Host Configuration Protocol [Dro97] and certain aspects of the DNS [Moc87a].

3.7 Proxy Privacy Issues

In Chapter 2 we discussed the privacy issues dealt with by a browser. A proxy has a more important role to play in matters of privacy. As an intermediary for many individual users, the proxy is aware of many details:

- The resources that are being accessed
- The frequency of such accesses
- The headers and body of the request
- The headers and body of the response

This knowledge affects the privacy of the user because there is a potential for privacy violation. However, a proxy is often viewed as a *trusted* intermediary if users configure their browsers to go through it. The users would know who is accountable for the information being gathered. As we will see in Section 3.8, there are scenarios in which users are not aware of the fact that their requests and responses are going through a proxy. In such cases, not knowing about the presence of an intermediary leads to added concern about who may have access to information regarding users' access.

Proxies know the IP address of the client. If the client is a single-user machine or if the same `User-Agent` field is present in the user's requests, the proxy may be able to determine that a set of requests are from the same user. A proxy may not always know exactly who is accessing Web resources through it. If the proxy is placed in front of a shared multiuser machine, it might not be able to identify precisely which user sent the request. In a shared machine environment, other information, such as system information about the time when users log in and out, can be used to identify the user. Such efforts are commonplace in situations involving breaking of the law. Police in some parts of the United States have used logs to trace users. Knowledge of what resources are being accessed is another sensitive unit of information. Selective examination of the kind of resources accessed from large sites can help create a profile of the user. People looking for information about a specific health condition or looking at certain Web sites advertising open job positions may face a certain degree of risk.

The contents of a request may have revealing information such as the user's date of birth and credit card number. Forms are routinely filled in by users accessing sites to register for conferences or buying books and plane tickets or trading stocks. An obvious solution, increasingly adapted by many Web sites, is the reliance on SSL, forcing the proxy to act as a tunnel and providing end-to-end encryption. Similarly, the contents of a response provide information about the user.

3.8 Other Kinds of Proxies

We have examined different roles of proxies in which the meaning of the term proxy has been clear. New kinds of proxies have emerged from the commercial world. Two kinds of proxies we consider are *reverse* and *interception* proxies. We examine the motivations for these proxies and see how they differ from the traditional proxies that have been described so far in this chapter. It is important to note that, although terms such as reverse and interception proxies have become prominent, these proxies do not always obey the HTTP protocol specification. More important, it may not be possible to test their behavior in practice, because their behavior has not yet been standardized.

3.8.1 Reverse proxies or surrogates

Initially, proxies were positioned close to users. Administrators configured proxies for local area networks or users within small organizations. As the Web began to increase in popularity, a few Web sites began to attract a significant portion of the traffic. Proxies had to be positioned closer to the origin server to reduce the load on them. Such proxies were labeled "reverse proxies" because they were on the other end of the request-response chain compared with traditional proxies that are close to users. Another reason to position a proxy in front of an origin server (or a collection of servers representing a site) is to ensure that origin servers are not the visible front end to all incoming requests. Reverse proxies prevent the origin server from being vulnerable to direct attacks from the outside world. An intermediary in front of an origin server site could also help in balancing the load between the set of servers comprising a busy site. The intermediary could redirect requests to different back-end machines, depending on their load. A reverse proxy is seen by a client as an origin server. A reverse proxy acts as a front end to one or more origin servers, which may be behind a firewall. The client's request is sent to the reverse proxy, which forwards it to origin servers. The reverse proxy may also have a cache. When forwarding a request, the reverse proxy acts as a tunnel; that is, the bits are relayed unchanged in both directions. The outside world would see only a single IP address—that of the reverse proxy.

Note that although the term reverse proxy has attained a measure of popularity, there is really no need for a separate term. From the point of view of a client, it is communicating with the origin server. A reverse proxy is simply a gateway, and the communication between the reverse proxy and the back-end origin server(s) is hidden from the client. In fact, the reverse proxy may not use HTTP to communicate with the origin server(s) behind it. Reverse proxies are now known by a new term in the industry—*surrogates*.

3.8.2 Interception proxies

If a proxy is explicitly designated to be in front of a Web client (i.e., the user agent treats the proxy as a server), then all the requests and responses to and from the client will flow through the proxy. Independent of the local network configuration, the proxy is able to see all Web-related network packets from the client to the Internet and vice versa. The client does not have the option to bypass the proxy and interact directly with origin servers. In many organizations, where the goal is to ensure that all accesses are seen by the proxy, this is often the default configuration. If, however, the clients have multiple routes to the Internet or if users are able to bypass the explicit proxy, then the proxy would not be in a position to see all requests and responses.

The Web portion of traffic can be extracted by examining network traffic. A proxy that either directly examines network traffic and intercepts Web traffic or receives redirected traffic flow from network elements performing traffic interception is known an as an *interception* proxy. The interception proxy then attempts to generate a response to the request locally or redirects the request to other places. For an interception proxy to see all requests and responses, the interception proxy must be placed in such a way that the only route to the Internet from the clients is via the interception proxy. An interception proxy requires policies tailored to specific portions of the network traffic to be introduced into the router. Because the interception is done at a lower layer in the protocol stack, it is not easy to permit certain requests to bypass the interception proxy. Clients do not play any role in deciding if and what portion of their requests and responses are redirected. As a consequence, no client configuration is required.

In Section 3.2 we introduced the term transparent proxy. The transparency of the proxy has to do with what happens to the message and not whether the presence of the proxy is transparent (i.e., invisible) to the client or user. Interception proxies were originally called transparent proxies in the industry. This has since been clarified, and there is a conscious attempt to call interception proxies by their proper name.

3.9 Summary

A proxy is a popular and useful intermediary on the Web that enables a large number of clients behind it to share access. Proxies aid in filtering requests and responses and in preserving a user's privacy. Caching helps in significantly lowering the user-perceived latency. Proxies ensure that the semantics of forwarded requests/responses are not modified while playing the roles of a client and a server. Because virtually all the popular ISPs use proxies, a large fraction of requests to Web servers come from proxies. Hierarchical proxies at a local, regional, and national level are popular on the Web.

4

Web Servers

A Web server is a program that generates and transmits responses to client requests for Web resources. This chapter describes the operation of Web servers, completing the three-part view of Web software components—the clients that initiate requests, the proxies that act as intermediaries, and the servers that generate responses. Handling a client request consists of several key steps—parsing the request message, checking that the request is authorized, associating the URL in the request with a file name, constructing the response message, and transmitting the response message to the requesting client. The server can generate the response message in a variety of ways. In the simplest case, the server simply retrieves the file associated with the URL and returns the contents to the client. In other cases, the server may invoke a script that communicates with other servers or a back-end database to construct the response message.

This chapter starts with an explanation of the differences between a Web *site* and a Web *server*. Then we explain how a server handles a client request, including a discussion of request authentication and techniques for generating dynamic responses. HTTP is a stateless protocol; therefore the server does not necessarily retain information across successive requests. We describe how the server can save some information to reduce the overhead of satisfying future requests. To handle multiple clients at a time, the server needs an effective way to alternate between servicing the various requests. We discuss and compare the two primary approaches, *event-driven* and *process-driven* servers, and various hybrid schemes. The system resources required by a server depend on the popularity of the Web site. We briefly discuss the challenges of hosting multiple servers on the same machine and managing replicas of a single site on multiple machines. To illustrate the operation of a real Web server, the chapter ends with a case study of the public-domain Apache Web server.

4.1 Web Site versus Web Server

A Web site consists of a collection of Web pages associated with a particular hostname, whereas a Web server is a program that satisfies client requests for Web resources. In this section, we examine the functionality of various kinds of Web sites and discuss the implications on the underlying Web server. We also explain the difference between a Web site and a Web server and distinguish the Web server from the underlying computing platform.

4.1.1 Web site

The user experience on the Web consists of downloading Web pages from various Web sites. Web sites vary substantially in terms of the type of information they provide:

- **University:** A university may have a Web site that provides information about the academic and research programs and includes photographs and contact information. The main university site may link to other Web sites for certain academic departments. These Web sites may include listings of offices and phone numbers, information about particular academic courses, and personal home pages for professors and students.
- **Business-to-consumer:** A company may have a Web site describing its products and job openings. The site may also permit customers to review detailed product and pricing information and place orders. This could be as simple as reproducing printed material online as a collection of static files and images. As an extension, the site could allow users to place orders for goods and services by interacting with a database that maintains inventory and ordering information. Furthermore, the site could allow users to search the database.
- **Corporate intranet:** Many companies also have internal Web sites that are not accessible to the general public. These sites may provide access to directory listings and information about employee benefits. A user name and password may be required to access per-employee information. Before the advent of the Web, these databases may not have been easily accessible to employees. Making these databases accessible on an internal Web site is an efficient way to conduct business inside a company and to provide employees with convenient access to important information.
- **Business-to-business:** Companies that depend on one another for services may also use Web sites to coordinate their joint activities, with lower cost and higher efficiency than interacting by paper or telephone. For example, one company (e.g., an auto maker) may place orders from another company (e.g., a steel producer) on a Web site. Performing these business-to-business transactions on the Web simplifies the process of placing orders and reporting billing information across company boundaries.

- **Special event:** Some Web sites relate to specific events, such as sporting events or national elections. These sites are usually relatively short-lived and have rapidly changing content. Consider a Web site for the Olympics. Few users would access the site until a few weeks before the competitions begin. Then the site might report the scheduled events and provide stories about the participants. Once the Olympics start, the site may include new stories and dynamically generated information about sporting events. During this period, the site may be extremely popular. The site may experience a sudden increase in the number of requests just before or just after a popular event. The requests may come from users all over the world at various times of the day.
- **Portal:** A portal site strives to create and maintain a long-term relationship with a large number of users by providing a central place for locating information. For example, a portal site may provide access to information about the weather, television listings, and news events. The portal may allow the users to customize the presentation of the material. For example, the user may want to see the weather in Tokyo, the latest baseball scores, and current prices of certain stocks. In addition, the portal site presents hypertext links organized by topic, providing easy access to users. The designers of the portal site categorize and verify these links.
- **Search:** Rather than navigating through a collection of hypertext links, a user may want to locate information that does not fall into an obvious category. A search engine allows a user to enter a query and returns a list of hypertext links to Web pages that contain the search strings. In contrast to Web sites that allow access to a particular back-end database, a search engine performs queries on an indexed set of Web resources acquired by spiders, as discussed in Chapter 2 (Section 2.7). A search engine's primary task is to generate responses based on user queries.
- **Gateway to other services:** Many Web sites provide other services, such as newsgroups, e-mail, bulletin boards, chatrooms, and instant messaging. For example, a Web site for network news allows users to subscribe to newsgroups and to read and post articles. This requires the site to keep information about the newsgroups and articles read by each user. Similarly, a Web site can provide a frontend to e-mail that presents a different view to each user and allows users to read, file, compose, and send messages. Chatrooms provide an opportunity for users to interact with each other. An online newspaper may provide a chatroom for readers to discuss their opinions about the latest news events.

The load on a Web site can be characterized in a variety of ways including the popularity of the site, the geographic diversity of the users, the number and size of the Web resources, the proportion of content that is generated dynamically, and the need to restrict access to certain users.

4.1.2 Web server

A Web server is a program that handles HTTP requests for particular resources. Creating and transferring a Web page may, in fact, require the involvement of multiple servers, scripts, and databases. Consider the canonical example of a user visiting the Web site `www.bar.com`. The resource `http://www.bar.com/foo.html` may reference several embedded images that are downloaded automatically by the browser. These embedded images do not have to reside at `www.bar.com`. For example, the HTML file at `http://www.bar.com/foo.html` could have an embedded image `http://images.bar.com/foo3.gif` that resides at `images.bar.com`. In fact, the image content could be hosted by a different company `www.images.com`, resulting in an embedded reference such as `http://www.images.com/fooimages/foo3.gif`. Hosting images at a separate server enables the base Web server to handle a large rate of requests for small, frequently changing HTML documents.

The Web server runs on an underlying platform that consists of a computer that has access to the network. The computer consists of one or more processors with memory and perhaps a disk for storing static documents and scripts. Platforms vary widely in terms of their computational power, network connectivity, and storage capacity, depending on the type of Web resources and expected rate of client requests. The Web server interacts with the processor, disk, and network connection via the underlying operating system. For high-end Web sites, the computer is dedicated to running the server. In other cases, the computer may run a variety of other applications, such as an e-mail or File Transfer Protocol (FTP) server or user applications. As part of satisfying a request, the server may invoke a script that interacts with other servers or back-end databases. The interactions with other servers may involve other protocols besides HTTP.

4.2 Handling a Client Request

Web servers provide access to a diverse collection of resources, ranging from static files to scripts that generate customized responses. In this section, we discuss the steps involved in handling a client request. We then discuss how Web servers authenticate users to limit access to certain resources. Next we describe how Web servers generate dynamic content by parsing HTML files and invoking scripts. Finally, we discuss the role of cookies in retaining state across a sequence of requests by the same user.

4.2.1 Steps in handling a client request

At a high level, a Web server proceeds through the following steps in handling an HTTP request:

1. **Read and parse the HTTP request message:** The server reads the request message sent by the client. The header of the message contains control information, such as the requested operation (e.g., GET) and the URL of the requested resource (e.g., /foo.html). The server can extract other header fields that affect the construction of the response message.

2. **Translate the URL to a file name:** The server converts the URL into the file name of the corresponding resource. The URL may have a direct relationship to the structure of the underlying file system. For example, Web resources may be located in a base directory, such as /www, where the URL http://www.bar.com/foo/index.html corresponds to the file /www/foo/index.html.

3. **Determine whether the request is authorized:** Before generating a response message, the server checks that the client has permission to access the resource. Although many Web resources are available to all users, the server may limit access to some resources based on authorization information in the HTTP request header.

4. **Generate and transmit the response:** The server generates a response message that includes a header to convey status information (e.g., an error indicating an unauthorized request or nonexistent resource, a redirection for the client to repeat the request with a different URL, or a successful response that includes the requested resource). In addition, the header may include metadata about the resource, such as the length and format.

At some point in handling a request, the server may record information about the request and response messages in a log. For example, the server may generate the log entry before or after transmitting the response message.

As an example of handling a request, consider the canonical example presented earlier, in Chapter 2 (Section 2.3.1). The client sends an HTTP request for http://www.bar.com/foo.html to the www.bar.com server. The server reads the request message to determine the name /foo.html of the requested resource. Then the server identifies the associated file /www/foo.html and determines that authorization is not required for access to this resource. Next the server invokes system calls to learn the key attributes of the resource, such as the file size and the last time it was modified. These attributes appear in the HTTP response header (e.g., the Content-Length and Last-Modified header fields), along with other information such as the status of the response, the identity of the server, and the current time. After composing the response header, the server transmits the header and the contents of the file to the requesting client.

Upon receiving the response message, the client parses the HTML file and issues HTTP requests for each of the embedded images foo1.gif, foo2.gif, and foo3.jpg. The server handles these requests in the same manner as the request for foo.html. In responding to each request, the server retrieves the associated file, constructs a response header, and transfers the header and the data. The contents of any of these files can change without affecting the operation of the server. In addition, the server does not impose any relationship between the resources in the Web page. Rather, the author of `foo.html` imposes these relationships by referencing each of the images within the HTML file. The browser initiates the retrieval of these images by sending HTTP requests to the server, and the server handles each of the requests independently.

A response message from a server does not always transmit a resource. For example, suppose that the browser has a cached copy of `foo.html`. Not knowing if the resource has changed at the server, the browser can send a request to validate the cached copy. The browser includes the last modification time of the cached resource in the request header. Upon receiving the request, the server determines the last time that the file `/www/foo.html` was modified. If the two times match, the resource has not changed since the browser's previous request. The server sends a response message with a header that indicates that the requested resource has not been modified, instructing the browser to use the cached copy. In this case, the response message does not include the contents of the resource. On the other hand, if `/www/foo.html` had changed, the server's response message would include the latest contents of the file.

4.2.2 Access control

A Web server may limit which users can access certain resources. Access control requires a combination of *authentication* and *authorization*. Authentication identifies the user who originated the request, and authorization determines which users have access to a particular resource. We describe how a Web server authenticates a user with the help of the user agent. Then we discuss how the Web server determines whether a user can access the requested resource.

AUTHENTICATION

Most client-server systems authenticate a user by asking for a name and password. In this model, the server maintains a password file, which lists the names and passwords for all authorized users; the passwords may be stored in an encrypted form to protect the information. The user enters the name and password information as part of establishing a session with the server. The server checks that the name and password correspond to a valid user and remembers the identity of the user for the remainder of the session. At some point, the user or the server terminates the session. Further access requires the user to initiate a new session with the server, which involves entering the name and password again.

The Web does not have a notion of a session between the user and the server. The user has the illusion of having an ongoing session with the Web site, consisting of a sequence of requests for Web pages. However, the server simply sees a stream of independent HTTP requests. In a sense, each request belongs to its own session. Hence, the Web server must perform authentication for *every* request for a resource that has access restrictions. However, the user may find it annoying to enter a name and password for every HTTP request, including requests for embedded images. Instead, the server instructs the user agent to include the name and password information in the HTTP request header. The user enters the name and password, and these are stored until the user closes the browser. Having the user agent remember the name and password enables the server to perform authentication while still treating each request independently. Any intermediaries between the user agent and the origin server simply forward the authentication information.

For example, suppose that a user clicks on a hypertext link that corresponds to a protected resource at the server `www.bar.com`. The browser sends an HTTP request to the Web server. The server recognizes that the requested resource has access restrictions. The server returns an HTTP response that indicates that the request requires authorization. The response also identifies what *kind* of authentication is required. The server may select from a variety of types of authentication, such as basic or digest access authentication [FHBH+99]. The response also identifies the *realm*—a string that associates a collection of resources at the server. Each collection may have its own authentication scheme, with different names and passwords. To complete the authentication process, the browser prompts the user for a name and password and includes this information in subsequent requests. HTTP authentication is discussed in more detail in Chapter 7 (Section 7.10).

AUTHORIZATION

The authentication process enables the server to identify the user responsible for an HTTP request. To control access to Web resources, the server must employ an authorization policy. The server needs an effective way to know *which* authenticated users should be permitted to access a particular resource. These policies are specified as part of server configuration. A policy is typically expressed in terms of an *access control list* that enumerates the users who are granted or denied access to the resource. The exact details of how to specify access control lists and how to store user passwords and names depend on the server software. Rather than have a separate access control list for each resource, the server may have a default configuration for all resources in each directory or all resources at the server. Resources requiring authentication could be located in a single directory (e.g., `/www/private`).

Authorization refers to the process of enforcing these access control policies. As part of handling a request, the server must determine if the requested resource is protected by an access control list. For example, `http://www.bar.com/private/index.html` may be associated with an HTML file stored at

`/www/private/index.html`. Each subdirectory may be limited to particular users. Hence, the server must inspect the access control policy of each directory in the path to the requested file. If a directory is configured to restrict access, the server must parse the list of users to determine if the request can proceed. In addition to checking the user name, the server may allow or deny access to the resource based on other information associated with the HTTP request, such as the host name or IP address of the requesting client. However, an authorization policy based on the client name or address is risky because some requests may be sent by a proxy rather than the user agent. In fact, a user that is denied access to a resource could configure the browser to send requests through a proxy that is permitted to access the resource.

Authenticating HTTP requests can impose a heavy load on the Web server. The server must validate the user name and password to authenticate the user and must parse the authorization information in each directory in the path of the requested resource. Complex server configuration makes the authorization process more expensive. Overhead can be reduced by performing these functions only when necessary. For example, the policy for a high-level directory such as `/www/public` may specify that none of the subdirectories requires access-control checks. This allows the server to skip the check for configuration information in the subdirectories. The server administrator can limit authorization to a small handful of sensitive resources, which may be placed in a special subdirectory. This helps minimize the overhead of authentication and authorization, while still protecting access to sensitive data.

4.2.3 Dynamically generated responses

In addition to delivering static content, the Web provides access to dynamically generated resources. This feature differentiates the Web from earlier file-transfer services on the Internet. Dynamically generated responses are created in a variety of ways. A *server-side include* instructs the Web server to customize a static resource based on directives in an HTML-like file. In contrast, a *server script* is a separate program that generates the requested resource. The program may run as part of the server or as a separate process that communicates with the server. Dynamic generation of the response message gives content creators a great deal of flexibility, at the expense of a heavier load on the server, as well as introducing potential security risks.

SERVER-SIDE INCLUDES

Content creators often want to personalize a Web page for the requesting user. For example, the Web page may display the current time or the IP address of the client. The creator of the content does not have this information at the time an HTML file is created. Instead, the file could include directives, or macros, that instruct the server to insert the information at the time of the request. In responding to the client request, the server parses the file and substitutes text for each macro. The macros are special tags in the file that are interpreted by the server. For example, the file could contain the macro

```
<!-#echo var=''LAST_MODIFIED''->
```

to include the file's last modification time in the response sent to the client. The information appears in the *body* of the response, as part of the text in the HTML, and would be displayed to the user. This is independent of the server's inclusion of metadata in the HTTP response header.

The macros can refer to a wide variety of variables, including information in the HTTP request message. In addition to simple substitutions, a macro could request that the server insert another file into the document. For example, /www/foo.html could have a macro that includes the current contents of another file /www/infoo.html inside the HTML in the response message. More generally, the macro could instruct the server to invoke a program and include the output in the document; the server invokes the program identified in the macro, rather than a program identified by the URL in the request message. Server-side includes offer a relatively simple way for content creators to customize their documents with minor extensions to HTML. This obviates the need for the content creator to learn other techniques for dynamically generating the HTML content. However, server-side includes require the Web server to parse the HTML-like file and perform the operations requested by the macros. This results in higher latency for the user, compared with the traditional downloading of a static HTML file.

Parsing a file for every request would introduce unnecessary load on the server, especially if most files do not include macros. Instead, the server determines whether the file requires parsing, based on the URL. A common convention is that the name of the resource has the .shtml extension, instead of .html. Another popular file extension is .php for pages handled by PHP (Hypertext Preprocessor, or Personal Home Page). PHP is a cross-platform, HTML-embedded scripting language that has advanced features beyond simple substitutions. A Web server runs a PHP interpreter that parses and manipulates the files. A PHP file can incorporate data submitted by the user in an HTML form. For example, suppose a user supplies a name and telephone number. These variables can be included in the HTML file returned by the server. PHP also has flexible support for retrieving data from back-end databases. Another popular file extension is .asp for Microsoft's Active Server Pages (ASP) product. ASP, like PHP, embeds variables and references to scripts directly in the HTML file. However, ASP is available only on Microsoft server platforms.

SERVER SCRIPTS

Rather than embedding information in an HTML-like file, a separate program could generate the entire resource. In this situation, the URL in the HTTP request message corresponds to a program rather than a document. The program may perform a variety of tasks, such as accessing information from a database or creating a response that is customized to the requesting client. Supporting the execution of scripts is conceptually similar to allowing the users to log in to the server to run programs. Yet, there are several important differences. Rather than having direct access to the server machine, the user specifies the desired script and its arguments in an HTTP request message. The scripts produce output in a format (e.g., HTML) that can be interpreted by the Web browser. From the viewpoint of the client and the user, these dynamically generated responses are no different than static resources, except perhaps for the additional latency introduced by running the script.

Executing a script at the server is also different from downloading a program (e.g., written in Java) for execution at the Web browser. Running a program at the browser is more appropriate for applications that interact with the browser and the user. In contrast, server scripts have access to data that may not be available anywhere else. For example, a Web server may invoke a script to satisfy a user's query for books on a particular topic. Answering the query may involve accessing a large amount of potentially proprietary data. Handling the request at the client would require a copy of this data, as well as a program that can perform the actual search. Executing the program as a script at the server ensures that the software and raw data remain private. The program can be upgraded over time to fix mistakes and incorporate improvements without requiring users to download the new software. Likewise, the data can change over time, transparent to the user.

In theory, the code that generates the dynamic response could be integrated with the software for the Web server. This is not desirable because it would require changes to the server every time a new feature is added. In addition, each application developer would need to have intimate knowledge of the server software. Instead, it is preferable to have one set of programmers who develop the Web server software and have another, potentially larger, set of programmers who write applications that generate dynamic content. Having a clear separation between the server and the script is critical. The main role of the Web server is to associate the requested URL with the appropriate script and to pass data to and from the script. The main role of the script is to process the input from the server and generate the content for the client. The server can interact with the script in several different ways, as follows:

- **Separate process invoked by the server:** The script can run as a separate process invoked by the server to create the requested resource. Having a separate process isolates the server from the operation of the script, at the expense of extra overhead for creating and destroying a process for each request. This is the traditional approach taken by the Common Gateway Interface (CGI).

- **Software module in the same process:** The script can be a separate software module that executes as part of the Web server. Calling a module within the server avoids the overhead of creating a separate process, at the risk of consuming excessive system resources on the server. This is the approach taken by Netscape Server Application Programming Interface (NSAPI), Microsoft's Internet Server Application Programming Interface (ISAPI), Apache's *mod_perl* module, and Sun Microsystems' Java *servlets*.

- **Persistent process contacted by the server:** The script can be a separate process that handles multiple requests over a long period. The server communicates with the process to send arguments and receive the output. Having a long-running process obviates the need to create and destroy a process for each request; in addition, the process may maintain a connection to other services, such as a back-end database. This is the approach taken by FastCGI [Fcg].

Developing techniques for communicating between Web servers and scripts has been an area of significant commercial activity during the past few years. This has spawned a wide variety of application programming interfaces for writing scripts.

PASSING DATA TO/FROM THE SCRIPT

Decoupling the scripts from the Web server requires a well-defined interface for passing data between the two pieces of software. First, the server must determine that the requested resource identifies a script rather than a document. URLs that correspond to scripts typically include a "?" character or a string such as "cgi," "cgi-bin," or "cgibin." More generally, though, the association of a URL with a script is determined by the configuration of the server. For example, the server could be configured to assume that any URL with a particular extension (e.g., `.cgi`) or associated with a particular directory (e.g., `/www/scripts` or `/www/cgibin`) corresponds to a script. After identifying that the URL corresponds to a script, the server checks that the access permissions assigned to the script permit execution. Then the server invokes the script and awaits its completion before sending a response to the client.

Having a well-defined interface for exchanging data is crucial to making the server and the script work together. The exact interface differs from one scripting technique to another. Still, all of the techniques address a common need for the server to relay input data to and receive output data from the script. To illustrate, we describe the approach taken by the popular Common

Table 4.1. Example CGI environment variables

Type	Variable	Example
Server	SERVER_NAME	www.bar.com
	SERVER_SOFTWARE	Apache/1.2.6
	SERVER_PROTOCOL	HTTP/1.0
	SERVER_PORT	80
	DOCUMENT_ROOT	/www
	GATEWAY_INTERFACE	CGI/2.0
Client	REMOTE_ADDR	10.9.57.188
	REMOTE_HOST	users.berkeley.edu
Request	CONTENT_TYPE	text/html
	CONTENT_LENGTH	158
	REQUEST_METHOD	GET
	QUERY_STRING	name=Noam+Chomsky
	ACCEPT_LANGUAGE	de-CH
	HTTP_USER_AGENT	Mozilla/2.0

Gateway Interface (CGI) [Gun96]. CGI defines interfaces for a variety of operating system platforms. Operating systems vary in how they exchange data between applications. This makes it difficult to have a single interface that applies to all platforms. A UNIX-based Web server would direct data to the script via standard input and environment variables and receive data from the script via standard output. Programming languages, such as Perl or C, have functions that return the value of a given environment variable. In the remainder of the discussion, we focus on the interaction between a UNIX server and a CGI script.

The Web server provides a variety of information to the script, as shown in Table 4.1. Information about the server includes the name (hostname or IP address), the name and version of the server software, the name and version of the protocol, the server port number, and the root directory for resources hosted at the Web site. Information about the client request includes the IP address and hostname of the client. Information about the request includes the content type of the request, the length of the request, and the preferred format for the requested resource. Other fields from the HTTP request message are available in variables starting with HTTP. For example, the HTTP request message may include a User-Agent header that identifies the type of browser that initiated the request; this information would be available in the HTTP_USER_AGENT environment variable. Similarly, the HTTP_COOKIE variable provides the cookie, if any, included in the HTTP request. The environment variables enable the script to customize its operations to the underlying server, the requesting client, and the request headers. For example, the script could read the file `neatdata.txt` in the root directory `/www` and transform the contents to generate an HTML file that announces the client's IP address and includes a text greeting in Swiss-German.

CGI also provides a way for a script to accept input from a user. Users enter data via HTML forms. Returning to the canonical example, suppose that the Web page `http://www.bar.com/foo.html` displays a box for the user to enter text and press a Submit button. Suppose the user types "Noam Chomsky" and clicks on the Submit button, which triggers the browser to send an HTTP `GET` request for `http://www.bar.com/book.cgi?name=Noam+Chomsky`, or a `POST` request with the URL `http://www.bar.com/book.cgi` and the arguments in the body of the message. Upon receiving the request, the server invokes the script `/www/book.cgi`. In addition to setting environment variables, the server passes the user's arguments to the script via an additional environment variable (QUERY_STRING, for `GET`-based forms) or standard input (for `POST`-based forms).

The script inspects the client input (if any) and the environment variables. In processing the request, the script may interact with other servers or databases. For example, the `/www/book.cgi` script may issue a query to a database to locate books written about Noam Chomsky. In writing the response message to the standard output, the script can generate HTTP headers on behalf of the server. For example, a script could generate a header that indicates the size and type of the body (e.g., a 3576-byte GIF image) or provides a URL that redirects the client to another Web page. A Web server can be configured to accept the response header provided by the script without modification; this is referred to as a *no-parse-header script.* Otherwise, the Web server parses the output of the script to include any missing information (e.g., a `Date` header with the current date/time) before forwarding the response to the client.

PERFORMANCE AND SECURITY IMPLICATIONS OF SCRIPTS

Running scripts at the server has important performance and security implications. Server resources are consumed by invoking the script and copying data back and forth. In addition, the script itself may perform computations, access databases, or contact other servers. These operations introduce delays in responding to the client request. Consider a user request that requires interaction with a database that runs on a different machine than the server. The script running on the server machine must contact the remote machine to issue a query to the database. The response is delayed by the network transmission and database functions. In addition, scripts are commonly written in languages, such as Perl, that are compiled at the time of execution. The overhead of compiling the script increases the response latency. Precompiled languages, such as

C, are more efficient but are typically more difficult to program, particularly for the string manipulations common in Web scripts.

Allowing a URL to trigger the invocation of a script substantially expands the functionality of the Web. However, a script can conceivably perform almost any function and may be written without an appreciation of the system resources it consumes. In the worst case, a renegade script may never finish and could consume considerable processor and memory resources. As a result, Web servers typically impose a limit on the processing and memory resources that can be consumed by a script. As an additional precaution, the administrator of the Web site could prohibit the use of scripts or impose limits on who is allowed to install new scripts. Scripts also introduce security risks. A script can perform numerous functions not envisioned by the developers of the Web server. A script may have access to a variety of files on the server machine. A poorly written script could alter this data or return private information to the requesting client.

Scripts that accept user input require additional precautions to ensure that the user cannot direct the script to perform sensitive tasks. Consider the extreme example of a script that allows the user to enter arbitrary commands for execution on the server machine. The user could direct the script to delete files on the server machine or send sensitive information to the user (e.g., via e-mail). These kinds of situations can be prevented in several ways. First, the script can be written in a way that limits the type of user input. For example, the Web page could allow the user to select from a set of predefined commands or enter a list of keywords, rather than a set of commands for execution on the server machine. Second, the script could preprocess the user's input to avoid performing operations that would access sensitive programs or data. Third, the site administrator can limit the access privileges of the scripts themselves. For example, the scripts could be denied access to files containing sensitive data (e.g., the password file) and to certain commands (e.g., sending e-mail or deleting files). The site administrator could also force a script to run with the same permissions as the person who wrote the script, which precludes the script from accessing files that the author cannot access.

4.2.4 Creating and using cookies

Cookies provide a way for a Web site to retain state about a user over time, as discussed in Chapter 2 (Section 2.6). Web sites use cookies to track users and store information about transactions that span multiple HTTP transfers. Cookies are typically created, used, and modified by scripts invoked to generate dynamic responses, rather than by the Web server.

A Web site may tailor its content to the requesting user. For example, an e-commerce site may return a Web page with a personalized greeting that includes the user's name and recommendations for possible purchases. Tracking the users also enables a Web site to compute profiles of individual users and aggregate statistics about user access patterns, such as the average length of time that users spend at the site. However, an HTTP request does not provide sufficient information to identify the user. Multiple users may browse the Web from the same machine or direct their requests to the same proxy. In addition, a machine's IP address may change over time if the user's Internet Service Provider (ISP) assigns a dynamic IP address when the user connects to the Internet. In theory, the site could require the user to provide a unique name, perhaps with a password, for each Web request, at the expense of irritating the user.

Instead, the browser can be instructed to include a unique cookie in each HTTP request. Returning to the canonical example, suppose the Web server receives an HTTP request for `http://www.bar.com/book.cgi?name=Noam+ Chomsky` that contains a cookie. The server invokes the script `/www/book.cgi` and passes the cookie in the HTTP_COOKIE environment variable. The script can use the cookie to determine which advertisements to include in the Web page. For example, the advertisements may relate to books on topics related to previous purchases by the same user. From the browser's viewpoint, the cookie is an arbitrary string of characters. In contrast, the script associates a particular meaning with the string. In the simplest case, the string simply represents a unique user identifier, such as a user number or name. If the request does not include a cookie, the script could create a new cookie and include the cookie in the header of the response message

```
Set-Cookie: Customer="user17"; Version="1"; Path="/book"
```

Subsequent requests from the same user would include the cookie

```
Cookie: Customer="user17"; Version="1"; Path="/book"
```

The script can use the cookie as a user identifier in interacting with a back-end database. For example, an e-commerce site may have a database that stores information about the past orders and the current shopping basket of each user. The database retains state across a sequence of requests, in contrast to the Web server that handles each request independently by invoking a script that interacts with the database.

In other situations, the cookie may encode additional information, such as the user's name and color preferences. This is useful for dynamically generated content that is customized based on these attributes. For example, a Web page may include a personal greeting that includes the user's name. The cookie may also contain information about the user's previous actions in browsing the Web site. Storing history information in the cookie may obviate the need to retain information about the user in a back-end database. For example, the cookie for an e-commerce site could contain current contents of the user's shopping basket.

Consider a user that visits an e-commerce site and submits various forms to order books. The user adds a book to the shopping basket, which triggers the browser to send an HTTP request that includes the cookie associated with that Web site. The script generates a response message that includes

```
Set-Cookie: Order="Chomsky_Bio"; Version="1"; Path="/book"
```

Then the user adds another book to the shopping basket, which triggers an HTTP request with

```
Cookie: Customer="user17"; Version="1"; Path="/book";
        Order="Chomsky_Bio"; Version="1"; Path="/book"
```

The process continues as the user selects more items. In this example, all of the critical data is encoded in the cookie. However, this approach could result in very large cookies. The browser may not be willing to store a cookie that exceeds some maximum length. To avoid generating large cookies, the script could simply use the cookie as a user identifier and maintain the user's shopping basket in a back-end database.

A typical browser treats the cookie as an opaque string sent on behalf of a single user. However, sophisticated users may share, create, or modify cookies. For example, suppose a Web site does not allow a user to download a certain resource unless the HTTP request contains a cookie. Users might construct their own cookies to prevent the site from tracking their requests over time. In addition, one user might guess a possible cookie for another user by modifying the string in the server's Set-Cookie response. Referring to the previous example, a savvy user might send an HTTP request that includes a cookie that replaces the string user8 with user17, under the assumption that the user8 cookie corresponds to a valid user. To address these problems, the cookie may include some encrypted information that prevents users from generating valid cookies on their own. As part of processing a request, the script could check that the cookie is valid. Although this prevents the use of bogus cookies, there is still a risk that a user may use a cookie that belongs to someone else. To prevent such actions, the cookie may be assigned an expiration time. Once the cookie has expired, the user would have to accept a new cookie to gain access to the site.

4.3 Sharing Information Across Requests

Although a Web server handles each HTTP request independently, the server may retain some information to reduce the overhead of handling future requests. As part of satisfying a request, the server may store the HTTP response body or parts of the HTTP response header in main memory for future use. Similarly, the server may save information generated in the process of handling the request. In each case, the server must take care to avoid sending out-of-date information to the client.

4.3.1 Sharing HTTP responses across requests

In practice, a small proportion of the resources at a Web site are responsible for most of the requests. The server can amortize the overhead of handling these requests by storing frequently requested resources in main memory. Suppose a server receives a request for `http://www.bar.com/foo.html`, a static HTML file. To handle the request, the server must open and read the file that corresponds to this URL. Reading the file triggers the copying of data from the disk to main memory. Accessing the disk imposes load on the system and results in delay in replying to the request. Ideally, the next request for `/foo.html` would not require opening and reading the file again. Instead, the server could transmit the data directly from main memory. This is referred to as *server-side caching* because data from the disk is cached in main memory at the server.

Caching a resource at a Web server is somewhat different than browser or proxy caching. The server stores data in main memory as a local performance optimization. The server needs to ensure that the copy in main memory is consistent with the data stored on the disk. If the file's contents change, the server should not transmit the copy that is stored in main memory. To avoid returning an out-of-date response, the server could check the last modification time of the file on the disk before returning the cached copy; if the file has changed, the server could remove the cached copy from main memory. Alternatively, the file system could notify the server whenever a file is modified. This would trigger the server to evict the cached contents from main memory. In this scenario, the server could send a cached response to the requesting client without explicitly checking the last modification time of the file.

In addition to caching static files, a Web server could also store dynamically generated responses in main memory. Consider a Web site that allows a user to enter a search string and receive a list of URLs for Web pages that contain the string. Many requests contain the same search string. Instead of satisfying each request independently, the server may store the results of common queries in main memory. The server can handle requests that match a cached query, rather than invoking a script to interact with a back-end database. The results of a query may span multiple Web pages, and the user may select the second page after inspecting the items on the first page. The server may satisfy the request for the second page from a cached list of results from the initial query, rather than generating the contents of the second Web page from scratch. Caching dynamically generated responses has the potential to reduce server overhead significantly, particularly for sites that primarily respond to user queries. As with static content, the server would need to ensure that the cached result is consistent with the primary copy of the information. Adding new data to the database should trigger the server to evict the results of previous queries from main memory.

4.3.2 Sharing metadata across requests

In addition to caching Web resources, the server could store the information generated in the process of handling an HTTP request, such as the following:

- **Translation of URL to file name:** The server must map the URL in the request message into the name of the corresponding file. Caching the translation obviates the need to repeat the translation for subsequent requests with the same URL. However, the server must ensure that the cached information is up-to-date; a reconfiguration of the server may change the association between the URL and the file name.
- **Control information about the resource:** The server may also cache the file descriptor that identifies the location of the file in the file system. In addition, the server may cache the basic attributes of the file, such as the size and the last modification time. This reduces the overhead for constructing the HTTP response header for future requests for the same resource. However, the server needs to ensure that the cached attributes are not used if the file has changed in the meantime.
- **HTTP response headers:** The server may cache a portion of the HTTP response header. Many of the headers in the response message convey the attributes of the requested resource (e.g., size, content type, and last modification time) or information about the server (e.g., server software version and configuration). Caching these headers obviates the need for the server to construct them for future requests. However, the server might not cache the entire response header because some fields (e.g., the date/time of the response) may change across successive responses for the same resource.

Caching information across successive responses for the same resource reduces the load on the server, allowing the server to handle a higher rate of requests.

In addition to caching information across multiple requests for the *same* resource, the server could cache certain information across requests for different resources:

- **Current date/time:** The current date/time appears in the HTTP response header and in the server log. Learning the current time requires invoking a system call (e.g., *gettimeofday()* in UNIX) that imposes an overhead on the server. The timestamp is typically recorded at the one second level. Yet, a busy server handles hundreds of requests every second. Rather than repeating the system call for every request, the server could use the same timestamp for a series of requests. For example, the server could invoke the system call after every few requests and when the server has been idle. However, caching the results of the system call for too long may limit the accuracy of the timestamp information available in the server logs.

- **Client name:** In some cases, the handling of a request may depend on the host name of the requesting client. For example, a server may restrict access to a resource or customize the response message for clients in certain domains (e.g., `.edu` or `.competitor.com`). Translating the client's IP address to a host name requires the server to invoke a system call (e.g., *gethostbyaddr()*). By caching this information, the server can avoid repeating the translation process on future requests from the same IP address. However, the translation from IP address to name may change over time. Using out-of-date information may be acceptable in some cases, such as customizing an advertisement on a Web page.

Caching information across requests for different resources offers further opportunities to improve the efficiency of the server.

4.4 Server Architecture

A Web server typically handles multiple client requests at the same time. These requests must share access to the processor, disk, memory, and network interface at the server. In this section, we discuss techniques for allocating system resources among competing client requests. An *event-driven* server has a single process that alternates between servicing different requests, whereas a *process-driven* server allocates each request to a separate process. Hybrid schemes attempt to capture the salient features of these two approaches. Although these approaches have been investigated in a variety of contexts before the advent of the Web, the handling of HTTP requests has important implications on the performance trade-offs.

4.4.1 Event-driven server architecture

The simplest way to structure a server is to have a single process that handles one request at a time. The process would accept a client request, generate a response, and transmit the response to the client before considering the next request. As a natural extension of handling one request at a time, the Web server could consist of a single process that alternates between servicing different requests. Rather than handling a single request in its entirety, the process periodically performs a small amount of work on behalf of each request. This event-driven approach is most appropriate when each request introduces a small, bounded amount of work. Processing a Web request subdivides nicely into a small number of steps—accepting the connection from the client, reading the HTTP request, locating the associated resource, and transmitting the response. In many cases, the server can complete each of these steps in a short period.

However, some of these steps may encounter delays that are beyond the Web server's control. For example, the server cannot start generating the response until the request message arrives from the client. Similarly, retrieving data from the disk may delay the transmission of the response message. While waiting for an operation to complete, the server should be able to switch to another request. This requires careful consideration of any operations that might block the server process. The Web server invokes system calls to instruct the operating system to perform low-level tasks that relate to network connections and disk transfers. To avoid waiting for these tasks to complete, an event-driven Web server typically performs nonblocking system calls that allow the calling process to continue executing while awaiting a response from the operating system. The completion of each operating-system operation constitutes an event that must be handled by the server process.

At any given time, the server may have one or more pending events relating to various Web requests. Handling an event may trigger additional system calls which, in turn, create new events. For example, consider a client that requests a static resource stored on the server's disk. After reading the client request and identifying the URL, the server triggers an event to retrieve the associated file from the disk. While waiting for the data to arrive from the disk, the server can handle another request. Handling all requests in a single process allows the server to serialize operations that modify the same data. This is particularly important in the Web context because HTTP requests may trigger the creation or modification of Web resources. For example, suppose two users attempt to overwrite the same resource. The event-driven server can easily ensure that one write operation completes before the next one starts. In addition, running the Web server as a single process facilitates sharing of data across different requests. For example, suppose two users issue a query with the same search terms. The server can cache the result of the first query and return the same response for the second request.

Structuring a Web server as a single, event-driven process makes the most sense when each event introduces small, bounded delay. For example, parsing an HTTP request is usually a relatively simple task. However, other operations, such as waiting for the arrival of an HTTP request, may incur a longer delay. Fortunately, the operating system performs these functions, allowing the server process to service other requests in the meantime. However, some HTTP requests introduce more substantial processing delays. Writing server software that explicitly alternates between requests introduces substantial complexity into the software design to store intermediate results for each request. For example, dynamically generated Web responses typically require the server to execute a script. The server may not know in advance how long the script must run. Allowing the script to run indefinitely could result in large delays for the other requests. Instead, the script may run as a separate process to enable the server to handle other requests.

An event-driven server must rely on efficient support from the operating system for nonblocking system calls. Support for nonblocking system calls varies across different operating systems. In practice, nonblocking operations that interact with the network interface exhibit good performance. Interactions with the disk subsystem are more complicated. For example, a nonblocking system call to read a file from disk may still block the calling process while performing the disk operation. This can degrade the throughput of the Web server and increase response latency. These operating-system limitations, coupled with the challenges of developing the server software, argue against an event-driven architecture. As a result, most high-end Web servers do not have an event-driven architecture. Still, several experimental Web servers employ the event-driven model, and elements of the event-driven approach arise in other architectures.

4.4.2 Process-driven server architecture

As an alternative to the event-driven architecture, the server could devote a separate process to each request. In this approach, each process performs all of the steps involved in handling a single request. Running multiple processes enables the server to service multiple requests at the same time. In contrast to the event-driven approach, the process-driven model depends on the underlying operating system to switch between the various requests. The operating system runs one process for a period of time (say, 10 ms or 100 ms) before switching to another process. This gives the illusion that each process runs on a separate computer. In addition, if a process blocks waiting for a system call to complete, the operating system starts running another process. For example, while one process waits to receive data from the disk, another process can execute.

A process-driven Web server typically has one master process that simply listens for new connections from clients. For each new connection, the master process creates, or *forks,* a separate process to handle the connection. After parsing the client request and transmitting the response, the process terminates. Terminating the forked process after handling a request protects the system from certain kinds of programming errors. A process that does not release memory resources could gradually consume increasingly more memory. This is referred to as a *memory leak.* As part of terminating a process, the operating system automatically reclaims any memory that has been allocated to the process. The simplicity of this approach allows developers to focus on the core of the server software (parsing requests and generating responses). Most early Web servers adopted this model, including the CERN and NCSA servers [KMR95].

The overhead of forking and terminating a process is significant relative to the work involved in handling an HTTP request for a small, static resource.

To reduce the overhead, a set of processes could be created when the server starts. Once created, a process handles one request after another. When a new connection arrives, the master process identifies an existing, inactive process to handle the request, rather than creating a new process. In addition to reducing server overhead, using an existing process reduces the latency experienced by the user. However, this approach is sensitive to programming errors that cause memory leaks. Even if the Web server software does not have such errors, many Web sites incorporate libraries or scripts written by third-party programmers. This software may have memory leaks. To address this problem, the server may terminate the process after handling a certain number of requests. Alternatively, the Web server could employ advanced memory-management techniques that limit the amount of memory consumed by each process, as discussed in more detail in the context of the Apache Web server in Section 4.6.1.

Despite the performance improvements offered by preforking processes, the process-driven approach has several limitations. First, switching from one process to another introduces overhead. The operating system must save information about the running process and update various tables and lists before loading information about the next process; in the event-driven approach, the data structures for the active requests are stored in a single process. In the process-driven model, switching to another process may require loading new data from the disk into main memory, or from the main memory into the processor's cache. Most Web requests do not require significant computation, making the switching between processes a more substantial portion of work performed by the server. Second, additional overhead arises when the processes need to share data. Each process is its own program, with its own address space. In the Web, a small number of resources account for the majority of requests. Storing these commonly requested resources in main memory avoids the expense of retrieving or generating the response from scratch for each request. In a process-driven server, sharing the resources in main memory requires coordination between the processes.

4.4.3 Hybrid server architecture

Hybrid server architectures attempt to combine the strengths of the event-driven and process-driven models. For example, the process-driven model could be generalized to permit each process to handle more than one request at a time. In effect, each process would become an event-driven server that alternates between a small collection of requests. This reduces the number of processes and lowers the overhead of sharing information across the set of requests directed to the same process. However, this approach inherits some of the weaknesses of the event-driven and process-driven approaches. Like event-driven servers, this approach requires care to ensure that handling a single request does not introduce substantial delay for servicing other requests. Limiting the number of requests associated with each process reduces the likelihood of encountering this problem. Like process-driven servers, the hybrid server incurs the overhead of switching between processes and sharing data between processes. Still, handling multiple requests in the same process reduces the number of processes and permits some sharing among the requests within a process.

A second approach addresses the overhead of switching between processes. Some operating systems allow a single process to have multiple independent *threads* of control. Each thread is a sequential flow of execution in the shared address space of the containing process. A multithreaded Web server could assign a thread to each request. The server would have a single process, like an event-driven server, with multiple distinct flows of execution, like a process-driven server. In contrast to an event-driven server, the multithreaded process does not need to coordinate the switching between threads explicitly. When one thread performs a blocking system call, the other threads in the same process can run. The overhead of switching between threads is lower than switching between processes because threads in the same process share a common address space. This enables the threads to share information across requests. For example, the threads could share access to popular resources and certain HTTP response headers. Still, the threads must employ some form of synchronization to access the shared data. Developing software for a multithreaded server is usually somewhat complicated. Threads running in the same process are not protected from each other; without careful coordination, one thread may overwrite data needed by another thread. In addition, the lack of support for threads in some operating systems makes it difficult to develop a multithreaded server that can run on a variety of platforms.

A third approach combines the salient features of the event-driven and process-driven models in a hybrid scheme [PDZ99]. The event-driven approach is well suited to handling requests that do not incur significant processing or disk overheads. Many Web requests result in short response messages that do not require disk access. For example, suppose a client requests a resource that does not exist. Recognizing that the URL does not correspond to any file or script at the site, the server would reply with a brief error message. In addition, the server may have many popular Web responses cached in main memory, obviating the need to access the disk. This suggests a hybrid server architecture that applies the event-driven approach by default. The server has a main event-driven process that handles the initial stages of every request. If a request requires significant computation (e.g., when the server must invoke a script) or a disk access (e.g., when handling a request requires retrieving a file from the disk), then the main process instructs a separate helper process to perform the time-consuming operation(s). The event-driven process can handle the transmission of the response to the client, using nonblocking system calls.

4.5 Server Hosting

Throughout the chapter, we have implicitly assumed that each Web server runs on a single machine and each machine runs a single Web server. However, this is not always true. In practice, a single computer may host content for multiple Web sites. In addition, a popular Web site may be replicated on multiple machines.

4.5.1 Multiple Web sites on a single machine

In the early days of the Web, an individual or institution that wanted a Web site would install Web server software on a single computer. Each Web site was administered locally. With the commercialization of the Internet, it is increasingly common to have Web sites operated by a separate hosting company. A Web hosting company could have a collection of computers in one or more locations. Separating the roles of the content creator and the hosting provider offers several important advantages:

- The hosting company takes care of all of the technical details of running and maintaining the servers, obviating the need for each institution to have in-house expertise in managing Web servers.
- The hosting company provides a computing and network infrastructure to support heavy demand for the Web site, obviating the need for the content creator to invest in these resources.
- The hosting company can amortize the cost of the computing and networking resources over a large number of Web sites.
- The owner of the content does not risk exposing its other data to the Internet by allowing access to its own machines. In addition, traffic to and from the Web site does not impart load on the institution's IP network.

However, the owner of the content becomes critically dependent on the hosting company to provide efficient, reliable access to the Web site. In addition, making changes to the content requires some coordination with the hosting company.

The hosting company typically hosts multiple Web sites and allows the content creators to update the content. Many Web sites are not popular enough to consume all of the processing, disk, and memory resources of a single computer. Some sites are very popular during certain times of the day and are relatively lightly loaded the rest of the time. For example, sites serving businesses may be active during the day, and entertainment sites may be more popular in the evening. Hosting multiple Web servers on a single computer offers an effective way for the hosting company to reduce cost. In addition, combining Web sites that stress different resources on the computer provides a good way to take advantage of the entire system. For example, a site with mostly dynamically generated content may consume substantial processing resources, whereas a site with a large amount of static content may task the disk subsystem. Running these two sites on the same machine makes efficient use of both the processor and the disk.

Running multiple sites on the same machine requires a way to direct client requests to the appropriate site. Consider a company, `hostmany.com`, that hosts content for companies `foo.com` and `bar.com` on the same computer. The simplest approach would be to have the machine run a single server `www.hostmany.com` that accepts requests to both sites. For example, the companies could have separate sets of files on the disk, and all URLs could start with `http://www.hostmany.com/foo/` or `http://www.hostmany.com/bar/` to indicate which set of files the server should access. However, this approach would not be acceptable to many content creators. Most content creators would prefer to have their own hostnames, which are visible to the rest of the Internet. For example, the two companies may want their Web sites to have hostnames `www.foo.com` and `www.bar.com`, respectively.

To allow separate hostnames, the hosting company could run multiple Web servers on a single machine. The servers are referred to as *virtual servers.* Each virtual server has its own document tree and configuration options and operates as if it were the only Web server on the machine. Suppose that `www.foo.com` and `www.bar.com` run on the same host. A request for `http://www.foo.com/index.html` would refer to the resource `/index.html` on the `www.foo.com` virtual server, whereas a request for `http://www.bar.com/index.html` would refer to the resource `/index.html` on the `www.bar.com` virtual server. As part of sending an HTTP request, a Web client must determine the IP address of the Web server. In the early days of the Web, each virtual server needed to have its own IP address to ensure that the client's HTTP request would reach the correct server. For example, `www.foo.com` and `www.bar.com` could be assigned 10.63.127.8 and 10.63.127.9, respectively, even though the two virtual servers run on the same machine.

Many operating systems include support for assigning multiple IP addresses to a single machine. Traffic sent to either address would reach the correct machine; then the operating system would direct the data to the appropriate virtual server. This approach is effective but not particularly efficient. First, the operating system may impose limits on the number of server processes or the number of IP addresses for a single machine. Second, assigning a separate address to every Web server consumes a large part of the Internet's currently limited address space. The rapid growth in the number of Web sites in the 1990s exacerbated both of these problems. This led to changes in HTTP to allow multiple virtual servers to have the same IP address, as discussed in Chapter 7 (Section 7.8).

4.5.2 Multiple machines for a single Web site

The most popular Web sites receive an extremely large number of client requests, well in excess of what a single machine can support. Handling a high rate of requests typically requires replicating the content on multiple machines. The simplest way to duplicate the content is to devote a separate name to each replica. For example, consider a Web site that allows users to download new software, such as the latest version of a Web browser. The user may be able to select from a list of *mirror* sites that can provide the content. This helps distribute the load over the collection of sites. The list may also indicate the geographical location of the various replicas, enabling the user to retrieve the content from a nearby server. This reduces the load on the network and the delay to download the content. For downloading large software packages, these benefits outweigh the inconvenience of requiring the user to select a particular replica manually.

However, having a separate server for each replica has several disadvantages. Manual selection of a particular server is tedious for the user, especially for conventional Web browsing. Ideally, the replication of the content at different machines would be transparent to the user. Manual selection does not necessarily balance the load. An individual user is not aware of the choices made by other users or the current load on the servers. Having a different name for each replica also consumes multiple hostnames and results in multiple URLs that refer to the same content. Consider a Web page bar.html that is replicated at two servers www1.big.com and www2.big.com. Suppose the resource http://www1.big.com/bar.html has been stored in the browser cache. In the future, the user may issue a request for http://www2.big.com/bar.html. However, the browser would not know that this URL refers to the same content and, hence, could not return the cached contents.

Using the same name for each of the replicas avoids these problems. However, this requires an effective way to deliver a client request to a single replica. The simplest approach is to assign a different IP address to each replica. For example, www.big.com could run on two hosts with IP addresses 10.198.3.47 and 10.198.3.48, respectively. The translation of the server name into a particular IP address is performed by the Domain Name System (DNS), as discussed in Chapter 5 (Section 5.3.5). As an alternative approach, the name www.foo.com could be associated with a single IP address that corresponds to a surrogate that resides in front of the Web hosting complex, as shown in Figure 4.1. This proxy could decide which replica should handle the client's request. The selection of the replica could be based on a variety of criteria, such as the load on the servers or the requested URL. Techniques for selecting the best replica are an active area of research, as discussed in more detail in Chapter 11 (Section 11.13).

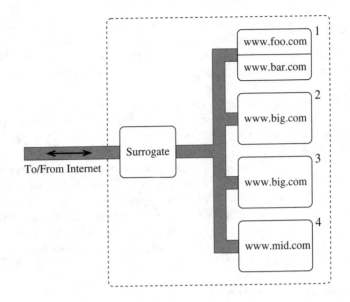

Figure 4.1. Hosting complex with surrogate in front of four server machines

Replicating the same content on multiple servers introduces several practical challenges. A sequence of requests from the same client might not be handled by the same replica. Having each replica generate the same response to the same request is extremely important. Each server must have each URL correspond to exactly the same content and trigger an identical HTTP response. If the content changes, the new data must be available from each replica. If each server retrieves resources from its own file system, any change to a file requires updating the copy at every replica. In addition, the replicas must have consistent access-control policies. A user should not be permitted access to a resource on one replica and denied access on another. This requires each server to have the same user-name and password information and access control policies. Similarly, if the Web site uses cookies, then the replicas must agree on how they generate and interpret cookies.

4.6 Case Study of the Apache Web Server

To illustrate the operation of a Web server, we present a case study of the popular, freely available Apache server software [Apa, LL99]. Released in 1995, the first version (0.6.2) of the Apache server was based on the earlier NCSA software [KBM94]. In fact, the name "Apache" refers to the fact that the software consisted of existing code along with some "patches" ("a patchy server").

The software was developed by volunteers who formed the original Apache Group [MFH00]. The Apache server has been the most popular Web server from 1996 onward [Netc]. Commercial server software, most notably from Netscape and Microsoft, are also commonly used, especially for large commercial Web sites.

In this section, we provide an overview of the basic operation of version 1.3.3 of the Apache server. Installing the Apache server can be as simple as copying the appropriate executable binary onto a machine. However, in most cases, Web administrators customize the software to the requirements of their server sites. This typically involves configuring parameters that affect the allocation of server resources, interpretation of HTTP requests, setting of HTTP response headers, access control, and server logging. The goal of this section is to convey, at a high level, how the server operates and to illustrate what kinds of configuration options are available to a site administrator. Although the discussion focuses on the Apache server, many of the same issues arise in any Web server software.

4.6.1 Resource management

The Apache 1.3.3 server assigns a separate process to each connection, in contrast to the recently developed Apache 2.0 server, which has a multithreaded implementation. File and memory resources are allocated in *pools* that are released automatically when a process terminates.

PROCESS MODEL

The Apache server follows the process-driven model, with a parent process that assigns a process to each new connection. Rather than creating a new process for every new connection, the parent preforks several child processes when the server starts. The number of initial child processes (**StartServers**) is one of several configurable parameters that relate to child processes, as summarized in Table 4.2. The server balances the trade-off between having too many processes or too few. The server imposes a limit on the number of simultaneous processes (**MaxClients**) that is configurable when the server software is compiled. In theory, the server could always have this many processes, even if many of them are idle, awaiting new connections. Keeping a set of idle processes avoids the overhead of forking new processes when more requests arrive. However, having a large number of idle processes consumes operating system resources unnecessarily.

The Apache server imposes a limit on the minimum and maximum number of idle processes (**MinSpareServers** and **MaxSpareServers**). Every few seconds, the parent process determines how many child processes are idle. Then the parent creates or terminates child processes, depending on whether the number is too low or too high. Killing idle processes returns resources to the operating

Table 4.2. Key configuration directives for child processes and network connections

Directive	Definition (default value in Apache 1.3.3)
StartServers	Initial number of child processes (5)
MaxClients	Maximum number of child processes (256)
MinSpareServers	Target minimum number of idle children (5)
MaxSpareServers	Target maximum number of idle children (10)
MaxRequestsPerChild	Maximum number of requests per child (30)
ListenBacklog	Maximum number of pending connections (511)
SendBufferSize	Size of the TCP send buffer (OS default)
MaxKeepAliveRequests	Max number of requests per connection (100)
KeepAliveTimeout	Maximum idle time for connection (15 sec)

system that can be used by active processes and reduces system overhead. When the number of idle processes is low, creating new processes prepares the server for future client requests. By spawning more processes before the requests arrive, the server ensures that process creation does not delay the handling of new client requests. This approach to creating and terminating processes is an effective way to achieve the dual goals of running with a relatively small number of idle processes and limiting the rate of creation of new processes. In addition to removing idle processes occasionally, the Apache server imposes a configurable limit on the number of HTTP requests handled by each child process (`MaxRequestsPerChild`). The child process is terminated after reaching this limit.

The Apache server has certain default settings for each of the configurable parameters. However, the appropriate parameter settings depend on the mixture of client requests. Consider a server that receives requests from a large number of low-bandwidth clients. This argues for allowing the server to have a relatively large number of active processes, for two reasons. First, the clients' bandwidth limitations require the server to transmit at a low rate, requiring a longer service time for each request. Second, the server needs to have a relatively large number of simultaneous transfers to make efficient use of its link to the Internet. As another example, consider a server that executes a script for nearly every HTTP request. Running a script consumes significant processing resources at the server. For a reasonable response time for client requests, the server may need to impose a relatively small limit on the number of simultaneous processes. Optimizing the server throughput and response latency requires tuning of the configurable parameters.

The Apache server has configuration options that relate to the underlying network connection handled by each child process. The Transmission Control Protocol (TCP) coordinates the delivery of request and response messages, as discussed in more detail in Chapter 5 (Section 5.2). A parent process listens for client requests to establish TCP connections. When each of the child processes has a connection, the operating system maintains a queue of pending connections. The Apache server imposes a limit on the number of queued connections (`ListenBacklog`). The operating system has a send buffer for storing outgoing data for each established connection. The Apache server can change the default size of this buffer (`SendBufferSize`). Increasing the send buffer size enables higher throughput, particularly when there is high delay between the server and the client. Finally, the server limits the number of HTTP requests on a single TCP connection (`MaxKeepAliveRequests`) and the maximum time a connection can remain idle (`KeepAliveTimeout`). When either of these limits is reached, the client process terminates the TCP connection.

RESOURCE POOLS

A Web server consists of software modules performing various tasks, such as listening for new connections, parsing requests, generating responses, and transmitting response messages. Like any other software, these modules consume operating system resources. For example, handling a request may require a process to allocate memory, access a file, create a child process to execute a script, and transmit data over the TCP connection to the client. One of the main challenges in designing a large server is to ensure that these operating system resources are used efficiently. Problems arise when application software does not release these system resources upon completing a task. If the available system resources diminish over time, then active processes cannot acquire the resources they need. This is not acceptable for a Web server that must run continuously for a long period. Instead, the system must reclaim resources as the tasks complete.

The Apache server addresses this issue with the *pool* abstraction. A pool is a data structure that tracks a group of operating-system resources that are created and destroyed together. Consider an erroneous request that results in an error condition. The process handling the request can simply destroy the associated pool to return the resources to the operating system for use by other modules. The pool abstraction isolates the allocation and deallocation of resources into a small, well-tested part of the server software. This protects the server from programming mistakes or error conditions that arise in other parts of the code. The utility of the pool abstraction rests on two main tenets—the routines that support the pool abstraction should work correctly, and the rest of the server software should not circumvent the use of pools by allocating or deallocating resources in some other manner.

Other parts of the server software interact with pools via an application programming interface (API). The API includes basic functions to create, initialize, or destroy a pool. Other functions provide information about the available resources in the pool or to allocate resources within the pool. For example, a pool created to handle a client request may allocate memory for storing the HTTP request message and for creating the HTTP response message. The API also includes specific functions for creating and manipulating strings. This is particularly useful in constructing HTTP response headers. For example, the server process may need to copy information from the client's request into another buffer or concatenate two strings. After completing the client request, the process can clear the pool to release these buffers and close any associated files or connections. Terminating a process also releases the system resources associated with the pool.

4.6.2 HTTP request processing

The Apache server proceeds through five key steps in processing an HTTP request: (1) converting the requested URL into a file name, (2) determining whether the request has permission to access the file, (3) identifying and invoking a handler to generate a response, (4) transmitting the response to the client, and (5) logging the request [Tha96]. Each phase is handled by one or more software modules. The Apache server includes various core modules. Additional modules can be written by third-party developers to provide alternative ways of performing each phase of request handling. The combination of open software and extensible modules has been a major factor in the widespread adoption of the Apache server.

TRANSLATING THE URL TO A FILE NAME

In the first stage of handling an HTTP request, the server associates the URL with a particular file name, if any. This can be a rather complicated process that depends on the configuration of the server. The core part of the server software performs basic preprocessing to canonicalize the URL. For example, many Web sites allow individual users to create Web pages. The URL `http://www.bar.com/~peter` may map to `/usr/users/peter/public_html/wwwfiles`. This would involve configuring the server to perform a conversion function on all URLs containing the "~" character. Similarly, the server may need to preprocess the URL to remove certain strings. For example, `http://www.bar.com//a.html` may be converted to `http://www.bar.com/a.html` by removing duplicate "/" characters. Similarly, `http://www.bar.com/b/../a.html` would also be converted to `http://www.bar.com/a.html` in response to seeing the ".." string.

Apache includes numerous configurable software modules for manipulating URLs. Each server has a configurable base directory where files are located. Consider a Web server, `www.bar.com`, with the root directory `/www`. The URL `http://www.bar.com/foo.html` would be translated to the file name `/www/foo.html`. To store files in different locations, the Apache server allows the specification of aliases. Aliases provide a way to decouple the directory structure at the server from the URLs visible to the outside world. Otherwise, a reorganization of the files at the server would invalidate existing URLs. In addition, aliases can be used to allow multiple URLs to map to a single resource. For example, the URLs `http://www.bar.com/~bala/kandr.ps` and `http://www.bar.com/~jrex/kandr.ps` may both correspond to the file `/www/book17.ps`. Mapping of the URL to a file name can also depend on when the server receives the request. For example, the server can be configured to map `http://www.bar.com/a.html` to `http://www.bar.com/morning.html` during the morning and `http://www.bar.com/afternoon.html` during the afternoon.

The Apache software includes an optional module for correcting common misspellings of "words" in the URL. The module can inspect the requested directory to see if any file's name has a close match with the requested file (e.g., including the addition, deletion, or transposition of a single character, or the change of lower and upper case). However, this feature introduces overhead to scan the list of files in the directory and identify a possible match. In addition, sending responses based on a partial match may inadvertently expose a file that was not meant to be available to requesting clients. The server also has a module that rewrites requested URLs based on a configurable set of rules. The rewriting module uses a regular-expression parser to match portions of the URL string. Manipulations can vary based on a variety of parameters, including HTTP request headers. For example, an HTTP request message may include a `User-Agent` header that provides information about the user's browser. Rewriting the URL based on this information enables a server to return a different resource to the user depending on the browser.

DETERMINING WHETHER THE REQUEST IS AUTHORIZED

Access control policies depend on the configuration of the server. For example, access to resource `http://www.bar.com/books/a.html` could be restricted to a particular set of clients. Requests coming from certain hostnames or IP addresses could be disallowed, or users could be required to provide a valid name and password. To avoid the tedium of specifying access control policies for each resource, a single policy may be applied to collections of resources. Configuration files consist of directives that control access to a Web resource depending on the URL, file name, directory, or virtual server. The configuration

```
<Directory /www/books>
AuthType Basic
AuthName specialuser
AutUserFile /www/let_them_in/users
require valid-user
</Directory>
```

restricts access to files in the directory /www/books to users that provide a valid
password for the specialuser realm. The file /www/let_them_in/users has
a list usernames and their (encrypted) passwords. The configuration

```
<Directory /www/cgi-bin>
order deny,allow
deny from all
allow from 10.9.57.188
</Directory>
```

accepts requests only for resources in /www/cgi-bin from a Web client with IP
address 10.9.57.188.

The Web site administrator can specify these policies in a central configuration file, with one directive per line. However, using a central configuration file
has two main disadvantages. First, any change to the configuration file requires
restarting the server. Second, configuring policies on behalf of a large set of Web
pages with different authors can become a burden for the site administrator.
To address these problems, the site administrator can allow individual users to
override the default configuration in the central file. Each directory can have an
.htaccess file that specifies policies for that directory and any subdirectories.
This enables a user named Viv with files in the directory /www/users/viv to
have a file /www/users/viv/.htaccess that overrides the default policies specified for /www/users. The main configuration file determines which directives
can be specified in individual .htaccess files. This enables the site administrator to constrain the access control policies applied by individual users.

After realizing that the URL corresponds to a particular file, the server
starts the *directory walk* process to determine which policies to apply to the
requested file. The server checks the central configuration file for any directives
that apply to the file. Then the server inspects the .htaccess files one directory
at a time. For the file /www/users/viv, the server checks the central configuration file, followed by /www/users/.htaccess and /www/users/viv/.htaccess.
At each step, the server may accumulate additional configuration directives that
apply to the requested file. Because the .htaccess files are evaluated for each
request, the configuration can be changed without restarting the server. However, looking for an .htaccess file in each subdirectory incurs an overhead on
the server in processing the request. The site administrator can limit the performance impact by constraining which subdirectories are allowed to override
the directives in the central configuration file.

GENERATING AND TRANSMITTING THE RESPONSE

As part of parsing an HTTP request, the server creates and populates a *request record* data structure that is used by various other software modules.
The request record contains information from the request itself, including the

URL, the HTTP protocol version, and the content type and content encoding of data sent by the client (if any). The record has a pointer to the pool that has been allocated for handling this request; the pool is cleared when the server completes the handling of the request. The record includes information gleaned from the previous stages of processing the request—the filename associated with the URL and the list of configuration directives associated with the resource. Other portions of the request record, such as the HTTP response headers, are assigned as the server generates the response message.

Apache has a collection of *handlers* that perform an action using the requested file, as summarized in Table 4.3. The handler is typically assigned based on the filename extension or location, as dictated by the configuration of the server. The Apache software has several built-in handlers. The default handler sends the contents of the file to the client, adding necessary HTTP response headers. Another handler can send the file "as is," with the HTTP headers included in the file. This is useful, for example, for returning a precomputed HTTP message that redirects the client when the requested resource has moved to a new location. Apache defines handlers for dynamic content that treat the file as a CGI script, a server-side include file, or an *imagemap* rule file for clickable maps. For example, consider a request for

```
http://www.germancities.de/imagemap/country?163,83
```

the numbers 163 and 83 reflect the location of the user's cursor when clicking on the map. The file `/www/imagemap/country` associates regions of the image with URLs. To handle the request, the server identifies the URL associated with the coordinates and sends a response that directs the browser to initiate another HTTP request using the new URL. The file can also be interpreted as *type map* that supports content negotiation by listing the names of files containing different variants of the resource (e.g., in English and in Spanish). Depending on information in the request header, the server determines which file and HTTP headers to return to the client. Other handlers relate to the management of the server, treating the file as server configuration information or a status report.

The configuration of the server also determines what metadata appear in the HTTP response header. The Web server associates certain filename extensions with particular attributes of the resource. The server can have a configuration file that defines the Multipurpose Internet Mail Extensions (MIME) type associated with each filename extension:

```
application/octet-stream     bin exe pax tgz jar
application/pdf               pdf
application/postscript        ai eps ps
audio/x-pn-realaudio          ram rm
audio/x-realaudio             ra
```

Table 4.3. Built-in handlers in Apache server and default file extensions

Handler	Purpose (file extension)
default-handler	Send the file as static content
send-as-is	Send the file as an HTTP response message (.asis)
cgi-script	Invoke the file as a CGI script (.cgi)
server-parsed	Treat the file a server-side include (.shtml)
imap-file	Treat the file as an Imagemap rule file (.imap)
type-map	Treat the file as a map for content negotiation (.var)
server-info	Get the server's configuration information
server-status	Get the server's status report

```
image/gif        gif
image/jpeg       jpeg jpg jpe
text/html        html htm
text/plain       txt
video/mpeg       mpeg mpg mpe
```

For example, a URL that corresponds to the file /www/index.html would trigger the default-handler that transmits the file's contents to the client. The file extension .html would lead the server to include the header the header `Content-Type: text/html` in the response message. Upon receiving the response, the browser uses the `Content-Type` header to select the appropriate helper application to display the response, as discussed earlier, in Chapter 2 (Section 2.4.3).

The browser's interpretation of the response message also depends on other metadata, such as the encoding format and the language. The server assigns these attributes based on configuration commands, such as

```
AddEncoding x-compress    Z
AddEncoding x-gzip        gz
AddLanguage en            .en
AddLanguage fr            .fr
AddLanguage de            .de
AddLanguage it            .it
```

A filename can have multiple extensions, each corresponding to different metadata. For example, the file /www/index.en.html.Z would correspond to a compressed HTML file in the English language. Configuration also determines whether the response header includes information related to caching. For example, suppose the site administrator knows that a particular set of resources changes at noon every day. Then the server could be configured to include the appropriate expiration time in the HTTP response header when these resources are requested. The requesting client could use this information to decide how long to cache the response.

4.7 Summary

In generating and transmitting responses to client requests, a Web server performs a variety of important tasks. The server associates the URL in the request message with a particular file and determines how to generate the response message. In addition, the server decides whether the request is authorized. Responding to the request may involve retrieving the requested file from the disk or invoking a script that generates the response. The script can create the response based on the user's cookie and information stored in a back-end database, without the involvement of the Web server. The server does not necessarily retain any state across successive requests, although storing some information may reduce the overhead of responding to future requests. A busy server typically handles requests from a large number of clients at the same time. Scaling a server to handle a high request rate requires careful consideration of the server architecture. The limitations of event-driven and process-driven architectures have led to the development of hybrid schemes. Handling the heavy demands on a popular Web site requires replicating the content on multiple machines. In contrast, a less popular site may share a single machine with other Web sites.

Part III

Web Protocols

5

Protocols Underlying HTTP

Web transfers depend on a suite of communication protocols. A protocol defines both the syntax and the semantics of the messages exchanged between senders and receivers. For example, the Hypertext Transfer Protocol (HTTP) defines the format and meaning of the requests sent by Web clients and the responses sent by Web servers. Networking protocols are typically developed in *layers* with each handling a specific aspect of communication. The protocol suite for the Internet consists of four main layers, as illustrated in Figure 5.1:

- **Link layer:** The link layer handles the hardware details of interfacing with the physical communication medium, such as an Ethernet, Asynchronous Transfer Mode (ATM), or Synchronous Optical Network (SONET).
- **Network layer:** The network layer handles the delivery of individual *packets* of data through the network. A network-layer protocol is implemented in routers and the end hosts.
- **Transport layer:** The transport layer coordinates the communication between hosts on behalf of the application layer. In practice, a transport-layer protocol is typically implemented in the operating system of the end host.
- **Application layer:** The application layer handles the details of specific applications. In practice, an application-layer protocol is typically implemented as part of the application software, such as a Web browser or Web server.

This division of functionality enables each protocol to focus on performing a single task with well-defined interfaces to the protocols in adjacent layers. The standardization of the protocols enables interoperability between components developed by different vendors.

In this chapter, we present a detailed overview of the three main protocols involved in the transfer of HTTP messages, starting at the network layer:

- **Internet Protocol (IP):** IP is a network-layer protocol that coordinates the delivery of individual packets (units of information) from one host to

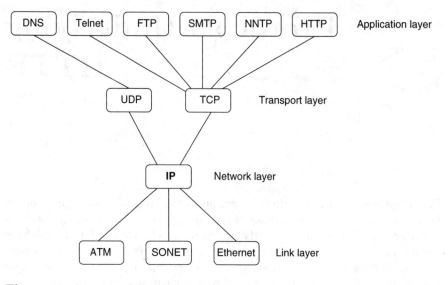

Figure 5.1. Layering of protocols

another, based on the IP address of the destination host. IP runs over a wide variety of link-layer technologies.

- **Transmission Control Protocol (TCP):** TCP is a transport-layer protocol that coordinates the transmission of IP packets in order to provide the abstraction of a reliable, bidirectional connection between two communicating applications. TCP is the primary transport protocol in the Internet, although some applications use the User Datagram Protocol (UDP).

- **Domain Name System (DNS):** DNS is an application-layer protocol that controls the translation of hostnames, such as `www.foo.com`, into IP addresses, and vice versa. DNS provides this general service to a wide variety of applications.

HTTP transfers depend on DNS for translating the server name into an IP address, TCP for sending the HTTP request to the server and the HTTP response to the client, and IP for delivering the individual packets. After a detailed discussion of IP, TCP, and DNS, we present a brief overview of four important application-layer protocols: Telnet, File Transfer Protocol (FTP), Simple Mail Transfer Protocol (SMTP), and Network News Transfer Protocol (NNTP). These protocols support applications that predated the Web and influenced the design of HTTP. In addition, these protocols have become a part of the Web because they can be invoked in the context of the Web browser.

5.1 Internet Protocol

The Internet Protocol (IP) is the network-level protocol underlying the Internet, a collection of interconnected networks spanning the globe. In this section, we describe how the Internet evolved from an experimental network connecting a small number of research institutions in the 1960s. Then we discuss the key design goals that influenced the specification of IP and explain the use of IP addresses to identify hosts. For completeness, we also present an overview of the information carried in the header of an IP packet.

5.1.1 Evolution of the Internet architecture

In the late 1960s, the United States had a small number of high-speed super-computers used for scientific research at various national laboratories. These machines typically executed large computations in a batch mode, with users submitting jobs and collecting the results later. Initially, these supercomputers could be accessed only by people at the same physical location. The large cost of these supercomputers motivated the Department of Defense's Advanced Research Projects Agency (ARPA) to find some way to share the computing resources across the national laboratories and university research groups. This led to the creation of the ARPANET network to interconnect the research organizations. In addition to providing remote access to supercomputers, the ARPANET facilitated collaboration across sites by allowing users to share files and exchange e-mail.

The growth of the ARPANET continued in the 1970s. An increasing number of universities and research organizations around the world began to connect to the network. In addition, communication protocols were developed for a variety of applications, including FTP. In 1980, the formalization of open, standard protocols for transmitting data over the ARPANET set the stage for the rapid growth of the number of hosts on the network. The IP and TCP standards were crucial to allowing communication between different types of computers over diverse networking technologies. Another important contribution was the implementation of IP in the Berkeley Software Distribution (BSD) version of the UNIX operating system. BSD UNIX was freely available to universities, enabling a larger set of users to access the ARPANET. In some cases, a single institution would have a local area network with multiple computers that needed access to the ARPANET. Increasingly, the ARPANET was used to interconnect a collection of *networks,* rather than computers.

Starting in 1988, the ARPANET was gradually replaced by the NSFNET, an Internet backbone funded by the National Science Foundation (NSF). As with the ARPANET, use of the NSFNET was initially limited to universities and research laboratories. Starting in the early 1990s, the NSFNET began to allow commercial traffic. During the mid-1990s, the Internet evolved into a large, commercial network, spurred by the rapid emergence of the World Wide

Web as the dominant application. In the United States, the government-funded network was replaced by a collection of backbone networks operated by large service providers. Still, the government played an important role by funding the creation of several Internet exchange points, where the commercial backbones meet to transfer traffic. By the end of the 1990s, the Internet consisted of a diverse collection of backbone networks interconnected via public exchange points and direct connections. The increasing amount of data transferred on the network has led to expansion of the network in terms of its size, speed, and scope, with nearly every country in the world having some Internet presence. More detailed discussions of the history of the Internet are available in other sources [Sal95, LCC+97, Abb99, ISO].

At the beginning of the 21st century, the Internet consists of a collection of networks, each operated by an institution such as a university, company, or government branch. Each institution has its own networking equipment for exchanging traffic between users and with the rest of the Internet. The network consists of routers that direct traffic across a collection of links. Links consist of a wide variety of different media, ranging from telephone lines to high-speed fiber optics. A router is a special-purpose computer that is devoted to directing traffic from its incoming links to its outgoing links. The routers run a suite of protocols standardized by the Internet Engineering Task Force (IETF). The fact that IP does not depend on the underlying link-layer technology has been critical to enabling Internet traffic to travel over a variety of types of links and between routers built by different equipment vendors.

Upon receiving traffic on an incoming link, a router must select an outgoing link to carry that traffic toward its ultimate destination. A suite of routing protocols coordinate the selection of routes for IP traffic to follow. Within a single network, routers communicate using intradomain protocols, whereas interdomain protocols are used to communicate among networks. The separation between intradomain and interdomain routing is similar in spirit to the delivery of postal mail. First, the letter is routed from the region that sent the letter to the region that is receiving the letter. Then the receiving region can handle the details of delivering the letter to the correct recipient. The letter may travel through several post offices in different states or countries. Still, the sender only needs to know the *address* of the receiver, not the entire path. In fact, any individual post office does not need to know the entire path, just the next step in the journey. Similarly, an IP router simply forwards Internet traffic to the next router (the "next hop") in its journey. The analogy of the postal system provides a useful way to explain a variety of concepts in IP networks.

5.1.2 IP design goals

IP evolved from a set of design goals [Cla88] for the ARPANET. The key idea of IP is to keep the network relatively simple and put any necessary intelligence

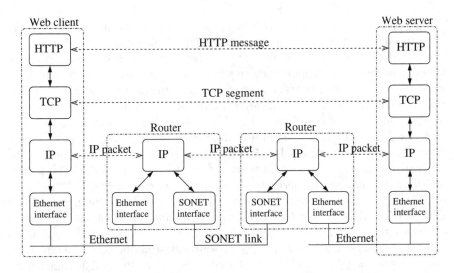

Figure 5.2. Protocols involved in transferring HTTP messages

in the end hosts. This is in sharp contrast to the telephone network, which has very complicated switches but simple edge devices (i.e., telephones). At the most basic level, IP provides a framework for sending individual *packets*. A packet is a unit of information—a certain number of bytes of data, as specified by the sender. In traveling from the sending host to the receiving host, a packet traverses a collection of routers that communicate via IP, as shown in Figure 5.2. Returning to the postal analogy, sending an IP packet through the Internet is analogous to sending a letter through the postal system. The postal system makes its best effort to deliver the letter in a timely manner. However, a letter may not reach its intended recipient or may experience an unusually long delay. A series of letters sent from one person to another may not arrive in order.

Similarly, the routers in the Internet treat each packet independently and do not need to retain state across successive packets. A sequence of IP packets traveling from one host to another may not traverse the same path through the network. Packets may be lost, corrupted, or delivered out of order. In this sense, the postal system and the Internet are both very different from the traditional telephone network. The telephone network determines the path for the call and allocates the necessary bandwidth before transmitting any data. For example, the network could dedicate 64 Kb/sec for each telephone call on each link in its route. The telephone connection is not established unless sufficient resources are available. This ensures that existing telephone calls are not affected by the decision to accept a new connection. In contrast, the postal system does not explicitly limit the number of letters that can be mailed; performance may degrade during busy periods, such as major holidays. The model of the Internet and the postal system is referred to as *packet switching,* in contrast to the *circuit-switching* model used in the traditional telephone network.

The differences stem from the fact that the Internet was designed for a very different purpose—to support remote access to shared computing resources. A user may spend several hours connected to a remote machine and have long periods of inactivity. Having a dedicated circuit for this traffic would be wasteful. Instead, Internet traffic is divided into IP packets that are sent as needed. Because traffic may be generated at any time, each packet must include a *header* identifying the destination. The header of an IP packet is analogous to the envelope containing a letter that is mailed via the postal system. The header information would not be necessary in a circuit-switched network. Despite the overhead of sending a header with every packet, packet switching is typically more efficient than circuit switching in transmitting bursts of data because a packet-switched network can interleave traffic from different source-destination pairs at the packet level. Typically, some source-destination pairs are idle while others are exchanging traffic. Packet switching allows the active transfers to consume the available network resources.

When the network is lightly loaded, an incoming packet proceeds directly to an outgoing link at each router in its path. However, the absence of a dedicated circuit implies that the network does not always have sufficient resources to carry each packet to its destination. Multiple source-destination pairs may be active simultaneously and impart a heavy load on certain links in the network. When a link is overloaded, the router temporarily stores the waiting packets in a queue. During heavy congestion, the router may have to discard one or more packets to avoid overflowing the queue. However, most Internet applications, such as Web downloads and file transfers, cannot tolerate missing data. The more stringent requirements of these applications seem to contradict the basic paradigm of unreliable packet delivery. The IP philosophy does not suggest that such weak guarantees are sufficient for building applications. These richer services are provided by transport-layer protocols running on the source and destination machines, rather than by the routers in the network.

Limiting the functionality of network routers was an important design goal in the early days of the ARPANET. Agreeing on a relatively simple network allowed the designers of the ARPANET to focus more of their attention on the development of new applications. In addition, the designers were concerned about how a more complex network would react to failures. The hardware and software components in IP networks were not very reliable, especially in comparison to the mature technology in the telephone network. In addition, the designers of the ARPANET wanted the network to continue to function even if a natural disaster or malicious attack caused individual components to fail. Later, as the ARPANET evolved into the Internet, it became increasingly important to enable the installation of new links and routers without disrupting the operation of the network. IP routers automatically adapt to changes in the network topology. When a router or link fails, the remaining routers eventually compute new routes and the traffic continues to flow. The failed router does not have any critical information that is needed to sustain the communication between the sender and receiver. The communication can continue as long as the sending and receiving machines do not fail and the network has at least one path between the two end points. At worst, the failure may result in a few lost packets.

The fact that IP offers such a simple packet-delivery service makes it easier to continue to provide the service in the presence of transient network failures. Building on top of IP, the end hosts implement transport-layer protocols that coordinate the end-to-end delivery of data between applications. The two main transport protocols are the Transmission Control Protocol (TCP) and the User Datagram Protocol (UDP). Both protocols have been standardized and implemented in a wide range of operating systems. TCP provides the main abstraction needed by most Internet applications—a logical connection that delivers a sequence of bytes from the sender to the receiver in an ordered, reliable fashion. Standardized in 1980, TCP provides the underpinning for Telnet, FTP, SMTP, NNTP, and, more recently, HTTP. TCP is the transport-layer protocol responsible for the vast majority of the traffic in the Internet. The ability of TCP to adapt to network congestion has been critical to the sustained growth of the Internet. We discuss TCP in more detail in Section 5.2.

UDP provides a simple abstraction of unreliable datagram delivery. The sending application instructs the operating system to send a collection of bytes to the remote application. The UDP datagram is sent in an IP packet directed to the receiving machine. The IP packet may be lost or delayed in the network. Retransmission of the lost datagram, if required, must be performed by the sending application. UDP is best suited to applications that can tolerate a certain number of lost packets. For example, many multimedia applications transmit audio and video content as a stream of UDP packets. A lost packet may degrade the quality of the audio or video as seen by the recipient. However, the application can still continue to function. Allowing the sender to decide whether to retransmit the data gives extra flexibility to the application. UDP is also used by other applications that transmit short query and response messages. Later in this chapter, in Section 5.3, we describe the use of UDP for DNS queries. The application can repeat its query if a response does not arrive within a certain period of time.

IP is at the center of a diverse collection of protocols at various layers, as shown earlier in Figure 5.1. Application-layer protocols, such as FTP and HTTP, rely on an underlying transport-layer protocol to deliver messages between the communicating hosts. Application-layer and transport-layer protocols are used to communicate between hosts. A network-layer protocol handles the delivery of each individual packet. All Internet applications rely on a single, pervasive network-layer protocol—the Internet Protocol. A network-layer protocol provides hop-by-hop communication between individual network components, such as hosts and routers. IP transmits packets over a wide variety of underlying link-layer technologies, such as Ethernet or SONET. The ability of IP to accommodate diverse link-layer and application-layer protocols has been crucial to the rapid evolution of the Internet and the Web to a world-wide infrastructure.

Despite the advantages of having a simple network-layer protocol, the decision to implement the transport protocols at the end hosts has important performance implications. The layering of TCP and UDP on top of IP implies that these transport-layer protocols must tolerate the delays and losses inside the IP network. In the early days of the ARPANET, most applications were not very sensitive to delay. A slight increase in the latency of running a batch job on a supercomputer or delivering an e-mail message was not especially visible to users. Although delay had a more significant impact on interactive applications such as Telnet, the small number of users of the original ARPANET did not have high expectations for the performance and reliability of the network. Users have become less tolerant of poor performance as the Internet continues to evolve. Like Telnet, the Web is an interactive application. Delays in delivering Web content frustrate Web users. In addition, new Internet applications, such as Internet telephony and multimedia streaming, have even more stringent performance requirements.

In response to these demands, the Internet is evolving to provide better support for applications that require predictable communication performance. Newer IP routers are able to differentiate between traffic from different users or applications to give better service to a subset of the traffic. For example, the routers could give preference to the packets transmitting audio data for an IP telephony application over the packets transmitting an e-mail message. In addition, the Internet Service Providers (ISPs) may promise better performance to high-paying customers at the expense of low-paying customers. Over time, the Internet could conceivably evolve to resemble more closely the traditional telephone network, which provides very predictable and reliable service. However, there has been considerable resistance to changing the Internet into a circuit-switched network because this would sacrifice the simplicity and robustness of a decentralized, connectionless network. Most of the proposed changes to the Internet preserve the basic notion of IP packet-delivery service.

5.1.3 IP addresses

Internet hosts are identified by numerical addresses. Returning to the postal analogy, sending an IP packet is similar to mailing a letter. The letter is placed in an envelope that provides the address of the intended recipient. The postal system forwards the letter based on the addressing information; the contents of the letter have no impact on the delivery process. Two people may exchange a sequence of letters as part of an ongoing correspondence. The letters may be sent over a long period. The postal system is completely oblivious to the relationship between these letters. Each letter is forwarded independently. The sender and receiver are responsible for recognizing that the sequence of letters form a single conversation and for deciding if or when to send a reply. IP networks have a similar separation of responsibility. The header of an IP packet includes all the information necessary for a router to deliver the enclosed contents to the appropriate destination.

The destination address is a 32-bit number that usually refers to a particular machine, such as a Web server. In an IP header, the destination address is represented as a 32-bit binary number. The binary representation can be easily interpreted by the routers. The 32-bit address allows 2^{32} destinations. Internet addresses are allocated in a hierarchical manner. Again, this is analogous to the postal system, where residents of the same neighborhood share a common postal code. The letter can be forwarded to a post office associated with the postal code. Then this post office can consider the remainder of the address to route the letter to the destination. Similarly, an IP address can be divided into a *network* part and a *host* part. Routing through the Internet is based on the network portion of the address. Most routers in the Internet do not need to know how to reach the individual hosts. Once the packet reaches the destination network, the host portion of the address is used to direct the packet to the appropriate destination machine.

Institutions are allocated IP addresses in contiguous blocks of various sizes. Initially, IP addresses were allocated in three main block sizes, or classes, based on the number of 8-bit *octets* devoted to the network and host portions; two other address blocks are reserved for multicast traffic and for future use. Figure 5.3 illustrates the division of the 32-bit IP address into network and host portions:

- **Class A:** Class A addresses start with a 0 in the first bit and use the first octet for the network address, leaving three octets (24 bits) for the host address. Hence, the first octet of a class A address has a value between 0 and 127 (i.e., binary numbers 00000000 and 01111111, respectively). A class A network consists of $16,777,216$ (2^{24}) IP addresses.

- **Class B:** Organizations that did not require such a large number of hosts could be allocated a Class B address. A Class B address starts with 10 in the first two bits and uses the first two octets for the network address and the last two octets for the host address. A Class B network consists of 65536 (2^{16}) addresses.

- **Class C:** Even smaller organizations could be allocated Class C addresses that start with 110 in the first three bits and use the first three octets for the network address and only the last octet for the host address. The Internet has a large number of Class C networks, each with 256 addresses.

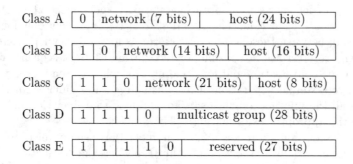

Figure 5.3. Five classes of 32-bit IP addresses

- **Class D:** The remainder of the IP addresses are class D (starting with 1110), used for multicast traffic sent to a collection of machines.
- **Class E:** Class E addresses (starting with 11110) are reserved for future use.

The division along octet boundaries motivated the representation of IP addresses in dotted-decimal notation, which represents each octet as a decimal number ranging from 0 to 255 (or, $2^8 - 1$). For example, 122.5.208.78 is a valid IP address, but 373.57.7.300 is not. The class A network 12.0.0.0 consists of IP addresses ranging from 12.0.0.0 to 12.255.255.255.

Restricting IP addresses to 32 bits imposes a major limitation in the number of hosts on the Internet. The rapid increase in the number of computers on the Internet in the 1990s led to a depletion of available address space. Increasingly, devices such as telephones, vending machines, and toasters have their own IP addresses. In contrast, the original ARPANET was designed to support a relatively small number of hosts. At the time, the Internet was not viewed as a general, pervasive, global infrastructure. Allocating 32-bit addresses in three main classes seemed reasonable at the time. The version of the IP protocol with a 32-bit address space is referred to as version 4 (IPv4). The draft standard RFC 2460 [DH98] for version 6 of the Internet Protocol (IPv6) calls for a 128-bit address space [Hui98]. However, IPv6 requires significant changes throughout much of the Internet. As this book goes to press, widespread deployment of IPv6 has not occurred. Instead, people have found alternative ways to limit the depletion of the IPv4 address space.

A variety of techniques have been applied to limit the explosion in the number of IP addresses. For example, some organizations assign IP addresses to machines dynamically, to avoid allocating an IP address to a machine that is not communicating with the rest of the Internet. For example, suppose an Internet service provider has 500 modems and 20,000 customers. At any given time, at most 2.5% of the customers are connected to the network. The service provider can operate with a much smaller pool of IP addresses by assigning an IP address to a user when the modem connection is established. Similarly, companies often have a large number of computers that communicate within the corporate network and may have a single machine (a firewall or a proxy) that coordinates communication with the rest of the Internet. The computers inside the corporate network are not visible to the rest of the Internet; thus they do not need unique IP addresses. Multiple companies can assign IP addresses to their computers from the same block of IP addresses.

Still, these mechanisms do not fundamentally resolve the problem of IP address depletion. To slow the depletion of IP addresses, the Internet infrastructure evolved to support greater flexibility in the allocation of blocks of IP addresses. The restriction of having fixed address block sizes was abandoned with the introduction of classless interdomain routing (CIDR) in the early-to-mid 1990s [RL93, FLYV93, FRB93]. CIDR allows the division between the network and host portions of the IP address to occur at *any* point in the 32-bit number. Thus the size of a block of IP addresses could be any power of 2. A CIDR network, then, is identified by a network address and a mask length that indicates how many bits are devoted to the network part of the address. For example, consider the network 204.70.2.0/23. The 23-bit network address leaves 9 of the 32 bits for representing the 512 (2^9) hosts on that network. The last 9 bits can vary from 000000000 to 111111111. The third octet can have a 0 or a 1, allowing numbers ranging from 00000010 to 00000011. Hence, the IP addresses in this block range from 204.70.2.0 to 204.70.3.255.

The move to CIDR had two important advantages. First, the allocation of IP address blocks became more flexible, allowing more efficient use of the 32-bit address space. For example, an organization needing 512 addresses could be assigned a block with a 23-bit mask (i.e., allowing $2^9 = 512$ addresses), rather than allocating an entire class B network (with $2^{16} = 65536$ addresses). Second, CIDR enabled service providers to aggregate their networks into larger blocks for the purposes of routing. Suppose an ISP has been assigned the 12.0.0.0/8 network. This large block of addresses could be divided into smaller blocks and allocated to specific customers of this ISP. For example, one customer might have the 12.45.0.0/16 network and another might have the 12.194.34.0/23 network. The allocation of address blocks may depend on the size of the customer. A large address block such as 12.45.0.0/16 may be allocated to a large customer, whereas a smaller block such as 12.194.34.0/23 may suffice for a smaller customer.

The ISP would need to know how to reach each of these separate networks. The rest of the Internet only needs to know how to reach the ISP responsible for these address blocks. Rather than store separate routing information for 12.45.0.0/16 and 12.194.34.0/23, the routers in the rest of the Internet could each store a single route for the entire 12.0.0.0/8 block. Upon receiving a packet

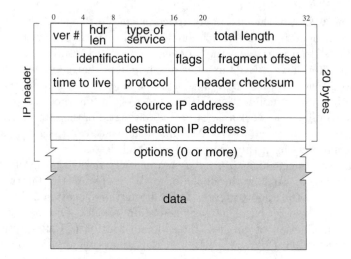

Figure 5.4. Format of an IP packet

destined to an address in this larger block, the router needs to forward the packet toward the ISP responsible for the 12.0.0.0/8 block. The router does not need to be concerned about which customer (let alone which host) would ultimately receive the packet. Returning to the postal analogy, the postal code is used to forward a letter to the correct destination post office. Then the street name and house number are used to direct the letters to the intended recipient. Packet forwarding in IP networks follows a similar hierarchical approach. The main difference in CIDR networks is that the number of levels in the hierarchy, and the number of bits used at each level, is flexible. Several books provide a more detailed overview of IP routing [Hui00, HM00, Ste99].

5.1.4 IP header details

Each IP packet has a header, as shown in Figure 5.4. The fields of the IP header are typically set by the operating system on the sending machine. Although an IP router forwards a packet based on the destination address, the header includes additional fields that are important for successful communication between the sender and receiver:

- **Version number (4 bits):** The 4-bit version number typically has a value of 4, corresponding to IPv4. Knowing the version number enables the routers and the receiving host to interpret the rest of the header correctly. Any other version of the protocol, such as IPv6, may have a different header format.

- **Header length (4 bits):** The 4-bit header length indicates the number of 4-byte words in the header. The basic IP header is 20 bytes long (five 4-byte words), but longer headers are possible when *IP options* are used. The length of the IP header is always a multiple of 32 bits.

- **Type of service (8 bits):** The 8 type-of-service (TOS) bits were originally included in the IP header to influence the path the packet follows through the network. For example, paths may have different performance properties, such as low-delay, high-throughput, or high-reliability. A packet from an IP voice call should travel on a low-delay path because interactive audio applications are sensitive to latency. In contrast, a packet from a large file transfer might be forwarded on a high-throughput path because file transfer delays depend on the bandwidth available between the sender and receiver. However, most routers did not implement TOS routing, so these bits were rarely used. Growing interest throughout the 1990s in supporting predictable communication performance has led to renewed interest in using the TOS bits to affect how routes share buffer and link resources across different classes of traffic.

- **Total length (16 bits):** The 16-bit total length field indicates the total number of bytes in the packet. An IP packet can be up to 65536 (2^{16}) bytes long. However, most link-layer technologies cannot handle such large packets and therefore may impose a smaller *maximum transmission unit* (MTU). For example, many local area networks use Ethernet, which has an MTU of 1500 bytes. The limitation on the MTU can be handled in two ways. In the first approach, the sending machine avoids sending IP packets that exceed the MTU of the links along the path to the receiving machine. But, typically the application does not know the MTU values in advance. In the second approach, an oversized IP packet is divided into two or more *fragments* by the sender or a downstream router. The fragmentation of IP packets is supported by the next three fields in the IP header—the 16-bit identifier, the 3-bit flags, and the 13-bit offset.

- **Identification (16 bits):** The 16-bit identifier field contains a unique value for each IP packet from the sender. Before forwarding a packet to an outgoing link, an IP router checks that the packet size does not exceed the link's MTU. A packet that is too large can be fragmented by the sender or an intermediate router. Each fragment of the packet has the same identifier. This enables the destination to recognize that the fragments belong together. The fragments are reassembled at the destination, and a single IP packet is delivered to the higher-layer protocol, such as TCP or UDP.

- **IP flags (3 bits):** Two of the three 1-bit flags relate to the fragmentation process; the other bit is reserved for future use. The "more fragments" bit is set to 1 for all but the last fragment of a packet. This ensures that the destination can determine whether all of the fragments have arrived.

Fragmentation can be disabled by setting the "don't fragment" bit. Upon receiving an oversized packet with the "don't fragment" bit set, the router discards the packet and notifies the sender. The notification is sent using the Internet Control Message Protocol (ICMP) [Pos81], a protocol for conveying error messages and making routing suggestions.

- **Fragment offset (13 bits):** The 13-bit fragment offset field contains the offset (in 8-byte units) of this fragment from the beginning of the original IP packet. Using 8-byte units enables the 13-bit field to identify offsets within an IP packet that is up to 2^{16} (8×2^{13}) bytes long, the maximum size permitted by the 16-bit packet length field. For each fragment, the 16-bit length field in the IP header is set to the number of bytes in that fragment. Together, the offset and length enable the destination to determine what range of bytes is covered by this fragment. Once all of the fragments have arrived, the destination can reassemble the packet.

- **Time-to-live (8 bits):** The 8-bit time-to-live (TTL) field limits the number of hops in the path traversed by the packet. The sender sets the TTL field to an initial value. Then each router along the path decrements the field either by one or by the number of seconds that the packet stayed at the router. When the TTL reaches 0, the packet is discarded, and an ICMP error message is sent to the sender. This procedure addresses a potential robustness problem in IP routing. Sometimes a misconfigured router or a link failure can cause a temporary routing loop. As a result, some packets may repeatedly travel over the same set of links, not making progress toward the destination. Packets stuck in a loop consume link and router resources. The packet may eventually reach the destination long after the two end points have stopped communicating. The arrival of a very old packet may confuse the recipient. Discarding packets with expired TTLs avoids this problem.

- **Protocol (8 bits):** The 8-bit protocol field identifies the higher-level protocol responsible for sending the IP packet. Reserved values include 1 for ICMP, 6 for TCP, and 17 for UDP. Knowing the protocol is important for the recipient of the packet to interpret the data after the IP header. The IP header is typically followed by another header associated with the higher-level protocol. This is similar to placing a letter inside one envelope, which is then placed inside an additional envelope. The first header is used to reach the correct destination machine, and the second header is used to direct the IP packet to the appropriate application running on that machine. Each higher-level protocol has a different header format.

- **Header checksum (16 bits):** The 16-bit checksum provides a way to detect if any of the bits in the header is corrupted as the packet travels through the network. Noise on a transmission link could corrupt one or more bits in the header, turning a 0 into a 1 or a 1 into a 0. A corrupted destination address could cause the network to deliver the packet to the wrong machine. Before transmitting the packet, the sender computes the 16-bit sum of the bits in the IP header and includes the result in the header checksum field. An IP packet with an incorrect header checksum is discarded by the receiving machine. Routers along the path update the header checksum as part of forwarding an IP packet to account for any changes in the header, such as decrementing the TTL field. It is important to note that the checksum applies only to the IP header and not to the contents of the packet. IP does not detect whether the data were corrupted. Checking for corrupted data can be provided by the higher-level protocol, such as UDP or TCP, with a separate checksum.

- **Source IP address (32 bits):** The IP header includes the 32-bit address that identifies the sender of the packet. Including the source address in the IP header allows the recipient to identify the sender. For example, the receiving application may want to send a reply message. In addition, the routers along the path may need to know the source address to send ICMP error messages (e.g., when a TTL expires). In addition, many routers can be configured to discard traffic from unwanted sources. This involves filtering packets based on the source address field.

- **Destination IP address (32 bits):** The 32-bit destination address is necessary to identify the intended recipient of the packet. Upon receiving a packet, a router uses the destination IP address to determine the "next hop" en route to the destination.

- **IP options (variable length):** The final field of the IP header contains a variable-length list of optional information, ending on a 32-bit boundary. IP options can be used to exercise additional control over routing or security or to have routers add a timestamp to the packet. For example, the "source routing" option allows the sender to specify the route for the packet. The route is specified as a list of IP addresses for the routers in the path. The "source routing" option starts with 3 bytes that include the option code, the length of the option, and a pointer to the next address in the list, followed by the list of router IP addresses. Because most routers are optimized for the common case of a fixed-format 20-byte header, packets with IP options typically receive much slower service. In practice, most options are rarely used, and many hosts and routers do not support all of the options that have been defined.

The sender of the IP packet controls the contents of the header. Over the years, the headers have been used for purposes that were not part of the initial design of the protocol:

- **Spoofing source addresses:** The source IP address typically corresponds to the IP address of the sending machine. However, the sender could conceivably put an arbitrary value in the source address field. Such *spoofing* of the source address is usually done when the sender wants to attack the destination host or the network. Using an incorrect source IP address makes it difficult to determine who launched the attack. Although the sender would not receive any reply messages sent by the receiver, the sender would succeed in burdening the destination host and the network with unwanted traffic. This is referred to as a *denial of service attack.*

- **Discovering the MTU of a path:** The "don't fragment" bit in the IP header plays an important role in learning the maximum packet size permitted by the routers along a path through the network [MD90]. Fragmenting a packet is undesirable for several reasons [KM87]. Performing fragmentation and reassembly imposes a burden on the router and the destination host, respectively. In addition, losing one fragment (e.g., because of a full buffer in a downstream router) results in the loss of the entire IP packet because IP does not provide a mechanism for the retransmission of lost fragments. Avoiding fragmentation requires the sending host to know the MTU size for the path to the receiver. The ICMP message for oversized packets provides a useful way for a sender to learn the MTU of the path to the destination. The sender can experiment by sending packets of various sizes with the "don't fragment" bit set to see whether any of the routers along the path generates an error. In practice, differences in MTU values across the various link technologies do not pose a significant problem. The communication software on most computers imposes a de facto MTU (e.g., 576 or 1500 bytes) that is small enough to avoid fragmentation inside the network.

- **Identifying the hops along a path:** As with the "don't fragment" bit, the TTL field provides a useful way for the sender to learn about the path to the destination. To learn the identity of the first router in the path, the sender can transmit a packet with a TTL of 1. Then the first router would send an ICMP error message that includes the identity of the router. Repeating this process for increasing TTL values allows the sender to identify subsequent routers along the path. This is the basis of the popular `traceroute` tool [Jac], which is used to diagnose and debug routing problems. However, `traceroute` does not always provide an accurate view of the *end-to-end* path. Because IP does not guarantee that successive packets follow the same route, packets with different TTL values may not identify routers on the same path. Similarly, IP does not guarantee that packets from machine A to machine B will follow the same path as the reverse traffic from B to A. Therefore `traceroute` provides information only about the forward path from A to B and not the reverse path from B to A. Learning about the reverse path from B to A requires performing a `traceroute` from machine B.

IP offers a simple and robust packet-delivery service that operates over a variety of link-layer technologies and provides the underpinning for transport-layer protocols.

5.2 Transmission Control Protocol

The Transmission Control Protocol (TCP) coordinates the transmission of data between a pair of applications. Applications communicate by reading from and writing to a *socket* that presents data as an ordered, reliable stream of bytes. TCP provides a logical connection between two end points by building on top of IP's packet-delivery service. The TCP sender divides data into *segments* and transmits each segment in an IP packet along with a TCP header. Before transmitting data, the two end points must coordinate to establish the TCP connection. During the data transfer, the end points cooperate to control the flow of data and retransmit lost IP packets. In addition, each end point adapts its transmission rate in response to congestion to avoid overloading the network. The TCP header includes the information necessary to coordinate the ordered, reliable delivery of segments. Several books provide a detailed overview of TCP [Ste94, KR00].

5.2.1 Socket abstraction

The socket abstraction provides reliable, bidirectional communication between two applications, typically running on different machines. Writing applications that directly transmit and receive IP packets would be very complicated. Instead, transport-level protocols coordinate the transfer of IP packets to provide richer service semantics. Many applications need to send or receive data across the network in the same way they would write or read a file. If the sender transmits 5000 bytes, the receiver should receive 5000 bytes. The transmission process should not corrupt the data or change the order of the bytes. That is, the sending and receiving applications should be allowed to assume that they communicate over a channel that provides an *ordered, reliable byte stream*. IP does not provide this service. Instead, this abstraction is provided by the Transmission Control Protocol (TCP), which typically is implemented in the operating system of each host connected to the Internet.

An application uses TCP by creating a socket, much like opening a file. Both end points need a precise way to identify the socket. Knowing the IP addresses of the two machines is not sufficient. A single machine may run multiple applications, and a single application such as a Web server may have multiple sockets. Each socket is associated with a *port* number at each end point. The port number is a 16-bit integer, ranging from 0 to 65535. The numbers below 1024 are *well-known ports* reserved for particular application-level protocols, such as port 80 for HTTP. The assignment of port numbers to applications is

managed by the Internet Assigned Numbers Authority (IANA). The remaining
port numbers, ranging from 1024 to 65535, can be used by any application.
However, in some cases, a new Internet service that does not have a well-
known port is developed. This application may select a particular unreserved
port number, resulting in a de facto standard for that application.

By default, a Web client such as a browser creates a socket that connects
to port 80 on the server machine. However, there is nothing special about
the choice of a particular port number. For example, a Web server could be
configured to listen for client requests on port 8000. In this case, the client
would need to know to request a connection to port 8000 instead of port 80.
This is achieved by having the port number in the URL. For example, if the user
requests the resource `http://www.foo.com:8000/bar.html`, the client would
request a socket that connects to port 8000 rather than port 80 at the server.
The client also needs a port number for its end of the connection. Otherwise,
the server would not know how to direct data to the client. As part of creating
the socket, the operating system on the client machine assigns an ephemeral
port number (between 1024 and 65535) to the client application. The socket
is identified by five pieces of information—two IP addresses (for the machines
running the two applications), two port numbers (for the two application end
points), and the protocol (TCP).

Applications create sockets via system calls implemented in the operating
system. Consider the example of an application A (e.g., a Web client) establishing a socket to a remote application B (e.g., a Web server). Application
A initiates the creation of the socket by invoking a system call. In the UNIX
operating system, the *socket()* function is used to create a new socket [Ste98b].
Then the application invokes the *connect()* call to associate the socket with the
IP address and port number for application B. As part of executing the *con-
nect()* call, the operating system also selects an unused local port number (from
1024 to 65535) for application A. At this point, the operating system running
application A knows the two IP addresses and two port numbers that uniquely
identify the bidirectional connection between the two applications. Then the
operating system initiates establishment of the TCP connection to application
B. After the connection has been established, the *connect()* call returns and
application A can begin reading data from and writing data to the socket.

In contrast, application B initially plays a passive role in establishing the
socket. Application B listens on a particular port for requests to establish a
connection. In UNIX, this involves creating a socket and calling *bind()* to assign a local port number (e.g., port 80). Then application B invokes the *listen()*
system call. This signifies B's intent to wait for connections from remote applications. This triggers the operating system to respond to any requests to
establish TCP connections to this port. The application learns about these
new TCP connections by calling *accept()*. By default, the *accept()* call waits
until at least one new connection is available. Once a connection is available,

the system call completes the creation of the socket. At this point, application B can begin reading data from the socket and writing data to the socket.

Once the connection has been established, either application can read or write data. In fact, both applications could read and write at the same time because the socket provides a bidirectional communication channel. In the Web, the client (application A) initiates the communication. The client writes the HTTP request into the socket. The server (application B) waits for data to reach its socket. Then once the data has arrived, the server reads the HTTP request from the socket. After processing the request, the server writes the HTTP response into the socket. In the meantime, the client waits for data to reach the socket. Then the client reads the response from the socket. This pattern is typical of client-server applications. TCP provides a much more general service that supports arbitrary bidirectional communication between the two applications. In general, either A or B could write data first, or both applications could read and write data at the same time.

The operating system handles the details of establishing a logical connection between the two applications and coordinating the transfer of IP packets. For application A, the operating system executes *socket()* and *connect()* functions. If the remote host does not respond, the operating system informs application A that the request to create a socket has failed. For application B, the operating system executes the *socket()*, *bind()*, *listen()*, and *accept()* functions. As part of creating the socket, each host allocates memory for transmitting and receiving packets. When the application writes to the socket, the operating system directs the data to the remote IP address and port. Likewise, when packets arrive, the operating system directs the data to the appropriate socket based on the port numbers. The application can then read the data from the socket. Underneath the two communicating applications, the operating system coordinates the sending and receiving of packets to create the abstraction of an ordered, reliable stream of bytes.

5.2.2 Ordered reliable byte stream

A TCP connection delivers data as an ordered, reliable stream of bytes. Each IP packet has header information that identifies the sending and receiving machines. The information in the IP header is sufficient for the routers in the network to forward the packet to the appropriate destination machine. However, the IP header does not provide enough information to associate the incoming IP packet with the correct socket. To address this problem, the TCP sender creates a second header inside the IP packet that includes additional information. Returning to the postal analogy, this is similar to having one envelope contain another. The postal system does not need to know about the inner envelope; the information on the outer envelope is sufficient to determine the address of the intended recipient. From the viewpoint of the postal system, the inner envelope is simply part of the contents of the outer envelope. The recipient can open the outer envelope and inspect the information in the inner envelope.

Similarly, TCP is layered on top of IP. The TCP header appears in the data portion of an IP packet. The routers inside the network need not inspect the bits in the TCP header. Once the IP packet reaches the destination machine, the operating system inspects the TCP header to direct the data to the appropriate socket. The socket is identified by the two 16-bit port numbers, which are included in the TCP header. The separation of responsibilities between IP and TCP is very important. The TCP header must convey sufficient information for the sending and receiving machines to provide the socket abstraction to applications. TCP must deal with the fact that IP packets may be lost, corrupted, or delivered out of order. These challenges are addressed by cooperation between the TCP sender and TCP receiver.

Consider the transmission of a message from one application to another. The operating system on the sending machine divides the message into segments; each segment is a contiguous set of bytes that fits into a single IP packet. The TCP header identifies the connection associated with the segment. To handle packets that arrive out of order, the sender also labels each segment with a sequence number. The recipient is responsible for reordering the packets that arrive out of order. If packet 2 arrives before packet 1, the operating system on the receiving machine knows to wait for packet 1 before delivering the data to the receiving application. The sender also includes information to help the recipient determine if the data has been corrupted during transmission. In particular, the TCP sender computes a checksum over the contents of the packet and includes the checksum in the TCP header; the receiver recomputes the checksum and discards the packet if the results do not match.

The sender is not certain if the packets reached the recipient. To address this problem, the recipient sends acknowledgments to the sender, indicating that the packets have been received. For example, after receiving segments 1 and 2, the recipient could inform the sender that the first two segments have arrived. If the recipient has data awaiting transmission, the acknowledgment and the outgoing segment could be included in a single packet. The sender knows that the recipient acknowledges the reception of packets. If no acknowledgment arrives, the sender eventually assumes that packet 1 was lost. In reality, the delivery of the packet may have been delayed, the packet may have been corrupted, or the acknowledgment may have been lost. However, the sender cannot distinguish among these situations. Instead, the sender simply sends another copy of the data, including the sequence number. If no acknowledgment arrives, the sender may transmit yet another copy. Upon receiving at least one (uncorrupted) copy of the letter, the receiver sends an acknowledgment to the sender. If more than one copy arrives, the recipient simply discards the extra copies.

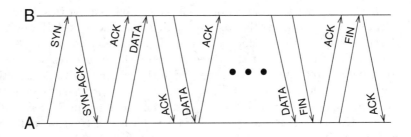

Figure 5.5. Timeline of a TCP connection

5.2.3 Opening and closing a TCP connection

The SYN, ACK, FIN, and RST flags in the TCP header are used in opening and closing a TCP connection. Packets with these flags set are sent in response to system calls that open or close the corresponding socket. When application A creates a socket, the operating system coordinates the establishment of the TCP connection with application B on the remote machine. Establishing a TCP connection involves a *three-way* handshake, as shown in Figure 5.5:

1. **SYN from A to B:** A initiates the connection by sending a packet with the SYN bit set to 1. The SYN packet includes the *initial sequence number* for the stream in the 32-bit sequence number field. That is, the SYN packet *synchronizes* the sequence number. The SYN packet itself counts as part of the stream and consumes the first sequence number. For example, suppose the SYN packet has a sequence number of 4500. Then the first data packet from A would have a sequence number of 4501 to identify the first byte of data.

2. **SYN-ACK from B to A:** After transmitting the SYN packet, A waits for a response from the remote host. Suppose application B is listening for a request to establish a TCP connection on a particular port. The arrival of a SYN packet from A would trigger both the creation of the socket and the transmission of an acknowledgment packet from B to A. B sends a packet to A that sets both the SYN and ACK flags. The SYN flag initiates the reverse direction of the connection (from B to A), and the ACK flag acknowledges receipt of A's SYN packet. The acknowledgment number in the TCP header is set to the value one larger than the initial sequence number in A's SYN packet. As with A's SYN packet, B's SYN-ACK packet includes an initial sequence number. This sequence number marks the beginning of the stream of bytes traveling from B to A and is unrelated to the initial sequence number for the traffic from A to B.

3. **ACK from A to B:** Once the SYN-ACK packet has arrived, the connection from A to B is complete, and the operating system can inform

application A that the connection has been established. At this point, application A can begin writing to and reading from the socket. However, at this point, application B does not know if A has received the SYN-ACK packet. The third part of the three-way handshake involves sending an ACK packet from A to B to acknowledge the creation of the connection from B to A. The ACK packet from A has the acknowledgment number set to the value one larger than the initial sequence number in B's SYN-ACK packet. Upon receiving this packet, application B can transmit data over the socket to A.

Across time, the operating system selects different initial sequence numbers for TCP connections. Consider what could happen if every TCP connection used an initial sequence number of 0. Suppose that a TCP connection between A and B had an outstanding packet inside the network that experienced a long transmission delay. Eventually the packet would be retransmitted and delivered to the receiver. Suppose that A and B close the TCP connection once the data transfer has completed. Later, A and B might establish a new TCP connection with the same port numbers as the old connection. Suppose that, after the new connection has been established, the duplicate packet from the old connection finally reaches the destination. In this situation, the recipient might mistakenly associate the old packet with the new connection and deliver the data to the application. If the new connection had a different initial sequence number, then the recipient could recognize that the delayed packet does not belong to the same ordered byte stream.

Either end point can terminate the TCP connection. An application triggers the closing of the TCP connection by closing the associated socket. Connection termination typically involves a *four-way* handshake. If application B closes the socket first, as shown in Figure 5.5, the four steps consist of

1. **FIN from B to A:** Application B closing the socket initiates the transmission of a packet with the FIN flag set to 1. At this point, B does not transmit any new data. Still, B is responsible for completing the ordered, reliable delivery of the previous data sent to A. That is, the operating system running application B continues to retransmit lost packets from earlier in the stream. In addition, B may continue to receive and acknowledge packets from A. Like the SYN packet, the FIN packet from B consumes one byte in the sequence number space.

2. **ACK from A to B:** Upon receipt of this packet, A transmits an ACK packet with an acknowledgment number that is one higher than the sequence number in B's FIN packet. Dedicating a sequence number to the FIN flag enables the A to acknowledge the reception of the flag even when the FIN packet does not contain any data.

3. **FIN from A to B:** After application A reads all of the bytes from the socket, the next read operation indicates that the end-of-file has been reached. At this point, application A would know that B does not intend to transmit any additional data. As such, application A would typically close its socket, which triggers the transmission of a FIN packet to B.

4. **ACK from B to A:** Upon receiving the FIN packet, B transmits an ACK packet to acknowledge the closure of the connection from A to B. Upon receiving the ACK packet, A knows that B has received the FIN packet. At this point, the connection is closed. Transmitting any new data between A and B would require opening a new TCP connection.

Note that it is possible that both applications initiate the closure of the connection at the same time. In this case, both applications would send their FIN packets in parallel. Both of these FIN packets would be acknowledged to complete the closure of the connection.

The four-way handshake of FIN and ACK packets is the normal way to close a TCP connection. However, the TCP header also includes an RST flag for resetting a connection in anomalous situations. Suppose a host receives a TCP data packet for a connection that does not exist. That is, the IP addresses and port numbers in the IP and TCP headers, respectively, do not match any active socket at that host. Then the host would reply with an RST packet. Similarly, consider an application that sends a SYN packet to another host at a particular port. If no application is listening for requests on that destination port, then the host would reply with an RST packet. For example, suppose the machine www.foo.com is not actually running a Web server. If no program is listening to requests on port 80, then the host would send an RST packet back to the sender that is trying to open a TCP connection. The operating system on the sending machine would notify the application that the attempt to create a socket had failed.

5.2.4 Sliding-window flow control

The TCP sender limits the transmission of data to avoid overflowing the buffer space at the receiver. In theory, TCP could transmit data whenever the application writes data into the socket. However, TCP limits the transmission of data for two important reasons. First, the sender should not transmit more data than the receiver can store in its buffers—transmitting excess data would overflow the buffer at the receiver and result in lost packets. Second, the sender should not transmit data more quickly than the network can handle—sending too aggressively can overload the network, creating congestion that increases communication latency and the likelihood of lost packets. Each TCP sender limits the number of outstanding (unacknowledged) bytes in the network, using *sliding-window* flow control. To avoid overflow of the buffer at the receiver, packets from B to A include the *receiver window* in the TCP header.

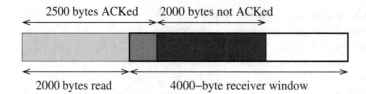

Figure 5.6. Example of a 4000-byte receiver window

The receiver window indicates the number of bytes that A can send beyond the last byte acknowledged by B. For example, suppose that the operating system running application B has allocated a 4000-byte receive buffer for storing incoming data for this TCP connection, as shown in Figure 5.6. Further, suppose that B has received and acknowledged 2500 bytes from A, and 2000 of these 2500 bytes have been read by application B. Then the receive buffer still has 500 bytes of data. B cannot handle more than 3500 additional bytes of data. The ACK packet to A would acknowledge the receipt of the first 2500 bytes and would indicate a receiver window of 3500 bytes. Upon receiving the ACK packet, A can continue transmitting data. However, A cannot send more than 3500 more bytes of data. Otherwise, A may overflow the receive buffer at B. Suppose A sends an additional 2000 bytes, for a total of 4500 bytes. The first 2000 bytes have been sent, received, acknowledged, and read. The next 500 bytes have been sent, received, and acknowledged, but they have not been read by application B. Because the next 2000 bytes have been sent but not acknowledged, A does not know that they have been received.

The next 1500 bytes are eligible for immediate transmission. A cannot send any remaining data without the risk of overflowing the buffer at B. At any given time, A cannot transmit beyond the end of the current receiver window, which is indicated by the sum of the last acknowledgment number and window size from B. The default size of the TCP receive buffer is a configurable operating system parameter. In practice, most operating systems allocate an 8 KB, 16 KB, or 32 KB buffer. Applications can usually invoke a system call to increase the size of the receive buffer. For a host pair with a large round-trip time (e.g., a client and server in different parts of the world), the size of the receive buffer can still limit the achievable throughput. For example, suppose that a pair of hosts have a 500 ms round-trip time and receiver B has an 8 KB buffer. Sender A cannot transmit more than 8 KB (64 Kb) of data every half second. This translates into a maximum throughput of 128 Kb/sec, regardless of the bandwidth available on the path from A to B. More generally, TCP throughput is inversely proportional to the round-trip time between the sender and receiver.

5.2.5 Retransmission of lost packets

The retransmission of lost packets plays a crucial role in how TCP provides reliable delivery of a stream of bytes. IP does not inform the TCP sender when the packet is lost. Instead, the sender must infer that a packet has been lost based on the response (or lack of response) of the receiver. The receiver acknowledges receipt of data from the sender by transmitting acknowledgment packets—packets with the ACK bit set, with the acknowledgment number indicating the next byte expected in the stream of bytes from the sender. If the receiver has a segment to transmit, the acknowledgment information can be piggybacked with the data. The sender infers that a packet has been lost in two ways: a retransmission timeout or duplicate acknowledgments. The sender sets a retransmission timer after transmitting data to the receiver. If the timer expires before an acknowledgment arrives, the sender assumes that the packet was lost en route to the receiver. Selecting the appropriate value for the retransmission timeout (RTO) is a delicate process. Setting RTO too low results in a false alarm, and the sender unnecessarily retransmits a packet that was not actually lost. Setting RTO too high postpones the detection of a lost packet, resulting in unnecessary delay in retransmitting the packet.

The right value for the retransmission timeout depends on the distance between the sender and receiver, as well as the network congestion. Hosts that are five seconds apart should use a larger RTO than hosts that are 200 ms apart. The appropriate RTO varies from one situation to another, and the TCP sender *learns* the appropriate RTO value by observing the delay experienced in transmitting data to the receiver. The TCP sender estimates the round-trip time (RTT) to the receiver—the time between transmission of a packet and receipt of the acknowledgment. Based on these measurements, the sender can estimate the average RTT, as well as the variance. The RTO is set to the average RTT plus an additive factor that depends on the variability of measured delay to avoid triggering unnecessary retransmissions [PA00]. The RTT estimate becomes more accurate as the sender and receiver exchange more traffic.

In some cases, the sender can infer that a packet has been lost without waiting for the retransmission timer to expire. Consider a sender that has transmitted several packets to the receiver. Suppose that the second packet has been lost but that the third, fourth, and fifth packets reach the receiver. After receiving the first packet, the receiver sends an ACK packet. The acknowledgment number is set to the first byte expected in the second packet. However, because the second packet has been lost, the receiver receives the third packet next. The receiver sends another ACK packet. The acknowledgment number still indicates the first byte of the second packet because this field is set based on the reception of a *contiguous* stream of bytes. After the arrival of the fourth data packet, the receiver sends another ACK packet with the same acknowledgment number. At this point, the sender has received three ACK packets with the same acknowledgment number.

Receiving *duplicate acknowledgment* packets allows the sender to infer that the second data packet was lost. Still, the sender should not react too quickly. It is possible that the second packet was delayed but not lost. That is, the third and fourth data packets may have been delivered out of order. Receiving three duplicate ACKs (four identical ACKs) is a strong indication that the second data packet was actually lost. Rather than waiting for the retransmission timer to expire, the sender performs a *fast retransmission* of the second packet. Fast retransmission results in much quicker recovery from packet loss. The likelihood of fast retransmissions, relative to retransmission timeouts, depends on a variety of factors, including the length of the data transfer and the degree of congestion on the path from the sender to the receiver.

For the most part, the fast retransmission mechanism reduces the delay in recovering from packet loss without introducing unnecessary retransmissions. However, duplicate acknowledgments also arise when packets from the same TCP sender are delivered out of order. These duplicate acknowledgments can mislead the TCP sender into assuming that a packet has been lost. Out-of-order delivery can occur when the IP packets traverse different paths through the network en route to the receiver. For example, suppose packet 7 traverses a slower path than packets 8, 9, and 10, causing packet 7 to arrive after packet 10. The TCP receiver transmits duplicate acknowledgments upon receiving packets 8, 9, and 10. The third duplicate acknowledgment triggers the TCP sender to retransmit packet 7. Out-of-order packets degrade TCP performance. Although the IP protocol does not guarantee in-order packet delivery, packets tend to arrive in order. However, fluctuations in routes and the use of multiple routes between a pair of hosts do cause out-of-order packets to occur in practice [Pax97a, Pax97b].

5.2.6 TCP congestion control

TCP senders adapt to network congestion by decreasing the transmission rate. This adaptation is crucial to sustaining the rapid growth of the Internet. Otherwise, a collection of aggressive TCP connections would overload the network, resulting in a large number of lost packets. Retransmissions of these packets would only exacerbate the congestion. However, the connectionless nature of the IP protocol makes it difficult for the routers inside the network to control congestion. Instead, the responsibility for congestion control is relegated to the end hosts. Because IP does not provide explicit feedback about network congestion, the TCP sender must infer that the network is congested based on indirect observations of performance [Jac88]. The TCP sender paces data transmissions based on a sliding window that depends on both the available buffer space at the receiver and the available bandwidth in the network, represented by the *receiver window* and the *congestion window,* respectively. The sender transmits data based on the minimum of these two values to avoid overflowing the receiver buffer and to prevent network congestion. Congested links result in lost IP packets. Upon detecting that a packet has been lost, the sender decreases the size of the congestion window to lower the transmission rate. In the absence of packet loss, the TCP sender gradually increases the congestion window to transmit data more aggressively.

TCP implements an *additive increase, multiplicative decrease* algorithm to change the size of the congestion window, as dictated by RFC 2581 [APS99]. In the absence of packet loss, the sender gradually (linearly) increases the congestion window, one time per window of data. In particular, the sender increases the window by the maximum segment size (MSS) for the TCP connection. For example, a maximum transmission unit (MTU) of 1500 bytes would result in an MSS of 1460 bytes to allow for the two 20-byte headers for IP and TCP. In response to a loss event (one or more packets lost in a window of data), the sender quickly (multiplicatively) decreases the congestion window to reduce the load on the network. Upon receiving the third duplicate ACK, the congestion window is set to half of the current window size. The additive increases and multiplicative decreases result in fluctuations in the size of the congestion window across time, as illustrated in Figure 5.7. The plot has a sawtooth shape, with gradual increases in the congestion window, until the connection experiences a packet loss.

The process of increasing and decreasing the size of the congestion window amounts to experimenting with the network to determine the appropriate transmission rate. For example, suppose that four TCP connections travel over a shared busy link. For simplicity, assume that the connections have the same round-trip times and that the receiver window does not limit the transmission rate. On average, each connection would consume one quarter of the link bandwidth. If one connection stops transmitting data, the other three connections would increase their window sizes to consume one third of the link bandwidth, on average. Similarly, if a fifth connection starts transmitting data on the link, each of the connections would eventually decrease its congestion window to consume one fifth of the bandwidth, on average.

TCP provides an effective way to adjust the transmission rate of each connection in response to network congestion. However, a *new* connection does not have any information about the state of the network. Starting with a large congestion window would introduce a significant amount of traffic into the network in a single burst. This traffic could exacerbate network congestion. Instead, TCP forces new connections to begin with a *slow-start* phase, as shown in Figure 5.7. At the beginning of the slow-start phase, the TCP sender has a small *initial congestion window* of one or two MSSs. That is, the sender can transmit only one or two maximum-size packets to the receiver. The congestion window increases by one MSS with the reception of each acknowledgment packet from

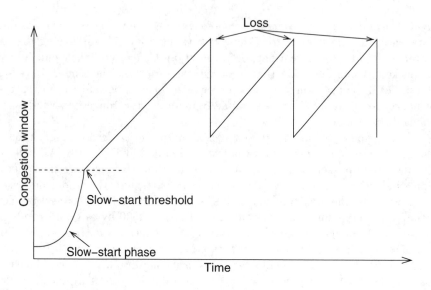

Figure 5.7. TCP congestion window across time

the receiver. This increases the congestion window by a factor of two after an entire window of acknowledgments has been received. As a result, during the slow-start phase the congestion window grows *multiplicatively,* rather than linearly. This enables the connection to reach a larger congestion window more quickly.

Despite the multiplicative increase in the window size, the sender transmits data relatively slowly for the first few round-trip times. During this period, the TCP connection cannot fully exploit the bandwidth available on the path from the sender to the receiver. The slow-start phase terminates when the congestion window reaches the *slow-start threshold.* The TCP sender adjusts the value of the slow-start threshold in response to packet-loss events [APS99]. Once the congestion window reaches the slow-start threshold, the TCP sender switches to the regular *congestion-avoidance* phase that increases the congestion window linearly. The additive increases and multiplicative decreases continue until the TCP sender experiences a retransmission timeout. When a retransmission timeout occurs, the sender assumes that network congestion has changed significantly. As a result, the TCP sender resets the congestion window to its initial value of one or two MSSs and repeats the slow-start phase.

TCP's congestion control mechanisms are fairly complicated, and the exact details vary somewhat across different versions of TCP [FF96]. Improving TCP congestion control remains an active research area [APS99, MMFR96, FF96, AFP98, RF99, Flo94, Flo00]. Most proposed extensions to TCP try to make congestion control less conservative in the hope of improving application

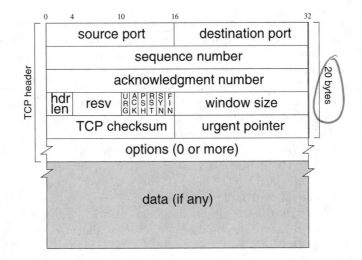

Figure 5.8. Format of a TCP segment

performance. Still, the basic operation of congestion control remains the same. In general, new connections and connections that experience a retransmission timeout proceed through the slow-start phase. The slow-start phase implies a small initial congestion window and a multiplicative increase in the size of the congestion window as packets are acknowledged. After the slow-start phase, the connection enters the congestion-avoidance phase, in which the congestion window undergoes additive increase (on ACK) and multiplicative decrease (on detecting congestion). The TCP sender paces data transmissions based on the minimum of the congestion window and the receiver window to avoid overloading the network or overflowing the receive buffer, respectively.

5.2.7 TCP header details

The TCP sender transmits each segment in a single IP packet, along with a TCP header. As shown in Figure 5.8, the TCP header includes

- **Source port number (16 bits):** The 16-bit port number associated with the TCP sender. The sender's IP address is available in the IP header.
- **Destination port number (16 bits):** The 16-bit port number associated with the TCP receiver. The receiver's IP address is available in the IP header.
- **Sequence number (32 bits):** The 32-bit sequence number identifies the position of the first byte of the segment contained in the packet. The receiver uses the sequence number to identify where the segment fits in the byte stream and to reorder segments that arrive out of order. Before

transmitting the first segment, the sender selects an *initial sequence number* that represents the beginning of the ordered byte stream. The sequence numbers for all other segments are relative to this initial sequence number.

- **Acknowledgment number (32 bits):** To acknowledge the receipt of data, the TCP header includes a 32-bit acknowledgment number. This field indicates the next byte that the receiver expects to receive, and is valid only if the ACK flag is set to 1. When A transmits data to B, the TCP header includes the sequence number of each segment and the packets from B to A acknowledge the receipt of these segments.

- **Header length (4 bits):** The 4-bit header length indicates the number of 32-bit words in the TCP header. The header is usually 20 bytes long, corresponding to five 32-bit words. Longer headers occur when the sender uses *TCP options* that contain additional control information.

- **Reserved (6 bits):** The 6-bit reserved field is allocated for future use.

- **TCP flags (8 bits):** The TCP header also includes an 8-bit field with six 1-bit flags. These flags correspond to various control operations:

  - **URG:** The URG (urgent) flag instructs the TCP receiver to inspect the portion of the segment identified by the 16-bit urgent-pointer field in the TCP header.

  - **ACK:** The ACK (acknowledge) flag is set when sending an acknowledgment. When the ACK bit is set, the 32-bit acknowledgment field indicates how much data has been received by the sender. Once data transfer begins, the TCP sender almost always sets the ACK bit.

  - **PSH:** The PSH (push) flag indicates that the TCP receiver should immediately deliver the incoming data to the application's socket.

  - **RST:** The RST (reset) flag is set when aborting a TCP connection.

  - **SYN:** The SYN (synchronize) flag is set when establishing a TCP connection. When the SYN bit is set, the value of sequence-number field identifies the initial sequence number.

  - **FIN:** The FIN (finish) flag is set when the sender has finished transmitting data. The FIN translates into an end-of-file character when the receiving application reads from the socket.

The SYN, ACK, FIN, and RST flags are discussed in more detail later in this section. In practice, most operating systems do not provide a way for the sending application to set the PSH flag or for the TCP receiver to react to the flag. The URG flag is used to alert interactive applications, such as Telnet, to the presence of control characters (e.g., cntl-C) that may affect the handling of the previous bytes in the stream.

- **Receiver window (16 bits):** The 16-bit receiver window indicates the number of additional bytes the receiver can handle beyond the data that

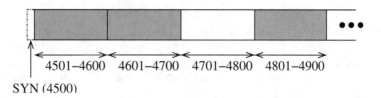

Figure 5.9. Four segments in a TCP connection (third segment lost)

have been acknowledged thus far. To avoid overflowing the receiver buffer, the TCP sender does not transmit data in excess of the receiver window.

- **TCP checksum (16 bits):** The 16-bit checksum aids the TCP receiver in detecting corrupted packets. In contrast to the header checksum in the IP header, the TCP checksum covers *both* the header and the data. The checksum enables the receiver to detect whether the TCP segment has been corrupted during transmission. The sender computes the checksum over the header and data. The receiver recomputes the checksum and compares it with the value in the TCP header. If the answers differ, the receiver discards the corrupted packet. The receiver does not acknowledge the receipt of the corrupted packet. Hence, the sender would eventually retransmit the missing data.

- **Urgent pointer (16 bits):** When the URG flag is set, the 16-bit urgent pointer directs the receiver's attention to a particular portion of the incoming data (e.g., a cntl-C character that interrupts an ongoing transfer). The 16-bit urgent pointer identifies the last byte of urgent data in terms of an integer offset from the sequence number in the TCP header.

The IP header contains some of the information necessary for the TCP connection, including the source and destination IP addresses and the packet size. The size of the IP packet is the sum of the lengths of the IP header, the TCP header, and the TCP segment. The IP header length is included in the IP header, and the TCP header length is included in the TCP header.

When a packet arrives, the receiver determines the range of bytes spanned by the TCP segment, based on the sequence number and the length. Suppose that the sender starts with an initial sequence number of 4500 and transmits data in 100-byte segments, as shown in Figure 5.9. The sequence number 4500 represents the opening of the TCP connection. The first segment has sequence number 4501 and length 100 and spans bytes 4501 to 4600. The second segment has sequence number 4601 and length 100, and so on. Suppose that B receives the first, second, and fourth segments; the third 100-byte segment has been lost or delayed. Because B has received only 200 contiguous bytes of the stream, an acknowledgment packet from B to A would have an acknowledgment number of 4701 (4501+200). Byte number 4701 is the sequence number of the next byte that B expects to receive. It is important to note that the sequence number field corresponds to the transmission of the segment, and the acknowledgment number field corresponds to the reception of the data. A and B may be transmitting data to each other simultaneously. For any packet, the sequence number and acknowledgment number fields are unrelated because they do not correspond to the same direction of communication.

5.3 Domain Name System

The Domain Name System (DNS) coordinates the translation of hostnames to IP addresses and IP addresses into hostnames [Moc87b, Pos94]. In this section, we describe how an application interacts with a DNS resolver that issues queries to a local DNS server. Then we describe the hierarchical and distributed structure of DNS, followed by a discussion of the DNS protocol. Next we consider how Web clients, proxies, and servers issue DNS queries and how DNS is used to balance the load across multiple replicas of a Web site.

5.3.1 DNS resolver

IP routers forward packets based on the 32-bit destination address in the IP header. However, numerical addresses are inconvenient for users and applications. Instead, machines on the Internet have host names, such as `ftp.foo.com` or `cs.berkeley.edu`, that consist of strings separated by periods. Remembering a hostname is much easier than remembering an IP address. In addition, the IP address associated with a hostname may change over time. For example, a Web site's IP address may depend on what company is hosting the content; if the Web site moves to a new hosting service, the IP address may change. If the URLs for the Web site's content included the IP address (e.g., `http://10.187.56.3/bar.html`) rather than the hostname (e.g., `http://www.foo.com/bar.html`), the URLs would have to change every time the IP address changes. In addition, any attempts to use the old URL (e.g., from a browser's list of bookmarks) would fail. Finally, the same Web site may be available on multiple hosts, each with a different IP address. Identifying the site by name provides flexibility in deciding which server to contact. In addition to translating names into IP addresses, an application may need to determine the hostname associated with a particular IP address. For example, an FTP server may check that an FTP client has a hostname with an `.edu` extension.

The translation of hostnames into IP addresses and IP addresses into hostnames is coordinated by DNS. Internet applications, such as Web browsers, access DNS through a *resolver,* a software library that is linked with the application. A DNS resolver performs two main functions. The *gethostbyname()* function converts a hostname to an IP address, and the *gethostbyaddr()* function converts an IP address to a hostname. The resolver interacts with one or more DNS servers to perform these functions on behalf of the application. To bootstrap the process, the resolver must know how to contact at least one DNS server. A machine using the Internet is typically configured with a list of IP addresses, each of which corresponds to a local DNS server. The machine may learn the IP addresses of the local DNS servers automatically using the Dynamic Host Configuration Protocol [Dro97]. Network administrators typically try to place the local DNS servers close to the requesting clients. For example, a university department may have a single Ethernet for interconnecting its computers, including its local DNS servers. An ISP may place its DNS servers close to the bank of modems where users connect to the network.

For example, suppose a user enters the URL `http://www.foo.com/a.html` at the Web browser. The browser software would extract the domain name `www.foo.com` from the URL. To contact the Web server, the browser must translate `www.foo.com` into an IP address. The browser software would invoke the *gethostbyname()* function, which would contact one of the local DNS servers. The reply from the DNS server includes the Web server's IP address, which is returned by the *gethostbyname()* function. Then the browser can initiate communication with `www.foo.com`. In some cases, the application invokes *gethostbyname()* with a *fully qualified domain name* that identifies the complete hostname, such as `zippy.bar.com`. In other cases, the application refers to the host with a shortened name, such as `zippy`. The client machine is configured with a default domain name to use in DNS queries. For example, suppose the client machine is configured to use the default domain name `bar.com`. If the user enters the URL `http://zippy` at the Web browser, the *gethostbyname()* function would ask the local DNS server to determine the IP address associated with the fully qualified domain name `zippy.bar.com`.

Nearly every Internet application performs a *gethostbyname()* before initiating communication with another machine. For example, sending an e-mail message to `buddy@zippy.bar.com` or transferring a file from `ftp.foo.com` requires the application to learn the IP address of the remote machine. The application running on the remote machine may need to send a response. This requires the receiving application to know the IP address of the sender. The sender's IP address is available in the header of the IP packet. Thus the remote machine does not necessarily have to contact a DNS server before replying to the sender. However, the receiving application does not know the hostname of the machine that sent the message. Knowing the hostname is useful if the remote application performs logging or authentication. For example, suppose the administrators of `ftp.bar.com` do not want any users from `zippy.bar.com` to Telnet in to their machine. Then the Telnet application at `ftp.bar.com` would need to determine the hostname of the sending machine before granting access. The Telnet application would convert the sender's IP address into a hostname by invoking the *gethostbyaddr()* function.

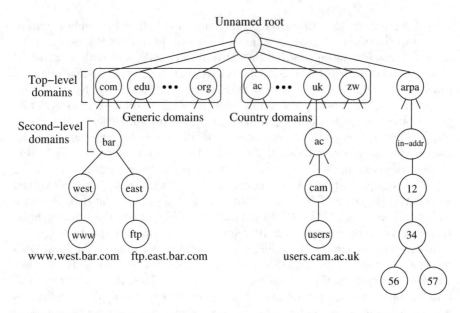

Figure 5.10. DNS hierarchy

5.3.2 DNS architecture

In the early days of the ARPANET, the translation of hostnames into IP addresses was handled in a centralized manner. A single master file listed the IP address associated with each hostname. The file was updated a few times a week. Each organization connected to the ARPANET was responsible for updating its local copy of this file. This approach was sufficient when the network was very small. As the network grew larger, maintaining consistent copies of the master file became unwieldy. Developed to address this problem, DNS is a distributed database that consists of a hierarchical set of name servers, each responsible for a portion of the domain names and address space. The DNS architecture reflects the hierarchy of hostnames and of IP addresses. The responsibility for translating hostnames into IP addresses is assigned based on the strings in the hostname. Similarly, the responsibility for translating IP addresses into hostnames is assigned based on the numbers in the IP address.

DNS has a hierarchical name space with an unnamed root, as shown in Figure 5.10. The first layer of the tree contains the top-level domains. The names of the top-level domains reflect the history of the Internet's evolution from the ARPANET developed in the United States. The top level includes the three-character *generic* or *organizational* domains:

- Commercial organizations (`.com`)

- U.S. educational institutions (.edu)
- U.S. government (.gov)
- U.S. military (.mil)
- Networks (.net)
- Other organizations (.org)

Although .edu, .gov, and .mil are reserved for U.S. institutions, the remaining generic domains include many organizations outside of the United States. Seven new generic domains were introduced in November 2000:

- Air-transport industry (.aero)
- Businesses (.biz)
- Nonprofit cooperatives (.coop)
- Unrestricted use (.info)
- Museums (.museum)
- Individuals (.name)
- Accountants, lawyers, and physicians (.pro)

The top level also includes the two-character *country* domains, ranging from Ascension Island (.ac) to Zimbabwe (.zw). A separate .arpa domain controls the translation of IP addresses into domain names, a process described in more detail later in this section.

Until the late 1990s, groups operated by the U.S. government were responsible for managing the DNS and for assigning IP addresses and domain names. At the end of the 1990s, this control began its transition into the hands of the Internet Corporation for Assigned Names and Numbers (ICANN) [ICA]. The top-level domains are handled by a collection of root servers. Suppose a Web user enters the URL http://www.east.bar.com/a.html at a browser. The resolver contacts the local name server to translate www.east.bar.com into an IP address. Unless the information has been cached, the local name server contacts the root server to learn the IP address of the .com DNS server. Then the local DNS server contacts the .com DNS server to learn the IP address of the DNS server responsible for the bar.com *zone.* Each zone is a subtree of the DNS hierarchy that is administered separately. A zone typically has a primary server and several secondary servers that can replace the primary in the event of a failure. Depending on the size of the institution, the domain may be divided into multiple zones, corresponding perhaps to different buildings or geographic locations.

The early approach of listing all hostnames and IP addresses in a single file could never have handled the large set of hostnames in the Internet today. The separation of administrative responsibility is crucial to supporting the rapid growth of the Internet. An organization does not need to notify others when a host is added or removed from its network. Similarly, the bar.com organization may decide to have separate zones for east.bar.com and west.bar.com. The company may have two main locations in the United States, one on the east coast and one on the west coast. By dividing `bar.com` into two zones, each location can update its mapping of hostnames to IP addresses without consulting the other. Individual hosts need only know the IP address of one or more local DNS servers and do not need to be informed when other hosts are added or changed. The only time an organization needs to update its parent zone is when a DNS server is added or removed. This does not occur very often.

The hierarchy of domain names does not correspond to the hierarchical structure of IP addresses. Although `www.east.bar.com` and `www.west.bar.com` both have `bar.com` in their names, their IP addresses could be completely different. Efficient mapping of IP addresses to hostnames requires a *separate* hierarchy based on IP addresses. At the beginning of the twenty-first century, the allocation of IP addresses is supported by three regional Internet registries—APNIC (Asia-Pacific Network Information Centre), ARIN (American Registry for Internet Numbers), and RIPE NCC (Réseaux IP Européens Network Coordination Centre)—with new registries proposed for Africa and Latin America. ICANN distributes portions of the IP address space to each of these organizations which, in turn, allocate addresses to organizations within their regions. Allocating a fixed set of addresses to each region helps promote fair and efficient allocation of the remaining IPv4 addresses. In addition, allocating large blocks of IP addresses along geographic lines facilitates aggregation of IP addresses. Ideally, a router in one part of the world would not need to know how to reach each individual organization in another part of the world.

Upon obtaining a block of IP addresses, an organization becomes responsible for a portion of the `in-addr.arpa` name space. The `in-addr.arpa` name space is a hierarchy based on the octets in the 32-bit IP address, starting with the beginning of the addressing hierarchy—the leftmost octet of the address. For example, finding the hostname associated with the IP address 12.34.56.78 would involve contacting a server for `12.in-addr.arpa`. This domain may be further divided into subdomains, including `34.12.in-addr.arpa`. The division of responsibility along octet boundaries reflects the historical allocation of IP addresses with fixed prefix lengths of 8, 16, and 24. Under CIDR, an organization may have a block of IP addresses that does not match with octet boundaries. For example, suppose the address block 12.34.56.0/23 is allocated to a single company. Then the DNS server responsible for `34.12.in-addr.arpa` would delegate both `56.34.12.in-addr.arpa` and `57.34.12.in-addr.arpa` to this company. The company would be responsible for mapping individual IP addresses in 12.34.56.0/23 to domain names.

5.3.3 DNS protocol

The DNS protocol governs the communication between a DNS client and a DNS server. A DNS client sends a *query* for information (e.g., the IP address

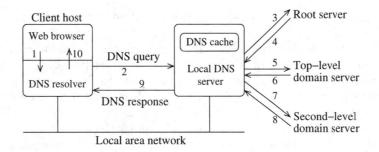

Figure 5.11. DNS resolver and local DNS server

associated with a particular hostname) to a DNS server, and the DNS server returns a *response* with the requested information (e.g., the IP address). The local
DNS server sends responses to resolvers and issues queries to other DNS servers.
The root DNS servers send responses to queries generated by other DNS servers
and do not issue queries of their own. Suppose that an application invokes the
gethostbyname() call to determine the IP address of `www.foo.bar.com`. The resolver contacts the local DNS server, which sends a query to a root DNS server
to learn the IP address of the `.com` DNS server. Then the local DNS server
sends a query to the `.com` DNS server to learn the IP address of the `bar.com`
DNS server. The local DNS server next sends a query to the DNS server for
the `bar.com` zone. If this zone has been subdivided, an additional query may
be issued to the `foo.bar.com` domain, which responds with the IP address for
`www.foo.bar.com`. Similarly, mapping the IP address 12.34.56.78 into a hostname results in a series of DNS queries to various DNS servers in the `in-arpa`
part of the hierarchy.

 DNS queries can be *recursive* or *iterative*. A recursive query requests that
the receiving DNS server resolve the entire request itself. For example, the
resolver issues a recursive query to the local name server to translate a hostname
into an IP address. As shown in step 1 in Figure 5.11, the resolver is invoked
by a system call from the application. Then the resolver sends a DNS query to
the local DNS server (step 2) and waits for the reply (step 9). The local DNS
server handles the steps involved in satisfying the resolver's query. An iterative
query requests that the receiving DNS server respond directly to the DNS client
with the IP address of the next DNS server in the DNS hierarchy. Root servers
handle only iterative queries. The local DNS server sends a query to the DNS
root server (step 3) to learn the names and IP addresses of the DNS server(s)
for the zone at the next level (step 4). This is preferable to burdening the root
servers with the responsibility of completing the resolution process. Then the
local DNS server can send a query to the next DNS server in the chain (steps
5 and 6, and steps 7 and 8). Ultimately, the local DNS server responds to the

resolver (step 9), and the resolver provides the IP address to the application (step 10).

DNS servers employ caching to reduce the latency in responding to queries and to reduce the amount of DNS traffic in the Internet [DOK92]. The local DNS server has a cache that stores the response sent to the resolver. In addition, the cache can store the IP address of each of the DNS servers involved in satisfying the query. For future queries, the local DNS server may be able to avoid contacting the root server and instead contact the first-level or second-level DNS server directly, based on the cached information. For example, as part of learning the IP address of `www.foo.com`, the local DNS server would learn the IP address of the `.com` top-level DNS server and the `foo.com` second-level DNS server. The local DNS server could satisfy a future query for `ftp.foo.com` by contacting the `foo.com` DNS server directly. The resolver does not perform caching because the information would last only for the duration of the application and could not be shared with other applications running on the same machine or with other hosts on the same network.

A DNS server caches responses to queries based on a TTL field. Each DNS response includes a TTL indicating the number of seconds that the response could be cached. DNS caching substantially reduces the latency for translating host names to IP addresses. The first request for `www.foo.com` may incur high latency for contacting the root server and the zone server, but future requests should be satisfied directly by the local DNS server. After the TTL expires, the information is removed from the cache and is fetched again upon receiving another query to translate `www.foo.com` into an IP address. DNS servers also cache negative information about failed queries. For example, suppose a user made a typographical error and entered the URL `http://www.boo.com` instead of `http://www.foo.com`. If `www.boo.com` does not exist, the local DNS server receives a negative response to its query and returns an error message to the resolver. The local DNS server remembers that the query for `www.boo.com` was unsuccessful so it can respond more quickly in the future with a failure indication.

DNS primarily uses UDP for sending queries and responses, although TCP may also be used. Using UDP enables the resolver and the DNS servers to communicate via single-packet messages without the overhead of establishing a connection. This is very useful because most DNS queries and responses are very short. However, the UDP packet may be lost inside the network. The sender of the DNS query retransmits the query if no response arrives after some period. If the timer expires before the response is received, the query is issued again. TCP is used instead of UDP for longer transfers. For example, an organization may have a secondary DNS server that provides backup service if the primary DNS server fails. The secondary DNS server needs a copy of the information available at the primary server. TCP is typically used for copying this data from the primary server to the secondary server.

5.3.4 DNS queries and the Web

A Web client performs a *gethostbyname()* query to convert a hostname into an IP address before establishing a transport connection to the Web server. For example, suppose a Web user enters a URL `http://www.foo.com/a.html` at a browser. Unless the resource is available in the browser cache, the browser must contact the Web server. In some cases, the client may not need to perform a DNS lookup of `www.foo.com`:

- **Request directed to a proxy:** The client may be configured to send requests to a downstream proxy. Establishing a TCP connection to the proxy requires the client to know the IP address of the proxy, not of the origin server. If the client is configured with the proxy's hostname, then a *gethostbyname()* call may be necessary to determine the proxy's IP address. A client that is configured with the proxy's IP address does not need to invoke the *gethostbyname()* call.

- **Request satisfied by the client cache:** Before issuing an HTTP request, the client looks for the Web resource in its local cache, based on the URL. If a fresh copy of the requested resource is available in the cache, the client does not need to contact the Web server. Otherwise, the client must contact the Web server to validate the cached resource or fetch a new resource from the server.

- **Using the result of a previous query:** The client may fetch several resources from the same server. In satisfying a request for `http://www.foo.com/a.html`, the client determines the IP address of `www.foo.com`. If the Web page has embedded images, the client may establish additional TCP connections to the server to fetch these resources. To avoid repeating the *gethostbyname()* call, the client may reuse the IP address learned from the previous call. Storing the results of the *gethostbyname()* call differs from DNS caching at the local DNS server because the *gethostbyname()* call does not return the TTL associated with the response to the DNS query. To reduce the risk of using expired information, the Web client should not store `www.foo.com`'s IP address for very long (e.g., beyond a few minutes).

Although the Web client needs to learn the IP address of the Web server, the Web server knows the IP address of the client when receiving a request because the client's IP address is included the header of each IP packet. The server can learn the hostname associated with this IP address by invoking the *gethostbyaddr()* function. Knowing the client's hostname can be useful for a variety of purposes, including logging, authentication, and targeted advertising. For example, recording the hostname in server logs enables the site administrators to know which requests came from users at particular institutions. The Web server may also wish to restrict access to certain resources, based on the hostname of the requesting client. Alternatively, the server may customize the HTTP response messages based on the client's hostname. The most common example of customization is targeted advertising, in which the embedded images in a Web page are tailored based on the domain name of the requesting client.

The mapping of the Web client's IP address to a hostname is controlled by the DNS server(s) at the Web client's institution. The Web client may have an incentive to spoof its hostname. For example, suppose a Web client has IP address 10.34.56.78 and hostname `a.badclient.com`. The IP-to-hostname mapping in the Web client's local DNS server could be set to map 10.34.56.78 to the name `b.goodclient.edu`. Supplying an invalid hostname could trick a Web server into granting access to the wrong client. As a precaution, the Web server could follow the *gethostbyaddr()* call with a *gethostbyname()* call. The *gethostbyname()* call would determine the IP address associated with `b.goodclient.edu`. In the example, the DNS mapping would be controlled by a different institution and would presumably return a different IP address, say 122.33.205.4. Realizing that the two IP addresses are different, the Web server could reject the HTTP request.

Mapping the client's IP address into a hostname often incurs significant delay. Invoking the *gethostbyaddr()* function results in a query to the Web server's local DNS server. This DNS server is unlikely to have information about the client's IP address in its cache, unless the client recently issued a Web request to the same Web server. Hence, the query must proceed to the root server and through the various zone servers in the `in-addr.arpa` domain. It is not uncommon for the query to fail. Many clients have dynamically assigned IP addresses or IP addresses that reside behind a corporate firewall. These addresses are typically not mapped to a hostname that is visible in the Internet; these queries incur delays in traversing the DNS hierarchy and fail to return useful information. Even if the query succeeds, performing a subsequent *gethostbyname()* call to check the validity of the IP-to-hostname mapping would further increase the latency.

In addition, the DNS queries consume resources at the Web server. The process that is invoking the *gethostbyaddr()* function must wait until a reply is generated. This increases the length of time that a process runs on behalf of an HTTP request, which, in turn, increases the number of processes running on the server. To avoid this overhead, a Web server that handles a large number of simultaneous requests may skip the step of converting the client's IP address into a hostname. Depending on the Web site, knowing the hostname of the requesting client may not be important to the correct operation of the server. However, in some cases, the Web server may perform customization or authentication based on the hostname of the client. To maximize efficiency, the server could be configured to limit the application of *gethostbyaddr()* to Web requests that require this information.

5.3.5 DNS-based Web server load balancing

DNS also plays an important role in directing HTTP requests to a collection of Web servers that provide access to the same content. Although a hostname typically corresponds to a single IP address, a busy Web site may be replicated on multiple machines that have the same hostname, as discussed in Chapter 4 (Section 4.5.2). The replicas may be necessary to support the heavy request load. In addition, the replicas may be located in different geographical locations in order to provide better service to a diverse set of clients. For example, the name www.big.com may correspond to four machines with the IP addresses 10.198.3.47, 10.198.3.48, 10.34.99.1, and 10.34.99.2. To support hostnames with multiple IP addresses, a DNS server can provide a list of IP addresses in response to a DNS query. In response to a query for the IP address of www.big.com, a local DNS server would learn all four IP addresses. The local DNS server selects one of these IP addresses to return to the resolver responsible for originating the DNS query.

In a traditional DNS implementation, the local DNS server would select the first IP address in the list. This would result in a heavy load of HTTP requests on the machine with IP address 10.198.3.47. To avoid this problem, the DNS server responsible for www.big.com could vary the order of the IP addresses for each query. For example, the reply to the first DNS query would return 10.198.3.47, 10.198.3.48, 10.34.99.1, and 10.34.99.2, whereas the next reply might use 10.198.3.48, 10.34.99.1, 10.34.99.2, and 10.198.3.47. Such *round-robin* sequencing helps distribute the load across the various replicas. However, this technique does not consider the current load on each of the machines or on the network. In addition, it does not consider the proximity of the client machine to each of the replicas. Extensions to DNS server implementations have addressed these limitations without requiring changes to the DNS protocol. These changes can be applied on the DNS server receiving the query or on the DNS server sending the response.

First, consider changes in the software of the DNS server *issuing* the query. Suppose a local DNS server receives a query from a resolver to determine an IP address for www.big.com. A list of four IP addresses is provided by the DNS server responsible for www.big.com. Rather than returning the first IP address to the requesting resolver, the local DNS server could determine which machine is most appropriate. This decision could be based on a variety of factors, such as the round-trip time to contact the server machine or the length of the route to the server. The local DNS server may measure these statistics over time to develop a more accurate estimate. Then the resolver is given the IP address of the "best" replica. These techniques do not require changes to the resolver code or the software running on the DNS server responsible for www.foo.com. Only the software for the local DNS server would need to change. However, maintaining an up-to-date estimate of the round-trip times introduces overhead on the local DNS server and the network.

Next consider changes in the software of the DNS server responding to the query. The DNS server responsible for www.big.com could try to select the "best" of the four IP addresses. This DNS server may have access to up-to-date information about the current load on each of the www.big.com machines. In addition, the DNS server responsible for www.big.com may try to estimate which replica is closest to the local DNS server that issued the query. The DNS server for www.big.com does not know the IP address of the Web client that sent a query to the local DNS server. In selecting the best replica of the Web site, the DNS server for www.big.com might assume that the Web client is near the local DNS server. Proximity to the Web client reduces the latency in satisfying Web requests and lowers the amount of network resources required to carry the IP packets. The decision of which IP address to return can be based on a variety of factors, including the proximity to the client, load on the network, and load on the server replicas.

Traditionally, a response to a DNS query can be cached for a long period, depending on the value of the TTL field. TTLs of days or weeks are not uncommon. However, large TTLs do not allow the big.com DNS server to exercise much control over which replicas of www.big.com are accessed. To gain more control, the DNS responses can use a smaller TTL value, on the order of minutes. This ensures that the local DNS server cannot cache the response for very long. After a cache entry expires, the local DNS server cannot satisfy the next resolver request without contacting the big.com DNS server again. This gives the big.com DNS server an opportunity to respond with a different IP address for www.big.com. However, this also requires the Web browser to wait longer for the *gethostbyname()* call to return when the cached information at the local DNS server has expired. In addition, the small TTL values result in a higher load on the system as a whole. DNS was not designed as a general infrastructure to support server load balancing. The growth of the Web and the decrease in TTL values have raised concern about the scalability of the DNS infrastructure. Techniques for directing client requests to an appropriate replica are discussed in more detail in Chapter 11 (Section 11.12).

5.4 Application-layer Protocols

Applications execute on end hosts and communicate via application-level protocols. An application-layer protocol defines both the syntax and the semantics of the messages exchanged between the end systems. The syntax defines the format of the messages, whereas the semantics dictate how the applications should interpret the messages and respond to the sender. In this section, we describe the protocols underlying four key Internet applications—Telnet, file transfer, e-mail, and network news—that predate the emergence of the Web. We describe how the design of each application-level protocol relates to the motivating application and discuss the interaction with the transport layer.

5.4.1 Telnet protocol

Telnet [PR93] permits a user to connect to an account on a remote machine. A client program running on the user's machine communicates using the Telnet protocol with a server program running on the remote machine.

THE TELNET APPLICATION

In the early days of the ARPANET, the primary purpose of the network was to permit a user in one location to access a machine in another location. The user would have an account on a local machine and an account on a remote machine. The user invokes a Telnet client on the local machine to establish a connection to the Telnet server on the remote machine. For example, suppose the user types "`telnet big.foo.gov`." The Telnet client would perform a *gethostbyname()* call to determine the IP address of `big.foo.gov`. Then the client would create a socket to communicate with the Telnet server. The server prompts the user for a login identifier—the name of the user's account on the remote machine— followed by a password. For the most part, Telnet users interact with the remote machine in the same way they would interact with their local machine. The Telnet client and server simply relay the data back and forth.

THE TELNET PROTOCOL

The Telnet client program performs two important functions—interacting with the user terminal on the local host and exchanging messages with the Telnet server. By default, the Telnet client connects to port 23 on the remote machine because this TCP port number has been reserved for Telnet servers. The TCP connection persists for the duration of the login session. The client and the server maintain the TCP connection even when the user interrupts the transfer of data (e.g., by hitting cntl-C or Delete). For interoperability between different platforms, the Telnet protocol assumes that the two hosts run a general Network Virtual Terminal (NVT). The NVT is a very simple character device with a keyboard and printer—data typed by the user on the keyboard is sent to the server, and data received from the server is output to the printer. The NVT terminals on the two hosts exchange data in the 7-bit U.S. variant of the ASCII format, with each character sent as an octet with the first bit set to 0. Some control information, such as the end-of-line indication, is sent as a two-octet sequence.

Each Telnet control message starts with a special octet (i.e., 8 bits of 1s) to ensure that the recipient interprets the subsequent octets as a command.

Otherwise, each octet is interpreted as data (e.g., a user keystroke). Sending control messages on the same connection as the data is referred to as *inband signaling*. The initial control messages between the client and the server are used to exchange information about their capabilities. For example, the client may indicate the type and speed of its terminal and whether data should be sent one character at a time or one line at a time. After the capabilities exchange, the server instructs the client to send a login identifier and password. Once the authentication completes, the user interacts directly with the remote machine. The client application relays user keystrokes to the server, and the server relays any output back to the client. However, the client and server must scan every byte they receive to look for commands (starting with the 11111111 octet). A Telnet sender uses TCP's urgent-pointer field to direct the receiver's attention to Telnet commands.

5.4.2 File Transfer Protocol

FTP [PR85] allows a user to copy files to and from a remote machine. The client program sends commands to the server program to coordinate the copying of files between the two machines on behalf of the user.

The FTP application

The FTP client connects to the remote machine and prompts the user to enter a login identifier and a password. However, some users may not have their own accounts on the remote machine. To grant access to a broad set of users, many FTP servers have a special account (e.g., "anonymous") that does not require the user to know a password. The FTP server coordinates access to a collection of files in various directories. An FTP server typically has a special directory, with one or more subdirectories, that can be accessed by FTP clients. Many FTP clients have a simple command-line interface. The user can log in to the FTP server, traverse through the directories of files, and send and receive files. The interface may allow the reader to send or receive *multiple* files with a single command. Recent FTP client implementations provide a menu-based graphical user interface. In fact, a Web browser allows users to specify the desired file as a URL (e.g., `ftp://ftp.foo.com/bar/neatfile`). The browser performs the low-level tasks of connecting to the FTP server as an anonymous user and sending a sequence of FTP commands to fetch the requested file.

The FTP protocol

FTP uses separate TCP connections for control and data. By default, the FTP client connects to port 21 on the remote machine. The client uses this control connection to send commands and receive replies, and the connection persists across multiple commands. The specification of FTP includes more than 30 different commands, which are transmitted over the control connection in NVT ASCII format. The commands are not case-sensitive and may have arguments; each command ends with a two-character sequence of a carriage return (CR) followed by a line feed (LF). These commands differ from the commands typed by the user at the interface provided by the client. Transferring a single file involves a single user-level command that triggers the client to send a sequence of FTP commands to the server. The FTP server responds to each command with a three-digit reply code (for the FTP client) and an optional text message (for the human user). The first two digits provide information about the type of the reply; the third digit does not have any particular meaning. For example, the 200 ("command okay") has a "2" to indicate positive completion of the command that is followed by a "0" to indicate that the response relates to syntax.

The control connection persists across a sequence of commands and replies as the client and server continue their dialogue. The typical interaction between a client and server starts with a command that identifies the account (e.g., anonymous) on the server machine, followed by another command to send the user password (e.g., the user's e-mail address, for anonymous FTP). The arguments for these two commands are gleaned from the user's input. The server uses this information to decide which files the client can access. For example, an anonymous user may have restricted access to a small subset of the files. At the beginning of a session, the FTP client can see the root directory exported by the FTP server. The next action by the client depends on the request initiated by the user—to read a file, to write a file, to list the files in the current directory, to move to another directory, to see the name of the current directory, and so on.

File transfers use a separate connection established by the host sending the data. If the user wants to retrieve the file `foo.txt`, the server initiates the creation of the TCP connection. However, the server does not know what port number to use as the destination port for the FTP client. Before sending the command to retrieve `foo.txt`, the FTP client asks its underlying operating system to allocate a port number (above 1023). The FTP client uses the control connection to inform the server of the selected port number for the data connection. The server creates the data connection, writes the contents of the file `foo.txt`, and closes the connection. The FTP client reads the bytes from its socket up to the end-of-file (EOF) character. In practice, some organizations have firewalls that disallow outside hosts from initiating TCP connections. To allow clients behind firewalls to retrieve data from FTP servers, FTP has a command that forces the server to play a passive role in the establishment of the data connection.

A file is typically transmitted as a stream of bytes, with the closure of the TCP connection indicating the end of the transmission (EOF). The FTP specification also describes a *block mode* that allows a sender to transmit the file as a series of data blocks; each block starts with one or more header bytes. Block mode enables the sender to transfer multiple files on the same data connection, with each file ending at a block boundary. However, block mode is not widely implemented. In practice, each data transfer requires a separate TCP connection. In contrast, the control connection can persist across multiple data transfers. FTP includes a command for aborting an ongoing data transfer without terminating the control connection. This allows the user to terminate the copying of a file without requiring the client to repeat the process of connecting to the server and authenticating the user.

Although Telnet restricts data transfer to 7-bit ASCII characters, FTP permits a wider range of data types, including binary files. However, the FTP server does *not* provide information about the data type of each file. Instead, the FTP client must request the data transfer in a particular form. For example, suppose the user wants to copy the file `picture.gif` from the local machine to the remote machine. The user would need to request a binary transfer. This would trigger the FTP client to issue a command to the FTP server to switch to binary mode. The client and the server cannot infer the format of the file without help from the user because the local file is not directly associated with additional attributes. The `.gif` extension in the file name does not necessarily indicate the media type of the file. After copying the file, the user can invoke a separate program to display or modify the contents of the file, based on the user's knowledge of the media type. For example, the user could invoke *ghostview* to display a PostScript file.

5.4.3 Simple Mail Transfer Protocol

SMTP [Pos82] supports the transfer of e-mail. SMTP is used to send an e-mail message from a local mail server to a remote mail server. In addition, SMTP may be used to send an e-mail message from the user's mail agent to the local mail server.

THE ELECTRONIC MAIL APPLICATION

Delivering an e-mail message from one user to another involves several components. A user invokes an e-mail agent to send and receive e-mail messages. The agent may also support a variety of other features, such as mail folders, e-mail aliases, and an editor for composing messages. In addition to providing an interface to the user, the e-mail agent coordinates the interaction with a local mail server. The local mail server maintains each user's mailbox and coordinates the exchange of messages with mail servers in other locations. For example, suppose a user named Viv has her own computer and receives e-mail at `viv@foo.com`; the mail server maintains the mailbox `viv`. The separation of functionality between the user agent and the mail server is valuable—the mail agent provides rich features for a single user, and the mail server provides reliable service for multiple users.

In contrast to transferring files, sending and receiving e-mail is not an interactive application. In sending an e-mail message, the mail agent does not necessarily know if and when the message reaches the recipient's mail server or mail agent. In fact, the sending user may terminate the mail agent before the local mail server completes the delivery of the e-mail message to the remote mail server. In practice, many users send and receive e-mail via their Web browsers. This occurs in two main ways. First, the Web browser may act as the mail agent that communicates with the local mail server and provides an interface for reading and composing messages. Second, the browser may be used to visit a Web site that allows users to read messages (by retrieving an HTML file) and send messages (by submitting an HTML form). In this situation, the Web server coordinates the communication with the mail server. For example, the server may invoke scripts to retrieve the e-mail messages sent to the user and send the e-mail messages submitted by the user.

An e-mail message consists of a header and a body. The body represents the text sent by the user. Each header field starts on a separate line and consists of a single string, followed by a colon and another string (e.g., `Date: Sat Oct 28 2000 11:29:32 GMT`). Some of the fields, such as `To` and `Subject`, depend on user input. Others, such as `Date` and `Message-Id`, are set by the user agent or by the local mail server that sends the message. The header and the body consist of text lines in U.S. 7-bit ASCII format. Each line ends with a two-character sequence—a carriage return (CR) followed by a line feed (LF). Initially, e-mail messages could contain only text data. Later, the Multipurpose Internet Mail Extensions (MIME) [FB96a, FB96b] provided a standard way to convert other types of data into text format for inclusion in e-mail messages. MIME includes additional headers that indicate the size and encoding of the contents of the message.

THE SMTP PROTOCOL

SMTP was developed in 1982 to replace FTP for transferring e-mail messages from one mail server to another. Under SMTP, the sending mail server establishes a TCP connection on port 25 on the receiving mail server. The combined header and body are transmitted from one mail server to another using a sequence of commands. In transmitting e-mail messages, the mail servers do not distinguish between the header and the body. The only function performed on the message is the prepending of additional header fields, such as `Received`. This enables the recipient to identify the sequence of mail servers involved in transferring the message. Similar to FTP, SMTP is text oriented and command based. The sender issues a sequence of commands, one at a time, and receives replies consisting of a three-digit reply code and a textual string.

The local mail server determines the identity of the remote mail server by performing a special kind of DNS query. The local mail server issues a query for MX (Mail Exchanger) information for the fully qualified domain name in the right-hand portion of the e-mail address (e.g., `users.foo.com` in `viv@users.foo.com`). The DNS reply contains the name of one or more hosts acting as mail servers for the given fully qualified domain name. After selecting a remote mail server (e.g., `bigmail.foo.com`), the local mail server performs an additional DNS query to learn the IP address of the remote mail server. Then the local mail server establishes a TCP connection to the remote mail server. Problems may arise at either stage. First, the DNS query may return an error. For example, the message may be directed to a domain that does not exist (e.g., `viv@users.foo.com`, where `users.foo.com` does not exist). This would cause the local mail server to return an error to the sender of the message. Second, suppose that the local mail server learns the IP address of the remote mail server but is unable to establish a TCP connection. This could happen if the remote server is temporarily offline or a network failure has disconnected the two hosts. In these situations, the local mail server stores the message and attempts the transmission again in the near future. In the meantime, the sender may be informed that the message transfer has been delayed.

The communication between the two servers starts with a greeting message from the remote mail server. Then the local mail server issues commands to transfer the e-mail message. A typical exchange involves separate commands to

- Identify the local mail server
- Identify the sender of the e-mail message
- Identify each recipient of the e-mail message
- Send the actual e-mail message

In contrast to FTP, SMTP uses a single TCP connection for both the command-reply exchanges and the transfer of the e-mail message. The sender identifies the end of the message with a CRLF, followed by a period (".") and another CRLF. However, the e-mail message may include a line that starts with the "." character, which may confuse the recipient. Therefore the local mail server adds a second "."—sending ".." instead of "."—to these lines. The extra "." is removed by the recipient before displaying the message to the user.

In addition to transferring the message between the mail servers, delivering an e-mail message requires two additional steps involving the mail agent—the transfer of the message to the local mail server and the reception of the message from the remote mail server. The sender's user agent initiates the transfer of the e-mail message to the local mail server. This transfer may also involve SMTP, although the mail agent could use other protocols instead. Sending an e-mail message involves transmitting data from a mail agent to a mail server. In contrast, retrieving a message from a mailbox involves retrieving data from a mail server. The reception of e-mail messages typically does not involve SMTP. HTTP may be used to access a mailbox on the Web. Other protocols, such as the Post Office Protocol (POP3) and the Internet Message Access Protocol (IMAP), have been specifically designed for retrieving e-mail messages from the mail server. A detailed overview of the protocols used for exchanging e-mail is available elsewhere [Joh00].

5.4.4 Network News Transfer Protocol

NNTP [KL86] supports the transfer of articles associated with electronic newsgroups. A user agent uses NNTP to communicate with a local news server, which uses NNTP to communicate with a central repository of news articles.

THE NETWORK NEWS APPLICATION

In addition to exchanging messages between a pair of users, e-mail is sometimes used to distribute messages to a group of users over a period of time. For example, an organization could create a mailing list for distributing messages on a particular topic. Interested users can subscribe to the list. However, mailing lists are not an efficient way to reach a large and changing set of users. Each member of the list receives a separate copy of the message, which consumes network resources and storage space. In addition, the manager of the mailing list must update the list of recipients as users come and go. In practice, this process can be automated by having users send e-mail to a special e-mail account that corresponds to a program that handles the details of adding and removing members from the list. The manager's mail server may also have difficultly reaching all of the intended recipients, particularly if users neglect to unsubscribe from the group before terminating or changing their e-mail accounts.

The difficulties associated with mailing lists motivated the creation of the USENET news system, developed in 1979 and standardized in 1983 [Hor83]. The key idea is to store the messages in a central database instead of having a separate copy in each subscriber's mailbox. The database consists of a collection of *newsgroups* (e.g., `soc.culture.indian`), each associated with an ordered list of messages. Newsgroup names consist of strings separated by periods. The naming scheme is hierarchical. For example, a variety of related groups starts with `soc` or `rec`. The database supports requests to retrieve newsgroup articles and supports indexing, cross-referencing, and aging of the articles. The system administrator can specify expiration policies for removing old articles to conserve storage space at the Netnews server.

Like an e-mail message, an article in a newsgroup includes several header lines. For example, an article includes header lines such as

- E-mail address of the person who posted the article
- Subject matter of the article

- Date/time when the article was generated
- Number of lines of text in the article
- Unique message identifier for the article
- List of newsgroups receiving with the article

Newsgroups are replicated at various places in the Internet. For example, a company or university may have its own news server to support a collection of users. The local news server may not replicate all of the newsgroups and may support special newsgroups tailored to its user community. For example, a university may exclude newsgroups on certain subjects and may support additional newsgroups for various academic courses taught at the school.

Users read and post articles via a user agent that coordinates interaction with the local news server. The user agent provides an interface that displays article summaries that list a subset of the header lines and supports reading and posting of articles. Most Web browsers can communicate with a local news server. On the Web, a newsgroup is identified by a URL that includes the name of the group (e.g., `news:soc.culture.indian`). In addition to displaying text, some user agents can parse and display formatted data. In addition, the user agent remembers which newsgroups the user reads and which messages have been read or deleted. This information is typically stored in a local file that can be read the next time the user invokes the agent. Some Web sites provide access to Netnews articles, allowing users to read articles (by retrieving HTML files) and to post articles (by submitting an HTML form). In this situation, the Web browser communicates directly with a Web server that coordinates the interaction with the Netnews system.

THE NNTP PROTOCOL

NNTP was introduced in 1986 to replace the use of the UNIX-to-UNIX Copy Protocol (UUCP) for transferring Netnews articles. NNTP coordinates the transfer of messages between the local news server and the central repository. NNTP may also be used between the user agent and the local news server. An NNTP client establishes a single TCP connection to port 119 at the NNTP server. Like FTP and SMTP, the NNTP client issues commands to a server that returns a three-digit reply code and an optional textual message. Depending on the reply code, NNTP responses may include additional parameters. The number and type of these extra parameters are fixed for each response code to simplify interpretation of the response by the NNTP client. In processing commands, the NNTP server keeps track of the current newsgroup name and article number accessed by the NNTP client.

NNTP has a variety of commands that perform different types of functions. One set of commands provides general information about the NNTP server and the various newsgroups, including the following:

- Summary of the commands understood by the NNTP server
- List of the valid newsgroups, including information about the first and last article in each newsgroup and whether the newsgroup allows users to post articles
- List of newsgroups created since a particular date/time
- List of articles posted to a particular newsgroup since a particular date/time

Providing information about changes since a particular date/time enables the NNTP client to update its view of newsgroups and articles without requiring the NNTP server to store information on behalf of each client. Other commands are used to move to another newsgroup (referred to by its name), move to another article (referred to by message identifier or its number within the newsgroup), move backward by one article within the current newsgroup, and move forward by one article within the current newsgroup.

Other commands return the entire article or just the headers or the contents. For each of these commands, the article is identified by its message identifier or a number that indicates its position in the newsgroup. NNTP also has commands related to the creation of new articles. The client sends a request to post an article. If the server responds successfully, the client sends the article on the existing TCP connection, following the same convention as SMTP. The end of the article is identified by a single period "." on a line. Upon receiving the article, the central repository creates a unique message identifier and adds the article to the newsgroup. Another command supports the copying of existing messages between two NNTP servers. NNTP also includes a command for the client to terminate a session. After sending a reply to the termination command, the NNTP server closes the TCP connection.

5.4.5 Properties of application-layer protocols

New application-level protocols arise to support new ways of communicating over the Internet. Telnet arose to support user interaction with an account on a remote machine, and FTP addressed the need to copy files between accounts. As e-mail grew in popularity, SMTP replaced the early use of FTP for transferring e-mail messages. Similarly, NNTP arose to support the transfer of Netnews, as an alternative to mailing lists. As a result of this heritage, Telnet, FTP, SMTP, and NNTP have important similarities and differences, as follows:

- **Command/reply:** Telnet clients and servers send commands in binary format, starting with a special octet (11111111). In contrast, under FTP, SMTP, and NNTP, commands are text-based and are sent by the client. The commands have a well-defined, fixed format, and the server responds with a three-digit reply code and an optional text message. Some NNTP responses include additional information in a fixed format, depending on the reply code.

- **Data types:** Telnet, FTP, SMTP, and NNTP transmit textual data in the standard U.S. 7-bit ASCII format. FTP also supports the transfer of data in binary form, when indicated by the client. SMTP and NNTP incorporate the MIME standard to support the conversion of non-ASCII data into ASCII format and to convey type information to the recipient.
- **Transport:** All four protocols rely on a reliable transport protocol, typically TCP. Telnet, SMTP, and NNTP use a single TCP connection for transmitting commands/replies and data, and the connection persists across multiple transfers. In contrast, FTP uses separate connections for control and data. The control connection persists across multiple command/reply exchanges; successive data transfers typically use different connections.
- **Directionality:** FTP and NNTP can transfer data in both directions— copying data or posting articles from the client and retrieving files or articles from the server. SMTP is used to transmit e-mail messages from the client to the server. In Telnet and FTP, the client is typically an agent that interacts directly with a user. In SMTP and NNTP, the client may be a local server that exchanges data (an e-mail message or Netnews article) with a remote server.
- **Statefulness:** Under all four protocols, the server retains information about the session with the client. For example, a Telnet server stores information about NVT terminal settings. An FTP server remembers the client's current directory and the current mode of data transfer (binary or text). An SMTP server remembers information about the sender and recipients of an e-mail message while waiting for the `DATA` command to transmit the message contents. An NNTP server remembers the current newsgroup and article number for the client.

Telnet, FTP, SMTP, and NNTP were mature application-level protocols before the advent of the Web. Therefore several key elements of HTTP relate to these earlier protocols. Yet, HTTP also differs in many important ways, as discussed in the next two chapters.

5.5 Summary

The Internet Protocol provides a basic packet-delivery service over a wide variety of link-layer technologies. Having a simple, open standard facilitated the rapid evolution of the Internet into a worldwide communication infrastructure. More complex services are deferred to the transport-layer and application-layer protocols that are implemented at the end hosts. Each layer performs a specific task without depending on the implementation details of the other layers. The Transmission Control Protocol provides the abstraction of a socket that delivers an ordered, reliable stream of bytes between two hosts. This serves as a primary building block for a wide variety of Internet applications. Hosts can be represented by names and IP addresses. The Domain Name System provides a simple and scalable way to translate between these two representations. Together, IP, TCP, and DNS support a wide range of Internet applications, including Telnet, file transfer, e-mail, and network news. These applications rely on protocols, such as Telnet, FTP, SMTP, and NNTP, that predated the emergence of the Web and influenced the design of HTTP.

6

HTTP Protocol Design and Description

A protocol is a language with a grammar, syntactic structure such as message formats, and semantic rules indicating how the fields of the messages are interpreted. The Hypertext Transfer Protocol (HTTP) is the request-response protocol underlying the World Wide Web. It is an application-level protocol like File Transfer Protocol (FTP) and Telnet. However, unlike those protocols, HTTP is stateless. HTTP was conceived in 1990 and has been the protocol carrying a significant portion of the traffic on the Internet since 1995.

It is important to understand the difference between HTTP and the World Wide Web. As discussed in Chapter 1, the Web consists of three semantic parts: the HTTP protocol, the Hypertext Markup Language (HTML), and the Uniform Resource Identifier (URI) naming scheme. The Web has a few significant software components (browsers with a graphical interface, proxies, and origin servers) that communicate between each other using the HTTP protocol. Web components also use HTTP as a communication mechanism for accessing resources available via other protocols such as FTP or Telnet.

HTTP is used to transmit information in multiple formats, languages, and character sets. The HTTP message syntax is based on MIME—Multipurpose Internet Mail Extensions [FB96a, FB96b]. The contents of an HTTP message body are treated blindly by the protocol—no interpretation is done.

This chapter is based on the Informational Request for Comments RFC 1945 [BLFF96], which introduced the key concepts and terminology that are essential for understanding HTTP. RFC 1945 described the common use of HTTP in the mid-1990s. The current version of the HTTP protocol as this book goes to press is HTTP/1.1. The next chapter focuses on HTTP/1.1 and the differences between HTTP/1.0 and HTTP/1.1. Our decision to present the details of HTTP/1.0 and HTTP/1.1 in separate chapters is deliberate. Examining HTTP/1.0 first gives readers an opportunity to see the salient aspects of the protocol and the remarkable degree to which it succeeded in the presence of other competing protocols. Examining HTTP/1.1 next provides a historical perspective of the protocol evolution process.

In this chapter, we examine how HTTP evolved from the early days of the Web. We begin with an overview of the HTTP protocol, examining its origin, its basic features, and its chief influences. The HTTP protocol was developed by learning from other systems that were in vogue at the time of creation of the Web and adopting several ideas from them.

The next section examines the building blocks of the protocol: the language elements—objects, request methods, headers[1] used in HTTP messages, and the various classes into which responses are divided. The current set of popular applications on the Web, such as searching and remote command execution, are a small subset of the operations facilitated by HTTP. Understanding the basic elements of the protocol provides insight into its capability and the range of possible applications.

After examining extensibility issues of the protocol, we look at a few security issues associated with Web interaction using HTTP. The Secure Socket Layer (SSL) and the use of SSL in Web exchanges are examined. Like other communication protocols, HTTP has several rules that aid in the construction of interoperable implementations. We examine the protocol compliance rules associated with the HTTP protocol and the meaning of the protocol version number. We conclude with an examination of principles and practice associated with HTTP/1.0.

6.1 Overview of HTTP

An overview of HTTP can be appreciated via a historical timeline. The HTTP protocol evolved along with the Web and its two other components—URI and HTML. HTTP evolved in two distinct phases:

- From the first HTTP/0.9 specification to the HTTP/1.0 version over a period of four years
- From HTTP/1.0 to HTTP/1.1 in another four years

Table 6.1 shows a partial timeline of the various standards documents and their earlier draft versions.

HTTP was proposed by Tim Berners-Lee in March 1990 at the CERN laboratories, as a sufficiently powerful mechanism to access documents anywhere in the Internet and to help navigate between them via *hypertext* [Nel67] links. The earliest version of the protocol, named HTTP/0.9[2], was first described in January 1992 in the www-talk mailing list [BL92a], although it had actually been implemented in 1990. The specification of HTTP/0.9 led to codification of the rules of interaction between clients and servers, as well the expectations the two

---

[1]Note that this chapter uses the terms *header* and *header field* interchangeably.

[2]It is typical in protocol evolution to label an initial version with a value less than 1 before it is widely discussed and improved.

Table 6.1. Historical timeline of HTTP-related documents

Date	Document
Mar 1990	CERN labs document proposing Web
Jan 1992	HTTP/0.9 specification
Feb 1992	W3 and WAIS/X.500
Dec 1992	Proposal to add MIME to HTTP
Feb 1993	UDI (Universal Document Identifier) for the Network
Mar 1993	HTTP/1.0 first draft
Jun 1993	HTML (1.0 Specification)
Oct 1993	URL specification
Nov 1993	HTTP/1.0 second draft
Mar 1994	URI in WWW
May 1996	HTTP/1.0 Informational, RFC 1945
Jan 1997	HTTP/1.1 Proposed Standard, RFC 2068
Jun 1999	HTTP/1.1 Draft Standard, RFC 2616
2001	HTTP/1.1 Formal Standard

components have on each other. Specific details of syntax and semantics were enumerated, and HTTP/0.9 was labeled as a subset of the more detailed protocol being planned. Attention was focused primarily on dealing with searching, because searching was the primary function provided by competing systems such as Gopher and Archie.

Hypertext had become popular in the 1980s as a system to navigate between linked documents. We defined hypertext in Chapter 1 as nonlinear writing; that is, text that is not constrained to be linear. The reader can move from one part of a document to another point in the same document or an entirely different document. Such nonlinearity is explicitly enabled via hypertext. A hypertext document may consist of just a collection of pointers to other hypertext documents.

In December 1992, discussion arose in the `www-talk` mailing list about the potential for making information retrieval systems like Wide Area Information Servers (WAIS) and the Web compatible with MIME. MIME, an evolving Internet standard at that time, classified data formats and supported multipart messages in order to send multipart documents via e-mail. HTTP responses could be returned in extended MIME messages. The first draft specification of HTTP/1.0 was made in March 1993. In June 1993, the draft specification [BLC93] of the Hypertext Markup Language (HTML) proposed HTML to be a MIME content type. Later that year, in October, the first Internet Draft specification of Uniform Resource Locators (URL) was published [BL93b] after discussions within the URI working group.

Several drafts of the HTTP/1.0 documents followed. In May 1996, in order to capture the state of HTTP implementations, an Informational Request For Comments, RFC 1945 [BLFF96] was released. This has served as the basis for most HTTP/1.0 component implementations. The next three years saw furious activity in trying to upgrade HTTP/1.0 to fix a variety of problems. RFC 2068 was introduced as the Proposed Standard in January 1997 and in June 1999, RFC 2616 [FGM$^+$99] was released as the Draft Standard for HTTP/1.1. The formal standard of HTTP will appear in 2001.

The rest of the section provides an overview of the HTTP protocol along two tracks:

- **Protocol properties:** Here we examine HTTP's dependence on the URI infrastructure, the request-response nature of HTTP, the absence of state maintenance across requests, and the notion of metadata (information about a resource).
- **Protocol influences:** In this part we examine the influences on HTTP by MIME, as well as some of the other protocols popular at the time of the birth of HTTP. We also compare HTTP against other application-level protocols that predated the Web.

6.1.1 Protocol properties

In this section we examine a few key properties of HTTP. They are

- **Global URI:** HTTP relies on the URI naming mechanism. HTTP uses URIs in all its transactions to identify resources on the Web.
- **Request-response exchange:** HTTP requests are sent by clients and result in responses from servers. The direction of the flow is from clients to servers; the server does not initiate Web traffic.
- **Statelessness:** No state is maintained by clients or servers across requests and responses. Each pair of request and response is treated as an independent message exchange.
- **Resource metadata:** Information about resources are often included in Web transfers and can be used in several ways.

RELIANCE ON A GLOBAL URI

HTTP relies on the notion of a Uniform Resource Identifier (URI) [BLFM98]. The naming mechanism permits resources to reside anywhere on the Internet and separates the notion of a resource from that of a response. A resource can have the same URI attached to it forever, although the resource's representation and contents change several times during its lifetime. A URI is thus a formatted string from the protocol's point of view. A URI simply denotes a resource independent of its current location or the name by which it is known. In this sense, a URI is a combination of a Uniform Resource Locator (URL) [BLMM94,

Fie95] and a Uniform Resource Name (URN) [SM94]. A URI is a superset of both URL and URN and can be represented by either or by both. The most popular form of a URI is a URL.

As an example of distinguishing among a URI, URL, and URN, consider this book. The book has an International Society of Book Numbers (ISBN) number, 0-201-71088-9, assigned by the Library of Congress in the United States of America. The ISBN number is guaranteed to be globally unique, different from that of the books already published, and will persist even when millions of other books are published. The Library of Congress alone decides how to assign the unique number to this book. The ISBN number is the URN for this book; it names the book but does not provide information on where the book can be obtained. A URI for this book can represent the contents of this book if the entire contents are available via a machine accessible protocol. Suppose the contents of this book were placed on a Web server and made accessible via HTTP. The book's location could be specified via the URL `http://www.research.att.com/books/kandr.ps.gz`. The book could also be made available via anonymous FTP in the directory `pub/bala` on the machine `ftp.research.att.com`. Thus it has an alternate URL `ftp://ftp.research.att.com/pub/bala/kandr.ps.gz`. A URL thus gives the location of a copy of the resource. The book's URI is therefore any of the URLs mentioned above or the URN (ISBN).

A URI is considered to be *absolute* if the string starts with a *scheme* and is followed by a string representing the resource that can be obtained via that scheme. A *scheme* simply designates the protocol that should be used to access the resource. A *relative* URI does not start with a scheme name. The very first specification of the HTTP protocol—later known as `HTTP/0.9` [BL92a]—listed five schemes—`file`, `news`, `http`, `telnet`, `gopher`. It also anticipated the use of at least two more (`WAIS` and `X-500`) and reserved schemes for them.

Although a scheme name maps to a specific protocol, more than one protocol may be involved in accessing a resource named by a URL. A Web request for a resource typically requires multiple protocols, such as Domain Name System (DNS) to look up the host name where the resource resides and Transmission Control Protocol (TCP) to fetch it over a transport link. Similarly, there may be more than one scheme to identify a single resource.

The most common scheme in use on the Web today is `http`. Each scheme has its own syntax, and all schemes have a mechanism to name resources. By separating the scheme from the internal syntax of the particular protocol, the naming mechanism of the Web enabled it to easily overlay itself on top of several other systems. Because the same resource can be accessed using different protocols, other systems could overlay themselves on top of HTTP. Resolving non-HTTP URIs, that is, resources that are accessible by protocols *other* than HTTP, was necessary because such an ability was becoming common at the time of the Web's creation. Separation of scheme from syntax led to the Web being a uniform front end for accessing resources that may typically be accessible only by other protocols such as `ftp`. Examples of non-HTTP URI include `rtsp://clips.foo.com/preview/audio`, `telnet://ox.aciri.org`, and so on. When faced with a non-HTTP URI, the browser parses the scheme name up to the ":" character and invokes the appropriate protocol handler—RTSP (Real Time Streaming Protocol) and Telnet, respectively.

REQUEST-RESPONSE EXCHANGE

The HTTP protocol specifies the syntax and semantics by which the components of the Web, such as clients and servers, communicate with each other. An HTTP message is a structured collection of octets in a specific syntax. HTTP is a request-response protocol—a *request* is a message sent from a client to a recipient server. The recipient server may be the origin server—the server on which resources reside or are generated, or an intermediary, such as a proxy. The recipient server sends a *response* message back. The client can be a *user agent*—someone who initiates a request—or anyone in the path between the initiator and the final receiving server. The protocol specifies a set of extensible request *methods* that are used by the client to perform operations such as requesting, altering, creating, or deleting a *resource*. A resource is an object, service, or collection of entities that can be clearly identified and located anywhere on the network [BLFM98].

Consider the following HTTP request:

```
GET /foo.html HTTP/1.0
```

The string `/foo.html` identifies the resource being requested via the `GET` method. The version number of the HTTP protocol, which in the above example is 1.0, is used to identify the capabilities of the sender. The purpose of the request is to retrieve the current contents of the resource identified by the string `/foo.html` from the server. More technically, the request causes the `GET` method to be applied to the resource identified by `/foo.html`. In general, a request message consists of a method, a URI, a protocol version identifier, optional request header fields, and an optional entity—a representation of data sent with the request.

Upon receiving the request message, the server parses it and applies the method to the resource. The generated response is sent back to the client as a response message. For example,

```
HTTP/1.0 200 OK
Date: Wed, 22 Mar 2000 08:01:01 GMT
Last-Modified: Wed, 22 Mar 2000 02:16:33 GMT
Content-Length: 3913
..

<3,913 bytes of the current contents of /foo.html>
```

A response message consists of a numerical response code (e.g., indicating success or failure) and a reason phrase explaining the numerical code, optional response header fields, and an optional body. In the example, the first line, known as the *status-line*, has the version number of the HTTP server and a 200 OK response code signifying that the request was successful. The Date response header indicates the time at which the response was generated. The Last-Modified and Content-Length headers indicate the time at which the resource was last modified and the length of the entity included in the response message (3913 bytes), respectively. The HTTP/0.9 version of the protocol did not have a status line, nor did it have any headers.

Not all header fields are of informational nature. Some request header fields can modify the request by constraining the method to be applied under certain circumstances only. Such header fields are termed *request modifiers*. For example, a client might not want a response if it has not changed since the last time it was obtained from the server.

One way to understand the protocol is to imagine that the origin server contains black boxes representing resources denoted by URIs. An origin server applies the request method to the resource identified by the URI and generates a response. The common understanding of reading a resource from a file and writing the response back to the client is abstracted away in the black box view. This view generalizes the notion of a resource and separates it from the response sent to the client. Different requests for the same URI can result in different responses, depending on several factors: the request header fields, the time of request, or changes to the resource that may have happened.

HTTP is an application-layer protocol similar to FTP, Simple Mail Transfer Protocol (SMTP), and Network News Transfer Protocol (NNTP), described in Chapter 5. HTTP can use any underlying transport protocol to transmit the message from the sender to the recipient. In reality, virtually all known implementations of HTTP use the Transmission Control Protocol (TCP) as their transport-level protocol.

It is not possible for a server to respond *before* a request is received. The direction of the message exchange is from the client to the server first and then the responses from the server back to the client. It is also possible for an HTTP server *not* to respond to a request. In this sense, HTTP is similar to other application-level protocols such as Gopher [AAL+92] and WAIS [KM91].

We have outlined the basic nature of HTTP communication between a client and a server; in practice there are several other components that might participate in the message exchange altering the manner and content of the messages. The presence of other components, such as proxies, gateways, or tunnels, does not alter the basic notion that HTTP is a mechanism for exchanging messages between a sender and a recipient. However, proxies play an important role in HTTP apart from a level of indirection between an originating client and a final recipient server. Proxies allow for scale—several clients can participate in

HTTP interaction without causing excessive load on the network. Proxies are discussed in more depth in Chapter 3.

STATELESSNESS OF THE PROTOCOL

HTTP is a *stateless* protocol. Statelessness implies the absence of state maintenance across request-response pairs. Each new request for a resource triggers a separate application of the request method on the resource URI with a new response being generated. The components using HTTP can and do maintain state about past requests and responses. A browser sending several requests in a row might keep track of the delay between each response. A server might keep information about the IP address of the client that sent the past dozen requests. However, the protocol itself does not have any awareness of the previous request or response. There is no intrinsic support in the protocol nor any requirement for state to be maintained. Unlike HTTP, NNTP and FTP maintain some amount of state, as discussed in Chapter 5.

HTTP's statelessness was a design decision to ensure its scalability. At the time of the creation of Web, there were several competing systems employing stateless protocols. The competing systems were also aimed at enabling access to a large number of resources on the Internet. Adding state to HTTP was perceived to hamper the scalability of the Web. A protocol that required state maintenance across several unrelated connections could require significant amount of information to be stored on the part of a server.

As the Web has evolved, the absence of state in HTTP was perceived to be a problem for some applications. For example, e-commerce requires some state to be maintained across HTTP requests. A transaction consisting of a sequence of requests and responses should not have to be repeated in its entirety if one of the requests in progress was aborted. HTTP state management became a visible issue resulting in the introduction of cookies, discussed in Chapter 2 (Section 2.6).

RESOURCE METADATA

Metadata is information that relates to a resource but is not part of the resource itself. The concept of metadata was borrowed from the Simple Mail Transfer Protocol (SMTP [Pos82]), which included a facility to characterize the payload. A significant amount of metadata can be included with an HTTP request or response. Examples of metadata include: the size of a resource; the type of the content, such as `text/html`; and the last modification time of the resource. Depending on the resource, it is possible to include a variety of metadata. For example, dynamically generated responses are unlikely to have their content length included because this would add latency to the response. However, for a static resource, the information can be obtained easily. Likewise, the idea of last modification may make sense for a static resource and not for a dynamic resource. The metadata of a resource is returned in a response via several entity headers, defined later in this chapter. In fact, some metadata may have to be present in certain requests and responses.

The ability to include metadata leads to a rich interaction between senders and recipients. Among the several uses of metadata are

- Disclosing information about the encoding format of the entity can help in processing it.
- The content length metadata can serve as a way for the recipient to ensure that it received what was sent.
- The server can indicate the last modification time of the resource, which can help a cache decide if the response should be cached. Likewise, it can indicate when a response should be considered stale by a cache.

6.1.2 Protocol influences

As mentioned in Chapter 1, several systems competed with the Web for providing seamless access to resources on the Internet. The evolution of the HTTP protocol was influenced both by the competing systems such as Gopher and WAIS and by syntactical substrates available. In this section, we examine the external influences on HTTP and compare HTTP with other application-level protocols.

THE ROLE OF MIME IN HTTP

First proposed in 1992, Multipurpose Internet Mail Extensions (MIME), extended RFC 822, the Internet Mail Protocol, to facilitate sending multiple *objects,* both textual and nontextual, within a single message. MIME can be used to represent text in non-ASCII character sets. MIME defined a variety of multimedia data objects and created a way for future data formats to be registered with Internet Assigned Numbers Authority (IANA).

In June 1992, a suggestion [Con92] was made to add MIME capability to the Web, WAIS, and Gopher systems. An idealized view of the proposal was that all resources could be encapsulated by MIME and protocols such as Gopher and HTTP would only handle non MIME-compliant data. Although this ideal was not realized, some MIME concepts were deemed [BL92b] to be of interest to the Web:

- **Classification of data formats:** The primary MIME concept adopted in HTTP is the data format—different entities can be sent between senders and recipients using an augmentable set of ways. In HTTP, the data format is defined as a MIME type. HTTP is able to take advantage of MIME's extensibility mechanism.

- **Formats for multipart messages:** The ability of MIME to include multiple entities in a single message body (known in MIME as a "multipart" type) was adopted in HTTP to some extent.

Other MIME concepts were not adopted:

- The "rich text" markup mechanism for formatting representation: MIME's text markup mechanism was somewhat similar to the Standard Generic Markup Language (SGML) from which HTML was derived. The capabilities present in HTML were deemed to be the same or better.
- A way to address external documents: MIME's format for links to documents could be syntactically mapped to URIs (though at that time they were known by the acronym UDI for Universal Document Identifier).

The differences between MIME and HTTP can be categorized as follows:

- MIME was defined for exchanging e-mail messages. HTTP's goal was high performance over binary connections.
- The use and interpretation of certain header fields in MIME and HTTP are different. For example, HTTP's `Content-Length` header is used to indicate the size of the *entity body*—what follows header fields in a request or a response. In MIME, the corresponding header field is optional. When present, it is metadata about data that is *not* included in the message. MIME's `Content-Length` header is not a required field, but it is recommended that HTTP applications include this header whenever possible.
- There is no limit on the length of a line in HTTP messages, unlike as with MIME. Lines both in the headers and body of an HTTP message can be arbitrarily long.
- HTTP is not MIME-compliant. MIME does not have a notion of content-encoding as defined in HTTP/1.0 and HTTP/1.1. The `Content-Encoding` entity header in HTTP (discussed in Section 6.2.3) lists modifications to the underlying media type of the resource. HTTP does not use the `Content-Transfer-Encoding` header of MIME.
- The notion of entity in MIME and HTTP is different. MIME was defined for mail messages, and the entity was enclosed in a mail message. MIME had just two data types: entities and messages. It did not distinguish between the message sent between sender and receiver directly or in the presence of intermediaries. Initially, HTTP tried to adopt the entity model of MIME but soon ran into difficulties because of transformations that could be applied to the entity.

A certain tension is present in the goal of universality of the Web [BL] and the dependence on registration of MIME types with organizations such as the International Corporation for Assigned Numbers and Names (ICANN). Having a central formal repository requires that all implementations referring to the types be conformant. The creation of an online registry that can be electronically accessed for the addition of a new type would be a better alternative.

The introduction of MIME terminology made it harder to separate the roles of header fields used in different contexts, such as from client to server or vice versa. The set of HTTP header fields began to be treated as an arbitrary collection of ASCII strings that could be ignored by Web components that did not understand them. HTTP headers, as we will see in Section 6.2.3 and in Chapter 7 (Section 7.2.2), are used both to provide metadata and to modify the behavior and interpretation of HTTP methods.

HTTP VERSUS PROTOCOLS OF ARCHIE, GOPHER, AND WAIS

The design of HTTP was influenced by protocols that were popular around the time of the creation of the Web. In Chapter 1 (Section 1.1.1), we discussed the role played by Archie, Gopher, and WAIS in the evolution of the Web in general. Various aspects of the protocols underlying these systems influenced the design of HTTP. Specifically, Gopher [AML+93] had a stateless client-server protocol similar to that of HTTP. All the servers run on well-known TCP ports—70 in the case of Gopher, 210 in the case of WAIS, and 80 in the case of HTTP. The notion of a document type was rudimentary in Gopher. In HTTP, content type was significantly broadened.

The Prospero [NA93] protocol, which enabled a single view of a collection of files across the Internet, was used by Archie. Prospero was primarily a novel distributed file system letting users create private views of files located anywhere on the Internet. Prospero was lightweight in the sense that it separated the role of data access and data interpretation. However, it did not have a specific protocol for retrieving files—FTP, Gopher, and so on could be used to retrieve files on top of Prospero. Prospero itself runs over UDP and has an added reliability layer on top of UDP. In contrast, HTTP, Gopher, and WAIS typically run over TCP. Prospero, unlike Gopher, did worry about different levels of authentication. Archie had plans to start using URIs in later versions.

The primary goal of the Gopher protocol was to retrieve documents remotely. The main difference between Gopher and HTTP is the use of hypertext in conjunction with HTTP and text files and menus in Gopher. However, HTTP simply treats menus and text files as a special case of hypertext files [BL92a]. It would be unfair to compare Gopher with the more recent versions of HTTP because no significant improvements have been made to the Gopher protocol since the Web became the dominant system. Although the virtual directory listing capability allowed Gopher clients to cache past directory retrievals, there was no mechanism in the Gopher protocol to identify inconsistencies between cached directory entries and the current contents of the directory. Caching was purely an application-level decision that was beyond the scope of the Gopher protocol. The Gopher protocol was specifically constructed to have all the intelligence reside in the servers rather than be specified via the protocol. The burden of providing a broader set of services required improving the server with no changes to the protocol. Although this made for a much simpler protocol compared with HTTP, different server implementations could exhibit different behaviors. Gopher defined a set of type characters indicating whether the resource being accessed was a file, directory, binary file, and so on. The choice of a single character to identify the type of the resource naturally limited the number of different types that could be represented. HTTP later moved to the extensible set of MIME-type extensions, and arbitrary resource types could be understood by the various HTTP software components. Security issues were never discussed in the Gopher protocol.

HTTP AND OTHER APPLICATION-LEVEL PROTOCOLS

HTTP was also influenced by other application-level protocols that predated Archie, Gopher, and WAIS. HTTP has also influenced other application-level protocols. We examine one example of each of these two cases.

HTTP has adopted the idea of response classes (Section 6.2.4) from the application-level protocol SMTP [Pos82]. Rather than try to invent a new scheme to classify the various responses that could be generated, the *function group* concept of SMTP reply codes was adopted. A function group classified the responses into a small number of categories such as success, failure, or error. The list of classes was later augmented as the HTTP protocol evolved, but the basic scheme remains unchanged.

HTTP is only one of several application-level protocols, although it is currently the most popular one. There are already other application-level protocols that have adopted the syntax and some of the semantics of HTTP, including the Real Time Streaming Protocol (RTSP) [SRL98], discussed in Chapter 12 (Section 12.4).

6.2 HTTP Language Elements

In this section we examine the various building blocks of the HTTP/1.0 protocol. The HTTP/1.0 specification (RFC 1945) was a much more detailed specification than HTTP/0.9. The specification included a detailed terminology and grammar section, as well as a detailed breakdown of the components of an HTTP message. We first define a few basic terms used in the protocol specification before discussing the various language elements. As mentioned earlier, a protocol is a language, and the key elements of the HTTP protocol are methods, headers, and response classes.

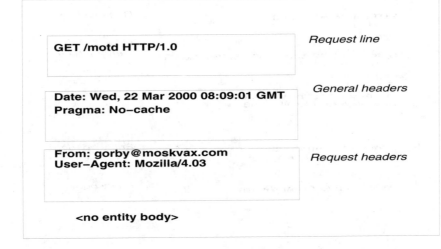

Figure 6.1. An HTTP request message

6.2.1 HTTP terms

Our definitions of the various HTTP terms are identical to those found in the two RFCs describing HTTP/1.0 and HTTP/1.1, RFC 1945 [BLFF96] and RFC 2616 [FGM+99] respectively. Where necessary, we provide additional context and examples. Most of the terms have been defined in Chapter 1. But we expand on four important terms here: message, entity, resource, and user agent.

MESSAGE

An HTTP message is a sequence of octets that is sent over a transport connection. A message is the fundamental unit of communication in HTTP. An HTTP message can be a request sent from a client to a server or a response sent from a server to a client. A request message begins with a *request* line, whereas a response message starts with a *status* line. Request and response messages can have zero or more message headers, separated from an optional message body by two characters—the carriage return (CR) and linefeed (LF) characters.

An HTTP request message, shown in Figure 6.1, has the following syntactic format:

```
Request-Line
General/Request/Entity Header(s)
CRLF
Optional Message Body
```

PUT /motd HTTP/1.0	*Request line*
Date: Wed, 22 Mar 2000 08:10:07 GMT	*General header*
From: gorby@moskvax.com **User–Agent: Mozilla/4.03**	*Request headers*
Content–Length: 23 **Allow: GET, HEAD, PUT**	*Entity headers*
Welcome to Comer's Vax	*Entity body*

Figure 6.2. Another HTTP request message

A request message begins with a request line and is followed by a set of optional headers and an optional message body. The request line consists of a request method, the URI being requested, and the protocol version of the client. For example, in the HTTP request

```
GET /motd HTTP/1.0
Date: Wed, 22 Mar 2000 08:09:01 GMT
Pragma: No-cache
From: gorby@moskvax.com
User-Agent: Mozilla/4.03
CRLF
```

also shown in Figure 6.1, the request method is `GET`, the resource being requested is `/motd`, and the client's protocol version is HTTP/1.0. The headers `Date` and `Pragma` are *general* headers, and such headers can be present in requests and responses. The `From` and `User-Agent` headers are request headers, and these headers only appear in request messages. The general, request, and entity headers are explained later in Section 6.2.3. This request message ends with the line break character sequence CRLF, which consists of the carriage return and linefeed characters. The above HTTP message has no message body.

Figure 6.2 shows a request message with a message body. The `PUT` method is used to create a resource `/motd`. The request method is followed by a single general header (`Date`) and two request headers (`From` and `User-Agent`). The

Figure 6.3. An HTTP response message

request message has two entity headers (`Content-Length` and `Allow`). The first entity header indicates the length of the content and the second specifies what methods may be applied to the resource `/motd`. The entity body consisting of the string *Welcome to Comer's Vax* follows.

A response message has the following syntactic format:

```
Status-Line
General/Response/Entity Header(s)
CRLF
Optional Message Body
```

A response message starts with a status line which includes the HTTP version of the server and a status code of the response. This is followed by optional general and response headers and an optional message body. Note that, because of the presence of intermediaries, the final message received will not necessarily reflect the origin server's protocol version number. Figure 6.3 shows the response message for the `GET` request described above.

```
HTTP/1.0 200 OK
Date: Wed, 22 Mar 2000 08:09:03 GMT
Server: Netscape-Enterprise/3.5.1
Content-Length: 23
CRLF
Welcome to Comer's Vax
```

The status line in the response message indicates that the server supports HTTP/1.0, and the response code is 200 OK, indicating that the request succeeded. The response message includes the general header Date and a response header Server. The entity header Content-Length presents the length of the entity body. After the CRLF line break sequence, the entity body follows, which in the above example is the string *Welcome to Comer's Vax.*

A message does not have an entity body unless it has a message body. A message body in a request and response is also referred to as a *request body* and *response body*, respectively. Not all messages are permitted to have message bodies.

ENTITY

HTTP/1.0 defines an entity as a representation of a resource that is enclosed in a request or response message. An entity consists of entity headers and an optional entity body. Entity headers consist of metadata about the entity. For example, the length of the entity body might be given in the entity header Content-Length. Obviously, a response with Content-Length of zero will not have an entity body. The definition of entity changed slightly between HTTP/1.0 and HTTP/1.1 primarily as a result of the introduction of content negotiation (described in Chapter 7, Section 7.9).

An entity body, when present, is in some sense the most important part of the HTTP message. In the case of a request message, the entity body could be the data the user typed in an HTML form. In a response message, the entity body is the body of the message; that is, the content of the response without the response headers.

RESOURCE

HTTP/1.0 [BLFF96] defines a resource as a "network data object or service that can be identified by a Uniform Resource Identifier (URI)," making the definition somewhat circular. The inclusion of the word "network" implies that the data object or service can be located anywhere in the world as long as it is accessible via a network connection. The decision to extend the definition of a resource to a service was a crucial one. A data object is static or dynamically generated, but a service can implement an arbitrary application that simply uses the Web as a transfer medium for initiating the service and handling the response. For example, consider a Web site that returns instant stock quotes. Stock prices change constantly, and the resource http://www.cnnfn.com/quote=T? will yield the current stock price of AT&T. The quote service can use any back-end mechanism to obtain the current stock price. It simply uses the Web as a mechanism to transfer the request (a particular subset of stocks) and the response (the current price of each of the stocks).

USER AGENT

A user agent is the client that *initiates* the request and can be a browser,
spider, or any other tool involved in generating the request. The distinction
between a user agent and a general client is important. Generally, additional
requirements are placed on the initiating component. The user agent is the
only party directly connected to the user if the request was initiated by a user.
The user agent can ignore error messages or present them to the user, offer
choices to the user such as retrying a request after an authentication failure,
redirect requests or choose a specified alternate location, or negotiate for the
best representation of a response. For example, a user agent should be able
to understand that a request lacked the necessary authentication based on the
response received from a server. The user agent can then prompt the user for
the proper authorization and resend the request with the authorization.

Often, information about the user agent is sent as part of the request in
the `User-Agent` header (described in more detail in Section 6.2.3). The header
includes information such as the name of the browser or the operating system
of the machine. Examples of common user agents include `Mozilla/3.01 (X11;`
`I; SunOS 5.5 sun4m)` and `Mozilla/2.0 (compatible; MSIE 2.1; AOL 3.0;`
`Mac)`. It is possible to identify the version of the browser (Mozilla/3.01 or MSIE
2.1) and the operating system used by the user (e.g., SunOS 5.5).

6.2.2 HTTP/1.0 request methods

A request method notifies an HTTP server what action should be performed
on the resource identified by the Request-URI (the URI specified in the request line). The most commonly used method is the `GET` method which fetches
the current value of the resource identified by the URI. Although HTTP/1.0
defined only three methods (`GET`, `HEAD`, `POST`), other methods were implemented in some versions of clients and servers claiming to be HTTP/1.0. These
are the `PUT`, `DELETE`, `LINK`, and `UNLINK` methods. All seven methods are explained to capture what was in the various implementations at the time of the
writing of the HTTP/1.0 informational RFC specification. Because `LINK` and
`UNLINK` methods are not part of the latest HTTP/1.1 standard, they will not
be discussed in detail.

It is hard to describe methods, header fields, and response codes in a
sequential manner because any discussion about one of the concepts necessarily
involves the other two. For now, it suffices to know the elements of a request-
response transaction at a high level:

- A request method is included in a client's request along with several headers and a URI.

- The method is applied to the resource by the origin server, and a response is generated. The response consists of a response code, metadata about the resource, and other response headers.

Note that an intermediary such as a caching proxy, receiving the request and returning a cached response, is *not* applying the method.

Two important properties of a method are safety and idempotence. A request method that merely examines the state of a resource (e.g., obtains its current value) is viewed as a safe method. A method that can alter the state of the resource is not safe. An idempotent method, on the other hand, has the property that the side effects of one request are the same as multiple identical requests. In other words, if several identical requests are issued in a row, either the result of applying the method on the resource produces no side effects, or the same side effect in each case. The predictability of the impact of a method on a resource is useful in deciding whether a resource should support the method. Additionally, if a sequence of requests are idempotent and if the connection were unexpectedly closed, then it would be reasonable for a client to reissue the set of requests.

The HTTP/1.0 methods are described next.

GET

The most popular method in use today is the GET method. A GET request is applied to the resource specified in the URI, and the generated response is the current value of the resource. This response is returned to the requesting client. If the URI refers to a static file, a GET request would result in the file being read and contents returned. If the URI refers to a program, then the data, if any, is returned as the body of the response. The GET method is safe and idempotent. A request for a CGI resource, for example, may cause the resource to change when the GET method is applied to the resource. Because such a side effect was not the user's *intent,* the method is considered safe.

A GET request could include arguments that are constructed based on the user's input. This is frequently the case when the request is for a CGI resource. For example,

GET http://www.altavista.com/cgi-bin/query?q=foo

includes the user's query string ("foo") in the resource http://www.altavista.com/cgi-bin.

A GET request that includes a request modifier may result in a different action. For example, the GET method can be constrained to fetch a resource only if the requested resource's last modification time is greater than the value specified in the If-Modified-Since header. Thus a GET request for a resource /foo.html from an HTTP/1.0 client

```
GET /foo.html HTTP/1.0
```

may yield a different result from

```
GET /foo.html HTTP/1.0
If-Modified-Since: Sun, 12 Nov  2000 11:12:23 GMT
```

depending on when the resource /foo.html was last modified on the origin
server. The request modifier If-Modified-Since is used to reduce both network usage and user-perceived latency in waiting for the response to be generated and sent from the origin server. If the resource was not modified since the
time specified in the If-Modified-Since header, the server sends a response
code indicating this, with no entity body accompanying the response. Note that
the notion of a last modification time is a simplified view of a resource assumed
to be a file that may change periodically. For a dynamically generated resource,
the notion of last modification time is not entirely meaningful. HTTP/1.0 has
a handful of request modifiers. Several more modifiers have been introduced in
HTTP/1.1, as we will see in the next chapter.

The GET request method has no request body. If a request body is present,
it is ignored by servers.

HEAD

The HEAD method was introduced to obtain just the metadata associated with a
resource. No response body is returned as a result of a HEAD request. However,
the metadata that a server returns should be the same metadata that would be
returned if the request method had been GET. For example, the HEAD request
to obtain the metadata associated with the resource /foo.html

```
HEAD /foo.html HTTP/1.0
```

might return

```
HTTP/1.0 200 OK
Content-Length: 3219
Last-Modified: Sun, 12 Nov  2000 11:12:23 GMT
Content-Type: text/html
```

The response consists of the status line (HTTP/1.0 200 OK), indicating the
request succeeded, and a set of headers representing the metadata for the resource /foo.html. In the example, the metadata includes information about
the length of the content and the resource's last modification time and type.
The HEAD method is safe and idempotent.

The primary uses of the HEAD method include debugging the server implementation at relatively low overhead to the server and determining whether
a resource has changed recently without actually retrieving it. The metadata
may be cached or used to update existing cached values if a change in the

resource can be detected. In HTTP/1.0, a change could be detected by examining the `Last-Modified` or `Content-Length` header field values. However, because a resource might change without changing its length, examining the `Content-Length` header field value alone does not guarantee detection of change.

HTTP/1.0 did not permit the `HEAD` method to be used with a request modifier such as `If-Modified-Since`. This restriction was eased in HTTP/1.1.

The `HEAD` request method also has no request body. If a request body is present, it is ignored by servers.

POST

Unlike the `GET` and `HEAD` methods, which are used to *retrieve* information, the `POST` method is used primarily to update an existing resource or provide input to a process handling data. The body of the request includes the data. The origin server, depending on the Request-URI, permits specific actions to be performed. The `POST` method could alter the contents of a resource, and therefore it cannot be viewed as a safe method. Because the side effects of a set of identical `POST` requests could each differ, `POST` is not an idempotent method.

To modify an existing resource, the user must have the necessary authentication. Not all users may have access rights to change a resource. If the user has permission to alter the resource, the origin server would accept a new version of the resource from the client. Another use of the `POST` method is to take the body of the request and use it as input to a program identified by the Request-URI. The program could be a mail handler or bulletin board manager that creates a file accessible by other applications such as a mail reader or news reader. It is possible that no resources are affected or created as a result of a `POST` request. In such cases, the body of the request is treated as input to a program that simply consumes the data.

Consider the example

```
POST /foo/bar.cfm HTTP/1.0
Content-Length: 143


<entity body>
```

If the receiving server could successfully apply the method to the resource, it would return a response indicating that the request succeeded. Suppose `/foo/bar.cfm` is a resource that does not exist on the origin server. The server would create this resource and send back a response indicating the resource was created. If, on the other hand, `/foo/bar.cfm` is a program that expects input, then the 143-bytes-long entity body is treated as input to the program. Any output generated by the program is sent back to the user as the entity body of the response. Note that the `Content-Length` header is required as part of a POST request so that the receiving HTTP/1.0 server would know that it has received the full request.

The GET method could also be used to submit input to a program. However, there are subtle differences between using the GET and POST methods for this purpose. In a GET-based form, the input is encoded in the Request-URI. Suppose a user wants to fill in two fields of a search form: a search string and the database to be searched. For example, the request

```
GET /search.cgi?string=iktinos?db=greek-architects HTTP/1.0
```

shows how a form can be encoded in the query component of the Request-URI. Here the resource being requested via the GET method is search.cgi, with values for two fields (string and db). The POST way to perform the same search is

```
POST /search.cgi HTTP/1.0
Content-Length: 34
CRLF
query iktinos
db greek-architects
```

Both requests will yield the same response. However, suppose there are proxies in the path between a client and the origin server. The proxy is likely to log requests that flow through it. However, while the Request-URI is likely to be logged, the entity body is not likely to be logged. The log would include the search string in the case of a GET-based form and not in the case of the POST request. Some proxies and servers limit the length of the URI they will process, and this might be another reason to opt for the POST method over a GET-based form.

PUT

The PUT method is similar to POST in that processing the method would typically result in a different version of the resource identified by the URI in the request. If the Request-URI did not exist, it is created, and if it already exists, it is modified. However, the resource identified in the PUT method *alone* would change as a result of the request.

HTTP/1.0 did not formally define the PUT method. By the time RFC 1945 was issued, several client and server implementations had begun to use this method and so PUT (along with DELETE, LINK, UNLINK) was briefly discussed in an appendix of RFC 1945. In Chapter 7 (Section 7.12.1), we present a broader discussion of the differences between the PUT and POST methods. The PUT method is not a safe method. The PUT method is idempotent because a sequence of identical `PUT` requests would have to include the same entity and thus the side effects would be the same in each case.

DELETE

The `DELETE` method is used to delete the resource identified by the Request-URI. The method is provided as a convenience to delete resources remotely. However, given the nature of the action, origin servers have control over if and when the requested action is actually performed. The server may send a successful response without actually deleting the resource. There are two kinds of successful response: one that indicates request acceptance for later processing and one that is an actual completion of the request. Such flexibility is crucial for origin servers to decide when and how to schedule the action and not be forced to hold the connection to the client open until the action has actually completed. The `DELETE` method is not a safe method. Like `PUT`, `DELETE` is idempotent.

LINK AND UNLINK

The `LINK` method permitted creation of links between the Request-URI and other resources. Once such a link was created, it was possible to request the resources by the same Request-URI. The `UNLINK` method was used to delete the links created via the `LINK` method.

Although these methods were defined in the appendix of HTTP/1.0, they were not implemented widely and were deleted in HTTP/1.1.

6.2.3 HTTP/1.0 headers

A header (or, more formally, header field) is a free-format ASCII string representing a name often with a value specified. Headers play an important role in the HTTP protocol and are the primary means to alter the handling of a request. Headers can be used to provide metadata about the resource, such as its length, encoding format, and language. Headers can be thought of as parameterizing or describing a request or a response. A response header can indicate whether the response can be cached or how to decode the message to obtain the original entity (what compression algorithm was used to transform it, for example).

As we saw in Chapter 5, each of the lower-layer protocols has headers. In contrast to the fixed-format headers in IP and TCP, application-layer protocols have a much freer format for representing headers. Lower-level protocols often are limited by the size of packets for performance reasons. The packets are also fixed in size. The fixed format of headers in lower-level protocols ensures that messages do not grow arbitrarily as a result of additional headers. Application-level protocols do not have this problem, and new headers are a typical way to add new features.

New headers can be defined in HTTP and can be of arbitrary length. The extensibility mechanism in the protocol (discussed briefly in Section 6.3) enables new headers to reflect new ideas as they emerge. Existing implementations that want to take advantage of new features can cooperate, and others can ignore the headers that they do not recognize. However, unrestrained growth in the number of header fields and length of headers adds to the overall size of messages and thus user-perceived latency and load on the network. Large numbers of new headers can also increase the complexity of the protocol. The interaction between features that depend on the various headers is a significant factor in the additional complexity.

An HTTP message can have any number of headers, each delimited by the CR and LF characters. There are specific rules associated with the forwarding and interpreting of headers in a message as the request or response flows through the network via proxies. Certain types of HTTP request-response message may have some required headers. Most of the headers are optional, and Web components add them for specific reasons. Web components can and do ignore optional headers. The headers defined in the specification are meant to be understood by all Web components: clients, proxies, and servers.

A header has a generic syntax of a name and value separated by the colon ":" character. For example, to indicate the time a message is generated, the `Date` header is included in the message as follows:

`Date: Thu, 23 Dec 1999 08:12:31 GMT`

The string "Date" is the header-field name, and the string "Thu, 23 Dec 1999 08:12:31 GMT" is the field-value. An example of a header with multiple field value is

`Accept-Language: de-CH, en-US`

The field-name is `Accept-Language`, and the field-values are *de-CH* and *en-US*.

HTTP defines a hierarchy of headers. The message header in HTTP/1.0 is a generic name for a header that could be

- A *general* header used in requests and response messages.
- A *request* header found in request messages to express preference on the nature of response, to include additional information with the request, or to specify a constraint on the server in handling the request.
- A *response* header found in response messages to provide additional information about the response or to request additional information from the user.
- An *entity* header found in requests and response messages. Entity headers are used to provide information about the entity, such as its modification

time. If a general header or a request-response header field is not recognized as such, then it is treated as an entity header field.

If a header is not recognized by a recipient of a message, it should be simply ignored. However, if the recipient happens to be a proxy, the proxy should forward the header.

Although the order of different header fields is not significant, it is common to have general-header fields, followed by request-header or response-header fields and then entity-header fields. For a given header field, if multiple field-values are specified, their order should not be changed by proxies forwarding the message.

GENERAL HEADERS

Headers that can appear in both request and response messages are called *general* headers. HTTP/1.0 defines only two general header fields: `Date` and `Pragma`. The general headers are significant only to the message itself and *not* to the entity that is part of the message. For example, suppose a resource `/foo.html` is requested. The `Date` header in the corresponding response message indicates that the message was generated at the indicated time and has no bearing on when the associated entity (the resource `foo.html`) may have been created or modified last.

- **Date:** The `Date` general header indicates the date and time of the message origination. The `Date` header has the same syntax as the date string in RFC 822 (the standard for Internet text messages, subsequently updated in RFC 1123). A date in this format looks as follows:

  ```
  Date: Tue 16 May 2000 11:29:32 GMT
  ```

  Although this is the preferred format, HTTP/1.0 also permits the date string in two other formats (specified in RFC 1036 and the ANSI C standard's *asctime()* format). The RFC 1036 format is as follows:

  ```
  Date: Tuesday, 16-May-00 11:29:32 GMT
  ```

  The RFC 1036 format suffers from the two-digit year problem. As the example shows, the year value would be treated as 0 instead of 2000. The error of permitting the second format based on RFC 1036 has been subsequently fixed in the newer version of the protocol (HTTP/1.1) as a result of the infamous Y2K problem. The ANSI C standard's `asctime()` format is as follows:

  ```
  Date: Tue May 16 11:29:32 2000
  ```

  HTTP/1.0 requires that clients and servers generate date strings in either the first or second format. However, HTTP clients and servers should be able to accept all three formats, which is necessary because some senders may be non-HTTP applications and are not bound by the HTTP specification. The protocol specification states the rules for Web components to talk to each other. However, because the components are exposed to non-HTTP applications, the component's interface to them must be defined as well.

- **Pragma:** The `Pragma` header permits directives to be sent to the recipient of the message. A directive is a way to request components to behave in a particular way while handling a request or a response. In general, directives are optional as far as the protocol is concerned although in reality several specific directives are obeyed by most components. The distinction is important because, although the protocol requires components to forward the directives, it does not mandate components to obey them if they are not relevant. The only directive defined in the protocol is

```
Pragma: no-cache
```

which informs proxies in the path not to return a cached copy; that is, the sender is interested in getting a response directly from the origin server. HTTP/1.0 does not define the meaning of the `Pragma: no-cache` directive in a response message.

REQUEST HEADERS

A *request header* can be used by the client to send information with the request or to specify constraints on the server handling the request. The information sent can be additional information about the client, such as identification of the user or the user agent, or credentials, such as the authorization necessary for the request to be processed by the origin server. HTTP/1.0 defines five request headers:

- **Authorization:** The `Authorization` header is used by the user agent to include appropriate credentials required to access a resource. Some resources cannot be accessed from servers without proper authorization. An example of an `Authorization` header is

```
Authorization: Basic YXZpYXRpS29IDizM1NA==
```

The *Basic* refers to an authentication scheme in which the credentials are in the form of userid and password. The string `YXZpYXRpS29IDizM1NA==` is an encoding of a userid and a password in Base64 format [FB96a]. The format uses a simple encoding and decoding algorithm, and the encoded data is not significantly larger than the original data. Other authentication schemes are permitted in HTTP, including transport level encryption.

- **From:** The `From` request header lets the user include his/her e-mail address as an identification. This is useful for client programs running as agents (robot agents in a spider, for example) to identify the user responsible for the program. An example of a `From` header is

```
From: gorby@moskvax.com
```

Note that general use of the `From` header is discouraged because it violates the privacy of the user, especially when sent without the consent of the user.

- `If-Modified-Since`: The `If-Modified-Since` header is an example of a conditional header, indicating that the request may be handled in a different way based on the value specified in the header field. If the previous response from the server had been been cached at a client or a proxy, the value specified in the `Last-Modified` *response* header is used in a subsequent GET request as the argument in the `If-Modified-Since` header. For example, for the following request:

```
GET /foo.html HTTP/1.0
If-Modified-Since: Sun, 21 May 2000 07:00:25 GMT
```

the server would compare the value specified in the `If-Modified-Since` header with the current value of the last modified time of the resource. The last modified time of a resource may be available at the application level, depending on the server. In many servers, this value is obtained via a simple operating system level system call (for example, *stat()* or *fstat()* in UNIX). If the resource had not changed since `Sun, 21 May 2000 07:00:25 GMT`, then the server would simply return a `304 Not Modified` response. For resources that do not change often, this can help reduce needless transmitting of data. The server does not have to regenerate the resource, and user-perceived latency is lowered because the client can obtain the contents locally.

- `Referer`: The `Referer` [3] header field lets the client include the URI of the resource from which the Request-URI was obtained. For example, suppose that the user is visiting the Web page `http://www.cnn.com`, and clicks on a reference in that page to the resource `http://www.disasterrelief.org/Disasters/worldglance.html`. The `Referer` header in the request sent to `http://www.disasterrelief.org` will have the string `http://www.cnn.com`, as follows:

```
GET /Disasters/worldglance.html HTTP/1.0
Referer: http://www.cnn.com
```

Benign use of the `Referer` field includes locating obsolete links. More frequently, it is a source of violation of a user's privacy. In earlier chapters

---

[3] Among the somewhat comical aspects of the HTTP protocol are the typos, such as `Referer` instead of *Referrer*, which must stay that way because of widespread deployment.

(Chapter 2, Section 2.6.4, and Chapter 3, Section 3.7), we discussed the issue of privacy loss because of presence of cookies and proxies. The `Referer` field is a header that can be used by origin servers via server logs to track the behavior pattern of a user.

Worse yet, suppose a GET-based form (discussed in Section 6.2.2) is used in an online transaction, and the user fills out a credit card number. Let us say that the form is itself transmitted in a secure way (say, using SSL), and the resulting page from the form request contains a link to another page, possibly on a different server, S. Now, if the user visits this page, the server log of server S will have an entry with the `Referer` field that contains the user's credit card number.

Additionally, a server can check the `Referer` field to deny requests for certain resources if references for resources are found in pages not under the control of the server. For example, suppose the reference to an embedded image `onlymine.gif`, originally in resource A, is copied to another container document, B. Now, if the browser tried to display B, it would generate a request for the embedded resource `onlymine.gif` and include a `Referer` field-value of B. The server could refuse to honor the request since the `Referer` field did not have the value A.

- User-Agent: The `User-Agent` field can be used to include information about the particular version of the browser software being used, the client machine's operating system version, and possibly the hardware details. Some examples of `User-Agent` headers are

    ```
    User-Agent: Mozilla/4.03 (Macintosh; I; 68K, Nav)
    User-Agent: Mozilla/4.04 [en]C-WorldNet  (Win95; I)
    ```

There are good uses for this information. For example, one can identify the popular set of browsers to see if there are problems in requests coming from a particular version. A server can send back an alternate version of the resource if it knows that a particular browser software has difficulty displaying the default version. Questionable uses of this header include tracking the user, a potential invasion of a user's privacy. For example, suppose several users using different versions of browser software on a large time-shared system send requests to an origin server. Then the `User-Agent` field can be used to help isolate the user who made certain requests.

RESPONSE HEADERS

Just as request headers send additional information about the requests, response headers are used to send more information about the response and the server that originated the response. The syntax of the status line is fixed the header cannot include additional information. If a response header is not recognized, it is assumed to be an entity header.

HTTP/1.0 defines three response headers, as follows:

- `Location`: The `Location` header is used to redirect the request to where the resource can be found and is useful in the redirection class response (Section 6.2.4). A `Location` header has the following syntax:

  `Location: http://www.foo.com/level1/twosdown/Location.html`

  Because different variants of a resource might be chosen in response to a request, the `Location` header provides a way of identifying the location of the chosen variant. If a set of resources is replicated in multiple mirror sites, the `Location` header can be used to indicate the proper site from which the client should obtain the resource. If a new resource was created as a result of a request (such as `POST`), the `Location` header identifies the resource that was created.

- `Server`: The `Server` response header is analogous to the `User-Agent` request header. The `Server` header has information about the origin server software's version number and any other configuration-related information. Some common examples of `Server` header are

  ```
  Server: Apache/1.2.6 Red Hat
  Server: Netscape-Enterprise/3.5.1
  Server: Apache/1.x.y mod_perl mod_ssl mod_foo mod_bar
  ```

  The value specified in the `Server` header is useful to help debug problems found in responses and for statistical purposes such as identifying the most popular versions of servers. On the downside, once a server version is identified as having problems, others might be tempted to attack other sites known to run the same version of software. Similar to the `User-Agent` header, the `Server` header is optional, and it does not have to be included in responses.

- `WWW-Authenticate`: The `WWW-Authenticate` header is used to issue a challenge to the client seeking access to an authenticated resource. This is returned along with a `401 Unauthorized` response, and the client can retransmit the request with the appropriate credentials in the `Authorization` header. For example, a server could send a challenge such as

  `WWW-Authenticate: Basic realm="ChaseChem"`

  and the client can include the proper authorization necessary in its request, as explained earlier in this section.

ENTITY HEADERS

An *entity* header is used to include information about the body of the entity or the resource in the absence of an entity body. An entity header is not a property of the request or response message, but of the specific resource being requested or sent. Entity headers may be found in requests and in responses. An unrecognized general, request, or response header is treated as an entity header. In other words, the protocol specifies a hierarchy of interpretation of header fields. A new header can be introduced in a request or a response message as a way to add new metadata about the entity without fear of it being interpreted as a general, request, or response header.

There are six entity headers defined in HTTP/1.0, as follows:

- `Allow`: The `Allow` entity-header is used to indicate the list of valid methods that can be be applied to a resource. This can be used in both requests and responses. For example, the `PUT` method could include an `Allow` header in the request listing the methods that could be applied to the resource. An origin server, upon receiving a request for applying an invalid method on a resource, would send an `Allow` header in the response with the list of valid methods for that resource. The `Allow` header could also be used in a successful response to indicate the full list of meaningful methods for that resource.

As an example of `Allow` entity-header in a request message, consider

```
PUT /foo.html HTTP/1.0
Allow: HEAD, GET, PUT
```

The request informs the server where the resource `/foo.html` is going to be stored, and that the methods `HEAD`, `GET`, and `PUT` are permitted to be used with that resource. Other request methods may be tried by clients, and the origin server is not required to support them.

- `Content-Type`: The `Content-Type` header indicates the media type of the entity body, such as `image/gif`, `text/html`, or `application/x-javascript`. A `POST` request may include a form with the following `Content-Type`:

```
POST /chat/chatroom.cgi HTTP/1.0
User-Agent: Mozilla/3.0C
Content-Type: application/x-www-form-urlencoded
```

The various media types used in the `Content-Type` must be registered with IANA.

- `Content-Encoding`: The `Content-Encoding` header indicates how the resource representation has been modified and how it could be decoded into the format indicated in the `Content-Type` entity header. Content coding is performed on documents to transform them without information loss. Compression is a common encoding technique. The corresponding decoding technique should be known to the recipient in order for the response to be transformed back into its original format. A message whose entity has been compressed using *gzip* may include the header

```
Content-Encoding: x-gzip
```

New media types and content-codings can be defined by registering with
the IANA, as per RFC 1590.

- Content-Length: The Content-Length header indicates the length of the
  entity body in bytes. The content length is important for ensuring that
  the entity body sent was received in its entirety by the recipient. The
  Content-Length value may be used as a *validator* to compare a cached entry against the current entry. Note that Content-Length header is present
  both in requests and responses. Without Content-Length header in a request, a client would have to close the connection to indicate it has finished
  transmitting the request. In Section 6.2.2, we saw an example of a POST
  request using Content-Length. In the case of dynamically generated responses, the entire response must be generated before the content length
  is known. Because Content-Length is a header and must be inserted in
  the response message before any of the response body, this adds latency to
  the recipient. Typically the Content-Length header is omitted in dynamic
  responses. If a dynamically generated response had been buffered before
  being sent, the content length may be known. HTTP/1.0 uses closing of
  connection as the end-of-entity indicator.

- Expires: The Expires header is a way for a sender to state that the
  entity should be considered stale after the time specified in the header. A
  client must not cache a response beyond the date specified in the Expires
  header. The distinction between *storing* a resource in a cache and *caching*
  is important. A response may be stored (i.e., kept) in a cache past its
  expiration time, but it cannot be *returned* as a response without validating
  it with the origin server. The reason Expires is an entity header and not
  a response header is that the expiration refers to the associated entity and
  not to the message itself. A server could send

```
HTTP/1.0 200 OK
Server: Microsoft-IIS/4.0
Date: Mon, 04 Dec 2000 18:16:45 GMT
Expires: Tue, 05 Dec 2000 18:16:45 GMT
```

indicating the resource is going to expire in a day.

- Last-Modified: The Last-Modified header specifies the time at which
  the resource was modified last. If the resource is a static file then the file system last-modified time could represent this value. A dynamically generated
  resource may have the same Last-Modified time as the time of server's
  response message origination. In fact, the Last-Modified time can never
  be later than the message origination time. The protocol does not state
  rules for how expiration values should be computed. The Last-Modified
  header in a response is a hint to the recipient to compare against the
  Last-Modified value of its cached version to see if the cached response
  is stale. The presence of Last-Modified header was treated by several

HTTP/1.0 caches as an indication that the content was *not* dynamically generated because a `Last-Modified` header would not have much meaning for dynamically generated content. In Chapter 7 (Section 7.3.2), we discuss the significance of such cache-related headers in more depth.

A server could send a response as follows:

```
HTTP/1.0 200 OK
Date: Sun, 21 May 2000 08:09:12 GMT
Last-Modified: Sun, 21 May 2000 07:00:25 GMT
```

6.2.4 HTTP/1.0 response classes

Every HTTP response message begins with the `Status-Line`, which has three fields: the server's protocol version number, the response code, and a natural language reason phrase. A request processed at a server might succeed, fail, or be redirected to another server. There could be syntactic errors in the request message or problems with the server handling the request. The various kinds of responses are grouped into a set of *response classes*. In HTTP, each of the five classes of responses has several response codes, each of which is a three-digit integer. The five classes of responses are the informational class, with response codes being three-digit integers beginning with 1 (written as 1xx); success class (2xx); redirection class (3xx); client error class (4xx); and server error class (5xx).

The notion of response class was borrowed from the SMTP [Pos82] mail protocol. The FTP protocol [PR85] has a similar notion of reply codes. Response codes were called *reply codes* in SMTP and *replies* in FTP. Initially, there were only four classes in HTTP, but later the informational class (1xx) was added. The choice of the initial four classes of response is somewhat arbitrary because the HTTP protocol is different from the mail protocol. However, adoption of a well-understood mechanism from a very widely used application serves as a good starting point. Although in theory, the protocol permits additional classes to be created, in practice the implementations may not handle entirely new classes of responses gracefully. Proper implementations should treat a response code belonging to an unknown response class as an error.

Along with the numerical response codes, a short natural language descriptive phrase called the *reason phrase* is included in HTTP for the benefit of debugging by the implementors. The reason phrase is similar to that of the text associated with a SMTP reply code. Some browsers display the reason phrase. However, there are differences between SMTP reply codes and HTTP response codes. Each of the three digits of a SMTP reply code has a special significance, as indicated in Appendix E of RFC 821. The first digit is the class of the response, the second digit gives slightly more detailed information about the reply, and the third digit gives the finest level of detail. Unlike the first and second digits, the third digit does not have a specific meaning with its value. The second digit in SMTP reply codes has values of 0 for syntax, 1 for additional information responses, 2 for communications channel related, and 5 for mail related. However, in HTTP neither the second nor third digits have any additional classification. The response codes in each class were allocated serially as the need arose.

Whereas the response codes are standardized, the reason phrases are *not* standardized. Different string equivalents can be used in different installations without affecting how the response code is interpreted. For example, a 404 Not Found response is just as meaningful as a 404 Missing Resource or 404 Kaanavillai.

It should be noted that, although not all response *codes* are understood by all HTTP applications, the response *class* to which the code belongs must be understood. The class can be gleaned from the first digit of the code. Each class of response x has x00 as the default response. If an application receives a response code that it cannot understand, it will behave as if it received the default response code. Suppose an HTTP/1.0 proxy receives a 206 Partial Content response code that was defined in HTTP/1.1. An HTTP/1.0 proxy is not expected to know how to interpret such a response properly. However, the proxy must treat this as a 200 OK response code, except that it must not cache the response. An HTTP application such as a browser or a proxy should behave *reasonably* even when it receives an unrecognized response code. Note that such a definition implicitly prohibits addition of new classes of response codes because older HTTP applications would not know how to interpret response codes in the new class. We examine the five response classes in detail next.

INFORMATIONAL CLASS RESPONSES

Even though the informational class of response was defined in HTTP/1.0, no actual response codes were allocated until HTTP/1.1. This is an example of anticipation of future needs and concerns about extensibility, both of which are a sign of good protocol design. This class of response was explicitly set aside for experimental applications. By the time HTTP/1.1 was formalized, informational class response codes that were useful within regular Web transactions were defined and are now used. The 1xx class of response status codes is discussed in more depth in Chapter 7 (Section 7.2.3).

SUCCESS CLASS RESPONSES

After a server has received and accepted the HTTP request for processing, it generates a success class response. This does not indicate that the result will meet the client's expectation. The server has understood the request and includes the appropriate response based on the request method. A successful response code does not have any implication on presence or absence of message

body. For example, a response code of 200 OK could still have an empty body
because the message body may be of zero length.

The four 2xx response codes in HTTP/1.0 are as follows:

- 200 OK: The 200 OK response is returned when the request was successful.
  Depending on the request method, a varying amount of detail is included in
  the response. For example, the GET request results in the response returned
  by the origin server applying the GET method to the resource. In the case
  of a HEAD request, a 200 OK response would include only the metadata in
  the response.
- 201 Created: This response is returned when a resource has been successfully created as a result of a POST request. Although not officially defined
  in HTTP/1.0, the PUT method can also return a 201 Created response
  when the Request-URI does not already exist and is created successfully.
- 202 Accepted: The 202 Accepted response informs the client that the
  request has been received but not yet handled fully. Although the request
  may fail later, the primary intent of this response code is to let the user
  agent continue with its task without waiting for the action to complete on
  the origin server. 202 Accepted was specifically introduced to handle cases
  in which the origin server knew that the response would not be created
  immediately. For example, a request might trigger a program that could
  take a long time to complete on the origin server, or it might schedule
  a process to be triggered later. Along with the response code, the origin
  server should provide some indication of when the action might actually be
  completed. Assuming that a meaningful estimate can be generated, such
  an indication, in a natural language, should be in the response body.
- 204 No Content: 204 No Content is feedback from the origin server to
  acknowledge completion of request handling and does not require a change
  in what a user might actually see. Suppose a user clicks on an imagemap
  maintained on the origin server that has only certain active parts; that
  is, clicking on the active parts might trigger a response. If the user clicks
  on *other* parts of the imagemap, there should be no change to what is
  displayed to the user. This is accomplished by the server sending back a
  204 No Content, which the browser interprets as "no change required."

REDIRECTION CLASS RESPONSES

The redirection class of response codes is used to inform the user agent that
additional action is needed to complete the request. A redirection response
code may eventually lead to a successful response. There is also a risk of an
infinite loop in multiple redirections, which is prevented by limiting the number
of redirections. The actual limit is governed by server policy. There are four
redirection class response codes, as follows:

- **300 Multiple Choices:** The 300 Multiple Choices was defined largely to fill the role of the default response code. Applications are not actually expected to use this response code. Information about the availability of the resource in a different location is included with the 300 Multiple Choices response via the Location response header. A user agent uses the location information and automatically attempts to fetch the resource from the new location.
- **301 Moved Permanently:** The 301 Moved Permanently is used to indicate that the resource being requested has a new home. This is useful for GET and HEAD requests automatically being redirected to the new site but not for the POST method. The POST method, unlike GET or HEAD methods, might require explicit confirmation from the user because it potentially changes contents on the origin server.
- **302 Moved Temporarily:** The 302 Moved Temporarily is a variation on the 301 Moved Permanently response in that the requested resource has moved but not permanently. Unlike the 301 Moved Permanently response, clients should continue to use the old URL in future requests. Whereas 301 Moved Permanently responses are cacheable by default, 302 Moved Temporarily responses are not.
- **304 Not Modified:** The 304 Not Modified response code is returned if the modification time of a resource being validated has not changed since the last modification time included in the request. This has particular significance to caching and is explored in more depth in Chapter 11.

CLIENT ERROR CLASS RESPONSES

The 4xx class of response codes is used for identifying errors assumed to have been made by clients. User agents display the error codes and reason phrases to the user who can take corrective action. HTTP/1.0 has four client error codes, as follows:

- **400 Bad Request:** This response indicates that the syntax of the request was either incorrect or unrecognizable by the origin server.
- **401 Unauthorized:** If the request lacks the necessary authorization, then the server returns the 401 Unauthorized error code. This could happen if the request did not include any authorization information or included invalid authorization information. HTTP/1.0's default challenge-response authentication is discussed in Section 6.4.
- **403 Forbidden:** A response code of 403 Forbidden is returned when the server will not accept the request. Note that the request has been understood by the server and the server is deliberately refusing to service it. The reason for refusing the request may be included in the entity body by the server.

- **404 Not Found**: Given the large number of requests for nonexistent resources, the most widely known client error code is 404 Not Found, which is returned when an origin server is unable to locate the requested resource. The error might be due to the fact that the resource is unavailable temporarily. HTTP/1.0 does not have provision to indicate when the resource might become available again.

SERVER ERROR CLASS RESPONSES

The 5xx class of response codes is used for returning errors related to the server or if the server knows it cannot perform the request currently. The distinction from the 4xx class of codes is that the error is in the server and the client cannot send alternative requests to solve the problem.

There are four response codes in the 5xx class, as follows:

- **500 Internal Server Error**: The generic error in the 5xx class is 500 Internal Server Error which is returned if the server is unable to determine the precise error condition.
- **501 Not Implemented**: If the server knows that it is missing the ability to handle a specific request method, it can return the 501 Not Implemented error code. For example, a server receiving a request method that was defined in a later version of the protocol would return this code.
- **502 Bad Gateway**: The 502 Bad Gateway response code is used when a server currently acting as a proxy or gateway is unable to process a response received from another server. This indicates that the responding server was not the source of the error.
- **503 Service Unavailable**: When a server is temporarily unable to respond but believes it can respond at a later time, it uses the 503 Service Unavailable response code . The server may be temporarily busy. This response is an indication to the client that it may want to retry the request later.

6.3 HTTP Extensibility

One of the early design decisions in HTTP was the notion of extensibility. There is no preset list of acceptable methods. New request methods, response classes, and response codes could be introduced as the protocol evolves. As we will see in Chapter 7, several new methods, headers, and response codes were added in HTTP/1.1. Resources can be in any media and content type. The avoidance of needless restriction in the protocol can help novel applications that may not have been envisioned as a possibility at the time of the protocol creation. An example of this is the introduction of streaming media on the Web (as we will see in Chapter 12).

In the early days of the Web, several different browsers were popular and new versions of browsers were introduced periodically. The new users on the Web would begin with the latest version of the browser. It was thus possible to introduce new features that were browser-dependent. Once the number of people on the Web became very large, it became harder to expect all users to switch to the latest version of the browser. Thus it was not practical to introduce new features that were dependent on the capabilities of the latest version of the browser. Compatibility with the older browsers became a serious requirement.

Extensibility does not imply that the protocol is perfect or that the implementations of components do not introduce some restrictions. The principle of *separation of concerns* states that a protocol need not be concerned about the specifics of how it is implemented. The reality of the marketplace ends up dictating the actual evolution of the protocol. In Chapter 7 we will see examples of how far a protocol can evolve in the face of reality.

6.4 SSL and Security

Concerns about network security issues arose from the time computer networks began to be interconnected. More information is accessed via the Web, and more commerce is being conducted on the Web now. The issue of security was taken seriously relatively early in the Web context. A well-known issue with security is that complex software is harder to secure and browsers and Web servers are becoming quite complex. Modern browsers and servers consist of tens of thousands of lines of complex code. There are several software entities involved in a typical Web transaction. In the presence of multiple intermediaries, some of them unknown to the originating user agent or the Web server, secure Web communication cannot be achieved simply by securing the client and the server application. Any of the intermediaries could alter the message or be vulnerable to interception.

The HTTP/1.0 protocol had its own security mechanisms. But rather than depend on the HTTP protocol or on each of the Web applications to provide its own notion of security, a relatively early attempt was made to provide security for Web communication at a layer below that of the application. This is the Secure Socket Layer mechanism, known widely as SSL [SSL95]. We discuss both SSL and its use in conjunction with HTTP in this section. We also look at the stand-alone security mechanism of HTTP/1.0.

6.4.1 SSL

SSL was introduced in 1994 by Netscape and is the basis for the IETF standard of Transport Layer Security standard (TLS [DA98]). SSL is a protocol between the transport and applications layers. Different application-level protocols, such as HTTP, LDAP, and Internet Message Access Protocol (IMAP [IMA]), can all use SSL. SSL Version 3.0 [SSL], which was derived after security flaws in earlier versions were found and fixed, is the current version of SSL and is the basis for TLS. SSL is supported by the most prominent browsers in use today.

The primary purpose of SSL is to enable a client using TCP/IP as its transport layer connection to transport bits securely to a server that is capable of understanding SSL. The security stems from an encrypted connection between an authenticated client and server. A message in its native form is converted via encryption into a form that is readable only by someone who can reverse the encryption process. The conversion of plaintext to what is known as *ciphertext* (the unreadable encrypted version) is accomplished using an algorithm and a *key*. Any number of mathematical techniques serve as choices for encryption algorithms and the strength of the encryption (i.e., how hard is it for an interloper to be able to retrieve the plaintext from ciphertext) depends on the algorithm *and* the choice of a key. The key is often a password known only to the software involved in the communication and is not part of the message. The strength of the key is determined by the number of bits needed to represent it because determined intruders might simply guess all possible keys. An extremely complicated algorithm with a very small key represented in a dozen bits requires examining 2^{12} (i.e., 4096) values and can be done trivially by any computer. However, a computer costing several millions of dollars would take 10^{25} years to explore all possible values of a 128-bit key by brute force techniques. The length of the encryption/decryption process is not directionally proportional to the length of the keys. Note that a poor algorithm with a large key is much weaker than a complicated algorithm with a small key.

An encrypted message can thus be transmitted on a network that might be vulnerable to interception. Even if the intercepting parties obtain a copy of the ciphertext and know the exact algorithm used to encrypt the plaintext, they do not possess the key required to convert the ciphertext to plaintext. The range and capabilities of the various encryption algorithms are beyond the scope of this book. Readers are encouraged to read further on this topic (e.g., [Ste98a, RGR97]).

Public-key cryptography and a certificate authority are used for a server to authenticate itself. A certificate is basically a file identifying a person or an organization. A client can ensure that the server is indeed who the server claims to be by checking the certificate of a trusted third party. A server, likewise, can ensure the client's identity by checking the client's certificate against a trusted third party. In practice, a server rarely checks a client's certificate. Both client and server may have only a small list of such trusted third parties.

The two parts of the SSL protocol are the record and handshake protocols. The handshake protocol is similar to TCP's handshake protocol and is used to set up a connection. The handshake phase uses subprotocols to set up a record layer and to authenticate endpoints. The format in which data is exchanged during the handshake is decided by the record protocol.

The data transmission format is agreed upon in the record protocol that handled the necessary encryption, compression, and reassembly. The key contribution of the record protocol is that both parties can be assured that the data to be exchanged will be encrypted and message integrity will be preserved. The record protocol breaks data into chunks no larger than 16 KB, optionally compresses it before computing an integrity check, encrypts the result, and sends it with a header. When the message returns from the Web server, the steps are reversed: decryption, checking of integrity, optional decompression, and delivery to, say, a browser.

Note that the record protocol does not in any way interfere with anything happening at the higher (application) layer. For example, the choice of certificates is independent of any HTTP/1.1-level authentication.

The first step of an SSL communication is the choice of encryption methods. Not all encryption methods are equally strong, and not all pairs of communicating clients and servers support all methods. Thus the client and server first choose the method with the maximal strength that both can understand. Virtually all SSL clients and servers use certificate-based authentication, and so the server sends a signed certificate to establish its identity with the client. In some cases, the server might require the client to do the same, although this is relatively rare. E-commerce sites tend to base their certification of a user's identity through the credit card information supplied. The server site has a third party (the credit card issuing bank) to function as the certifying agency and is less concerned about the user's identity. However, in some instances there may be reasons for requiring clients to certify themselves. For example, a site that might want to lower its exposure to risk and be indemnified might insist on verifying the client's certificate.

The client and server then exchange a message similar to TCP's SYN message, indicating that they are ready to start exchanging the actual message. To ensure that none of the exchanges thus far have been compromised, they also exchange a hash function of the set up messages. From now on, the message flow proceeds in the manner of encryption chosen.

A discussion of encryption protocol strength and certificate authorities is beyond the scope of this book. Readers should consult any of the several books (e.g., [Ste98a]) on Web security for this.

6.4.2 HTTPS: Using SSL in Web exchanges

HTTPS is a protocol that uses SSL for transporting the HTTP message. Everything in the communication between the client and the server is encrypted, including the Request-URI. Packet monitors that capture traffic on the wire will not be able to know what resource was accessed (and with what arguments, if any), and requests are thus immune from privacy and security violations, as long as the encryption used is sound. Unlike HTTP, which usually runs on TCP port 80, HTTPS runs typically on TCP port 443. The need for a separate port is because a dedicated TCP/IP socket is needed to transport the HTTP messages.

The most common use of SSL is in conjunction with HTTP, although other application-level protocols can use it. Users often do not even notice that the browser is using SSL. The primary differences are that URLs start with `https:` instead of `http:`, and if the SSL negotiation sequence fails, no actual data is transferred between the client and the Web server.

Note that although HTTP is stateless and an HTTP connection may be closed by closing the TCP connection, SSL-related information may be retained and reused. In other words, the client and server pair can continue communicating securely if another resource on the same site is accessed by the same browser client without having to go through the SSL handshake. Currently, the keys agreed upon can be used up to a day without renegotiation.

Many versions of popular browser clients such as Netscape and Internet Explorer support SSL, as do many popular Web servers. Browsers permit users to choose among a set of cryptographic protocols (e.g., SSL 2.0 or SSL 3.0). After choosing a protocol version, additional customization as to the choice of encryption is possible. For example, the Netscape browser provides several choices for SSL V3.0, ranging from the Data Encryption Standard (DES) of the United States National Institute of Standards and Technology (NIST) to several invented by the RSA Company [RSA], such as RC2 and RC4.

It is debatable whether most users of a browser are savvy enough to distinguish between versions of the SSL protocol. It is even less likely that they will be able to make informed choices between specific encryption mechanisms. The default settings on a site are thus important and end up dictating the actual level of security of users on that site. Browsers also have the option of warning users about certificate authority sites that may not be trustworthy or may have expired certificates.

Typically browsers display an icon (closed lock) if the connection is using SSL.

6.4.3 Security in HTTP/1.0

Because not all HTTP transactions use SSL, there is a security mechanism in HTTP/1.0. Security considerations in HTTP/1.0 primarily deal with safety of the various methods, client authentication, and secure transfer of data. Minor issues covered include dealing with pathname-based attacks, such as users exploiting the pathname feature of files to access files that may not have been explicitly linked to a visible URL by the site. For example, although the URL `http://www.1729.org/unit1/f1` may have a link from an external page, a user might try to access the URL http://www.1729.org/unit1/f2. If the URL happens to exist, an external user might be able to access it even though the owner of the site www.1729.org may not have intended for this to occur. Such attempts stem from the common knowledge that many resources are organized in related parts of a file system and many users use similar pathnames for related URLs. It is also possible to make more educated guesses about existence of URLs that are not officially linked to from the outside world. Many users assume that a URL must be linked from the outside world in order for it to be accessible. Of course, it is possible to create resources and require authentication for every resource, preventing open access to any of the resources.

The potential for misuse of information present in server logs (described in more detail in Chapter 9) whereby a user's privacy can be violated by revealing the nature, frequency, and patterns of actual accesses, was covered in the protocol specification. The Referer and From headers (discussed in Section 6.2.3) are examples of headers whose misuse enables violation of a user's privacy. The Referer field could be used to glean a pattern of browsing of a user, and the user's identification may be transmitted without their consent via the From header. HTTP/1.0 strongly recommends that implementations provide a way to let users opt out of such violations of their privacy.

One of the basic security issues associated with HTTP is due to the popular CGI script mechanism (Chapter 4, Section 4.2.3). CGI scripts serve as the primary means of remotely invoking scripts, and there are significant security problems associated with them. The risks include side effects of scripts invoked, for example, by malicious users with arguments crafted to take advantage of buffer overflows.

A method was deemed safe if it resulted in retrieving only a resource and did not cause any side effects on the origin server. Notably, the GET and HEAD methods are considered safe. However, it is quite conceivable that a request that invoked a script on the origin server (e.g., a CGI script) could result in a resource being created, modified, or deleted. The point about safety is that the *user* is not responsible for the side effects. It should be noted that there is no restriction on the methods being used in a fashion that could cause side effects.

Client authentication in HTTP/1.0 relied on a typical challenge-response scheme and was known as the *Basic Authentication* scheme. A client wishing to access a resource is presented with a challenge (in the WWW-Authenticate response header from the server). The client has to respond with a valid set of *credentials* which is, basically, a password. The credentials are returned in the Authorization header, and, if they are acceptable to the server, the resource is sent. However, if the credentials are not acceptable, the server typically sends back either a 403 Forbidden or a 401 Unauthorized response. Unfortunately, in HTTP/1.0, the credentials were sent in cleartext, making it insecure. This was fixed in the later version of the protocol.

At one of the very early IETF meetings discussing HTTP/1.0, a separate subgroup was formed to move security discussions out of the core protocol group [HTT94]. Although security was not an afterthought in HTTP/1.0, not much attention was paid in the form of laying down stringent requirements in the specification. This was rectified partially in HTTP/1.1, as we will see in the next chapter.

6.5 Protocol Compliance and Interoperability

A protocol specifies syntax and semantics for communication between two or more parties. The rules associated with the various messages, the headers that can and should be included in messages, and the response codes expected in return all form an integral part of the specification of a protocol. Interoperability is one of the primary reasons for specifying a protocol. A component with a particular version of the protocol (e.g., HTTP/1.0) implies a certain level of capability when it comes to interacting with other components. In the presence of new versions of the same protocol, various components must continue to be backward compatible.

A protocol compliance requirement might be as simple as stating that the string in a version number of a protocol not have leading zeros—in other words, a simple syntactic requirement. However, it can also be more complex: A server, supporting multiple organizations that do not trust each other, must check values of specific headers generated under the control of the organizations to ensure that the identification of a user or address has not been altered. Not all rules specified in the protocol are as vital as others; for example, although it is important that each HTTP request contain a method, it is not essential that each request include an identification of the user or the user agent.

We will first examine how version numbers in the message headers are interpreted and then examine the different levels of compliance requirements. Note that only RFCs in the standards track have compliance requirements. For example, RFC 1945 describing HTTP/1.0 is an informational RFC and consequently does not include compliance requirements. RFC 2616 describing HTTP/1.1 is in the standards track, and thus the state of HTTP/1.1 protocol compliance will be examined in Chapter 15 (Section 15.3).

6.5.1 Version number and interoperability

When HTTP components communicate with each other, the version number in the messages signifies the capability of the sender and the receiver. An HTTP server must be able to interpret all messages with version numbers that are smaller or equal to its own. The requirement to interpret messages covers both syntax (format of messages) and semantics (capabilities and features of that version of the protocol). The response from a server must be in a version of the protocol that the client can understand. An HTTP client must properly specify its own version number and interpret messages from a server in a format equal to or less than its own.

HTTP version numbers have a major and a minor component. For example, HTTP/1.0 has a major number of 1 and a minor number of 0. The rules are relatively straightforward for changing the major and minor numbers. Suppose the capabilities of the sender are augmented by adding to the HTTP message semantics but require no change to the message parsing algorithm. The minor number can be changed (a version number change implies adding one to the current value) without changing the major number. However, if the message format requires changes, then the major number must also change. Changing the major number has serious consequences on interoperability.

The details of interpreting version numbers is explained in depth in RFC 2145 [MFGF97]. Communicating in a safe manner requires components to have a clear understanding of the interpretation of version numbers in a message. As we will see in the next chapter, proxies introduced significant problems with the interpretation of version numbers.

6.5.2 MUST, SHOULD, MAY requirement levels

To make sure that implementations of the protocol specification follow the rules, a variety of *levels of requirement* are specified. This is common to many protocols, and the language for specifying the rules has been formalized in RFC 2119 [Bra96a]. RFC 2119 defines the levels of requirement used in Internet protocol specifications. There are three primary requirement levels: MUST, SHOULD, and MAY. The negations MUST NOT and SHOULD NOT also exist.

The levels of compliance requirement are an important part of specification of any protocol. Without them it is possible to have arbitrary implementations that cannot interoperate with each other. Developers of components such as clients, servers, and proxies can readily identify the features of the protocol that have to be implemented and the ones that are optional. The division into different levels of compliance makes the task of an implementor easier because some implementors may care about implementing only portions of the protocol that are absolutely required.

A MUST-level requirement implies that compliance is absolutely essential. An implementation of the protocol that does not have that feature is *not compliant* with the protocol specification. If even one of the MUST-level requirements is not met, the implementation is *not* compliant. A SHOULD-level requirement is treated as a recommendation, and an implementation can be *conditionally* compliant with the specification without implementing the feature. However, the recommendation is meant to indicate that the feature should be implemented if at all possible. An implementation satisfying all the MUST- and SHOULD-level requirements is said to be *unconditionally* compliant. Often an implementation may have to be fully compliant to be used in certain sites or for certain applications.

A MAY-level requirement is purely optional, and although such a feature may be present in some implementations, it is not necessary. An implementation meeting the MUST- and SHOULD-level requirements will be considered compliant even if it does not implement the MAY-level requirements.

The various levels of compliance requirements have a strong impact on the overall set of features one would expect to find in the various implementations of a Web server, proxy, or client. Although several features are optional, implementors of Web components should pay close attention to the MUST- and SHOULD-level requirements. The absence of compliance on the part of one component is a fundamental problem in a complex system such as the Web because this could lead to other components interpreting the result incorrectly. For example, suppose a server ignores a MUST-level requirement and generates an incorrect response. A downstream proxy might assume that it has received the correct response and cache it. The incorrect response will be forwarded as a valid response to many clients requesting the same resource in the future.

There are generic compliance rules for HTTP clients and servers transmitting version numbers. For example, an HTTP server MUST NOT send a version number for which it is not at least conditionally compliant. If the server knows that the client is buggy, then it MAY send a lower version number. Likewise, if the client suspects that the server it is communicating with is buggy, it MAY send a lower version number.

6.6 Summary

Although the current version of HTTP is HTTP/1.1 (described in the next chapter), it is useful to examine the evolution of the HTTP protocol during the initial days of the World Wide Web. More important, there are several clients, proxies, and servers on the Web that are still using HTTP/1.0. A significant portion of the traffic on the Web is in HTTP/1.0. Embedded HTTP/1.0 clients are still being written. Some of the design decision for HTTP/1.0 was related to the popularity of the other systems that were in vogue in the late 1980s and early 1990s. The introduction of hypertext links enabled the explosive growth of the Web and the codification of the HTTP protocol. Codifying common practices and enumerating the methods, headers, and response codes helps the Web components interface smoothly with each other.

The initial version of a protocol is rarely the best version, and many lessons were learned as a result of deploying HTTP/1.0 clients, proxies, and servers. Anticipating a success disaster is quite rare, and HTTP/1.0 was not an exception. Fortunately, key ideas such as response code classes were borrowed from more established protocols, which helped avoid other problems. The decision to keep HTTP stateless led to a rich set of headers, enabling the protocol to be extended in different directions, as we will see later in the book.

The use of HTTP/1.0 in practice led to several improvements, ranging from long-lived connections to security. These improvements are the motivation for HTTP/1.1. Although some popular Web browsers and many of the Web servers run on popular Web sites have migrated to HTTP/1.1, HTTP/1.0 is still in wide use.

7

HTTP/1.1

In the previous chapter, we examined the origins and early evolution of the HTTP protocol leading up to the version that became known as HTTP/1.0. In this chapter, we take an in-depth look at the current version of HTTP, a draft standard as the book goes to press that is likely to be fully standardized by 2001. Although some minor changes are still possible between now and the final standardized version, we do not expect any significant high-level features to change. The primary references on which this chapter is based are RFC 2616 [FGM+99], RFC 2617 [FHBH+99], and the archive of the thousands of e-mail messages exchanged on the HTTP Working Group mailing list [WG-99] between September 1994 and the time the book went to press.

This chapter begins with an overview of the evolution of the HTTP/1.1 protocol. The problems with HTTP/1.0 and intermediate nonstandard implementations led to the proposal of several enhancements. We enumerate the problems with HTTP/1.0 and map them to the key semantic changes in HTTP/1.1 presented in the rest of the chapter. The enumeration of the syntactic differences between HTTP/1.0 and HTTP/1.1 along the lines of methods, headers, and response codes is necessary to understand the various semantic differences. The major semantic changes are then discussed individually along with the purported motivations for the changes. Specific examples illustrating the new or altered features are used to clarify the presentation. Where possible, the effects these changes are likely to produce when practical implementations of HTTP/1.1 components become widely available are also discussed. The role of proxies that have to meet both client- and server-side requirements of HTTP/1.1 rounds out the chapter.

7.1 The Evolution of HTTP/1.1 Protocol

By the time RFC 1945 was issued to describe the then-current practice of HTTP/1.0, there were already hundreds of thousands of Web sites, millions of users, and terabytes of Web data flowing on the Internet. HTTP had already become the dominant protocol on the Internet in terms of packets and bytes. The widespread prevalence of Web documents with embedded images led to the increase in the number of bytes downloaded by users. Text was rapidly becoming a smaller part of the overall number of bytes. HTML documents often reference a dozen or so embedded images, ranging from small Graphics Interchange Format (GIF) images (such as buttons or icons) to larger inline images such as illustrations and photographs. The Web had become an integral part of popular culture and e-commerce was growing rapidly.

Unfortunately, some of the basic design decisions in HTTP/1.0 had severe side effects. For example, one problem was that the application-level protocol HTTP ran on top of the most prevalent transport-layer protocol, TCP. Although TCP was the transport protocol of choice in the early days of the Web, even the original version of HTTP—labeled as HTTP/0.9—did not require the use of TCP. The 1992 article introducing what later became known as HTTP/0.9 [BL92a] specifically included the following:

> Note: HTTP currently runs over TCP, but could run over any connection-oriented service.

Because TCP has been the dominant transport protocol since the early 1980s, it is not surprising that virtually all HTTP implementations have run on top of TCP. TCP, however, was *not* optimized for short transfers; most Web transfers in the early days of the Web (around 1994) were of files that were under 10K [BC94]. In this section we see a complete list of such problems in HTTP/1.0.

We begin with the history of HTTP/1.1's evolution and a look at the Internet Engineering Task Force (IETF) protocol standardization process. We then examine the various problems with HTTP/1.0 that led to changes in HTTP/1.1. The new concepts in HTTP/1.1 are then explored.

7.1.1 History of evolution

Between January 1995 and June 1999, the HTTP Working Group made a significant effort to address the various problems in HTTP/1.0. The four-plus years of evolution from HTTP/1.0 to HTTP/1.1 saw several draft versions of the protocol. The discussions in the HTTP Working Group during these years are available in an online archive [WG-99]. Some of the key changes in the protocol that resulted from these discussions have been captured in a paper [KMK99]. The evolution was driven by the early impact of HTTP/1.0 on the Internet and the desire to introduce features based on the experiences of developers of the various Web components. The explosion of the Web's popularity occurred during this period.

The change from HTTP/1.0 to HTTP/1.1 has been neither smooth nor easy. Several browser and server implementors had introduced features that neither adhered to the common usage of HTTP/1.0 nor had attained a consensus in the HTTP Working Group discussions. Once new features became part of common usage, the need for backward compatibility drove the negotiations in the Working Group. Several of the known problems of HTTP/1.1 can be traced back to the desire for backward compatibility and the lack of extensibility in HTTP/1.0. However, the protocol did evolve in significant ways and addressed a wide variety of issues.

Many browsers are still not HTTP/1.1 compliant and there are relatively few HTTP/1.1 proxies. Because of commercial interest, a significant amount of nontechnical pressure was applied on the protocol community. Several prominent companies had popular products. Corporations that had a specific interest in retaining a feature or in advancing a particular point of view were outspoken on matters of specific interest to them. However, the protocol evolution process did complete without any particular corporation succeeding in having specific points of views forced on the entire Web community. Even when a single product had a large portion of the market share, the final version of the protocol does not appear to have been swayed by views prevalent in that product. One reason for this is the IETF process of protocol evolution based on consensus of views. The other is the diligence of the HTTP Working Group. However, existing implementations influenced the addition of some features. An example of this is the range request feature, which we discuss in Section 7.4.1. Separate from the standardization of HTTP/1.1, the issue of state management in HTTP [KM00] also faced implementational pressures.

Attempts to standardize or upgrade a protocol go through the following stages; a detailed outline of the process is presented in RFC 2026 [Bra96b].

1. A draft document is written and discussed electronically and at face-to-face meetings of the IETF held three times a year. Such a draft document is referred to as an Internet Draft and is made available electronically at the IETF Web site.

2. An Internet Draft may be assigned to one of three tracks: Informational, Experimental, or Standard by the IESG (Internet Engineering Steering Group). If the IESG approves the Internet Draft to become a Request For Comment (RFC) document, the RFC Editor assigns an RFC number. An Informational document is not meant to be an implementation guide nor should it be viewed as a standard. For example, RFC 1945, which described the state of HTTP/1.0, is an Informational RFC. Similarly, the recent Internet Printing Protocol specification outlined in RFC 2565 [HBMT99], is an Experimental document and not part of the Standards track. Most standardization efforts require multiple versions of Internet Draft documents at each stage in the Standards track.

3. A draft document in the Standards track goes through three stages: Proposed Standard, Draft Standard, and Internet Standard. A Proposed Stan-

dard is the first stage for a protocol specification and is considered to have a clear design, reviewed by the community, but not requiring implementation and operational experience. A Draft Standard must have two interoperable implementations that have been independently implemented. The implementations must cover the various features and options of the specification, ensuring that only mature and stable specifications attain Draft Standard. Finally, a specification reaches the Internet Standard status after significant testing is done and there is widespread acceptance of the specification's usefulness to the Internet community. Such a specification has both an RFC number and a number in a separate series named STD (short for Standard). An IETF protocol document spends a certain amount of time in each standardization stage as the IETF gathers comments from the community. After attaining the Proposed Standard stage, a document has to wait a minimum of six months before becoming eligible for advancement to Draft Standard, although in practice it may take much longer. At Draft Standard stage, a document has to wait for four months or at least one IETF meeting (whichever is later) before it can be moved to Internet Standard.

The HTTP evolution process was complicated because of the intermediate Proposed Standard RFC 2068 [FGM+97], which captured the then-current state of HTTP/1.1 discussions. The draft document of HTTP/1.1 submitted for Proposed Standard unfortunately stayed as a draft for longer than usual before it became a Proposed Standard in January 1997. Partly as a result of bad timing, a major release of a browser coincided with the release of RFC 2068. Soon, several client and server implementations, by and large compatible with the specification as outlined in RFC 2068, began claiming to be "HTTP/1.1," even though the HTTP/1.1 protocol specification was only at Proposed Standard and not Internet Standard stage. The version number quickly became a running joke because Web servers were claiming to implement the HTTP/1.1 "standard" that did not exist (and does not exist at the time of writing this book). Thus although problems were discovered with the specification (and captured to a very large extent in Section 19.6.3 of RFC 2616), the software implementing the specification did not change quickly. However, the issuance of RFC 2068 did lead to testing of the various software components implementing the specification.

Attempts to standardize the HTTP/1.1 protocol thus had the additional burden of ensuring compatibility with implementations of browsers and servers that were compatible with RFC 2068, a Proposed Standard. RFC 2616 [FGM+99] was issued in June 1999 as a Draft Standard. It is expected to become a full Internet Standard in 2001. One reason for the delay is that an IETF standard cannot be formalized until "non-normative" references have been removed. In the case of HTTP/1.1, this includes the reference for the MIME E-mail Encapsulation (MHTML, RFC 2110 [PH97]) which has been subsequently obsoleted by RFC 2557 [PH99].

7.1.2 Problems with HTTP/1.0

Changes to HTTP/1.0 were deemed necessary in a variety of areas. RFC 2616 (in Section 19.6.1) listed a few of the changes between HTTP/1.0 and HTTP/1.1. A broader catalog of differences was presented in [KMK99], and an extended version of that taxonomy is used here. The set of problems related to HTTP/1.0 are as follows:

- Lack of control with respect to cache duration, cache location, and selection among cached variants of specific requests and responses
- Full contents of a resource downloaded when only a small part was needed, and inability to continue with interrupted transfers
- Poor use of TCP for short responses, which were typical in the Web
- Absence of guarantee of full receipt of dynamically generated responses
- Extensibility problems and inability to learn about intermediate servers
- Depletion of IP addresses at an alarming rate, because of the popularity of top-level domain names for Web businesses
- Inability to take preferences of clients and servers into account and tailor request and response messages accordingly
- Poor levels of security compounded by the rapidly growing needs of secure communication over the Web and the fact that HTTP/1.0's basic authentication scheme sent passwords in the clear
- Ambiguity of rules for dealing with proxies and caches
- Miscellaneous problems with various methods, headers, and response codes

Considerably longer overall network delays, increased user-perceived latency, and heightened security concerns brought some of the problems with HTTP/1.0 to light. In some cases, workarounds and alternative means were available (e.g., Netscape's Secure Socket Layer [SSL] provided end-to-end security). However, significant problems remained to be addressed. The HTTP Working Group made several improvements by paying attention to the proper use of requirement levels (as per RFC 2119 [Bra96a]), eliminating any specific dependency on TCP as the only transport-level protocol for HTTP and deleting largely unused methods (discussed in the appendix of RFC 1945).

7.1.3 New concepts in HTTP/1.1

Apart from attempts to fix the known problems in HTTP/1.0, some new concepts were introduced in HTTP/1.1. The key concepts proposed to improve the protocol include the following:

- A hop-by-hop mechanism

- Transfer coding
- Virtual hosting
- Ensuring semantic transparency in caching
- Support for variants of a resource

We examine the first two ideas in this section—hop-by-hop mechanism and transfer coding. These two ideas apply broadly to the HTTP message exchange protocol. The other ideas are narrower and are discussed in later sections. Virtual hosting (discussed in Section 7.8) enables multiple Web servers to run on the same machine without requiring a separate IP address for each server. Support for semantic transparency was made a priority in HTTP/1.1. A caching proxy, when it receives a request from a client, cannot return a response in its cache without proper revalidation. Because multiple versions of a resource might be present in origin servers with different variants being appropriate for different clients (e.g., preference for a particular language or character set), it was necessary to let caches be able to select the suitable variant. Support for semantic transparency and handling variants has been added in HTTP/1.1 and is discussed in detail in Section 7.3.3.

THE HOP-BY-HOP MECHANISM

From a user's point of view, a request is sent to the origin server and a response is returned to the user agent. This is an end-to-end view of a Web transaction. This may not always be the case because of the presence of caches or proxies. In other words, the HTTP message travels through several intermediaries. HTTP/1.0 headers are sent from sender to receiver in either direction. Proxies in the path, even when they did not understand header fields, were expected to forward them (this point is stressed in Section 7.1 of RFC 1945 and RFC 2616).

Given the widespread presence of intermediaries in the Web, it is possible that a pair of adjacent intermediaries in the path could use an alternate way to exchange HTTP messages. For example, they may be capable of using a better compression algorithm not available to other components in the message exchange chain. These adjacent components would have to include specific metadata about their special ability via headers. However, these headers could not be sent further down the chain because other downstream recipients may not understand the special ability possessed by this pair. A mechanism whereby an arbitrary set of headers could be safely sent *only* to certain intermediaries became necessary. This led to the introduction of *hop-by-hop* headers—headers that are valid only for a single transport-level connection. The `Transfer-Encoding` header introduced in HTTP/1.1 originally arose to enable hop-by-hop compression [Fie97]. Hop-by-hop headers cannot be stored by caches or forwarded by proxies. The recipient of hop-by-hop headers strips them before forwarding the rest of the message. Intermediate servers delete hop-by-hop headers and could add new ones. HTTP/1.1 uses a new `Connection` header to list headers that are meant to be hop-by-hop, that is, meant just for the immediate connection and not to be forwarded down the chain. For example,

`Connection: header1, header2`

implies that the server receiving the message must remove the headers `header1` and `header2` before forwarding the message.

An understanding of the hop-by-hop mechanism is necessary to answer questions about the percentage of network traffic that uses HTTP/1.1. It is not enough to examine the clients and origin servers that are HTTP/1.1. If the intermediaries between the client and the origin server are not using HTTP/1.1, the message would be downgraded to an earlier version of HTTP. Thus the end-to-end traffic would not be HTTP/1.1.

TRANSFER CODING

In HTTP/1.1, the notion of an entity was distinguished more clearly from that of a message, as follows:

- **Message:** The unit of communication in HTTP with headers and (optional) body.
- **Entity:** What is actually transferred by a message. An entity is separated into entity headers and entity body.

A notion of *transfer-coding* values was introduced in HTTP/1.1 distinct from HTTP/1.0's content coding. In HTTP/1.0, there was no way to distinguish between an encoding transformation applied to the entity and one applied just to the entity-body. Content coding is applied to the whole entity, whereas transfer coding refers to the encoding transformation applied to entity-bodies. The transformations themselves are indicated by transfer-coding values.

A content-coded document is often transmitted from the sender to the recipient without any alteration by the intermediaries. The recipient decodes the content coding. For example, a common content coding is compression; the sender compresses the document and the recipient uncompresses it. Transfer coding, on the other hand, transforms the entity-body in order to transport it safely through the network. Transfer coding is only a property of the message and not of the original entity. Being a property of the message, transfer coding can be added or removed by any of the intermediaries. In fact, transfer coding can be applied to a message that has been content coded. A transfer coding is not aware of the semantics of the message. The choice of a particular content coding, say the compression algorithm, may depend on the particular content

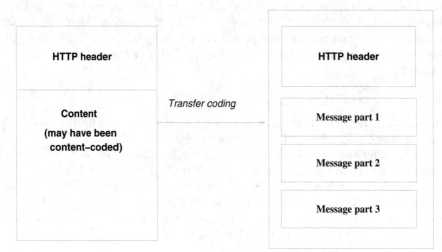

Figure 7.1. Transfer coding of a message

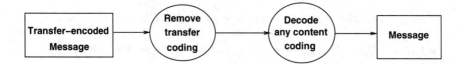

Figure 7.2. Removing transfer coding and any content coding in a message

type. However, transfer coding transforms the message blindly, independent of
the content.

In terms of HTTP message syntax, removing message headers leaves us
with the message body. But if we remove the message headers and any transfer
encodings that may have been applied, then we are left with the entity body.
In HTTP/1.0, removing the message headers yielded the entity body directly.

Figure 7.1 shows how a message is transfer-coded. Note that the coding
is independent of the semantics of the content. The content may already have
content encoding applied to it before being transfer-coded.

Figure 7.2 shows how a message that has been transfer-coded can be decoded to obtain the original message. First, the transfer coding that has been
applied is removed. Next, if any content coding has been applied, it is removed
to obtain the original message.

Transfer-coding manifests itself in HTTP/1.1 via two new headers, as follows:

- The request header `TE`, used by a sender to indicate what transfer codings are acceptable to it in responses
- The general header `Transfer-Encoding`, used to specify what transfer coding has been applied to the message

The transfer-coding mechanism itself is a hop-by-hop mechanism because intermediaries can remove the transfer coding or add their own transfer coding. Both `TE` and `Transfer-Encoding` are hop-by-hop headers. Uses of `TE` and `Transfer-Encoding` are described in Section 7.4.3 and Section 7.12.2, respectively.

7.2 Methods, Headers, Response Codes in 1.0 and 1.1

In this section we enumerate the differences between HTTP/1.0 and HTTP/1.1. The differences are categorized into three parts dealing with old and new request methods, headers, and response codes. The trio of methods, headers, and response codes form the bulk of the protocol syntax. Examining the new request methods, headers, and response status codes yields a quick understanding of the scope and magnitude of differences between HTTP/1.0 and HTTP/1.1. Addition of headers, reduction of ambiguities in selecting the right header, and stating the rules when multiple headers are present all add to the size and complexity of a protocol. The semantics of the changes are discussed in succeeding sections. The tables here serve as an index to the sections where the semantic changes are discussed.

7.2.1 Old and new request methods

HTTP/1.0 had only three request methods (`GET`, `HEAD`, and `POST`) as shown in Table 7.1. Four other methods (`PUT`, `DELETE`, `LINK`, `UNLINK`) were used in some HTTP/1.0 implementations and are described in the appendix of RFC 1945. However, these methods are not available in many implementations. In fact, even in the implementations that included them, they were not provided consistently. Two of these four methods (`PUT` and `DELETE`, marked with a dagger in Table 7.1) have been retained in HTTP/1.1 and formally specified. The other two methods, `LINK` and `UNLINK`, were removed in HTTP/1.1. Three new request methods were introduced in HTTP/1.1 (`OPTIONS`, `TRACE`, and `CONNECT`). The changes in the HTTP/1.0 methods are significant enough to warrant separate discussion, and so we indicate the later sections of this chapter where they occur.

Being an informational RFC, RFC 1945 does not indicate the requirement levels of the methods. RFC 2616 does state the requirement levels associated

Table 7.1. HTTP/1.1 request methods. Numbers in third column refer to section numbers in this chapter. '*' denotes HTTP/1.0 methods and '†' denotes non-standard HTTP/1.0 methods.

Method	New/changes in HTTP/1.1	Section
GET*	Requesting parts of entities	7.4.1
HEAD*	Conditional request headers allowed	7.12.1
POST*	Connection management,	7.5,
	message transmission	7.6
PUT†	Method formalized	7.12.1
DELETE†	Method formalized	7.12.1
OPTIONS	New method, extensibility	7.7
TRACE	New method, extensibility	7.7
CONNECT	New method, future use	7.12.1

with the various methods in HTTP/1.1. *Only* the GET and HEAD methods are a MUST-level requirement. In other words, a browser that implements these two methods correctly could communicate with a Web server (also implementing just these two methods) and both of them could label themselves HTTP/1.1 compliant. Of course, the server must respond with a proper error code for methods it does not implement. In practice, most browsers and servers implement many more than just these required two methods.

7.2.2 Old and new headers

Headers are the primary means for altering the behavior of a request and provide metadata about the resource. In the following sections, we examine general, request, response, entity, and hop-by-hop headers.

GENERAL HEADERS

HTTP/1.0 defines only two general headers (Date and Pragma). HTTP/1.1 has seven additional general headers. General headers can be used in requests and responses and typically deal with a broader concept than request or response headers. Table 7.2 lists the general headers and maps them to their primary semantic concepts. We discuss the new general headers later in this chapter.

The Date and Pragma headers, as discussed in Chapter 6 (Section 6.2.3), were present in HTTP/1.0. The list of acceptable date and time formats was changed to remove the previously acceptable RFC 1036-based date format. RFC 1036 permitted two-digit year strings, which is clearly unacceptable in light of the Y2K problem (years requiring four digits to be represented instead of two). Thus, although clients and servers are still permitted to accept dates

Table 7.2. HTTP/1.1 general headers. '*' denotes HTTP/1.0 general headers.

Header	Definition/semantic concept(s)	Section
Date*	Message generation date/time	6.2.3
Pragma*	Message directive	6.2.3
Cache-Control	Caching directives	7.3.3
Connection	Hop-by-hop, connection management	7.1.3, 7.5
Trailer	List of headers at end of message	7.6
Transfer-Encoding	Transformation to message body	7.6
Upgrade	Upgrading to other protocols	7.7
Via	Learning about intermediate servers	7.7
Warning	Error-notification	7.12.2

in all three formats (RFC 822/1123, RFC 850/1036, and ANSI C's *asctime()* format), they can only generate date strings in the RFC 1123 format.

There is no change in the semantics of the Pragma general header, and no new directives were added. Handling of Pragma directives is not a requirement imposed by the protocol. HTTP/1.0 defined Pragma: no-cache only for request messages, and HTTP/1.1 did not extend it to response messages. HTTP/1.1 permits the use of Pragma for backward compatibility and introduced a more general cache control mechanism via the Cache-Control general header. The Cache-Control header is used to send directives in requests and responses and constrain behavior of cache components.

REQUEST HEADERS

HTTP/1.0 has only 5 request headers, whereas HTTP/1.1 has 19, as shown in Table 7.3. The 5 request headers from HTTP/1.0 (Authorization, From, If-Modified-Since, Referer, and User-Agent) have all been retained in HTTP/1.1, though some of their semantics have changed. Specifically, access authentication described by the Authorization header has been expanded significantly in HTTP/1.1. There is a separate RFC describing Basic and Digest Authentication [FHBH+99]. The If-Modified-Since request modifier was permitted to be used only with the GET method in HTTP/1.0 but can be used with any method in HTTP/1.1.

We divide the request headers into four classes, as follows:

- **Response preference:** Headers used to express preference on responses such as language or character set.

Table 7.3. The HTTP/1.1 request headers. Numbers in last column refer to section numbers in this or the previous chapter. '*' denotes HTTP/1.0 request headers.

Class	Header	Brief description (Section)
Response preference	`Accept`	Preferred media types (7.9)
	`Accept-Charset`	Preferred character sets (7.9)
	`Accept-Encoding`	Preferred content-codings (7.9)
	`Accept-Language`	Preferred natural languages (7.9)
	`TE`	Preferred transfer-codings (7.4.3)
Information sent with request	`Authorization*`	User agent's credentials (6.2.3)
	`From*`	User's e-mail address (6.2.3)
	`Referer*`	URI from which Request-URI obtained (6.2.3)
	`User-Agent*`	Information on user agent software (6.2.3)
	`Proxy-Authorization`	Client authorization with proxy (7.11.3)
Conditional request	`If-Modified-Since*`	Comparison with last modified time (6.2.3)
	`If-Match`	Comparison against entity tags (7.3.3)
	`If-None-Match`	Comparison against entity tags (7.3.3)
	`If-Unmodified-Since`	Comparison with last modified time (7.4.1)
	`If-Range`	Send range only if entity unchanged (7.4.1)
Constraint on server	`Expect`	Expected server behavior by client (7.4.2)
	`Host`	Host of resource being requested (7.8)
	`Max-Forwards`	Limit forwarding hops (7.7.1)
	`Range`	Request byte ranges of an entity (7.4.1)

- **Information sent with request:** Headers used to send additional information with the message, such as identification information about the user and/or the browser.
- **Conditional requests:** Headers used to make the request conditional, leading to a server interpreting the request method in a different way.
- **Constraint on server:** Headers used to make the server behave in a particular way.

The 14 new request headers in HTTP/1.1 are explained in the relevant sections later in this chapter.

RESPONSE HEADERS

Response headers are used to give additional information about the server or the response. Response headers have been enhanced in HTTP/1.1 in two ways: the existing response headers from HTTP/1.0 (`Location`, `Server`, and `WWW-Authenticate`) have been clarified, and six new response headers have

Table 7.4. HTTP/1.1 response headers. '*' denotes HTTP/1.0 response headers.

Concept	Header	Brief description	Section
Redirection	Location*	Alternate location for URI	6.2.3
Information related	Server*	Server identification	6.2.3
	Retry-After	Delay before retrying request	7.12.2
	Accept-Ranges	Partial request	7.4.1
Security related	WWW-Authenticate*	Challenge for authentication	6.2.3
	Proxy-Authenticate	Challenge for authentication	7.11.3
Caching related	ETag	Opaque validator	7.3.3
	Age	Time since response generated	7.3.3
	Vary	Selecting resource variant	7.3.3

been added. The `Location` response header has been distinguished from the new `Content-Location` entity-header.

The complete list of response headers in HTTP/1.1 is shown in Table 7.4.

ENTITY HEADERS

Entity headers are used to provide additional information about the resource or the entity body and have the same semantics as in HTTP/1.0. In addition to the six entity headers already available in HTTP/1.0 (`Allow`, `Content-Encoding`, `Content-Length`, `Content-Type`, `Expires`, `Last-Modified`), HTTP/1.1 has four new entity headers in HTTP/1.1. Although the protocol does not have to change in order for new header fields to be defined, recipients may not recognize the new header fields. Unrecognized entity header fields (like all unrecognized headers) are ignored by recipients. Proxies can ignore but still must forward unrecognized headers. Table 7.5 shows the list of entity headers in HTTP/1.1.

HOP-BY-HOP HEADERS

The eight hop-by-hop headers of HTTP/1.1 are `Connection`, `Keep-Alive`, `Proxy-Authenticate`, `Proxy-Authorization`, `Trailers`, `TE`, `Transfer-Encoding`, and `Upgrade`. The rest of the headers are end-to-end and they *cannot* be made into a hop-by-hop header simply by listing them in a `Connection` header and expecting the next connection to strip them. New headers can be introduced and be made hop-by-hop by specifying them in a `Connection` header. For example, if a new header `Volume` is defined, it will be treated as an end-to-end header and forwarded by intermediaries even if they do not understand the header. However, by adding

```
Connection: Volume
```

Table 7.5. HTTP/1.1 entity headers. '*' denotes HTTP/1.0 entity headers.

Header	Brief description	Section
Allow*	Methods applicable to resource	6.2.3
Content-Encoding*	Content coding(s) applied to entity body	6.2.3
Content-Length*	Length of entity body	6.2.3
Content-Type*	Entity body's media type	6.2.3
Expires*	Entity body's freshness duration	6.2.3
Last-Modified*	Resource's last modification time	6.2.3
Content-Language	Natural language of entity	7.9
Content-Location	Alternate location for resource	7.9
Content-MD5	Integrity check of entity body	7.10
Content-Range	Location of range in entity body	7.4.1

the header will be stripped once it gets to the next hop.

7.2.3 Old and new response codes

The 16 response status codes of HTTP/1.0 (as discussed in Chapter 6, Section 6.2.4) are still meaningful in HTTP/1.1. There are a total of 41 response codes in HTTP/1.1 as shown in Table 7.6.

HTTP/1.1 has defined several new status codes in every class. We examine some of the important new status codes and explain why they were introduced in HTTP/1.1. However, no new status code *classes* were defined—new classes would not be understood by HTTP/1.0 clients or proxies. HTTP/0.9 clients could not understand response codes because they only received entity bodies.

The response status codes are not always the same for a given situation: it is possible for a server to send a different status code based on the current situation and the server policy for the request. The choice of which status code may even be guided by the server's desire not to reveal too much about the particular reason for an error response.

It is difficult to uniformly classify response codes into specific semantic categories. HTTP/1.0 does not provide specific guidelines for which response code should be returned for a given scenario. To a large extent, neither does HTTP/1.1. Thus, although there is leeway on which code within a class is actually returned, there is no doubt about the class of response code that would be appropriate in a specific situation. For example, the 200 OK, 201 Created or 204 No Content could be sent when a PUT request succeeds. Likewise, a server that does not wish to let the client distinguish between a nonexistent resource and one for which the client lacks proper authorization could use a 404 Not Found response rather than a 403 Forbidden response. If information about a specific user agent's behavior is known, a server may be able to send a different

Table 7.6. HTTP/1.1 response status codes. '*' denotes HTTP/1.0 response codes.

100 Continue	404 Not Found*
101 Switching Protocols	405 Method Not Allowed
200 OK*	406 Not Acceptable
201 Created*	407 Proxy Authentication Required
202 Accepted*	408 Request Timeout
203 Non-Authoritative Information	409 Conflict
204 No Content*	410 Gone
205 Reset Content	411 Length Required
206 Partial Content	412 Precondition Failed
300 Multiple Choices*	413 Request Entity Too Large
301 Moved Permanently*	414 Request-URI Too Long
302 Found*	415 Unsupported Media Type
303 See Other	416 Requested Range Not Satisfiable
304 Not Modified*	417 Expectation Failed
305 Use Proxy	500 Internal Server Error*
306 (Unused)	501 Not Implemented*
307 Temporary Redirect	502 Bad Gateway*
400 Bad Request*	503 Service Unavailable*
401 Unauthorized*	504 Gateway Timeout
402 Payment Required	505 HTTP Version Not Supported
403 Forbidden*	

response code. For example, several user agents created before HTTP/1.1 do not understand the 303 See Other response, but when they receive a 302 Found response, they react in the same way the specification says they should for a 303 See Other response. This information can be used to send a 302 Found response instead of a 303 See Other response to such user agents.

HTTP/1.1 INFORMATIONAL CLASS (1XX) RESPONSE CODES

HTTP/1.0 in RFC 1945, did not define any informational class (1xx) codes, whereas HTTP/1.1 defined two new 1xx response status codes, as shown in Table 7.7. HTTP/1.0 correctly anticipated the need for this class of responses and included it. In fact, RFC 1945 even included constraints on 1xx responses (e.g., responses could not include a body), even though a specific 1xx status code was not conceived at that time.

Table 7.7. Informational class (1xx) response status codes

Status code and reason phrase	Brief description	Section
100 Continue	Permit request transmission	7.4.2
101 Switching Protocols	Switch to other protocol	7.7

Table 7.8. Success class (2xx) response status codes. '*' denotes HTTP/1.0 response codes.

Status code and reason phrase	Brief description	Section
200 OK*	Request accepted	6.2.4
201 Created*	Addition of variants	7.3.3
202 Accepted*	Temporary answer	6.2.4
203 Non-Authoritative Information	Metadata not definitive	7.12.3
204 No Content*	No user view change	7.12.3
205 Reset Content	User view change	7.12.3
206 Partial Content	Successful range request	7.4.1, 7.12.3

HTTP/1.1 SUCCESS CLASS (2XX) RESPONSE CODES

There are seven response codes in the 2xx class, of which four are from HTTP/1.0. Table 7.8 shows the old and new codes and the places where the semantics of the new response codes are discussed.

HTTP/1.1 REDIRECTION CLASS (3XX) RESPONSE CODES

The 3xx class of response codes is used to specify alternative actions that can be taken by the user agent in order to complete the request. An older redirection class response status code in HTTP/1.0, 300 Multiple Choices, has a more direct application in HTTP/1.1. The meaning of another HTTP/1.0 status code, 302 Found, was slightly changed. Additionally, there are four new redirection class status codes added in HTTP/1.1. Table 7.9 shows all the 3xx class of response codes and indicates where the semantic changes are discussed.

Although user agents may not display the reason phrase (a short natural language descriptive phrase explaining a status code) associated with a response, such phrases are a useful way to provide a clearer description of the response status codes. The reason phrase for the status code 302 was changed between HTTP/1.0 and HTTP/1.1. The original reason phrase in early discussions and implementations was Found, but in RFC 1945 it was inadvertently listed as Moved Temporarily. The new reason phrase in HTTP/1.1 is Found.

Table 7.9. Redirection class (3xx) response status codes. '*' denotes HTTP/1.0 response codes.

Status code and reason phrase	Brief description	Section
300 Multiple Choices*	Base response code	7.9
301 Moved Permanently*	New home for resource	6.2.4
302 Found*	Reason phrase change	6.2.4
303 See Other	Mishandled 302 responses	7.12.3
304 Not Modified*	Revalidation response	6.2.4
305 Use Proxy	Request again via proxy	7.12.3
306 (Unused)	Formerly used code	7.12.3
307 Temporary Redirect	Temporary location of URI	7.12.3

HTTP/1.1 CLIENT ERROR CLASS (4XX) RESPONSES

There are 14 new HTTP/1.1 client error class response status codes reflecting the significantly widened range of feedback given to clients when they are suspected to have erred in the request. The changes primarily fall into five broad categories, as shown in Table 7.10. The first category consists of the four HTTP/1.0 response codes. The four new categories are as follows:

- **Clarification status codes:** These four response codes clarify some of the older response codes available in HTTP/1.0. The changes are relatively small, but the new response codes were created to handle certain situations.
- **Negotiation status codes:** Because some Web resources are available in several variants (language, character set, etc.), HTTP/1.0 introduced content negotiation, a mechanism by which a client can inform the server the set of languages and/or character sets acceptable to the user. A key change in HTTP/1.1 is the extension of the negotiation capability between sender and receiver: Negotiation can be driven by both user agents and servers.
- **Length-related codes:** There are two codes in this category. Notion of length arises in two contexts: the content length of the message and the length of a Request-URI. Servers might insist on taking certain actions based on the absence or presence of length information.
- **New requirements status codes:** This class consists of four response status codes, present as a result of significant feature additions in HTTP/1.1. They differ from the above two categories in that HTTP/1.0 does not offer any of the features necessitating these codes.

Table 7.10. Client error class (4xx) response status codes. '*' denotes HTTP/1.0 response codes.

Classification	Status code and reason phrase	Section
HTTP/1.0 error codes	400 Bad Request*	6.2.4
	401 Unauthorized*	6.2.4
	403 Forbidden*	6.2.4
	404 Not Found*	6.2.4
Clarification of HTTP/1.0 codes	405 Method Not Allowed	7.12.3
	407 Proxy Authentication Required	7.11
	408 Request Timeout	7.12.3
	410 Gone	7.12.3
Using negotiation capability in HTTP/1.1	406 Not Acceptable	7.9
	415 Unsupported Media Type	7.12.3
	413 Request Entity Too Large	7.12.3
Length related	411 Length Required	7.10
	414 Request-URI Too Long	7.10
New codes for other features in HTTP/1.1	402 Payment Required	7.12.3
	409 Conflict	7.12.3
	412 Precondition Failed	7.3.3
	416 Requested Range Not Satisfiable	7.4.1
	417 Expectation Failed	7.4.2

HTTP/1.1 Server error class (5xx) responses

The 5xx response status codes are returned when the server is unable to handle the request or has committed a mistake. There were four 5xx response status codes in HTTP/1.0, whereas there are a total of six in HTTP/1.1. The 5xx response codes are shown in Table 7.11.

HTTP/1.1 formalized the use of the informal `Retry-After` header with `503 Service Unavailable` in HTTP/1.0. Two new status codes were introduced: `504 Gateway Timeout` and `505 HTTP Version Not Supported`.

With this high-level overview of changes to HTTP/1.1 in terms of methods, headers, and response codes, the following sections describe the various semantic changes in detail.

7.3 Caching

A cache is a store of responses for later reuse. HTTP specifies several important rules related to caching. The rules relate to cacheability, validation, and coherence of cached responses. However, policy decisions, such as cache replacement,

Table 7.11. Server error class (5xx) response status codes. '*' denotes HTTP/1.0 response codes.

Status code and reason phrase	Brief description	Section
500 Internal Server Error*	Unexpected server condition	6.2.4
501 Not Implemented*	Functionality lacking	6.2.4
502 Bad Gateway*	Upstream server error	6.2.4
503 Service Unavailable*	Temporary inability to handle request	6.2.4
504 Gateway Timeout	Upstream server's delay in response	7.3.3
505 HTTP Version Not Supported	Unsupported protocol version	7.12.3

and heuristics for evicting potentially stale responses are beyond the scope of the protocol. In this section, we restrict ourselves to discussing protocol-related issues of caching. A more in-depth discussion of caching in general can be found in Chapter 11. We begin with a brief terminology of both protocol- and policy-related terms related to caching and examine caching in HTTP/1.0. The new cache-related headers in HTTP/1.1 are then discussed.

7.3.1 Caching-related terms

Several terms related to caching are used throughout the protocol specification. A response that has been obtained from an origin server may be stored in a cache for a certain duration of time. The cached response may be returned when a subsequent request for the same resource is received, subject to several criteria. The terms commonly associated with caching are as follows:

- **Age:** The age of a response is either the time since the entity was sent by the origin server or the time since it was revalidated as fresh by the cache. It is expressed in seconds.
- **Expiration time:** The expiration time of a cached entity is set by the origin server as the time after which the cache *must* revalidate the entity before returning it as a response. If the origin server does not set an expiration time, a cache may assign its own *heuristic* expiration time to the cached entity. The expiration time is also expressed in seconds.
- **Freshness lifetime and staleness:** A response is generated at the origin server at a certain time. The origin server can decide how long that response can be considered *fresh*, that is, when it is not proper to treat the response as current. Once the age of a response has crossed its freshness time, the response is considered *stale*, regardless of whether the resource has actually changed on the origin server. Thus the freshness lifetime is the

length of time between response generation and expiration time. Freshness is a duration, whereas expiration time is a particular point in time.

- **Validity:** Caches can check with the origin server to see if the cached copy of the resource is fresh. This check is called *revalidation*. Revalidation may be done against a proxy, not just an origin server.
- **Cacheability:** A cache must decide if a response should be stored. The cacheability of a response depends on a variety of factors, such as an origin server permitting the response to be cached and the absence of an explicit expiration time. Even if an entity is cached, validation may be needed to ensure its freshness. Cacheability and validity of a response are related, but different, concepts. Not all responses are cacheable, and not all cached responses can be returned as a valid response from a cache.
- **Cache maintenance:** A cacheable response is stored in a cache and returned later. Maintaining a cache requires dealing with issues such as cacheability of a response, duration of time a response can be cached, and deciding on the need for a cached response to be revalidated.

7.3.2 Caching in HTTP/1.0

Caching had already become an issue during the early discussions of HTTP/1.0. By the time RFC 1945 was complete, caching was supported in minimal form in HTTP/1.0. The need for caching arose because of latency problems associated with low connection speeds and the large number of requests for a small proportion of resources that were popular. If a resource does not change between requests, the time spent in fetching the same resource, the consumption of network bandwidth, and the load on the server are all wasted.

HTTP/1.0 provided caching control in the following three ways:

- A request directive (`Pragma: no-cache`)
- A modifier to the `GET` request (`If-Modified-Since`)
- A response header (`Expires`)

HTTP/1.0 permitted the `Pragma: no-cache` request directive, whereby clients could request that the response be obtained directly from the origin server. The `Pragma` directive could be ignored, but typically recipients adhered to it. Clients could bypass any caches and obtain the current copy of the resource the origin server.

HTTP/1.0 also provided an `Expires` entity-header to let origin servers indicate that the resource can be cached safely until the time of expiry.

The other caching mechanism in HTTP/1.0 is the conditional `GET` request using the `If-Modified-Since` request modifier (discussed in Chapter 6, Section 6.2.3). If a cached copy of the response was still fresh, the server would send back a `304 Not Modified` response with no response body. The sender of the request could use its cached value instead. If the last modified time of the resource was newer than what was in the request, the server would return an appropriate status code (often 200 OK) with the full response body. Note that responses returned with response codes other than 200 OK are also cacheable. Suppose a proxy sent a request and received a 304 Not Modified response. The proxy would return either the cached response to the client or a 304 Not Modified response, depending on whether the request sent by the client had an If-Modified-Since header.

Several HTTP/1.0 implementations had misused the Expires header by using values that forced immediate expiry of the resource (thus preventing the response from being cached). This is known as *cache busting*. There are good and bad reasons for an origin server to bust caches. If the origin server has reason to believe that a cache might be returning stale resources, the origin server might try to ensure that a resource is not cached in the first place. A *cache hit* (successful location of a requested response in a cache) by a client behind a caching proxy will not be seen by the origin server. An origin server may be generating pages that include advertisements in the form of separate GIF images. To increase ad revenue, the server might want to ensure that advertisements are sent to clients each time a page is visited. The origin server will not be able to demonstrate that the advertisement carried on their pages was actually seen by such users. If the resource had not been cached, the client's request for the page would result in the advertisement GIFs being retrieved from the origin server, thus increasing the number of advertisements delivered by the origin server.

The Last-Modified header typically implies that the resource was not dynamically generated, and several HTTP/1.0 caches used this as a way to decide if the response was cacheable. However, such a deduction is not always true. Several dynamically generated responses may be the same each time they are generated. A Common Gateway Interface (CGI) script that generates the nth digit of pi presumably generates the same answer each time. In other words, depending on the request and the argument, the dynamically generated response may still be cacheable. A caching proxy may not be able to make deductions about the nature of the script being executed.

All time comparisons in HTTP/1.0 depended on absolute clock values. This turned out to be a design flaw that required repair in HTTP/1.1, as we will see next.

7.3.3 Caching in HTTP/1.1

The soaring popularity of the Web, the popularity of just a few resources at a site, and the similarity of request patterns of users within a particular administrative domain all led to a significant increase in the desire for caching. At the same time, the need for *semantically transparent* caching was widely felt.

A cache must be able to return a cached response without fear that the origin server would return a different response.

Some key guidelines followed in designing the changes related to caching in HTTP/1.1 were as follows:

- Separating the issues of what is cached and whether a cached response could be used safely. The protocol's role is in ensuring correctness but not in worrying about policy guidelines regarding how long an object can be cached and when/how cached contents should be replaced.
- Ensuring correctness, even if there was a cost associated with it. A cache should not *unknowingly* return a stale value. The specification permits relaxation of semantic transparency under some circumstances. The client or origin server can relax transparency explicitly. A cache could warn the user when a response does not meet the desired level of transparency (with a warning header, as we will see later in Section 7.12.2).
- Allowing the server to provide more information about the cacheability of a resource and give users more control over what is cached.
- Not depending on absolute timestamps or a requirement of synchronization between the clocks at the client and server.
- Providing support for caching negotiated responses.

A few other minor issues were considered, such as separating caching from the history mechanism in a browser (discussed in Chapter 2, Section 2.3). The history mechanism simply moves the user through past accesses independent of the freshness or staleness of any resource presented to the user. The protocol does permit user agents to give information about staleness of a particular resource to a user. Some browsers actually reload pages that may have expired since the time the page was cached.

Because HTTP/1.0 already had a notion of expiration (via the `Expires` header), changes related to caching had to be compatible with how the expiry time was used. Distinct mechanisms were introduced in HTTP/1.1 to handle the issues of cacheability and semantic transparency. Furthermore, with additions of features to the caching mechanism, explicit rules for handling combinations of headers had to be defined. The protocol does not spell out rules for handling every possible combination of headers. The combinatorial explosion resulting from examining each pair of header combinations renders this impossible. Faced with handling combinations of headers, implementations have to be resilient and follow a set of ground rules. Among the principles that are often cited is the robustness principle outlined in RFC 791 [Jon81]. The robustness principle, an oft-quoted expression in several contexts, is

> Components should be liberal in what they accept and conservative in what they send.

For HTTP, the interpretation of this aphorism is that the receiving component should be tolerant of incorrect, confusing, or unforeseen header combinations but should strive to send only meaningful combinations of headers.

HTTP/1.1 states some specific rules about combining headers in order for proper generation of responses from caches. Upon receiving a response from an origin server, a caching proxy has to decide what to send to the client that originated the request. If the origin server sent a 200 OK response with, presumably, a new copy of the resource, then the cache can store the new response and send it on to the client. However, suppose the response is 304 Not Modified, that is, the cache is permitted to use its cached response to send to the client. The cache is *not* permitted to use the end-to-end headers in the cached response. Instead, the cache *must* use the end-to-end headers in the response it just received from the origin server. This is important because the origin server may send a 304 Not Modified response with updated headers such as Expires and Cache-Control.

The four new headers in HTTP/1.1 that are associated with caching are: Age, Cache-Control, ETag, and Vary. Their semantics are discussed next.

THE AGE HEADER

The server uses the Age header to indicate how long ago the response was generated on the origin server. If the server is a caching proxy (i.e., not an origin server), this value could be the time since the cached response was revalidated. Proxies are obligated to generate an Age header. The value specified in an Age header is in seconds and cannot be negative.

THE CACHE-CONTROL HEADER

HTTP/1.1 offers more fine-grained control, unlike HTTP/1.0's caching model. To provide more control to both senders *and* recipients over caching, HTTP/1.1 added the new general header Cache-Control. Several cache-control directives are possible in requests and responses, and the set is extensible. Origin servers can insist that a response be private to a single user. Also, when a certain amount of time has passed, caches could be obligated to validate cached responses before returning them to requesters. Intermediaries have to forward the directives because they could apply to all the proxies and gateways present in the request-response chain. Note that the directives are a MUST-level compliance requirement and all caches have to obey them. It is important to note that protocol compliance requirement does not imply that caches *will* actually obey them. In Chapter 15 (Section 15.3), we will examine the impact of noncompliance of Web components.

Although some directives are common to requests and responses, the presence of a request directive has no bearing on presence or absence of a similar

Table 7.12. Cache-control request directives

Directive	Brief description
no-cache	Forcible revalidation with origin server
only-if-cached	Obtain resource only from cache
no-store	Caches are not permitted to store request, response
max-age	Response's age should be no greater than this value
max-stale	Expired response OK but no staler than stated value
min-fresh	Response should remain fresh for at least stated value
no-transform	Proxy must not change media type
extension tokens	New tokens representing new request directives

response directive. We next examine the cache-control request and response directives.

Cache-control request directives The cache-control request directives are a way for clients to override the default handling of their requests by caches. Table 7.12 presents the set of cache-control request directives. Clients may want to ensure that their requests bypass caches and protect the privacy of the requests. Clients may also want the response to come only from caches and to ensure that intermediaries do not transform the response in any way. Note that even though a variety of request directives exist, browser implementations may not permit users to set all of them. The various request directives are explained next.

- no-cache: The no-cache request directive serves the same function as the HTTP/1.0's Pragma: no-cache directive; that is, any proxy in the path between the sender and the origin server is not permitted to return a cached response. Instead, a proxy is obligated to forward the request to the origin server. This is known as an "end-to-end reload." For example, when a user clicks on the Reload button of the Netscape browser (with the Shift key pressed), the browser sends the Pragma: no-cache directive. The user receives the current copy of the resource, independent of what may be in any of the intermediate caches.
- only-if-cached: The flip side of the no-cache directive is the directive only-if-cached. Instead of ensuring that the request not be satisfied by a cached value, the sender *only* wants a response from the cache. A sender might be concerned about the delay in the network or not be particularly concerned about the freshness of a cached response. A cache could send the response if the request constraints are met but can return the 504 Gateway Timeout response code otherwise. A proxy may knowingly return a stale response, but only if the request has no other constraints, such as an

`If-Modified-Since` header. Semantic transparency requirements simply require that proxies do not return a stale response without knowing that it is stale.

- `no-store`: The `no-store` request directive prevents the request and response from being cached. A user may not want the request to be recorded even for a short time. The `no-store` directive is a useful aid to meet such privacy requirements. This directive enjoins the cache to not store the request message or any response to the request. However, there is no guarantee that a request (or response) won't accidentally be stored somewhere. A better choice for the user might be to encrypt the request.

- `max-age`: To decide if a cached response is stale, a user agent can alter the default expiration mechanism used via the `max-age` cache-control directive. The response should be younger than the time value specified (in number of seconds) in the `max-age` directive. Thus a `max-age=0` directive forces an end-to-end revalidation.

- `max-stale`: The `max-stale` directive expresses willingness on the part of the client to accept responses that may have expired in the cache. However, responses cannot exceed the expiration time by the argument specified (if any). If no arguments are specified, the client is willing to accept any response. Specifying `max-stale` permits clients to bypass the policy guidelines of the proxy. A `max-stale=60` directive implies that the user agent is willing to accept a response that may be stale but by no more than a minute.

- `min-fresh`: The `min-fresh` directive expresses the willingness of a client to accept a response that will be fresh at least for the number of seconds specified. If a value of 60 is specified as the argument for the `min-fresh` directive, the expectation is that the response will not be considered stale after 60 seconds.

- `no-transform`: The `no-transform` directive prevents a cache from modifying the media type (such as `text/html`, `image/gif`) of the entity body. Transformation of an entity body could involve changing its content coding (e.g., compressing the entity body), content type (altering an image in GIF format to Joint Photographic Experts Group (JPEG) format), or integrity check (a checksum). One reason to transform an entity body is efficiency—compressing a response speeds up its transfer. However, in some cases, a response should not be transformed: altering the granularity of a medical image might lose some crucial information. If a recipient of the entity body is relying on its checksum to verify correctness, even a simple alteration would cause the integrity comparison to fail.

The intermediate cache is not given the right to overrule the end-to-end considerations of the sender and the receiver. The `no-transform` request directive restores control to the sender (and to the receiver in the case of a response directive). However, caches can and do ignore end-to-end con-

Table 7.13. Cache-control response directives

Directive	Brief description
public	OK to cache response anywhere
private	Response for specific user only
no-store	Caches are not permitted to store response, request
no-cache	Do not serve from cache without prior revalidation
no-transform	Proxy must not change media type, etc.
must-revalidate	Can be cached but revalidate if stale
proxy-revalidate	Force shared user agent caches to revalidate cached response
max-age	Response's age should be no greater than this value
s-maxage	Shared caches use value as response's maximum age
extension tokens	New tokens representing new response directives

siderations while making decisions that are locally optimal. One example in which a cache may have a legitimate reason to ignore a directive is an academic site's cache ignoring requests for loading fresh copies of resources from sites of questionable educational value. But when a cache ignores any explicitly stated request directives (such as no-cache), it has to include a warning in the response to indicate potential staleness of response.

- *extension tokens:* The presence of an extension mechanism in the set of cache-control directives permits the additions of new request directives. However, if caches do not understand or do not want to implement the new directives, they can safely ignore them. The protocol insists (with a MUST-level requirement) that unrecognized cache-control directives be ignored. At all times, the semantic transparency of the cache is the overriding factor.

Cache-control response directives   The cache-control response directives are a way for a server to ensure that caches in the path of the response behave in a particular way. The various cache-control response directives are listed in Table 7.13. The response directives permit the server to limit cacheability of responses. Control of caching ranges from whether a response can be cached at all to which part of the message can be cached and who has access to a cached response.

We examine the various cache-control response directives next.

- public: The control related to caching is mostly symmetrical in HTTP/1.1. Servers have as much control over cacheability of responses as clients. The server can specify the cacheability of a particular response, and such specifications have precedence over any default policy used by caches. For example, whereas a cache might decide not to store certain responses for fear of violating privacy, a server, by including the `Cache-Control: public` response header, can indicate that this particular response may be cached.

- `private`: The `private` response directive narrows the cacheability of the response to just a single user. The word "private" was probably not the best choice because this directive does not govern the privacy of the message in any way. The designers were looking for an antonym for "shared," because the `private` directive prevents a shared cache from storing the response. Additionally, the specification of `private` can be narrowed to just parts of the message rather than the entire message by adding a field name argument. For example, the inclusion of

```
Cache-Control: private = "CustomerID"
```

in the response would ensure that the contents of the `CustomerID` field alone are not stored in a public cache.

- `no-store`: The `no-store` response directive, similar to the request directive, is used to prevent the response from being cached. When this directive appears in a response, neither the request nor the response message must be stored in a cache.

- `no-cache`: Unlike the `no-store` directive, the `no-cache` directive does not prevent a response from being stored. However, the `no-cache` directive effectively prevents a response from being cached by forcing the cache to validate the response with the origin server before responding to a request. The primary purpose of this directive is to significantly lower the possibility of some caches returning stale responses. The response can still be cached, but the cache must guarantee the response's freshness by revalidating it. Although revalidation increases latency, network bandwidth could still be saved if the revalidation is successful.

A `no-cache` directive may be used with or without header field-names. If the directive includes one or more header field-names, the directive only applies to those header fields. For example, suppose the response is as follows:

```
HTTP/1.1 200 OK
Server: Apache/1.2.6 Red Hat
Date: Thu, 24 Feb 2000 18:13:36 GMT
Content-Type: text/html
Location: http://kinghascome.com/ads/elvis_has_left.gif
Cache-Control: no-cache=Location

   ...
```

The meaning of the `no-cache` response directive is relaxed in the presence of additional header fields in the directive. The rest of the contents of the response excluding the `Location` header may be reused, thus reducing bandwidth wastage and user-perceived latency. Yet, the origin server has a measure of control over the response. The cache must remove the Location header field before sending the response to the client. The origin server is able to have nuanced control over the resource without an all-or-nothing model for caching a response. Similarly, by using Cache-Control: no-cache=set-cookie2, the origin server can suppress the caching of the Set-Cookie2 header [KM00].

- no-transform: The no-transform response directive, similar to the request directive, is used to prevent a cache from altering the response (e.g., shrinking the resolution of an image resource).

- must-revalidate: The must-revalidate directive allows an origin server to indicate that for certain responses it might be too risky for a cache to return potentially stale values. The directive forces the cache to revalidate the resource with the origin server. More importantly, if the proxy is unable to revalidate with the origin server (e.g., if the proxy is unable to reach the origin server), the cache must return an error instead of a stale response to the client. The difference between the must-revalidate directive and the seemingly similar no-cache directive is that caches are not likely to cache responses that include the no-cache response directive. If the response includes a must-revalidate directive, the response can be cached, but it must be revalidated upon becoming stale. A no-cache directive forces the cache to validate regardless of when the response becomes stale. In practice, because caches are not likely to store responses that include a no-cache directive, a request for such an entity will translate to a retrieval from the origin server and not just a revalidation. Using must-revalidate saves bandwidth compared with using the no-cache directive. However, a user using a shopping basket in an e-commerce application would prefer to either know the precise contents or receive an error message rather than a stale value.

Suppose a cache is dependent on the next-hop server for a response and does not receive the response after a certain amount of time. If this would cause the cache to disobey the must-revalidate directive, then the cache is obligated to generate the new HTTP/1.1 response code 504 Gateway Timeout (as in the case of the only-if-cached directive). The server can select the specific timeout period. The 504 Gateway Timeout is a more meaningful response than the generic 500 Internal Server Error.

The cache-control response directive no-store is to ensure that a request-response is not even stored, whereas no-cache may result in storage but ensures no stale responses are returned. The must-revalidate directive may result in a response being stored, but it ensures that a stale response is revalidated. However, a response considered fresh by a cache may have actually changed on the origin server. This distinction is crucial in order to understand the need for both no-cache and must-revalidate directives. The no-store directive precludes caching entirely. With no-cache, there is a possibility of caching but no risk of returning a response that has changed. With `must-revalidate`, there is a real possibility of caching and no possibility of staleness, though there is potential for returning a response that has changed.

- `proxy-revalidate`: The `proxy-revalidate` response directive is less restrictive than the `must-revalidate` directive. Whereas the latter applies to all caches, the `proxy-revalidate` does not apply to nonshared user agent caches. A user agent cache (unlike a proxy's cache) can return a cached response without having to revalidate. Some actions, such as authentication, can be done safely by a user-agent cache once and remembered. However, a shared cache implies potential of multiple users, and thus actions done on behalf of one user may not apply to another. Consequently, revalidation of responses in shared caches may be required. Such finer-grain level of control in caching is typical of the improvements in HTTP/1.1.

- `max-age`: The `max-age` response directive is the preferred way to specify the expiration time of an entity. The presence of a `Cache-Control: max-age` response directive overrides any value in the `Expires` header when calculating the freshness lifetime of a cached response. This is an example of a new feature of HTTP/1.1 to provide greater flexibility to newer components: an HTTP/1.1 cache that receives a `max-age` directive would adhere to the expiration time, whereas an HTTP/1.0 cache would ignore the `max-age` directive.

- `s-maxage`: The `s-maxage` header applies to shared caches only and is used to override both `Expires` and `max-age` directives' values. As discussed previously, shared caches are obligated to revalidate a response with an expired `s-maxage`.

- *extension tokens:* Cache-control response directives can also have new tokens defined and used by participating caches.

THE ETAG HEADER

Entity tags (`ETag`) were introduced in HTTP/1.1 primarily as an opaque validator [Mog95] for comparing a cached entry against a possibly newer version. A given resource may have different versions, and each version will have a distinct entity tag. An entity tag is always associated with a specific resource and should not be used to compare across different resources. The construction of an entity tag is deliberately opaque in the sense that recipients should not be required to infer anything by examining the entity tag string.

The guarantee offered by an entity tag is simple: If there are different entities associated with the same resource, the entity tags differ. Consequently, for the same resource, if entity tags are identical, the versions of the resources can be considered identical.

Entity tags decouple cache validation (ensuring that the cached resource is still fresh) from expiration (whereby a server explicitly sets a time after which the resource cannot be considered fresh). Also, resources, when they change, may not always have an entirely new value: some versions of a resource may have existed in the past. The problem of nonsynchronous clocks (on the cache and server machines) and the fact that some resources may revert to an earlier version were not given serious consideration before the introduction of entity tags. Being able to reliably identify versions of resources below the one-second granularity was another motivating factor.

A response for a resource `foo.html` could include an entity tag, as follows:

```
HTTP/1.1 200 OK
Date: Sun, 26 Dec 26 1999 18:12:26 GMT
Server: Apache/1.2.6 Red Hat
Last-Modified: Fri, 24 Dec 1999 06:21:42 GMT
ETag: cc678-12d12-66394036
Content-Length: 15044
Content-Type: text/html
...
<contents of foo.html>
```

HTTP/1.1 takes into account the fact that multiple versions of resources exist and a request could be made for any of them. The new request modifiers in HTTP/1.1 `If-Match` and `If-None-Match` use entity tags. Specifically, these request modifiers can be used along with entity tags to indicate interest in specific versions of a resource. The `If-Match` request modifier lets the client specify one or more entity tags to see if they match the current variant on the server. For example, a sender using the `PUT` method to update a resource might use a conditional `PUT` specifying the version of the resource it wants to change, to make sure that the resource has not changed meanwhile. If the resource has a different version, the attempt would fail and the server would return a `412 Precondition Failed` status code.

For example, suppose a client sends the following request:

```
PUT /big.html HTTP/1.1
If-Match: "er82s1poy", "weoi2re"

<new contents for big.html>
```

The server would compare the entity tag for the current version of `big.html` to see if it matches either "er82s1poy" or "weoi2re." If the entity tag matched either of them, the server would perform the requested method. In this case, the requested method would result in updating the version of `big.html` that matched the entity tag. If neither of the entity tags in the request matches the current version, the server would *not* perform the request. Instead it would send back a 412 `Precondition Failed` response status code.

The new `If-None-Match` request-header can also be used with entity tags. A good use of this header is preventing a method from accidentally modifying an existing resource. For example, including an `If-None-Match: *` header with a `PUT` method ensures that the request will not succeed if the resource existed.

The HTTP/1.1 specification distinguishes between *strong* and *weak* entity tags. A strong entity tag changes whenever entities are not byte equivalent, that is, if the two entities differ in the slightest. However, an origin server may change a strong entity tag even when the bytes of the variant do not. A weak entity tag, on the other hand, changes only when there is a semantic difference. A weak entity tag is expected to not change if the origin server does not believe there is a semantic difference between the variants.

Unlike in HTTP/1.0, 201 `Created` responses in HTTP/1.1 can include an entity tag. The `ETag` response header included with a 201 `Created` response has the entity tag of the variant that was created (often as a result of a `POST` request).

THE VARY HEADER

When a response is cached in HTTP/1.0, the URI is used as the key to store and retrieve the response from the cache. However, multiple representations of the same resource make the URI an inadequate key. Content negotiation permits the choice of response based not just on cached content but on the representation choices (such as language and character set). If negotiated responses are cached, the cache must select from the variants. The `Vary` response header is used to list a set of request headers that should be used to select the appropriate variant from a cached set.

The server specifies what criteria must be used to choose the appropriate variant. For example, consider an origin server that sends the following response:

```
HTTP/1.1 200 OK
Date: Sun, 26 Dec 26 1999 18:12:26 GMT
Server: Apache/1.2.6 Red Hat
Last-Modified: Fri, 24 Dec 1999 06:21:42 GMT
ETag: cc678-12d12-66394036
Content-Length: 15044
Content-Type: text/html
Vary: Accept-Language
```

A cache caching this response must also store the value in the request headers listed in the `Vary` response header (`Accept-Language` in this example). If a subsequent request made to the cache is about to yield a cached response, the cache must ensure that all the headers in that request that are listed in the `Vary` header are identical to what were in the original request. Thus, if the original request, which resulted in the response with the `Vary` header, had

> `Accept-Language: en-us`

then in order for the cache to return the cached response for a subsequent request, that subsequent request must have `Accept-Language: en-us`. If a subsequent request has

> `Accept-Language: en-cockney`

then the cache cannot return the cached response and instead must forward the request to the origin server.

7.4 Bandwidth Optimization

Shortly after the Web began to grow in popularity, the following factors led to the dramatic increase in bandwidth usage on the network:

- Resource sizes began to grow and images became much more common. The sizes of image resources were often larger than textual ones.
- Images were often embedded in a text document. A typical page averaged nearly a dozen embedded images.
- Many more users were on the Web, with increasingly better connectivity to the net.
- A popular browser in the mid-1990s, Netscape, used multiple connections to download resources in parallel.

The need to save bandwidth led to examining the various ways in which a resource could be transformed, reduced, or not sent at all. The three categories of changes to HTTP related to optimizing bandwidth are as follows:

- If the entire resource need not be transmitted (e.g., if the user was only interested in portions of a resource), this would save bandwidth. The protocol needed to support ways to specify the necessary parts of a resource and transmit them.
- If the sender knew *a priori* that the receiver could not handle the message body, it would be best not to send the resource at all. Exchange of control information that could verify this would be a way of eliminating transmission of unnecessary bits.
- One way to save bandwidth is to transform the resource before sending and reconstruct it faithfully on the receiving end. The transformation would preferably reduce the size of the resource before sending.

The new *range request* mechanism was introduced to address the first of the three categories outlined above. The *Expect/Continue* mechanism addresses the second, and compression addresses the third. We examine each of these three ways by which HTTP/1.1 attempts to help minimize bandwidth usage.

7.4.1 Range request

Users' network connectivity has not kept pace with the popularity of the Web. Many users had (and still have) low-bandwidth connections to the Internet. The slow downloading of resources led to frustration on the part of users, who often aborted connections in progress with only portions of resources downloaded. If there was a caching proxy in the path between the origin server and the client, or if there was caching at the browser level, the partially downloaded portion of the resource would have been cached. However, a new request for the same resource would result in the full download of the resource. This wasted bandwidth and increased overall latency.

The original suggestion [Din95] for range requests was made in early 1995 as improvements over FTP and cited two specific reasons: (1) avoiding complete transfers when resuming from an interrupted long transfer and (2) clients might be interested in only part of a document. Resumption from interrupted transfers was already possible in FTP. The more interesting distinction between FTP and HTTP was that FTP was rarely used to transfer dynamically generated documents. If the transfer of a dynamically generated response was aborted, the response would have to be regenerated, adding to the latency. In the latter case, specific files could be extracted from archived collections of files (which are quite common on the Internet). Before this suggestion, experimental servers had already implemented such features [Fra95].

Requesting only portions of a resource can be useful in other situations. For example, user agents can selectively request a particular part in the middle of a potentially large resource without downloading the earlier and later portions. Users are not always interested in the entire resource. For example, if a resource is continuously growing, users may only be interested in the new portion. Or if the resource is a structured document (say, a book with chapters, sections, pages, etc.), selective requests for a part of the resource is a natural user expectation.

Some media types can use range request effectively and easily; Adobe's Portable Document Format (PDF), for example, indicates the start and end byte locations of each of the pages in the document. A client could establish multiple parallel connections and fetch different pages simultaneously and reconstruct the resource.

In fact, the need for browsers to be able to retrieve subranges in Adobe's PDF documents was one of the driving forces behind the proposal of range requests in its final form [FL95].

These problems can be solved if requesters (i.e., user agents or proxies) are able to indicate the specific portions of the resource of interest to them. The ability to specify interest in parts of a resource is provided by the HTTP/1.1 *range request* mechanism.

For example, using a Range header, a client can specify that it is interested in the byte range 2000-3999, and even if the entire resource is 100,000 bytes, only 2000 bytes are sent by the server. For example:

```
GET bigfile.html HTTP/1.1
Host: www.justwhatiwant.com
Range: 2000-3999
```

The GET method is thus modified to request only portions of a resource.

The following request would result in a response from a server capable of handling range requests:

```
HTTP/1.1 206 Partial Content
Date: Thu, 10 Feb 2000 20:02:06 GMT
Last-Modified: Wed, 9 Feb 2000 14:58:08 GMT
Content-Range: bytes 2000-3999/100000
Content-Length: 2000
Content-Type: text/html
```

The Content-Range entity header (new in HTTP/1.1) helps the recipient place the partial body being included in the proper place inside the full entity.

The 206 Partial Content response code indicates to the client that the response received is not a full response. The client can also request just the last N bytes of a resource by indicating it is interested in the *suffix* of the resource. For example, the following request seeks just the last 1000 bytes of the resource:

```
GET bigfile.html HTTP/1.1
Host: www.justwhatiwant.com
Range: -1000
```

If the client did not know the current size of the resource but had the initial portion cached, a range request could still be issued. For example, to get all the bytes of the resource after byte position 9120 in the resource, the client could send the following request:

```
GET bigfile.html HTTP/1.1
Host: www.justwhatiwant.com
Range: 9120-
```

A set of ranges, rather than just a single range, can be requested. The reason for wanting request sets of ranges is obvious: once a client knows specific and distinct portions of a resource that it wants, it can request all of them in a single request and the server can send them as a multipart response. The server uses a different media type for such a response—*multipart/byteranges*. Such a media type includes two or more parts, and each of the parts includes its own `Content-Range` header indicating the byte range of that part.

The syntax to retrieve sets of ranges is flexible. The sets of ranges are specified with commas separating them. A client wanting a set of ranges would send a request as follows:

```
GET bigfile.html HTTP/1.1
Host: www.justwhatiwant.com
Range: 0-100, 2000-2400, 9600-
```

The response would be the first 101 bytes, 401 bytes in the middle of the resource, and all bytes after byte position 9600. The response would appear as follows:

```
HTTP/1.1 206 Partial Content
Date: Thu, 10 Feb 2000 20:25:23 GMT
Server: Apache/1.2.6 Red Hat
Last-Modified: Fri, 24 Dec 1999 06:21:42 GMT
ETag: cc678-12d12-66394036
Content-type: multipart/byteranges; boundary=----ROPE----

----ROPE----
Content-Type: text/html
Content-Range: bytes 0-100/15044
...the first 101 bytes of the resource...
----ROPE----
Content-Type: text/html
Content-Range: bytes 2000-2400/15044
...401 bytes from middle of the resource...
----ROPE----
Content-Type: text/html
Content-Range: bytes 9600-15043/15044
...all bytes after byte 9600 of the resource...
----ROPE------
```

The separator string (----ROPE----) is referred to as the *boundary* string and is used to separate the various ranges. The message is terminated with the boundary string with two extra dashes. The `multipart/byteranges` media type is self-delimiting and does not require servers to provide the content length.

HTTP/1.1 introduced `416 Requested Range Not Satisfiable` response to handle range requests made on byte ranges when none of the ranges could be returned from the current resource. For example, if a client issued a request

```
GET /small.html HTTP/1.1
```

```
Host: www.justwhatiwant.com
Range: 10000-12000, 14000-19000
```

for a resource `small.html` smaller than 10000 bytes, the `416 Requested Range Not Satisfiable` status code would be returned. Along with this response code, the current length of the resource is sent back as follows:

```
HTTP/1.1 416 Requested Range Not Satisfiable
Content-Length: 9600
```

HTTP/1.1 does not mandate that servers be able to handle range requests, though it is suggested that they should do so if possible. A server capable of accepting byte range requests for a resource can indicate its capability via a

```
Accept-Ranges: bytes
```

response header. However, it is possible for clients to make a range request without ever having seen such a response header from a server for a resource. A server unable to handle range requests simply returns a full response and a `200 OK` response code. Servers can use the `Accept-Ranges` header to indicate unwillingness to accept any form of ranges for a resource by stating

```
Accept-Ranges: none
```

Clients would know not to send requests for partial entity bodies.

The syntax of the range request evolved over time. Initially, a syntax for specifying byte ranges as part of the URL was proposed. For example,

```
http://www.halfway-svc.com/partial/firstpage;byterange=0-49
```

would be a way to request the first 50 bytes of the resource identified by `http://www.halfway-svc.com/partial/firstpage` and

```
http://www.halfway-svc.com/partial/firstpage;byterange=1500-
```

would be used to request all but the first 1500 bytes of the resource.

However, because retrieving parts of a resource concerns *transporting* bytes and not *naming* of the resource, this is not an appropriate syntax for the partial requests mechanism. Also, some caching proxies used the URL as a key for storing responses, and having range information embedded in the URL would cause problems. Manipulating the URL implies that servers that could not handle range requests would have to return a failure response, rather than, say, the entire response. Instead, by adding a new header, servers that do not understand byte ranges can ignore the header but still send a success code and the full response. The care with which extensions are constructed in a protocol is reflected in the ability to handle such design questions.

The range request can be intelligently combined with conditional requests. Suppose a range request has been made for a resource in a cache, but the full range is not part of the cached entry. It is possible that the resource has not changed on the origin server, in which case it might be enough for the cache to obtain the missing part. However, if the resource has changed on the origin server, the entire resource must be obtained. Typically this would require two requests: one to ensure that the resource has not changed and another with a range request if it has not changed. To accomplish this task in a single request, HTTP/1.1 provides a new header field—If-Range. The semantics of the If-Range header are as follows: If the resource has changed, the full resource is returned in the response; otherwise, only the requested byte ranges are sent back. The If-Range header specifies the variant of the resource against which the conditional request is evaluated.

For example, consider the following request:

```
GET bigfile.html HTTP/1.1
Accept-Language: en-us
Accept-Encoding: gzip, deflate
Range: bytes=1300-1500
If-Range: cc678-12d12-66394036
User-Agent: Mozilla
Host: www.notonline.com
```

If the entity tag of the resource on the origin server matches the entity tag present in the If-Range header, the server would just send back the 201 bytes in the requested range 1300-1500, or else it would send the entire resource.

The new response header If-Unmodified-Since in HTTP/1.1 can be used in conjunction with range requests to obtain portions of a resource, *only* if the resource has not changed. For example, the client request

```
GET /ads/game03.gif?0CYES HTTP/1.1
Host: www.theads.com
Range: bytes=8353-
If-Unmodified-Since: Tue, 26 Oct 1999 10:54:20 GMT
```

is used to obtain all bytes of the resource /ads/game03.gif?0CYES starting from byte position 8353, if it has not changed since the specified date. If the resource has changed, the client would want the full range. If the resource has not changed since the specified date, the server could respond as follows:

```
HTTP/1.1 206 Partial content
Server: Microsoft-IIS/3.0
Date: Wed, 27 Oct 1999 18:17:29 GMT
Content-Type: image/gif
Last-Modified: Tue, 26 Oct 1999 09:54:20 GMT
Content-Length: 14255
Content-Range: bytes 8353-22607/22608
```

Table 7.14. Examples of range requests in a 1000-byte resource

Range syntax	Interpretation
100-300	201 bytes from 100 to 300
10-30, 50-100, 300-600	373 bytes from 10 to 30, 50-100, and 300-600
920-950, 951-1000	81 bytes from 920 to 1000
920-970, 951-1000	81 bytes from 920 to 1000
920-	81 bytes from 920 to 1000
-450	Last 450 bytes from 551 to 1000
0-0, 1000-1000	First and last byte
0-0, -1	First and last byte
950-1100	Illegal range (exceeds 1000)
950-900	Illegal range (first byte offset greater than last)

Table 7.14 presents a variety of range requests that can be issued on a 1000-byte-long resource. The syntax of range requests is quite flexible. Table 7.14 shows how to request single or multiple ranges, all bytes after a particular byte position, specific number of bytes from the end, and so on. Examples of illegal ranges, whereby a server cannot unambiguously extract the requested bytes, are also presented.

The initial idea of byte ranges [FL95] went beyond simple byte ranges and suggested ways of requesting lines in a document or chapters in a book, that is, ranges were meant to be independent of document type. Although the current standard for HTTP/1.1 permits only byte range requests, in the future, this might be extended to more semantically significant ranges. For example, one could imagine requesting sections of a book, segments of audio resources or movie clips. The protocol leaves open the possibility for such extensions in the future. In fact, the Real Time Streaming Protocol (RTSP [SRL98]) permits range requests based on time units instead of bytes, as discussed in Chapter 12 (Section 12.4).

7.4.2 The Expect/Continue mechanism

If an HTTP server is unable to handle large requests, it would be useful for the client to know about this *before* the request is sent. A client would benefit by knowing its expectation would be met before sending large requests. Consider the example of a Web server's handling of large PUT or POST forms. Although there is no protocol-specified limit on the size of the included entity body, Web servers have their own internal ceiling based on handling and storage limitations. However, by the time the user agent learns that the server is going to reject a (potentially large) request, it is too late. The user may have spent considerable effort and time in filling the form. User agents may have an estimate of typical sizes of completed forms. Additionally, once the request has been sent, bandwidth has been wasted. A mechanism whereby the user agent can know the possible limitations of a server before submitting a (large) request body would thus be useful for the client and save potentially wasted bandwidth.

The **Expect** mechanism provides precisely such a solution. It lets the client know whether the server would be able to meet the expectation of the client with respect to the particular request. If the server can meet the desired expectation and handle the request, it can indicate this using the 100 `Continue` response. A server unable to handle the request can send a suitable response code based on the specific inability in handling the request. If the request is too long, the server could send a 413 `Request Entity Too Large`. If the client was forbidden to make the request, the server could send a 403 `Forbidden`. If the server receives an unexpected **Expect** token or if it knows that its upstream server will not be able to handle the **Expect** mechanism, it sends the 417 `Expectation Failed` status code response. The response is sent before any request body is actually sent to the origin server.

For example, consider the following request, sent with an **Expect** header. The client indicates that it plans to send a 23248-bytes-long request body.

```
POST /foo/bar HTTP/1.1
Content-Length: 23248
Expect: 100-Continue
```

The server could send the following:

```
HTTP/1.1 100 Continue
```

indicating that it believes it can handle the request, and so the client could go ahead and send the (large) entity body on the already open connection. If the server does not believe it could handle such a request, it would send the following and may close the connection:

```
HTTP/1.1 417 Expectation Failed
```

Clients may include additional values with an expectation header. For example, a client might send the authentication information of the user issuing the request. If the server accepts the authentication, it would send the 100 `Continue` response and the client could send the body of the request message, as follows:

```
POST /secure.txt HTTP/1.1
Host: www.topsecret.org
Authorization: Basic ZGufaWP6J29atWU=
Expect: 100-Continue
```

If the server sends back the interim response code

```
HTTP/1.1 100 Continue
```

the client can continue with the request. If the server instead sends back

```
HTTP/1.1 401 Authorization Failed
```

the rest of the request would not be sent. The client would have to either send a new authorization value or not send the request.

Examining how a protocol is used in practice is one way for protocol designers to further develop the protocol. The usefulness of some of the features of the protocol may be unclear, and thus actual usage data on earlier versions of the protocol can help in protocol revision. Unfortunately, several incompatible versions of so-called HTTP/1.1 implementations existed already, making it necessary for the protocol specification to be more tolerant in dealing with the Expect mechanism. It is possible for a client that sends an `Expect:` `100-Continue` header to wait forever for a `417 Expectation Failed` or a `100` `Continue` response. To avoid this, the client should be able to time out and send the request body after a certain period of time (the actual timeout period may vary with the client implementation). The protocol prohibits a client from having to wait an indefinite amount of time, although it does not specify a timeout period. A client thus uses a probabilistic timeout rather than a deterministic timeout period.

The Expect mechanism is hop-by-hop. Expectation is only up to the next hop, and if the next hop server cannot meet the expectation, that server should return a `417 Expectation Failed` failure status code. However, the `Expect` request header is an end-to-end header. If the next-hop server (say, a proxy) does forward the request because it is not able to handle the request itself, the `Expect` request-header must also be sent along.

Even though the `Expect` mechanism was introduced to handle long request bodies associated with `PUT` and `POST` methods, it can be used in the future for other extensions. Servers that do not (yet) understand the new extensions are obligated to send back the `417 Expectation Failed` response status code. A possible extension of the `Expect` mechanism is an improvement to the negotiation scheme of HTTP/1.1.

It is interesting to note that the `Expect` header was introduced not as a client-driven expectation but to deal with a problem associated with the `100` `Continue` response. The `100 Continue` response was proposed almost two years before the introduction of the `Expect` header. The `100 Continue` response was introduced to enable a server to send an interim response code if it wanted to continue reading input from a client. The client may have a legitimate reason not to send its entity body before ensuring that the origin server would accept its request. If the origin server did not want to continue reading, it could send an error response. For example, if a client's `POST` request included a `Content-Length` header and the server knew it could not handle a request of that size, it could send back an error response. If it was able to handle the request, it could send a 100 `Continue` response. This, however, requires the client to pause before continuing to send the entity body. However, a sender could wait for a very long time before realizing that the server was not going to send a 100 `Continue` or an error response. An initial proposal was to have a five-second timeout, but soon it was realized that any arbitrary time for pausing by the client would not work in all cases. More importantly, HTTP/1.0 clients would not be able to understand a 100 `Continue` response because it was defined only in HTTP/1.1.

To avoid problems such as these, the `Expect` header was added, making a 100 `Continue` response possible *only* when the `Expect` header was present. Not all clients have to wait for a 100 `Continue` response. The final rules for HTTP/1.1 clients and servers include the following: a client has to send an `Expect` header if it intends to wait for a 100 `Continue` response and a server must send either a 100 `Continue` or a final error response. If the client has never received a 100 `Continue` response from an origin server in the past, the client does not have to wait for an indefinite amount of time and could go ahead and send the request body.

7.4.3 Compression

A good way to conserve bandwidth is to compress the response in a manner acceptable to the receiver. Compression has been used in many application-level protocols and was part of HTTP/1.0. Several popular image data formats are precompressed. For example, GIF and JPEG are popular image formats, and their data representation format is already compressed. Compressing such resources again is not likely to be very useful. However, many other responses that are typically stored in uncompressed format (e.g., ASCII text) can be compressed by the origin server before transmission. Likewise, clients including large entity bodies in their requests could compress the entities. It might even be feasible to compress the request and response headers, but the benefit of such compression is not clear given the intermediaries in the path. HTTP does not perform header compression.

Content codings were available in HTTP/1.0 (via the `Content-Encoding` entity header) and indicated how the resource was transformed on an end-to-end basis. Because HTTP/1.0 did not distinguish between hop-by-hop and end-to-end mechanisms, it was not possible to provide compression on a hop-by-hop basis. Suppose two intermediate servers understand a good compression algorithm that took less time to compress and provided better compression than other algorithms. These servers might want to use this algorithm to encode the message on the connection between them. The other servers in the path between the sender and the recipient do not have to understand that algorithm. Also, if there was a choice between different compression algorithms, a server might want to express a preference. Both of these are possible in HTTP/1.1.

The *transfer-coding* mechanism is a hop-by-hop mechanism to indicate the transformations applied to the entity body. Just as a client can include the `Accept-Encoding` header to indicate what content codings are acceptable, it can use a `TE` request header to indicate the transfer-codings it prefers. For example,

$$\texttt{TE: vdcomp;q=0.9, compress;q=0.1}$$

means that the sender is willing to accept `vdcomp` transfer coding with a (high) quality value of 0.9 and `compress` with a (low) quality value of 0.1. The client's choices of quality values (0.9 for `vdcomp` and 0.1 for `compress`) may be driven by several reasons, such as the availability of such programs and the speed of these algorithms. A server receiving such a request would not pick any algorithm for which the client specified a `qvalue` of 0 (i.e., viewed as unacceptable by the client) and would try to pick the highest quality value specified in the request. The choice expressed in the request is a preference—there is no guarantee that the server is able to oblige. In the above example, a server might choose a cached value in `compress` representation, ignoring the fact that the requester may prefer a `vdcomp` representation. A server unable or unwilling to comply with the specific transfer coding does not transform the response. The `TE` header applies only to the immediate connection, and thus any two servers who understand the `vdcomp` compression mechanism can benefit by including this header.

7.5 Connection Management

Virtually all known implementations of HTTP use TCP as the transport protocol. However, TCP was *not* optimized for the typical short-lived connections common in an HTTP message exchange. The use of TCP as transport protocol required a three-way handshake to establish the connection and another four packets to close the connection (Chapter 5, Section 5.2.3). An HTTP message would often fit in 10 packets. Thus, 7 out of 17 packets are overhead. This also meant that Web transfers never got past the TCP slow-start phase [Jac88] (discussed in Chapter 5, Section 5.2). Before the TCP window size could be increased significantly, the connection was closed, implying that the available bandwidth was never fully used.

As the Web grew in popularity, Web pages began to include embedded images. Downloading a *container* document—that is, text and images combined— required several HTTP transactions and thus multiple TCP connections. Before the full document could be displayed, the user experienced delay as a result of each of the serialized connections. One popular early browser (Mosaic) had such an implementation. One way to reduce the latency was the introduction of parallel HTTP connections. First used by Netscape, up to four connections were opened in parallel to download the images, thus speeding up the downloading of the complete document. However, this added to the overall network congestion, and the server had to pay the overhead of accepting multiple TCP connections.

Another way to solve the problem was to examine whether the TCP connection, once established, could stay open beyond a single request-response exchange. This led to the introduction of *persistent connections* in HTTP/1.1. The basic idea behind persistent connections was reducing the number of TCP connections opened and closed. With each reduced TCP setup and teardown, the number of packets on the network is reduced, which in turn reduces congestion. Giving additional time to a TCP connection helps it to learn about the congestion state of the network. More packets can be sent if there is less congestion, and a sender can ensure that it does not contribute to congestion by sending too many packets. Subsequent responses on the same connection benefit from the lowered congestion. Also, user-perceived latency is significantly reduced because the subsequent requests do not have to pay the penalty of delay of teardown of the previous connection, the setup delay of the new connection, or the repeating of the TCP slow-start phase each time. Errors with a request can be reported on the same connection without having to close the TCP connection.

In this section we trace the evolution of the persistent connection mechanism in HTTP to its current standardized state:

- Section 7.5.1 examines the older `Keep-Alive` mechanism in some of the implementations of HTTP/1.0.
- Section 7.5.2 looks at a few early suggestions for persistent connections in HTTP/1.1, as well as the multiple parallel connections approach that had already become popular. The goals of the persistent connection mechanism that was actually introduced in HTTP/1.1 are then examined.
- Section 7.5.3 examines the role of the `Connection` header in HTTP/1.1 persistent connections, especially with regard to the header's flexibility in keeping connections open or in closing them.
- Section 7.5.4 examines the role of pipelining on a persistent connection and issues related to unexpected closings of connections in the middle of handling a set of pipelined requests.
- Section 7.5.5 explores the decision clients and servers must make before closing a persistent connection. The protocol does not provide specific guidelines on how long a persistent connection should remain open.

The semantic changes regarding connection management are discussed in more depth because of its importance.

7.5.1 The `Connection: Keep-Alive` mechanism of HTTP/1.0

The ability to maintain HTTP connections beyond a single request-response was not originally a part of HTTP/1.0. However, as the popularity of the Web grew, some implementations of HTTP/1.0 introduced a form of persistent connection. Some browsers would include a `Keep-Alive` request header to request the connection to remain open past the current request. Servers willing to let the connection persist would honor this header and not close the connection after sending the response.

The `Keep-Alive` idea was similar to what became persistent connections in HTTP/1.1. A client interested in keeping the connection open would in effect request that the origin server not close the connection. This was done as follows:

```
GET /home.html HTTP/1.0
...
Connection: Keep-Alive
```

If the server was also interested in keeping the connection open, it would send a response, as follows:

```
HTTP/1.0 200 OK
...
Connection: Keep-Alive
...
<response body>
```

However, if an HTTP/1.0 server was transferring dynamic content, there was no way for the receiving client to detect the end of the response without the server closing the connection. Dynamically generated content typically does not include a `Content-Length` header because waiting to compute the length of the content would add latency to the client.

Simple extensions permitted the server to indicate (via header fields) how long the connection would stay open after the last request on that connection or the maximum number of requests that will be handled on a single connection. A client could examine the header fields and decide not to send more than a certain number of requests on that persistent connection.

7.5.2 Evolution of HTTP/1.1 persistent connection mechanism

Various attempts were made to make HTTP connections persist beyond a single request-response sequence, before the introduction of the current persistent connection mechanism in HTTP/1.1. They can be classified into two broad approaches: (1) new HTTP methods that could be used to get more than one resource and (2) using multiple parallel connections to fetch resources. The first approach included variations on a multiple `GET` mechanism related by the desire to support multiple requests on the same transport connection. The second approach explicitly advocated using different transport connections in parallel to fetch a group of resources. The mechanism that was standardized as the persistent connection mechanism in HTTP/1.1 began as an attempt to avoid having to make multiple parallel connections.

New HTTP methods approach: MGET, GETLIST, GETALL The first approach proposed new HTTP methods for sending multiple requests on the same transport connection. The three main proposals were MGET, GETLIST, and GETALL. None of these proposals survived the protocol evolution process and are not part of HTTP/1.1. However, it is useful to examine the design alternatives that were proposed.

The suggestion for introducing a new method, MGET, was made in [Fra94a, Fra94b]. MGET is similar to FTP's mget command whereby multiple files matching a particular pattern could be fetched via a single command on an open FTP connection. In FTP, an *mget* did require multiple data connections, that is, separate TCP connections. The proposed HTTP MGET method avoided the need for multiple TCP connections by listing a set of resources of interest in the request. The complete request would then be handled serially by the origin server. The following example of an MGET request, adapted from [Fra94a], lists multiple URIs along with request modifiers:

```
MGET HTTP/1.0
URI: /image1.gif
URI: /image2.gif
If-Modified-Since:  Saturday 29-Oct-94 20:04:01 GMT
URI: /image3.gif
CRLF
```

A server would reply to the MGET request by sending the responses to each of the resource requests preceded by the resource's size and a distinct content encoding that enabled proper parsing of the response by the receiving client:

```
HTTP/1.0 200 OK
URI: /image1.gif
Content-Type: image/gif
CRLF
2200
... 2200 bytes consisting of image data
CRLF
HTTP/1.0 304 Not Modified
URI: /image2.gif
CRLF
HTTP/1.0 200 OK
URI: /image3.gif
```

```
Content-Type: image/gif
CRLF
7180
... 7180 bytes consisting of image data
CRLF
```

The client would read each response up till the CRLF and extract the different responses. Obviously, obviating the need for establishing several sequential connections to send requests results in reduced latency and network costs.

The MGET suggestion arose in the context of discussions of obtaining a page along with its embedded images. With information about the layout of the images, a browser could start rendering the page while the contents of the images were still being downloaded. However, a browser requiring just the image layout information (which requires considerably less bandwidth) could obtain it via language or server support. For example, information could be included about inline images in the HTML source of the container document. However, this would require the protocol to know about a particular content type (HTML), which is not desirable. Alternatively, the server could include this information in a response header. However, dependence on the Web server is troublesome because the server may not always be able to provide the necessary information. For example, the images may not all reside on the same origin server as the enclosing document.

GETLIST and GETALL [PM95] are similar in spirit to MGET. Using GETLIST, a client could request a specified list of resources. To request all resources (the container document and all its embedded resources), the GETALL method would be used. The single request method GETALL would automatically transfer the entire document without requiring separate GET requests. One advantage of GETLIST over GETALL was that the client could be selective about which of the embedded resources it requested. A container document may have the same resource embedded multiple times, and it might not make sense to request such a resource more than once.

Simultaneous parallel connections approach   An alternative approach to using the same connection to fetch several resources simultaneously is the use of multiple parallel connections. A browser could open *several* connections in parallel and download each of the embedded images separately but simultaneously. An early version of the Netscape browser implemented parallel connections in 1994. Taking a limited view of the Web experience purely in terms of user-perceived latency, such an approach might be warranted. Although the user would feel that the data is being downloaded rather quickly, there is a downside to this approach: opening several connections in parallel imposes a considerable load on the network. There are a lot of packets because of the TCP setup and teardown that add to the congestion in the network. If too many clients started using parallel connections and in effect acquired as much bandwidth as they could, the result would be congestion. Additionally, there will be a spike in the load experienced by the server. If many clients requested resources containing embedded images from the same origin server, and each client used multiple parallel connections, the server might experience unacceptable load. The basic problem is that given the finite bandwidth, multiple connections in parallel by one client reduces the bandwidth that can be allocated to another client. In an attempt to grab more bandwidth, the multiple connections actually reduce the effective throughput.

However, there is a more serious drawback to the parallel connection approach because of requests that are aborted. Consider the following scenario: an origin server has a resource with a dozen embedded images, and the browser establishes several parallel connections to begin downloading them. If the user decided to abort the connection, all the parallel connections must be aborted. The considerable cost of establishing the connections has been paid already and is wasted.

Separate from aborted requests, parallel connections do not always improve the latency perceived by the user for downloading the original document. Each of the parallel retrievals is independent of the other, and each retrieval must separately pay the price of establishing a TCP connection and getting past the slow-start phase (as described in Chapter 5, Section 5.2.6).

Persistent connections in HTTP/1.1 With a variety of solutions being offered, an approach to providing persistent connections by letting the client and server indicate that connections could persist was designed and implemented [PM95]. This proposal can be divided into two parts: reusing existing transport connection and making some modest changes at the application (HTTP) level. The notion of reusing transport connection was similar to the earlier suggestions and had three goals:

- Reducing TCP connection costs (fewer setups and teardowns)
- Reducing latency by avoiding multiple TCP slow-starts
- Avoiding bandwidth wastage and reducing overall congestion

The suggested change at the HTTP level was modest. If several requests were sent on a persistent connection without having to wait for individual responses from the server, there could be additional reduction in latency. This is known as *pipelining* and is explained in Section 7.5.4. Separately, there can be a reduction in the overall number of connections if proxies used persistent connections. The needs of several individual clients could be met by fewer connections between a proxy and a server if the proxy maintained a persistent connection with the server.

A significant step in ensuring that persistent connections are deployed and used widely was the making of persistent connections the *default* in HTTP/1.1. In contrast, `Keep-Alive` was optional in the HTTP/1.0 implementations. The implementation of persistent connections is a SHOULD-level requirement in the HTTP/1.1 specification. Although nothing prevents a Web site administrator from turning persistent connections off as default, the protocol's SHOULD-level requirement increases the probability that administrators of compliant server implementations will leave persistent connections turned on as default. Web server administrators must take explicit action to turn off persistent connections in HTTP/1.1 server configurations. Because most sites tend to leave the default configuration as is, the benefits of persistent connection are likely to be available to more users.

The `GETALL` and `GETLIST` proposals developed into the persistent connection mechanism that became part of the HTTP/1.1 standard. None of the method suggestions (`MGET`, `GETALL`, etc.) survived the protocol finalization. Although multiple parallel connections are quite common, there is general acceptance that persistent connection with pipelining makes the most efficient use of network resources in achieving low user-perceived latency.

Another issue in dealing with persistent connections is the presence of proxies and caches. Should a connection persist on an end-to-end basis (between a client, a chain of proxies, and a server)? Care must be taken about proxies that run HTTP/1.0 and may not understand persistent connections. This issue is discussed in depth in Section 7.11.

7.5.3 The `Connection` header

Some implementations of HTTP/1.0 use the `Connection` header to indicate that a connection should be kept alive beyond a single request-response exchange. However, in HTTP/1.1, in keeping with a trend toward providing better control to both the sender and receiver, the `Connection` header could be used to indicate that one of the parties wanted to *close* the connection. The server might not want to maintain too many open persistent connections, or the sender (e.g., a proxy) might know that it had no further reason to keep a connection open with that particular server. Both sides could include a header `Connection: close` to indicate that they intended to close the present persistent connection independent of the wishes of the other side.

The `Connection` general header was described earlier as having a broader purpose: to list the set of headers that are meaningful only for the current transport-level connection to the next-hop server. In other words, a server receiving a `Connection` header would parse that header and remove all the headers listed in it. The `Connection: close` was introduced as a way to be compatible with the older (HTTP/1.0) form of persistent connections. Some implementations of HTTP/1.0 had included the `Connection: Keep-Alive` feature. Rather than invent a new header whose semantics overlapped with those of the Connection header, the HTTP/1.1 Connection mechanism absorbed Keep-Alive as one of many possible tokens that could appear in the Connection header. The notion of protecting a header (i.e., ensuring that the header was not forwarded by proxies) was retrofitted onto the existing Keep-Alive token as well. Because the default behavior in HTTP/1.1 is persistence, it is as if a Connection: Keep-Alive were included in each message. The problem in maintaining a persistent connection with proxies that do not understand Connection headers is discussed in Section 7.11.3.

7.5.4 Pipelining on persistent connections

The establishment of a persistent connection reduces the number of TCP setup and teardown packets. A client sending a request and waiting for a response before it sends the next request on the same persistent connection incurs additional latency. Instead, if the client could send a set of requests *without* waiting for the response (under the assumption that the requests will be handled in order), then the round-trip delay of waiting for each response is avoided. In fact, a key gain of the persistent connection mechanism is due to pipelining [Pad95].

For example, consider the requests for four images on the same persistent connection:

```
GET /foo1.jpg HTTP/1.1
CRLF
GET /foo2.jpg HTTP/1.1
CRLF
GET /foo3.jpg HTTP/1.1
CRLF
GET /foo4.jpg HTTP/1.1
CRLF
```

The example shows requests for four resources, foo1.jpg, foo2.jpg, foo3.jpg, and foo4.jpg, pipelined in a single HTTP connection. The client took advantage of the fact that it was going to request the four resources anyway and chose not to wait for each of the responses to be returned before sending the next request.

The requests over a persistent connection, whether pipelined or not, must be handled by the server in the order they were received. If the requests were not handled in order, the sender might not get the most recent value of a resource. The protocol specification suggests that only idempotent methods (Chapter 6, Section 6.2.2) should be used in sequence. For example, if a GET request followed an earlier PUT request, the expectation would be to receive the latest value for the resource (potentially changed by the PUT request). However, this assumes that both of the pipelined requests were processed without any interruption.

If the underlying transport connection was prematurely closed (say, because of an abort), the expectation might not be met.

HEAD OF LINE BLOCKING

If one of the earlier requests for a resource in the pipeline takes a considerable amount of time, the other requests on the same connection are going to be delayed. The problem is exacerbated when the server being contacted is a proxy that relays the pipelined requests to *different* origin servers. A pipelined request ahead in the queue may request a very large resource, and although the next request is to a different origin server and for a very small resource, it cannot be serviced until the first (long) request is handled. This is known as "head of line" blocking [Get97]. Thus, if a sender knows that earlier requests may take a significant amount of time, it should probably not pipeline the later requests behind the slower ones. A sender, however, might not always know how long a particular request might take.

Although it might be possible for a server to figure out a better order to send responses, avoiding head of line blocking in some cases, the protocol requires that responses be sent in the order of requests received. This is the easiest for the server to implement. Protocol specifications tend to err on the side of simplicity.

UNEXPECTED CLOSES IN A PIPELINED REQUEST STREAM

There are many ways in which an HTTP connection can be aborted. A user can explicitly abort the connection by clicking on the Stop button on a browser or by clicking ahead on a link while the page is being downloaded. The server can abort the connection if it believes its resources are being abused. A network failure can occur, causing the existing connection to terminate.

Persistent connections suffer from all the drawbacks related to aborted connections of simple requests but also introduce additional problems. In the case of a single request being aborted, the user can simply retry the request (if the user did not initiate the abort) or ignore the aborted request (especially if the user issued the abort). There is no state across requests, and an abort does not introduce state maintenance problems for safe methods such as GET and HEAD. However, in the case of PUT and POST, there might have been an attempt to update the server. Suppose a sequence of requests are pipelined and the user aborts the requests before all the responses arrive. The user agent has to determine how many requests had received a response and resend the other requests.

The protocol specifies that clients must be able to recover if the connection is closed for any reason. For example, the client may have to reopen the connection and send all the requests that were not fully handled. Normally, this is not a problem. However, if the requests had a certain semantic ordering (i.e., there is a dependency on the order in which the requests were processed), the user agent may need to consult the user and optionally reissue the aborted requests. For example, the part of the request stream that was processed may require the entire set of requests to be reissued.

The lack of communication between the transport layer and the application layer is the reason for the poor handling of aborts in the middle of a pipelined request stream. If there was a way in the HTTP layer to indicate aborts without closing the transport layer, then this problem would be avoided. But it would be a poor design for an application-layer protocol to have dependencies on a lower-layer protocol. This issue is discussed in more depth in Chapter 8 (Section 8.2.1).

7.5.5 Closing persistent connections

Once a persistent connection has been established, the natural question that arises is when to close the connection. The protocol does not play any role in this decision, leaving it to the individual components to decide. The only recommendation in the protocol is that the default mode of connection be persistent. This forces the client or server to explicitly choose not to keep the connection open. However, there are no recommendations relating to how long a connection should persist or how many requests a server should handle on a single open persistent connection before closing it.

Several competing interests must be resolved, as follows:

- A server may want to serve many different clients. Keeping a persistent connection open with a client might hinder the server's ability to serve other clients and provide fair access to all clients.
- A server may choose to handle more requests on the existing connection from a client because the client might just try to reestablish a new connection if the current connection is closed.
- A server might want to close a connection once a certain time limit has been reached, to ensure fairness. The time limit may apply to the total time the connection has remained open or the idle time between any two connections. This also prevents a client trying to get more than a fair share of the time of the origin server and the network bandwidth.
- A server might be communicating with a special client (or proxy) and want to have connections with such clients to persist longer than others; for example, it might want to differentiate service between clients.

These issues and others were discussed to a reasonable extent before the HTTP/1.1 version of the protocol was standardized. A variety of proposals were made that suggested the addition of parameters to a persistent connection (both in request and response). Among the options were:

- `timeout`: to indicate how long before a persistent connection will be closed
- `max`: to specify the maximum number of requests that would be handled on a given persistent connection
- `state`: to indicate which headers need to have their state stored

However, these additional parameters had problems. A timeout parameter did not make sense in a world where round-trip estimates were not known or where intermediate proxies might have to introduce their own values for the parameters. A timeout notion, even if optional, would remove control from the server of when to close the connection. For example, a client might optimistically use a large timeout value, hoping to keep the connection open for a long period of time. However, if the client then becomes idle and does not use the connection, the server must decide unilaterally when to close the connection. The `timeout` and `max` options were actually implemented in an early version of the NCSA server [Sin95]. Because each request was going to appear serially, knowing the maximum number of requests was not helpful (this was before pipelining was implemented). The `state` option was suggested to not have to resend headers that did not change with each message. The specific example used in proposing the `state` option was large `Accept` headers. But the `state` option adds significant overhead, and no one was able to quantify the advantages of savings resulting from maintaining state. Thus all these options were dropped from the persistent connection mechanism.

The specification is necessarily silent about how long a connection should be open. Each server might use its own heuristic to decide when to close a persistent connection. In fact, implementations of persistent connections in servers often take into consideration a collection of factors before deciding if a persistent connection should be closed.

HTTP/1.1 imposes specific requirements on certain methods in dealing with prematurely closed connections. For example, HTTP/1.1 requires that POST requests be able to recover from a premature close. The client must immediately stop transmitting the body of the message as soon as it learns that the connection has been closed. The client should retry the request if it has not seen a response status from the server. The retry can take place after a certain amount of time has passed and may be repeated a few times unless a error status code (4xx or 5xx) is received.

7.6 Message Transmission

A key goal in exchanging HTTP messages is to ensure that the parties recognize that they have received the full message without any loss. Transporting the message safely through the network is essential for maintaining integrity of the transaction. The length of a response is a useful indicator for a receiver to know when the full response has been received. The only mechanism by which HTTP/1.0 origin servers could indicate the size of the entity body was through the `Content-Length` field. The length of a static resource could be easily determined by its length (often by an operating system call). The origin server has to wait for a dynamically generated response to be fully generated before computing its length. The `Content-Length` header field cannot be filled until the entire response is generated. Thus the origin server could not start sending the response until this header field is filled. This requires buffering of the entire response, thus adding latency to the end user.

In HTTP/1.0, the server indicated the end of dynamic content by closing the connection. If closing the connection was the only way to indicate the end of response, persistent connections would not be possible. Thus an alternative way was needed to indicate the end of a message without closing the connection.

HTTP/1.1 solves the basic problem of safe message transmission by introducing a transfer-coding termed *chunked*, which lets a sender break a message body into arbitrary size *chunks* and ship them separately. Each chunk is preceded by the length of that chunk, enabling the receiver to ensure that it received the chunk fully. More importantly, the sender generates a zero-length chunk at the very end, and receipt of this indicates that the entire message has been transported safely. The chunking of the message obviates the need for arbitrarily large buffers that might be necessitated if a proxy is going to store the response before forwarding to an older (say, HTTP/1.0) client. It also eliminates the latency of waiting for the generation of the full response before addition of the `Content-Length` header (as discussed in Section 7.6).

Consider the following example of a response being encoded into chunks:

```
HTTP/1.1 200 OK
Server: Apache/1.2.7-dev
Date: Tue, 07 Jul 1998 18:21:41 GMT
Connection: Keep-Alive
Transfer-Encoding: chunked
Content-Type: text/html
691
        <...1681 bytes of chunk data...>
76
        <...118 bytes of chunk data...>
0
```

The `Transfer-Encoding` header (with a value of `chunked`) indicates to the recipient that the response is chunked and thus the response should be parsed differently from nonchunked responses. The chunked response in the examples has three chunks, the first of length 1681 bytes (which is 691 in hex, the required format for the length), preceded by a chunk-size indicator, followed by a chunk of 118 bytes (76 in hex), also preceded by the corresponding chunk-size indicator. Finally, a zero-length chunk (chunk-size indicator of 0, with no body following it) is found, which informs the recipient that the response has ended. The recipient verifies the length of the individual chunks and upon receiving the zero-length chunk knows that the full response has been safely received. In the case of dynamic responses, the server can send chunks as and when they are generated. This reduces latency by not having to wait for the full response to be generated before sending any part of it.

Chunking a message at the HTTP level has no bearing on how the transport layer may treat the HTTP message. A single chunk may span multiple packets, or multiple chunks may fit in a single packet. Chunking is a mechanism that is targeted purely at the application level. Both request and response messages can be chunk-encoded.

A response message that is chunk-encoded ends with a zero-length chunk. However, the message can be followed by an optional *trailer*. The trailer is separate from the body of the response, and a receiving server or user agent will know that the full body has been received before processing the trailer. The trailer in a chunked response can consist of only entity header fields and values. Suppose a response is dynamically generated and the sender needs to compute a digest of the full response (a digest can be thought of simply as a checksum). For example, a sender may want to include an integrity checksum (e.g., using the Message Digest algorithm MD5 [Riv92]) with the response, but until all the bytes of the response are processed, it would not be possible to generate the checksum. However, by deferring the MD5 header to the trailer of the response, the chunks of the response body could be sent as they are generated without increasing the latency. Similarly, the trailer could include `Authentication-Info` header as discussed in the Digest Authentication RFC [FHBH+99].

To warn recipients of the additional information present, a `Trailer` header is used to list the headers that are going to appear in the trailer of the message. Trailers can include both necessary and optional information. The willingness to accept trailers on the part of a client implicitly indicates that it will buffer all the information preceding the trailer if necessary. For example, an origin server could include some authentication information in the response, which could determine whether the receiving proxy should forward the response or not. However, this implies that the receiving proxy would have to buffer the entire response. In keeping with the spirit of symmetrical control, HTTP/1.1 requires that necessary trailers be sent in a chunked response only if the proxy had earlier indicated its willingness to buffer the entire response if needed. This is accomplished by including a `TE: trailers` request header.

The sender sends the following request to indicate its willingness to accept trailer fields in the chunk-encoded response:

```
GET /foo.html HTTP/1.1
Host: www.checktrailers.com
TE: trailers
```

The server sends back a chunk-encoded response with a `Trailer` header indicating what headers the recipient should look for at the end of the response, as follows:

```
HTTP/1.1 200 OK
Trailer: Splinfo
Transfer-encoding: chunked
CRLF
691
        <1681 bytes of chunk data>
76
        <118 bytes of chunk data>
0
Splinfo: vol=7; pe="u4,895527629,5465";
CRLF
```

The chunk-encoded response has the normal set of chunks, with chunk length followed by the zero-length chunk. Immediately after the zero-length chunk, the server includes the trailer with the `Splinfo` header (specified in the `Trailer` header) and a set of values for that header. The last line has the carriage return and linefeed (`CRLF`) characters required to be at the end of a chunked message.

Whereas HTTP/1.0 required a valid `Content-Length` be present in all `POST` requests, HTTP/1.1 does not. In HTTP/1.0, there was no other way to delimit an entity body, whereas this is now possible in HTTP/1.1 with chunk encoding. Note that messages that are chunk-encoded should not have a `Content-Length` header because the message length of such messages will be computed from the chunks. Suppose an HTTP/1.1 server sends a chunk-encoded message to an HTTP/1.1 proxy, which must forward it to an HTTP/1.0 client. If the message included a `Content-Length` header, the HTTP/1.1 proxy would ignore the header. Because an HTTP/1.0 client would not understand chunked encoding, the HTTP/1.1 proxy parses the chunks to create a regular message and forward it to the HTTP/1.0 client with a valid `Content-Length`.

7.7 Extensibility

Protocol designers often leave room for changes by keeping extensibility in mind during the specification. It is inevitable that any protocol will need to evolve. Although some changes may be anticipated at the time of protocol specification, it is unlikely that all changes will be foreseen. In the case of HTTP, there was an additional problem: Several popular implementations of various Web components based on intermediate "standards" had been created. The HTTP/1.1 version had to ensure that any changes made were compatible

with existing implementations. This was done to ensure that browsers and
servers compatible with older versions would continue to work as new versions
of components became popular. Older versions are not likely to disappear for
several years.

Learning from the experience of the past, the designers of HTTP/1.1 decided to leave several openings for *future* extensions. Features were created
without limiting them just to the application that was responsible for its origination. Rather than limit the possible values a particular parameter could have
to a narrow set, care was exercised to leave open other sets of values. Given
the set of compatibility problems that HTTP/1.1 designers faced, they tried to
limit future difficulties for later versions of the protocol.

As discussed in the following sections, HTTP/1.1 attempted to enhance
extensibility in the following three key ways:

1. By introducing methods to learn about a server's capability before making
   requests and to learn what the server actually received
2. By adding a new header to learn about intermediate servers in the path of
   a Web transaction
3. By adding support for upgrading to other protocols

7.7.1 Learning about the server

Two new methods were introduced in HTTP/1.1 to learn about a server. They
are the OPTIONS and TRACE methods. We examine them in detail here.

THE OPTIONS METHOD

HTTP/1.0 had no provision for a client to learn about the abilities of an origin
server. The OPTIONS method was introduced in HTTP/1.1 to achieve this goal.
Consider the following situations:

- A client might want to know if an origin server would accept a method
  that is not mandated by the protocol (anything that is not at a MUST
  requirement level). Suppose a large PUT request was sent by the client and
  refused by the server because of its inability to handle the method. The
  transmission of the large request would have wasted network bandwidth.
- A client might want to know if there are any specific requirements associated with a particular resource of interest.
- A user agent might want to know about the capabilities of a proxy in the
  path to the origin server.
- A proxy might want to probe an upstream server claiming to be HTTP/1.1
  to see if it can handle a specific HTTP/1.1 feature, such as the Expect
  mechanism.

For all these reasons, a new method—OPTIONS—was introduced in HTTP/1.1. The target of an OPTIONS request is not just an origin server but can be any server along the path from the sender to the recipient. The OPTIONS method is a safe method, like GET and HEAD.

For example, to obtain a list of methods understood by a server, a client would send an OPTIONS request, as follows:

```
OPTIONS * HTTP/1.1
Host: foo.com
```

The server could reply with

```
HTTP/1.1 200 OK
Allow: HEAD, GET, POST, TRACE, OPTIONS
```

This response indicates that the server is able to handle the five methods listed in the Allow entity header of the response. Note that the URI specified in the example is "*". This means that the client is interested in the capabilities of the server, not for any specific URI. For a specific URI, the Allow response header would reflect the set of methods applicable to that resource.

For a user agent to learn about a specific proxy in a request chain using the OPTIONS method, the user agent must ensure that the request is handled by that proxy. Proxies normally forward requests that they cannot handle toward the origin server. For clients to specifically target a proxy in the chain for a response, a new request header was introduced in HTTP/1.1. The client includes a value in the new Max-Forwards request header causing each proxy in the chain to decrement its value until it gets to zero, whereupon that proxy must reply to the OPTIONS request. The Max-Forwards header was created for both targeting a proxy and detecting loops in a chain of proxies. It is similar to the Time to Live (TTL) field in IP packets (as discussed in Chapter 5, Section 5.1.4).

Consider the following example used to limit forwarding:

```
OPTIONS /bar HTTP/1.1
Host: foo.com
User-Agent: Mozilla/2.0
Max-Forwards: 1
```

Such a request would be sent to the first recipient, which would subtract one from the Max-Forwards header and forward it to the next recipient, which would have to reply to the request because the value of Max-Forwards is now zero.

Some extensible features of this new method were defined. For example, a body included in an OPTIONS request could be optionally used by the origin server to respond in a broader manner. The actual syntax of possible bodies in an OPTIONS request has not been specified and has been left open for extensions in the future. This is another example of letting the protocol evolve gracefully without placing undue demands on Web components to implement all the changes in a single step.

In the discussions preceding the standardization, attempts were made to let responses to OPTIONS requests return compliance information such as compliance with a particular version of the standard or noncompliance with respect to a particular feature. However, because of the ambiguity involved in the term *compliance* and the increased complexity, this ability was not added to HTTP. The extension has been added in the form of a DAV: header in the distributed authoring and versioning extension of HTTP named WebDAV [GWF+99], discussed briefly in Chapter 15 (Section 15.5.2). WebDAV extension allows remote Web content authoring operations via a set of methods, headers, and request and response entity body formats. A WebDAV server receiving an OPTIONS request can indicate its capabilities via the DAV header. For example, DAV: 1 implies that the server is able to meet all the MUST-level requirements but does not support locking. The header DAV: 1, 2 implies that the server also supports locking.

THE TRACE METHOD

The TRACE method introduced in HTTP/1.1 enables a client to know the contents of the message that was actually received by the receiver. Unlike the OPTIONS method, which enables a client to learn about the ability of a server, TRACE triggers an action on the part of the server—sending back a copy of the message received.

In the TRACE method, the entire contents of the request message are returned to the sender by the server as the contents of the response body. For example, if the client made the following request:

```
TRACE /bar HTTP/1.1
Host: foo.com
User-Agent: Mozilla/2.0
```

it should result in this response:

```
HTTP/1.1 200 OK
Content-type: message/http

TRACE /bar HTTP/1.1
Host: foo.com
User-Agent: Mozilla/2.0
```

The body of the response must be the full HTTP message the target server received. Of course, as in any HTTP response, there are response and entity headers. The Content-type entity header is used to indicate that the response to the TRACE method is of the media type message/http. The media type `message/http` indicates that the response body is an HTTP request or response and that it obeys the relevant MIME conventions for such media types (such as line length limit and valid encodings).

This kind of application-layer loopback (sending a request out and receiving the same back) is not a new concept introduced in HTTP. Other protocols have somewhat similar mechanisms—the best-known one is `traceroute` [Jac] (see Chapter 5, Section 5.1.4). The `traceroute` command traces the route followed by an IP packet destined for a host, by sending UDP probe packets with a maximum TTL value and then listening for an Internet Control Message Protocol (ICMP) `TIME_EXCEEDED` response from gateways along the way.

7.7.2 Learning about intermediate servers

HTTP/1.1 pays more attention to the intermediaries in the request-response transaction chain. An HTTP/1.1 intermediary (proxy or gateway) adds identification information about itself and the server from which it received the message, in the new `Via` header.

The `Via` header is an extensibility and interoperability mechanism for HTTP/1.1 clients and servers. When a user generates a Web request, the request may travel through several intermediate servers en route to the origin server. The intermediate servers could be proxies, gateways, or front ends to servers. Likewise, the origin server might be interested in knowing the various intermediate servers involved in the request. In fact, any of the servers in the path might be interested in learning about the intermediate servers. This has a historical parallel to some commands that exist in the lower layers of the protocol stack. The ability to trace the various hosts involved in the path of an IP packet was provided by the `traceroute` [Jac] tool almost a decade before the emergence of the Web. The `Via` header is a reproduction of a part of this capability at a higher layer of the protocol stack. The `Via` header itself was fashioned after the `Received` field as defined in RFC 822 (the standard for the format of Internet text messages [Cro82]). It is also similar to the mechanism in the Border Gateway Protocol (BGP) [RL95, Ste99] where each Autonomous System adds its number (ASN) to the AS-PATH attribute.

Before the `Via` header proposal, there was a proposal for a different header, named `Forwarded` [FFBL95]. This header was meant for indicating the steps between the client and origin server in both directions. But this only included the names of the servers between the client and origin server. With the addition of the capability to learn about the protocol version as well, the `Forwarded` header was renamed `Via`.

All HTTP/1.1 proxies and gateways are obligated to participate (i.e., it is a MUST requirement) in the Via mechanism. Intermediaries are required to identify their hostname and the version number of the *preceding* server from which the request or response arrived. If there is a privacy concern, an intermediary can use a pseudonym instead of the real hostname. HTTP/1.1 proxies or gateways (though, in practice, HTTP/1.0 proxies can also participate) append the identification information to the new `Via` general header, in sequential order, as the message flows between sender and receiver. The end recipient thus has information about a subset of the servers in the path. Although it is not uncommon to find some HTTP/1.0 proxies that have been selectively upgraded to add the `Via` header, many HTTP/1.0 proxies do not know about the `Via` mechanism.

For example, a server might see the following `Via` header:

```
Via: 1.0 M-PROXY3:8080 (Squid/2.1.PATCH2),
     1.0 t1.us.irc.net:3128 (Squid/2.3.DEVEL1),
     1.1 qd.us.ircache.net:3128 (Squid/2.3.DEVEL1)
```

indicating that there were three intermediaries that participated in the Via mechanism. The first entry in the `Via` header

```
1.0 M-PROXY3:8080 (Squid/2.1.PATCH2)
```

indicates that an HTTP/1.0 server was the connection immediately preceding the `M-PROXY3` machine and was running a Squid 2.1 proxy server on port 8080. The last of the intermediaries that participated in the Via mechanism is `qd.us.ircache.net`, which was running a Squid 2.3 proxy on port 3128, and its preceding link was an HTTP/1.1 server.

Upon receiving the request, the origin server knows how many HTTP/1.1 proxies/gateways were in the path and might also learn about HTTP/1.0 servers that are connected to HTTP/1.1 proxies. Again, the caveat of multiple same-version proxies under the same administrative control being aggregated for security reasons might interfere with learning the exact number of proxies in the path. The `Via` header is an end-to-end header, and thus all intermediate proxies forward it.

The `Via` header is used in conjunction with the `TRACE` method (discussed in Section 7.7.1) to learn about the path followed by an HTTP message. The `Via` header includes information about the various HTTP/1.1 proxies or gateways that may be in the path between the client and the origin server. The client does not have to send the `TRACE` request all the way to the origin server; instead, it can be sent to a proxy along the path. This may not be a one-shot process; a client may have to iterate a few times before being able to locate a specific proxy. Different proxies under the same administrative control that have the same version number are often aggregated and labeled by a single string in a `Via` header for security and privacy reasons. As in the `OPTIONS` method, the `Max-Forwards` header can be used to limit the number of hops of the request method.

The `Via` mechanism also can be used to avoid loops in the request path. Upon noticing its name in a `Via` header, a proxy could decide to stop forwarding the message.

7.7.3 Upgrading to other protocols

Because new versions of HTTP and other protocols are likely to be deployed in the future, HTTP/1.1 provides a way to help a current connection migrate to the newer protocol. A new hop-by-hop header, `Upgrade`, was introduced in HTTP/1.1. When a sender includes the `Upgrade` header and a set of protocols it supports, as possible ways of communicating, the recipient server could switch to one of those protocols for this or for any additional exchange(s) on the existing transport-layer connection. The server must indicate the protocol it switched to via the `101 Switching Protocols` response header.

Consider the following example, in which an HTTP/1.1 client and server wish to upgrade their connection to another protocol:

```
GET http://security.are.us/private-data HTTP/1.1
Host: chase.bronx.com
Upgrade: SafeBank/1.0
Connection: Upgrade
```

The client is requesting a resource, `security.are.us/private-data`, and indicating that it is capable of handling communication in another protocol—`SafeBank/1.0`. The server at `chase.bronx.com` can respond in HTTP/1.1 or alternatively switch to the `SafeBank/1.0` protocol and indicate that it has done so via the `101 Switching Protocols` response code:

```
HTTP/1.1 101 Switching Protocols
Upgrade: SafeBank/1.0
Connection: Upgrade

<response for client's request>
```

Any further communication on the *current* transport-layer connection can now be done using the `SafeBank/1.0` protocol. For future separate connections to use a protocol other than HTTP/1.1, the server should use appropriate redirection class (3xx) responses.

Being a hop-by-hop header, `Upgrade` is stripped by proxies before the message is forwarded. The recipient server, however, is free to ignore the `Upgrade` header if it does not understand the header or does not want to switch protocols. Note that because `Upgrade` is a hop-by-hop header, the impact of the upgrade is only on the immediate transport connection.

7.8 Internet Address Conservation

The Internet has been using version 4 of the Internet Protocol (IP), which permits a maximum of 2^{32} host addresses. For several years, the number of addresses permitted by IPv4 was considered to be more than adequate. However, the sudden popularity of the Web and the early recognition on the part of the business community that short Web site names are more likely to be remembered led to an explosion of Web site names of the form www.foo.com. These "pure" hostname URLs simply consisted of the hostname and were thus easy to remember. However, each hostname required a separate IP address because of a misfeature in HTTP/1.0 implementations.

When a client contacted an HTTP/1.0 server at www.foo.com to obtain the resource http://www.foo.com/bar.html, the first line of the request only had

```
GET /bar.hml HTTP/1.0
```

That is, the user agent stripped the server name in the URL from the HTTP request. The server name was needed to make the transport-level connection, and by the time the HTTP server received the message, the server name was no longer present in the message.

The popularity of the Web led to the notion of outsourcing Web hosting. A company that did not want to host its Web content would let another company manage its Web content. Such a Web-hosting company would manage Web content for several companies. However, each company wished to advertise its site by its own "vanity" URL (e.g., www.foo.com) rather than be seen as part of some other Web-hosting company (e.g., www.hostmany.com/foo). The combination of vanity URLs and the server's inability to extract the intended server name from the URL implied that all resources had to be hosted under the same hostname or a new "pure" hostname was needed. Consider, for example, a user requesting a resource http://www.serverA.com/bar.html. The Web server at the host www.serverA.com would receive the following request:

```
GET /bar.html HTTP/1.0
```

In this situation, it is impossible for another Web server to run at the same host under the different name www.serverB.com because there is an ambiguity in interpreting a request for /bar.html. The two servers may be equally capable of responding to this request, and there is no way to resolve the ambiguity.

The desire for vanity URLs led to the allocation of a separate IP address for each domain name corresponding to the vanity URL. The proliferation of Web sites and the increasing popularity of the Internet led to the rapid depletion of available IP addresses. At some point in the future, IPv6 [DH98] might help alleviate the depletion of IP addresses. IPv6 has 128 bit addresses, dramatically increasing the number of addresses available compared with the 32-bit address

range of IPv4 addresses. As this book goes to press, an appreciable portion of
the Internet has yet to adopt IPv6.

To avoid the erosion of Internet addresses, the Internet Engineering Steering Group (responsible for managing the standardization process of the Internet
Engineering Task Force) mandated that the HTTP Working Group help conserve IP addresses during the transition to HTTP/1.1. The Working Group
had the option of changing the request line to include the hostname, as follows:

```
GET www.foo.com/bar.hml HTTP/1.0
```

However, an existing HTTP/1.0 server would not be able to parse this request
line correctly. The interoperability requirement could not be violated in the
protocol evolution, and so a necessary compromise was introduced. An early
suggestion was the introduction of an `Original-URI` header, which would contain the complete URI (including the server name). During the protocol evolution discussion, it was decided that such a header would be long and contain
redundant information. Thus the `Host` header line was born. The above request,
in HTTP/1.1, would be

```
GET /bar.hml HTTP/1.1
Host: www.foo.com
```

All HTTP/1.1 requests *must* have the `Host` header field. A port number
could also be included, but if it is omitted (and the resource is an HTTP
URL), the default port number 80 is assumed. HTTP/1.1 servers that receive
a request from an HTTP/1.1 client that does not include the `Host` header are
obligated to reject the request. The hope is that such a strict requirement might
help reduce the proliferation of IPv4 addresses. Of course, because HTTP/1.0
clients are not expected to know about the `Host` header, HTTP/1.1 servers
would continue to accept HTTP/1.0 requests that do not have `Host` headers.

Web sites are no longer required to take up a separate IP address in order
to obtain a vanity URL such as `www.foo.com`. Multiple names (aliases) can be
mapped to a single IP address through DNS lookups. Such a "virtual hosting"
technique permits a front-end Web server to accept requests for several different
Web sites behind it and redirect the requests accordingly. However, name-based
virtual hosting will not work under SSL because the entire header is encrypted.
Note that there is no requirement that a client must be an HTTP/1.1 client
in order to send `Host` headers. In fact, popular browsers that are still using
HTTP/1.0 routinely include the `Host` header.

7.9 Content Negotiation

If there is a single representation of a resource, a simple HTTP request message
can be used to request the resource. But when there are different formats of a

resource, the client and server would have to negotiate for the client to try to obtain a preferred representation. Initially, resources on the Web were just in one language (English), and recent studies have indicated that even now most of the content is in English [LG99]. The content that was in a different language was available *only* in the different language (e.g., French, Dutch). With the growth of the Web and the same content being available in multiple languages, the natural issue of being able to choose variants of the same resource arose. Resources vary not just in language but in character sets and encoding formats as well. The list of possible character sets such as ASCII, or variants of the International Standards Organization (Latin or Cyrillic alphabet), and encoding formats (gzip, compression, etc.) are registered with the Internet Assigning Numbers Authority. HTTP's content negotiation is designed to help clients and servers negotiate between different formats of a resource.

The dimensions along which negotiation can proceed are extensible. The rules for content negotiation specified in HTTP/1.1 will apply to the additions. Content negotiation can be done dynamically. Clients can learn about the different representations in which content is available and choose the most suitable representations after negotiating with the server.

In 1993, an early draft of HTTP [BL93a] discussed content negotiation in a fair amount of detail. Several intermediate HTTP/1.0 drafts discussed various negotiation-related headers, such as `Accept` and `Accept-Charset`. The Mosaic browser included `Accept` headers in its requests, and early versions of the Apache server included support for negotiation. Extending negotiation was a topic of interest from the earliest days of HTTP Working Group [Sec95]. Because consensus was not reached by the time of finalization of RFC 1945 describing HTTP/1.0, the discussion related to the five request headers (`Accept`, `Accept-Charset`, `Accept-Encoding`, `Accept-Language`, and `Content-Language`) was moved to the appendix. HTTP/1.1 not only formalized the discussion on content negotiation but provided two different kinds of negotiation as follows:

- **Agent-driven:** In agent-driven content negotiation, the client receives a set of alternative representations of the response, chooses the best representation, and indicates that in the second request.
- **Server-driven:** In server-driven negotiation, the server chooses the representation based on what is available at the server, the headers in the request message, or information about the client, such as its IP address.

Delay in implementing general negotiation in a variety of clients and servers led to separation of this effort from the HTTP specification.

In HTTP/1.0, the lack of agent-driven negotiation resulted in less control for the user in choosing a particular variant of a resource. In HTTP/1.1, the sender can indicate, in the `Accept` header, the entity characteristics they are willing to accept (such as text or audio media type). Consider the following example:

```
GET /asterix.html HTTP/1.1
Host: www.getobelix.com
Accept-Language: en-us, fr-BE
```

A user agent requests a resource `asterix.html` and is willing to accept either the U.S. English variant of that resource or a French-Belgian version. The server can choose between the variants and send back a response as follows:

```
HTTP/1.1 200 OK
Content-Length: 23819
Content-Language: fr-BE

...

<response in French-Belgian>

...
```

The origin server has decided to select French-Belgian for the resource, as indicated in the `Content-Language` header. The `Content-Language` entity header indicates the natural language of the entity body and thus that of the intended recipient. When entities are available in different natural languages, this header is a useful way to distinguish between them. However, multiple languages can be listed in the header if the entity might be understood by more than one audience. An example of the use of `Content-Language` with multiple languages is

<code>Content-Language: en-cockney, x-pig-latin</code>

which says that contents are meant for people who can speak either the Cockney dialect of English or Pig Latin.

User agents can express their preferences in terms of what content types are acceptable in a header, but it is largely meaningless if the origin server is unable to furnish content in that form. User agents and clients can negotiate on other matters such as encoding, but the origin server is the sole arbiter for negotiation on matters related to content.

HTTP/1.1 permits a server to have its own algorithm for generating a list of formats and then use the information present in the request headers to optionally tailor the response. One motivation for the server to send the "best" response is to ensure that the client does not send a subsequent request for a different variant. If the requested format is not available, the server could send a `406 Not Acceptable` response. The `406 Not Acceptable` code was introduced for agent-driven negotiation. The server would also include information on the various characteristics governing the resource so that the sender could choose from among the available variants. The downside of the `406 Not Acceptable` response is the extra request that is needed to fetch an acceptable variant from the list. If servers have only a single variant, then they should be able to return it and ignore `Accept` headers. The specification suggests that sending a variant different from the ones listed as acceptable is preferable to sending a 406 Not Acceptable response.

It is hard for a user agent to send a selection algorithm with a request to the origin server, and therefore the origin server is the best place for selecting an algorithm. The server configuration file would be an appropriate place to specify the selection algorithm. In other words, the server maintains the algorithm that decides the best choice of response. However, server-driven negotiation is not always sufficient. The reliance on the user agent to have the user select from a menu of choices indicates that the server is unable to perform this task automatically.

The 300 Multiple Choices response code was broadened in HTTP/1.1 primarily as a result of the introduction of content negotiation. This code is used to indicate that a resource can be selected in a negotiated fashion from a variety of possible representations found in different locations. The origin server can indicate a *preferred* representation for the resource, but the redirection lets the user agent make the proper choice.

One way for user agents and origin servers to specify the extent to which they prefer a particular format is through quality values, known in HTTP as qvalue. As mentioned in Section 7.4.3, a *qvalue* is a number between 0.0 and 1.0 with a low quality value indicating lower preference and a high quality value indicating higher preference. Quality values were originally proposed in the first draft document describing content negotiation [BL93a] but were formalized in HTTP/1.1 after components with negotiation capability were implemented. The weight associated with a particular parameter can now be expressed on a per-request or a per-response basis. The meaning of a quality value of 0 is that content with that particular parameter is unacceptable to the client. Unfortunately, the term *quality value* was chosen before fully defining the range of its application; in reality quality values specify *lowering* of quality from the ideal. A quality value of 1.0 is ideal and 0.9 is 10% less than the ideal sought.

Content negotiation is flexible in that not only can multiple parameters be specified but each parameter can have various choices, each with its level of acceptability. For example, different quality values can be specified for encoding formats:

```
Accept-Encoding: vdelta;q=1.0, gzip;q=0.5, compress;q=0.1
```

The example indicates that the client has the highest preference for the vdelta encoding of the response. If the server cannot provide the client with this format, then it should attempt to provide the resource in gzip format and, failing that, in compress. In this example, the server can send the response in one of these formats or in its native form. If the client had instead specified

```
Accept-Encoding: vdelta;q=1.0, gzip;q=0.5, compress;q=0.1,
                 identity;q=0
```

then the server is limited to sending the response in one of the three formats (`vdelta, gzip, compress`) or sending a `406 Not Acceptable` response code. If the `identity;q=0` string was omitted, then the server could send an encoding of its choice.

Arbitrarily adding possible formats to the request or response header increases the number of bytes transmitted over the network. A popular early browser used to send large `Accept` lists in every request. Even if the arguments specified in the `Accept` header cannot be used by a recipient, the bytes have already been sent. There is a tension between the amount of information that is sent and what is actually used at either end. The server can be flexible in providing choices in responses. Likewise, the user agent can specify an arbitrary set of acceptable or preferred formats. Content negotiation is thus a powerful tool that needs to be used with care.

Cached negotiated responses require more careful handling. A cache might respond to a request for a variant of a resource with an alternate location. This is accomplished in HTTP/1.1 via the new `Vary` response header and the `Content-Location` entity headers. Recall that the `Location` header is used to redirect the request to where the resource can be found. The `Content-Location` header has an alternate location of the entity in the request; this is different from the requested resource's URI.

A combination of agent-driven and server-driven negotiation is called *transparent content negotiation.* A variant list is sent by the server, and the user agent selects the most suitable one. Rather than force the user agent to participate in selecting variants each time, the process can take advantage of caches in the path. The optimization of the negotiation process relies on caches in the middle caching the list of variants and the variants themselves. In effect, the negotiation is shifted from the server to a cache that acts on the server's behalf. Thus the agent-driven negotiation normally done by the user agent is done at a cache much closer to the client than the origin server. However, a cached negotiation policy is useful only as long as the server's negotiation stance does not change. This naturally raises questions of how the cache would stay current with changes at the server. The HTTP Working Group decided to leave transparent content negotiation out of the HTTP/1.1 specification, and work on it has proceeded independently [HM98]. Transparent content negotiation is discussed in more depth in Chapter 15 (Section 15.5.1).

7.10 Security, Authentication, and Integrity

Security is necessary to ensure that only authenticated users have access to resources. The messages being exchanged on the Web should not be vulnerable to interception by parties not involved in the exchange. Messages may be intercepted, and therefore the contents of the message should be opaque to everyone except the intended parties. Consider a letter sent in the mail from A to B:

- A and B should be sure that no one else reads the contents of the letter.
- B should be able to ensure that the letter did indeed come from A.
- The letter should be received intact by B (i.e., the contents sent by A should be unaltered).

All these expectations apply for HTTP messages.

Several authentication schemes are used. Some resources may require simple authentication schemes, whereby a client authenticates itself with a userid and password, which are exchanged as plaintext (in the clear, without encryption). Other resources may require a more complex level of authentication, in which the password itself is encrypted.

One common authentication method is a challenge-response scheme, in which a server sends a challenge string expecting a specific response from the client. A challenge may only be valid for a specific *realm*—a region of space where a user may be authenticated. This region may be a machine or a set of directories. Each server defines a *protection space* for a resource by combining a realm and the URI of the resource. Each protection space has its own authorization database. The advantage of protection spaces is that different authentication schemes can be applied to different resources.

We begin by discussing the problems with the security model of HTTP/1.0 and the attempts made to fix it in HTTP/1.1. We then examine the problems associated with maintaining the integrity of entity bodies. HTTP/1.1's solution was to introduce authentication information to be added to messages either as a header or in a trailer.

7.10.1 Security and authentication

Security became a key concern as the Web became more popular and e-commerce grew rapidly. HTTP/1.0 had minimal notions of security, notably a challenge-response scheme that enabled a client to receive a resource after satisfying a server that it has proper credentials. This is the *Basic authentication* mechanism described in Chapter 6 (Section 6.4).

The Basic authentication scheme of HTTP/1.0 was not a very secure method, because it relied on the fact that the connection between the client and server was trustworthy. This was known at the time of drafting the HTTP/1.0 specification not to be the case. HTTP/1.0 did not preclude the use of end-to-end encryption, but it also did not define any other security mechanism. The username and password sent by the client to the challenging server were sent in base64 encoding [FB96a]. Base64 encoding, for all practical purposes, is plaintext, and the username and password are vulnerable to anyone snooping on the network. The growth in e-commerce led to transmission of credit card numbers on the Web, which are also candidates for such snooping.

Another problem with HTTP/1.0 credentials is the lack of discrimination of scope. Unlike Basic authentication, Digest authentication permits limiting the scope of the credential in several ways by including the request method, the URI, and a limited lifetime in the checksum computation. Credentials in HTTP/1.0 have a lifetime longer than necessary: Essentially they last forever. This means that anyone who intercepts the credential can use it much later with impunity. Shortening the credential's lifetime is an obvious security enhancement. This was done in HTTP/1.1 by restricting the response to a single resource and method. Someone snooping on the network could only replay the same request for which the response has already been seen by them. The client is required to compute a checksum that involves the URI, request method, username, password, and a one-time nonce value. A *nonce* is a base 16 or base 64 string that is guaranteed to be unique every time a server sends a `401 Unauthorized` response (the `401 Unauthorized` response is sent when the server deems the credentials sent by the client as unsatisfactory). A nonce value is constructed by a combination of a server-generated timestamp, the entity tag of the resource, and a private key known only to the server. The nonce value is opaque to the client.

HTTP authentication is discussed in depth in RFC 2617, which is a companion to the HTTP/1.1 specification (RFC 2616).

7.10.2 Integrity

Message integrity is an essential component of security: what was sent must be transported intact to the receiver. The new `Content-MD5` entity header in HTTP/1.1 provides a somewhat primitive integrity check of the entity body. An MD5 [Riv92] digest is a 128-bit checksum. The digest's value in `Content-MD5` is encoded as per the base64 algorithm [MR95]. Generation of `Content-MD5` header is restricted to clients and origin servers because it is meant to be an end-to-end integrity mechanism. The digest permits all recipients including intermediate entities (such as proxies and gateways) to check that the received entity has not been modified accidentally during transmission. The digest cannot however help in detecting malicious alterations to the entity or to any headers, since the malefactor could also change the contents of the `Content-MD5` header making it impossible to detect the alteration.

A common threat on the Internet is a denial of service (DOS) attack. In the Web context, DOS attacks can take many forms, including sending large messages to a Web server. Large messages may overrun buffers and lead to security violations as well. DOS attack is a classic problem faced by servers; by knowing the length of a message *a priori,* a server can decide if it wants to spend its resources processing a request. The `411 Length Required` response code lets the client know that the server needs to know the content length of the message body before processing the request. This is a standard mechanism to ensure that a protocol does not force a server to accept arbitrarily large messages. However, if the message is chunk-encoded (see Section 7.6), content length need not be present in the message. An HTTP/1.1 server is obligated to parse chunk-encoded messages. However, the server can always decide that a message is too long and send a `411 Length Required` response code and then close the connection.

The new `414 Request-URI Too Long` response code can be sent if the server is not willing to parse a very long URI. Because the protocol does not specify the maximum length, individual implementations use their local constraints to set the value accordingly. A good use of this status code is when the server believes it might be under a common buffer-overflow security hole attack. Programs that have fixed string buffers and do not check for overflow might allow overwriting of other sections of their code, thus compromising security.

Security in HTTP/1.1 is given serious consideration through preventing plaintext transmission of passwords, limiting lifetime of credentials, and helping in preserving the integrity of messages. New response codes were created to make component implementors aware of security attacks.

7.11 The Role of Proxies in HTTP/1.1

One of the key improvements in HTTP/1.1 was the recognition of the important role played by the intermediaries between the sender and the receiver. Although tunnels and gateways are also intermediaries, the most notable intermediary is a proxy. The role of a proxy has become central to the Web architecture. The construction and details of proxies have been covered in Chapter 3. Specifically, issues relating to the proxy as a handler of HTTP requests and responses were discussed in Chapter 3 (Section 3.4.2). To focus attention on the role played by proxies, we divide our discussion of the changes into four parts, as follows:

- Types of proxies
- Syntactic requirements on an HTTP/1.1 proxy
- Semantic requirements on an HTTP/1.1 proxy
- Impact of other Web components on HTTP/1.1 proxies

7.11.1 Types of proxies

Proxies range from a single server located between a client and an origin server to significantly more complicated scenarios such as a set of hierarchical proxies that may serve an entire nation. As far as the HTTP/1.1 protocol is concerned, there are three different ways a proxy can behave:

- The proxy acts as an intermediary to other systems, speaking a variety of protocols such as WAIS, FTP, or Gopher.
- The proxy speaks HTTP and is an intermediary between an HTTP sender and an HTTP receiver.
- The proxy plays the role of an HTTP proxy or a client or a tunnel at various times based on the request.

For a proxy to act as an intermediary to other systems, no new requirements were introduced in HTTP/1.1. They continue to function as they did in HTTP/1.0.

In the second case, a proxy may reply to a request if it can do so *satisfactorily*; that is, the response meets the desired freshness guarantee. The freshness guarantee can be constrained by client or a server. If not, the proxy can pass the request further down the chain. When a response eventually comes back, the proxy could optionally cache the response before sending it on to the requesting party. A proxy could modify the request or response.

In the third case, a proxy may also switch to being a tunnel when the `CONNECT` method is used. Although the HTTP/1.1 specification simply reserves this method, this has been used in the initiation of Transport Layer Security (TLS) [KL00] over an existing TCP connection via the `Upgrade` mechanism.

7.11.2 Syntactic requirements on an HTTP/1.1 proxy

The two broad syntactic requirements on an HTTP/1.1 proxy are as follows:

- Requirement dealing with forwarding messages
- Requirement dealing with modifying existing headers or adding new ones

We examine the two requirements next.

FORWARDING MESSAGES

When forwarding a message, a proxy must consider the protocol version of the sender from which it received the message and the receiver to which it is forwarding the message. Suppose that an HTTP/1.1 proxy forwards a request message it received from an HTTP/1.0 sender. Even if the proxy receives an HTTP/1.1 response from its next-hop server, it cannot return that response to the original sender. The original HTTP/1.0 sender may not be able to understand some of the possible HTTP/1.1 aspects of the message. However, if the original sender spoke HTTP/1.1, the HTTP/1.1 proxy could return the HTTP/1.1 response intact. In fact, the specification suggests that a proxy cache the version number of its next-hop server so it can know what sort of message to send.

There are special rules associated with forwarding 1xx class responses. For example, the proxy cannot forward a 100 Continue response if the Expect header was added by the proxy (i.e., the `Expect` header was not present in the original message the proxy received). If the proxy receives a request with an expectation that it cannot meet, it is obligated to return a `417 Expectation Failed` response independent of whether the downstream server might be able to meet the expectation. This is due to the `Expect` mechanism being a hop-by-hop mechanism.

For the `TRACE` and `OPTIONS` methods, proxies must check to see if there is a `Max-Forwards` header (see Section 7.7.1) and ensure that its value is not zero and decrement the value before forwarding a message. Similarly, a request without a `Host` header from an HTTP/1.1 client should not be forwarded by a proxy; instead it should return a `400 Bad Request`.

Headers not understood by a proxy must still be forwarded by it unless they are protected by a `Connection` header (described in Section 7.5). Proxies must treat hop-by-hop headers and those protected by the `Connection` header carefully. Mistakenly forwarding headers meant for a single connection can cause problems. The proxy must remove any headers matching the connection tokens listed in a `Connection` header before the message is forwarded.

ADDING HEADERS OR MODIFYING EXISTING HEADERS

HTTP/1.1 proxies are obligated to add information about themselves to the `Via` header, as discussed in Section 7.7. Proxies also have to indicate the protocol version number of the upstream server from which the message was received. However, a proxy at the edge of a network (say, acting also as a firewall) must mask the identity of machines that are behind it and ensure that they are not added to the `Via` header.

HTTP/1.1 proxies cannot alter the order of field values in headers of messages because the semantics might be altered. Two content encodings in a row can have an entirely different meaning when applied in the reverse order. Several end-to-end headers (e.g., `ETag`, `Content-MD5`) and fields in the `Expires` headers should not be modified by transparent proxies. Additionally, the presence of the cache control directive `no-transform` prevents certain headers from being changed (e.g., `Content-Encoding`, `Content-Type`). A proxy should not modify the `From` request header (indicating the e-mail address of the user issuing the request) and the `Server` response header (identifying the software and version number of the Web server).

Proxies are not permitted to alter the fully qualified domain name present in the URI of a message. However, if a proxy receives a hostname that is not a fully qualified domain name, it is permitted to add its domain to the hostname. Proxies are not permitted to *generate* certain headers (e.g., the end-to-end integrity check entity header `Content-MD5`; see Section 7.2.2). The proxy can, however, use the value provided in the `Content-MD5` header to ensure that the entity body received by it is correct.

7.11.3 Semantic requirements on an HTTP/1.1 proxy

Semantic changes in HTTP/1.1 dealing with proxies are largely in four areas: caching, range requests, persistent connections, and security.

CACHING REQUIREMENTS ON A PROXY

Several changes in HTTP/1.1 relate to caching. Because proxies play a primary role in caching, the changes affect proxies considerably. For example, proxies must pay attention to entity tags that are sent as cache validators and ensure that semantic transparency is maintained when returning a cached value. A proxy is obligated to take into account the various fields in a conditional header before deciding on the appropriate cached value. In the presence of the cache control directive `Cache-Control: s-maxage=0`, a shared-proxy cache must revalidate a cached response.

When a proxy is acting as a cache and returns a cached response, it is obligated to send an `Age` header with its response to indicate that the response was not generated "first-hand." The `Age` header includes an estimate of the amount of time that has elapsed since the response was either originally generated at or revalidated with the origin server. The receiver could use the `Age` value to estimate how old the response was.

CONNECTION MANAGEMENT REQUIREMENTS ON A PROXY

HTTP/1.1 proxies that implement persistent connections must make sure that they maintain persistent connections for their upstream and downstream connections. There was an implementation of persistent connection in HTTP/1.0 (the `Keep-Alive` header) that required explicit negotiation. However, interaction between the `Connection` header and `Keep-Alive` header could result in a hung connection. This occurred because an HTTP/1.0 client could send a `Keep-Alive` header to a proxy that did not understand `Connection` but might mistakenly forward it. If the downstream connection also maintained a `Keep-Alive` connection, the proxy in the middle would never receive the closing of the response. To avoid such problems, HTTP/1.1 proxies are not permitted to establish a persistent connection with HTTP/1.0 clients.

Proxies may use a different set of guidelines (compared with a client or origin server) for deciding when to close a persistent connection. An origin server may have reasons to close persistent connections sooner because it serves a lot of clients. A proxy typically has fewer clients behind it than the number of clients accessing a popular origin server. Thus a proxy has a better idea of which connections should persist longer because it can keep track of the access patterns of the clients. The protocol does not specify how long (in units of time) a proxy should maintain a persistent connection but does state general guidelines for the *number* of persistent connections it should maintain in parallel to any given upstream server. The protocol suggests that a single-user client maintain no more than two persistent connections with any server or proxy. A proxy should limit itself to 2*n connections to another server or proxy where *n* is the number of simultaneously active users.

BANDWIDTH MANAGEMENT REQUIREMENTS ON A PROXY

HTTP/1.1 clients have the ability to make range requests. This imposes specific constraints on a proxy. If a proxy forwards a range request to a server and obtains the entire resource as the response, it should only send the requested range back to the client. A proxy should, however, store the complete response. However, a proxy cache that does not support range requests must not cache partial responses.

HTTP/1.1 proxies have additional rules for dealing with the *Expect* mechanism. The role of a proxy is harder because it is now dealing with a partial request from a client but must worry about the abilities of a downstream server. As per the discussion of rules for forwarding headers earlier in this section, HTTP/1.1 proxies are obligated to forward the `Expect` header with the request. However, if the proxy knows that the next-hop server's version is less than HTTP/1.1, the proxy should return a `417 Expectation Failed` response instead of forwarding the request. Likewise, if a proxy received a `100 Continue` response from a server, it should not forward the response to a client unless the client's request had included an `Expect` header.

SECURITY REQUIREMENTS ON A PROXY

Several headers and response codes were introduced to handle security requirements at a proxy. Among them are request headers such as `Proxy-Authenticate` and response codes such as `407 Proxy Authorization Required`.

The `Proxy-Authenticate` request header is needed when a resource is available only to authenticated clients. The client must provide the necessary credentials. The header specifies the authentication scheme being used and includes a challenge to enable a client to send back its credentials.

The `407 Proxy Authorization Required` response status code is similar to HTTP/1.0's `401 Unauthorized`. However, `407 Proxy Authorization Required` is a single-hop authentication unlike the `401 Unauthorized` end-to-end header. The `407 Proxy Authorization Required` is used by the proxy to inform the client that the authorization must actually be done with a proxy, whereas the `401 Unauthorized` response is used by the origin server to send a challenge directly to a client. The proxy sends a `Proxy-Authenticate` authentication header to the client with a challenge, stating the appropriate authentication scheme being used and the valid parameters for the URI being requested. The client must send its credentials for that URI to the proxy using the new `Proxy-Authorization` request header.

7.12 Other Miscellaneous Changes

Several other minor changes exist between HTTP/1.0 and HTTP/1.1. We examine the various miscellaneous changes not covered in the earlier set of categorization by dividing the changes into three parts: method-related, header-related, and response-code-related. The changes are discussed here to reduce the distraction from the more important changes covered earlier in the chapter.

7.12.1 Method-related miscellaneous changes

Several of the HTTP/1.0 methods had minor changes in their semantics. In some cases, minor clarifications were made to the interpretation of these methods. The affected methods were `HEAD`, `PUT`, `DELETE`, and `CONNECT`.

THE HEAD METHOD: MINOR CHANGE

In HTTP/1.0, it was not possible to modify a `HEAD` request with conditionals (such as `If-Modified-Since`), but HTTP/1.1 has no such restrictions. Conditional headers can be used with any method in HTTP/1.1. The HTTP/1.1 specification follows the principle of adding restrictions only when warranted and indicates the specific reasons for any restrictions that were added.

THE PUT METHOD: CLARIFICATIONS

The `PUT` method was partially described in RFC 1945 as part of HTTP/1.0. Subsequent discussions in the HTTP Working Group led to a consensus on its formal definition as a method in HTTP/1.1. An origin server processing a `PUT` request examines the Request-URI to decide if the request would modify an existing resource or create a new one. The origin server must verify the access rights of the user before applying the method to the resource. The formal definition added specific requirements for origin servers and caching proxies. For example, an origin server must respond with a 201 `Created` response if a resource was created as a result of a `PUT` request. If a resource associated with the `PUT` (as well as `POST` and `DELETE`) method was present in a cache, the cached response must be marked as stale. A caching proxy that observes a request method capable of changing the resource on the origin server must invalidate any entities in the cache that are associated with that resource.

The following example of a `PUT` request is used to either create or modify a resource `/foobar/foo.html`:

```
PUT /foobar/foo.html HTTP/1.1
```

```
User-Agent: Mozilla/2.0
Authorization: Basic ZHeadFuaYow29PinWU=
Content-Type: text/html
Content-Length: 433
Host: bar.com
...
<433 bytes of possibly new foo.html>
```

The request includes information about the content type and length, as well as credentials in the `Authorization` header. The credentials are needed by the origin server to ensure that the user has the necessary access rights to modify or create the resource. Assuming that the credentials are acceptable, the server would create or update `/foobar/foo.html` and return an HTTP/1.1 200 OK response.

PUT versus POST method: Differences   During the course of formalizing the definition of the PUT method, questions arose on the distinction between PUT and POST methods. To understand the difference between the PUT and POST methods, one must examine the interpretation of the URI in the request. PUT constrains the server to apply the request *only* to the enclosed URI and send back a redirection class response if the server cannot do so. The resource can be created or modified. The resource in the POST method, however, refers to the program that is going to handle the data included in the entity of the POST message. This is the case when a user fills out a form as part of submitting a request.

THE DELETE METHOD: FORMALIZATION

Like PUT, the DELETE method is discussed in the appendix of RFC 1945, but it was not formally defined. The DELETE method caused the resource associated with the requested URI to be deleted if the request was not overridden by some other means on the origin server. An origin server, for example, could verify access rights of the requester and decide not to delete the resource. In this case, the server should indicate to the requesting client that the request was not accepted by returning a 401 Unauthorized or a 403 Forbidden response.

In HTTP/1.1, the requirements on the part of components are specified clearly for dealing with the DELETE method. For example, the protocol specifies response codes to be sent by the origin server if the deletion is likely to succeed. A proxy that sees a DELETE request for a resource could mark its cached copy as stale.

THE CONNECT METHOD

The CONNECT method for tunneling between proxies was suggested by Ari Luotonen [Luo97] in 1998 in a (now expired) Internet Draft but was not formally standardized. A new method—CONNECT—was defined as a placeholder (i.e., to ensure that this method was not defined for some other use in the future) in HTTP/1.1. The method name is reserved for future use, although one particular use is mentioned in the RFC—a proxy being able to change itself into a tunnel for security purposes. In other words, a proxy would blindly start relaying the message it receives in either direction. The CONNECT method has been used to initiate Transport Layer Security (TLS) over an existing TCP connection within HTTP/1.1 [KL00], for establishing tunnels across proxies.

7.12.2 Header-related miscellaneous changes

Some HTTP/1.0 headers were changed in modest ways, and some new headers were added for narrow reasons. We examine these changes in three parts: general, response, and entity headers.

GENERAL HEADERS

If the message body has been modified in any way, then the manner of modification is indicated in the Transfer-Encoding header, so that the recipient will know how to parse the message body. In HTTP/1.0, there was no guarantee (in the absence of a Content-Length header) that the recipient actually received what was sent by a sender. Transfer coding helped ensure that the recipient received everything that was sent. The Transfer-Encoding header is a hop-by-hop header and is thus meaningful only for the current connection.

As a result of the introduction of Transfer-Encoding header, the definition of an HTTP request and response message changed between HTTP/1.0 and HTTP/1.1. To obtain the entity-body, only the headers in an HTTP/1.0 message had to be removed, whereas in an HTTP/1.1 message, any transfer codings applied must be removed.

RESPONSE HEADERS

One HTTP/1.0 response header (Retry-After) was changed in HTTP/1.1, and a new Warning header was added.

The Retry-After header is discussed in the appendix of the HTTP/1.0 specification in the context of inconsistent implementations of the protocol. However, the header was not made part of the HTTP/1.0 protocol specification. This header was introduced in HTTP/1.1 to clarify the semantics of the 503 Service Unavailable response code. The two reasons for this response code are: the server is offline for an indeterminate amount of time or is transiently

Table 7.15. HTTP/1.1 Warning codes

Warning code	Brief description
110 Response is stale	Cache indicates returned response is stale
111 Revalidation failed	Attempt to revalidate response failed
112 Disconnected operation	Cache is disconnected from the network
113 Heuristic expiration	Freshness lifetime chosen by a heuristic
199 Miscellaneous warning	Arbitrary warning to be displayed to the user
214 Transformation applied	Content-coding or media-type changed
299 Miscellaneous persistent warning	Arbitrary 2xx warning for display to the user

busy and is likely to become available in a short period of time. For the latter condition, if the server could notify the client that the service may become available at a later time, the client could retry the request after that period of time. The time value is indicated either as a relative time from now or at a specific time in the future. In HTTP/1.1, the `Retry-After` is used in several responses, including the `413 Request Entity Too Large` (discussed in Section 7.2.3) and various redirection class (3xx) responses.

The early error messages in HTTP/1.0 were not really meant for human reading. The 4xx and 5xx class of errors had short and simple natural language phrases (or *reason phrases*), but possible corrective actions could not be gleaned from these phrases. Unfortunately, the status code and reason phrase appear in the first line of the response (the `Status-Line`), and so multiple status codes could not be placed there. Multiple status codes would confuse recipients. Any additional information must appear in separate headers. This was fixed in HTTP/1.1 by the introduction of a `Warning` header. A message explaining the warning along with the code for the class of warning could be sent. Note that these warning codes are not general HTTP response codes. HTTP/1.1 has defined seven Warning codes, as shown in Table 7.15.

The Warning code classes enables extensibility; additional codes are possible in the future.

For example, suppose a resource was obtained in a particular content coding (say, `gzip`), but the proxy in the path has altered the response to some other format. It would be useful to indicate this in a warning message rather than simply forward the response in its transformed manner. The proxy could include a `Warning` header as follows:

```
Warning: 214 Transformation applied
```

Likewise, if a proxy was going to return a cached response as a result of being unable to contact the origin server, the proxy can indicate that the response is inconsistent, as follows:

```
Warning: 111 Revalidation failed
```

ENTITY HEADERS

Six entity headers were described in HTTP/1.0, while `Content-Language`, was discussed in the appendix of RFC 1945. Some of the HTTP/1.0 entity headers were changed in HTTP/1.1 to take advantage of the new capabilities of HTTP/1.1. For example, HTTP/1.1 clarified that multiple content codings may have been applied to the resource in the `Content-Encoding` entity header. Origin servers were enjoined to ensure that the `Last-Modified` value of an entity is close to the time they generate the `Date` value in the response. If the entity were to change just before the response is generated, the recipient would have a good idea of the entity's modification time.

7.12.3 Response-code-related miscellaneous changes

Many of the response classes had a few response codes whose semantics were slightly modified in the change from HTTP/1.0 to HTTP/1.1. We discuss the changes within the response class to which the codes belong.

2XX RESPONSE STATUS CODES

Of the four old 2xx response codes, only two have changed, and they have changed only slightly. The 200 `OK` response code includes a minor clarification that responses to `HEAD` requests send no *message body* (as opposed to *entity body,* in HTTP/1.0). In other words, entity headers could be included.

Some minor improvements were made to the HTTP/1.0's 201 `Created` response code. A `Location` header can be included in the response, indicating the specific URI for the created resource. A resource could have several locations, and the `Location` header would be used to indicate the specific location. Other characteristics specific to the resource, such as the content type, could also be included in the response header.

Of the three new 2xx response code status in HTTP/1.1, two are explained here. The third (206 `Partial Content`) was discussed in Section 7.4.1—we include a caveat regarding caching of 206 `Partial Content` responses here.

203 Non-Authoritative Information   This new response code is used to indicate that the metadata about the resource was obtained from places other than the origin server. The metadata is not likely to be identical to what the origin server would have sent. In cases in which it is possible to have additional metadata about the resource, the protocol permits the information to be included, but with a different response code.

205 Reset Content   The new response status code 205 `Reset Content` in HTTP/1.1 is used by the origin server to help the user agent give feedback to the user. There was no provision in HTTP/1.0 to do this. Suppose the user has submitted a form to a server. The server, by returning the 205 code, could cause the user agent to clear the form, indicating to the user that the form has been accepted by the server. The user could continue using the form to submit additional requests. This is an example of a change to the protocol that helps user agents use a response from the server to indicate change of state to the user.

206 Partial Content   Caches that do not support `Range` headers must not cache a 206 `Partial Content` response. Such a warning is an example of constraints placed on implementations that do not provide a new feature but could easily receive responses with status codes associated with the new feature. The protocol specification includes many such constraints, but implementations are not always tested against such constraints, leading to potential problems. A change in the protocol thus has implications on server and client implementations that are seemingly unaffected by the change.

3XX RESPONSE STATUS CODES

The four new response status codes in HTTP/1.1 are 303 `See Other`, 305 `Use Proxy`, 306 (`Unused`), and 307 `Temporary Redirect`. The 303 and 307 response codes were introduced so that Web components could indicate the desired behavior more clearly. The 305 response code was introduced in the intermediate (non-standard) specification RFC 2068. The 306 response code suggestion was made in an intermediate draft version of the protocol specification but was removed during the protocol standardization process.

303 See Other   The HTTP/1.0 302 `Moved Temporarily` response included a `Location` header indicating to the user agent where the URI can actually be found. The 303 `See Other` response is similar to the older 302 `Moved Temporarily` status code but was added specifically to fix a common problem with user agents that were mishandling a 302 response. This is an example of protocol evolution as a result of known bugs in existing implementations.

307 Temporary Redirect   The 307 `Temporary Redirect` response code informs the user agent that the resource can *temporarily* be found at the new URI given in the `Location` header of the response. In the presence of a redirection response, some user agents mistakenly use the GET request method to retrieve the resource from the new URI regardless of the request method in the original request. This is in spite of the fact that both RFC 1945 and one of the intermediate HTTP/1.1 specifications (RFC 2068) clearly indicated that request methods must not be changed because of a redirection. Redirection is used in conjunction with mirrored origin servers whereby a client's request can be redirected to a replica nearer to the client. This reduces the load on a particular origin server.

305 Use Proxy The 305 Use Proxy response code instructs the requesting entity to repeat the request via the indicated proxy specified in the Location header of the response. This was originally introduced to permit an origin server to deny access unless the request goes through a suitable proxy. The purpose of this was to reduce the load on the origin server. The origin server is also well positioned to indicate which proxy the client should use. Additionally, the intermediate specification RFC 2068 was not clear about the use of the 305 response code and created a possible security hole. Only one request could be redirected via a 305, and such a redirection could only be done by origin servers. If this were not the case, a man-in-the-middle attack became possible—an intermediate component could have requests redirected to an unfriendly proxy.

306 (Unused) The 306 response was introduced in an earlier draft version of the HTTP specification and removed later. A version of the Netscape proxy server expanded on the requirements for a 306 Switch Proxy response code, so that the recipient could use the proxy specified in a new Set-proxy hop-by-hop header, for future requests. The addition was primarily to add some missing functionality in the semantics of the 305 Use Proxy response code and to restrict the use of this response code only by proxies rather than origin servers. However, concerns about the security implications of this response (specifically, a man-in-the-middle attack) led to the elimination of 306 status code in HTTP/1.1. However, because simply eliminating would mean that older implementations would no longer work, the code has been reserved.

4XX RESPONSE STATUS CODES

Several new 4xx class response codes were created in HTTP/1.1. The response codes in Table 7.10 not discussed earlier can be examined in three categories: clarification, using negotiation capability in HTTP/1.1, and new codes for other features.

1. Clarification status codes: We discuss three new status codes under the clarification category.

405 Method Not Allowed   The 405 Method Not Allowed was introduced to give a slightly more detailed response when a request for a particular resource was denied. Rather than sending a generic 403 Forbidden
error response (as would be the case in HTTP/1.0), the server lists the
set of methods that *are* legal for the requested URI. This is done via the
entity header Allow. Note that the server is obligated to do this if a 405
Method Not Allowed response is sent. The sender can then change the
request method accordingly. Suppose a client had sent a TRACE request
to a server that did not implement that method. The server would send
back:

```
HTTP/1.1 405 Method Not Allowed
Allow: GET, HEAD, POST, PUT
```

The client thus learns the set of valid methods that the server is able to
handle.

408 Request Timeout   Another example of clarification is reflected in
the 408 Request Timeout status code. The server may not be willing to
wait forever for a client to send a request and might time out. Rather than
close the connection with an ambiguous error response, the server sends a
more nuanced code indicating that it is timing out.

410 Gone   If a resource is not found, an HTTP/1.1 server will return
the 404 Not Found response just as HTTP/1.0 servers do. However, if the
server knows that the resource has been removed or its new location cannot be determined, the new response status code 410 Gone can be used
to indicate this. The information that a resource is not likely to be found
later is known via internal configuration information that is available to the
server. The client, unlike when it receives 404 Not Found, knows not to
retry the request that yielded 410 Gone. With the presence of the DELETE
method, some resources are going to be permanently deleted. The difference between 404 Not Found and 410 Gone is similar to the difference
between 301 Moved Permanently and 302 Found.

2. Negotiation status codes: We discuss two new status codes under the negotiation category here.

   413 Request Entity Too Large   The 413 Request Entity Too Large
   response code is sent if the server cannot handle such a large request message. The server can permit the sender to try the same request later if
   there is a possibility of the server being able to handle a large entity. The
   Retry-After header is used to specify the time after which the request

should be tried again by the client. This response code is particularly useful in conjunction with the `Expect` mechanism—the client could send an `Expect` header with the size of the request entity, and if it receives a `100 Continue` response, it could send the rest of the request.

415 Unsupported Media Type   The `415 Unsupported Media Type` response code is used when the sender's request entity is in a format that is not supported by the server for the specified request. A different request method might alter the behavior of the server: suppose a `PUT` request included an entity in a format that the server did not support. The same format could be used in a `POST` request, and the server might be able to accept the entity and forward it to the program that is going to handle it.

3. New codes for other features in HTTP/1.1: We discuss two new response codes in this category here.

402 Payment Required   The `402 Payment Required` status code was added in anticipation of the growth of e-commerce on the Web. However, no semantics have been defined for this code. This is simply a placeholder for future use.

409 Conflict   The `409 Conflict` status code was introduced in an early draft of HTTP/1.0 for supporting version control but did not formally enter the specification until HTTP/1.1. If two users attempt to change a resource via `PUT`, the origin server can detect this as a problem and respond with a `409 Conflict` response. The response body includes an indication of what might have gone wrong if the request had completed. The `409 Conflict` response is sent when the server believes that the client can take remedial actions and resubmit the request. The body of the response can include information that can be used by the user agent to take the appropriate action.

5XX RESPONSE STATUS CODES

Of the two new response codes in the 5xx class, `504 Gateway Timeout` was described earlier in the context of cache control directives. The other new response code in this class is `505 HTTP Version Not Supported`. This is a specific error code indicating that the protocol version number in the request message is not supported by the server. Such lack of support may be due to something as simple as the server's inability to understand the format of messages in the sender's protocol version number. Alternatively, the server might not be able to meet the semantics and capabilities expected by the sender. The response could indicate what *other* protocols the server does support so that the sender can submit a suitable request.

7.13 Summary

After nearly a decade from the time it was conceived, the HTTP protocol has matured into the most widely used application-level protocol of our times. Current data worldwide on the measurable part of the Internet indicates that nearly three out of four packets are in HTTP—either HTTP/1.0 or HTTP/1.1. By any measure, this is a stunning statistic. Although there were several problems in HTTP/1.0, a significant fraction of the traffic in the Internet is still in HTTP/1.0. Many browsers and servers are in HTTP/1.1, but virtually all intermediaries are in HTTP/1.0. This implies that only a small portion of the end-to-end traffic is purely in HTTP/1.1. One reason for the improved hop-by-hop capabilities in HTTP/1.1 is to ensure that protocol enhancements can be used between any two components that speak HTTP/1.1.

This chapter has provided the rationale for the changes to HTTP/1.1 and, where appropriate, traced the evolution of the ideas behind the changes. The hope is that readers become familiar with the process by which protocols are evolved, often under difficult circumstances. The comparative presentation of the HTTP/1.0 and HTTP/1.1 language elements should help the reader appreciate the amount of work that went into evolving the protocol. The categorization of the key semantic changes should help readers focus on the important aspects of the protocol from a practical perspective. Readers should remember that although we have attempted to cover the myriad issues carefully, the IETF standards specifications have the final word on any questions regarding correctness. The next chapter examines how the transport-layer protocol interacts with HTTP.

8

HTTP/TCP Interaction

Although the Hypertext Transfer Protocol (HTTP) does not depend on any particular transport protocol, nearly every implementation of HTTP uses the Transmission Control Protocol (TCP). TCP was standardized in 1980, ten years before the emergence of the Web. Early application-layer protocols built on TCP differ markedly from HTTP. For example, Telnet is an interactive application that uses a single TCP connection to transfer data between a client and server over a period of time. In contrast, a Web client typically establishes multiple TCP connections to retrieve a collection of resources from a Web server. The File Transfer Protocol (FTP) maintains a single control connection between the client and server and transmits data on separate connections. In contrast, HTTP uses a single connection for transferring control and data. Compared with the files transferred by FTP, most Web request and response messages are relatively short. These unique characteristics of Web traffic have important implications for the efficiency of TCP.

This chapter discusses the interaction between HTTP and TCP and the implications for Web performance. First, we discuss how TCP implementations use the expiration of timers to trigger many key operations, such as the re-transmission of lost packets. Although these timers affect any application-level protocol built on top of TCP, the characteristics of HTTP traffic lead to more dramatic performance effects on the Web than on earlier Internet applications. Next we explore how the separation of functionality between the transport and applications layers influences Web performance. Certain TCP mechanisms were motivated by earlier application-level protocols, such as Telnet and Rlogin. These features interact in subtle, and often negative, ways with HTTP. Next we discuss the performance and fairness implications of Web clients that have multiple TCP connections to the same Web server at the same time. For example, a browser may establish multiple connections to download multiple embedded images in a Web page. Busy Web servers must handle a large number of simultaneous TCP connections to a collection of different clients. We discuss ways to reduce the overhead on Web servers of handling a large number of TCP connections.

8.1 TCP Timers

TCP implementations rely on timers to trigger key protocol operations, such as the following:

- **Retransmission of lost packets:** The expiration of the retransmission timer triggers a TCP sender to retransmit a (presumably) lost packet.
- **Repeating the slow-start phase:** Some TCP implementations force a TCP sender to repeat the slow-start phase of congestion control after a period of inactivity.
- **Reclaiming state from a terminated connection:** The TCP sender that initiates the closure of the connection removes the state associated with the connection after a period of time has elapsed.

In this section, we explain why the timers that control these three operations have a significant influence on Web performance. Later, in Section 8.2.3, we discuss another timer that controls the transmission of delayed acknowledgments.

8.1.1 Retransmission timer

Web downloads sometimes stall for several seconds in a row, typically at the beginning of the transfer. These delays often stem from the time required for the TCP sender to detect that an Internet Protocol (IP) packet has been lost. In this section, we explain how the creation of the TCP connection can be delayed for several seconds as a result of a large initial retransmission timeout (RTO) value. Then we explain why retransmission timeouts occur relatively often in the middle of HTTP transfers, compared with other Internet applications.

DELAY IN ESTABLISHING A TCP CONNECTION

From the user's viewpoint, clicking on a hypertext link translates directly into the display of the Web page in the browser window. Transparent to the user, the Web browser proceeds through several steps to retrieve the Web page—establishing a TCP connection, transmitting the HTTP request, receiving the HTTP response from the server, and rendering the resource. Because Web browsing is an interactive application, delay in any of these steps is visible to the user. This is in sharp contrast to noninteractive applications, such as the transfer of e-mail, in which the user does not expect an immediate reply. Although Telnet and FTP are interactive, these applications have a clear separation between establishing the connection and transferring the data. The typical user interacts with the remote machine for a relatively long period of time; therefore, a few seconds of additional delay in establishing the TCP connection and supplying a name and password do not necessarily have a considerable effect on the user's overall satisfaction.

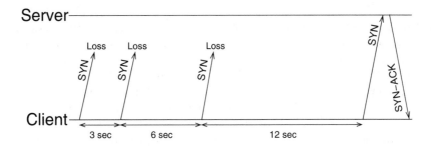

Figure 8.1. Client retransmitting lost SYN packet to server

Establishing a TCP connection requires a three-way handshake—a SYN from the client, a SYN-ACK from the server, and an ACK from the client. In the absence of packet loss, the client can transmit the HTTP request after one round-trip delay. However, the loss of the SYN or the SYN-ACK packet introduces a longer delay. TCP senders have two ways to detect a lost packet— duplicate acknowledgments and a retransmission timeout, as discussed in Chapter 5 (Section 5.2.5). However, the receiver does not send duplicate acknowledgments unless the TCP sender has transmitted multiple packets. At the beginning of the connection, a TCP sender has not transmitted any data packets, and the rate of packet transmission is limited by the small initial congestion window. In the absence of duplicate acknowledgments, the TCP sender must rely on the retransmission timer to detect a lost packet. Selecting the RTO value is a delicate process. A large RTO results in high latency in responding to lost packets, whereas a small RTO results in unnecessary retransmissions. To balance these trade-offs, the TCP sender selects an RTO based on estimates on the round-trip time (RTT) to the receiver.

However, at the beginning of a TCP connection, the sender has not accumulated any RTT measurements. This complicates the selection of an RTO for the initial packets of the connection. To address this problem, the TCP standard prescribes that the sender start with a default RTO of three seconds [PA00]. If the SYN-ACK packet does not arrive after the first retransmission of the SYN packet, the TCP sender increases the RTO from three seconds to six seconds and continues to double the timeout value after each successive retransmission, as shown in Figure 8.1. The combination of the large initial RTO and the exponential backoff avoids generating unnecessary retransmissions of the SYN and SYN-ACK packets when the hosts have a large RTT. If the SYN or SYN-ACK packet is lost, delaying the retransmission avoids overloading the already congested network. The conservative policy for retransmitting lost SYN and SYN-ACK packets does not have much effect on noninteractive applications.

Losing one or more SYN or SYN-ACK packets has a significant influence on Web performance. The loss of two successive SYN packets would result in a total delay of nine seconds before the transmission of the third SYN packet. Arguably, the likelihood of losing one or more SYN or SYN-ACK packets should be quite small. However, the advent of the Web has resulted in substantial network congestion and, consequently, higher packet loss rates (e.g., 5% or more) [Pax99]. Despite the deployment of high-speed links in many parts of the Internet, congestion still occurs on critical links. The links that connect a company, university, or even an entire country to the Internet may be very congested, particularly during the busiest hours of the day. The links between different Internet service providers are often heavily congested. Even if the network is lightly loaded, a busy Web server may lose SYN packets. The operating system on the server machine maintains a queue of pending TCP connections. If this queue is full, new SYN packets are discarded.

The high delay affects the behavior of Web users. The frustrated user may terminate the request by clicking on the Stop button on the browser. The user may then click on the Reload button to repeat the request. When the user clicks on the Stop button, the browser reacts by instructing the operating system to close the underlying TCP connection, as discussed in more detail in Section 8.2.1. When the user then clicks on the Reload button, the browser immediately initiates the creation of a new TCP connection. The operating system transmits a new SYN packet to the server and sets the RTO to its initial value (say, three seconds). If the new SYN packet reaches the server, then the TCP connection would be established much more quickly than waiting for a three-second or six-second timer to expire. The Web user's abort-and-reload behavior effectively triggers an immediate "retransmission" of the SYN packet. The user may also click on the Reload button without clicking on the Stop button. Clicking on the Reload button triggers both the termination of the existing TCP connection and the establishment of a new connection.

Stopping and restarting a stalled transfer typically reduces user-perceived latency, at the expense of higher load on the server and the network. For example, the operating system underlying a busy Web server may discard multiple SYN packets from different clients in a short period of time. If the users react by repeating their requests, each of these clients would send another SYN packet to the server. This exacerbates the already heavy load on the server machine. Similarly, user behavior can inflate the load on a congested network link. A heavily loaded link results in lost packets. Because most Web transfers are short, a relatively large fraction of the lost packets are SYN or SYN-ACK packets. If the lost packet causes the user to stop and restart the request, the client transmits a second SYN packet in a short period of time. This increases the amount of traffic that travels over the already congested link.

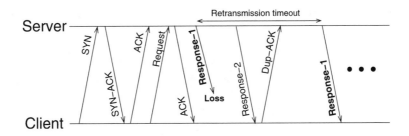

Figure 8.2. Client sending a single duplicate ACK to the server

DELAY IN THE MIDDLE OF A WEB TRANSFER

Compared with the beginning of a connection, long retransmission timeouts are less likely to occur in the middle of transferring a Web response for two reasons:

- **Smaller RTO value:** The TCP sender gradually refines the RTO value by observing the delay experienced by data packets. Over time, the RTO value becomes closer to the actual RTT between the sender and receiver. Consider a sender and a receiver with an RTT of 200 ms. At the beginning of the connection, the TCP sender has a three-second RTO. The TCP sender selects the RTO based on the average and variance of the RTT. Eventually, the RTO may drop to 250 or 300 ms.

- **Duplicate acknowledgments:** Retransmission timeouts are less likely to occur once the TCP sender starts transmitting data. As the data packets arrive, the TCP receiver sends acknowledgment packets that reflect the number of contiguous bytes that have arrived so far. Following a packet loss, the acknowledgment number does not increase for subsequent ACK packets. Upon receiving these duplicate ACK packets, the sender infers that the earlier data packet has not reached the receiver. The reception of three duplicate ACKs triggers the TCP sender to retransmit the missing packet without waiting for the retransmission timer to expire, as discussed in Chapter 5 (Section 5.2.5).

Both of these positive effects become more significant as the TCP sender transmits more data. The RTT estimate becomes more accurate as the hosts exchange more data, and the likelihood of duplicate acknowledgments increases as the TCP sender achieves a larger congestion window.

However, most Web responses involve a relatively small amount of data, in the range of 8 to 12 KB. These short transfers spend most, if not all, of their time in the slow-start phase of congestion control. The slow-start phase begins with a small initial congestion window of one or two packets, as discussed in Chapter 5 (Section 5.2.6). With a small congestion window, the likelihood of

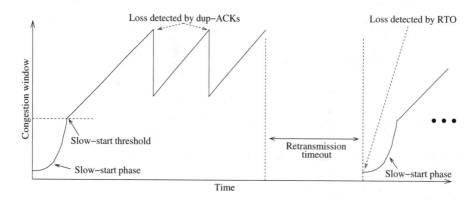

Figure 8.3. Repeating the slow-start phase after a retransmission timeout

successfully delivering multiple packets after a loss is very low. The TCP receiver is unlikely to generate the three duplicate ACKs necessary to trigger a fast retransmission of the lost packet [BPS+98]. For example, the loss of the first packet of a response message would result in a single duplicate acknowledgment triggered by the reception of the second packet, as shown in Figure 8.2. The small congestion window precludes the server from transmitting any additional packets until receiving an acknowledgment for the first packet. Waiting for the retransmission timer to expire stalls the transfer of data from the server. In addition, retransmission timeouts force the TCP sender to reset the size of congestion window to its small initial value, as shown in Figure 8.3. Retransmission timeouts can result in significantly long delays for Web transfers. Stopping and restarting the transfer may result in a faster response, compared with waiting for the retransmission timer to expire.

8.1.2 Slow-start restart

Persistent connections offer an attractive alternative to establishing a separate TCP connection for each Web transfer. Avoiding the slow-start phase of TCP congestion control is one of the purported advantages of reusing an existing TCP connection, as discussed earlier in Chapter 7 (Section 7.5). However, sending a response message on a previously idle persistent connection generates a large burst of packets. To avoid overloading the network, the TCP specification requires a TCP sender to repeat the slow-start phase of congestion control after a period of inactivity. Several techniques have been proposed to avoid repeating the slow-start phase without overloading the network.

IDLE PERSISTENT CONNECTIONS

A Web client often downloads multiple resources from the same Web site in a short period of time. For example, the user may download a Web page that contains multiple embedded images. The browser requests these images from the server after parsing the container HTML file. In addition, a user may click on hypertext links to browse through multiple pages at the same server. With persistent connections, these HTTP transfers can travel over a single TCP connection. The transfers may experience higher throughput by having a larger congestion window. Suppose a client requests an HTML file, followed by requests for four embedded images. The transfer of the HTML file starts with an initial congestion window of one or two packets. The congestion window grows as the transfer proceeds through the slow-start phase. By reusing the connection, the transfer of the embedded images benefits from the larger congestion window. In fact, the congestion window may continue to grow as the server transfers multiple responses.

However, using a large congestion window may overload the network if the persistent connection has been idle for a period of time. Consider a user who downloads a Web page from a server and, after spending five seconds reading the page, retrieves another page from the same server. Assume, for the time being, that the client and the server have both decided to retain the connection. Network congestion may have changed substantially during the five-second idle period. While this TCP connection was inactive, other TCP connections on the same path may have increased their congestion windows to consume the available bandwidth. Consider the simple case of a busy link that carries traffic for five active TCP connections with the same round-trip times. On average, each of the five connections has a throughput of around 20% of link capacity. If one of these connections is idle for several seconds, the other four connections would start sending more aggressively until they each consume around 25% of the capacity.

Allowing the previously idle connection to transmit at its old rate could introduce substantial congestion. The connection would immediately start sending data at a rate that would consume 20% of the link capacity, while the other four connections continue transmitting data at 25% of link capacity. This generates a large amount of additional traffic—20% above the link capacity. Many of the packets traversing the congested link would be lost. In fact, packet losses may force several of the connections to reduce their sending rates. After the connections lower their sending rates, the link may become underutilized. The underutilization persists while the connections gradually increase their congestion windows. In addition to degrading overall performance, sending too aggressively may lower the throughput of the aggressive connection as well. The network congestion may cause the connection to experience a high rate of packet loss, forcing the retransmission of one or more packets.

Repeating the slow-start phase

To avoid generating a sudden burst of packets, the TCP sender should transmit less aggressively after an idle period. The slow-start phase of congestion control was designed precisely to avoid sudden and unexpected bursts of network traffic. During the slow-start phase, the TCP sender increases its congestion window and attempts to estimate its fair share of the bandwidth on its path through the network. Allowing a previously idle connection to use a large congestion window is similar to allowing a new connection to start with a large initial congestion window. The burst of traffic could overwhelm the network links and cause high packet-loss rates. To avoid these performance problems, the TCP specification requires a connection to repeat the slow-start phase following an idle period. This is referred to as the *slow-start restart* mechanism.

A precise definition of the slow-start restart mechanism requires the clarification of two key issues: the beginning of an idle period and the resetting of the congestion window. The idle period starts once the TCP sender stops transmitting data and all previous data packets have been successfully acknowledged by the receiver. After receiving the last acknowledgment, the TCP sender sets a timer. Once the timer expires, the sender resets the congestion window to its initial value of one or two maximum-size packets. The TCP sender uses the current RTO value to define the duration of the idle period. That is, if the application does not introduce any new data during the RTO period, the underlying TCP sender resets the congestion window and repeats the slow-start phase of congestion control.

Slow-start restart would occur if a connection is idle for longer than a few RTTs—typically a few seconds, at most. Most automatically generated requests for embedded resources would arrive within this time interval. However, persistent connections may also handle requests generated by users as they browse through multiple Web pages at the same site. Users frequently introduce longer delays between successive requests. The characteristics of these interrequest times are discussed in more detail in Chapter 10 (Section 10.5.3). The larger spacing between user-generated requests can trigger the slow-start restart mechanism. Repeating the slow-start phase reduces the performance gains achievable with persistent connections. A server cannot fully exploit a high-bandwidth path to the client if successive requests must start with a small congestion window. However, repeating slow start is important for the overall health of the network.

Reducing the slow-start restart performance penalty

The slow-start restart mechanism prevents the previously idle TCP connection from generating a large burst of traffic that would congest the network. Several techniques have been proposed to reduce or avoid the performance penalties associated with slow-start restart [Hei97]:

- **Disabling slow-start restart:** The Web server could disable the use of the slow-start restart mechanism, at the risk of allowing a previously idle connection to generate a large, unexpected burst of traffic. The risk is reduced if the server closes connections after a short idle period. For example, the server may close a connection that has been inactive for more than 15 seconds to limit the total number of connections, as discussed later, in Section 8.4.2.
- **Using a larger slow-start restart timeout:** The operating system underlying the Web server could be configured to use a larger timeout parameter for triggering slow-start restart. However, the larger the timeout parameter, the more likely it is that the connection's previous congestion window is inconsistent with the current status of the network.
- **Gradually decreasing the congestion window:** Rather than an all-or-nothing solution, the TCP sender could *gradually* decrease the congestion window during the idle period. The TCP sender could reduce the congestion window in proportion to the length of the idle period. This adaptive approach becomes more conservative with the increasing uncertainty about prevailing network conditions.
- **Pacing the transmission of packets:** To avoid generating a burst of packets, the TCP sender could pace the transmission of packets into the network. Suppose the congestion window allows the sender to transmit four packets. Transmitting all four packets back-to-back would generate a large burst of traffic. Instead, the sender could introduce some delay after each packet transmission. This would reduce the likelihood of overloading the network links on the path to the receiver, while still allowing the sender to use the four-packet congestion window.

The TCP implementation on the Web server machine could employ a combination of these techniques. For example, the TCP sender could use a larger timeout, gradually decrease the congestion window, and pace the transmission of packets.

8.1.3 The TIME_WAIT state

Busy Web servers handle a high rate of requests for new TCP connections. Having a large number of TCP connections consumes memory resources and introduces overhead in processing incoming packets. Ideally, the operating system could reclaim these resources as soon as the connection closes. However, TCP requires one of the two hosts to retain information about the closed connection for a period of time. In this subsection, we explain why one host must enter the so-called TIME_WAIT state and why this responsibility often falls

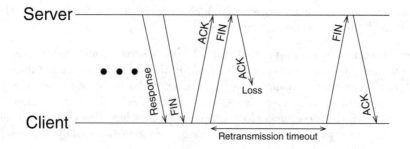

Figure 8.4. Loss and retransmission of final ACK packet from the server

upon the Web server rather than the client. Then we discuss several proposals for reducing the overhead of the TIME_WAIT state on Web servers.

RETAINING INFORMATION ABOUT CLOSED CONNECTIONS

Retaining information about closed TCP connections introduces significant overhead on a busy Web server. Consider a Web server that closes a connection after sending an HTTP response to the client. Closing the connection initiates a four-way handshake, starting with the transmission of a FIN packet, as discussed in Chapter 5 (Section 5.2.3). Upon receiving the FIN packet, the TCP implementation at the client sends an acknowledgment packet. Then the client reads the HTTP response. After the last byte of the response message, the client reads an end-of-file (EOF) character that signifies that the server has closed its end of the connection. The client then closes its end of the connection, which triggers the transmission of a FIN packet. Upon receiving the client's FIN, the TCP implementation at the server sends an ACK, completing the handshake. After receiving the ACK, the client knows that the connection has been terminated. However, the *server* has no way of knowing if the client ever received the ACK packet.

Suppose that the server's final ACK packet was lost in the network, as shown in Figure 8.4. If the ACK packet was lost, the client would eventually experience a retransmission timeout. After the timeout, the client would send its FIN packet again. If the retransmitted FIN packet is lost, the client would experience another timeout and send the FIN packet again. Because the server does not know whether or not its ACK has reached the client, the server does not know if the ACK packet must be transmitted again. In the meantime, the server cannot delete its information about the TCP connection. Suppose that the server removes all information about the connection, under the false assumption that the client has received the ACK packet. Later, when a retransmitted FIN packet arrives, the server would not know that this packet belonged to the closed connection. Thinking that the FIN packet was sent erroneously, the server would send an RST (reset) packet back to the client, rather than retransmitting the ACK packet.

A more serious situation arises when the connection has one or more outstanding packets in the network. Suppose that the server has received the entire request message and the client has received the entire response message. A duplicate (retransmitted) packet from this connection may remain in the network. That is, a packet may have been sent more than once, with one copy reaching the recipient and the other copy still traveling through the network. This packet may eventually reach the receiver. The handling of the duplicate packet depends on the status of the connection between the two hosts, as follows:

- **Connection is still open:** Suppose the duplicate packet arrives while the TCP connection is still open. The receiver inspects the sequence number of the packet and recognizes that this data has already been received. The receiver discards the duplicate packet.
- **Connection has been closed and no new connection exists:** Suppose that the connection has been closed and the two hosts have not established a new TCP connection. When the packet arrives, the operating system on the receiving machine inspects the port numbers in the TCP header to identify the connection associated with the data. No active connection matches these port numbers, so the receiver discards the packet.
- **Connection has been closed and a new connection exists:** Suppose that the connection has been closed and the two hosts have established a new connection using the *same pair* of port numbers. When the duplicate packet arrives, the port numbers are inspected by the operating system on the receiving machine. The port numbers match an existing connection, and the data is directed to the application associated with the new connection. This is a mistake, because the duplicate packet does not actually belong to this new connection.

To prevent the receiver from associating the duplicate packet with the wrong application, the two hosts must have a way to avoid creating a new connection with the same port numbers, at least for some period of time after the closure of the previous connection.

To prevent the establishment of a new connection with the same port numbers, at least *one* of the hosts must remember that the previous connection existed. The TCP specification assigns this responsibility to the host that sends the first FIN packet. On this host, the TCP connection enters the TIME_WAIT state. The operating system maintains information relating to the connection to retransmit the final ACK packet, if necessary, and to prevent creation of a new connection with the same IP addresses and port numbers. The connection must stay in the TIME_WAIT state long enough that no outstanding packets remain in the network. This is very difficult because IP does not provide a limit on the worst-case delay for delivering a packet. In practice, the time-to-live (TTL) field in the IP packet header should ensure that a packet does not remain in the network indefinitely, as discussed in Chapter 5 (Section 5.1.4). The 8-bit field permits a maximum TTL value of 255 seconds.

TCP requires the host to remain in the TIME_WAIT state for twice the *maximum segment lifetime* (MSL), an estimate of the worst-case delay. The TCP standard specifies that implementations should use an MSL of 2 minutes [J. 81], though common implementations use 30 seconds, 1 minute, or 2 minutes. On the one hand, a small MSL reduces the duration of the TIME_WAIT state, which reduces the amount of system resources devoted to retaining information about closed TCP connections. However, a small MSL also increases the likelihood that a duplicate packet remains in the network. Likewise, a small MSL increases the likelihood that the sender is unable to re-transmit a lost final ACK packet. On the other hand, a large MSL results in a long stay in the TIME_WAIT state. This results in a potentially large number of connections in the TIME_WAIT state at the same time, which could consume significant system resources on a busy Web server. In addition, a large MSL value could actually limit the achievable rate of communication between the two hosts.

Suppose a client creates a TCP connection with port 1025 to a server running on port 80 on a remote host. After sending the FIN packet to close the TCP connection, the server enters the TIME_WAIT state for four minutes. After receiving the ACK from the server, the client terminates the connection. The client may wish to establish another connection to the same server to request another resource. This new connection must use a different client port (such as 1026) because the server is still in the TIME_WAIT state for the old connection. The TCP header has a 16-bit field for the port number, which restricts the number of different ports that can be used by the client during the four-minute period. In practice, this would not impose a significant limitation on a typical Web browser. However, a busy proxy may need to establish TCP connections to a popular server at a very high rate. The restriction is even more significant if the proxy is configured to send all requests to a downstream proxy. The inability to establish new connections with the old port numbers limits how often the proxy can send requests to the next proxy in the chain.

EFFECT OF TIME_WAIT ON WEB SERVERS

Web servers often initiate the closure of a TCP connection and bear the overhead associated with the TIME_WAIT state. First, consider the case in which the client and the server do not maintain a persistent connection. In this situation, the server would typically close the connection (by sending a FIN packet) immediately after sending the HTTP response to the client. Second, consider the case in which both the client and the server keep the TCP connection open.

In this scenario, eventually either the client or the server closes the TCP connection. The server often has a stronger incentive to close the connection. For example, a busy Web server cannot afford to maintain a persistent connection for every client. In fact, a Web server typically applies an application-level timeout to close a TCP connection after a period of inactivity, as discussed later, in Section 8.4.2. In contrast, a Web browser may have little incentive to close a persistent connection because reusing the existing connection would reduce the latency experienced by the user over establishing a new connection.

In either of these two scenarios, the server closes the connection first and hence must enter the TIME_WAIT state. The situation becomes more complicated when the client is an intermediary, such as a proxy. A busy proxy has connections to a large number of clients and servers. A proxy may have as much of an incentive to close the connection as the server, if not more. If the proxy closes the connection, then the proxy incurs the burden of the TIME_WAIT state, rather than the server. The TIME_WAIT state imposes a heavy burden on busy proxies as well. In general, the TIME_WAIT state introduces an unfortunate trade-off—because busy hosts have an incentive to close connections, the busy hosts must bear the overhead of the TIME_WAIT state.

The overhead of the TIME_WAIT state is exacerbated by the fact that the TCP connections are relatively short-lived because most Web responses are small. Suppose a client requests a single resource from a Web server. The server may spend a few seconds sending the response message. After closing the connection, the server must stay in the TIME_WAIT state for four minutes. This is an extremely long time relative to the period that the connection was open. Earlier Internet applications, such as Telnet and FTP, typically used TCP connections for a longer period of time. Compared with an FTP server, a Web server has a larger proportion of its TCP connections in the TIME_WAIT state. The use of persistent connections partially addresses the problem. Using a single TCP connection for multiple HTTP transfers reduces the total number of TCP connections opened, and closed, at the server. This, in turn, reduces the number of TCP connections in the TIME_WAIT state. However, a busy Web server may still have a large number of connections at a time in the TIME_WAIT state.

REDUCING TIME_WAIT OVERHEAD

Reducing the burden of the TIME_WAIT state is extremely important for high-performance Web servers. Techniques for reducing this overhead fall into two main categories—lowering the system resource requirements for TIME_WAIT connections and shifting the responsibility for the TIME_WAIT state to Web clients. The operating system must retain information about each connection in the TIME_WAIT state. Storing this information consumes memory that could be used for other purposes, such as caching frequently accessed Web resources.

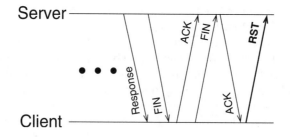

Figure 8.5. Client sending RST to free server from the TIME_WAIT state

Fortunately, the operating system does not need to retain as much information for TIME_WAIT connections as for active connections. Modern operating systems reduce the memory requirements to the bare minimum necessary for the operating system to retransmit the final ACK packet and to prevent the creation of a new connection with the same IP addresses and port numbers. Having a large number of connections in the TIME_WAIT state also increases the overhead for the operating system to check for expired TCP timers, such as the retransmission timer. Most operating systems check for expired timers by periodically scanning the list of TCP connections. Placing the TIME_WAIT connections at the end of this list reduces the processing time required to scan the list. Reducing the memory and processing requirements for TIME_WAIT connections results in a substantial increase in the throughput of busy Web servers [AD99].

Despite the benefits of reducing the memory and processing requirements, the TIME_WAIT state still imposes an overhead on Web servers. Several techniques have been proposed that shift the responsibility for the TIME_WAIT state to the client [FTY99], which presumably handles a relatively smaller number of TCP connections, as follows:

- **Change TCP:** The specification of TCP could be changed to have the *recipient* of the first FIN packet incur the burden of the TIME_WAIT state. For example, suppose the Web server closes a TCP connection and sends a FIN packet to the client. After receiving the server FIN, the client TCP implementation could transition to the TIME_WAIT state. To ensure that the server does not enter the TIME_WAIT state, the client could send an RST packet to the server, as shown in Figure 8.5. Receiving an RST packet triggers the operating system at the server to leave the TIME_WAIT state and reclaim the memory resources associated with the TCP connection. An alternative approach involves changing the procedure for establishing a TCP connection to require the two hosts to negotiate who should handle the TIME_WAIT state upon connection closure.

- **Change HTTP:** The specification of HTTP could be changed to have the client initiate the closure of the TCP connection. For example, a new response header could allow the server to instruct the client to close the connection after receiving the complete response message. A new request header could allow the client to express its willingness to assume responsibility for closing the connection. For example, the client could close the TCP connection after automatically downloading the embedded images in a Web page. However, relinquishing control to the client may not be an appropriate solution in practice. The client may not have an incentive to close the connection, or to assume responsibility for the TIME_WAIT state.

However, each of these approaches requires changes to TCP or HTTP. Neither of the proposed approaches offers an attractive solution to the performance problems associated with the TIME_WAIT state. Instead, administrators of busy Web servers typically modify the operating system to reduce the TIME_WAIT timeout (e.g., five seconds). This reduces the TIME_WAIT overhead, at the risk of establishing a new TCP connection with the same port numbers.

8.2 HTTP/TCP Layering

The transfer of Web resources draws on the application-layer functions provided by HTTP and the transport-layer functions provided by TCP. In some cases, it is not clear which layer should perform a certain function. This section discusses three examples in which functions implemented at the transport layer have a significant effect on Web performance:

- **Aborted HTTP transfers:** Because the HTTP protocol does not have a mechanism for terminating an ongoing transfer, aborting an HTTP request requires closing the underlying transport connection, as discussed in Section 8.2.1.
- **Nagle's algorithm:** Nagle's algorithm limits the number of small packets transmitted by a TCP sender, which may delay the transfer of the last packet of an HTTP message, as discussed in Section 8.2.2.
- **Delayed acknowledgments:** The TCP receiver may delay transmission of an acknowledgment in the hope of piggybacking the acknowledgment on an outgoing data packet, at the expense of increasing the latency in transferring an HTTP message, as discussed in Section 8.2.3.

Handling aborted transfers at the transport layer avoids the need for HTTP to have an intricate relationship with any particular transport protocol. Nagle's algorithm and delayed acknowledgments were included in implementations of

TCP to reduce the overhead of transferring data for interactive applications such as Telnet and Rlogin.

8.2.1 Aborted HTTP transfers

A user may abort an ongoing Web transfer by clicking on the Stop button or by clicking on a hypertext link to retrieve another page. Abort operations are a common part of conventional Web browsing. In some cases, the browser may display the contents of a page as the response message arrives from the server. This allows the user to read part of the page and, perhaps, click on a hypertext link before the page has arrived in its entirety. In particular, the user may click on a hypertext link before all of the embedded images have been downloaded. In other cases, a user may interrupt a transfer that is proceeding slowly and then hit the Reload button to attempt to download the page again. A user with slow network access, such as a telephone modem, may be more likely to abort Web transfers. Transfers of large resources are likely to be aborted before they complete. In this subsection, we explain why aborting a Web transfer requires closing the underlying transport connection and discuss the implications on Web performance.

Absence of an abort mechanism in HTTP

HTTP does not provide a way for the client to communicate its desire to terminate the ongoing transfer. The notion of aborting a request lies at the boundary between the transport and application layers. Including an abort mechanism in HTTP would have been difficult to do without specifying the interaction with the underlying transport protocol. Although Web transfers typically employ TCP, the HTTP specification is divorced from the details of any particular transport protocol. Other application-level protocols, such as Telnet, have faced the same challenges. Telnet chose a different solution. During a Telnet session, a user can type cntl-C or the Delete key to abort the current command. The sender can use the urgent pointer field in the TCP header to draw the immediate attention of the receiver, as discussed in Chapter 5 (Section 5.2.7). This avoids the need for the receiver to process the previous bytes of the stream. However, this optimization is tied closely to TCP.

HTTP/1.1 could have followed a similar approach by introducing an abort request method. However, introducing an abort request would complicate the handling of pipelined requests. Suppose that a client has sent several pipelined requests on a persistent connection, followed by an abort request on the same connection. The server would need to read ahead in the list of pipelined requests to learn that the client has requested an abort. If the client pipelines several requests, either the server would have to abort all of the pending requests or the client would need to indicate which requests should be aborted. Addressing these problems would have introduced substantial complexity to the protocol. Thus the specification of HTTP/1.1 does not include an abort mechanism.

Consequently, a Web client has no effective way to abort an ongoing HTTP transfer short of terminating the underlying transport connection. Consider a user that aborts the transfer of a 20 MB file after 5 MB have arrived. The client has two choices: terminating the TCP connection or receiving 15 MB of unnecessary data. Retrieving extra data imposes a burden on the network and consumes bandwidth that could be used to satisfy the user's next request. This increases user-perceived latency. Hence, most Web client implementations choose to terminate the TCP connection.

EFFECT OF ABORT OPERATIONS ON WEB PERFORMANCE

Aborting the TCP connection has important implications for Web performance. Consider an HTTP/1.1 browser that has a persistent connection to an HTTP/1.1 server. After retrieving an HTML file, the browser generates a series of pipelined requests for the various embedded images. Suppose that while the server is transmitting these images, the user clicks on a hypertext link to access another Web page at the same site. The browser terminates the TCP connection to abort the transfer of the embedded images. Terminating the TCP connection avoids the transfer of the remainder of the embedded images. However, the user must wait for the browser to establish a new TCP connection to the server before the next Web page can be retrieved. This requires the typical three-way handshake to open the new connection and the repetition of the TCP slow-start phase.

Aborted transfers can introduce additional problems when the HTTP request has a side effect. For example, the user's request could create a new resource, increment a variable, or trigger a script that purchases a product at an e-commerce site. If the TCP connection is terminated before the browser receives the server's response message, then the user does not know whether the request was completed at the server or not. HTTP does not provide any way for the server to unilaterally contact the client to indicate whether the request was processed. The Web site may maintain additional state that enables the client to determine whether the previous request was processed. Suppose a user visits an e-commerce site and sends a request that would add an item to a virtual shopping basket. Upon aborting the request, the user may not know if the item was successfully added to the basket. The Web site may allow the user to visit a Web page that displays the current contents of the shopping basket. This would allow the user to determine whether the previous request had completed before the TCP connection was aborted. Alternatively, the HTML form could include a unique transaction number that enables the script processing the request to recognize whether the transaction has already been performed.

Abort operations tighten the coupling between pipelined requests on the same TCP connection. Aborting one request in the pipeline requires aborting all of the pipelined requests that have not been processed yet. For example, aborting the downloading of a Web page terminates the transfer of all of the embedded images. This captures the intent of the user to abort the transfer of the entire page, rather than the downloading of a single Web resource. However, consider the case of a proxy that pipelines requests from two clients on a single persistent connection to a Web server. The proxy issues a request on behalf of client A, followed by a request on behalf of client B. If client A aborts its request, then the proxy has two choices. The proxy could keep the connection open and receive the server's entire response to the first request. This is wasteful because client A does not want to receive this data. Alternatively, the proxy could abort the connection. This would require the proxy to open a new connection and send client B's request a second time. Neither option is attractive. The proxy cannot avoid this problem without having a separate TCP connection to the server on behalf of each client.

The user-level abort operation does not immediately stop the transfer of data from the server. Consider a browser communicating directly with a Web server. When the user clicks on Stop, the browser initiates termination of the TCP connection by sending a FIN or RST packet to the server. In the meantime, the server continues to send data to the client. Depending on the propagation delay and the size of the Web response, the entire response may be transmitted before the server receives the RST/FIN packet. The problem is exacerbated when the client sends the request via an intermediary, such as a proxy. In this case, the HTTP transfer involves a TCP connection between the client and the proxy and a second TCP connection between the proxy and the server. Suppose that the server-proxy path has high bandwidth relative to the proxy-client path. This is a common scenario when the client has a low-speed modem. Because of the mismatch in network bandwidth, the transfer between the server and the proxy may proceed much more quickly than the transfer between the proxy and the client.

Consider a client that requests a 20 MB resource and aborts the transfer after receiving 5 MB of the response. The proxy may have received the entire resource from the server. The transfer of the last 15 MB is wasted, unless the proxy receives another request for the resource in the near future. If the client had communicated with the server over its slow connection, rather than through a proxy, the server would not have sent the additional 15 MB. Flow control on a single TCP connection between the client and the server would have prevented the server from sending so aggressively. Preventing the transfer of excess data requires some coupling between the server-proxy and proxy-client connections. The proxy could limit how much data it reads from the connection to the server. By not reading the data in the receive buffer, the proxy reduces the receiver window of the TCP connection. Reducing the receiver window size limits how much data the server can transmit. Deciding how much data to read from the receive buffer introduces a fundamental tension between avoiding excess traffic for aborted transfers and reducing latency for normal transfers.

DETAILS OF ABORTING THE TCP CONNECTION

The browser aborts an ongoing data transfer by invoking a system call to close the connection to the Web server. Depending on the browser implementation and the operating system, the system call may generate either a FIN or an RST packet. Assume that the system call triggers the transmission of a FIN packet. Upon receiving the FIN packet, the operating system on the server machine delivers an EOF to the server application. The operating system continues to transmit data from the send buffer to the remote client. After reading the EOF, the server stops writing new data into the send buffer. The data already in the send buffer and in the network would be delivered to the machine running the browser. Whether the browser application sees this additional data or not depends on how the connection was closed. If the browser has closed both the reading and writing ends of its connection, the operating system would discard the data. If the read direction of the connection remains open, then the operating system would deliver the data to the browser application. Continuing to receive data may be useful if the browser plans to cache the partial contents to satisfy future user requests.

Some UNIX implementations do not allow applications to initiate the transmission of an RST packet. For these systems, an abort would generate a FIN packet, whereas other operating systems may trigger an RST packet. Upon receiving an RST, the operating system on the server machine discards any remaining outgoing data for the connection, including data that the server application has already written into the send buffer. This is both good and bad. On the positive side, resetting the TCP connection avoids the transfer of additional data from the server. In addition, the RST packet causes the operating system on the server machine to discard any data residing in the receive buffer, rather than allowing the receiving application to read the data. This would obviate the need for the server to read any pipelined HTTP requests that might reside in the receive buffer. On the negative side, an RST does not close the connection in a clean manner. For example, suppose that some of the packets sent by the server machine had not reached the receiver. After receiving an RST, the operating system on the server machine would not retransmit these lost packets.

8.2.2 Nagle's algorithm

Interactive applications such as Rlogin and Telnet typically generate many small packets to transmit user keystrokes and short responses. Nagle's algorithm reduces the number of small packets by delaying the transmission of data [Nag84]. After discussing the motivation for limiting the number of small packets, we describe how Nagle's algorithm degrades the performance of Web transfers, particularly under persistent connections. Then we explain how the Web server can prevent the transmission of small packets even when Nagle's algorithm is disabled.

REDUCING THE NUMBER OF SMALL PACKETS

Consider the Telnet application that allows a user to interact with a machine in another location. This application coordinates the transfer of user keystrokes to the remote machine and the transfer of the machine's responses back to the user. Quick responses are necessary to give the user the illusion of interacting directly with the remote machine. However, the TCP sender underlying the Telnet application should not generate a separate IP packet for each keystroke. Otherwise, each keystroke would result in a 41-byte packet—a 20-byte IP header, a 20-byte TCP header, and 1 byte of data. Sending 41 bytes for every byte of data would introduce significant overhead, resulting in heavy congestion in the network. After receiving data from the application, the operating system should wait to accumulate additional data before transmitting a packet. Interactive applications are not tolerant of latency; therefore the operating system should not delay the transmission for very long. Nagle's algorithm addresses this trade-off. The algorithm ensures that the TCP sender transmits at most one small packet per RTT. In this context, a "small" packet is a packet containing fewer bytes than the maximum segment size (MSS) for the TCP connection (e.g., 536 or 1460 bytes).

Consider a TCP sender that has transmitted a packet and is waiting for an acknowledgment from the receiver. The TCP sender does not transmit any small packets until all outstanding acknowledgments are received. By this time, the sender may have accumulated additional data. On a wide-area connection with a large RTT, Nagle's algorithm avoids having multiple short packets in flight at the same time. On a local-area connection with a small RTT, the acknowledgment packets from the receiver almost always arrive before the sender has new data to transmit. Limiting the number of short packets in flight would not introduce any extra delay before sending the next data packet. In addition, Nagle's algorithm would not affect bulk-transfer applications because the transmission of a large file typically results in full-size segments. The approach has the most influence precisely when it is needed—for interactive applications communicating over a connection with a large RTT.

NAGLE'S ALGORITHM AND PERSISTENT CONNECTIONS

Nagle's algorithm can have a negative effect on Web performance when Web transfers result in the transmission of small TCP segments. Consider a Web

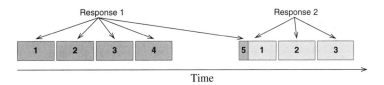

Figure 8.6. Server transmitting full-size packet containing end of response

server that transmits an HTTP response message by writing the response header followed by the response body, using two separate system calls. The underlying operating system might transmit the HTTP header in a single, small segment before the Web server has performed the second system call that writes the response body into the send buffer. Suppose the response body is also smaller than the maximum segment size. In theory, the operating system would have to delay the transmission of the response body, in the hope of accumulating more data. However, if the server application initiates the closure of the connection, the operating system does not expect the application to provide any additional data over the connection. This triggers the transmission of the small segment, regardless of whether the acknowledgment of the first packet has arrived. If the server does not close the connection, the operating system does not transmit the small second segment until the acknowledgment of the first segment arrives. In addition to the RTT for the acknowledgment to reach the server, the operating system at the client machine may delay the transmission of the acknowledgment packet, as discussed later in Section 8.2.3.

Even if the server writes the entire response message in one step, Nagle's algorithm can degrade the effectiveness of persistent connections [Hei97]. Consider a Web server that writes an HTTP response message into the send buffer. This would generate a relatively large amount (say, 8 to 12 KB) of data, typically in a short period of time. The operating system would transmit the response message as a series of full-size packets. At most, depending on the size of the response, there may be one small final packet at the end of the message. For example, consider a 6000-byte message that is transmitted over a TCP connection with an MSS of 1460 bytes. This would result in four 1460-byte segments and one 160-byte segment. The operating system would transmit the sequence of full-size packets and then delay the transmission of the small final packet. The transmission of the final packet is triggered by one of the following two events:

- **Writing of additional data into the send buffer:** The server application may write additional data into the send buffer, resulting in the transmission of a full-size packet, as shown in Figure 8.6. The packet contains the end of the first response message and the beginning of the second response message. However, the server does not necessarily have additional

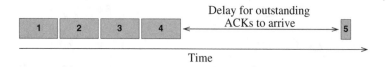

Figure 8.7. Server transmitting small packet after receiving ACKs

data to transmit to the client. For example, the server may not have additional requests from this connection to process at this time.

- **Receiving all outstanding acknowledgments:** Acknowledgments may arrive for all of the outstanding data that was transmitted to the receiver, allowing the operating system to transmit the small final packet. Figure 8.7 shows an example in which the server has an initial congestion window of two full-size packets and receives an ACK packet for every other data packet. Waiting for acknowledgments introduces an RTT delay. For small response messages, the round-trip delay in sending the small final packet may be a very significant part of the total latency.

Disabling Nagle's algorithm is an easy way to avoid these performance penalties. This is achieved by setting the appropriate option when establishing the connection. For example, the UNIX operating system has a *setsockopt()* function for setting options. Setting the TCP_NODELAY option in the *setsockopt()* call disables Nagle's algorithm. Web servers supporting persistent connections typically disable Nagle's algorithm. Web clients may also disable Nagle's algorithm. Otherwise, the transmission of large request messages, such as PUT and POST requests, may encounter performance penalties.

DISADVANTAGE OF DISABLING NAGLE'S ALGORITHM

On the surface, disabling Nagle's algorithm should not have any undesirable effects on Web performance. However, Nagle's algorithm provides important protection when the application writes data in small increments. Consider a Web server that performs a separate system call to write each line of the HTTP response header. With Nagle's algorithm disabled, each *write()* call could result in a separate packet. This would be very inefficient. For example, consider a 300-byte response header consisting of ten lines. The header should fit in a single IP packet. In fact, the packet could also include the initial part of the response body, if one exists. However, writing the header lines one at a time would result in up to ten packets when Nagle's algorithm is disabled. This problem was common in the early NCSA Web server, which invoked a system call to write each response header. A similar phenomenon has also been observed in a Network News Transfer Protocol (NNTP) server [MSMV99].

The likelihood of having a separate packet for each header depends on the load on the server. A heavily loaded server is less likely to send a large number of small packets. Consider a busy server that is generating and sending hundreds of responses at the same time. The transmission of IP packets is limited by the bandwidth of the underlying network connection. During periods of heavy load, the operating system must queue the data written by the server. Consider a server process that invokes ten system calls to write the headers of a single response message. On a heavily loaded server, the second system call may occur before the server transmits the data from the first system call. The operating system combines the data from the two system calls into a single packet. In fact, the operating system may transmit all ten headers in a single packet. If the server were lightly loaded, the operating system would transmit the ten headers as separate packets. Each of these packets would incur a 40-byte overhead for the IP and TCP headers.

The server can avoid generating small packets without enabling Nagle's algorithm by generating the entire response header and then invoking a single *write()* call to write the header into the transmit buffer. This ensures that the operating system does not create separate packets for each header line and also avoids the overhead of performing multiple system calls. In fact, the server could conceivably perform a single system call to send both the HTTP header and the response body, as discussed in more detail later, in Section 8.4.1.

8.2.3 Delayed acknowledgments

By design, TCP supports bidirectional communication between two hosts. When both hosts transmit traffic, TCP acknowledgments can be piggybacked on data transfers. Delaying the transmission of an acknowledgment increases the likelihood of piggybacking the ACK on a data packet. Although effective for two-way applications such as Telnet and Rlogin, delaying the transmission of acknowledgments increases the latency for Web transfers. If Nagle's algorithm is enabled, delayed acknowledgments can stall the downloading of the last portion of a Web page. In this subsection, we discuss the motivation for delayed acknowledgments and examine the implications on Web performance.

MOTIVATION FOR DELAYED ACKNOWLEDGMENTS

A TCP sender depends on acknowledgments from the receiver to pace the transmission of data. The congestion window controls the packet transmissions. Once the window is full, the sender cannot transmit new data packets before receiving an ACK from the receiver. Receiving ACKs in a timely manner is crucial to sustaining a high data-transfer rate. However, sending an ACK requires the receiver to transmit a 40-byte packet—a 20-byte IP header and a 20-byte TCP header, with the ACK bit set. This is very inefficient. Consider a sender that transmits 400-byte packets to the receiver. Sending a 40-byte acknowledgment packet for every data packet would increase the amount of traffic in the network by 10%. The amount of acknowledgment traffic can be reduced in two ways. First, the receiver does not necessarily have to send an ACK for every data packet. Second, the receiver could piggyback the ACK information (the ACK flag and acknowledgment number) while sending data packets of its own.

Piggybacking the ACK on an outgoing data packet avoids sending separate acknowledgment packets. This is very effective when the receiver has data of its own awaiting transmission. However, piggybacking is impossible when the receiver does not have data to send. To increase the likelihood of piggybacking, TCP allows the receiver to *delay* transmission of the ACK packet in the hope that the application will generate data soon. This is very effective for interactive applications. Consider a user running on machine A that has an Rlogin session with machine B. Suppose the user types one or more characters. These characters are sent over the TCP connection to B. Then the Rlogin application reads these characters from the connection. The application generates an echo of these characters to be displayed on the screen on machine A. The echo generates a data packet to be sent from B to A. Ideally, B would acknowledge reception of the initial characters and send the echo with a single packet. However, this is not possible if B generates an ACK immediately after receiving the data packet from A. Instead, the receiver could delay the ACK and piggyback it on the packet with the echoed characters.

The longer B waits to send the ACK, the higher the chance of piggybacking on an outgoing data packet. However, B should not wait too long. Acknowledging the receipt of the packet from A is important. A may not be able to send additional data if the transfer is not acknowledged. Hence, delaying the ACK could increase the latency of transfers from A to B. To balance this trade-off, TCP invokes a timer to trigger the transmission of the ACK, even if no outgoing data is available. Most TCP implementations send outstanding ACKs every 200 ms, although some implementations introduce a delay of up to 500 ms. To avoid delaying ACKs for busy connections, TCP requires that at least every other full-size packet must be acknowledged, even if the delayed-ACK timer has not expired. For example, if a Web server is transmitting a large response message to a client at high speed, the client would transmit an ACK packet immediately after receiving every other data packet, even if the client did not have outgoing data to send to the server.

INTERACTION OF DELAYED ACKS WITH HTTP TRAFFIC

Delayed ACKs reduce the amount of acknowledgment traffic in two ways: by piggybacking the ACK on an outgoing data packet and by sending an ACK for every other data packet, rather than every packet. Piggybacking of ACKs is very unlikely for Web traffic. A typical Web transfer involves a small HTTP request message from the client, followed by an HTTP response from the server.

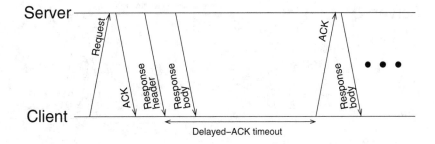

Figure 8.8. Client delaying the ACK of first two segments from server

It is very unlikely that *both* hosts would transmit data at the same time, except perhaps when a server is sending a response while the client is pipelining subsequent request messages. Delaying the transmission of an ACK packet rarely allows the client to piggyback the acknowledgment on an outgoing data packet. Instead, the 200 to 500 ms latency introduced by the delayed-ACK timer can degrade Web performance. This latency may be visible to the user. In addition, when the server's congestion window is full, delaying the transmission of acknowledgments stalls the transmission of the rest of the response.

The delayed-ACK mechanism can introduce unnecessary delay for Web traffic, depending on how the server software is written. Consider a Web server that transmits an HTTP response header and body in two separate steps. The HTTP response header is typically smaller than the MSS. The operating system may transmit the small packet before the application writes any additional data into the send buffer. Later, the server application starts writing the response body into the send buffer. If the server has disabled Nagle's algorithm, the operating system can start transmitting the packets containing the response body. Upon receiving the first full-size packet, the client has received two packets from the server. However, the client does *not* generate an ACK because the first packet (the HTTP header) was smaller than the MSS. The client must wait for the delayed-ACK timer to expire before sending an ACK. Depending on the congestion window size, the server may not be able to transmit additional data until the ACK arrives, as shown in Figure 8.8. To avoid this problem, some operating systems disable the delayed-ACK mechanism at the beginning of a connection. However, this does not prevent the problem from arising for subsequent response messages that use the same TCP connection.

Nagle's algorithm has a subtle interaction with the delayed-ACK mechanism when the server and the client maintain a persistent connection [Hei97]; the same phenomenon has been observed in an NNTP server [MSMV99]. Consider a Web server that has written an HTTP response into the send buffer. The operating system divides the response message into TCP segments, each

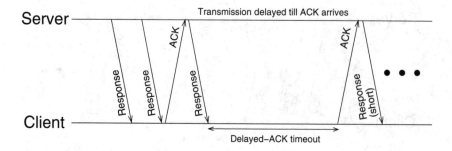

Figure 8.9. Interaction of Nagle's algorithm with delayed ACKs

transmitted in an IP packet. The operating system tries to send data in full-size packets, though the last packet is typically smaller than the others. For example, consider a 5000-byte message that is transmitted as three 1460-byte segments and one 620-byte segment. Following the delayed-ACK algorithm, the client acknowledges each pair of full-size packets. After receiving acknowledgments for the first two packets, the server transmits the third full-size packet. Upon receiving this packet, the operating system on the client machine does not transmit an acknowledgment packet, in accordance with the delayed-ACK mechanism. However, the operating system on the server machine does not transmit the final small segment until receiving all outstanding acknowledgments. The server transmission stalls awaiting an ACK from the client (because of Nagle's algorithm), and the client delays the acknowledgment (because of the delayed-ACK algorithm), as shown in Figure 8.9. Fortunately, disabling Nagle's algorithm at the server can prevent this situation from arising in practice.

8.3 Multiplexing TCP Connections

The previous two sections consider the dynamics of an individual TCP connection. However, a client often establishes *multiple* TCP connections to a server. Having multiple TCP connections at the same time has important performance and fairness implications. In this section, we examine the motivations for clients to establish multiple connections, discuss the resulting performance issues, and consider several ways to control the potential performance problems.

8.3.1 Motivation for parallel connections

A Web client has several incentives to have multiple TCP connections to a Web server at the same time as follows:

- **Simultaneous downloading of embedded images:** A Web browser typically establishes parallel connections to a server to retrieve multiple embedded images at the same time. The first few bytes of an image typically indicate the size of the picture. This allows the browser to start rendering the Web page before the images have arrived in their entirety. The JPEG and GIF formats also support *progressive* encoding, or *interlacing,* which enables the browser to display the image with increasing quality as the response message arrives from the server. A user may prefer to see a coarse-grain view of several embedded images rather than a fine-grain view of a single image, making parallel downloading of embedded images an attractive alternative to serializing the requests. Parallel connections also arise when a user issues requests from multiple browser windows at the same time.

- **Proxy acting on behalf of multiple clients:** A Web proxy may handle requests for multiple clients accessing the same Web server at the same time. The proxy could conceivably send all of the requests over a single TCP connection. This avoids the overhead of establishing a new connection, at the expense of coupling the performance experienced by different users. Suppose user A and user B configure their browsers to connect to the same proxy. Suppose user B requests a 100-byte HTML file just after user A requested a 100 MB file from the same Web server. If the proxy sends both requests over the same (persistent) connection to the server, then user B would have to wait for the transmission of the 100-megabyte file to complete before any part of the small HTML file would be sent. Having two connections to the server would allow the proxy to retrieve the files in parallel, resulting in a much better response time for user B.

- **Higher throughput by transmitting aggressively:** The client can achieve higher throughput by establishing multiple TCP connections to the server. Suppose a client communicates with a server over a path with a large RTT. Even if the network and the server are lightly loaded, the high RTT limits the TCP throughput. The maximum window size is limited by the client's receive buffer and the congestion window, and the server cannot transmit more than one window's worth of data before receiving acknowledgments sent by the client. In addition, the congestion window is small at the beginning of the connection because of the slow-start phase of congestion control. Transmitting responses over multiple connections can increase the overall throughput from the server to the client.

The HTTP specification suggests that a user agent should have at most two TCP connections to a server at a time, and a proxy that handles requests on behalf of multiple clients should limit itself to two connections per requesting client. However, client and proxy implementations often disobey these guidelines. In addition, a user agent may open multiple parallel connections to retrieve different parts of a *single* resource by issuing range requests, as discussed in Chapter 7 (Section 7.4.1).

8.3.2 Problems with parallel connections

Parallel connections increase overall throughput for an individual client, at the expense of the greater good. The use of parallel connections causes several problems, as follows:

- **Unfairness to other clients:** A client that issues requests on multiple connections at a time achieves higher throughput by claiming bandwidth that would normally be allocated to other clients. Consider two Web clients that send requests over the same path through the network to the same Web server. Suppose that client A has four parallel TCP connections, whereas client B has just one TCP connection. Client A may receive up to four times more server processing and network bandwidth than client B, which could result in significantly lower latency for client A. However, client B would receive lower throughput and experience higher latency. One way to counteract the unfairness is for client B to open multiple TCP connections as well. To receive a higher proportion of the bandwidth, each client has an incentive to open more connections than the other clients.

- **Higher network and server load:** In addition to introducing unfairness between users, parallel connections increase the load on the server and the network. Consider a client that opens multiple connections at the same time to download a collection of embedded images. This introduces a sudden burst of traffic that imparts a heavy load on the network and the server. Even if each TCP connection proceeds through the slow-start phase of congestion control, the aggregate traffic from the set of connections could be quite large. As an extreme example, consider a client that opens 20 TCP connections to the same server. The client would generate 20 SYN packets in a very short period, followed shortly by 20 HTTP request messages. The Web server would consume most of its system resources trying to receive and process the SYN packets and HTTP requests. For the network, the collective load generated by a large number of SYN packets can cause a sudden backlog of traffic, ultimately leading to packet loss.

- **Higher user-perceived latency:** In addition to competing with traffic destined to other clients, the parallel connections compete with each other for network and server bandwidth. Consider a client with a 28.8 Kb/sec access link to the Internet (e.g., a telephone modem). If the client opens 20 parallel connections, each transfer receives at most 1.44 Kb/sec. In retrieving embedded images in a Web page, slow progress on multiple transfers may be preferable to fast progress on a single transfer. In other cases, the user may prefer fast progress on a small number of transfers. For example, a user may download multiple Web pages in different browser windows. Having a large number of active transfers at the same time would force the user to wait longer to receive any of the Web pages.

These fairness and performance problems have several possible remedies, as follows:

- **Removing performance incentives for parallel connections:** Enforcing fairness typically requires the use of scheduling algorithms to arbitrate access to network bandwidth and the system resources at the server. For example, rather than performing first-in first-out scheduling, a network router could alternate between packets to or from different end points. Alternatively, the router could keep track of how much traffic has been sent to each destination or from each source and penalize the end points that send too aggressively. The penalty may involve discarding some proportion of the packets. However, these techniques increase the complexity of the routers. Similarly, the TCP implementation on the Web server machine could ensure that traffic destined to different clients receives a fair share of the network bandwidth. In addition, the Web server could allocate its processing, memory, and disk resources fairly across different clients.

- **Providing alternatives to parallel connections:** Persistent connections address some of the incentives for using parallel connections, as discussed in Chapter 7 (Section 7.5). Sending multiple responses over a single TCP connection avoids the overhead of establishing multiple connections. In addition, reusing an existing TCP connection typically avoids the need to repeat the slow-start phase of congestion control. However, persistent connections do not address the desire to download multiple embedded images at the same time. A client could conceivably retrieve a portion of each image on a single persistent connection by sending a series of range requests. As an alternative, the relationship between HTTP and TCP could change to allow interleaving of several independent transfers on a single TCP connection.

Techniques for fair bandwidth allocation have been an active area of research and development as the Internet continues to evolve from a best-effort environment to a network that supports a wide range of services [Kes97]. Recent proposals for changing how end hosts allocate bandwidth across a collection of Web transfers are considered in more detail in Chapter 15 (Section 15.1).

8.4 Server Overheads

Reading request messages, generating responses, and transmitting data to clients consume significant resources at Web servers. These operations require the server to perform several functions that relate to TCP. In this section, we describe how some of these steps can be combined or avoided. Then we consider the challenges of handling a large number of simultaneous connections. These performance issues apply to both proxies and origin servers.

8.4.1 Combining system calls

The Web server interacts with TCP through a series of system calls. Performing multiple steps in a single system call provides the operating system with additional information that can improve the efficiency of the data transfer. Consider a UNIX-based Web server processing a GET request for a static file:

1. **Listening for requests for new connections:** The server listens for requests for new connections, and the operating system maintains an accept queue of pending connections.
2. **Establishing a new connection:** The server acquires a new connection from the accept queue using the *accept()* call. At this point, the server has a connection for communicating with the requesting client. In preparation for transmitting data to the client, the server may perform a *setsockopt()* call to disable Nagle's algorithm.
3. **Generating the response message:** The server performs one or more *read()* calls to read the client's HTTP request message. Then the server parses the request message and identifies the requested file. The server opens the requested file, using the *open()* call. The server may invoke various other system calls to construct the HTTP response header (e.g., to learn the current time, as well as the file's size and last modification time).
4. **Sending the response message:** After constructing the HTTP response header, the server uses the *write()* call to write these bytes to the connection. Then the server can begin sending the file. This involves using the *read()* call to read from the file and the *write()* call to write the data to the connection. If the send buffer is full, the operating system may prevent the server application from performing additional *write()* operations until some of the earlier data has been successfully transmitted to the client.
5. **Closing the file and (optionally) the connection:** After writing the last byte of the response, the server can *close()* the file and optionally *close()* the TCP connection. If the server implements persistent connections, and the client did not request that the connection be closed, the server may keep the connection open for a subsequent transfer. Finally, the server can perform a *write()* to create an entry in the server log.

Executing a system call typically requires a context switch between the server application and the operating system. Having a single system call perform multiple operations avoids the overhead and delay associated with context switches. Combining multiple steps into a single system call also facilitates other performance optimizations related to TCP [NBK99], as follows:

- **Copy the file contents directly to the operating system:** In satisfying the GET request, the Web server must read a file and then write the contents to the send buffer. In many cases, the server does not inspect or manipulate the contents of the file. Reading the file, and then writing into the send buffer, introduces unnecessary overhead. The bytes are copied from the file system to user space and then from user space to the send buffer in the operating system. Instead, data could be copied directly from the file system to the send buffer using a single system call. Several operating systems include a *sendfile()* or *transmitfile()* system call to perform this function.

- **Send the response header and body with a single call:** The server could send the response header as part of the same system call, such as the *writev()* call. The server typically constructs the response header in a separate buffer. The combined system call would need to allow the application to specify a buffer (for the response header) and a file (for the response body) and then transmit the contents of the buffer followed by the contents of the file. This would avoid the need for separate system calls to write the header and the body to the socket, without requiring the application to first copy the header and body into a contiguous buffer. In addition, this enables the operating system to send the beginning of the response body in the same IP packet as the response header. Otherwise, if two system calls were involved, the operating system might send the header before the server performed a second call to send the body. Combining these two steps reduces the total number of packets and avoids potentially harmful interactions with the delayed-ACK timer, as discussed in Section 8.2.3.

- **Send the response and close the connection with a single call:** The server could close the connection as part of the same system call that writes the HTTP response. This would allow the server to write the HTTP header, send the response body, and close the connection in a single step. The operating system knows that the server wants to close the underlying TCP connection. Closing the connection involves sending a packet with the FIN bit set. The operating system has the option of piggybacking the FIN on the last data packet of the transfer, as shown in Figure 8.10. This is possible because the operating system already knows that the application wants to close the connection. Otherwise, the operating system may have already transmitted the last data packet before learning that the application intended to close the connection. For large response messages, the operating system typically would not have completed the transmission of the entire response before the second system call. However, smaller response messages are likely to require a separate FIN packet. Having a single system call for sending the response and closing the connection ensures that the operating system piggybacks the FIN. This reduces overhead by avoiding the transmission of the extra packet.

Extending the operating system to include new system calls can improve the performance of Web servers. In theory, the entire Web server could be

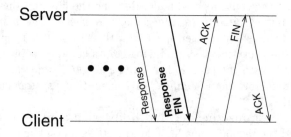

Figure 8.10. Server piggybacking the FIN on the last data packet

implemented in the operating system. Implementing an application in the operating system is common in small embedded systems that perform a single task. However, general-purpose operating systems usually do not implement entire applications. Executing time-consuming functions inside the operating system makes it difficult to share processor, memory, and disk resources across multiple tasks. As a result, operating systems typically have a small set of carefully chosen system calls. The needs of Web servers may motivate the addition of a few system calls or the improvement of the implementation of other system calls. However, individual applications usually do not warrant major changes in the set of functions provided by the operating system.

8.4.2 Managing multiple connections

The efficiency of a Web server depends on the number of TCP connections that are open simultaneously. Web servers control the number of connections in two main ways: by rejecting requests for new connections and by closing idle connections.

CONTROLLING NUMBER OF SIMULTANEOUS CONNECTIONS

Each TCP connection consumes a certain amount of memory at the server for storing TCP state information and the send/receive buffer. For example, each TCP connection has a control block that stores information such as the congestion window and RTT estimates. These memory requirements can grow quite high when the server has a large number of simultaneous TCP connections. Inactive connections in the TIME_WAIT state also consume server resources, as discussed in Section 8.1.3. In addition, a process-driven server has a separate process for each open connection, resulting in additional memory requirements. TCP and process state consume memory that could be used for other purposes, such as server-side caching of Web resources and their metadata, as discussed in Chapter 4 (Section 4.3). Server-side caching becomes much less effective when the server has a very large number of simultaneous connections. Cache misses introduce extra server overhead for fetching resources from disk and regenerating metadata.

The overhead for the operating system to handle an incoming packet grows with the number of open connections. When a packet arrives, the operating system must inspect the source and destination IP addressees and port numbers to demultiplex to the appropriate TCP connection. In some older operating systems, packet demultiplexing required a linear scan of the list of connections; as an optimization, the connections in the TIME_WAIT state could be placed at the end of the list because they are very unlikely to receive any packets. For a further reduction in latency, modern operating systems maintain a hash table that maps the source and destination IP addresses and port numbers to the appropriate connection. Still, the access latency and memory requirements for the hash table grow in the number of connections. In addition, for an event-driven server, a single process must listen (e.g., using the *select()* call) on all open connections for arriving packets. The overhead of this system call increases with the number of simultaneous connections, even when many of the connections are idle [BM98].

The optimal number of active TCP connections depends on the server architecture and the characteristics of the HTTP traffic. Generating and transmitting response messages consumes processor, memory, disk, and network resources at the server. Sharing these system resources across a large number of simultaneous requests results in higher delay in generating and transmitting the response messages. As an extreme example, consider a Web server that invokes a CGI script that requires two seconds of processing time to generate each response message. Allowing the processor to alternate back and forth between servicing each of the ten requests would result in a 20-second latency in generating each response. Higher user-perceived latency may cause the user to leave the Web site or abort the slow responses and initiate new requests. The poor performance irritates the users and wastes system resources at the server. In the worst case, the server becomes so overloaded that no productive work is performed. The number of simultaneous TCP connections must be carefully controlled to avoid this situation.

Despite the disadvantages of having too many simultaneous TCP connections, the server should not be unnecessarily restrictive. Limiting the number of simultaneous connections may block or delay TCP connection setup requests from new clients. When the server has reached the maximum number of connections, any arriving SYN packets are placed in a queue. The SYN requests are delayed until one of the existing connections closes. Once the accept queue is full, the server drops SYN packets, thereby rejecting requests for new connections. An overly conservative limit on the number of connections also results in underutilization of the server and network resources. The server needs a certain number of active TCP connections to exploit the available network bandwidth because the transmission rate for many connections is limited by round-trip delays and throughput limitations along the path to the requesting client. A Web server could send responses to a large number of low-bandwidth clients without exhausting the capacity of a high-bandwidth link to the Internet.

POLICIES FOR CLOSING PERSISTENT CONNECTIONS

As part of controlling the number of connections, an HTTP/1.1 server must also decide when to close a persistent connection. Keeping a persistent connection open allows the server to respond more quickly to subsequent requests by the same client and avoids the overheads of terminating and reestablishing the connection. Maintaining a connection beyond a single HTTP transfer increases the number of simultaneous connections at the server. The server can employ a wide variety of strategies for closing persistent connections. The simplest strategy is for the server to apply a timeout to close an idle connection. For example, the connection could be closed if no request has arrived in the last 15 seconds. If the connection has been idle for several seconds, the likelihood of receiving another request in the near future is very small.

However, even a relatively small timeout value may keep the connection open too long, especially because many clients request only one resource from the server. To handle this situation, the server can employ a hybrid timeout policy [PM95]. The server could use a small timeout after the first request and increase the timeout if the client issues additional requests. In addition to applying a timeout, the server may also limit the total number of requests allowed on a single connection. Otherwise, a client would have an incentive to generate periodic requests simply to keep the server from closing the persistent connection. For example, every ten seconds the browser might generate an HTTP request, even if the client is idle, in order to ensure that the connection remains open long enough to handle the client's next request. By limiting the number of requests per connection, the server avoids rewarding this behavior. However, this policy forces a well-behaved client to incur the overhead of establishing a new TCP connection after reaching the limit on the number of requests.

Policies based on timeouts and the number of requests are relatively easy to implement because they consider each TCP connection in isolation. In a process-driven server, these policies have the advantage of not requiring any coordination between processes. The server could conceivably implement more complicated policies by considering all of the open connections collectively. The server effectively has a cache of open TCP connections, and deciding which TCP connection to close amounts to a cache-replacement decision. For example, the server could close the connection that has been idle the longest. Similar to the timeout-based policy, this heuristic assumes that an idle connection is less likely to receive a request in the near future. Alternatively, the server could base the decision on the relative importance of the user. This may be a reasonable policy for a commercial site that wants to deliver good performance to high-paying customers. Similarly, the server may try to avoid closing connections to far-away clients that would experience high setup delay in opening a new TCP connection.

8.5 Summary

Despite the benefits of dividing communication tasks into multiple protocol layers, interactions between layers can have negative implications on end-to-end application performance. The timers that control key operations in TCP have a direct effect on HTTP performance. TCP features that were designed when Telnet and Rlogin were dominant applications can interact in subtle ways with Web transfers. Implementation decisions in Web software components can mitigate or exacerbate these effects. In contrast to earlier Internet applications, a Web client typically has multiple transport-layer connections at the same time to download multiple Web resources in parallel. Parallel connections increase network and server load and introduce unfairness across Web users. Busy proxies and servers handle a large number of TCP connections on behalf of multiple clients. The efficiency of proxies and servers depends on having effective policies for controlling the number of open connections.

Part IV

Measuring/Characterizing Web Traffic

Web Traffic Measurement

Measuring and analyzing Web traffic often plays an important role in designing Web sites, managing Web proxies and servers, and operating IP networks. In addition, measurements of Web transfers have been instrumental for identifying the key characteristics of Web traffic and evaluating new techniques for improving Web performance. Web traffic measurement consists of three main steps—monitoring the Web transfers at some location, generating the measurement records in a particular format, and preprocessing the records to prepare for subsequent analysis. In this chapter, we present an overview of Web measurement, starting with a discussion of the motivations for collecting these measurements. Then we discuss the five main techniques for monitoring Web traffic—client, proxy, and server logging; packet monitoring; and active measurement. Each technique has certain practical advantages and limitations, with important implications on the kinds of information available in the measurement records.

Although output formats for Web traffic measurements have not been standardized, most implementations of Web proxies and servers follow informal guidelines for logging formats. We present an overview of the de facto standards for proxy and server logging—the Common Log Format (CLF) and the Extended Common Log Format (ECLF). Client logging, packet monitoring, and active measurement are applied in an informal manner, and the output formats vary from one realization to another. We then discuss how the size and diversity of Web measurements introduce significant challenges in storing and analyzing the data. Preprocessing the measurement data provides an opportunity to remove erroneous records, filter unwanted fields, and transform the data into a form suitable for traffic analysis. Performing these preprocessing steps reduces the complexity of the analysis software and facilitates the use of a wide variety of tools for storing, analyzing, and displaying the measurement data.

Each traffic measurement technique has certain limitations that make it difficult to evaluate certain basic properties of the Web. Some information may not be available in a log or trace because of where the data is gathered or what fields are recorded. We discuss a variety of ways to draw inferences about missing information by exploiting the fields that are available in the measurement records. We then present four case studies that demonstrate the application of the traffic measurement techniques and the inference of specific performance metrics. These four studies investigate the characteristics of the workloads at Web servers, the variability of the traffic generated by Web clients, the benefits of caching Web resources at a proxy, and the frequency of modifications to Web resources. Rather than discussing the results of the studies, we emphasize the techniques for collecting, recording, preprocessing, and analyzing the traffic measurements.

9.1 Motivation for Web Measurement

Measurement of Web traffic has played a crucial role in characterizing user access patterns, the performance of Web software components, and the underlying network infrastructure. In this section, we discuss the motivations for collecting and analyzing Web data from the viewpoint of content creators, Web-hosting companies, network operators, and Web researchers. Some of these goals are difficult to achieve because of limitations in Web measurement data, as discussed later in the chapter.

9.1.1 Motivation for content creators

Content creators can glean valuable information from measurements of user browsing patterns. Consider an electronic commerce (e-commerce) site that sells books. Statistics about the number of visitors to the sites influence the advertising revenue for advertisements embedded in the Web pages. In addition, analysis of user access patterns can guide the process of redesigning the Web site. Suppose many users visit the home page and then click on a particular sequence of hypertext links to locate popular paperback books. This would motivate changing the home page to provide a direct link to a list of the most popular books. Knowing how long users stay at the Web site and how many pages they download is also useful. If many users leave after viewing one or two pages, the site may need better organization or more interesting material. Users jumping quickly between successive pages might not be finding the information they want. The content creator could address this problem by allowing users to search the site by topic.

A content creator may also be interested in knowing how users get to the Web site. For example, suppose that 25% of the requests for the book-seller's home page were issued by a user clicking on a hypertext link from a particular news site. Then the book-seller may continue to advertise at that news site. Measurements may also be used to characterize the performance of the Web site. Suppose that downloading the home page takes an average of eight seconds on a 56.6 Kb/sec telephone modem. This information may motivate the creation of a simpler home page with fewer embedded images. Measuring user-perceived latency may also be useful in judging the performance of the Web server that hosts the site. High latency or low throughput could motivate the content creator to redesign the site or switch to a different Web-hosting company. A large number of requests coming from clients in Italy would motivate replicating the site in Europe and perhaps creating new content directed toward these users.

9.1.2 Motivation for Web-hosting companies

Measurements also play an important role in managing a Web server. Consider a Web-hosting company that provides access to a collection of Web sites. By logging all accesses to the Web sites, the company can compute statistics on the number of response messages and the number of bytes transferred on behalf of each Web site. This information may be necessary for billing purposes and for deciding how to allocate system resources to each site. For example, a site that receives a large number of requests could be replicated on multiple server machines. A site that receives most of its requests during the day (e.g., a business site) can share a machine with a site that receives most of its requests at night (e.g., an entertainment site). In addition, measurements can be used to detect possible performance problems. Upon learning that many users experience high delay in accessing the Web sites, the hosting company can invest in a high-speed connection to the network and additional Web server machines.

Measurements can guide the selection of tunable parameters in the server software. Web servers have a wide variety of configurable parameters that affect the allocation of resources, as discussed in Chapter 4 (Section 4.6). For example, the benefits of enabling persistent connections on a server depend on how often a single client issues multiple requests in a short period. If persistent connections are enabled, the policy for retiring an idle connection can depend on measurements of how much time typically elapses between successive requests. Traffic measurements are also useful for comparing different vendors of Web server software. Web measurements can be used to benchmark server performance. Similarly, measurements can guide a decision to install a surrogate to reduce the load on the origin servers. For example, knowledge of user access patterns could be used to estimate what fraction of the requests could be satisfied directly by the surrogate without interacting with the origin server.

9.1.3 Motivation for network operators

Operators running a network also benefit from measurements of Web traffic. For example, a company with a local area network may benefit from installing a caching proxy. Measurements can be used to estimate what fraction of requests can be satisfied by a shared cache. Likewise, an Internet Service Provider

(ISP) could collect measurements to estimate how much bandwidth could be saved by installing a caching proxy in various locations in the network. A network provider could use measurement data in benchmarking the performance of proxy products available from different vendors. An ISP may monitor traffic to and from users with different network connections, such as low-bandwidth telephone modems and high-bandwidth cable modems. This helps the ISP gauge how much a higher-bandwidth connection reduces Web latency and, in turn, how lower latency affects user behavior. Based on these trends, an ISP can decide how much to expand network capacity to accommodate the increasing number of users with high-bandwidth connections.

Measurements of Web traffic can help the network provider identify the most popular Web sites among its users and to track the latency in transferring content from these sites. Poor performance for popular Web sites may motivate the provider to increase the capacity of the network or to change how traffic is routed to and from the Web servers. If the users download a large amount of content from a particular Web site, the network operator may negotiate to establish a direct network connection to the company that hosts that site. In addition, monitoring changes in access latency alerts the operator to potential problems in the network, such as a failed link or increased traffic from some customers. Traffic measurements can be used to evaluate potential changes to the configuration of the network. Because the Web is currently responsible for most of the traffic in the Internet, Web measurements are useful for stress-testing networking equipment, such as new routers, and for estimating the load on Domain Name System (DNS) servers.

9.1.4 Motivation for Web/networking researchers

Measurements of Web traffic have been invaluable to the research community for evaluating the performance of Web protocols and software components. In addition, characterization of Web traffic has been an active research area since the early days of the Web. Traffic measurements have played an important role in the evolution of HTTP. For example, analysis of measurement data played a major role in the decision to make persistent connections the default behavior of HTTP/1.1 servers. More recently, measurements have been used to estimate the penetration and effectiveness of the various new features in HTTP/1.1. For example, a study of Web traffic measurements influenced the decision to add persistent connections to HTTP/1.1 [PM95]. Measurements have been widely used to evaluate new policies and mechanisms for Web components. Web traffic measurements have played a key role in evaluating Web caching techniques, such as cache replacement, cache validation, and prefetching.

In addition to Web research, analysis of Web traffic has had a large impact on Internet research in general. Collecting and analyzing Web measurements has led to a much deeper understanding of the dynamics of Internet traffic.

This analysis has led to the development of more realistic traffic models that can be used to evaluate a wide range of networking protocols, as discussed in more detail in Chapter 10. Web measurements have been used to study the interaction between HTTP and TCP, and the implications of Web traffic on congestion in the Internet. Measurement continues to play a critical role for researchers striving to understand Web traffic dynamics and the implications on network performance. These efforts assume greater importance as the Internet evolves into a crucial part of the global economy.

9.2 Measurement Techniques

Web measurements can be collected in a variety of ways, with important implications on the type of information that is available. Web software components, such as browsers, proxies, and servers, can generate logs as part of handling requests. Traces of Web traffic can be collected by passively monitoring the links and routers in the network. In addition, a special Web client can initiate HTTP requests for the purpose of evaluating Web performance. In this section, we consider the effectiveness and limitations of each of these approaches to collecting Web traffic measurements.

9.2.1 Server logging

A Web server typically generates a log as part of processing client requests. Each log entry corresponds to an HTTP request handled by the server, including information about the requesting client, the request time, and the request and response messages. The developers of Web servers have followed informal guidelines for log formats, as discussed in more detail in Section 9.3. Similarities in log formats, and the dominance of a small number of server vendors, have facilitated the development of numerous commercial tools for analyzing server logs. Statistics derived from server logs provide valuable information to site administrators and content developers. In addition, server logs have given researchers a unique opportunity to study the access patterns of a group of clients to a set of resources. Server logs have formed the basis of most research studies that have characterized HTTP traffic or evaluated new techniques for improving Web performance.

Most Web servers perform logging by default. However, in practice, server logs do not provide very detailed information. Because recording the entire header of each request and response message would impose a significant overhead, most Web servers log only the request method, Request-URI, and response code. In addition, the server log typically does not provide fine-grain timing information. For example, the timestamp in the server log may refer to when the request was received, when the server started or finished processing the request, or when the server finished sending the response. A server log rarely includes all of these timestamps. In addition, the timestamps may be at a relatively coarse level of granularity, such as the one-second level. Coarse-grained timestamps make it difficult to have an accurate estimate of how long the server spends in handling a single request, or the elapsed time between successive requests. In fact, the log entries may not be listed in the order that the HTTP requests were received, depending on when the server creates the log entry.

On the surface, a server log could be used to analyze user access patterns and the relative popularity of the resources at a Web site. However, requests that are satisfied by a browser or proxy cache would not appear in the log. The server does not know how many requests are satisfied by caches. In fact, popular resources may be more likely to be returned from a cache. To ensure that all requests are logged, the server could be configured to restrict the caching of responses at clients and proxies. For example, each response message from the server could include a header that prohibits caching or requires the reval-idation of cached responses. However, such *cache-busting* techniques increase the amount of traffic in the Web by reducing the effectiveness of caching, as discussed later, in Chapter 11 (Section 11.11.1).

Each entry in the server log includes information about the client respon-sible for the request. For example, the server log typically includes the client's IP address or hostname. Associating requests with a particular user agent is important for studying browsing patterns. However, associating requests with users is difficult for a variety of reasons, as follows:

- **Proxies:** A request could come from a proxy, rather than a user agent. A single proxy could generate requests on behalf of multiple users, making it difficult to determine which requests originated from each user.
- **Shared client machines:** Many organizations have shared computing platforms with separate accounts for each user. The client IP address is not a unique identifier when multiple user agents run on a single machine.
- **Dynamic IP address assignment:** The IP address associated with a particular machine can change over time. Many users connect to the Inter-net via modem connections to an ISP. ISPs typically assign an IP address to each client from a pool of available addresses.

Over time, requests from a single user may come from a variety of IP addresses, and multiple users may send requests from the same IP address. To resolve these ambiguities, some Web sites track users by requiring client requests to contain cookies that uniquely identify the users.

Although server logs have played a key role in Web research, the character-istics of any one server log may not be representative of other servers. Web sites vary widely in their popularity and functionality. The Web site for an academic department at a university differs substantially from a popular e-commerce or portal site. The sites may have different types of resources and different user bases. In addition, members of the research community typically do not have access to the server logs for large commercial Web sites. Companies may view their server logs as containing sensitive customer data or other information that may be valuable to their competitors. As a result, many research studies of the Web have been based on logs from universities and nonprofit institutions. Unfortunately, it may be difficult to apply the results of these studies to commercial Web sites.

9.2.2 Proxy logging

Web proxies, like servers, typically create logs as part of normal operation. In contrast to a server log, a proxy log provides a record of requests to a wide range of Web sites, especially if the proxy is located near the requesting clients. For example, the proxy may handle all HTTP requests from the clients at a single company or ISP. The proxy log provides useful information about the access patterns of these clients as they visit various Web sites. The proxy often has more detailed information about the requesting clients than is available to origin servers. The first proxy in the chain from the user agent to the origin server can distinguish between requests from different users. Proxies later in the chain may not be able to distinguish between the users, unless the HTTP requests include cookies. Distinguishing between users is valuable for analyzing the demographics of the user community accessing particular Web sites.

A proxy log includes requests that are satisfied by the proxy's cache. The origin server would not see these requests. As such, proxy logs can be used to determine the relative popularity of different Web sites and the effectiveness of policies for Web caching. However, there is a tension between the diversity of the clients and servers in the proxy log, depending on the location of the proxy. A proxy close to the clients handles requests for a relatively small number of clients to a rather large number of servers. As an extreme example, the proxy may handle requests on behalf of a single user agent. A proxy close to the servers handles requests for a relatively large number of clients to a rather small number of servers. For example, a surrogate may handle requests on behalf of a single Web site.

Proxy logs have several of the same disadvantages as server logs. The proxy does not see the requests that are satisfied by the browser cache or other proxies closer to the user agents. The proxy does not see all, or even most, of the requests to any particular server. This makes it difficult to characterize certain properties of the Web, such as the request rate for popular sites and resources. In addition, the clients of any one proxy may not be representative of the rest of the clients in the Web. The proxy may have a rather homogeneous set of clients, in terms of geographical location and access bandwidth. Consider a proxy near a bank of telephone modems that service residential users in

Boston, Massachusetts. The access patterns seen by this proxy are likely to differ substantially from clients connecting the Internet on a high-bandwidth connection at a company in Paris, France. Finally, as with server logs, many commercial institutions do not make their proxy logs publically available.

9.2.3 Client logging

Collecting logs at the user agent has the potential to provide a detailed view of user browsing patterns. A browser could conceivably record timestamps for various points in the request-response exchange. The browser can record user actions that never translate into HTTP requests, including requests satisfied by the browser cache, as well as mouse and keyboard operations in the browser. The browser knows if, and when, the user terminates a request by clicking on the Stop button. An aborted request may not be logged at the origin server, depending on how much of the request is processed before the user aborts the transfer and when logging is done. Compared with proxies and servers, the user agent handles a relatively small number of requests at a time. Logging the full set of request and response headers would not impose as much of a burden on the browser.

In contrast to proxy and server logging, there is no de facto standard for the format of browser logs. Popular browsers do not generate logs by default; therefore collecting client logs requires modifying the browser software and distributing the modified browser to a collection of users. However, source code is typically not available for the recent versions of the popular Web browsers. In addition, a realistic study of browsing patterns requires a large number of sample users to employ the modified browser. These users might not be representative of other users. Several strategies have been developed to collect detailed logs of user browsing patterns without modifying the browser source code. For example, the logs could be collected by a proxy running on the user's machine. The browser could be configured to direct all requests to the proxy.

However, a typical proxy would not know about requests satisfied by the browser cache. To address this problem, the user's browser could be configured to disable caching or to perform revalidation whenever a requested resource is available in the browser cache. To avoid requiring the user to change the browser's caching policies, the proxy could force the user agent to bypass the cache for future requests by transforming HTTP response messages. The proxy could insert HTTP response headers (e.g., `Expires` or `Cache-Control: no-cache`) that lead the browser to think that the response should not be cached or that the cached response must be validated by the server. This ensures that the proxy sees every request. However, forcing the browser to generate an HTTP request for each resource may have a negative impact on performance, which may in turn affect the user's behavior. In addition, this approach may result in a substantial increase in the load on the proxy and the network.

9.2.4 Packet monitoring

Client, proxy, and server logging impose an overhead on the software components underlying the Web. In addition, logs collected at the application level have little or no information about network activity at the TCP and IP levels. Monitoring the traffic inside the network offers an attractive way to collect detailed traces without affecting the operation of the Web software components. However, collecting network traces requires a way to capture individual IP packets as they travel across a network link or through a router. Some link-level technologies are more amenable to packet monitoring than others. For example, many local area networks consist of shared media, such as Ethernets. In this case, a packet monitor can easily capture a copy of each packet on the link. Collecting packet traces on point-to-point links, such as a fiber optic cable, requires splitting the cable or having dedicated support in the router to ensure that the monitor receives a copy of each packet.

A packet monitor can produce detailed traces of Web activity at the HTTP, TCP, and IP levels. The monitor could conceivably record the timestamp of every IP packet on the link. In contrast, typical proxy and server logs have a single timestamp for each Web transfer. A detailed timeline of the request and response packets is invaluable for analyzing the delay, throughput, and loss properties of the Web transfer. With effective hardware support, a packet monitor can generate detailed timestamps at the millisecond level, or lower, compared to the one-second granularity in most proxy and server logs. Because packet monitoring does not interfere with the operation of the Web, the monitor can log very detailed information, such as the full HTTP headers for request and response messages. In fact, the monitor could conceivably log the entire message. In addition, packet traces include transport-level information such as when and how TCP connections terminate. This is useful for studying aborted HTTP transfers that are difficult, if not impossible, to analyze from proxy and server logs. Packet traces also provide detailed information about the throughput of the ongoing transfers traversing the link.

However, packet monitoring is not a panacea. Like a proxy, a packet monitor cannot capture requests satisfied by the browser cache or HTTP messages that have been encrypted using the Secure Socket Layer (SSL). In addition, packet monitoring becomes more difficult with increasing link speed. As the packets arrive, the monitor must be able to capture the packets, perform any necessary processing, and store the resulting data. Limitations in processor, memory, and disk speeds make it challenging to monitor high-bandwidth links. At any given time, a link may carry IP packets from a wide variety of different Web transfers. To generate traces at the HTTP level, the monitor must be able to associate the incoming packets with the appropriate HTTP transfer. HTTP messages usually span multiple IP packets, requiring the monitor to reconstruct the HTTP-level information from the underlying packet stream.

Developing robust software for reconstructing HTTP messages from packet traces is a challenging task, as we discuss later, in Chapter 14 (Section 14.1). In addition, monitoring a single link provides a somewhat limited view of the Web. Internet routing does not guarantee that the traffic between two hosts traverses the same set of links in both directions. Depending on the location of the link in the Internet, the monitor may not see both the request and response messages for a single transfer. Also, the traffic on any particular link may not be representative of the rest of the Web. Deploying packet monitors on a large number of links would be very expensive. Compared with client, proxy, and server logging, packet monitoring introduces additional concerns about violations of user privacy. The packet monitor has access to every packet on the link and is not a participant in the Web transfers. Users typically do not know if request or response messages travel by a packet monitor.

9.2.5 Active measurement

Client, proxy, and server logs and packet traces typically do not include enough information to evaluate the performance experienced by Web users. Consider the problem of characterizing the delay in downloading the Web page `http://www.foo.com`, including any embedded images. If one or more of the embedded images reside at a different server, the server log of `www.foo.com` would not provide information about all of the requests. Even if all of the requests are captured in a single proxy or server log, this log would not contain detailed timing information about the requests and responses. In addition, a proxy or server log would not capture the latency introduced by the DNS query to translate `www.foo.com` into an IP address. A client log, if available, would capture the experience of a single user contacting a particular set of Web pages; this client's experience may not be representative of other users. Packet traces would only capture the activity seen on a single link, and this link may not carry all of the traffic generated by a single request for a Web page.

Using client logs, proxy logs, server logs, or packet traces to study user performance has two main limitations. First, these measurement techniques capture an HTTP transfer at a single location. This makes it difficult to determine the performance as experienced by a user or to decompose the various components of delay. Second, these measurement techniques are passive in that they monitor HTTP transfers "in the wild," with no control over if or when requests occur. This makes it difficult to conduct a systematic investigation of Web performance. An alternative approach is to generate requests in a controlled manner and observe their performance. This is referred to as *active* measurement, in contrast to the *passive* collection of logs or traces. Active measurement of the Web employs a user agent to send requests and record information about the responses, such as timestamps and HTTP headers. In practice, the active measurements may be generated by a simplified user agent that does not support the full range of tasks handled by a browser. The user agent typically reads an input file that includes a list of Request-URIs and the time the requests should be generated.

Conducting an experiment based on active measurements requires addressing the following three key issues:

- **Where to locate the modified user agents:** Deciding where to locate the clients is a delicate matter. Web performance varies across client-server pairs. Clients differ in terms of access bandwidth, closeness to the server, and presence of proxies. A client on a high-speed local area network would not have the same experience as a client using a low-bandwidth modem. Similarly, a client in the United States would not have the same experience as a client in Russia in accessing a Web page in North America. When Web sites are replicated on multiple server machines, the two clients may not have their HTTP requests satisfied by the same replica. One replica could be heavily loaded while another is lightly loaded. Therefore, collecting active measurements that are representative of "typical" Web performance is extremely difficult.

- **What requests to generate:** Web performance varies across different Web sites. Web servers differ in terms of the hardware platform, the server software, the network connectivity, and the popularity of the site. In addition, two Web pages at the same site may differ in terms of the size of the page and the embedded images. One approach is to select a representative set of requests based on the popularity of the Web pages or the Web servers. For example, a list of popular URLs could be extracted from previous traffic measurements, such as packet traces or proxy logs. Then the modified user agent could replay these requests to measure user performance in accessing these pages. Alternatively, a list of the most popular Web sites could be used to determine which sites should be included in the measurement experiment. The notion of popular URLs and sites may depend on the scope of the experiment; for example, clients in Russia may access a different set of Web sites than clients in the United States. In addition, the selection of Web sites may be affected by other criteria, such as the desire to compare sites running different server software or configuration.

- **What measurements to collect:** Deciding what measurement data to collect at the time of the experiment has important implications for what performance issues can be studied. The modified user agents can log a variety of information about the requests, such as timestamps relating to the DNS query, the TCP connection establishment, the HTTP transfer, and the rendering of the response. However, the user agents do not have a complete view of the sources of these delays. For example, the log would not indicate what actions were taken by the local DNS server, whether a

packet loss caused a TCP timeout, and whether the HTTP request was
satisfied by the origin server or by a proxy along the path. Additional
measurements can aid in understanding the sources of delay. For example,
packet traces collected at the client would provide more detailed timing
information, and logs collected at other points in the path from the client
to the server would help identify which Web components contributed to
the latency.

Active measurement is an effective technique for studying user performance. However, the diversity and complexity of the Internet makes it difficult
to draw general conclusions from the measurement data. Characterizing Web
performance requires extensive experimentation over a wide range of times,
client locations, and server sites. This necessitates a wide-scale, global measurement infrastructure. In recent years, several research groups have deployed
software in a variety of geographical locations for the purpose of collecting active measurements of Web performance [BC99, KW00]. We discuss one of these
measurement platforms [KW00] in greater detail in Chapter 15 (Section 15.4).
In addition, companies such as Keynote Systems [Key] employ active measurement to evaluate the performance of various Web sites and ISPs.

9.3 Proxy/Server Logs

Most Web proxies and servers generate logs as a routine part of processing
requests. Each entry in the log corresponds to a single request-response pair
and includes a number of fields related to the requesting client, the time of the
request, and the HTTP request and response messages. Although no formal
standards dictate the log formats, most proxy and server implementations follow informal guidelines for what information to record. However, the number
of fields, as well as their format and interpretation, varies from log to log.

9.3.1 Common Log Format (CLF)

Each entry in a CLF log consists of the seven fields listed in Table 9.1, as
follows:

- **Remote host:** The remote host identifies the client's IP address or hostname, such as 10.245.131.2 or users.bar.com. The server can directly determine the client's IP address from the socket associated with the HTTP
  request. However, logging the client name requires the server to perform a
  DNS query to convert the IP address into a name. The server records the
  client's IP address if the DNS lookups are disabled or if the DNS query is
  unsuccessful. Web servers supporting busy Web sites typically disable the
  reverse DNS lookup, as discussed earlier, in Chapter 5 (Section 5.3.4).

Table 9.1. Common Log Format

Field	Meaning
Remote host	Hostname or IP address of requesting client
Remote identity	Account associated with connection on client machine
Authenticated user	Name provided by user for authentication
Time	Date/time associated with the request
Request	Request method, Request-URI, and protocol version
Response code	Three-digit HTTP response code
Content length	Number of bytes associated with the response

- **Remote identity:** The remote identity indicates the owner associated with the TCP connection on the client machine. The TCP connection is used to communicate with a specific application running under a particular account on the client machine. The name associated with this account is not normally available to the other end point of the TCP connection. RFC 1413 defines an Identification Protocol [St.93] for querying a remote host for this information. However, in practice, these queries are time-consuming and most hosts do not respond to them. Thus most Web servers do not issue these queries. Instead, this field usually appears as a "–" in a server log.
- **Authenticated user:** The authenticated user identifies the name of the user as provided in the `Authorization` header of the HTTP request. This field corresponds to the name entered by the user in accessing password-protected information. This field is logged as a "–" when the HTTP request does not include authorization information or if the server does not record this information.
- **Time:** The server log also includes the time of the request at the one-second granularity. The CLF guidelines do not define the format and interpretation of this field, resulting in significant differences from one log to another. The correct interpretation of the time depends on when the server performs the system call (e.g., *gettimeofday()*) to determine the time [Dav99]. Depending on the server implementation, the time may correspond to when the server starts reading the request message, starts generating the response, starts writing the response into the socket buffer, or finishes writing the response into the socket buffer. These four timestamps could differ substantially, particularly for large resources and for dynamically generated content. The server does not necessarily know when the operating system transmits the first or last packets of the response message.

```
10.245.131.2 - - [15/Oct/2000:00:00:25 -0400] "GET /img/logo.gif
    HTTP/1.0" 304 0
10.245.131.2 - - [15/Oct/2000:00:00:26 -0400] "GET /img/site.gif
    HTTP/1.0" 304 0
10.3.2.16 - - [15/Oct/2000:00:00:38 -0400] "GET /est/bybhi.html
    HTTP/1.0" 304 0
10.16.202.34 - - [15/Oct/2000:00:00:45 -0400] "GET /img/tday.gif
    HTTP/1.0" 200 3699
```

Figure 9.1. Example CLF log with fictitious client IP addresses

- **Request:** The request field corresponds to the first line of the HTTP request header, which consists of the request method, the Request-URI, and the protocol version.
- **Response code:** The response code indicates the three-digit code included in the HTTP response header, such as 200 for the 200 OK response.
- **Content length:** The content length indicates the number of bytes associated with the response. Depending on the server implementation, this field may correspond to the size of the entity body, the size of the response message, or the number of bytes transferred by the server. If the server records the size of the entity body, the content length would be 0 or "–" for responses that do not include an entity body (e.g., 304 Not Modified). The size of the response message differs from the number of bytes transferred if the server does not transmit the entire response message. For example, an aborted transfer may result in a transfer length that is smaller than the content length.

Figure 9.1 shows four records in a CLF log. In each record, the second and third fields are "– –" because the server does not log the remote identity or the authorized user. The time field includes the day, month, and year, followed by the local time; the "–0400" indicates that local time is four hours behind Greenwich Mean Time.

9.3.2 Extended Common Log Format (ECLF)

Server logs may include a variety of other fields, as summarized in Table 9.2. The exact set of fields depends on the configuration of the server. The ECLF format does not indicate exactly which additional fields are included in the log. Typical fields include the following:

- **User agent:** This field reports the value of the User-Agent request header, which reports the name and version number of the software responsible

Table 9.2. Fields that may be included in extended logs

Field	Meaning
User agent	Information on user agent software
Referer	URI from which Request-URI was obtained
Request processing time	Time spent processing the request
Request header size	Number of bytes in the request header
Request body size	Number of bytes in the request body
Remote response code	Response code from the server
Remote content length	Size of the response from server
Remote response header size	Size of the response header sent by server
Proxy request header size	Size of the request header sent to server
Proxy response header size	Size of the response header sent to client

for the request, as discussed in Chapter 6 (Section 6.2.3). In practice, the `User-Agent` header often includes additional information, such as the name of the operating system running on the user's machine.

- **Referer:** This field reports the value of the `Referer` request header, if present. The `Referer` request header indicates the URI of the Web page where the user issued the request, as discussed in Chapter 6 (Section 6.2.3). For example, suppose the user initiates the request by clicking on a hypertext link at a Web page from a search engine; the `Referer` field would contain the URI of the search engine's Web page.
- **Request processing time:** This field indicates how many seconds the server spent generating the response. This field is particularly useful if the server spends considerable time processing certain requests, such as requests that trigger the execution of a script.
- **Request header size:** This field indicates the number of bytes in the header of the HTTP request message sent by the client.
- **Request body size:** This field indicates the number of bytes in the body of the client's HTTP request message. A request message typically does not have a body, unless the client sends a `PUT` or `POST` request.

Together, the request header size and request body size indicate the total size of the client's request message.

The remaining fields listed in Table 9.2 relate to proxies. In contrast to user agents and origin servers, a proxy acts as both a client and a server. In handling a single transfer, the proxy receives a request from the upstream client and may direct a request to a downstream server. As a result, a proxy may log additional fields that are not available in a log generated by an origin server. For example, a proxy may record the following:

- **Remote response code:** This field indicates the three-digit code included in the `Status-Line` of the HTTP response header sent by the server to the proxy. The remote response code may differ from the *response code* field, which indicates the response code sent from the proxy to the client.

- **Remote content length:** The remote content length is the number of bytes in the response message sent by the server to the proxy. The remote content length may differ from the *content length* field, which records the length of the message sent by the proxy to the client.
- **Remote response header size:** The remote response header size is the number of bytes in the header of the response message sent by the server to the proxy.
- **Proxy request header size:** The proxy request header size is the number of bytes in the header of the request message sent by the proxy to the server. This may differ from the *request header size* field, which records the size of the request header sent by the client to the proxy.
- **Proxy response header size:** The proxy response header size is the number of bytes in the header of the response message sent by the proxy to the client.

These additional fields may be useful in analyzing how the proxy performs as an intermediary between clients and servers.

9.4 Preprocessing Measurement Data

Collecting measurements of Web traffic often results in a large amount of data that may be analyzed in a wide variety of ways. Preprocessing involves the following three steps:

- Parsing the data to identify erroneous records
- Filtering the data to remove unnecessary fields
- Transforming the data into a format that is amenable for analysis

Having a cleaner representation of the data facilitates the use of a wide range of software tools for storing, analyzing, and visualizing the data. However, preprocessing should preserve the key information from the measurement data to avoid imposing unnecessary restrictions on the subsequent analysis. A case study of preprocessing Web server logs is presented in Chapter 14 (Section 14.2).

9.4.1 Parsing measurement data

As the first step in preprocessing the measurement data, parsing considers the syntax of the data independent of the semantics. Measurement data typically consists of a collection of records consisting of one or more fields. For example, the CLF log in Figure 9.1 contains four records each with seven fields. Packet traces may have a more complicated format. Parsing involves identifying the boundaries between successive records in the log, as well as the distinct fields within each record. For example, records may be separated by a newline character or by blank lines, and fields may be separated by blank spaces or tabs. Variable-length records may include a special length field that indicates how to locate the beginning of the next record. Each field also has a particular format, such as a timestamp within brackets (e.g., `[15/Oct/2000:00:00:25 -0400]`) or a request line within quotations (e.g., `"GET /img/logo.gif HTTP/1.0"`).

The parser could be written in a variety of different programming languages. The choice of a programming language depends on the complexity and size of the measurement data. For example, a CLF server log does not require very complex parsing relative to a packet trace. The parsing code can identify records and fields that violate the expected syntax. For example, a record may not have the correct number of fields, or a field may not have the correct format. The parsing code can identify and discard these records, allowing the rest of the preprocessing and analysis software to assume that all of the data is syntactically correct. The code that parses the measurement data may generate a collection of records in a more convenient form. Alternatively, the code may assign the fields of each record to variables for future processing. In addition, the parsing code can hide the variations in data formats from one set of measurements to another. For example, different Web server implementations often produce CLF logs with variations in syntax. Handling these differences in the parsing code allows the rest of the software to operate on a wider variety of server logs.

9.4.2 Filtering measurement data

The next preprocessing step involves filtering the measurement data to remove unnecessary fields and records. In some cases, certain fields may be omitted from each record because they do not convey useful information. For example, every record in the CLF log in Figure 9.1 has a "–" character for the remote-identity and authenticated-user fields because the server disabled the Identification Protocol and did not employ authentication (or did not record the authenticated user). A reduced log could exclude these fields. In addition, the filtering software could delete fields that are not needed for analyzing the data. For example, consider a packet trace that includes the full request and response header for each HTTP transfer. Extracting the first line of the request and response headers may be sufficient for many analysis tasks. Omitting the rest of the header would substantially reduce the overhead of storing the measurement data. However, deciding to remove information requires careful consideration of the full range of analysis tasks that might draw on the measurement data.

Filtering may also involve removing entire records based on the contents of one or more of the fields. Records with invalid fields may be disruptive to future analysis. For example, a CLF record may have a timestamp field that is syntactically correct but does not fall in the time interval covered by the log. In addition to omitting erroneous records, filtering may be used to remove records that are not relevant to the subsequent analysis. For example, an analysis of accesses to resources at a server may not need to process the requests that return certain error response codes. Similarly, an analysis of image resources could focus on records with Request-URIs with filename extensions that correspond to common image formats (e.g., `.gif` and `.jpg`).

9.4.3 Transforming measurement data

The final preprocessing stage transforms the data to produce a new collection of records for subsequent analysis. The transformed data may have a simpler syntax that is more amenable to processing. For example, the request-line field in a CLF log could be converted into three separate fields: the request method, Request-URI, and protocol version. Likewise, fields that are case-insensitive could be converted to a single format. For example, `Content-Length` and `Content-length` should be recognized as the same header. In addition to minor syntactic conversions, transformation may involve converting a field into different units. A timestamp represented in a log as a year, month, day, hour, minute, and second could be converted to a single number, such as the UNIX representation of time (i.e., the number of seconds since midnight on January 1, 1970). As another example, a client IP address in dotted decimal notation (10.34.197.3) could be converted to a 32-bit unsigned integer to save storage space.

Other transformations change the semantics of a field to add or suppress information in each record. For example, the CLF log in Figure 9.1 includes the IP address of the requesting client. The IP address could be converted to a hostname by issuing a DNS query. Performing this conversion after the log is created avoids the overhead for the server to determine the name-to-address mapping as part of handling the HTTP request. However, the mapping should be performed as soon as possible after the data are collected to have the most accurate information. Performing the transformation as part of preprocessing also avoids the need to convert IP addresses into names multiple times during the subsequent analysis tasks. Other transformations may obscure information to protect user privacy. For example, the preprocessing software could apply a function that encrypts the client IP address.

The proper programming language for transforming the data depends on the complexity of the operations. Scripting languages may be suitable for simple syntactic changes and conversions. More complex functions, such as DNS queries, may be implemented as system calls. The software for preprocessing the measurement data produces a new collection of records that can be analyzed in numerous ways. The records could be stored in a database that supports a variety of queries. The records could also be entered into a generic spreadsheet program or specialized log-analysis software. Alternatively, scripts written in awk or Perl could compute statistics about the data, or more complicated analysis programs could be written in C. In any of these situations, starting with a clean and consistent set of records greatly simplifies the analysis of the traffic measurements.

9.5 Drawing Inferences From Measurement Data

Traffic measurements do not always contain all of the information necessary to provide an exact answer to basic questions about the characteristics of the Web. Some of these limitations stem from the fact that the measurement data does not include all of the relevant fields, such as specific timestamps or HTTP headers. In other cases, the necessary information is not available where the measurements are collected. This section discusses techniques for drawing inferences about HTTP headers, client/server identity, user actions, and resource modifications, despite the limitations of measurement data.

9.5.1 Limitations of HTTP header information

The headers of HTTP request and response messages provide a wealth of information about Web transfers. However, some Web logs and traces do not include the full set of HTTP headers. Most server logs capture the request line and response code but not the header fields in the request and response messages. Collecting more detailed logs requires reconfiguring or modifying the server. A packet monitor or a client, proxy, or server could conceivably capture the header of each message and the entire message body. However, this is often infeasible in practice. Many measurement studies rely on proxy and server logs that record a small number of fields related to the HTTP header. In some cases, a request listed in a log can be *replayed* by issuing a new request to the same server and observing the response. However, this approach is not appropriate if the requested resource has changed at the server or if the HTTP response depends on headers in the HTTP request.

Some missing header information can be inferred from the fields, such as the request method, the Request-URI, and the response code, which are available in the server log. The Request-URI can be used to infer the `Content-Type` of the requested resource. For example, URIs ending in `.html` or `.htm` are likely to correspond to HTML files, whereas URIs ending in `.gif` or `.jpg` are likely to correspond to images; however, some images may have different file extensions, and some URIs ending in `.gif` or `.jpg` may not correspond to images. Similarly, the Request-URI or the request method may indicate whether the request invokes a script at the server. A Request-URI that includes the string "`cgi`" or "`cgi-bin`" typically corresponds to a script. `GET` requests with arguments listed at the end of the Request-URI and `POST` requests typically correspond to HTML forms. These heuristics can be used to compute basic statistics from a server log, such as the proportion of responses that return dynamically generated content or particular content types.

Certain response codes imply the existence of particular headers in the HTTP request. For example, the 206 `Partial Content` response implies that the client requested a subset of a resource, using the `Range` header. Similarly, a 304 `Not Modified` response implies that the request included validation information, such as the `If-Modified-Since` header. However, a `Range` or `If-Modified-Since` request may also result in a 200 `OK` response that returns the entire entity. Inferences based on the response code provide a lower bound on how often certain types of requests occur rather than an exact count. Some analysis tasks may use the response code to determine which requests to ignore in computing certain statistics. For example, consider the problem of counting the number of unique resources requested from a Web server based on the information in a server log. A Request-URI that always results in a 404 `Not Found` response should not be included because the requested resource could not be generated at the Web site during the period of the log.

9.5.2 Ambiguous client/server identity

Associating a collection of HTTP transfers with the same user, resource, or Web site is difficult in practice. For example, the client IP address logged by a server is not necessarily a unique identifier of a user. A single client may send requests on behalf of multiple users, and a single user may browse the Web from multiple client IP addresses, as discussed in Section 9.2.1. Similarly, the server IP address recorded in a packet trace is not a unique identifier of a Web server. A single machine may run multiple Web servers, and a single Web site may be replicated on multiple machines. The hostname of the server may be available from the Request-URI or the `Host` header of an HTTP/1.1 request, assuming that the measurement data includes this field. However, HTTP/1.0 requests do not include the hostname. In some cases, the IP address of the server could be converted to a hostname at a later stage by issuing a DNS query. However, the DNS information may be out of date by the time the packet trace is analyzed.

Identifying unique resources is also difficult in some cases. As part of handling a request, the server converts the Request-URI into a filename. Consider the problem of identifying the number of unique resources requested from a Web server, based on the Request-URI field in the server log. In some cases, multiple valid Request-URIs correspond to the same resource. For example, `http://www.foo.com/` and `http://www.foo.com/index.html` typically refer to the same file (`/www/index.html`). Although URIs are case-sensitive, a Web server could be configured to treat the Request-URI `http://www.foo.com/INDEX.HTML` as an alias for `http://www.foo.com/index.html`. Some conversions involve relatively trivial operations, such as removing duplicate "/" characters. Request-URIs that differ in simple ways can be detected as part of processing the server log. In other situations, the server may treat certain Request-URIs as aliases for another URI. Without access to the server configuration information, recognizing aliases is virtually impossible. Most studies typically assume that different Request-URIs correspond to different resources.

9.5.3 Inferring user actions

Analyzing Web traffic measurements often involves determining when, and how often, particular user events occur. Studying user behavior involves identifying when a user clicks on a hypertext link. Even if a client can be associated with a single user, identifying and classifying user clicks is difficult in practice. Information from the HTTP request and response messages, as well as the size and time of the transfer, can be used to draw inferences about key events. For example, the time field in a server log provides a useful way to identify the sequence of requests by the same client. The time between successive requests can be used to infer which requests might belong to a single "visit" to a Web site and which of these requests correspond to a user clicking on a hypertext link, as opposed to embedded resources automatically downloaded by the browser.

The stateless nature of HTTP makes it difficult to determine which requests belong together because the client does not have a session with the Web server with a fixed starting or finishing time. Instead, the beginning of a client's visit to a Web site can be inferred based on measurements in a log or trace. The first request corresponds to the beginning of the visit. A request that occurs within a few tens of seconds of the previous request by that client could be viewed as part of the same visit to the site. Stronger inferences are possible with additional information about the structure of the Web site. For example, the new Request-URI may correspond to a hypertext link on one of the earlier pages, increasing the likelihood that the request was generated by clicking on an earlier page. Information about the hypertext references on earlier pages may be available from the `Referer` field in the HTTP request message. Alternatively, the hypertext structure could be determined by inspecting the Web pages at a later stage; however, the contents of the Web pages may have changed in the meantime.

A single user action, such as clicking on a hypertext link, may trigger multiple HTTP requests to download a Web page and embedded images. Isolating the effects of user actions required an effective way to distinguish between user clicks and automatically generated HTTP requests. Although a browser log could differentiate between these two kinds of requests, a proxy/server log or a packet trace would not necessarily have this information, unless the full contents of the Web page are available. Instead, a heuristic may be used to classify the requests based on the time between successive requests—a request that occurs less than, say, one or two seconds after a previous request by the same client is generated automatically by the browser. The inference is stronger if the Request-URI references an image, such as a GIF or JPEG file. The requested resource is even more likely to be an embedded image if the Request-URI has the same path as the original HTML file. For example, a request for `http://www.foo.com/bar/pict.gif` that closely follows a request for `http://www.foo.com/bar/index.html` probably refers to an embedded image.

Larger interrequest spacings could be classified as a user "click," especially if the request accesses a resource that is not in image format. Estimating which requests stem from user clicks is important for studying the typical user experience in visiting a Web site, including statistics such as the average number of clicks per visit and the time between successive clicks. The time between clicks can be thought of as quiet time or think time. In general, these heuristics based on request spacing are somewhat simplistic. A user may spend more than a few minutes "thinking" about a Web page before clicking on a hypertext link or may click on a hypertext link after less than one second. Alternatively, a user may leave the computer for a period of time and then continue browsing the Web site. In addition, a single client may issue a collection of requests on behalf of multiple users. Still, these time-based heuristics sometimes provide the only way to develop models of user behavior from traffic measurements.

9.5.4 Detecting resource modifications

Identifying when Web resources are created, modified, and deleted is useful for analyzing changes in a Web site. In addition, statistics about how often a resource changes may have implications for Web caching policies. Ideally, Web servers would generate records for the creation, modification, and deletion of resources in addition to the logging of client requests. However, studying changes to resources is difficult because Web traffic measurements typically do not include this information. Resources that are never requested do not appear in a log or trace. In addition, a resource may be modified multiple times between successive requests, and server logs typically do not include information about the age of a resource or its last modification time. Still, statistics about resource modifications may be inferred from the HTTP headers, response sizes, and timestamp(s) recorded for each measurement record. In some cases, this information is sufficient for estimating the age of a requested resource and the time between successive modifications.

Consider the problem of determining the age of a resource at the time of a request, based on information from the HTTP headers. The age is the difference between the request time and the last modification time. Although most server logs include the request time, the last modification time is usually not recorded. Yet, a packet monitor or browser log may record the `Last-Modified` and `Date` headers from the HTTP response message. The age of the resource is the difference between these two times. If the measurements do not include the time from the `Date` header, the time of the request could be noted where the measurement takes place. For example, a packet trace or proxy log might note the time the request was observed. However, the measurement of the request time does not necessarily reflect the time at the origin server, where the `Last-Modified` header is generated. The clocks running on various machines in the Internet may not agree exactly. If it is possible to correct for the differences between the clocks, or the difference is known to be small, then this may not pose a significant problem.

Another approach to studying the modifications to Web resources involves comparing the `Last-Modified` headers of successive responses for the same resource. If the response messages have different `Last-Modified` times, the resource changed at least once during the time between the two responses. The difference between the two `Last-Modified` times provides a lower bound on the time that elapsed between the changes to the resource. For example, suppose one response had a `Last-Modified` time of 1 pm and the second response had a `Last-Modified` time of 2 pm. The previous version of the resource existed for no more than one hour. If the resource changed more than once between the two responses, the time between modifications might be less than one hour. This approach to measuring the time between changes is not sensitive to differences in clocks between the origin server and the component that measures the responses because both `Last-Modified` times were typically set by the same machine—the origin server.

HTTP response messages do not necessarily include the `Last-Modified` header. In some cases, the response message may include another header, such as an `ETag`, that can be used to identify separate instances of the same resource. This provides an indication that a resource changes between successive responses, without providing information about the time that the change took place. In other cases, changes to a resource can be detected from changes in the `Content-Length`. If two responses for the same Request-URI have different content lengths, the two resources are different. However, the reverse is not true. A resource may be modified without changing its size. Still, comparing the `Content-Length` headers of two responses provides a conservative estimate of the frequency of modifications.

However, the `Content-Length` header may not be available from certain measurements. For example, a server log may record the *transfer length* of the response, rather than the content length. Depending on the server, the transfer length may or may not include the length of the response header. The transfer length differs across successive responses for the same Request-URI if some transfers are aborted before they complete or if the response messages have different transfer codings. In some cases, it may be possible to infer which responses were aborted. Consider a server log that records 20 responses for a particular Request-URI. Suppose 1 response has a smaller transfer length than the other responses, and the other 19 responses have the same transfer length. The 1 log entry with a short transfer length may have stemmed from an aborted response. However, the resource may have been modified twice, with the second modification returning the resource to its original size. Another heuristic exploits the fact that some proxies and servers write response messages into the socket buffer in fixed-size blocks (e.g., 4096 bytes or 8192 bytes). Transfer lengths that are multiples of the block size are more likely to correspond to aborted transfers.

9.6 Measurement Case Studies

In this section, we present four case studies that illustrate how to work around the inherent limitations of the measurement techniques to draw meaningful conclusions about the characteristics of Web traffic:

- **Saskatchewan server log study:** A collection of six server logs from 1995 were analyzed to identify the basic properties of Web workloads [AW97].
- **British Columbia proxy log study:** A collection of seven proxy logs from 1996 and 1997 was used to simulate the performance of a caching proxy under a variety of configurations [DMF97].
- **Boston University client log study:** Client logs collected from university students in 1995 were used to study user browsing patterns and explain the characteristics of the resulting network traffic [CBC95, CB97].
- **AT&T packet trace study:** A packet trace from 1996 was used to analyze the frequency of modifications to Web resources, as well as the nature of the changes to the modified resources [DFKM97].

Because relatively little work has been done on active measurement in the Web, we defer the case study of active measurement to Chapter 15 (Section 15.4). Throughout the presentation, we emphasize the measurement and analysis methodology rather than the specific numerical results of the studies because the numerical results depend on the places and times that the data were collected.

9.6.1 Saskatchewan server log study

A study of server logs at the University of Saskatchewan had the broad goal of identifying the key properties of Web workloads [AW97]. The search for invariant characteristics required analysis of multiple logs from different kinds of Web servers. The analysis drew on six server logs from three universities, two scientific organizations, and one ISP. The researchers did not have control over the fields available in the server logs. The six CLF logs included the name of the requesting host, the request time, the Request-URI, the response code, and the number of bytes transferred in the response, in the following format:

```
hostname - - [dd/mmm/yyyy:hh:mm:ss:tz] request status bytes
```

Table 9.3. Key metrics of Saskatchewan study of server logs

Category	Metric
Basic statistics	Number of distinct Request-URIs
	Average/median transfer size
	Frequency of each response code
Access patterns	Time between successive requests
	Popularity of each requested resource
	Time between requests for the same resource
Inferences	Content types of requested resources
	Average/median resource size
	Frequency of resource modifications
	Frequency of aborted transfers

The log did not include information on the elapsed time for generating or transferring the response or on the actual size of the response message. In addition, there was no information on the complete set of files available at the servers or which requests were generated by users or by proxies or spiders. Still, some properties could be studied based on the information available in the server logs, as shown in Table 9.3. Several basic statistics were computed for individual fields in the log. For example, the study reported the number of distinct Request-URIs and the average transfer size, as well as the proportion of log entries with particular response codes.

Statistics about access patterns were computed by looking at the relationship between multiple log entries. Looking across the consecutive entries in the log made it possible to study the time between HTTP requests at the server. This provided an estimate of the request load on the server over time. Focusing on individual Request-URIs allowed the study to determine the frequency of requests for the most popular resources and the time between successive requests for the same resource. The properties were important to study because of their implications for the effectiveness of Web caching. Other information was inferred from the fields available in the log. For example, the Request-URI was used to infer the content type of the requested resource. The transfer sizes associated with a Request-URI over time were used to infer the resource size, as well as the frequency of resource modifications and aborted transfers.

9.6.2 British Columbia proxy log study

Researchers at the University of British Columbia conducted a study of Web caching based on seven proxy logs from 1996 and 1997 [DMF97]. The seven proxy logs represented a diverse set of institutions in different parts of the world, including universities, companies, and one national proxy. All of the organizations were running the Squid proxy server, discussed in Chapter 11 (Section 11.10.1). The information available in the proxy logs varied across the seven proxies. Each log entry included the client IP address, the request time, the Request-URI, and the response size. To protect user privacy, the client IP address was disguised by converting the address to another representation. Two of the servers used a different conversion function every day, making it impossible to determine if the same user visited the Web site on multiple days; the other five servers used the same conversion function across the entire collection period. Six of the logs came from caching proxies. These logs included an additional field indicating the action taken by the cache, such as whether the request was satisfied by the cache or not. Entries in the other log did not have this field but included the `Last-Modified` and `Expires` times, when available in the HTTP response message from the server.

In contrast to the previous case study, the British Columbia study did not focus on statistical characterization of the measurement data. Instead, the logs were used to evaluate the effectiveness of proxy caching based on simulations. The goal was to experiment with different cache sizes, request rates, and cache-coherency policies by using a simulator that was based on the Squid cache. Simulation was a valuable alternative to experimenting with different cache configurations in the operational proxies. First, reconfiguring the operational proxies at the seven institutions would not have been practical. Second, using a simulator enabled the study to experiment with cache sizes and cache-coherency policies that may not be available in the operational proxies. Third, using a simulator enabled the study to repeat the experiments, using the same log to drive multiple experiments with different proxy configurations.

The simulations evaluated a variety of cached configurations and computed four main performance metrics. Cache performance was judged by the proportion of the proxy's response messages and response bytes that came from the cache instead of the origin server. A request was satisfied by the proxy if the simulated cache had an up-to-date copy of the request resource, identified by the Request-URI. The simulations also recorded the likelihood that a cached response could not be returned from the proxy because the resource had changed at the origin server. In addition, the study also considered how much of the benefit of proxy caching came from sharing resources across multiple clients, rather than from satisfying successive requests by the same client. These metrics were studied under a range of cache sizes and client request rates. Varying the request rate involved sampling the proxy log to extract the sequence of requests from a randomly chosen subset of the clients. This emulated an environment in which the proxy served a smaller community of users with browsing patterns similar to those of the clients in the original log.

Missing information in the measurement data introduced several challenges. For example, ambiguous client identifiers made it difficult to study how frequently the proxy cache was used to share resources among multiple users, as opposed to satisfying successive requests by the same user. However, associating a set of requests with a user required having a unique identifier for the requesting client over the duration of the log. In two of the proxy logs, each client IP address was associated with a different identifier every day. These two proxy logs had to be omitted from the portion of the study that focused on resource sharing. For the other five institutions, each client machine had a single (disguised) identifier. In studying these five logs, the study had to assume that each client corresponded to a single user. This would not have been true in cases in which multiple users shared a single machine or a single user accessed the Web from multiple machines.

Incomplete data about caching-related headers made it difficult to know when the simulated cache had an out-of-date copy of a resource. In reality, a resource may have changed over time. However, six of the logs did not indicate if and when these modifications occurred. Yet, in some cases the logs could be used to infer that a resource remained fresh between two consecutive requests. The proxy log indicated whether or not the proxy satisfied a request from the cache. If a request was satisfied from the cache, then the cached resource was fresh at that time. Then this inference was applied to the simulated proxy cache. When the request was applied to the simulated cache, the simulator assumed that the resource was fresh and, hence, could be returned from the cache.

9.6.3 Boston University client log study

Researchers at Boston University collected browser logs to analyze Web browsing patterns and their impact on network traffic [CBC95]. At the time, Mosaic was the most popular Web browser. The software was in the public domain and could be modified to generate client logs. The browser was instrumented to produce logs of user requests and was distributed to a collection of workstations connected to a local area network in the Computer Science Department at Boston University. The browsers collected logs of user activity and sent reports to a central machine for processing. By the end of the measurement study, the popularity of Mosaic had been usurped by commercial browsers that could not be modified to collect measurement data. As a result, studies based on browser logs are difficult to replicate in today's Web environment. In addition, the browsing patterns of Computer Science students on a local area network may differ from the broad base of users accessing the Web today.

Each log entry corresponded to a single request and included the machine name of the client, the request time (in microseconds), the requested URI, the response size, and the retrieval time (in seconds). The browser logs were used to analyze basic properties of Web traffic [CB97], including many of the same statistics as in the Saskatchewan study, such as response sizes and resources sizes. In addition, the study analyzed the retrieval latency and its relationship to response size, as well as the relationships between a resource's content type

Table 9.4. Key metrics of Boston University study of browser logs

Category	Metric
Basic statistics	Resource size Response size Retrieval latency Resource content type
Timing	Time between automatically generated requests Time between requests generated by the user Aggregate load on the shared network

and its size, as summarized in Table 9.4. The study also examined the time between successive requests by the same user, even if the user's requests were directed to different Web sites. This was possible because the browser captured all requests by the user, including requests to various Web sites and requests satisfied by the browser cache. This information would not be available in a conventional proxy or server. In addition, the detailed timing information made it possible for the study to consider the time between the end of one response and the beginning of the next request. This captures the time the user spent inspecting the Web page before issuing the next request.

The study also considered the time between requests generated by the user versus the time between requests generated automatically by the browser. In hindsight, it would have been useful for each entry in the browser log to identify whether the request was triggered by a user action. In the absence of this information, the study had to infer which requests were automatically generated based on the elapsed time since the previous request. The presence of multiple, fine-grain timestamps for each log entry made these estimates more accurate than they would have been otherwise. Finally, the study exploited having measurement data for a collection of machines on the same network. In addition to characterizing user access patterns, the study considered the aggregate traffic generated by the collection of users on the shared network. Because the client logs recorded the request time at the microsecond level, the study was able to analyze the network traffic imposed by these requests on a relatively small time scale.

9.6.4 AT&T packet-trace study

Designing effective strategies for Web caching requires an understanding of which resources change, how frequently they change, and how much they change. These questions motivated a detailed study of the rate of change of Web resources [DFKM97]. Analyzing a small number of server logs would have given insight into the frequency of modifications to the resources at those sites. However, this would not have provided a good indication of how frequently resources change throughout the Web. Instead, the study focused on measurements collected from locations near a large number of requesting clients at two companies. The study drew on a proxy log from Digital Equipment Corporation and a packet trace from AT&T. We focus on the collection and analysis of the AT&T packet trace to contrast with the other three case studies.

The packet traces were collected on an Ethernet link connecting AT&T Research's internal network to the rest of the Internet in November of 1996. The packet monitor collected TCP packets with a source or destination port number of 80, corresponding to HTTP. The entire contents of each packet were logged to disk. After collecting the data, a separate program associated the packets with the appropriate request and response streams and reassembled the HTTP messages. Reconstructing HTTP request and response messages from packet traces is a complicated task, as discussed in detail in Chapter 14 (Section 14.1). The full HTTP request and response messages were recorded for every request, which generated nearly 20 GB of measurement data in a 17-day period. Recording the entire data transfer provided access to all HTTP headers. In addition, comparing the bodies of the response messages enabled the study to identify when and how the resources changed over time. Having access to the entire message allowed the researchers to study the HTTP transfers at a level of detail that would have been impossible with conventional proxy or server logs.

The study analyzed the age of requested resources and the frequency of modifications based on various timestamps, as discussed in Section 9.5.4. The Date header and the Last-Modified header (when present) provided information about the age of the resource. Across multiple responses for the same Request-URI, the Last-Modified header indicated if the resource changed between successive accesses. In some cases, the HTTP response did not include a Last-Modified header, making it difficult to infer when the resource had changed. In this situation, it was helpful to have access to the entire response message. Comparing the checksums of the entities in the HTTP response messages provided a way to determine if a resource has changed between successive responses for the same Request-URI. Having access to the entity body enabled the study to consider two other issues. First, comparing checksums across responses for *different* URIs identified situations in which the same content was available via more than one URI. Second, when a resource changed across successive responses, a direct comparison of the entity bodies could show *how* the resource changed. For example, text and HTML resources were inspected to determine if they were modified in relatively minor ways (e.g., change in a phone number or a hypertext link).

9.7 Summary

The four case studies illustrate the kinds of information that can be gleaned from measurements of Web traffic. Each of the measurement techniques offers a valuable glimpse of the characteristics of the Web. Yet, each technique has limitations that stem from where and how the measurements are collected and what fields are recorded. Capturing information about every component in a Web transfer is extremely difficult. In addition, the heterogeneous nature of the Web makes it difficult to generalize results from any one measurement study. Despite these impediments, measurement plays an extremely important role in evaluating Web software components and the HTTP protocol and analyzing user behavior and the basic properties of Web resources and Web sites. Measuring traffic in multiple places and times, and drawing careful inferences from the traces and logs, can compensate for some of the limitations of the measurement data. Analyses of a diverse collection of Web traffic measurements drive our presentation of Web workload characteristics in the next chapter.

10

Web Workload Characterization

Understanding and evaluating Web performance is difficult in practice. Important performance metrics, such as user-perceived latency and server throughput, depend on the interaction of numerous protocols and software components. Latency, in turn, affects how users react; for example, slow responses may cause users to abort requests. Evaluating system performance in a controlled manner requires a way to decouple the offered load from the underlying system. A *workload* consists of the set of all inputs a system receives over a period of time. Quantitative models that capture the main properties of the workload can drive a variety of performance evaluation techniques, such as benchmarking and simulation. For example, Web workload models are used to generate request traffic for comparing the performance of different proxy and server implementations. In addition, Web workload models drive simulation experiments that evaluate new techniques for improving Web performance.

This chapter focuses on the characteristics of Web workloads. Developing a workload model involves three main steps: identifying the important workload parameters, analyzing measurement data to quantify these parameters, and validating the model against reality. Our discussion starts with a motivation for workload characterization and an overview of Web workload parameters. Constructing a workload model requires an understanding of statistical techniques for analyzing measurement data and representing the key properties of Web traffic. Although characteristics such as Web resource sizes or the number of embedded images in a Web page vary from one measurement study to another, certain statistical properties persist across the studies. Analysis of traffic measurements reveals the substantial diversity of the Web in virtually every respect. Probability distributions provide an effective way to represent this variability in a concise manner. Hence, before discussing Web workload characteristics in detail, we present a brief overview of probability distributions.

We describe the key properties of Web workloads, based on the results of numerous studies of Web traffic measurements, as follows:

- **HTTP message characteristics:** HTTP defines several request methods and a variety of response codes. The relative popularity of certain request methods and response codes illustrates how the protocol is used in practice. A realistic model of Web workloads must have a representative mixture of request methods and response codes.
- **Resource characteristics:** Web clients request resources with diverse properties in terms of content type, size, popularity, and modification frequency. In addition, the number of embedded resources varies across different Web pages. These characteristics have important implications on the overhead of storing and transmitting Web resources.
- **User behavior:** In visiting a Web site, a user retrieves one or more Web pages, with some time between successive downloads. The browsing habits of users have significant impact on the request load experienced by Web proxies and servers, as well as the traffic load imparted on the underlying network.

Along the way, we discuss how the continued evolution of the Web could ultimately change these workload properties. Then we discuss how to combine the workload parameters to generate a stream of HTTP requests that captures the key properties of Web traffic. These synthetic workload models have been applied in a variety of benchmarks for evaluating the performance of Web proxies and servers in a controlled environment. Accurate benchmarks depend on having a detailed understanding of Web resources and user behavior. Despite the value of analyzing Web traffic measurements, gaining deeper insight into browsing patterns has the potential to violate users' privacy. The chapter closes with a broad discussion of the tension between user privacy and workload characterization.

10.1 Workload Characterization

A workload model consists of a collection of parameters that represent the key features of the workload that affect resource allocation and system performance. In this section, we discuss the motivations for characterizing Web workloads and identify key parameters of Web workload models.

10.1.1 Applications of workload models

Workload models can be applied to a variety of performance evaluation tasks, such as the following:

- **Identifying performance problems:** A Web server may exhibit performance problems, such as high latency or low throughput, under specific load scenarios that occur during the busiest period of the day. Identifying the cause of the problem requires the testing of the server under a realistic workload. Detecting the problem and evaluating potential solutions may involve subjecting the server to the same workload multiple times.

- **Benchmarking Web components:** The decision to purchase a particular proxy or server product typically depends on the price and performance. Comparing the performance of different proxies and servers requires applying a common, reproducible workload to each product. The workload should capture the key properties of Web traffic to ensure that the performance results are representative of how the products would perform in practice. Benchmarks may also be used to evaluate new features in a proxy or server implementation before deployment.

- **Capacity planning:** Web performance depends on the network bandwidth, CPU capacity, disk space, and memory available to Web proxies and servers. For example, a busy Web site may need to be replicated on several server machines. Deciding how many machines to devote to the site requires balancing the trade-off between cost and performance. Estimating the performance of a particular proxy or server configuration depends on having an accurate model of the expected workload.

Workload models have several advantages and disadvantages over other popular techniques for evaluating Web performance. One natural approach constructs requests directly from an existing log or trace, maintaining the same time between requests as seen in the original measurements. Replaying a trace or log has the advantage of reproducing a known workload and avoiding the intermediate step of analyzing the traffic. This approach is particularly useful to gain insight into specific scenarios that have caused performance problems in the past. However, replaying a trace does not provide much flexibility for experimenting with changes to the workload. In addition, a trace does not offer a clear separation between the offered load and the performance. The timing of the requests recorded in a trace depends on the performance of the system at that time. Applying the trace to a new scenario with different performance properties may not be appropriate. For example, a trace from an overloaded server might exhibit long delays between successive requests and a small number of clicks per user session. However, these properties may be by-products of the poor performance of the server rather than intrinsic aspects of the workload.

Another approach involves sending requests as fast as possible to evaluate a proxy or a server under heavy load. Stress testing is an important part of evaluating a new system. However, the performance of the system under this workload may not represent how the system would perform under realistic traffic patterns. Generating a request stream from a workload model overcomes some of the disadvantages of the other two approaches. Unlike trace-driven workloads, a synthetic workload derives from an explicit mathematical model that can be inspected, analyzed, and criticized. Unlike stress testing workloads, a synthetic workload has the potential to represent the key properties of real Web traffic. Most importantly, workload models offer the possibility of exploring system performance in a controlled manner over a range of scenarios by changing the numbers associated with each probability distribution. These experiments can lend insight into how a particular parameter affects system performance and how the system might perform as the characteristics of the workload change.

10.1.2 Selecting workload parameters

To ensure that a workload model is representative of real workloads, the parameters of the model should have certain properties, as follows:

- **Decoupling from the underlying system:** The parameters of a workload model should be decoupled from the details of the underlying system, such as a proxy or server implementation. A workload model would not include statistics such as user-perceived latency, server throughput, or the packet loss rate, because these performance metrics depend on the server platform and network congestion. However, traffic generated from a workload model may be used to evaluate these metrics on a particular platform.
- **Proper level of detail:** The parameters should represent the workload at the appropriate level of detail for evaluating the system. For example, a network-level workload model might include parameters relating to the size of IP packets and the number of packets in a transfer. A Web workload model might include the time between successive client HTTP requests and the size of HTTP response messages, but not the contents of the entity body.
- **Independence from other parameters:** Dependencies between workload parameters complicate the effort to have a succinct, simple workload model that accurately represents real Web traffic. However, identifying a small number of independent parameters is difficult in practice. For example, the size of a resource is typically related to the content type. The model can introduce additional parameters to capture these dependencies. For example, the model could have separate parameters for the sizes of HTML and image resources.

Workload models mature over time as the understanding of the system evolves. Table 10.1 summarizes the workload parameters identified over several years of studies of Web traffic measurements. The first category captures the basic characteristics of HTTP messages—the request methods and the response codes—that illustrate how the protocol is used in practice. The second category captures the key properties of Web resources, such as content type, size, and popularity. The third category captures the behavior of users visiting a Web site, such as the time between the arrivals of different users and the number of

Table 10.1. Examples of Web workload parameters

Category	Parameter
Protocol	Request method
	Response code
Resource	Content type
	Resource size
	Response size
	Popularity
	Modification frequency
	Temporal locality
	Number of embedded resources
Users	Session interarrival times
	Number of clicks per session
	Request interarrival times

"clicks" per visit to a Web site. These parameters dictate the timing of request arrivals at a Web proxy or server. In practice, the various parameters in Table 10.1 are not independent of each other. For example, the time between two user clicks may depend on the size of the response to the first request. Future studies may provide a deeper understanding of the dependencies between parameters. After a brief introduction to statistics and probability distributions, we describe the current understanding of the characteristics of Web workloads.

10.2 Statistics and Probability Distributions

Workload characterization involves associating each parameter of the workload model with quantitative values based on analysis of measurement data. Although simple statistics such as the mean, median, and variance suffice for some workload parameters, probability distributions provide a more general way to capture how a parameter varies over a range of values.

10.2.1 Mean, median, and variance

Statistics such as the mean, median, and variance capture the basic properties of many Web workload parameters. Consider a server log that records the request method and response code for each Web transfer. Determining the proportion of requests using the GET method or the proportion of responses with the 200 OK code involves counting the number of transfers of each type. Other parameters, such as the size of Web response messages, have a much wider range of values. Reporting the proportion of response messages with each possible size would be very tedious. Instead, the characteristics of response sizes can be represented with statistics, such as the average size. In practice, though, the average, or *mean,* does not capture the inherent variability of most of the Web workload parameters.

In fact, when a parameter varies widely, the mean is a very misleading statistic that may be skewed by a small number of large values. For example, consider a server that generates five response messages of sizes 4100, 4700, 4200, 20,000, and 4000 bytes, respectively. Based on these five responses, the average response size is 7400 bytes. Yet, this value does not provide an accurate representation of the typical response sizes. An alternative statistic is the *median,* the size of the "middle" resource; half of the resources are smaller than the median and the other half are larger than the median. In this example, the median resource size is 4200 bytes, which is a better indication of the typical size. However, the median does not hint at the possibility of having a very large response message. A sequence of 4100, 4700, 4200, 4800, and 4000 bytes would have the same median of 4200.

Computing both the mean and the median provides a better picture. The fact that the median is much smaller than the mean suggests the presence of a relatively small number of very large responses. For example, the first sequence has a mean of 7400 and a median of 4200, suggesting the possibility of having a large response. In contrast, the second sequence has a mean of 4360, which is very close to the median of 4200. This suggests that the second sequence of response sizes does not vary much. Besides the mean and the median, other statistics such as the variance or standard deviation attempt to quantify how much the parameter varies from the average value. A small variance implies that the parameter stays close to the mean value, whereas a large variance implies that the parameter may have values that differ substantially from the mean. Still, like the mean and the median, the variance and the standard deviation provide only a crude characterization of the parameter. These summary statistics do not provide enough information to generate a workload that is representative of how the parameters vary in practice.

10.2.2 Probability distributions

Probability distributions capture how a parameter varies over a wide range of values. Consider the distribution $F(x)$ of response sizes. $F(x)$ is the proportion of responses that are larger than x bytes. This is referred to as the *complementary cumulative distribution function.* The values of $F(x)$ can be determined directly from the measurement data, as shown in Figure 10.1. For the sequence 4100, 4700, 4200, 20,000, and 4000, $F(x)$ stays at 1 for x from 0 to 3999, dropping to 0.8 by $x = 4000$ and decreasing by 0.2 at x of 4100, 4200, 4700, and 20,000, reaching a value of 0 by $x = 20,000$. In this example, $F(x)$ changes values in a small number of points. However, in practice, a large set of response sizes could result in a function $F(x)$ that changes many times. As a result,

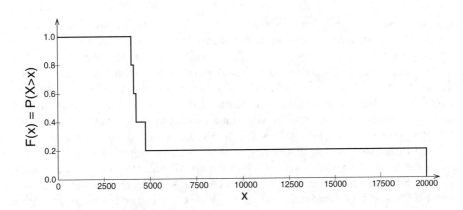

Figure 10.1. Example of a complementary cumulative distribution

working directly with the measured distribution may be difficult. Representing the distribution with an equation makes it easier to characterize the workload parameter and incorporate the results in a benchmark or an analytic model.

Several probability distributions have been widely studied and applied to workload characterization. Each distribution can be represented by a relatively simple equation with one or more variables. One of the most popular probability distributions is the exponential distribution with the form

$$F(x) = e^{-\lambda x}$$

with a mean of $1/\lambda$, where x can take on any value greater than or equal to 0. Other distributions have different equations with one or more variables that control the shape of the function.

Relating a measured distribution to an equation requires justifying the hypothesis that the equation is capable of accurately representing the measured data. Justifying this hypothesis consists of two key steps. First, the measured data is fitted with the equation to determine the value of each variable. For example, the value of λ in the exponential distribution can be set based on the average response size in the measured data. Second, statistical tests are performed to compare the resulting equation with the measured distribution. These tests quantify the "goodness" of the fit of the equation to the measured data. If the goodness-of-fit test fails, another distribution may be considered. For example, the exponential distribution cannot accurately represent most of the Web workload parameters in Table 10.1. In some cases, no single well-known distribution matches the measured data. Instead, it may be necessary to represent different parts of the measured distribution with different equations. For example, small responses may follow one distribution and large responses may follow another. Fitting measured data with distributional models and testing the goodness of the match has been an active area of statistics research for many years. These issues are discussed in detail in a variety of books [DS86, LK99].

Characterizing a diverse and evolving system such as the Web is very difficult. Measurements collected in different parts of the Web may lead to very different conclusions about workload characteristics. For example, the distribution of response sizes among low-bandwidth wireless clients may differ markedly from the distribution of response sizes for high-bandwidth clients. In addition, the emergence of new applications and services can change the workload characteristics. In some cases, changes in a workload parameter affect some of the variables of a probability distribution without altering the underlying distribution. For example, although the mean response size may vary between low-bandwidth and high-bandwidth users, the variability of the response sizes may be similar in the two scenarios. In the discussion of the workload parameters, we discuss how the characteristics have varied over time and search for key invariant properties. In addition, we discuss how changes in Web applications could have significant impact on certain workload parameters in the future.

10.3 HTTP Message Characteristics

The basic properties of HTTP request and response messages give an indication of how the protocol is used in practice. Statistics about the request methods and response codes can guide the creation of realistic Web workloads and identify possible problems with particular Web sites. The popularity of particular request methods and response codes is likely to change over time with the emergence of new Web applications and the growing penetration of HTTP/1.1.

10.3.1 HTTP request methods

Knowing which request methods arise in practice is useful for optimizing server implementations for the most common methods and developing realistic benchmarks for evaluating Web proxies and servers. HTTP/1.1 defines the GET, HEAD, POST, PUT, DELETE, OPTIONS, TRACE, and CONNECT methods, as discussed earlier in Chapter 7 (Section 7.2.1). A small number of the methods account for the vast majority of HTTP requests.

Traffic characteristics   Across a wide variety of measurement studies, the overwhelming majority of Web requests use the GET method to fetch resources and invoke scripts [AJ00, PQ00]. A small fraction of HTTP requests use the POST method, typically to submit data in forms. The other request methods do not occur often, because they are not triggered by typical user actions at the browser. Measurements show a small number of HEAD requests, which may be generated manually as part of testing an operational Web server. Despite the dominance of GET requests, the exact distribution of request methods varies from site to site. Sites that have an unusual mixture of request methods may have different performance trade-offs than other sites. For example, consider a Web site that allows users to send and receive e-mail messages. To send an e-mail message, the user enters the text in a form in the browser window and clicks on a button to submit the message. This Web site may receive a relatively large number of POST requests, and these request messages may include a large amount of data. A benchmark that assumed that most, or all, requests use the GET method to retrieve data from a site would not accurately represent the workload experienced by this Web site. Knowing that a site has an unusual mixture of request methods can identify situations when a traditional server benchmark would not provide an accurate indication of how the servers would perform for this Web site.

Future trends   In the future, the distribution of request methods may change based on the evolution of Web applications. Numerous Web sites allow users to submit forms for a variety of purposes, such as issuing queries to search engines or sending e-mail. If sites that allow users to submit data become more common, the proportion of POST requests would increase. Over time, a wider range of applications may allow clients to create new resources. For example, Web Distributed Authoring and Versioning (WebDAV) allows a collection of users to collaborate in writing and editing a document, as discussed later, in Chapter 15 (Section 15.5.2). If this application becomes popular, the number of PUT and DELETE requests would increase. WebDAV also introduces new methods that become more common as the application increases in popularity. In addition, existing applications may start using request methods in new ways. For example, a browser or a proxy could use the HEAD method to check whether or not a cached response is up to date, in advance of receiving a request for the resource. We discuss this application in more detail later, in Chapter 13 (Section 13.1.2). Likewise, the emergence of tools for testing and debugging Web components may increase the use of the TRACE method.

10.3.2 HTTP response codes

Knowing how servers typically respond to client requests is an important part of constructing a realistic model of Web workloads. HTTP defines a wide range of response codes divided into five classes, as discussed in Chapter 7 (Section 7.2.3).

Traffic characteristics   Sent in response to a successful request, the 200 OK code accounts for 75% to 90% of responses [AJ00, PQ00]. The next most common response code is 304 Not Modified, typically responsible for 10% to 30% of the responses. Of the remaining response codes, the other redirection

(3xx) codes and the client error (4xx) codes are the most common. For example, a 404 Not Found response is returned when the server cannot generate the requested resource. Some Web sites use redirection responses as a way to balance request load over a collection of replicas. For example, the frequency of 302 Found responses varies from site to site. These statistics suggest that benchmarks should not assume that all requests result in a 200 OK response.

Various factors account for the wide variety in response codes from different Web sites. The 304 Not Modified response code arises when a client wants to validate a cached copy of a resource. Web sites that are dominated by uncacheable content would not receive many requests to revalidate a cached resource and, as such, would not send many 304 responses. Otherwise, the frequency of 304 Not Modified responses depends both on the frequency of resource modifications and the likelihood of requests for cached resources. Web sites with mostly static content, such as HTML files and embedded images, are likely to return a relatively large number of 304 Not Modified responses. This is especially true if the site does not make effective use of the caching-related response headers (e.g., Expires) to indicate how long a client can safely return the cached response. Without this information, the client may have to revalidate the cached response with the server. This would increase the number of 304 Not Modified responses, particularly if the resource is requested by a large number of users.

A large number of client error class (4xx) responses may indicate a problem with the organization of a Web site, or with other Web pages that have hypertext links pointing to the Web site. For example, consider what happens when a Web administrator reorganizes the content at a Web site. Some URLs may no longer point to valid resources at the server. These URLs may still appear in other Web pages or in users' bookmarks. A large number of 404 Not Found responses would suggest that many requests still use the old URLs. Based on this information, the site administrator may configure the server to treat an old URL as an alias for the new URL or return a redirection response with the new URL. In some cases, the administrator may be able to identify other Web pages that still have hypertext links to the old content. The 404 Not Found error may also identify cases in which an HTML file has a hypertext link with a typographical error, such as a missing letter in the URL or a common misspelling of a "word" in the URL (e.g., http://www.bar.com/necesary.fig instead of http://www.bar.com/necessary.fig).

Future trends   Certain response codes do not arise unless the client uses particular request headers. Hence, the popularity of a response code may depend on the level of sophistication of Web clients. As an example, consider the 206 Partial Content response code that is used when the server returns a range of bytes from the requested resource, as discussed earlier, in Chapter 7

(Section 7.4.1). Range requests may become more common once HTTP/1.1 proxies are widely deployed. In addition, a browser may invoke a handler that generates range requests. For example, a handler that displays PDF files may issue range requests to access the pages in a document one at a time. New techniques for improving browser and proxy performance could also increase the frequency of range requests. For example, a client may cache a portion of a large resource and issue a range request to fetch the remaining part [SRT99]. Clients that issue range requests, coupled with servers that return byte ranges, could increase the frequency of the 206 `Partial Content` response code.

The frequency of 302 `Found` redirection responses varies from site to site. Some Web sites use redirection responses as a way to balance the request load over a collection of replicas. As part of handling the Web request, the server would select the "best" replica for satisfying the client request, based on the load on the replica or the proximity to the client. The redirection response instructs the client to repeat the request to this alternate server. The growing size and scale of the Web suggests that replicated servers will become increasingly common, especially for popular Web sites. However, HTTP-level redirection is just one way to control which server handles a client's request. If other approaches become more popular, the frequency of redirection responses may decrease rather than increase over time. We discuss the various approaches to directing client requests to replicated servers in more detail later, in Chapter 11 (Section 11.12). The 302 `Found` response code may also arise at Web sites that return a default Web page when an HTTP request attempts to access a resource that does not exist, in lieu of returning a 404 `Not Found` response.

10.4 Web Resource Characteristics

Understanding the characteristics of Web resources is an important part of modeling Web workloads. Resources vary in terms of how big they are, how popular they are, and how often they change. In addition, HTML pages vary in terms of the number of embedded references they have. In summarizing the characteristics of Web resources, we discuss content type, resource size, response size, resource popularity, modification frequency, temporal locality, and the number of embedded resources.

10.4.1 Content types

Web sites provide access to a wide variety of resources with different content types. Statistics about the content types provide an indication of the kinds of data available on the Web. Content type also has a direct relationship to other key workload parameters, such as resource size and modification frequency. In addition, certain types of content, such as text, are amenable to compression to reduce the size of response messages, whereas other content types, such as images, are often encoded in a compressed form.

Traffic characteristics   For most Web sites, the overwhelming majority of resources are text content (e.g., `text/plain` and `text/html`) and images (e.g., `image/jpeg` and `image/gif`) [AW97, DFKM97, AJ00]. The remaining content types constitute a relatively small portion of the resources. These content types include documents such as postscript and PDF, software such as JavaScript or Java applets, and audio and video data. However, the mixture of content types may vary dramatically from site to site. For example, a Web site that archives documents may have a large number of postscript or PDF documents. Other sites may make heavy use of applets. In addition, the popularity of certain content types may vary depending on the user community. Users with a low-bandwidth connection to the Internet may be less likely to download images or large documents, whereas technical users on UNIX-based systems may be more likely to access large postscript files. In some cases, the mix of content types seen by a client may depend on the policies of its proxy. For example, a proxy may filter responses based on the content type to prevent the downloading of applets that may compromise security.

Future trends   The emergence of new applications can have a sudden and profound influence on the distribution of content types. For example, the growing availability of multimedia content on the Web has led to an increase in the number of sites with audio and video data [AS98].

10.4.2 Resource sizes

The sizes of Web resources affect the storage requirements at the origin server and the overhead of caching resources at browsers and proxies. In addition, the size of a resource affects the load on the network and the latency in delivering the response message.

Traffic characteristics   Although the exact distribution of resource sizes varies across servers and across time, analysis of Web measurements show several common characteristics. In general, the average resource size is relatively small, although a small proportion of resources are quite large. Text, HTML, and image resources dominate many Web sites. Text, HTML, and images tend to be smaller than other types of content, such as audio and video data. The average size of an HTML file is around 4 to 8 KB, whereas the average size of an image is around 14 KB, though the exact numbers differ from site to site [Pit99, AJ00]. Although most HTML, text, and image files are small, some of these files are very large. HTML files have a median of about 2 KB, much smaller than the average size of 4 to 8 KB. This suggests a wide variability in

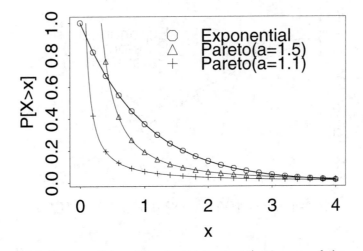

Figure 10.2. Exponential and Pareto distributions (with mean of 1)

the sizes of HTML files. Image sizes also vary substantially depending on the origin or purpose of the picture. Corporate logos, navigational aids, and advertisements are typically quite small, whereas photographs can be quite large. The variability in resource sizes holds for the other content types as well. In addition, a Web site typically has a mixture of different content types, which results in even greater variability in resource sizes. For example, a site with a mixture of text, image, and multimedia data may have resource sizes ranging from a few hundred bytes to several gigabytes.

Although the median captures the size of a typical resource, the probability distribution provides a better indication of the variability in resource sizes. Knowing the distribution of resource sizes at Web sites is useful for deciding how to allocate memory or disk space at a server or proxy. In addition, benchmarks for evaluating Web servers and proxies should capture the inherent variability in resource sizes. The high variability in resource size is typically captured by the *Pareto* distribution, where

$$F(x) = (k/x)^a, \quad x \geq k$$

with a *shape* parameter a and a *scale* parameter k. The distribution has a mean of $ka/(a-1)$ for $a > 1$. Figure 10.2 plots the Pareto distribution for two different a parameters—1.1 and 1.5—with a mean of 1. In the plot for $a = 1.5$, about 80% of the resources are smaller than 1. The remaining 20% of the resources are large enough to result in an average size of 1. The plot for $a = 1.1$ shows

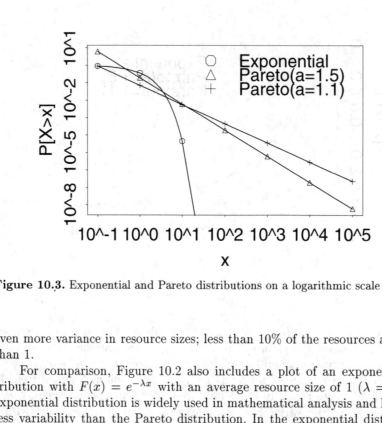

Figure 10.3. Exponential and Pareto distributions on a logarithmic scale

even more variance in resource sizes; less than 10% of the resources are larger than 1.

For comparison, Figure 10.2 also includes a plot of an exponential distribution with $F(x) = e^{-\lambda x}$ with an average resource size of 1 ($\lambda = 1$). The exponential distribution is widely used in mathematical analysis and has much less variability than the Pareto distribution. In the exponential distribution, only 60% of the resources are smaller than 1. Although the remaining 40% of resources are larger than 1, very few of these resources are larger than 4 or 5. This is more readily apparent in Figure 10.3, which plots these same three distributions using a *logarithmic* scale on both the x-axis and the y-axis. The curve for the exponential distribution drops below 10^{-10} by the time x reaches 40, implying that only one in ten million resources is larger than 40. In contrast, the two Pareto curves only drop to 10^{-3}, implying that one in a thousand resources is larger than 40. Very large resources arise much more often for the Pareto distribution than an exponential distribution with the same mean.

The Pareto distribution is a *heavy-tailed* distribution for values of a between 0 and 2. The heavy tail refers to how slowly $F(x)$ decreases for larger values of x. The Pareto distributions decrease linearly in the log-log plot in Figure 10.3. The slope of the log-log plot relates to the value of a. A smaller value of a results in a lower slope, resulting in more variability in resource sizes. For example, in Figure 10.3, the plot for $a = 1.1$ lies above the plot for $a = 1.5$ for large values of x. Numerous measurement studies have shown that the tail of the Pareto distribution captures the variability in the sizes of Web resources.

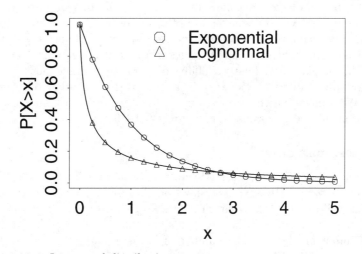

Figure 10.4. Lognormal distribution

Although the value of a differs from one set of measurements to another, most studies conclude that a is around 1.0 to 1.5 [AW97, CB97, BBBC99]. The mean of the distribution is very large for values of a close to 1, making the mean a difficult metric to use in characterizing Web resource sizes.

Despite providing an accurate characterization of the *large* resources, the Pareto distribution is not a good match for the remaining resources in the body of the distribution. Hybrid models that combine multiple distributions provide a better fit with the measured data. The body of the distribution is better represented by a *lognormal* distribution [BC98]. A *normal* distribution refers to a probability distribution with a traditional bell-shaped curve centered at the average value; half of the values are less than the average, and half of the values are more than the average. In the lognormal distribution, the logarithm of x has a normal distribution. Taking the logarithm increases the proportion of values that are below the average, as shown in Figure 10.4; for comparison, the graph also plots an exponential distribution with the same mean. The lognormal distribution accurately captures characteristics of Web resources, except for the very large resources in the tail of the distribution. Together, the lognormal and Pareto distributions model the full range of resource sizes in the Web.

Future trends The size of Web resources is likely to change over time. Users with high-bandwidth connections to the Internet tend to download larger resources [AFJ99]. This, in turn, may encourage content developers to create larger Web pages. However, a trend toward larger pages does not necessarily imply an increase in the *variability* of resource sizes. Changes in the mixture of content types can have a dramatic impact on the size of Web resources. For example, audio and video resources are often quite large. An increase in the amount of multimedia content available on the Web could change the distribution of resource sizes. Still, despite changes in the kinds of resources available on the Web, the extremely high variability of resource sizes has persisted over time. Heavy-tailed distributions arise in a wide variety of other contexts besides the Web, including the distribution of file sizes on UNIX machines and the execution time of programs on computers [HBD97].

10.4.3 Response sizes

The distribution of resource sizes reflects the variability in the sizes of files stored at Web servers. However, the load on the server and the network depends on which of these resources are actually sent to requesting clients. In analyzing the server and network performance, the size of response messages is a more important factor. The number of bytes in a response message determines the amount of bandwidth consumed in satisfying a client request. In addition, the response size affects the throughput available from the underlying TCP connection. The small congestion window during TCP's slow-start phase limits the transmission rate for many response messages. The response size also determines the relative importance of the various sources of delay in satisfying a client request. The overheads for determining the server's IP address and establishing a TCP connection are a major portion of the latency for short transfers. In contrast, long transfers are much more sensitive to server and network congestion.

Traffic characteristics   Response sizes may differ from resource sizes for a variety of reasons. First, some HTTP response messages do not transfer a resource. For example, 204 No Content and 304 Not Modified responses do not have a message body. These responses consist of a few hundred bytes of HTTP header, at most. The 304 Not Modified response code accounts for a significant portion of response messages, as discussed earlier in Section 10.3.2. Second, some Web resources are never requested and, hence, do not contribute to the set of response messages. Some studies have shown that larger resources are less popular than smaller resources, on average. For example, users who browse through a collection of Web pages may not casually download postscript and PDF files. Third, some responses are aborted before they complete, resulting in shorter transfers. Users are more likely to abort long transfers. All of these factors suggest that the size of a typical response message is smaller than the size of a typical resource.

In fact, studies show that the median of the response size distribution is several hundred bytes smaller than the median resource size [BBBC99, AFJ99].

Still, resource size is the primary factor affecting the size of response messages. The two probability distributions are very similar. Like resource sizes, response sizes can be represented by a combination of the lognormal and Pareto distributions [BC98, BBBC99]. In addition, like the resource size distribution, the response size distribution has a heavy tail. The variable a in the Pareto distribution demonstrates the heaviness of the tail. Both probability distributions have a in the range of 1.0 to 1.5, indicating a very heavy tail [Mah97, CB97, AFJ99]. This demonstrates that response sizes, like resource sizes, vary dramatically over a wide range of values.

Some client requests are satisfied by caching proxies without the involvement of the origin server. Any dependence between resource size and the likelihood that a resource resides in a proxy cache could change the mixture of response sizes at origin servers. Requests for popular resources are more likely to be satisfied by a cache. The higher popularity of small resources suggests that these responses are more likely to reside in a cache. In addition, caches with limited storage space may decline to store large response messages, further increasing the likelihood that requests for large resources are handled by the origin server. However, studies suggest that small resources are not much more popular with users than large resources, and Web caches often have sufficient memory or disk space to store large resources. As a result, caching does not appear to cause a significant difference between the sizes of responses sent from caches as compared with origin servers.

Future trends The exact relationship between resource size and popularity may depend on the situation. Low-bandwidth clients are much less likely to request large resources, and proxies serving these clients may decide not to cache large responses. On the other hand, more and more users access the Internet over high-bandwidth connections, such as cable modems and Digital Subscriber Lines. Users with higher bandwidth are more willing to download large resources. This may weaken any existing correlation between a resource's size and its popularity. All of these competing factors suggest that it is unwise to assume that the distribution of response sizes is the same as the distribution of resource sizes. Instead, realistic models of Web workloads must consider the characteristics of both metrics and track how the relationship between these two parameters changes over time.

10.4.4 Resource popularity

The popularity of the various resources at a Web site has important performance implications. Caching at browsers and proxies is most effective when a small number of resources account for the majority of requests. Similarly, clients may prefetch popular resources in anticipation of future requests. Popularity also affects the server overhead for responding to requests. The most popular

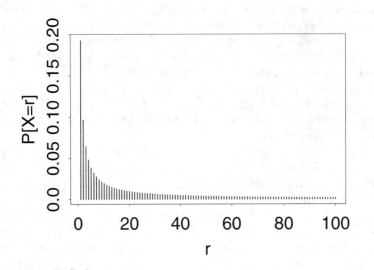

Figure 10.5. Zipf's law

resources are likely to reside in main memory at the origin server, obviating the need to fetch the data from disk. Similarly, the server may be able to store popular responses generated by scripts. For example, a search engine may receive the same query multiple times. The results of popular searches may be stored at the server. In practice, a server may not have sufficient space to store a large number of responses. The trade-off between storage space and performance benefit depends on the differences in popularity across the resources.

Traffic characteristics   Popularity is measured in terms of the proportion of requests that access a particular resource, and the resources are ranked from highest to lowest popularity. The *probability mass function* $P(r)$ captures the proportion of requests directed to each of these resources. For example, consider a Web site with 100 resources. If all 100 resources were equally popular, then $P(r) = 0.01$ for $r = 1, 2, \ldots, 100$. Steeper curves, such as the plot in Figure 10.5, imply that some resources are much more popular than others. In the example, the most popular resource accounts for nearly 20% of the requests to the set of 100 resources. The second most popular resource accounts for nearly 10% of the requests. The site receives very few requests for the least popular resources. The graph in Figure 10.5 is typical of popularity distributions in the Web.

The proportion of requests for a resource is inversely proportional to its rank. The distribution follows *Zipf's Law* [Zip49], where

$$P(r) = kr^{-1}$$

where k is a proportionality constant that ensures that $P(r)$ sums to 1. Zipf's law applies to a wide variety of situations, such as the popularity of different words in a document; words such as "the" and "and" occur much more often than words like "jejune." More generally, a *Zipf-like* distribution has the form

$$P(r) = kr^{-c}$$

for some constant c. Smaller values of c correspond to smaller differences in popularity across the set of resources. The extreme case of $c = 0$ corresponds to all resources having equal popularity.

The value of c varies across different Web proxies and servers [CBC95, ABCdO96, BCF+99, PQ00]. Early studies of requests to Web servers found c values close to 1. More recent studies show values in the range of 0.75 to 0.90, suggesting a trend toward less variability in popularity across the collection of resources. Caching at browsers and proxies tends to decrease the number of requests that reach the origin server for the most popular resources. However, requests for uncacheable resources cannot be satisfied by browser or proxy caches, making these resources a larger part of the mix of requests to origin servers. Relative to Web servers, the requests seen by proxies exhibit smaller values of c, suggesting even less skew in popularity. Proxies handle requests for a diverse collection of Web sites, which typically results in a larger number of resources with comparable popularity. In addition, the effectiveness of browser caching tends to limit repeat requests by the same client for the same resource. Still, resources returned from proxies and servers exhibit a wide variation in popularity.

Similar results hold for Web sites—a small number of popular Web sites receive most of the requests. The skew in site popularity has important implications on Web performance. First, the Web client's local DNS server is likely to have a cached copy of the name-to-IP-address mapping for the most popular domain names. This avoids the delay and overhead for the local DNS to contact other DNS servers, except when the cached DNS record becomes stale. Second, in practice, the busiest Web sites may be replicated at many locations in the Internet to move content closer to the requesting clients. Because these sites contribute a significant fraction of the traffic on the Internet, effective replication schemes for this small number of sites can offer a substantial reduction in network load and user-perceived latency. Third, new techniques for improving server or protocol performance do not have to be deployed at a large number of sites to have a significant impact. Selective deployment at the small number of popular sites offers most of the potential gain.

Future trends Zipf-like distributions have arisen in a wide variety of measurement studies since the inception of the Web, and these distributions have been a key property of numerous human systems besides the Web. However, the exact parameters of the Zipf-like distribution change over time and vary from site to site. Changes in the popularity distribution of resources at a Web site, or across Web sites, have impact on the effectiveness of caching. Less skewed distributions, with a smaller proportion of requests directed to the most popular resources, make caching less effective. If user communities become fragmented, there is a possibility that a larger fraction of the resources available on the Web would be relatively popular. For example, as more people throughout the world connect to the Web, new Web sites emerge that provide content for these user communities. These Web sites may be extremely popular in certain countries or regions. However, other social factors may argue for even larger skew in popularity distributions over time as users throughout the world have easy access to content throughout the world. In either case, these changes in the popularity distributions would affect the ability of Web caches to alleviate the load on origin servers and the network.

10.4.5 Resource changes

Web resources change over time as a result of modifications at the origin server. The frequency of changes, and the differences between successive versions of a resource, have important implications on a variety of Web applications. For example, many search engines depend on spiders to retrieve copies of Web pages for indexing. If the Web pages have changed at the origin servers, the search engine returns out-of-date results in response to user queries. Knowing how often the resources change at a site and the significance of these changes can help determine how often Web pages should be retrieved by the spider. Similarly, modifications to resources affect the performance of Web caching. Knowing that certain kinds of resources change more often than others can guide the caching policies at browsers and proxies. For example, resources that change less often may be given preference in caching or revalidated with the origin server less frequently.

Traffic characteristics   Any resource could change between successive requests, and scripts could generate dynamic responses of any type. In practice, though, the frequency of changes to resources varies based on the content type. At most Web sites, images do not change very often. In fact, some Web sites store their embedded images on a separate machine dedicated to delivering static content, as discussed in more detail later, in Chapter 11 (Section 11.13). For example, the HTML file http://www.foo.com/index.html may have an embedded image http://images.foo.com/pic.gif. Like image resources, text and HTML resources are often stored as static files at the origin server; these resources only change if the files are modified. However, text and HTML files change more often than images. Some text and HTML resources are generated by scripts in response to user input. For example, a user may visit a search engine Web site to search for information based on keywords. In response, the search engine may return an HTML file with hypertext links pointing to related Web pages. Repeating the HTTP request the next day may result in an HTML response containing a different list of hypertext links.

Some resources change in a periodic fashion—every minute, every 15 minutes, every hour, or every day [DFKM97, PQ00]. This reflects the presence of Web resources such as stock "tickers" that are updated over time. Similarly, news stories or comic strips may change once a day. The site administrator can capitalize on the periodic nature of these updates to reduce load on the server. Effective use on the caching-related response headers in HTTP/1.1 can reduce the frequency of requests for validating a cached copy of a resource. For example, the Expires header could indicate the next time that the resource would change. This would ensure that caches can return the response until the expiration time without the possibility that the resource has changed at the origin server. After the expiration time, any request for the resource would proceed to the origin server for the latest copy. Accurate timing information in the HTTP response message can reduce the load on the origin server as well as the user-perceived latency for accessing the resource.

An accurate model of Web workloads needs to consider the frequency of resource changes. For some Web applications, the nature of the changes to resources also matters. For example, an HTML file may include a counter that identifies the number of accesses to the Web page. This counter changes with every request. In some cases, a change is not semantically important. Users do not necessarily need to know the exact value of the counter on a Web page. Weak entity tags were included in HTTP/1.1 to address cases in which two variants of a resource are not semantically different, as discussed in Chapter 7 (Section 7.3.3). Knowing that a resource changes in minor ways could guide the Web site administrator in using weak entity tags to increase the effectiveness of browser and proxy caches. In other cases, the change to a resource may be semantically significant but not involve many bytes. For example, some text and HTML resources are modified to change a reference to an embedded image or hypertext link, or to modify a small amount of text, such as a phone number. This argues for finding ways for HTTP response messages to convey the *differences* between successive versions of a resource, rather than transferring the entire resource. We discuss this topic in more detail later, in Chapter 15 (Section 15.2).

Future trends   The frequency and type of resource modifications may change as the Web continues to evolve. The increasing use of the Web to issue queries to databases may influence the frequency of modifications to resources. If the information in a database changes over time, the queries may result in different responses. Just as stock quotes and daily cartoons are updated on a regular basis, new applications may result in new periodicities for changes to resources. The evolution of tools for authoring Web content may also affect the trends. For example, an authoring tool could assign a new URL for each variant of a file and eventually retire the old URL, rather than associating the same URL with all of the versions. This would reduce the likelihood that the individual Web resource would change over time. The client could send the updated resource to the server in the body of an HTTP request message. Finally, in the future, new content types may arise that naturally change more often or less often than existing content types. These trends would affect applications, such as spidering and caching, that are influenced by changes in Web resources.

10.4.6 Temporal locality

The time between successive requests for the same resource has a significant affect on Web traffic. Whereas resource popularity dictates the frequency of the requests without indicating the spacing between the requests, temporal locality captures the likelihood that a requested resource will be requested again in the near future. When a sequence of requests exhibits high temporal locality, there is a higher chance that a requested resource already resides in main memory at the origin server or in the proxy cache. Accurately capturing the temporal locality in a stream of references is an important part of modeling the workload of a proxy or server. Testing a server with a benchmark that has low temporal locality would underestimate the potential throughput that would be achieved if the actual request stream exhibits high temporal locality. High temporal locality also increases the likelihood that a request is satisfied by a browser or proxy cache and reduces the likelihood that a resource has changed since the previous access.

Traffic characteristics Temporal locality captures a different property of Web workloads than resource popularity. For example, consider requests for resources a and b. The request sequences (a, b, a, b, a, b, a) and (a, a, a, a, b, b, b) have the same number of requests of each of the two resources. The temporal locality is stronger in the second stream because the requests for each resource are closer together. Temporal locality can be measured by sequencing through the stream of requests, putting each request at the top of a *stack*, and noting the position in the stack—the *stack distance*—of the previous access to each resource. The sequence (a, b, a, b, a, b, a) would start with a stack (a). Then the second request would go on top of the stack, resulting in a stack (b, a). The third request accesses resource a, which appears in the second position in the stack. Hence, this request has a stack distance of 2, and the new stack is (a, b, a).

A small stack distance suggests high temporal locality. For example, the stream (a, a, a, a, b, b, b) would start with a stack of (a). The second, third, and fourth requests for a would have a stack distance of 1. Similarly, the second and third requests for b have a stack distance of 1. The temporal locality of a resource can be characterized by considering the distribution of stack distances over an entire sequence of requests. Studies of Web traffic have shown that the stack distances for requests for a resource follow a lognormal distribution [AW97, BC98], shown in Figure 10.4. Most requests access a resource that was requested in the recent past, resulting in small stack distances that suggest a strong degree of temporal locality. A small, but significant, proportion of the requests access resources that have not been requested for a while, if ever.

10.4.7 Number of embedded resources

A single user action, such as clicking on a hypertext link, often triggers multiple HTTP requests to download an HTML file and its embedded resources. These embedded resources include images, JavaScript programs, and other HTML files that appear as frames in the containing Web page. The number of embedded references in a Web page has significant impact on the server and network load. The client issues a separate HTTP request for each embedded resource unless a cached copy is available. The automatically generated requests introduce a burst of load on the server and the network. In fact, the client may open multiple parallel TCP connections to retrieve multiple embedded resources at the same time. In addition, multiple requests may be pipelined on a persistent TCP connection. A workload model that does not include the automatic downloading of embedded resources would not capture the sudden increases in load on the server and network. In addition, the number of embedded resources affects the effectiveness of persistent connections. Having a large number of embedded resources increases the likelihood that a single TCP connection handles multiple HTTP requests.

Traffic characteristics   Studies of Web measurements have shown that Web pages have a median of 8 to 20 embedded resources [CP95, Mah97]. The distribution has high variability, following the Pareto distribution [BC98]. A small, but significant, number of Web pages have a much larger number of embedded resources. In addition, the number of embedded images has tended to increase over time as more users have high-bandwidth connections to the Internet from work and from home. A large number of embedded resources does not necessarily translate into a large number of requests to the Web server. First, an embedded resource may be referenced in multiple Web pages, increasing the likelihood that a cached copy is available. Second, some embedded images do not reside at the same Web server as the containing Web page. For example, a Web page may include advertisements or images that are provided by a different server, as discussed in Chapter 11 (Section 11.13). This would decrease the number of requests for embedded resources directed to the server that delivered the containing Web page.

10.5 User Behavior Characteristics

Web workload characteristics depend on the behavior of users as they download Web pages from various sites. The arrival of users to Web sites, the number of pages they download, and the time they wait between successive downloads all contribute to the traffic patterns seen at Web proxies and servers.

10.5.1 Session and request arrivals

The workload imposed on proxies, servers, and the network depends on the timing of the HTTP requests issued by clients. The workload introduced by a single user can be modeled at three levels: session, click, and request. Although Web servers do not have explicit sessions with users, the series of requests by a single user to a single Web site could be viewed as a logical *session*. The user session begins with the first request and ends after the last request, followed by a period of inactivity. In the course of a single session, a user performs one or more *clicks* to request Web pages. A click corresponds to a user action, such as selecting a hypertext link, submitting a form, or typing a URL into the browser. Each click triggers the browser to issue an HTTP *request* for a resource, followed by automatically generated requests for the embedded resources referenced in that page.

From the viewpoint of the server, each session arrival brings a new user to the site. Some actions, such as the creation of a cookie, may occur at the session level. Each user click triggers a burst of HTTP requests for the server to handle. The client may establish a new TCP connection for a request or send the request on an existing TCP connection. An accurate workload model should capture the characteristics of arrivals at the session, TCP, and HTTP levels. Session arrivals can be studied by considering the time between the start of one user session and the start of the next user session. Studies have shown that the session interarrival times follow an exponential distribution [LNJV99, Fel00b]. This is one of the rare cases in Web workload modeling in which the exponential distribution arises. Exponential interarrival times correspond to a *Poisson process,* where users arrive independently of one another. The Poisson process has been widely studied in literature on queuing theory [Kle75].

However, the exponential distribution is *not* an accurate model of inter-arrival times of TCP connections and HTTP requests. HTTP requests often arrive in a burst because of user browsing behavior and the automatic down-loading of embedded resources. To capture these effects, the workload model can include the number of clicks in a user session, the time between successive clicks, and the number of embedded resources for each Web page. Each of these parameters introduces burstiness in the arrival of HTTP requests. The high variability implies that the average request rate is not a good indication of the load at a Web server. A server may receive requests at a much higher rate during certain periods. Handling bursty arrivals in an efficient manner requires additional capacity at the server and in the network. A workload model that assumes that HTTP requests arrive as a Poisson process would significantly underestimate the possibility of these heavy-load periods and would therefore overestimate the potential performance of the Web server.

10.5.2 Clicks per session

The number of clicks associated with user sessions has considerable influence on the load on a server. If a typical user downloads a large number of pages, the load introduced by each session would involve numerous transfers over a period of time. On the other hand, if most users access only one page, each session would involve the transfer of a single Web page and its embedded images. In this case, the server would not benefit from maintaining a persistent TCP connection past the transmission of the embedded images, because of the low likelihood of receiving additional requests from this client. In addition, the number of clicks per session has implications on the effectiveness of browser caching. Consider a Web site that has certain embedded images that appear in several Web pages. If a user visits multiple pages at the site, these images would be available in the browser cache. In contrast, if each user session consists of a single click, the server might have to transfer the entire set of embedded images for each page.

Users vary widely in the number of pages they browse at a Web site. Some users visit the home page of a Web site and do not download other pages. Other users may spend an hour or more looking at various pages at the Web site. Most sessions involve a small number of clicks, in the range of 4 to 10 clicks [Mah97, LNJV99]. However, the results vary from site to site. For example, e-commerce sites try to retain users, whereas a search engine directs users to content at other locations. In addition, browser and proxy caching reduce the number of HTTP requests that reach the origin server. The number of clicks follows a Pareto distribution [LNJV99], suggesting that some sessions involve a much larger number of clicks than others. As a result, a small proportion of the visitors to a site are responsible for the bulk of requests. When these users visit a site, the large number of requests may degrade the performance seen by other users. Hence, a realistic workload model should capture the impact of these heavy users on the network and server.

10.5.3 Request interarrival time

The time between successive requests by each user has important implications on the server and network load. A browser typically issues requests for embedded resources while receiving and parsing the container HTML file. However, the time between successive clicks depends on user behavior. In some cases, a user browses through Web pages very quickly, spending a short amount of time inspecting the contents of each page. In other cases, the user may spend several

minutes reading a page before requesting another page. The time between the
downloading of one page and its embedded images and the user's next click is
referred to as *think time* or *quiet time.* The characteristics of user think times
influence the effectiveness of policies for closing persistent connections. A simple
server policy would terminate the TCP connection after an idle period during
which no new HTTP requests arrive. If the think time exceeds this time period,
then the next HTTP request would require the establishment of a new TCP
connection.

The typical time between clicks varies from site to site, though most inter-
request times are less than 60 seconds. A small proportion of the think times are
very large, relative to the average think time. Measurement studies have shown
that think times follow a Pareto distribution with a heavy tail, with a around
1.5 [BC98]. Think times are not quite as variable as response sizes, which have
a in the range of 1.0 to 1.5. Overall, Web traffic exhibits variability in several
dimensions. Heavy-tailed distributions apply to numerous properties of Web
traffic—resource sizes, response sizes, the number of embedded references in a
Web page, the number of clicks per session, and the time between successive
clicks. In effect, a Web session can be modeled as a sequence of on/off periods, in
which each on period corresponds to downloading a Web page and its embedded
images and each off period corresponds to the user's think time. The durations
of on and off periods both follow a heavy-tailed distribution.

Web traffic consists of the superposition of multiple sequences of on/off
periods, each corresponding to a different user. As a result, the load on Web
servers and the network exhibits a phenomenon known as *self similarity,* in
which the traffic varies dramatically on a variety of time scales from microseconds to several minutes [LTWW94, WTSW97, CB97]. This suggests that the
average load is not a good estimate of the typical demand on the network or the
server. Web servers and network components typically must be engineered with
extra capacity to handle periods of excessive load. The variability of Web traffic
also has important implications for how servers and network components are
evaluated. Benchmarks applied to Web proxies and servers should capture the
inherent variability in traffic load. Similarly, evaluation of network protocols,
such as TCP, should consider the variability in transfer sizes and offered load
over time.

10.6 Applying Workload Models

A deeper understanding of Web workload characteristics can drive the creation
of a workload model for evaluating Web protocols and software components.
Generating Web traffic from the model involves creating a stream of HTTP
requests that adhere to the various workload parameters and applying these
requests to operational proxies or servers.

Table 10.2. Probability distributions in Web workload models

Distribution	Workload parameter
Exponential	Session interarrival times
Pareto	Response sizes (tail of distribution)
	Resource sizes (tail of distribution)
	Number of embedded images
	Request interarrival times
Lognormal	Response sizes (body of distribution)
	Resource sizes (body of distribution)
	Temporal locality
Zipf-like	Resource popularity

10.6.1 Combining workload parameters

Generating synthetic traffic involves sampling the probability distribution associated with each workload parameter. Consider a workload model that incorporates the parameters and distributions discussed in the previous two sections, as summarized in Table 10.2. User session arrivals follow a Poisson process with some mean arrival rate. Each new session arrives some time after the start of the previous session. The interarrival times can be chosen by computing a random number between 0 and 1 to correspond to the value of $F(x)$ from the exponential distribution. This value, in turn, can be used to compute the value of x for the interarrival time. For example, an exponential distribution with mean $\lambda = 1$ and a random number 0.3679 would correspond to $x = 1$ because $e^{-1} = 0.3679$. Repeating this procedure generates a sequence of times for new sessions to start. Each user session consists of some number of clicks, which can be computed from the Pareto distribution. Each click generates a request for a Web page, which includes an HTML file and some number of embedded resources. After downloading the Web page, some think time elapses before the next click; this think time can be derived from a Pareto distribution.

Resource characteristics can be generated in a similar manner. For example, a collection of synthetic Web pages could be generated in advance and stored at the server. Consider the task of generating 1000 Web pages for a synthetic workload for a Web server. The probability distribution for the size of HTML resources can be used to determine the number of bytes in each of the 1000 HTML files. Then the distribution for the number of embedded resources can be used to associate the page with some number of embedded resources. The size of each embedded resource would also stem from a probability distribution. Each of these resources is associated with a URL, which would appear in HTTP requests issued from the Web clients. In addition, the Zipf distribution for resource popularity is used to determine the proportion of client requests directed to each resource. In the end, each Web page at the server consists of an HTML file with a particular size and popularity that is associated with some number of embedded resources, each with some size.

Generating a synthetic workload requires integrating the resource characteristics with the timing of the client requests. For example, a request could be associated with a particular URL based on the popularity distribution. This ensures that the client visits each page in proportion to its popularity. However, this approach does not capture the temporal locality of successive requests for the same resource. Additional techniques can be employed to ensure that the client request stream matches both the popularity and temporal locality distributions [BC98]. Another important issue is to model resources that are modified at the server to capture the impact of changes in resource sizes and a realistic mix of cache validation traffic. For example, resource modification times could stem from a probability distribution. At each modification time, the resource could be changed at the server. Future requests for this URL would require the server to transmit the new resource rather than a 304 Not Modified response.

10.6.2 Validating the workload model

Generating synthetic traffic that accurately represents a real workload is very challenging, especially with such a large number of interdependent parameters. A synthetic workload does not necessarily capture all of the important features of Web traffic. However, using a synthetic workload for performance evaluation is based on the premise that the system would exhibit the same, or similar, performance under a real workload. As a result, validation of the synthetic workload is an important step in constructing and using a workload model. Validation is often confused with verification. Verification involves testing that the synthetic traffic has the statistical properties embodied in the workload model, such as the correct distribution of resource sizes and think times. This verifies the correctness of the implementation of the workload model. In contrast, validation requires demonstrating that the performance of a system subjected to the synthetic workload matches the performance of the same system under a real workload, according to some predefined performance metric.

The need to validate models arises in a wide variety of applications. Whenever the performance of a system is evaluated with synthetic input or an abstract model of the system, the validity of the results comes into question. However, models are rarely subjected to rigorous validation tests. Validating the model may be difficult, time-consuming, or simply overlooked. In other cases, a model that was validated for certain applications is mistakenly applied in a different context. Typically, a workload model is constructed for a specific purpose, such as evaluating server throughput and user-perceived latency. Using the same workload model to evaluate a different performance metric, such as the load on the server's CPU, may not be appropriate. Ideally, each of the key performance metrics is available for the Web server operating under real client requests. The same server could be evaluated under the synthetic workload, facilitating a direct comparison between the performance statistics.

Synthetic workload models are also used to test servers over a range of scenarios that might not have happened in practice. In this case, testing against a real workload may not be possible. Several techniques can increase confidence that the synthetic model reflects realistic scenarios. As a qualitative test, people with experience in observing Web traffic can examine the workload model to see if it captures the salient features of real workloads. Then analysis of real Web traffic can verify the underlying assumptions of the workload model. For example, suppose that a Web workload model assumes that the size of an HTML file is independent of the number and size of the embedded images on the Web page. Analysis of Web measurements could determine whether or not this assumption is an accurate reflection of reality. In addition, investigating the sensitivity of system performance to small changes in the workload model is very important. If minor changes in the input parameters have a significant impact on system performance, this suggests that small inaccuracies in modeling the real workload would compromise the utility of the synthetic model.

10.6.3 Generating synthetic traffic

Applying a synthetic workload to a Web proxy or server introduces several practical challenges. Testing a high-end server requires generating a high rate of requests from a large number of synthetic clients, with each client issuing requests based on the workload model. However, dedicating a separate computer to each client would be expensive and difficult to manage. Ideally, multiple synthetic clients could run on a single machine [BC98, BD99]. However, sharing the machine may introduce interference between the various clients. Clients running on the same machine must compete for access to the processor, memory, and disk, as well as the connection to the network. To prevent interference between the synthetic clients, the number of clients per machine must be limited, based on testing that identifies when the system cannot handle any additional clients without affecting the traffic patterns. Supporting a large number of clients on a single machine requires a system with a large amount of memory and an efficient implementation of TCP [BD99].

Generating synthetic traffic provides an opportunity to evaluate a proxy or server in a controlled manner. Collecting performance statistics is a crucial part of this process. However, measuring and recording these performance metrics may interfere with the operation of the client and the server. For example, the synthetic client may log the delay in receiving the server's response to an HTTP request. The overhead of measuring the time and recording the statistic may interfere with the sending of future requests. The interference can be reduced by writing statistics into memory, rather than into a file on the disk. However, depending on the system, the main memory may be a precious resource. Interference can also be reduced by limiting the number of clients running on each machine. The server may record performance metrics, such as processing load or the number of TCP connections over time. Limiting the frequency of acquiring and recording these statistics can limit the overhead on the server.

The properties of the underlying network have a significant impact on the performance of a Web proxy or server. The Internet exhibits high variability in packet delay and loss probabilities, which interacts with TCP congestion control. A realistic evaluation of a Web server should capture these interactions. A collection of clients with a high-bandwidth, low-latency connection to the server would produce a very different traffic load than low-bandwidth, high-latency clients spread throughout the world. Low bandwidth and high latency results in longer-lived TCP connections at the server, which increases the number of connections that must be handled at the same time. In addition, retransmission of lost packets increases the amount of data transmitted by the server. The ideal solution to this problem is to distribute the synthetic clients throughout the Internet. However, this may be expensive in practice. An alternative is to direct client requests and server responses through a machine that *emulates* the properties of the network by intentionally delaying or dropping packets [BD99].

Web performance depends on the interaction between user behavior, resource characteristics, server load, and network dynamics. Capturing all of these factors in a workload model is extremely difficult in practice. However, synthetic workloads help address the need to evaluate and compare Web software components in a controlled manner. A variety of benchmarks have been used to compare various proxy and server implementations [Wbe, TS95, Spea, Pol, MCS98, AC98]. These benchmarks typically consist of a suite of software for creating synthetic clients, installing synthetic workloads on proxies or servers, and collecting and analyzing performance statistics. Often, the synthetic workloads in these benchmarks have default parameter settings to apply the same workload to each of the implementations. Over time, the commercial benchmarks have become more sophisticated to capture the diversity of workload parameters and the newer features of HTTP. In addition, the benchmarks are evolving to incorporate other important aspects of Web traffic, such as dynamically generated resources and error responses.

10.7 User Privacy

Collecting and analyzing Web traffic provides important insight into the operation of the Web. However, Web requests and responses include potentially sensitive information about the end users and their browsing habits. In this section, we discuss the kinds of personal data that are available and who has access to this data. Then we discuss how characterizing the measurement data may result in violations of user privacy.

10.7.1 Access to user-level data

User actions, such as clicking on hypertext links and submitting forms, translate into a sequence of requests. The browser satisfies a user request by retrieving a response from its cache or by contacting a proxy or server. The browser also initiates requests automatically to download embedded images and repeat requests that receive redirection responses. Furthermore, the browser may invoke a helper application, such as a document previewer, that may initiate additional HTTP requests. Users may not be aware of the full set of requests sent on their behalf. The requests reveal the Web pages the user has visited, the searches the user has performed, the online purchases the user has made, and the text the user enters in applications that use forms. The contents of the HTTP request and response messages may be stored by the parties involved in the exchange, as well as by other components that intercept the network traffic. For example, an HTTP response message may be stored in the browser cache or captured by a packet monitor.

The Web provides the illusion of anonymity. However, an HTTP request message may contain a variety of information that identifies the user. In sending request messages, the browser may insert various HTTP headers that compromise personal information and enable tracking of user requests. The `From` header provides the user's e-mail address for logging or identification purposes. The `User-Agent` header indicates the browser and perhaps the operating system running on the user's machine. Other request headers, such as `Accept-Language`, may provide additional information about the user or enable the server to track successive requests by the same user. The browser sends HTTP requests and receives HTTP responses over a TCP connection. The IP address of the user's machine is associated with the browser end point of the TCP connection and appears in each IP packet in the transfer. A simple DNS query can translate the IP address into the host name of the user's machine, which may reveal the user's identity or the user's company, university, or ISP.

The loss of anonymity depends on how much another party can infer about the user. The company or service provider of the user may be sensitive information. For example, consider an employee of a company that visits a Web site that allows users to search a database of patents based on a set of keywords. Knowing that a company is interested in patents on a particular topic may be useful to its competitors. The name or e-mail address of the user is even more sensitive. For example, knowing that `viv@foo.com` has visited a Web site with reports about a particular disease may be useful information for the company that provides Viv's medical insurance. Knowing the specific request issued by the user is even more sensitive. Suppose that Viv downloads a Web page that lists job openings at another company. This information would be useful to Viv's employer. In addition, any details about the user's browsing patterns could be used to select the advertisements that Viv sees when visiting the Web site. The administrators of the Web site could also sell Viv's e-mail address and browsing information to other companies.

The request message may also include an `Authorization` header that indicates the user name and password at the remote server, as discussed in Chapter 7 (Section 7.10). The user's password is not encrypted under the Basic authentication scheme in HTTP/1.0. Any party that records the Base64-encoded password could impersonate a valid client. HTTP/1.1 addressed these problems by supporting Digest authentication. In addition to an `Authorization` header, an HTTP request may include a `Cookie` header that enables the server and other parties to track successive requests by the same user. The server may associate the cookie with the user's name, e-mail address, postal address, credit card number, and purchasing history. The information in the `Authorization` and `Cookie` headers applies to individual Web sites. However, administrators of Web sites may collaborate to share information and track users across accesses to different sites. Users may unknowingly retrieve resources from other Web servers as a result of automatic requests for embedded images and redirection responses.

The `Referer` request header identifies what resource referenced the Request-URI, revealing the previous step in the user's browsing patterns. This can reveal how the user moves from one Web site to another. In addition, the `Referer` field can inform others of the existence of an otherwise private URL. For example, suppose that someone creates a stand-alone Web page and sends the URL to a select group of people. No other pages have hypertext links that point to this Web page. Yet, if a user clicks on a link from this Web page, the private URL would appear in the `Referer` field. Any measurement data that includes the contents of the `Referer` field would have a record of this URL. In addition, requests for the private URL may be logged at a proxy. In addition, a client may be able to discover the private Web page by sequencing through a collection of URLs to see which requests return Web pages. In practice, the only way to control access to a private Web page is to perform password authentication for all requests for the private URL.

The user has control over the type of personal information that is made available to others. For example, the user provides the e-mail address that appears in the `From` header by configuring the browser, although this header is typically not included in HTTP requests in practice. In addition, the user can configure the browser's policies for accepting cookies. Most browsers can be configured to reject all cookies, limit cookies to certain Web sites, or receive approval from the user before accepting a cookie. The amount of personal data associated with a cookie depends on what the user reveals in submitting information to the Web site; for example, the user may decline to include an e-mail address when submitting a form. Users can limit the amount of personal information transmitted in HTTP headers by directing requests to an anonymizing proxy. When the request must contain personal information, such as a credit card number, the use of SSL and HTTPS provides an effective way to prevent intermediaries and packet monitors from inspecting the contents of the HTTP messages.

10.7.2 Information available to software components

User privacy depends on who has access to the sensitive information present in HTTP request and response messages. The browser has the most complete information about user preferences, user actions, and the contents of HTTP request and response messages. Compared with other Web components, the browser is a trusted entity to the user. However, the browser may provide other software components with personal information via the headers in HTTP request messages. This happens for several reasons. First, the server may use this information to customize the HTTP response messages. Second, browser and server software are often developed by the same companies, creating an incentive to have browser implementations that populate the HTTP request headers. Third, an ISP may also distribute a preconfigured browser to each user in order to direct requests through proxies and include particular headers in HTTP request messages.

A proxy may also be a trusted entity, as discussed in Chapter 3 (Section 3.7). For example, the proxy may be deployed by the user's employer or ISP as a way to improve user performance, reduce the overhead on the network, and filter inappropriate content. However, the proxy has access to all of the HTTP requests transmitted on behalf of the user to a wide range of servers. In addition, the network provider typically has access to additional information, such as the IP address or domain name of the user's machine, that can associate each request with a particular person. In some cases, the institution may have an incentive to track the browsing patterns of individual users. For example, a company may want to identify users who are looking for information about new jobs or particular illnesses. An ISP may monitor user browsing patterns to identify potential customers for new services. In addition, the ISP may have an incentive to provide information about the user's interests to interested third parties.

For the most part, a Web server is operated by an institution that is not affiliated with the requesting users. The server is typically not a trusted entity to the user. Based on HTTP request headers, the server may recognize that a collection of requests came from the same client. Compared with a proxy, a server often has greater difficulty associating a sequence of requests with a *particular* user. However, if the user submits personal information to the Web site, the script handling the user's request can associate that data with a cookie.

By receiving this cookie in future HTTP requests, the script can identify the specific user. Similarly, the script may associate personal information with the `Authorization` header. In some cases, the user may not mind entrusting the Web site with the personal information. For example, many companies have Web sites that provide their employees with access to proprietary data about salaries or benefits. In addition, some Web sites have privacy policies that describe how the site uses the data and whether or not the information is made available to third parties.

As participants in Web transfers, browsers, proxies, and servers have direct access to the HTTP request and response messages. However, other components may have access to the messages without the knowledge of the key parties. As the Web traffic flows through the network, packet monitors and interception proxies may capture the IP packets underlying the HTTP transfers. By gathering the sequence of packets, these components can reconstruct the HTTP messages, as well as other IP traffic such as e-mail messages and File Transfer Protocol (FTP) downloads. Depending on where the traffic is observed, the client IP address may reveal the identity of the requesting user. These components have access to the same information that is available to a proxy configured in the Web browser. In addition, these components may be installed by the user's company or ISP. However, in contrast to an explicit proxy, the user typically does not know whether a packet monitor or interception proxy lies on the path of the HTTP messages.

10.7.3 Application of user-level data

Despite having access to the full HTTP messages, most software components do not record all of this information. In practice, Web proxy and server logs contain a relatively limited number of fields. A network administrator could reconfigure or modify the software to record additional fields, at the expense of overhead on the proxy or server. Privacy policies also may limit which fields are recorded and in what form. For example, a trace or log may omit or encrypt fields that reveal the identity of the user. Associating a sequence of requests with a single user is an important part of analyzing Web workloads. Yet, this analysis does not require knowledge of the identity of each user. Similarly, Web measurements may be used to customize the Web site's content or advertisements based on the user's browsing patterns. This does not necessarily depend on knowing the identity of the requesting user.

In addition to limiting the fields in the log, privacy policies may restrict who has access to the data and for what purposes. For example, an ISP may decide to use packet traces or proxy logs to improve user performance and network efficiency. Likewise, the administrator of a Web site may use server logs to tune the configuration of the server or to customize and reorganize the Web content. Particularly sensitive information, such as customer names, postal addresses, purchasing histories, and credit card numbers may be stored separately in a secure database. Server logs may be used internally, with limited distribution to others. Logs that are distributed outside of the institution may have certain fields omitted or encrypted. Selling of user-level information to third parties may be explicitly restricted in the site's privacy policies.

New technologies can address the heightened concerns about user privacy on the Web. For example, the World Wide Web Consortium is developing the Platform for Privacy Preferences (P3P) [P3P]. P3P provides a way for users to record their personal profiles and privacy preferences and for Web sites to specify their privacy policies in a standard, machine-readable form. Based on the user's preferences and site's policies, the user or the browser can decide whether to access the Web site and what personal information to reveal. Ultimately, the key to protecting privacy is to ensure that users consciously decide what information to reveal, rather than having personal information revealed without their explicit consent. Requiring users to explicitly "opt out" of divulging information is not a viable model when a large number of users are not deeply familiar with the interworkings of the Web. Technologies such as P3P help by enabling users to "opt in" when they want to reveal selective information, rather than having to explicitly "opt out." New technical developments can help balance the trade-offs between the need to protect user privacy and the desire to collect data for personalizing the user's Web experience and analyzing Web workloads.

10.8 Summary

Evaluating the performance of Web protocols and software components requires an understanding of the characteristics of Web workloads. Capturing the variability inherent in Web workloads is a crucial part of developing an accurate workload model. Although Web workloads vary over time and location, the basic characteristics of most parameters are relatively stable. Most changes in workload characteristics manifest themselves as changes in the values of variables in a probability distribution, rather than an entirely different distribution. In addition, the relationship between a parameter and its implications on Web performance remains relatively stable. The diversity of Web workload characteristics, and the shifts over time and location, highlight the importance of evaluating Web protocols and software components over a range of scenarios. Synthetic workloads that combine the various workload parameters provide a way to compare the performance of different systems. These workload models have played an important role in benchmarking different proxy and server implementations. Finally, despite the many positive motivations for analyzing Web traffic measurements, collecting information about HTTP requests and responses may violate user privacy. HTTP headers include identifying information about individual users, and Web proxies and servers can employ a variety of techniques to track a sequence of requests by the same users. In addition, packet monitors and interception proxies that are not official parties in the request-response exchange may also acquire information about the users. Giving users control over what personal data they reveal is an important part of addressing the tension between user privacy and workload characterization.

Part V

Web Applications

Web Caching

With the rapid increase of traffic on the Web, caching was the first major technique that attempted to reduce user-perceived latency and reduce transmission of redundant traffic on the network. The pattern of the traffic also showed a remarkable tilt: many clients in an organization appeared to visit the *same few* sites. Within a few years, caching became a major industry. In this chapter, we provide an overview of caching in two parts, as follows:

- **The basics and mechanics of caching:** The overview part of the chapter begins with the historical evolution of caching and its high-level goals. The next four sections address the why, what, where, and how of caching. The *why* section addresses the motivations for caching at each stage of the request from the user through their Internet Service Provider (ISP) to the Internet, across different layers of the protocol stack (DNS, TCP, HTTP), to the origin server and back. The *what* section examines the issues involved in deciding if a message[1] is cacheable. A semantically transparent cache, one that returns a response that would be the same if it had been obtained from the origin server, must adhere to HTTP protocol restrictions. The *where* covers the places where caching is done on the path between the user and the origin server. The *how* examines the actual steps a piece of caching software must go through in caching a response and maintaining a cache. The overview continues with a look at cache replacement and cache coherency, before concluding with a look at how the rate of change of resources affects caching decisions.

- **The practice of caching:** The practice part of the chapter begins with a look at how caches pool information with other caches and the various protocols used by them to communicate with each other. We then examine specific software and hardware approaches used in caching. The software part consists of a brief case study of the popular public domain Squid caching system, and the hardware part examines industry practice

---

[1] We use the term *message* rather than *response* because request messages can also be cached.

along two axes: redirectors and appliances. A set of problems associated with caching at the commercial and social level is examined next. This is followed by a look at replication, a concept similar to caching, but with different goals and performance. We briefly examine two new topics: content distribution and content adaptation.

Caching is also discussed in other places in the book:

- Chapter 2 briefly discusses browser caching
- Chapter 3 briefly examines the role of proxies in caching
- Chapter 7 discusses HTTP/1.1 protocol issues dealing with caching, largely in Section 7.3
- Some recent advances in caching appear in the research perspectives section in Chapter 13

This chapter provides a comprehensive overview of the topic. Note that we use the terms *object* and *response* interchangeably in this chapter.

11.1 The Origins and Goals of Web Caching

RFC 2616, the draft standard of HTTP/1.1, defines a cache as a local store of response messages. A loose definition of caching is the movement of Web content closer to the users. Web caching is probably the most widely studied application on the Web. Several commercial products from a variety of companies in the form of software and hardware appliances exist on the market today. We begin with a brief history of caching, followed by an examination of its design goals and the list of problems that caching attempts to solve.

The first Web server *httpd* (built at the CERN Lab in Geneva, Switzerland) had an associated proxy server that included a cache [LA94]. One of the earliest Web caching projects began with Harvest [BDH+94], which indexed information across the Internet. Harvest sought to cache and replicate information gathered via different tools. A hierarchical object cache was a fundamental component of the Harvest architecture. A server registry enabled information to be gathered about other caches. The registry responded to queries about locations of caches. Colocated caches could pool their resources. After the development of Harvest, several caching projects and systems began to evolve.

Caching had already become an important and necessary aspect of the Web by the time of the HTTP/1.0 specification. Early caching experiments and measurements, some as early as 1994 [BC94], demonstrated the potential of a significant reduction in the number of bytes transferred. Caches began to store a variety of information associated with documents, such as the content type, size, and mean time between modifications. Cache consistency issues and delivery of cached responses to authenticated clients became important. Groups of caches were organized into hierarchies, which grew to span regions and nations. Caching was the first major Web application used on a daily basis as part of a typical user's daily Web experience.

The goals of caching are to reduce

- The user-experienced latency between the time of the initial Web request and the time the response is displayed by the user agent
- The load on the network, which could be a local area network or the Internet, by avoiding repeated transmission of the same response
- The load on the origin server by having an intermediary on the path between the client and the origin server handle the requests

The first goal is often the most widely cited goal of caching. Reducing user-perceived latency has important implications not just for the user's Web experience, but also for content developers. Studies have shown that when users receive responses quickly at a Web site, they tend to spend more time there. Many users still have relatively low-bandwidth connections to the Internet. Obtaining a page quickly increases the user's expectation of obtaining more information from the same site quickly.

The second goal primarily affects the network, but it has an interesting side effect. Transferring only *necessary* information (i.e., avoiding the retransmission of content that the user could have obtained closer to the client's location) reduces the overall congestion in the network. Reduction of congestion leads to improved performance for everyone using the network, because fewer packets are lost and there is less need for retransmission resulting from packet drops.

The third goal implies that an origin server can handle more requests from a diverse set of clients. The increased number of requests handled is reflected not just at the application layer, but also at the transport layer. There can be a reduction in TCP connections that are refused as a result of the wait queue being full and a shorter delay for the pending requests.

11.2 Why Cache?

We begin by examining the motivations for caching. Web-hosting companies must pay for the bandwidth they use and might want to increase cacheability to reduce costs. All participants in the Web message exchange can benefit from caching. The end users gain significantly from caching, because their latency in obtaining a response is lowered, enhancing their Web experience. A significant fraction of the aborts occurring during a user's session is typically the result of a user's frustration in not getting responses quickly. The bandwidth wasted as a result of redundant data transmitted on the network on a repeated basis is large. Given that the congestion is seen at various points on the Internet, reducing traffic or moving it to the edge of the network and away from the backbone would be beneficial. The benefits to the network are twofold: only necessary data traverses the network, and there is bandwidth available for other data. The distance of the cache from the user is also a significant factor in measuring the benefit of a cache to a user. A cache that is very close to the user could significantly lower user-perceived latency compared with a cache that is closer to the origin server.

We examine the various components of delay in fetching a resource and its impact on the user, the network, and the origin server. A resource cached at the user's browser or at a proxy near a user lowers the delay in bringing the response to the user. The notion of bringing content closer to the user is an attempt to reduce several of the components of delay in obtaining a response. As discussed in earlier chapters, from a user's point of view the components of delay in fetching a resource are affected by the following several factors:

- The network connectivity of the user to their ISP and the connection between the ISP and the Internet
- Unless the DNS lookup is cached, the DNS lookup time to locate the server to contact, even if the server being contacted is a proxy
- The congestion in the network and the bandwidth available on the path between user and origin server
- The load on the origin server
- The time to generate the response
- The time to render the response by the browser

These delay factors trace the path of a request sent from a browser to the origin server until the response is rendered back at the browser. We examine the impact of caching on each of these delay factors next.

Network connectivity   The connectivity between a client and the ISP is subject to less variability than the delays on the Internet. If content is brought closer to the service provider, there can be some degree of predictability in the latency experienced by the user. If the connection speed between the user's ISP and the Internet is high, the responses would be brought to the edge of the ISP's network quickly. However, if the connectivity to the Internet is slow, moving the response to the edge of the ISP's network might dominate the overall latency experienced by the user. As a secondary impact, if the connection between the user's ISP and the origin server is down at the time of the request, a cache at the ISP might be able to satisfy the request. The response may be stale, but, depending on the response, this might not be a serious factor. This should be tempered by the fact that many of the responses may be personalized and thus not available in the ISP's cache.

DNS-related delay   Increasing the time-to-live (TTL) value of DNS lookups can help reduce overall latency, assuming that bindings between names and addresses do not change often. As discussed later, in Section 11.13, some caching solutions may actually increase overall DNS lookup time but locate content closer to the user. Being closer might mean that the network distance (number of hops) traveled by the Web response is significantly less. A caching proxy's DNS cache is likely to have frequently accessed domains and can aid in reducing future DNS-related delays.

Network congestion and bandwidth issues   Reducing the number of hops might improve the throughput between the client and the server where content is located. If TCP is the underlying transport mechanism for HTTP, then reductions in round-trip time (RTT) improve throughput. TCP's throughput is inversely proportional to the RTT. Fewer hops might also reduce the likelihood that the transfer is subjected to the vagaries of end-to-end congestion delay. As we saw in Chapter 5 (Section 5.2.6), more packets on the network can cause congestion and lead to packet loss. The dropped packets must be retransmitted. If there is a decrease in the utilization of the network as a result of caching, the rest of the data on the network can be transmitted faster. The TCP sender can increase the congestion window size to use the network to its full capacity.

Origin server load   The origin server can also benefit from caching. The load on the origin server can be reduced if caching of frequently requested resources results in fewer requests to the origin server. The origin server is able to handle the requests of more individual users without having to queue the transport-level connections (e.g., the TCP accept queue) or to delay the processing of the HTTP requests. The origin server migrates the task of serving requests to several satellite helper sites—the caching proxies. The origin server can also maintain persistent connections with fewer inbound clients, and these connections can stay open longer. The time to generate redundant responses is eliminated, leaving more time for the server to perform other tasks.

Time to generate response   The time to generate the response for requests can be reduced depending on the Web server's architecture. If fewer of the server's resources (i.e., CPU cycles) are spent handling incoming requests, more resources could be devoted to response generation. If response generation was a significant fraction of the overall latency experienced by users, and caching obviated it entirely, this delay component could be the most significant one. Additionally, if the Web server's architecture serialized handling of requests, generating a long response would negatively affect handling of other requests on the same connection.

Browser rendering of response   A browser must parse and display the response. The time to render the resource by the browser cannot really be reduced by caching unless the entire rendered version of the page is in the volatile memory of the browser. Even if the response is stored at the browser's cache, reading and rendering the response can add to the delay. However, because the entire contents of the document are available locally, a different technique might be used to display the response. For example, a browser could alter the process of displaying the container document if all the embedded images were already available. Most Web pages are rendered as they are read in by the browser, therefore progressive rendering appears much slower than displaying from a memory cache.

Apart from delay issues, caching has financial ramifications. Caching reduces load inside an ISP's backbone. A *flash crowd*, caused by one or more resources on a site becoming suddenly popular, can lead to sudden spikes in the load of an ISP. For example, Web events, such as release of an eagerly awaited legal judgment, a popular sporting event, or a special Web cast, cause flash crowds. It may be cheaper to buy caches than to increase capacity inside a backbone. The bandwidth that has been freed as a result of caching can permit an ISP to support additional customers within the existing infrastructure.

Even in the absence of sudden spikes, ISPs are typically obligated to pay their upstream Internet providers based on the bandwidth, independent of the fraction of the bandwidth that is actually used. By reducing the number of bytes that they must download, ISPs may be able to reduce their overall costs. ISPs *peer* with each other if they exchange roughly similar amounts of bytes. Peering arrangements typically require that there be symmetry in the amount of traffic between the peers. There is thus a strong financial incentive to reduce the number of bytes that enter the ISP's network from outside. Large providers, in turn, have peering arrangements with other large providers. Caching can help differentiate an ISP from others in a crowded marketplace. New services can be added without fear of significant reduction in the quality of service experienced by an ISP's customers.

11.3 What is Cacheable?

A cache can decide whether a response is cacheable based on two factors: HTTP protocol-related requirements and the content under consideration. The protocol-specific caching considerations require that a cache obey the various directives regarding cacheability of a message. The content-specific requirements deal with issues that are divorced from protocol issues. The content-specific requirements are affected by the business requirements of a cache and policies that affect the frequency of cache revalidation—verifying whether a cached response is still fresh.[2] The policies in turn may be affected by attributes of the message, such as size or content type.

---

[2]The terms *cache revalidation* and *validation* refer to the same task.

11.3.1 Protocol-specific considerations

A well-behaved Web cache must abide by the constraints imposed by HTTP. The HTTP/1.1 draft standard defines simple rules for what responses are cacheable; the request method, request header fields, response status, and response headers all have to indicate that the response is cacheable. A constraint on the part of any of them makes the response uncacheable. For example, responses to the OPTIONS, PUT, and DELETE methods (described in Chapters 6 and 7) are not cacheable. Responses to the POST method are not cacheable *unless* the response has the necessary Cache-Control and Expires headers. If a cache does not support the Range header, any response that has a response status code of 206 Partial Content cannot be cached.

Some responses include resource-specific information from the origin server that may preclude caching of the message. Such information is of two kinds: cacheability information and cache directives. If the response includes cacheability information, the decision to cache should be driven by that. For example, the server might provide explicit freshness duration via headers such as Expires. If the time specified in Expires is a short time away from the time the response was received, the resource may not be cached. The Cache-Control directive may preclude caching of certain responses. For example, a Cache-Control: private directive states that a shared cache must not cache the response. A response message that includes the cache control directive

```
Cache-Control: no-store
```

should not even be stored. The cache control response directive

```
Cache-Control: no-cache
```

lowers the probability that a cache would store the response, because the cached response would have to be revalidated each time before it is returned as a possible cache hit. The directives do not have to be response directives specified by the origin server. They could be request directives specified by the requesting client. For example, Cache-Control: no-store can appear in a request or response. The protocol provides these directives to better maintain the privacy of a response, as well as to indicate that the resource may be volatile and change shortly after being sent. A cache would have to heed such cache directives if it is going to provide semantically transparent caching.

The presence of certain request headers such as Authorization or response headers such as Vary might lower the chances of a response being cached. The Authorization request header typically indicates that the requested resource is unlikely to be available for everyone. This lowers the potential for the response to be shared by many users. Similarly, the presence of a Vary header indicates that an acceptable cached response would be constrained by the values specified in the Vary header.

The conflicting goals of the various parties involved in caching were known to the HTTP protocol developers. The protocol standard may not lend itself to an optimal solution for all the parties involved in the transaction. However, the protocol designers focused on increasing semantic transparency in caching while providing control to all parties involved in the transaction.

11.3.2 Content-specific considerations

A cache may have its own set of rules for deciding on cacheabilty of a response, separate from protocol restrictions. In other words, just because a response is cacheable does not mean that it will be cached. Messages could be large, dynamically generated, or include cookies, all of which could affect cacheability of a message. Cache policy may be driven by factors other than protocol restrictions, such as attributes of a message. For example, the frequency with which caches revalidate resources with the origin server might be dictated by their policies on the cacheability duration of the resources. On the other extreme, if a cache provider is paid on the basis of the number of bits they deliver to users, they might opt to ignore last modification timestamps and send full bodies of responses instead of simply sending `304 Not Modified`. A shared cache may not want to cache responses to queries that have personalized information (such as cookies) embedded in them. Active server pages (ASPs) and requests for documents triggering authentication are examples of pages that are probably not good candidates for caching.

Businesses may be able to reduce the cost of transfer by ignoring certain cache-related restrictions. Caches may store resources that they are not supposed to cache, such as when the `Cache-Control: private` directive is used. The user's goal of reducing latency and the network provider's reduction of number of bits transferred may not coincide with that of cache companies' business incentives, leading to protocol constraints being ignored.

Caches may take storage overhead into account and not cache large resources even though they may be cacheable. If a message is too large, many objects may have to be evicted from the cache. In terms of latency, the cost to fetch smaller resources from the respective origin servers may be higher than the cost of obtaining them from a cache. Thus a cache might decide not to cache larger objects. On the other hand, a large cached response, if requested a few times by clients behind the cache, may yield significant savings in terms of bandwidth. For example, suppose a new version of a popular piece of software is made available on the Web. This resource is both large *and* likely to be requested quite often. Caching this resource would yield significant benefits. Part of the reason is that some service providers must pay on the basis of the total number of bits they download and would prefer instead to use a cache and download the resource just once.

Many caches forgo caching all responses to scripts, under the assumption that the parameters to the queries are not likely to be used again. Even deciding that a response was generated as a result of invocation of a script is based in a heuristic. The basic assumption in caching is that the same response is likely to be generated in the future, and a request for such a response might occur in the near future. A script might trigger a computation that is more likely to return a different result each time, compared with a request for a static resource that changes infrequently. However, the presence of cacheability information in a dynamic response such as an `Expires` or `ETag` header may indicate that the resource is actually cacheable. For example, consider a Common Gateway Interface (CGI) script that returns the nth digit of π. The response is not going to change as long as the argument is n. Many queries often result in the same answer, and some caches already take this into account. This is particularly true in the context of search engines, where a very large number of queries are for single search terms and often the same search term (e.g., "mp3," "sex"). If the search engine does not update its collection of pages more than once daily, for example, the CGI search query is going to return the same answer. Also, in general, it is not always possible to tell whether the response returned was dynamically generated or not.

The myth that responses for CGI queries and other dynamically generated pages should not be cached seems to be disappearing. Another category of response that may be viewed as uncacheable is responses that include data tailored to a specific user. For example, responses with cookie information in them are considered uncacheable by proxies, because they are expected to differ across users. But several messages with cookies may still be cacheable if they return the same response for different cookie values [WM99]. Note that some content types that are considered typically cacheable (e.g., images—GIF or JPEG formats) may actually include tailored data or not have any freshness information, rendering them uncacheable.

The decision to cache is affected by the rate of change of resources. Several resources change infrequently, if ever. Examples of resources that may never change include electronic copies of books. Some static resources may change over a period of time. Users' home pages change periodically with no particular frequency. Thus, examining the rate of change of a resource is a valid metric for deciding cacheability. One early heuristic for deciding on the cacheability of a resource was the last modification time of a resource. The assumption was that if a resource had not been modified in a long time, it was also less likely to change in the near future. This made the resource a better candidate for caching. If a resource was indeed cached, the last modification time was also used in deciding when to revalidate the cached response. Conversely, this approach also assumed that if a resource has been modified recently, there is a higher probability that it would change again soon. Thus the resource is not likely to stay fresh in the cache for a long time. At the same time, the frequently changing nature of a resource might indicate high interest in the resource and thus a higher rate of access, which argues for caching the resource. Because the overall benefit of caching springs mainly from the number of times a cached resource is actually accessed, the access rate of a resource should be considered in caching decisions.

The load on a cache may also have an impact on whether a response should be cached. For example, a busy cache could serve cache hits but simply forward cache misses and not store responses for the cache misses.

11.4 Where is Caching Done?

Caches are found in browsers and in any of the Web intermediaries between the user agent and the origin server. Typically a cache is located in a proxy, in addition to in a browser. It makes sense to cache in multiple locations rather than in just a single location:

- A browser cache can avoid having to refetch pages the user examined during the same session. However, a browser cache does not take advantage of frequently requested resources by other users in the same local environment.
- A caching proxy can help dozens, if not hundreds, of users. A browser cache, however, can store a reasonable set of recently received responses for a longer time than a caching proxy. A caching proxy, being a resource shared by hundreds of users, may have to evict some responses sooner than a browser cache.
- A regional cache can help several geographically colocated caches in one or more administrative entities. A national cache can group a set of regional caches and help reduce costs in countries facing high tariffs for moving data across national boundaries. With each geographical step away from the client, there is an added performance penalty, even when there is a cache hit.

In Chapter 3 (Section 3.8) we briefly examined reverse and interception proxies. A reverse proxy acts as a front end to one or more origin servers and can include a cache. In a reverse proxy, caching occurs on behalf of origin servers and not on behalf of users. Caching in a reverse proxy reduces the load on origin servers, although the issues faced by a reverse proxy are similar to the ones faced by a cache closer to users. The most popular resources requested at the origin servers are likely to reside in the cache of the reverse proxy. A reverse proxy forwards a request to the origin server if the resource is not found, except that the forwarding is done via a tunnel; that is, the proxy acts as a blind relay.

Interception proxies can be placed anywhere on the network and can examine the network and transport layer of the protocol stack. Interception proxies intercept the HTTP request and explicitly receive the response. Typically interception proxies are placed close to the clients. Note that interception proxies do not have to be directly in the path of the packets. A device that can examine packets at the transport layer could redirect traffic to an interception proxy. Once the packets are extracted, the request, optionally, can be redirected to nearby caches under the same administrative control as the interception proxy. Such interception is generally transparent to the user, who would notice only reduced latency, assuming the response was located in the cache. Unfortunately, some interception proxies do not adhere to the HTTP protocol, and the response received may not be the same as one might get from a compliant caching proxy or an origin server.

11.5 How is Caching Done?

We now discuss exactly *how* caching is done—the issues that must be considered in implementing a cache. First, a cache must decide whether the message is cacheable, then decide if space is available and, if not, how to replace some of the existing cached objects. The cache, upon receiving a request must decide whether it can satisfy the request and, if so, return the cached response while updating some information. The cache must have a coherency policy for maintaining freshness information of the cached resource.

11.5.1 Deciding whether a message is cacheable

A cache must first decide whether a message should be cached. Different caches have different ways to decide cacheability of a message. As discussed in Section 11.3, the common criteria used to decide on cacheability of a message are as follows:

- Are there protocol requirements that prevent the response from being cached?
- Is the content typically uncacheable (e.g., dynamic data or of a particular content type)?
- Is the cached response likely to be reused again?
- Will the decision to cache a particular response lead to replacement of one or more resources?

A cache would use some or all of these criteria to decide whether it should cache a message.

11.5.2 Cache replacement and storing the response in cache

After deciding to store a message, the cache checks to see whether the message can be stored without evicting other objects from the cache. If not, the cache replacement algorithm is triggered. Cache replacement introduces some overhead, especially if many small cached objects must be removed (we examine the cache replacement issue in more detail in Section 11.6). Additional overhead is caused when future requests for replaced objects are made—new connections must be established to retrieve them. Often, resources known to be stale are evicted from a cache even if the cache is not full. This reduces the need for triggering the cache replacement algorithm at the time a request is being handled, thus lowering user-perceived latency.

Once space becomes available, the cache extracts information about the message, such as last modification time, and expiry-, or staleness-related information. Message headers such as `Expire` and `Cache-Control: max-stale` carry information about expiration. These header fields help the cache comply with the HTTP protocol restrictions on the length of time a cached response can be returned as a semantically valid response. A cache that is compliant to the protocol is obligated to ensure that any responses it returns would still be considered as fresh by the origin server. Chapter 7 (Section 7.3.3) discussed the various semantics of cache-related headers. In the absence of specific expiration time information in the message, the cache uses a heuristic expiration time to decide when the message becomes stale. The heuristic expiration time could be based on the `Last-Modified` time associated with the resource. For example, a cache could add a fixed amount of time, say ten minutes, to the `Last-Modified` value and use that as a freshness interval. Finally, a key is generated for use in future lookups. The key is typically a hash value based on the URL of the request. When the cache receives a new request, it uses the URL to look up the resource in the cache.

11.5.3 Returning a cached response

When a response corresponding to the key looked up is found in the cache, a "cache hit" is said to have occurred. Then, depending on the policy of the cache and any constraining cache-related headers, a revalidation may be performed to ensure that the cached response is still fresh (revalidation and general cache coherency issues are discussed later, in Section 11.7). If revalidation indicates that the response is still fresh, the request is satisfied from the cache. Otherwise, the cache gets a new copy of the resource and uses its caching policy to decide whether that response should be cached while forwarding it to the client. If the request is not found in the cache (i.e., a "cache miss"), the request is forwarded.

11.5.4 Maintaining a cache

Periodically, a cache may check to see if the objects in the cache are still fresh and trigger eviction of stale objects. A cache may also examine the rate of requests for cached objects to decide which resources are popular and perform special activities on their behalf. For example, a cache might want to *prevalidate* popular resources to ensure that more frequently requested objects are fresh. Such prevalidation could be done via the HTTP `HEAD` request that requests only the metadata of a resource be sent back. A cache could also proactively contact the origin server to see if the resource has changed and, if so, *prefetch* it to update its cache. Such approaches trade off bandwidth against latency: increased traffic between a cache and an origin server to prevalidate or prefetch a resource costs additional bandwidth but has the potential for significantly reducing the user-perceived latency.

11.6 Cache Replacement

Once the cache is full, objects must be removed to make room to cache new responses. Several approaches for replacement have been examined over the past several years. Some of them are borrowed from traditional caching approaches in the file system world, and some are specifically tailored to Web caches. One well-known approach is the simple LRU (Least Recently Used) approach— replace the object that was the least recently used. Books on shelves that have not been examined in a long time may have more dust on them than recently examined ones. The longer the duration of time since last examination, the more the dust. The goals of caching, such as lowering the number of bits transmitted over the network and reducing the user-perceived latency, lead to complex cache replacement decisions. The complex approaches consist of a combination of a set of metrics that includes the size of cached objects, their content type, and even a notion of network distance to the origin server.

The usefulness of retaining a response in the cache can be gauged by numerous factors, including the following:

- **Cost of fetching the resource:** The cost to fetch a resource from an origin server is determined by the connectivity of the cache and the distance a resource must travel before it is brought to the cache. By replacing a resource that was expensive to fetch, a similar high cost has to be paid if the resource is requested in the future.
- **Cost of storing the resource:** A cache has a fixed size, and retaining a cached object means there is less space for other objects. A large resource takes more space, but, if it were replaced, fetching it again would also be more expensive.
- **The number of accesses to the resource in the past:** An object that has been accessed many times in the past is likely to be accessed again and might merit caching for a longer period.
- **The probability of the resource being accessed in the near future:** If a resource is likely to be retrieved again in the near future, it would not make sense to remove it from the cache. The probability of access to a resource may be known *a priori* or estimated based on past access patterns.

- **The time since the last modification of the resource:** A resource that has not been modified for a long time is less likely to change in the near future. A resource that was generated very recently might be a dynamic resource or likely to change again in the near future. Resources that are likely to change again are likely to be popular; such resources may be changed as a result of their popularity and are thus good candidates for caching. However, the cached response may have to be replaced frequently with the changing resource. The last modification time of a resource might thus be used to decide on the candidate for replacement.
- **The heuristic expiration time:** If there is no server-specified expiration time, the cache decides on a heuristic expiration time. If no expired resources are available as candidates, then resources that are close to their expiration time are prioritized as candidates for replacement.

Each of these factors plays a role in deciding which cache replacement mechanism would be the best suited for the mixture of objects in a cache.

The various factors taken into consideration for replacing objects in a cache gave rise to a variety of cache replacement algorithms. *One-level* algorithms use a single metric, whereas *two-level* algorithms use a combination of algorithms with primary and secondary metrics. Combination algorithms take a weighted approach rather than a straightforward hit-ratio approach. If the complexity of the replacement algorithm increases, there is a risk of diminishing returns. This is because of the overhead of adding a resource to a cache that is likely to be evicted soon. The algorithmic overhead is considered as cost and is a factor in the overall usefulness of the algorithm. We present a brief overview of the various algorithms proposed and in use for cache replacement.

Least Recently Used (LRU)   One of the oldest and most time-tested algorithms is LRU, which simply removes the oldest object (in terms of the time at which it was last accessed) from the cache. The idea is straightforward: Objects that have been accessed more recently are likely to be accessed again, and so less accessed objects should be evicted before removing any of the newer resources. A variety of research studies [AW97, ASA+95, WAS+96, CI97] has shown that this is not the best algorithm for maximizing the object hit ratio. Among the reasons are the absence of temporal locality in references to documents and that many objects are referenced just once.

Least Frequently Used (LFU)   LFU is another simple algorithm that ranks the objects in terms of frequency of access and removes the object that is the least frequently used. An LFU policy based on frequency count for cached resources was examined in [WAS+96, SSV97].

Size of object (SIZE) Another criterion for choosing an object to be replaced is its size. By deleting the largest object presently in the cache, it is possible to make space for many (smaller) objects.

Hyper-G (LFU/LRU/SIZE) The Hyper-G [AKMS95] combines the LFU, LRU, and SIZE policies. The first consideration for replacement is least frequently used, and if there is more than one resource that meets this criterion, the cache chooses the least recently used among them. If this still does not give a unique object to replace, the largest object is evicted.

GreedyDual-Size The GreedyDual algorithm [You94] was proposed in the context of page replacement in computer memories. All pages were considered to be of the same size, and the cost of fetching a page from secondary storage was a key ingredient. Subsequently, the algorithm was extended [CI97] to incorporate the varying sizes of Web resources. The modified algorithm associates a *utility* value and replaces the resource that has the lowest utility. Apart from the cost of bringing the resource into the cache and its size, the utility also takes into account an age factor that is updated as resources leave the cache.

Cache replacement was an issue in the early days of caching. With the steadily falling cost of storage, caches have become larger. Cache replacement has generally faded from the practical arena for the following four main reasons:

- Steadily falling cost of storage leads to caches of sizes large enough to hold most of the resources requested.
- An overall reduction in the fraction of traffic that is cacheable.
- The "good-enough" algorithms that satisfy most situations in which cache replacement is used. Algorithms such as Greedy Dual-Size and Hyper-G are in the good-enough category.
- Change in resources over time reduces the value of having a large cache that can store them longer.

11.7 Cache Coherency

An origin server decides the freshness duration of a cached response. A cache may have to ensure that the cached response is still fresh before returning it to a client requesting the resource. Cache coherency is a well-studied problem in all forms of caching on computers. Coherency was a problem in computer memories—a cached copy of a file may have changed on the disk. Attempts have been made to minimize the amount of work required to verify coherency, but the costs vary depending on the context. Various cache coherency algorithms have been introduced over the last few years for Web caches. The need for cache coherency may depend on the resources and policies in place at the cache. Caches may simply return an older cached value, along with a reason for the staleness of the response. Among the reasons are the connection to the origin server being down or the cache being busy. HTTP/1.1's `Warning` header (discussed in Chapter 7, Section 7.12.2) can be used to indicate that a potentially stale cached value is being returned. A user agent could make such information available to the user.

In the distributed file system world, caching was an issue that was studied in depth. The Web differs from the distributed file system world in many ways. Updates of resources on the Web occur in only one place—the origin server. In a distributed file system, updates may occur in different places. However, on the Web, the presence of multiple proxies and the potential for caching *partial* responses alter the picture. Additionally, the cost of checking coherency may be higher in the Web because of its loosely connected model and the overhead of establishing connections to the origin server.

The HTTP/1.1 protocol provides several ways for caches to maintain coherence. If an origin server sets a specific expiration time for a resource, a proxy that provides semantically transparent caching is obligated to adhere to the expiration time. The only exception to this is a constraint placed by the client's request via a `Cache-Control: only-if-cached` that forces the proxy to return a cached response without revalidating with the origin server. If the origin server does not set an expiration time, the proxy can use a heuristic expiration time. Heuristic expiration is often combined with coherency checks. The most common approach in the Web to check coherency is to send a `GET` or a `HEAD` request with an `If-Modified-Since` request header (discussed in Chapter 6, Section 6.2.3). The `If-Modified-Since` header carries with it the last modification timestamp of the resource, as indicated by the origin server. In some cases, the response generation time may be the last modified time. HTTP/1.1's entity tags, in conjunction with the `If-Match` header, can be used to perform coherency checks against specific variants of a resource (discussed in Chapter 7, Section 7.3.3). The origin server might respond with a complete copy (and a `200 OK` response code) or the `304 Not Modified` response code with no response body. A coherency check, however, requires a complete HTTP request-response exchange.

If a caching proxy sends a revalidation request each time a cache hit occurs, the policy is called *strong consistency.* If the cache uses a heuristic to decide whether the cached response is still fresh, without consulting the origin server each time a cache hit occurs, such a policy is called *weak consistency.* Depending on the cache and the typical set of responses cached, either the strong or weak approach may be appropriate. A lease-based heuristic and variations on time-based heuristics are among the weak consistency approaches. The two weak consistency approaches differ in which component takes the primary responsibility for deciding the freshness interval of a resource. The two heuristics are

1. **A lease-based approach:** A cache agrees to store a response for a fixed amount of time (the lease period) without revalidating. However, the server promises to notify the cache if a cached resource changes *within* the lease period. If the lease period expires, the cache can revalidate the resource and decide to renew the lease. This approach, outlined in [LC97], shifts the overhead of revalidating to the server, which now must keep track of all the caching proxies that it has promised to notify. This approach does not scale if an origin server must notify hundreds of thousands of proxies. Note that this is a proposal, and the server's cooperation is needed in order to notify the caches about lease expiry. Lease-based algorithms are discussed widely in the literature, although they are yet to be seen in cache products to any appreciable extent. One reason is that lease-based approaches require caches and servers to cooperate.

2. **A time to live (TTL) approach:** Responses have a cache expiration time associated with them. When the time interval passes, the responses are considered stale. During the TTL period, the cache does not revalidate the response and thus saves potentially unnecessary bandwidth use at the risk of staleness. The TTL value can vary with the response and can be based on the following factors:

   The expiration time specified in the response header field: The cache may directly adopt the value or modify it based on its policy. If there is no expiration time specified, the cache might assign a uniform TTL value for resources that have the same content type.

   The frequency of request for a cached resource: Resources requested frequently may be assigned a larger TTL value.

   Mobile environment: The disconnected nature of operations and the lower bandwidth of users in mobile environments [HL96] might suggest a variable TTL for responses likely to be accessed by such users.

   The last modification time of the resource: An adaptive TTL algorithm may assume that a recently modified resource is likely to change again [Cat92]. Hence, a cache might assign a smaller TTL for a recently modified resource. A cached response could be assigned a larger TTL value if a resource has not changed on the origin server for a very long time. The modification time information is gleaned from the `Last-Modified` response header.

   TTL-based approaches are quite popular.

Maintaining consistency can have a serious impact on cache response time because each revalidation request has the overhead of contacting the origin server [Joh99]. The dominance of the connection cost to the origin server points to the need for reducing the number of revalidation requests. As discussed in Chapter 10 (Section 10.3.2) and in several studies [AFJ99, KW97], the 304 Not Modified responses are a considerable fraction (10% to 30%) of all responses. In Chapter 13 (Section 13.1), we examine some techniques for reducing the number of 304 Not Modified responses. These techniques lower the need for separate connections for revalidations by using hints from the origin server that indicate when resources change.

11.8 Rate of Change of Resources

The rate at which different resources on the Web change varies widely. Many resources are created once and never modified. Some resources change with each access. The rate of change of resources raises important questions that affect caching, such as the following:

- What responses should be cached?
- Is there a correlation between the rate of change of a resource and the frequency of its access?
- How long should a response be cached?

Detecting changes in resources corresponding to files is easy. But caching proxies are not aware of how often dynamically generated resources change on origin servers. Often they may examine the URL to glean hints. For example, if a URL has the "cgi" string or the "?" character embedded in it, the cache might guess that the response was dynamically generated. However, this may not always be the case. Likewise, many resources that do not have *cgi* or "?" characters may well be dynamically generated. A dynamically generated resource may result in the same response each time. Some resources that might be considered non-dynamic may change with a very high degree of frequency. For example, a site such as www.cnn.com updates its pages frequently whenever a new news item is added to the page. Some pages change every time they are accessed; for example, they may have a counter indicating the number of accesses. Thus a notion of the *rate of change* of a set of resources can help in deciding whether a response should be cached and for how long.

The impact of rate of change of resources on caching can be examined by categorizing resources, as follows:

- **The content type:** Image resources tend to change less frequently than textual resources and thus could be assigned a longer freshness interval.
- **The frequency and periodicity of the changes:** If a cartoon (e.g., www.dilbert.com) were known to change only once a day, it could be cached as fresh until the next day. No freshness checks need be made on

such resources because they are guaranteed to remain fresh until the stable expiration interval.

- The size of the resource. If smaller resources tend to change often, this factor can be examined jointly with the rate of access of such resources to decide on their cache duration.

If resources have stable expiration times, then heuristics regarding rate of change would not be necessary. However, origin servers may not include a specific expiration period for resources. Among the reasons are that they may not know what a proper expiration period is, and, in some cases during the expiration period, there might be reduced traffic from a caching proxy. Reduced traffic lowers the number of "hits" an origin server receives, which in turn could lower advertisement revenue.

11.9 Cache-related Protocols

Depending on how the caches are organized, they may send and receive information about resources in which they are interested. Such communication is external and separate from the request and response messages that flow between clients and origin servers. Inter-cache communication can use HTTP but typically uses customized lighter-weight protocols. If a set of caches is arranged in a hierarchy, a cache can contact the other caches at the same level to see if the requested object is present in other caches. A query for a missing resource can be answered by one or more caches that happen to have the resource. Often, getting a copy of the resource from a local cache is better than obtaining it from the origin server. However, waiting for a response from all the caches in the hierarchy may increase the latency to the user. We next examine a few well-known solutions to reduce inter-cache communication costs.

Although we discuss several protocols below, they are not equal in sophistication, importance, or level of deployment. The primary purpose in discussing these protocols is to examine the various approaches taken thus far to help caches communicate with each other. We discuss four protocols: Internet Cache Protocol (ICP), Cache Array Resolution Protocol (CARP), Cache Digest Protocol, and Web Cache Coordination Protocol (WCCP).

11.9.1 Internet Cache Protocol (ICP)

A cache that does not have the requested object may want to check with another nearby cache. Such communication is distinct from the more traditional request for a resource from an origin server. Here, caches are the source and destination of the message exchange. A separate protocol was needed for inter-cache communication. One of the earliest protocols that was introduced for caches to communicate with each other is the Internet Cache Protocol

(ICP) [WC97b, WC97a]. ICP is an example of a query protocol—the message sent by a client cache is a query asking if the peer has a cached copy of a particular response needed by the client cache. ICP's current popularity stems from the fact that it is used in Squid [WC98], the freely available and widely used caching software.

ICP lends itself well to hierarchies—sets of caches connected together as peers and linked to a common parent. This process is repeated, and moving up the hierarchy corresponds to moving to a more central cache. Thus a set of local area caches may be linked to a central cache, which may peer with other central caches for other local areas. The central caches may have a regional cache as a parent, and a set of regional caches may have a national cache as their parent. Suppose a cache OriginalCache does not have the requested resource. OriginalCache would send ICP requests (typically, a UDP message) to all of its peers simultaneously. A successful response would indicate that the peering cache has the resource, and OriginalCache could request the resource using HTTP. If none of the peers have the resource, OriginalCache would have to send another ICP request to its parent. It is also possible that none of the peering caches respond within a specific amount of time, forcing OriginalCache to timeout. The parent of OriginalCache would repeat the process. If none of the caches have the response, OriginalCache would contact the origin server. The assumption underlying the ICP protocol is that sending a set of ICP queries to caches, even multiple times at various levels of the hierarchy, is faster than contacting the origin server. Additionally, several optimizations help reduce the overall cost. For example, when a response comes back from the origin server or one of the parent/peer caches, the intermediate caches on the path can store the response for future use. An unresponsive neighbor provides an indication of its connectivity to the OriginalCache.

Although regional and national proxies can help a large number of users by reducing the distance traversed to fetch resources, each application-layer hop can degrade performance. If the resource is not found at a hop, there is a significant addition to the overall delay. Even if there is a cache hit in a national proxy, there is a delay before the response percolates to the original client that generated the request.

11.9.2 Cache Array Resolution Protocol (CARP)

The Cache Array Resolution Protocol (CARP) [CAR] defines a mechanism by which a set of caching proxies can effectively function as a single logical cache. The set of responses that is collectively cached between the group ("array") of proxies is treated as one large cache. A hash function is used to partition the URLs across the caches. A client trying to locate a cached resource can target the request to an appropriate cache by applying a hash function. The hash function uses the request URL and the identity of the proxy members to construct a *resolution path.* Compared with ICP, CARP has a *deterministic* request resolution path, thus eliminating the need for any query messages. There are fewer duplicated cached responses in CARP than the query-based ICP. CARP uses both HTTP and a remote procedure call interface to let proxies communicate with each other. CARP associates a proxy with a load factor, which can be taken into account before a request is directed to the proxy. CARP [CAR] has been implemented by a major software vendor and is available as a product.

When the configuration of the caching system changes as a result of adding or deleting a proxy server, the cached URLs must be reassigned. The hash functions are recomputed when cache replacement occurs. A URL cannot be present in multiple caching proxies, and thus balancing load across proxies is difficult. Popular URLs would result in a small subset of caching proxies receiving a significant percentage of the requests. If a lookup of a cache entry fails, the proxy must be viewed as inactive for a duration of time.

11.9.3 Cache Digest Protocol

Cache Digest [HRW98] is an extension provided to ICP. The basic idea in Cache Digest is to permit the exchange of a *digest* of a cache's contents. A digest can be thought of as a terse description of the cache's contents. It is an indicator of the collection of objects in a cache. When a cache has a digest of all its peers, it can quickly check in the digest to see if the object of interest is available. If the lookup in the digest of a particular cache succeeds, that cache would be a candidate for receiving a request for the object. The requesting cache may even decide to choose *one* of the caches whose digests yielded a successful match. If a check in the digest fails, that cache is not contacted, reducing the need for sending multiple messages to all the peers.

One obvious problem is the staleness of a digest and the corresponding false hits. An object may be removed from a cache after the cache's digest has been constructed. Another problem is the size of the digests and their exchange among the peers. With many peering caches, the digest size can become very large. Recent work has led to smaller digest sizes [FCAB98].

ICP's UDP-based scheme can be used to exchange digests between the peering caches. However, for reliability, digests are exchanged using standard HTTP messages on top of TCP. A digest can be considered as a normal resource, and the revalidation techniques of HTTP (such as the `Expires` and `If-Modified-Since` headers) can be used to verify freshness of digests.

11.9.4 Web Cache Coordination Protocol (WCCP)

Unlike higher-level protocols such as ICP and CARP, the Web Cache Coordination Protocol (WCCP) [WCC99] is a coordination mechanism that is closely connected to the network layer. The purpose of WCCP is to intercept the HTTP request and redirect it to the cache engine. Because the request would fail if the cache is inaccessible for any reason, a coordination mechanism is needed. The coordinator's task is to load balance across multiple caches, ensuring that heartbeat information is available for them. By periodically checking that a cache is alive, the mechanism ensures that packets are not sent to a cache that is not responding to a heartbeat check.

Such a coordination mechanism is at the heart of the WCCP protocol, which is implemented as part of the Cisco Cache Engine. The cache engine is configured to receive Web requests redirected to it by the router. The router that has WCCP enabled is capable of examining all IP headers, and a TCP packet destined to port 80 (the default port for HTTP) is redirected to a cache engine. In addition, WCCP-enabled routers periodically communicate with the cache engines to ensure that they are accessible.

11.10 Cache Software and Hardware

Caching can be provided via software on intermediaries such as proxies, as described in Chapter 3. The software solution requires adding a piece of software to a proxy. Caching can also be provided via hardware designated specifically for caching. In the first part of this section, we examine the widely used Squid caching software as an example of a software solution. In the second part, we examine a variety of hardware solutions that require new physical devices to be configured and installed.

11.10.1 Cache software: The Squid cache

The Squid [WC98] cache is a widely used, open-source caching system that runs on most operating system platforms, including UNIX, Solaris, Linux, FreeBSD, NetBSD, and OS/2. Other popular caching systems include NetApp [Neta], Inktomi [Ink], and Novell Bordermanager [Nov]. Squid is capable of handling a variety of protocols apart from HTTP (e.g., FTP, SSL, Gopher, and WAIS). Squid is a configurable cache: users can specify what rules must be followed for caching responses (in terms of content type, duration of caching, etc.). To get a better idea of how Squid works, readers should consult the Squid Users Guide [Pea97].

As with any other caching proxy, a Squid cache must be configured at a client site. A browser's configuration can be edited to set the proxy field for any of the protocols that Squid supports (as discussed in Chapter 2, Section 2.4.2). For example, the port number in the HTTP field is set to be 3128, because Squid uses TCP port 3128 for communicating with Web clients by default.

Squid caches can talk to other peer caches, and Squid has adopted ICP as the protocol of choice. The communication with other caches is on UDP port 3130 by default, although communication can also use HTTP. The parent and sibling relationships between caches are specified via configuration files, and the hierarchy can be local, regional, national, or even international. Conditional caching can be configured across domain boundaries. For example, a single Squid cache can be the cache for a variety of national domains, such as .fr and .au. Caches near a particular site are located via a central registration database.

The Squid cache contacts a set of peers using UDP and assumes that the first cache to respond with a cache-hit is also likely to respond quickly to the actual request. In other words, Squid gathers information regarding the network load based on the response time. A response received from a sibling cache does not have to be cached at the querying cache. Instead, the querying cache could simply let the sibling cache serve as the cache for that object, if the caches are on a common network with high bandwidth and low latency. If none of the sibling or higher-level caches have a fresh copy of the requested resource, the Squid cache forwards the request to the origin server. The server's response is optionally cached before being returned to the client.

Squid is capable of working in a clustering environment: multiple caches on the same network segment (subnet) act as siblings. The advantages of a cache cluster include redundancy in the face of failure of a cache and the lower cost of a set of small machines over a single large server. The DNS server participates in a cache clustering scheme. The resolution of the cache server's address is done in such a way that a browser's lookup of a machine can reach the various caches in the cluster.

Squid uses Access Control Lists (ACLs) to decide which clients should be able to access it as a proxy. A list of IP addresses (at a prefix level) is used to filter incoming requests. Different addresses can be enabled for specific protocols. For example, a group of clients can use Squid as a cache for HTTP requests but not FTP requests. Squid can also be configured to disable access to certain Web servers; the ACL in this case consists of a set of destination domains. The specification of such access control is relatively straightforward. For example, consider the specification of an access control list (*acl*) labeled dumb consisting of two destination domains notbright.com and nitwit.com:

```
acl dumb dstdomain notbright.com nitwit.com
http_access deny dumb
```

This specification would prevent requests to any URLs in the two domains from clients behind the Squid cache.

A Squid cache also has the ability to function as a Web server *accelerator*: It can sit in front of one or more origin servers and act as the front end to incoming requests. The Squid server would have to run on the default HTTP port of 80 to function as a front-end server. The Squid server is then configured to be a front end for one or more origin servers and redirects incoming requests to the back-end origin server(s). Squid can handle the Host header of HTTP/1.1

(discussed in Chapter 7, Section 7.8) to decide which origin server should receive the request. The Squid server may exhibit better performance than the origin server. When the Squid server is configured as an accelerator, it can take care of updating its cache when the resources change on the origin server. The Squid accelerator acts as a mirror and is able to keep up with changes. The Squid server does not have to handle all the requests. An interesting technique is to separate the set of resources in an origin server into cacheable and non-cacheable ones. One server handles the requests for cacheable resources, and the Web server running on the nondefault port number handles the noncacheable resources. For example, the Squid cache can forward all CGI requests to the origin server. By making just the Squid server visible to the external network, it can prevent attacks on the origin server behind it. For example, the following configuration specification in a Squid server

```
acl safe dstdomain safe1.com safe2.com
http_access deny !safe
```

ensures that only safe1.com and safe2.com are reachable. The caching proxy would deny requests to any other domain.

Like many other caching proxies, Squid originally utilized a time-to-live model of expiration when resources entered the cache. Recent versions of Squid use a different model based on refresh rate. Instead of expiring resources automatically, an object's freshness is checked only when necessary. At the time of request, the resource's expiration status is checked, and, if the object is stale, it is revalidated with the origin server. A new version is obtained if necessitated as a result of the revalidation. Squid abides by the Cache-Control and Expires headers, if any, present in the request and response headers. Preference is given to the client's request header (e.g., Cache-Control: max-age) over the Expires header in the server's response. It is possible for the Squid cache to be configured to override adhering to the expiry time specified in the Expires response header.

Squid has recently introduced cache digests as well. The new version of Squid is able to handle some of the features of HTTP/1.1, such as persistent connections and proxy authentication. Squid is able to take advantage of recent enhancements to popular operating systems, such as the presence of thread libraries. In the case of interception proxies, whereby packets destined to a particular port are redirected by a proxy in the path, a Squid cache can act as the destination for the redirected packets. Squid can also understand WCCP (discussed in Section 11.9.4).

11.10.2 Cache hardware

Caching can also be provided with the help of dedicated hardware. Proxy caching, whereby a specific machine is configured to be the cache, has a few problems, as follows:

- A browser must be configured to contact a particular caching proxy.
- In the presence of multiple caches, inter-cache communication is required to prevent duplication of data across the caches.
- If the proxy is currently unavailable, the browser would have to be reconfigured.

An alternative way to solve the caching problem is to deploy specific pieces of hardware that rely on the networking infrastructure. Such solutions depend on the ability to intercept network traffic at various levels (network, transport, and application). The intercepted traffic is redirected to one or more machines acting as caching proxies. Hardware-based caching solutions can be classified into two broad categories: redirectors and appliances. A redirector, which can be a router or a switch, has to intercept the request. An appliance includes a redirection device but presents an all-in-one solution.

INTERCEPTORS AND REDIRECTORS

A redirecting device relies on being able to intercept the traffic between the requesting clients and the origin server. Cache hardware can use the networking infrastructure to intercept the traffic. Interception devices are often at the edge of the network of the ISP and are capable of seeing all the packets between the set of requesting clients and the Internet. Interception eliminates the need for the client to configure a proxy. Both Web and non-Web traffic is examined during interception, potentially adding delay for non-Web traffic that does not benefit from the interception.

The end user has no control over interception proxies. As we mentioned in Section 11.4, users are not aware of the presence of an interception proxy. A user receiving a response from an interception proxy assumes that it came from the origin server. Suppose the interception proxy's cache is not behaving properly and the response was either stale or not generated in a manner compliant with the HTTP protocol. The user has no way of knowing where the problem might have occurred. Interception proxies add to privacy concerns—users may be unaware of the potential of their privacy being violated by them.

Interception proxies have become fairly common on the market. Interception and redirection can be done via routers or switches. A *router* may have a specific policy to examine one or more ports (e.g., 80 for HTTP) and redirect that traffic. Such a setup can be thought of as an L3/L4 switch, that is, level 3 or level 4 of the protocol stack (network and transport layers). An L4 switch can examine the TCP SYN packet and decide if the request should be redirected. Cisco implemented policy routing in its routers to enable interception of the network traffic on port 80. Blindly forwarding traffic on a particular port, however, can lead to performance degradation because many messages are non-cacheable. For example, a dynamically generated response is unlikely to be in a cache. A Web *switch* is a network device that has software for intercepting Web traffic and redirecting it to one or more proxies. A switch typically operates at the transport layer (L4) and only intercepts TCP/IP packets meant for port 80. Non-Web traffic is not affected as a result. L4 switches may also be placed at the edge of the network. Switches are simpler, cheaper, and typically have less functionality than routers.

Switches can examine the *content* of the traffic, beyond just inspecting the port number. An intelligent switch can examine parts of the application-level headers. Examining content requires more work because the intercepting proxy must locate the HTTP header. The switch then uses a heuristic to decide whether the requested content is cacheable, and, if not, the switch sends the request directly to the origin server without redirection to the cache. Beyond examining content type, a switch can selectively redirect URLs of specific domains, filtering out domains that are unlikely to contain cacheable objects. Content-examining switches are viewed as examples of level 4+ (level 5 or level 7) switches.

Examining application-level headers (HTTP headers in this case) can help in making intelligent decisions about caching. Several of the HTTP headers—the version number of the protocol, `Cache-Control` directive headers, `Cookie` header—can be examined to make the appropriate decisions. For example, if the `Cache-Control: no-cache` header is set, then there is no point in redirecting the request to the cache. However, to view the application-level headers, the L5 switch necessarily terminates the transport-level (TCP) connection from the client. The distribution of requests to different caches to balance the load can be done via hash functions based on the URLs.

In general, examining application-level headers before deciding how to process the request can be problematic. Postponing action until the application-level headers are examined could add latency. The examination may reveal no interesting headers to help with the decision. Next, as we have discussed before, the URL may not be a good indicator of cacheability. A decision based on the fact that the URL contains the string `cgi` may not be sound. Whether or not the examination of headers and the URL is useful, the transport connection has already been terminated, and a separate transport connection must be made with the downstream server.

Typically, the boxes that actually deal with the caching of content are separate from the interceptor devices. There can be one or more caches, and the switches can redirect the requests to the appropriate cache. Separating interception from caching implies multiple caches can be added for load balancing and avoiding single points of failure.

Because the intercepting proxy is on the path of all traffic between the client and the network, clients may be cut off from the Internet if the proxy fails. Among the ways to avoid the single point of failure are using a heartbeat mechanism in the caches and turning off the interception mechanism, allowing client requests to go directly to the origin server when the heartbeat fails. An even more robust mechanism (employed by Foundry) [Fou] repeats the request to the origin server if the cache did not see a corresponding TCP SYN/ACK for a SYN.

APPLIANCES

Some ISPs prefer to buy appliances that handle all their caching needs. The primary benefit of an appliance is the reduced need for administration, compared with redirectors. The caching appliance model uses a proprietary operating system combined with a specific hardware platform. The typical installation is rack-mounted equipment requiring no maintenance on the part of the customers.

The two subcategories of appliances are those that require a separate redirection device and those that redirect internally. The latter category, for example, does not require a separate L4 or L5 switch. Hybrid versions have modules that can do switching at Layer 4. Upon detecting a cache failure, the appliance can send requests directly to the origin server.

The appliance approach does not always provide the necessary flexibility because of the proprietary nature of the underlying operating system. Specialized kernels and modified file systems are typically provided with the appliance. Change in traffic conditions might require reconfiguration of the cache setup. The ability to reconfigure a cache (add or remove caches) is dependent on the interface provided by the appliance. A customer may not be able to gather detailed measurements about their cache traffic. The customer is generally dependent on the kinds of measurement provided by the appliance. Generic measurement techniques do not work because of the novel kernel and/or file system of the appliance.

However, appliances are quite popular and have a reasonable penetration in the marketplace. They provide the necessary functionality of a caching infrastructure with minimal maintenance required on the part of the customers. As long as their application needs are met, customers might be satisfied with the measurement information that is provided by the appliance.

11.11 Impediments to Caching

Although caching helps reduce user-perceived latency and load on the network and origin server, there are several impediments to caching. We will examine some of the cache-related problems and attempts to overcome them. We begin with a look at cache busting, a deliberate attempt by some origin servers to prevent caching of responses. We then discuss the potential privacy violations that might occur as a result of caching of requests or responses.

11.11.1 Cache busting

Not all origin servers are interested in having cached content delivered by proxies. Not all responses are cacheable, and servers might want to have control over which resources are cached. When a proxy delivers cached content, it is possible for the content to be stale. The HTTP/1.1 protocol gives considerable control to the server to express its preference on the cacheability of particular resources. However, in the early days of the Web, the protocol was not flexible enough and servers had to resort to techniques outside the protocol to ensure that improper caching did not interfere with functioning of their Web site.

More importantly, the origin server has no way to know the desired number of times the same content is delivered to clients. Even origin servers that are interested in offloading content may want to obtain a count of the number of requests to their servers. In the case of Web pages that carry advertisements, origin servers may want to have an exact count of the number of clients who download their pages and thus a count of how many "eyes" see the advertisements. Many Web sites receive revenue based on the number of page views, that is, individual users who see their advertisements.

For these and other reasons, some servers participate in "cache busting." Cache busting is a technique to prevent responses from being cached. Initially this was viewed as a benign mechanism to ensure control on the part of the server. In the broadest sense, cache busting is any technique that prevents a resource that could normally be cached from being cached at proxies or browsers. Typical cache busting techniques include setting the cache parameters to values that effectively disable caching. For example, setting the `Expires` header to a value in the past guarantees that the response expires as soon as it arrives at the cache. The cache would not store such objects. An origin server can include the `Cache-Control: no-cache` or `Cache-Control: no-store` directive in the response to prevent caching. Another technique to bust caches is to deliberately alter the appearance of a page without actually changing the contents. For example, the advertisements on a page might just be rotated around parts of the page by altering the layout of the content.

We discuss two attempts made to reduce cache busting. The first attempt used an HTTP header to reduce the incentive for cache busting on part of the origin server, and the other suggested moving images normally served by an origin server to a proxy.

One attempt to solve the problem of cache busting was the proposal of a technique referred to as *hit-metering* [ML97]. The proposal introduced a new

HTTP header, named `Meter`, which would be used by a cache to report the number of cache hits for a particular resource. The main purpose of the `Meter` header was to inform the origin server of the approximate number of users who accessed a cached document. The hope was that the reporting of the hit count would reduce the incentive for cache busting. In fact, origin servers could explicitly direct a compliant proxy to serve a cached response a finite number of times before the proxy was obligated to contact the origin server. A proxy could report the count whenever it contacted the origin server, say during revalidation, via the `Meter` header. If a proxy removed a response from the cache, the proxy was obligated to report to the origin server about the hit count of that resource. A `HEAD` request was used for this purpose, which still requires a separate connection to the origin server. Hit-metering has not been successful. There have not been significant implementations of hit-metering in Web components. Site administrators did not appear to believe that the cache hit numbers reported would be correct. Cache busting, in some sense, was the path of least resistance and thus the easiest choice for origin servers.

The second technique, *ad-insertion* [Ami99], suggested that a proxy add advertisements to a page and relieve the origin server of this task. Such an approach would require that the proxy coordinate with the origin server so that the origin server is convinced that insertion is actually happening. The user agents and proxies gain in two ways. First, the cache is not busted, which increases the potential for cached responses to be used for a longer period. Second, users do not have to wait for the transfer of the advertisements from the origin server because the proxies do the insertion.

Another technique by which advertisements can be delivered without busting the cache is by using "clear GIFs." Clear GIFs, also known as "Web bugs," are small images invisible to users, which are placed on a page to serve as a counter. Most users permit browsers to download images that are embedded in a container document. By examining the contents of the Web page's HTML, it is possible to locate their presence. Note that this is a benign interpretation of a clear GIF. Downloading clear GIFs may result in cookies being exchanged. An advertising network using clear GIFs can augment the user's profile and decide on advertisements to be shown.

11.11.2 Privacy issues in caching

One topic that is not widely discussed in relation to caching is the violation of privacy. A user's requests for resources on the Web can be used by a proxy to construct a profile of the user. A response from an origin server could be cached at intermediaries along the response path against the wishes of the origin server, who might have wanted the response to be sent to just the requesting user. The privacy of the requesting user and the content provider could thus be violated. HTTP/1.1 introduced new headers and mechanisms to protect privacy. For example, the cache control request and response directive `no-store` prevents a message from being cached anywhere along the path of the request-response chain. The cache might be private (just for a single user) or shared (many users share the cache), and this distinction might be important. Such directives actually stem from legal considerations of caching related to protecting privacy on the Web. However, most HTTP messages from caches do not necessarily include such control directives, and components may not honor the directives when they are present. The client does not have any way of knowing for sure if the request is being cached along the way. Similarly, the origin server is not sure if the response is being cached or not.

An interesting alternative view of how caching might aid privacy is that when clients obtain cached responses from a proxy, they are actually shielded from origin servers. Origin servers that are interested in tracking users will receive only the IP address of proxies. Clients rely on proxies to protect their privacy because the proxies have detailed and accurate information on the requests issued by all the clients behind them.

The introduction of interception proxies that are largely invisible to the users adds another level of potential privacy violation. Whereas some origin servers might consider making the information maintained about users available, the interception proxies cannot be approached for information, because their presence is not known to the users. Thus users would not know that information is being maintained about them by interception proxies.

The popularity of the Web and the ease with which privacy could be violated have brought more attention to this problem. Privacy is slowly being taken seriously. There are legislative attempts in the European Union to protect the privacy of users and content providers. Several corporations in the United States now have a Chief Privacy Officer, whose role is to ensure that the privacy of customers is not violated.

11.12 Caching versus Replication

Replication can be viewed as an alternative to caching. In caching, requested resources are moved closer to the user. In replication, the contents of an origin server are copied to mirror sites. Clients can access a mirror site directly, or requests can be redirected to the clients. The advantage of replication is that *all* resources may be available at all times at the mirror sites, instead of just the responses cached at proxies nearer to clients. Cache mirrors can use a protocol other than HTTP to update the mirrors and keep them synchronized tightly to eliminate staleness of resources. However, there are several cache mirrors where only some of the resources—possibly the frequently requested ones—are present. Others are migrated on demand.

One advantage of replication over caching is the distribution model. The updating of resources in replication is outside the HTTP protocol. The list of replicas is known beforehand by the mirror administrators; therefore, it is possible to multicast a set of resources to the replicas. A single copy is sent on the network to the replicas. Additionally, when the resource is altered, the changes can be multicast as well.

Novel techniques can also be employed to send the differences directly to the mirrors. As we discuss in Chapter 15, Section 15.2, introducing new mechanisms to transmit only the changes of resources to caches requires considerable work at the protocol level to deal with backward compatibility issues. Distribution in replication can occur without such complications. Likewise, the resource encoding can take advantage of the software at the mirror sites. For example, mirror sites may be able to handle a novel format not generally available on the Web. Additionally, because the origin server has control over the resource and knows when a resource changes, it can immediately push changes or changed resources to the mirror sites without waiting for requests. Staleness actually can be eliminated, although at some cost because some resources may change frequently.

Reaching a mirror site is accomplished in different ways, as follows:

- Sites explicitly list a set of mirror sites, and users can chose a nearby mirror site, where "nearby" is a geographical notion. The assumption is that clients in New Zealand are in general better off going to an Australian mirror site than to a site in the United States. Requests to a site are essentially partitioned at the client level. The overall latency for users can be reduced by the clients accessing resources from nearby mirror sites. This is typically done in sites that provide access to large pieces of software.
- Redirection at HTTP level can be done via the 302 `Moved Temporarily`, 303 `See Other`, or 307 `Temporary Redirect` response-codes when a request is received at an origin server. The client uses the information in the `Location` header to contact the replica. The redirection at the HTTP level is not always transparent to the users, because users might be able to notice the additional latency caused by the two separate connections.
- Users can be redirected to mirror sites in a transparent manner. At the time of DNS lookup of a server name, the DNS server can resolve the server name to a different IP address depending on the origin of the request. All client requests for a site in New Zealand, may be directed to a mirror site in Auckland, New Zealand rather than the main site in India. Users do not need to configure explicit mirror site addresses in their browsers. The additional advantage of dynamic binding is that the DNS resolution can balance the load and redirect requests to different sites (as discussed in Chapter 5, Section 5.3.5).

11.13 Content Distribution

Content distribution is simply selective mirroring. The basic idea behind content distribution is to offload the work done by the origin server. This can be done by serving some or all of the contents that would be typically served by an origin server via a set of replicas. Several techniques can be used to redirect requests to replicas, including the use of the DNS. One way of partitioning a resource is into *base* and *embedded* components. A base document is the container document, and the embedded components are the image documents or scripts that are part of the Web page. The servers used to serve the non-container part of the resource are termed *content distribution servers*. They may be located close to the origin server or at different locations around the world, with embedded content replicated among them. At the time of the request, the content distribution service attempts to locate the content distribution server *closest* to the user to deliver the embedded images. The term "closest" could refer to geographical distance, network distance, and latency metrics. Such an approach reduces the load on the base server and potentially improves the response time for the end user.

The goal of content distribution is no different from that of caching. Both approaches move content closer to the user in order to reduce user-perceived latency and load on the origin server. With caching, proxies must worry about consistency and revalidate cached resources. With content distribution, the origin servers have control over the content and can make separate arrangements with servers that distribute content on their behalf.

In cache mirroring, large portions of a site are mirrored in several places on the Internet. In the content distribution approach, the origin servers decide which resources must be mirrored and, most importantly, offload the mirroring task to a different organization. Origin servers are obligated to notify the content distributing company whenever their resources change, similar to the mirroring case.

As an example, we consider the content distribution solution offered by Akamai [Aka]. A site that wishes to have parts of its resources distributed by Akamai would agree to rename those URLs with a specific prefix. The prefix includes a hostname string, for example, a1025o.akamaitech.net. Resolving the hostname string using DNS yields the IP address of an Akamai mirror server that is likely to have a copy of the resource. The decision to return a suitable IP address is made by the DNS server of Akamai. By design, the specified Akamai server is likely to be closer to the local DNS server of the client that made the request. The expectation is that the client is close enough to its DNS server in terms of network distance, and thus the resource has to travel a much shorter distance overall. Because the the server string has to be resolved, it is possible for Akamai to use its DNS server to help identify a suitable Akamai machine that has the requested resource. For example, consider a request for the container document `http://www.cnn.com/` that includes an embedded resource `/secdef.gif`. The embedded image's URL `http://www.cnn.com/secdef.gif` would be renamed as `http://a138g.akamai.tech.net/cnn.com/secdef.gif`. The prefix `a138g.akamai.tech.net` is the Akamai server that has control over this resource. When a client resolves `a138g.akamai.tech.net` using DNS, an IP address, say `1.2.3.4`, would be returned; this is the address of an Akamai machine near the client's local DNS server that potentially has the image `secdef.gif`. If not, the Akamai server `1.2.3.4` would request the resource using an internal protocol from either another Akamai server or the base server `www.cnn.com`. The Akamai server would then cache the resource to handle future requests. Another client in a different part of the Internet requesting the same container document will have an identically renamed link `a138g.akamai.tech.net/cnn.com/foo.gif`, except that the resolution of `a138g.akamai.tech.net` by that client might yield the IP address `5.6.7.8`, an Akamai server nearer to that client's DNS server.

Content distribution mirroring along the lines of Akamai must ensure that the DNS lookup tries to yield the nearer mirror site. Although the algorithm is proprietary, the mechanism is not. The DNS TTL values must be set in such a way that DNS responses are not cached too long. Otherwise, a Web client looking up the host `a138g.akamai.tech.net` might use an older IP address of an Akamai mirror server, which might no longer be the best choice for the resource requested. There is a trade-off between locating the best choice each time and incurring the overhead of DNS lookups. Although changing the TTL value of a DNS server of Akamai does not affect lookups of other sites, there is added DNS traffic on the network. The impact of this has yet to be studied fully.

Some problems exist with the content distribution approach. The origin server does benefit from the reduced load, and users benefit from obtaining some resources from "nearby" servers. However, the location of the content distribution servers can be a problem for a set of clients. It is possible for some clients to have better network connectivity, in terms of RTT to the origin server, than a content distribution server selected to deliver the content. Chapter 15 (Section 15.4) examines some recent research that measures the role of content distribution sites in the end-to-end Web performance.

Technically, the content distribution sites are working on behalf of the base server. Clients establish direct contact with the content distribution servers, and they expect the content distribution servers to be compliant with the HTTP protocol. Content distribution sites use different protocols in their communication with the base servers and might employ other means to ensure that they are delivering fresh content. The manner in which they ensure this is largely opaque to the outside world.

Among companies providing content distribution solutions are Adero [Ade], Akamai, Cisco [Cis], Digital Island [Dig], Exodus [Exo], Mirror Image [Mir],

Netcaching [Netb], SolidSpeed [Sol], Speedera [Speb], and Unitech [Uni]. Adero is an example of a Content Distribution Network that delivers the entire content of a site rather than letting the origin server serve the container document. Technical differences exist between the approaches taken by the various companies, but they do not appear to be significant. Some content distribution products can handle streaming media as well.

11.14 Content Adaptation

Recently, some new ideas have been proposed to offload additional work from the origin server by moving some of the work done by origin servers closer to the client. *Content adaptation* includes converting resources to different formats, translating between natural languages, or performing expensive computations. Content adaptation is at a conceptual stage as this book goes to press, and the ideas have not fully matured. The role of content distribution is to move content delivery closer to the user and away from the origin server. Content adaptation continues in the path of offloading work from the origin server by offering to move the heavier task of content adaptation closer to the user.

The Internet Content Adaptation Protocol (ICAP) [ICA01] draft suggests separating the role of a caching proxy from that of a content adaptor client. The content adaptor client sends HTTP messages to a content adaptor server. The protocol used between a content adaptor client and a content adaptor server is HTTP/1.1. The ICAP client can be colocated at a proxy and play the role of both an HTTP proxy and an ICAP client. In some sense, the ICAP client's location shows that some of the tasks performed by a proxy are being offloaded.

As an example of content adaptation, consider a resource available in a particular format: a video snippet with accompanying audio in the Tamil language. Suppose a few users behind a proxy are interested in getting a still collection of still pictures with the audio in the Dutch language. The choice of language is driven by their personal preference; the conversion of video to a series of still images could be due to their connectivity or absence of a multimedia player. It is possible that the origin server could maintain different versions of a resource in terms of both language and content formats. However, converting a Tamil video snippet into a series of still images with Dutch audio is going to require extensive alteration to the response. An origin server may not be interested in either maintaining a plethora of formats or in doing the conversion. The origin server might want to let some other trusted party perform such conversions. A traditional proxy might be a candidate, except that proxies might be too busy to spend a considerable portion of their resources to do necessary adaptation. A content adaptation server's role would be to offload work from both the origin server and the proxy to perform such computationally expensive tasks. However, the components performing adaptation need a way to learn of client interests in adapted content, communicate with origin servers to ensure that they obtain the proper instance of a resource to adapt, and deliver it to the proxy in front of the client. Content adaptation is still in its infancy, and it is early to discuss potentials for widespread adoption.

11.15 Summary

In this chapter, we have presented an overview of the vast area of Web caching. Caching is mature technology, with products being offered by dozens of companies. A cache that does not provide semantic transparency runs the risk of either delivering stale data to the user, or worse yet, not being sure whether the data is stale. We have explored a variety of issues related to caching, including what is cacheable, how to cache, and where to cache. We have briefly touched on newer issues related to content distribution and adaptation. Caching is a growing segment of Web businesses, and although other ideas are likely to be introduced, the basic idea is relatively stable—that of bringing content closer to the user.

Delivering Multimedia Streams

The Web provides users with access to a wide variety of resources without regard to the format or location of the data. In the early days of the Web, most Web sites were dominated by text and image resources. Web caching arose as a way to reduce the overhead of delivering popular resources to requesting clients. In recent years, audio and video content have become very popular, especially for users with high-bandwidth connections to the Internet. An audio or video stream consists of a sequence of sounds or images spanning a period of time. Like traditional text and image data, multimedia data can be stored as a file on a server and delivered in its entirety to requesting clients. This approach is common for transferring copies of movies or songs for future playback. However, many multimedia applications, such as video-on-demand and teleconferencing, allow the user to watch or listen to the stream of data as it arrives. Overlapping the playout of the data at the receiver with the transmission by the sender is referred to as multimedia *streaming*. Multimedia streaming applications impose strict performance requirements on the delivery of the data.

This chapter focuses on the protocols for delivering multimedia streams. First, we present an introduction to the unique characteristics of audio and video data and an overview of popular multimedia streaming applications. Drawing on this discussion, we describe the challenges of delivering multimedia content over the Internet. Although the Hypertext Transfer Protocol (HTTP) can be used to transfer multimedia content, most audio and video transfers are simply initiated via HTTP. The browser invokes a helper application (a media player) that communicates with a multimedia server using different protocols that are better suited to delivering audio and video streams. Next we survey the suite of Internet protocols that support a wide range of applications, such as multimedia-on-demand, teleconferencing, multiplayer games, and television distribution.

The rest of the chapter covers protocol support for multimedia-on-demand applications in greater detail. On-demand streaming of prerecorded audio and video content follows the same client-server model as the Web. These applications typically use the Real Time Streaming Protocol (RTSP) as an alternative

Table 12.1. Hierarchy of multimedia content

Term	Definition
Pixel	Picture element
Frame	Two-dimensional grid of pixels
Stream	Sequence of frames over time
Session	Synchronized set of streams
Presentation	Set of multimedia sessions

to HTTP. Defined in RFC 2326 [SRL98], RTSP coordinates the delivery of multimedia streams from a media server to the requesting client. The syntax and semantics of RTSP draw heavily on HTTP/1.1. We discuss the similarities between the two protocols to illustrate the generality of many of the concepts embedded in HTTP/1.1. In addition, we examine the differences between the two protocols to highlight the unique communication requirements of multimedia streaming applications. The discussion of RTSP also illustrates how the various multimedia protocols work together to deliver multimedia streams.

12.1 Multimedia Streaming

Multimedia streams differ from traditional Web resources in terms of the format of the data and the performance requirements for the delivery of the data. In this section, we present a brief introduction to the representation of audio and video content. Next we provide an overview of the diverse multimedia streaming applications that are popular on the Internet. Then we identify the common requirements that these applications impose on the delivery of multimedia streams. More detailed overviews of multimedia streaming are available in several books [CHW99, SR00].

12.1.1 Audio and video data

Compared with traditional Web content, multimedia streaming applications introduce complex relationships within and between streams. For example, a video *stream* consists of a sequence of images, or *frames,* which, in turn, each consist of a grid of *pixels,* as summarized in Table 12.1. Each pixel, or picture element, corresponds to a small square region of the image. The size of the image is expressed in terms of the number of pixels in each dimension. A 640 × 480 image has a width of 640 pixels and a height of 480 pixels. The color or intensity of each pixel is represented by a number. For example, true color uses 24 bits for each pixel, devoting 8 bits to express the intensity of each of the three primary colors—red, blue, and green—that can be perceived by the human eye. Representing every pixel in an image would require a large number of bits—a

640×480 image at 24 bits/pixel would require more than 7 Mb (i.e., $640 \cdot 480 \cdot 24$). Fortunately, an image can be compressed by capitalizing on redundancy in the picture, such as large regions with a single color. Compressed image formats, such as GIF and JPEG files, are very common on the Web.

Each frame in a video stream corresponds to a sample of the moving picture captured at a particular instant of time. Similarly, an audio stream consists of a sequence of audio samples. A media stream proceeds through the following stages before it is displayed to a recipient:

- **Capturing:** The audio or video stream must be captured from an analog device, such as a microphone or a video camera, and converted to a digital form.
- **Encoding:** An encoder converts the raw digital data into a particular audio or video format. The frames may be encoded as they are captured, rather than waiting until the entire stream has been captured.
- **Storing:** A server may store the encoded stream for future transmission.
- **Delivering:** The stream is transmitted to one or more recipients. A live stream may be transmitted as it is captured and encoded, whereas a prerecorded stream is transmitted by a server.
- **Decoding:** The receiver decodes and displays the data as they arrive. Alternatively, the receiver may store the entire stream before initiating playback.

The receiver plays the samples or frames in a manner that preserves their temporal spacing. To display a video stream that was encoded at 30 frames per second, the media player would show a new frame every 1/30th of a second. Video streams typically involve a large amount of data. Displaying thirty 640×480 images per second would require a bandwidth of 210 Mb/sec. Like image and text data, multimedia streams can be compressed. In fact, audio and video data introduce an additional opportunity for compression—exploiting redundancy across the sequence of samples or frames. Some video compression schemes generate small frames that represent the difference between successive images. Video compression schemes can also exploit regularity of the motion of objects in the picture from one frame to the next. Effective compression techniques can reduce the size of a video stream by a factor of 25 or 100. Video formats in the Web include RealVideo, AVI (Audio Video Interleave), QuickTime, and MPEG (Moving Pictures Expert Group) [AS98]. Common audio formats include RealAudio, AU (Audio), WAV (Waveform Audio), and MP3 (MPEG Audio Layer 3).

The encoding of audio and video streams introduces a fundamental trade-off between the amount of data and the quality as perceived by the user. This trade-off does not exist for traditional text content. The video streams available on the Web today typically have poor quality in many respects as follows:

- **Low frame rate:** A video stream with a low frame rate results in very abrupt motion. Frame rates below 24 or 30 frames/sec are distracting to the human eye. However, many Internet multimedia streams use lower frame rates, in the range of 10 to 15 frames/sec.
- **Small dimensions:** Most video streams available on the Web have small dimensions, typically a few inches high and wide.
- **Poor resolution:** The individual frames may have poor quality because of a coarse-grain representation of the pixels or aggressive compression of the data.

Each of these compromises in quality results in a reduction in the number of bits in the video stream. Similar compression techniques can be applied to audio data. However, in practice, humans are much more sensitive to degradation in the quality of audio content. In addition, audio streams require much less bandwidth than video streams, making it less critical to reduce the size in exchange for a drop in quality.

Many multimedia applications involve more than one stream. For example, a single multimedia *session* might consist of an audio stream and a video stream. Although the two streams may employ different encoding and compression techniques, they are linked by a common notion of time. The playback of the audio and the video streams must be coordinated to preserve the temporal properties that existed at the source. That is, the media player must play each stream at the appropriate rate, and the sound and images should be synchronized with each other. Finally, a single multimedia *presentation* may consist of multiple sessions over time and on different parts of the screen. Consider a university professor lecturing to a remote audience over the Internet. The presentation may include the video and audio of the speaker, an image of the current transparency, and a video of the audience in the other location.

12.1.2 Multimedia streaming applications

A wide range of multimedia applications play, or display, audio and video data as they arrive. Although many of these applications exist separately from the Web, the Web browser provides a common interface for invoking these applications. The desire to support a diverse collection of multimedia applications has had a direct influence on the design of the protocols for delivering multimedia streams. Popular classes of multimedia applications include the following:

- **Multimedia on demand:** In multimedia-on-demand applications, a client issues a request to a server to stream multimedia content for immediate playback. For example, the client may request a movie clip, a news story, or a song and play the data as they arrive. Multimedia-on-demand applications follow the same client-server model as traditional Web browsing.

In fact, a user may trigger a request for a multimedia session by clicking on a hypertext link on a Web page.

- **Internet telephony:** In "IP telephony" or "Voice over IP," users talk to each other in real time. The main motivations for IP telephony are the low cost of transferring audio data over the Internet and the possibility of integrating telephony with other IP applications. As in the traditional telephone network, one party initiates the call with the other. Once the call has been established, audio data flows in both directions. Each participant runs an application that can encode and decode audio data and interact with the network. Users may talk and listen via their computers or regular telephone handsets.

- **Teleconferencing:** Closely related to IP telephony, teleconferencing applications involve a group of people participating in a meeting. The simplest teleconference involves a collection of users exchanging audio, and perhaps video, data in real time. The application may also include support for a shared workspace, such as an online whiteboard, as well as floor-control functions for coordinating which participant should speak next. IP teleconferencing applications, such as CU-SeeMe [Dor95] and the vic/vat tools used on the MBone [Eri94], predate the emergence of the Web.

- **Radio/television:** Radio and television applications enable a user to tune in to a particular station or program. Multiple users around the world may watch the program at the same time. Just as IP telephony supplants the traditional telephone network, Internet radio and television applications circumvent the traditional radio and TV distribution networks. The Internet enables content providers to reach a large, global audience at a relatively low cost and without restrictions on broadcast frequencies.

- **Multiplayer games:** Gaming applications enable a distributed collection of users to participate in a single multiplayer game. Gaming applications typically allow users to join and leave the game over time and may present the users with customized views of their locations in the game. For example, a user may navigate around a playing field and encounter other players within a certain distance of the current location.

- **Virtual reality:** Similar to gaming applications, virtual reality allows a user to navigate through a simulated environment. For example, the user could take a simulated walk through a neighborhood, including a three-dimensional view of the various buildings on the route. User actions, such as turning to the left or moving forward, change the view seen by the user. Some virtual reality applications have multiple users navigating in the same environment.

The protocols for delivering multimedia streams try to accommodate the common requirements of these applications and also support new services that combine aspects of multiple classes of applications. For example, a user might initiate the playback of a prerecorded video stream into an ongoing video tele-conference.

12.1.3 Properties of multimedia applications

Multimedia applications have certain characteristics that have important im-plications for the transfer of multimedia data across the Internet.

Start-up delay   Once the receiver starts playing a multimedia stream, the successive frames should arrive in a timely manner. However, transferring the stream across the network introduces latency that may vary from one packet or frame to the next. The receiver typically introduces a small delay before playing the first frame to avoid disrupting the playback of the stream if subsequent frames experience higher latency. The player must allocate a small amount of buffer space to store the incoming data. Multimedia applications differ widely in how much start-up delay they are willing to introduce. For some applications, the media player may wait for several frames to arrive before initiating playback. A user may not mind waiting a few seconds before watching a prerecorded video stream or a live sporting event. In some cases, the user may be willing to wait several hours for a video clip, allowing the server to transmit the data at a much lower rate. Other applications, such as telephone calls and distributed games, cannot tolerate long delays. A delay of more than a few hundred milliseconds is extremely disruptive for such interactive applications. Willingness to tolerate delay may depend on the user. Users actively participating in a teleconference cannot tolerate long delays, whereas users simply listening to the teleconference could tolerate a delay of several seconds in exchange for higher quality or lower cost.

Content generation   Live streams are encoded and transmitted as they are generated. In contrast, a prerecorded stream is captured and encoded before transmission. Aggressive compression of the stream is possible for prerecorded streams because the data are available in advance of transmission. Prerecorded streams also give the server more flexibility in transmitting data to the client. The server may support Video Cassette Recorder (VCR) functions, such as pause, rewind, and fast-forward, to allow users to browse through the prere-corded data. Some applications have a mixture of live and prerecorded content. A television station that broadcasts a sporting event may also record the stream to play again later. Similarly, in the midst of watching a live event, a user may decide to record the remainder of the stream. In addition, prerecorded content, such as a television commercial, may be introduced into a live stream.

Number of receivers   Multimedia applications vary in the number of re-ceivers. In the simplest case, a user visits a Web site and requests a prerecorded multimedia session. The multimedia server transmits the requested audio and video streams to the single user. Other applications involve bidirectional communication. For example, most telephone calls involve two participants, though each direction of the call has a single recipient. In contrast, a videocast of a live sporting event or a prerecorded television show may involve hundreds or even thousands of recipients. Transmitting a multimedia stream to multiple receivers can introduce substantial overhead on the sender and the network. *Multicast* communication allows the sender to transmit a single copy of the stream to multiple receivers. Recipients receive the data by subscribing to a multicast group, identified by its IP address; the network ensures that each recipient receives a copy of the data. A portion of the IP address space is allocated to these multicast groups, as discussed in Chapter 5 (Section 5.1.3).

Session establishment   Multimedia applications vary in how the user initiates reception of the streams. In a multimedia-on-demand application, the user may trigger a request for a session by clicking on a hypertext link; the server satisfies the request by initiating the transmission of the requested stream(s). In an IP telephony application, the user may receive a message that signals the establishment of communication between the two hosts. At some point, before receiving the signaling message, the user must express willingness to receive such messages. The party initiating the call must have a way to locate the intended recipient and exchange signaling messages. In contrast, a television broadcasting application may announce the existence of a multicast group associated with the session. This provides the necessary information for users to join the multicast group to receive the transmission at the appropriate time.

12.2 Delivering Multimedia Content

In contrast to the handling of traditional text and image data, multimedia streaming imposes strict timing constraints on the delivery of data to the receiver. This section examines the unique performance requirements of multimedia streaming applications. Then we discuss why it is difficult to satisfy these requirements in traditional IP networks. Lastly, we consider the limitations of using HTTP as the application-layer protocol for streaming applications.

12.2.1 Performance requirements

The delivery of multimedia streams has different performance requirements than the transfer of text and image content.

Delay   Web users experience latency in downloading text and image content. In some cases, the Web browser displays text and image data as they arrive, showing more of the text and a higher-quality version of the image over time. Although frustrating to users, this delay does not affect the quality of the content once it has been received in its entirety. Delays on the order of a few tens or hundreds of milliseconds do not have a significant impact on the user. This is not the case for multimedia streaming. Once the playback of an audio or video stream begins, the successive audio samples or frames must arrive in a timely manner. Otherwise, the media player must compensate for the missing data. For example, the player might have to pause playout (awaiting the arrival of the next frame) or replay the previous frame. Either approach is disruptive to the user. Latency for audio streams causes even more performance degradation. The media player typically buffers a handful of frames before initiating playback of the stream in order to tolerate longer delays in receiving the subsequent frames.

Loss HTTP request and response messages are transmitted in their entirety, unless the transfer is aborted. HTTP assumes that messages are delivered via a reliable transport protocol, such as the Transmission Control Protocol (TCP). Reliable delivery is not an appropriate goal for many multimedia applications, because retransmitting a lost packet may introduce too much delay in delivering the data. A retransmitted packet is of limited use if it arrives after the media player has displayed the associated frame. In addition, the media player would not be able to receive subsequent data from the underlying socket buffer until the lost packet has been successfully retransmitted. The User Datagram Protocol (UDP) is often used as an alternative to TCP for the transport of multimedia streams. Many multimedia applications can tolerate the loss of a small amount of data. For example, a video player may be able to correct for a missing portion of a frame based on nearby pixels in the same frame, or the same set of pixels in the previous and subsequent frames. However, because lost or delayed packets degrade the quality of the stream, some applications still include limited support for recovery from lost data. This is typically achieved through selective retransmission of lost packets by the sender or the transmission of some redundant data to aid the receiver in recovering from lost information.

Throughput Most Web responses are small, with an average size of 8 to 12 KB. In contrast, audio and video streams are usually quite large. Streaming audio and video data requires high, sustained throughput. For example, uncompressed telephone-quality speech requires 64 Kb/sec; effective compression techniques can reduce the throughput requirements to around 10 Kb/sec. The bandwidth requirements for video streams vary widely, depending on the quality, frame rate, and image size. High-quality, compressed video requires as much as 4 to 6 Mb/sec, resulting in about 200 MB of data for a five-minute stream. Although brief periods of low throughput are acceptable for traditional Web content, the stringent delay requirements of multimedia streams make it difficult to tolerate variations in throughput. For prerecorded streams, the server may be able to send extra data during periods of high network throughput to tolerate periods of lower throughput in the future. For live streams, the sender has limited ability to exploit periods of high throughput.

12.2.2 Limitations of IP networks

The Internet was not designed with multimedia applications in mind. The combination of IP and TCP provide a best-effort, reliable, congestion-controlled transport model that is well-suited to most Internet applications. These very characteristics are problematic for multimedia streaming:

Quality of service IP provides a best-effort, connectionless service, where packets may be lost, delayed, or delivered out of order, as discussed in Chapter 5 (Section 5.1.2). Multimedia applications can tolerate minor variations in the delay, loss, and throughput properties of the underlying network. However, wide fluctuations in network performance cause significant degradation in the playback quality at the receiver. Providing better, and more predictable, communication performance requires changes to the network infrastructure or the deployment of additional capacity. Router vendors and network providers have begun to support basic differentiation of traffic on the Internet. This has the potential to improve the delay, throughput, and loss properties of the network.

Congestion control The growing popularity of multimedia applications has raised concerns about the demands imposed on the Internet infrastructure. Multimedia streams require sustained throughput over a period of time. In addition, a single stream may be transmitted to multiple recipients, by using IP multicast or by performing multiple unicast transfers. This further increases the load on the network. Multimedia applications typically use UDP as the underlying transport protocol. A UDP sender does not necessarily react to network congestion by decreasing the transmission rate. As a result, UDP transfers can overload network links and deny bandwidth to well-behaved TCP connections. This degrades the performance of TCP-based applications, such as Web transfers using HTTP. In recent years, there has been a considerable effort to develop approaches for *TCP-friendly* congestion control [FF99] for UDP traffic, including multicast transfers. The goal of TCP-friendly congestion control is to ensure that multimedia streams share network bandwidth fairly with other Internet traffic, without forcing multimedia applications to use TCP as their transport protocol.

Multicast In contrast to traditional Internet applications, many multimedia applications transmit the same data to multiple recipients. Supporting multicast in IP routers offers the potential for a significant reduction in the overhead on the sender and the network. Network support for multicast has been an active and challenging area of research for many years. Although many router products include support for multicast communication, IP multicast has not been widely deployed in operational networks. Application-level multicast is a popular alternative that provides efficient distribution to multiple receivers without requiring the routers to support multicast. Under application-level multicast, the sender performs unicast transfers to a small collection of proxies. Each proxy, in turn, may send the data to other proxies. Some of the proxies transmit data to the end hosts interested in receiving the stream. These proxies effectively form an *overlay* network built on top of the IP network. The Multicast Backbone (MBone) is an early example of an overlay network used for video conferencing. In recent years, application-level multicast has been proposed as a general solution for distributing multimedia content to a collection of recipients. In addition to relaying data, the proxies can perform a variety of other functions, such as caching or content adaptation.

12.2.3 Multimedia-on-demand over HTTP

Initially, the Web treated multimedia streams in the same way as traditional text and image content. A client would send an HTTP request to a Web server, and the server would transmit the requested resource to the client. The `Content-Type` header in the HTTP response message would indicate the encoding format (e.g., `Content-Type: video/mpeg`). Based on the `Content-Type`, the browser would invoke the appropriate helper application to interpret the response, as discussed earlier, in Chapter 2 (Section 2.4.3). For audio and video data, the helper application is typically a media player that decodes and displays the response. The player may also provide a graphical interface with control knobs for adjusting the volume and performing VCR functions such as pause, fast-forward, and rewind. From the browser's point of view, the media player is no different from any other helper application—the browser simply directs the data to the helper.

Handling multimedia content in the same way as text and image data has several advantages. All of the data can be stored at a Web server and accessed using a single protocol—HTTP. In addition, multimedia content could be cached at Web proxies on the path from the server to the client. However, treating multimedia streams like traditional Web data has the following disadvantages:

- **Start-up delay at the media player:** Depending on the implementation, the browser may not invoke the media player until the entire HTTP response has been received from the server. This introduces significant start-up delay for long audio/video clips. To avoid the start-up latency, the browser must direct the data to the media player as the packets arrive.

- **Copying data between the browser and the player:** The multimedia data must be transferred from the browser to the player as they arrive from the server. Depending on the implementation, this may require copying a large amount of data between the two processes on the client machine. The player must receive the data in a timely manner to permit continuous playback.
- **Interleaving of audio and video streams:** A helper application operates on the contents of a single response message. Consider an HTTP request for a multimedia session that includes both audio and video data. The Web server must interleave the audio and video content in a single response message to enable the player to play the data as they arrive. In some cases, the audio and video data are already combined together in a single file.
- **Overhead of reliable transport:** HTTP assumes an underlying reliable transport protocol, such as TCP. Streaming multimedia data over TCP introduces inherent inefficiencies. Detecting and retransmitting lost packets translate into additional delay for displaying the multimedia content. This may disrupt the playback at the media player.
- **Difficulty of VCR functions:** Treating the media player as a helper application complicates the handling of VCR functions. The player can provide limited pause, rewind, and fast-forward functionality by accessing data that has been received from the browser. Indexing to an arbitrary point in time in an audio or video stream is more complicated. This would require the player to issue a new HTTP request for the appropriate range of the data.

HTTP is not particularly well suited for transferring streaming multimedia content; alternative approaches have evolved to address these limitations.

Instead of receiving data from the browser, the media player could interact directly with the server. This interaction does not necessarily have to use HTTP. The player could interact with a multimedia server using a protocol that is more suitable for multimedia streaming. In parallel with the development of standard protocols, vendors implemented their own approaches for coordination between the player and the server. Typically, HTTP is used to initiate the multimedia transfer. In reply to the HTTP request, the server returns a small response containing metadata about the multimedia stream. For example, the HTTP response body may include a URL-like string with the name of the multimedia server and the desired content (e.g., `pnm://media.foo.com/clip`). The browser invokes a helper application that handles the response by establishing its own communication with the multimedia server.

The media player must understand the format of the metadata in the HTTP response body. In addition, the player must know how to communicate with the multimedia server. Early multimedia streaming companies, such as

RealNetworks, developed and sold multimedia servers and provided the media player to interested users free of charge. Controlling both the server and the player enabled the use of vendor-specific protocols for communicating between the player and the server and for representing the metadata in the HTTP response body. The development and deployment of standard protocols are necessary steps in decoupling the metadata, the player, and the multimedia server. Initial variants of the standard protocols have been implemented in some media players and servers.

12.3 Protocols for Multimedia Streaming

Multimedia streaming has unique requirements that are not addressed by HTTP. In this section, we discuss the suite of protocols designed to address these requirements, as follows:

- **Data transport:** Multimedia streaming requires the ability to deliver data with timing properties to one or more receivers. Transport of a stream is handled by two closely related protocols. The Real-time Transport Protocol (RTP) divides the stream into packets that each include a timestamp, a sequence number, and information about the sender [SCFJ96]. The RTP specification also defines the RTP Control Protocol (RTCP) that provides feedback about the quality of the transmission and the identity of the participants in the stream.
- **Session establishment:** Multimedia streaming requires a way for senders and receivers to express their interest in participating in a multimedia session. The appropriate protocol depends on the application. The Session Initiation Protocol (SIP) is used to invite a user to join a session [SSR99]. The Session Announcement Protocol (SAP) is used to advertise a multicast group that clients may join [HPW00]. The Real Time Streaming Protocol (RTSP) allows the client to send a request message to a multimedia server [SRL98].
- **Session description:** The participants in a session need to receive metadata such as the transport and encoding parameters of the constituent streams, the time duration, and the name and purpose of the session. This information is conveyed by the Session Description Protocol (SDP) [HJ98].
- **Presentation description:** The creation of multimedia documents requires an effective way to orchestrate the playback of sessions over time. As an alternative to HTML, the Synchronized Multimedia Integration Language (SMIL) provides control over when, where, and how the multimedia sessions are displayed [Syn98, Hos00, Smi].

RTP, RTCP, SIP, SAP, RTSP, and SDP are defined in Request for Comments documents produced by the Internet Engineering Task Force (IETF), whereas the World Wide Web Consortium (W3C) is responsible for the specification of SMIL.

12.3.1 Data transport

RTP and RTCP coordinate the delivery of a multimedia stream to one or more receivers. RTP [SCFJ96, Tho96] satisfies the basic requirements for the transport of multimedia streams for a variety of applications, such as multimedia-on-demand, IP telephony, and teleconferencing. The data in an RTP packet is associated with a particular audio sample or video frame in a stream; a single sample or frame may be spread across multiple RTP packets. The RTP header aids the receiver in interpreting the data.

Timing   The receiver needs timing information to coordinate the playback of the stream. The spacing of frames can be determined from the RTP header without requiring the sender and the receiver to synchronize their clocks. The RTP header includes a 32-bit timestamp field that represents the instance in time when the first byte of the data was sampled. All packets from the same audio sample or video frame have the same timestamp value. The first RTP packet in a stream has a random timestamp, similar to the random initial sequence number for the first packet of a TCP transfer. The timestamp increases linearly across the sequence of samples or frames in the stream. This enables the receiver to play the data with the appropriate spacing between successive samples or frames.

Sequencing   RTP does not include mechanisms for reliable delivery or flow control. The delivery of RTP packets depends on the underlying transport protocol. RTP does not assume that the underlying transport protocol provides an ordered, reliable byte stream, because retransmission of lost packets is not desirable for many multimedia applications. In fact, RTP typically runs over UDP, with each RTP packet transferred in a single UDP packet. As an alternative, TCP can be used to provide reliable transport or to transmit a stream across a firewall that discards UDP packets. However, IP packets may be lost or arrive out of order, and UDP does not perform any retransmitting or re-ordering of packets. The RTP header includes a sequence number to enable the receiver to process the incoming packets in the correct order and to determine when packets have been lost. The receiver can maintain packet-loss statistics to provide feedback to the sender. These statistics may trigger the sender to adjust its transmission rate.

Source identification   In addition to timing and sequencing information, the RTP header identifies the source(s) responsible for the data in the packet. This is particularly useful for applications that may have multiple sources transmitting data (e.g., teleconferencing). Each source is identified by a 32-bit number. Each RTP packet has a single *synchronizing source* responsible for defining the timestamp and sequence number for the data. In some situations, the synchronizing source generates the data with the help of one or more *contributing sources*. Consider a teleconferencing application with multiple participants. Each participant generates an audio stream and directs the RTP packets to an intermediate system, a *mixer*. The mixer combines the packets from the various participants and generates a single audio stream. The mixer is the synchronizing source for the new stream. The original participants are the contributing sources. As part of combining the separate audio streams, the mixer generates the list of contributing sources from the synchronizing sources of the constituent streams. By including the identifiers of the contributing sources in the RTP header, the mixer informs the recipients about all of the parties responsible for the combined stream.

Media format   The interpretation of the RTP data at the receiver depends on the encoding format. The RTP header includes a 7-bit payload-type field to identify the format of the multimedia data. The payload type is associated with the name and description of the encoding, including the frequency of the timestamp clock. The payload format defines the syntax and semantics of the RTP data, including media-specific headers. An initial set of payload types is defined in RFC 1890 [Sch96]. New encodings and their payload types are registered with the Internet Assigned Numbers Authority (IANA). The details of each payload type are described in archival documents, such as RFCs, to aid developers in supporting the encoding scheme. Payload types have also been defined for generic multimedia services, such as RTP mixers and redundant audio codings that are resilient to packet loss. For flexibility and extensibility, RTP also supports the use of dynamic payload types that have not been registered with IANA.

Although RTP provides most of the information necessary to transmit multimedia data from a sender to one or more receivers, some additional control information is sometimes necessary. Defined in the same RFC as RTP [SCFJ96], RTCP performs the following three functions:

- **Feedback:** RTCP provides feedback about the reception quality (e.g., packet-loss statistics) of the RTP packets at the receiver. This aids the RTP sender in detecting performance problems and adapting the transmission rate accordingly.
- **Identification:** RTCP associates each source identifier from the RTP packets with a unique canonical name. This allows the receiver to associate a collection of streams, possibly with different 32-bit source identifiers, with a single sender.

- **Synchronization:** RTCP associates a real wall-clock time with the time-stamps in the RTP packets. This enables the receiver to synchronize the playback of a collection of streams, such as audio and video, that belong to same session.

12.3.2 Session establishment

Senders and receivers must have a way of expressing their interest in participating in a particular multimedia session. The details of establishing communication between two or more parties varies depending on the type of application, as discussed earlier in Section 12.1.3. This has resulted in several different protocols, as follows:

- **Session Initiation Protocol (SIP):** SIP [SSR99, SR99] supports applications such as IP telephony, in which the recipient receives a personal invitation to participate in a session. The party initiating the session can use SIP to locate one or more users and invite them to join a session. SIP performs five basic functions: (1) deciding which host to contact, (2) identifying which media parameters to use, (3) determining whether the user is willing to receive calls, (4) establishing the connection to the user, and (5) handling the transfer and termination of the call.

- **Session Announcement Protocol (SAP):** SAP [HPW00] supports applications such as Internet radio, in which the identity of the intended participants is not known in advance. Rather than having the senders contact the receivers, interested users send a request to join the multicast group associated with the session. However, a user may not know which multicast group corresponds to a particular multimedia session. A SAP announcer periodically sends an announcement packet, containing a description of the session, to a well-known multicast address and port number (9875). This is similar to having a television station that lists the television programs and channel numbers for other stations. A SAP listener receives this announcement by joining the well-known multicast group. SAP listeners may themselves act as announcers to distribute the session information to others.

- **Real Time Streaming Protocol (RTSP):** RTSP allows a user to retrieve multimedia content on demand by issuing a request to a multimedia server, similar to sending an HTTP request to a Web server. Multimedia sessions and their constituent streams are identified by URLs. The client issues RTSP requests to acquire information about the server and the multimedia session and to play, pause, record, or browse the streams. RTSP provides the abstraction of a "network remote control" for multimedia servers. RTSP typically does not deliver the data. Instead, RTSP is used to select the transport mechanism (e.g., RTP and RTCP), the underlying transport protocol (e.g., unicast UDP, multicast UDP, or TCP), and the specific port numbers (e.g., ports 6970 and 6971). The RTSP specification draws heavily on the syntax and semantics of HTTP/1.1, as discussed in more detail in Section 12.4.

12.3.3 Session description

Regardless of how a multimedia session is established, the participants need to receive a description of the session. For example, participants may need to know the name and purpose of the session, the media parameters of the underlying audio and video streams, and IP addresses and port numbers. This information is conveyed in a standard format defined by SDP [HJ98]. In reality, SDP is not a protocol but rather a language or format for conveying information about a session. Session descriptions are transferred via other protocols, such as SIP, SAP, RTSP, and HTTP. For example, an HTML file could have a hypertext link that points to an SDP file. From the user's viewpoint, clicking on the hypertext link initiates transmission of the audio and video data. In reality, the Web browser sends an HTTP request to the Web server to retrieve the session description and then invokes a media player to handle the HTTP response message (i.e., the SDP file). Then the media player parses the SDP file and contacts one or more multimedia servers to retrieve the audio and video streams.

An SDP description consists of one or more lines of ASCII text. Each line consists of a one-character *type* and a text-string *value,* separated by an equal sign. The format of the value string depends on the type. The description has one or more lines of session-level information, which may be followed by additional information about the individual streams in the session. The session-level information applies to the entire session and to each of the media streams. The session-level information includes the name and purpose of the session, expressed as text strings, such as

```
s=Web Seminar
i=What everyone needs to know about the World Wide Web
```

The session-level section may also include the name, e-mail address, and phone number of the person responsible for the session, as well as a URL with more details. In addition, the session-level section can include information about encryption keys necessary to participate in the multimedia session or receive the individual streams. The description also includes the start and finish time of the session, in Network Time Protocol (NTP) format [Mil92], and an optional indication of the bandwidth requirements.

The SDP description also includes information about each media stream, such as the media type and encoding format (e.g., video in MPEG format). In addition, SDP specifies the details of how the stream is delivered. This includes information about the transport protocol (e.g., UDP) and media framing (e.g.,

RTP). For a multicast stream, the session description includes the multicast IP address and port number. The recipient uses this information to join the appropriate multicast group. For a unicast stream, the session description contains the hostname or IP address of the data source. The recipient can issue a DNS query to convert the hostname into an IP address and then contact the remote host to establish communication. The description may also indicate the bandwidth requirement for the stream. The recipient could use the bandwidth parameter to determine whether or not to receive the stream.

12.3.4 Presentation description

The creation of multimedia content requires a standard way for authoring presentations. The Hypertext Markup Language (HTML) serves this purpose for traditional Web content. However, HTML does not have constructs for controlling the temporal properties of a multimedia presentation. Developed by the W3C, SMIL is a markup language for building time-based streaming media presentations that combine audio, video, text, and image data [Syn98, Hos00, Smi]. SMIL enables developers to specify *what* content to display (and where it is located), *where* the content should displayed on the screen, and *when* the content should be displayed. Similar to HTML, SMIL allows authors to embed hypertext links that are followed when the user clicks in the appropriate location on the screen.

The author of a SMIL file can define the layout of the screen as a collection of *regions*. Each region is a rectangle with certain dimensions and placed at a particular location on the screen. Each region is associated with media data. Consider the example of a university professor lecturing to a remote audience. The presentation could associate different regions of the screen with the video of the professor, an image of the current slide, and a video of the audience at a remote location. The three media each consume a particular portion of the screen and may be retrieved from different locations, using different protocols and encoding formats. SMIL supports embedding of hypertext links; for example, clicking on the image region in the professor's presentation could trigger an HTTP request for a Web page that displays detailed information about the topic of the current slide. More generally, a hypertext link can be associated with a specific part of a region and a portion of time.

In addition to associating media with regions of the screen, SMIL enables the author to specify the timing properties of the presentation. The SMIL file can indicate when to start playing a stream and what portion of the stream to play. SMIL includes constructs for synchronizing different streams or sessions. Separate streams may be played in sequence, with the playback of one stream starting after the previous stream has completed. Alternatively, several streams may be played at the same time. The player handles the details of determining when all of the parallel streams have completed and when the next stream in a sequence can be played. The parallel and sequential approaches may be combined to allow one long stream to be played in parallel with a sequence of shorter streams.

Authoring multimedia content is complicated by the fact that the clients may vary widely in terms of bandwidth, screen size, player capabilities, and user preferences. For example, one user may have a 21-inch, high-resolution monitor and a high-bandwidth Internet connection. Another user may have a palm-top device with a wireless link. A user with a hearing disability may prefer to receive a text transcript of a speech rather than the audio stream. A SMIL file can specify a range of different presentation options, corresponding to different media streams. The media player determines which streams to retrieve and how they should be displayed. This is a convenient alternative to requiring the client to negotiate with the server to determine the appropriate parameters for the streams. The SMIL file can also specify a range of presentation options for a particular region that specify how a user can interact with the presentation. For example, the region may support zooming in and out on an image.

12.4 Real Time Streaming Protocol

The Real Time Streaming Protocol (RTSP) enables a client to request live or prerecorded streams from multimedia servers, similar to the way HTTP enables clients to issue requests to Web servers. In fact, RTSP borrows much of its syntax and semantics from HTTP/1.1 because, on the surface, the two protocols perform similar functions. The similarities highlight the generality of many of the concepts embedded in HTTP/1.1. However, the protocols have several key differences that illustrate the unique requirements of multimedia streams and the limitations of HTTP/1.1 for transferring multimedia data. In this section, we compare and contrast RTSP and HTTP. Then we describe the RTSP request methods, response codes, and headers in comparison with and in contrast to HTTP/1.1. This discussion draws on the overview of HTTP/1.1 syntax in Chapter 7 (Section 7.2).

12.4.1 Similarities and differences

The RTSP specification has significant overlap with the HTTP/1.1 specification. At a high level, the two protocols have a similar goal—to allow a client to request content from a server based on a Request-URI. Historically, the design of RTSP began after the initial work on the specification of HTTP. Basing RTSP on HTTP exploits the many commonalities between the goals of these two protocols. Streaming of multimedia content follows the same basic model as HTTP—resources identified by URIs, a request-response protocol, and the possibility of one or more intermediaries along the path between the client and the server. The protocols have comparable requirements for security and for proxies, two areas that required substantial design effort in the development of HTTP/1.1. Reusing these concepts, including specific protocol headers and response codes, reduces the overhead of designing and implementing RTSP. In addition, both protocols play a role in Web-initiated transfers of multimedia streams. The similarities between the two protocols provide significant flexibility in deciding which protocol should handle any particular function.

Either protocol could conceivably handle the entire task of retrieving a description of the multimedia session and requesting the multimedia data. Although HTTP may not be the best protocol for all of these steps, HTTP may be used to transfer the session description. In response to a user click on a hypertext link, the browser may issue an HTTP request for session description information (e.g., `http://www.foo.com/bar.sdp`). The Web server's response would include the session description information in SDP format, as follows:

```
HTTP/1.1 200 OK
Content-Type: application/sdp

v=0
o=- 2890844526 2890842807 IN IP4 192.16.24.202
s=RTSP Session
m=audio 0 RTP/AVP 0
a=control:rtsp://foo.com/bar/audio
m=video 0 RTP/AVP 31
a=control:rtsp://foo.com/bar/video
```

At this point, the Web browser could invoke a media player to perform the remaining steps, as discussed in Section 12.3.3. In addition, the media player may provide an interface for the user to select multimedia sessions. In this case, the media player may interact directly with the RTSP server to retrieve session descriptions without involving the Web browser.

Despite the many similarities between the two protocols, RTSP differs from HTTP in several key ways.

Separate control and data connections In contrast to HTTP, an RTSP server relegates the transfer of data to a separate connection. In this sense, RTSP more closely resembles FTP. The client and server exchange RTSP messages on the control connection. Other protocols, such as RTP and RTCP, handle the task of transferring the data. This separation permits the client and server to continue exchanging RTSP messages during the data transfer, in order to adapt the ongoing transmission or to initiate additional transfers. In addition, the control and data transfers may use different underlying transport protocols. RTSP messages typically travel over a TCP connection, although

UDP may be used. RTP and RTCP packets are typically exchanged over UDP, although TCP may be used as well.

Different format for Request-URIs   Port 554 has been reserved for RTSP. The choice of UDP or TCP can be specified in the scheme portion of the Request-URI. The schemes `rtsp` and `rtspu` correspond to TCP and UDP, respectively. For example, `rtsp://foo.com/bar` identifies a session that should be requested and controlled using RTSP over a TCP connection. In contrast, `rtspu://foo.com/bar` indicates that the client should issue the RTSP request over UDP. The RTSP Request-URI may refer to an entire session or an individual media stream. The request line of an RTSP request must include the absolute path of the URI, including the hostname. This avoids ambiguity about which RTSP server should receive the request. In contrast, HTTP/1.1 has a separate `Host` header for this purpose to retain backward compatibility with HTTP/1.0, as discussed earlier, in Chapter 7 (Section 7.8).

Stateful protocol   In contrast to HTTP, an RTSP server retains state across successive requests. A client may send multiple RTSP messages with regard to a single session or stream. This is required because a client may perform a variety of VCR functions, such as play, pause, fast-forward, and rewind, over a single session. The server must be able to interpret these requests in the context of the associated stream. To satisfy certain requests, the server may also have to retain information about the ongoing transmission of the stream. Consider a client request to pause the stream, followed by a play request. The server must continue the transmission at the appropriate point in the stream. Having a stateful protocol is also useful for transmitting and receiving content that consumes significant disk and network resources. Under RTSP, the client must issue a request for the server to allocate system resources for the multimedia session. This enables the server to determine whether sufficient system resources are available in advance.

Different methods, headers, and status codes   RTSP has a different set of request methods than HTTP, including methods used by the *server* to transmit request messages to the client. RTSP adopts many of the HTTP/1.1 response codes, although additional codes are defined to indicate various error conditions that do not arise in HTTP. Many of the HTTP headers have been adopted by RTSP, with several important additions and deletions. For the most part, the headers that were not adopted reflect the fact that RTSP does not transmit the actual multimedia data. Most RTSP response messages do not include an entity, except to convey session description information. The new headers defined for RTSP relate primarily to (1) the timing properties of the media streams, (2) the existence of separate protocols for data transfer, and

Table 12.2. RTSP request methods

Direction	Method	Description
Client to server	SETUP	Allocate system resources for stream
	PLAY	Start data transmission for stream
	TEARDOWN	Free resources associated with stream
	DESCRIBE	Return a session description
	PAUSE	Temporarily halt stream transmission
	RECORD	Start recording a stream
Bidirectional	OPTIONS	Return list of supported methods
	ANNOUNCE	Register a presentation description
	GET_PARAMETER	Retrieve value of named parameter
	SET_PARAMETER	Assign value of named parameter
Server to client	REDIRECT	Direct client to another server

(3) the allocation of state at the client or the server. These issues relate to the key differences between RTSP and HTTP, which stem from the unique requirements of multimedia data.

12.4.2 RTSP request methods

RTSP servers must support the four key methods used by clients to retrieve multimedia sessions—OPTIONS, SETUP, PLAY, and TEARDOWN. At a high level, the OPTIONS header enables the client to determine the capabilities of the server, such as the RTSP version number and supported methods; this method has the same behavior as the HTTP/1.1 OPTIONS method. The remaining three methods manipulate state at the server to coordinate the transfer of the multimedia data. The client uses the SETUP method to establish a transport connection for each stream in the session. The PLAY method is used to initiate transmission of the stream(s). The TEARDOWN method is used to terminate the transmission. These four methods are summarized in Table 12.2, along with the other RTSP methods.

In contrast to HTTP, an RTSP server allocates state in response to client requests. In addition to the SETUP, PLAY, and TEARDOWN requests, the RECORD and PAUSE methods also affect the state of a session. The RECORD method requests that the RTSP server receive and store a stream at the Request-URI for future playback. The PAUSE method temporarily halts a transmission without releasing the system resources at the server. A subsequent PLAY (or RECORD) request triggers the server to continue transmitting (or recording) the stream. Both the client and the server maintain state on behalf of each stream. The PLAY, RECORD, PAUSE, and TEARDOWN methods can be applied to an individual

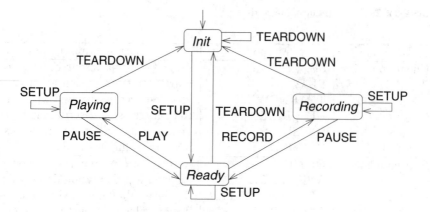

Figure 12.1. RTSP state machine for clients and servers

stream or to an entire session, depending on whether the URI in the RTSP request corresponds to the stream or session, respectively. A request method applied to a session affects each of the constituent streams. The SETUP method applies only to an individual stream.

The client and server state machines are summarized in Figure 12.1. The server changes state as part of processing the request method; the client changes state after receiving the response from the server. The SETUP method triggers a transition from the initial, *Init,* state to the *Ready* state. The TEARDOWN method returns the client and the server to the *Init* state. The PLAY and RECORD methods initiate *Playing* and *Recording,* respectively, and the PAUSE method causes a transition back to the *Ready* state. Data transmission occurs only in the *Playing* and *Recording* states. While in one of these two states, the client may initiate a SETUP request to change the transport parameters for the stream. The server continues streaming the multimedia data, perhaps using a different transport protocol or different set of ports.

The remaining RTSP methods do not affect the RTSP state machines at the client and the server and thus do not appear in Figure 12.1. For example, a client can issue an OPTIONS request to learn the server's capabilities without affecting ongoing transmissions. Likewise, the client can send a DESCRIBE request at any time to receive description information about a session or stream. RTSP also includes an ANNOUNCE method that allows the server to send a new description to the client. Consider a server hosting a live session that initially consists of a single audio stream. Suppose that a video stream becomes available. The server may send an ANNOUNCE request containing an updated session description to the clients listening to the ongoing audio feed. Based on this information, a client may initiate a request for the video stream by sending a SETUP request and a subsequent PLAY request. RTSP also allows a client to send an ANNOUNCE request to the server to create a new session description to the server; this is similar to the PUT method in HTTP.

In allowing servers to send requests to clients, RTSP differs from the traditional client-server model. Although support for the server-to-client requests is not required, these methods enhance the flexibility of the server. For example, the REDIRECT method allows the server to instruct the client to connect to another server location, based on a URI. After receiving the REDIRECT request, the client must issue a TEARDOWN of the current session and issue a SETUP request to the new server. The server may have a variety of motivations for redirecting the client. The redirection may improve performance if the new server is closer to the client or has lower load. Alternatively, the new server may provide different content, such as an advertisement, that is not available at the original server. In a sense, the REDIRECT method is similar to the redirection class of response codes in HTTP/1.1. However, an RTSP server can redirect the client at any time during the transfer of the multimedia stream.

In order to issue requests, a server needs to know what methods, if any, are supported by a particular client. For this, a server may send an OPTIONS request to the client. In addition to the OPTIONS and ANNOUNCE methods, RTSP includes two other methods that can be sent by both clients and servers. The GET_PARAMETER and SET_PARAMETER methods allow the sender to learn and alter the parameters of the multimedia session or stream associated with a particular Request-URI. These two methods provide general support for reading and writing an arbitrary set of variables, depending on the client and server implementations. For example, the server could use the GET_PARAMETER method to inquire about the number of data packets received by the client for a particular stream. This provides an alternative to using RTCP for receiving feedback on the quality of data transport. Alternatively, the client could send a SET_PARAMETER request to ask the server to reduce the transmission rate. These methods provide a flexible and extensible way for the client and server to cooperate in controlling the contents of the multimedia stream.

Most of the request methods relate to supporting a client that requests the playback of a stream from the multimedia server. However, an RTSP server may also permit the recording of multimedia content by supporting the optional ANNOUNCE and RECORD methods. Consider a user who wants to record a video teleconference at the RTSP server for future playback. In this case, the client sends a description of the conference to the server in an ANNOUNCE message. Then the client would send a SETUP message for each stream in the session to inform the server of the transport parameters, such as the IP address and port numbers. The Request-URI in the SETUP message indicates the name that the client wants to associate with the recorded content. Then the client would send a RECORD request to initiate the recording of the streams. At some later time, the client could contact the server to watch the recorded conference.

12.4.3 RTSP headers

At the time RFC 2326 for RTSP was written, the reference point for HTTP/1.1 was RFC 2068 rather than the Draft Standard RFC 2616. Many of the RTSP headers are borrowed from RFC 2068. HTTP includes request, response, general, and entity headers, as discussed in Chapter 7 (Section 7.2.2). The subsequent tables in this section have an asterisk (*) to identify the headers that were borrowed from HTTP/1.1. At the end of this subsection, we discuss the HTTP/1.1 headers that were not incorporated into RTSP.

GENERAL HEADERS

General headers can appear in request and response messages. RTSP borrows four general headers from HTTP/1.1 and introduces six new general headers, as summarized in Table 12.3. The Session and CSeq headers identify a sequence of RTSP messages associated with a single session. RTSP does not depend on having a single dedicated transport-layer connection for the duration of a session. An RTSP session may span multiple TCP connections, or the client and server may communicate using UDP. Each RTSP message that affects the session state includes a session identifier—an opaque string assigned by the server. The RTSP server assigns the identifier after receiving the SETUP request and returns the value in the Session header. Subsequent request and response messages concerning this session include the Session header. The CSeq header indicates the sequence number associated with each RTSP message. The need for sequence numbers stems from two key factors that differentiate RTSP from HTTP. First, because RTSP is stateful, multiple request-response pairs may arise in the context of a single session. Second, because RTSP messages can be transferred over UDP, the protocol cannot assume reliable, ordered delivery of the messages. The sequence number is incremented by one for each distinct request; the corresponding response message bears the same sequence number. When RTSP messages travel over UDP, the client and the server are responsible for retransmitting lost UDP messages, if desired. Any retransmitted request bears the same sequence number as the original message.

The Transport header is used in the SETUP request and response messages to coordinate the selection of the transport protocol and parameters for a media stream. In the request message, the header

```
Transport: RTP/AVP/UDP;unicast;client_port=18366-18367
```

requests that the server deliver the stream using RTP over UDP with the AVP (Audio Video Profile) payload type [Sch96]; the client selects port 18366 for the RTP connection and port 18367 for the RTCP connection. In the request message, the Transport header could include several sets of transport options. The header can include a variety of other parameters, such as the destination

Table 12.3. RTSP general headers (HTTP/1.1 headers marked with '*')

Header	Description
Session	Session identifier
CSeq	Message sequence number
Transport	Negotiation of transport parameters
Range	Selection of range of time for playback
Scale	Negotiation of playback rate
Speed	Negotiation of transmission rate
Date*	Message generation date/time
Via*	List of intermediate servers
Connection*	List of hop-by-hop headers
Cache-Control*	Caching directives

address for a multicast group, the RTSP request methods supported for the session, and the data compression scheme. The Transport header in the server response message confirms the parameters chosen by the client

```
Transport: RTP/AVP/UDP;unicast;client_port=18366-18367;
           server_port=16970-16971
```

and includes the server port numbers.

The Range, Scale, and Speed headers relate to the timing properties of the multimedia streams. The Range header is used to index to a particular point within a stream. Consider a media player that allows the user to scroll to an arbitrary part of an audio clip. The user may want to skip the first 30 seconds of the clip. Rather than receiving the entire stream, the RTSP PLAY request can include a Range header to indicate the desired range of time. This is conceptually similar to the Range request header in HTTP/1.1. However, HTTP/1.1 range requests identify a subset of bytes of a resource, whereas RTSP range requests identify a subset of the time duration of a stream. For example, the client's PLAY request could include

```
Range: npt=30-
```

to request that the server start transmitting data 30 seconds into the stream (NPT refers to Normal Play Time where the beginning of the stream corresponds to 0 seconds). In practice, indexing by time is more difficult than indexing by bytes, because frame sizes may vary across the duration of the stream. The 30-second point in a 60-second stream may not correspond to the exact middle of the sequence of bytes. In addition, some frames in the stream are encoded relative to earlier and later frames, making it difficult to start playing a stream precisely at that point in time. Because the RTSP server may not be able to start transmitting data from an arbitrary point in the audio or video stream, RTSP allows the server to initiate transmission from a nearby point in time. The server indicates the chosen time range in the Range header of the response message. The RTSP specification does not provide a bound on how much the Range indicated in the response message may differ from the Range requested by the client.

The Scale and Speed headers support fast-forward and rewind functions for the PLAY and RECORD methods. Scale relates to the speed of playback at the media player, and Speed relates to speed of transmission from the server. The normal playback rate corresponds to a scale of 1. Larger positive values correspond to fast-forwarding, and smaller positive values correspond to playing the content in slow motion. A negative value indicates that the stream should be played in the reverse direction. The client conveys the desired playback rate in the Scale header. The server tries to support the desired playback rate and returns the chosen rate in the Scale header of the response message. The server adapts the transmission of the stream to avoid increasing the data rate. For example, when the client requests a fast-forward operation on a video clip, the server may deliver a subset of the frames. Although selecting a subset of the frames avoids increasing the bandwidth requirement, the fast-forwarded stream would appear choppy to the user.

The client and server can also negotiate the bandwidth used for data delivery. By default, the transmission proceeds at the bit rate of the stream. This corresponds to a speed of 1. A higher value corresponds to a faster rate, and a lower value corresponds to a slower rate. The client requests the desired transmission rate in the Speed header in the request message, and the server returns the chosen rate in the Speed header in the response message. The Speed header can be used in conjunction with the Scale header to coordinate transmission of a stream during fast-forward or rewind operations. The client can use the Speed header to express a willingness to receive the stream at a higher data rate rather than to have the server decrease the quality of the stream during the period of faster playback.

The remaining four general headers are borrowed from HTTP/1.1. The Date header indicates the time the message was generated. The Via header is used to identify the sequence of proxies in the path between the client and the origin server. The Connection header lists the hop-by-hop headers that should be removed by the next recipient in the path. The Cache-Control header is used for sending caching directives. However, the interpretation of the Cache-Control header differs in RTSP. In contrast to HTTP, most RTSP responses are not cacheable, except for the session description information returned in response to a DESCRIBE request. In RTSP, the Cache-Control directives refer to the media stream, which is transferred via a different protocol. The Cache-Control header appears only in the SETUP request and response messages that establish the transport parameters. As in HTTP/1.1, the various

Table 12.4. RTSP request headers (HTTP/1.1 headers marked with '*')

Header	Description
Bandwidth	Estimated bandwidth available to the client
Blocksize	Desired packet size for transmission of data
Conference	Identifier of conference associated with stream
Require	Query whether features are supported by server
Proxy-Require	Query whether features are supported by proxy
From*	User's e-mail address
User-Agent*	Information about user agent software
Authorization*	User agent's credentials
Referer*	URI from which Request-URI was obtained
If-Match*	Positive comparison with entity tags
If-Modified-Since*	Positive comparison with last modified time
Accept*	Preferred media types
Accept-Encoding*	Preferred content-codings
Accept-Language*	Preferred natural languages

Cache-Control directives provide several ways for a client to express freshness requirements and for the server to express cacheability of the data.

REQUEST HEADERS

RTSP borrows nine request headers from HTTP/1.1 and introduces five new request headers, as summarized in Table 12.4. The new request headers relate to timing and resource allocation. The client uses the Bandwidth header to provide an estimate of the available network resources, in bits per second. The server can use this information to select a transmission rate for delivering multimedia data to the client on the separate transport connection. Similarly, the client may use the Blocksize header to indicate the desired maximum packet size for transferring the data. The packet size does not include the lower-layer headers, such as the IP, UDP, and RTP headers. The server may select a packet size less than or equal to the size requested by the client. The Bandwidth and Blocksize headers address issues that simply do not arise in HTTP, because an HTTP server transmits an entity over an ordered, reliable byte stream at a rate controlled by the underlying transport protocol.

The Conference header establishes a logical connection between the RTSP stream and an existing conference, established by another protocol, such as SIP. From the viewpoint of the RTSP server, the conference identifier is an opaque string. Associating an RTSP server with an ongoing conference is useful for a variety of purposes. For example, suppose a client wants to play a prerecorded audio clip in the existing conference. The client can include the Conference header in the SETUP request in order to identify the associated conference. The SETUP request would also include a Transport header to convey information about the ongoing conference. For example, the transport header could indicate the IP address of the multicast group, as well as the port numbers. After receiving the response to the SETUP message, the RTSP client can issue a PLAY request to initiate the streaming of audio content from the RTSP server to the multicast group.

The Require and Proxy-Require headers provide an efficient and extensible way for the client to learn what features are supported by the server. The argument of the header is a feature tag that names the features that the client wishes to use (e.g., Require: unusual-feature). If the server does not recognize and support the feature listed in the Require header, the RTSP response returns a negative acknowledgment to the client ("Unsupported Header"). In contrast, HTTP does not have request headers for querying about features at the server. HTTP servers can safely ignore certain headers that they do not support. The Require header enables the client to issue the RTSP request before learning whether or not the server can support the required feature. The user agent uses the Proxy-Require header to indicate that the features must be supported by each of the proxies along the path as well.

RTSP incorporates several HTTP/1.1 request headers related to client identification and authorization (e.g., From, User-Agent, Authorization, and Referer), caching (e.g., If-Match and If-Modified-Since), and content negotiation (e.g., Accept, Accept-Encoding, and Accept-Language). However, RTSP does not include the full set of HTTP/1.1 headers related to caching and content negotiation. Most RTSP methods do not return an entity, because the multimedia streams are transmitted on separate transport connections. An entity is included in an ANNOUNCE request and in the response to a DESCRIBE request. The entity is a session description, which can be represented in various languages (e.g., English or Swiss-German) and content types (e.g., SDP).

RESPONSE HEADERS

RTSP borrows seven response headers from HTTP/1.1 and introduces two new response headers, as shown in Table 12.5. The RTP-Info header plays an important role in coordinating the reception of media streams. Appearing in the server's response to the PLAY request, the RTP-Info header declares the value of RTP-specific parameters. For example,

```
RTP-Info: url=rtsp://foo.com/bar/audio;seq=47;rtptime=2894,
          url=rtsp://foo.com/bar/vidio;seq=184;rtptime=6674
```

Each media stream consists of a sequence of RTP packets, with random values for the base sequence number and base timestamp, as discussed earlier, in Section 12.3.1. For an RTSP-initiated transfer, the client learns these base

Table 12.5. RTSP response headers (HTTP/1.1 headers marked with '*')

Header	Description
RTP-Info	RTP-specific parameters for PLAY request
Unsupported	Feature not supported by the server
Server*	Server identification
Location*	Location of resource
Retry-After*	Delay before retrying redirected request
Vary*	Selecting resource variant
Public*	List supported methods (Allow in HTTP/1.1)
WWW-Authenticate*	Challenge for authentication
Proxy-Authenticate*	Challenge for authentication

values from the RTP-Info header. The first RTP packet in the stream would have these base values. The sequence number and timestamp would increase over successive RTP packets.

RTSP also includes the Unsupported response header for replying to request messages with the Require and Proxy-Require headers. Required options that are not supported by the server are identified in the Unsupported header of the response message. This provides a way for the server to explain why the client's request could not be performed, beyond simply returning an error code. The response headers borrowed from HTTP/1.1 relate to server identification (Server), request redirection (Location), retrying a request Retry-After), caching (Vary), and authentication (WWW-Authenticate and Proxy-Authenticate). The Public header, used to list the options supported by the server, derives from RFC 2068 and was not included in RFC 2616. The Public header in HTTP was replaced with the Allow header, as discussed earlier, in Chapter 6 (Section 6.2.3). Allow is an entity header in HTTP/1.1.

ENTITY HEADERS

RTSP borrows nine entity headers from HTTP/1.1 and does not introduce any new entity headers, as shown in Table 12.6. Compared with HTTP, RTSP has a fairly simple notion of message entities. An RTSP message entity, when it exists, represents session description information. In RTSP, any message that contains an entity must have a Content-Length header to ensure that the recipient can identify the end of the message. HTTP/1.1 has several other ways to detect the end of a message; for example, the entity in an HTTP/1.1 message may be transfer coded or represent multipart/byteranges. RTSP does not support these features. The Content-Base header provides a base URI for resolving relative URIs within the entity body. Although Content-Base was defined in the Proposed Standard of HTTP (RFC 2068), the Draft Standard for HTTP/1.1 (RFC

Table 12.6. RTSP entity headers (HTTP/1.1 headers marked with '*')

Header	Description
Content-Length*	Length of entity body (mandatory for nonzero entities)
Content-Type*	Entity body's media type
Content-Language*	Natural language of entity
Content-Encoding*	Encodings applied to entity body
Content-Location*	Alternative location for resource
Content-Base	Base URI for resolving URIs in entity (in RFC 2068)
Expires*	Session description staleness time
Last-Modified*	Session description modification time
Allow*	Methods applicable to the resource

2616) does not include this header. The Expires and Last-Modified headers in RTSP relate to caching of session description information. The Expires header indicates how long the session description can be cached without revalidating the information. The Last-Modified header indicates the last time the session description was changed. The argument of the Last-Modified header may be used in future If-Modified-Since requests to validate a cached copy of the entity. The Allow header lists the methods that are supported for the Request-URI.

OMITTED HTTP/1.1 HEADERS

Several of the HTTP/1.1 headers were not included in the RTSP specification. The omitted headers fall into several categories that relate to the differences between the two protocols, as summarized in Table 12.7. Most of the headers relate to the HTTP's support for diverse entities in request and response messages. In contrast, RTSP messages do not contain entities, except to convey session description information. Session descriptions are relatively short text documents. Compared with HTTP, RTSP does not have sophisticated support for the transfer of entities. The RTSP client and server do not negotiate the character set or transfer coding for a session description. RTSP messages do not include an MD5 checksum of the entity body, and no headers are listed after the entity of a message. Similarly, RTSP has less support for validation of the resources conveyed in RTSP messages.

　　RTSP does not include several of the HTTP/1.1 headers related to range requests. In HTTP/1.1, a client may use the Range request header to request a subset of the bytes in a resource. If the Request-URI does not permit range requests, an HTTP response returns the entire resource along with an Accept-Ranges: none header. In contrast, an RTSP server that does not

Table 12.7. HTTP/1.1 headers not included in RTSP

Concept	Header	Definition
Entity transfer	`Accept-Charset`	Acceptable character sets
	`TE`	Acceptable transfer codings
	`Transfer-Encoding`	Transformation to message body
	`Content-MD5`	Integrity check of entity body
	`Trailer`	List of headers at end of message
Validation	`ETag`	Opaque validator
	`Age`	Time since response generated
	`If-None-Match`	Comparison against entity tags
	`If-Unmodified-Since`	Comparison against last modified time
	`If-Range`	Conditional range request
Range requests	`Accept-Ranges`	Unwillingness to accept range requests
	`Content-Range`	Location of range in entity body
HTTP/1.0	`Host`	Host of resource being requested
	`Pragma`	Message directive
Miscellany	`Upgrade`	Upgrading to other protocols
	`Warning`	Error notification
	`Max-Forwards`	Limited request forwarding
	`Expect`	Expected server behavior by client

support a range request does not automatically transmit the entire multimedia stream to the client. Instead, the server responds to the client with an error code. Thus the `Accept-Ranges` header is not necessary. HTTP and RTSP have slightly different ways of responding to a successful range request. An HTTP/1.1 server indicates what byte range has been returned in the `Content-Range` entity header. In RTSP, the server indicates the time range that has been selected in the `Range` header; this range does not have to match the requested range. The difference in header names reflects the fact that, in RTSP, the time range refers to the multimedia stream, delivered on a separate transport connection, not the RTSP entity.

RTSP does not include the `Host` and `Pragma` headers that are included in HTTP/1.1 for backward compatibility with HTTP/1.0. An HTTP/1.1 client uses the `Host` header to indicate the domain name of the server, because this information is not available in the Request-URI. In contrast, an RTSP Request-URI has the absolute path, obviating the need for a separate header to convey the server name. The `Pragma` header was introduced in HTTP/1.0 for message directives, such as `Pragma: no-cache`. HTTP/1.1 introduced a different approach for conveying caching information—the `Cache-Control` header. How-

Table 12.8. New RTSP status codes

Category	Status code and reason phrase
System resources	250 Low on Storage Space 453 Not Enough Bandwidth
Unknown identifier	451 Parameter Not Understood 452 Conference Not Found 454 Session Not Found 462 Destination Unreachable
Unsupported feature	455 Method Not Valid in This State 456 Header Field Not Valid for Resource 457 Invalid Range 458 Parameter Is Read-Only 461 Unsupported Transport 551 Option Not Supported
Session/ stream	459 Aggregate Operation Not Allowed 460 Only Aggregate Operation Allowed

ever, maintaining backward compatibility with HTTP/1.0 requires HTTP/1.1 clients and servers to understand the `Pragma` header. Because RTSP does not have these backward-compatibility issues, the `Host` and `Pragma` headers are not necessary. The `Upgrade` and `Warning` headers are also omitted. RTSP also does not include the `Max-Forwards` header that relates to an HTTP/1.1 request method and the `Expect` header that did not exist in RFC 2068.

12.4.4 RTSP status codes

Each response message includes a status code to indicate the outcome of the request. RTSP status codes fall into the same five categories as HTTP response codes—informational (1xx), success (2xx), redirection (3xx), client error (4xx), and server error (5xx). RTSP introduces several new status codes, as summarized in Table 12.8; RTSP also incorporates many status codes from RFC 2068, as summarized in Table 12.9. To avoid conflicting with any new HTTP/1.1 response codes that might arise in the future, the RTSP-specific codes start at x50. The new codes fall into several main categories:

- **System resources:** Transmitting or receiving a media stream may consume significant system resources at the server. In a response to a `RECORD` request, the 250 Low on Storage Space status code warns the client that the server has limited storage space for recording the stream. The server may reject a client's request to play or record a stream with a 453 Not Enough Bandwidth response.

- **Unknown identifier:** The client request may include a variable or address that the server does not recognize. Upon receiving a SET_PARAMETER request that refers to an unknown parameter, the server sends a 451 Parameter Not Understood response. Similarly, the server sends a 452 Conference Not Found or 454 Session Not Found upon receiving a request with an unfamiliar Conference or Session identifier, respectively. If the server is unable to establish a connection for streaming data to the client, then the server sends a 462 Destination Unreachable response.

- **Unsupported feature:** The client request may have a method or header that is not supported for the Request-URI. For example, some methods are not valid depending on the current state (455 Method Not Valid in This State), and some headers are not valid for particular Request-URIs (456 Header Field Not Valid for Resource). A PLAY request may attempt to jump to a nonexistent portion of a stream (457 Invalid Range), or a SET_PARAMETER request may attempt to write a read-only parameter (458 Parameter Is Read-Only). The Transport header in a PLAY request may not include a supported transport specification (461 Unsupported Transport), or the server may not support a feature listed in the Require or Proxy-Require headers (551 Option Not Supported).

- **Session/stream operations:** The client request may violate the hierarchy of stream and session. That is, the client request may attempt to perform a stream-level operation on a Request-URI that corresponds to a session (459 Aggregate Operation Not Allowed) or a session-level operation on a Request-URI that corresponds to a stream (460 Only Aggregate Operation Allowed).

Most of the new status codes are client errors (4xx), except for 250 Low on Storage Space and 551 Option Not Supported, which are success and server-error codes, respectively.

In summary, RTSP is a multimedia streaming protocol that derived from HTTP/1.1. The protocol supports the playback of multimedia data from a server and the recording of multimedia data at a server. RTSP and HTTP have a similar underlying framework of applying a request method to a resource identified by a URI, in which a request or response message includes headers and an optional entity. The RTSP specification draws heavily on how HTTP/1.1 defines caching, proxies, and authentication. These similarities manifest themselves in a large number of RTSP headers and status codes that were borrowed from HTTP/1.1. Yet, RTSP differs from HTTP in several important ways. RTSP is a stateful control protocol that relegates the transferring of requested data to other protocols. In addition, RTSP defines additional headers and status codes that relate to the unique timing requirements of multimedia streaming and to the hierarchical relationship between frames, streams, and

Table 12.9. RTSP status codes borrowed from HTTP/1.1

100 Continue	406 Not Acceptable
200 OK	407 Proxy Authentication Required
201 Created	408 Request Time-out
300 Multiple Choices	410 Gone
301 Moved Permanently	411 Length Required
302 Moved Temporarily	412 Precondition Failed
303 See Other	413 Request Entity Too Large
304 Not Modified	414 Request-URI Too Large
305 Use Proxy	415 Unsupported Media Type
400 Bad Request	500 Internal Server Error
401 Authorized	501 Not Implemented
402 Payment Required	502 Bad Gateway
403 Forbidden	503 Service Unavailable
404 Not Found	504 Gateway Time-out
405 Method Not Allowed	505 RTSP Version Not Supported

sessions. These application characteristics manifest themselves in the addition of new request methods, headers, and status codes.

12.5 Summary

Audio and video streams differ from traditional Web content in three key ways. First, audio and video data have timing properties that affect how the helper application receives and plays the streams. Second, multimedia streaming requires the server to devote a significant amount of bandwidth over an extended period. Third, most multimedia streaming applications are resilient to a modest amount of lost data. These unique characteristics, coupled with the diversity of multimedia applications, has led to the development of a suite of protocols for multimedia streaming. The convergence of multimedia applications and the Web is still in its infancy. In the coming years, multimedia streaming applications and the suite of underlying protocols will continue to evolve.

Part VI

Research Perspectives

Research Perspectives in Caching

Caching is a rapidly changing research area—within a short time nearly a hundred papers have been published in a variety of conferences and dozens of companies have been formed. In the chapter devoted to caching (Chapter 11), we examined the various technical issues related to caching. Most of the ideas discussed in that chapter have been proposed in the last few years and have been evaluated to a reasonable degree. In this chapter, we look at more recent issues: research ideas that may not stand the test of time and may not have been evaluated enough to be reflected in documents such as the Internet Engineering Task Force's (IETF) Request for Comments (RFCs) or in commercial products.

We noted in Chapter 11 that the three main reasons for the introduction and success of caching were reduction of user-perceived latency, network load, and load on the origin server. Not surprisingly, most of the research work in caching has revolved around reducing these three factors. Rather than attempt to provide an exhaustive survey on the various research efforts related to caching, we look at a small but select subset of them, primarily because of the biases of the authors. More attention has been paid to some of the topics in cache research. For example, a lot of effort has been expended in the area of cache validation, once it was recognized to be a significant part of Web traffic. The need for reduction of the high cost associated with connections and exploration of prefetching techniques to reduce latency are other areas we will consider. This chapter is divided into the following three parts:

- **Cache revalidation/invalidation:** In the absence of explicit expiration times, cache revalidation is necessary to guarantee delivery of fresh responses to clients. Revalidation with the origin server ensures that the cached copy of the resource is the same as the version the origin server would have returned. Cache invalidation is a technique whereby the cache is notified that a cached response is no longer fresh. There is cost associated with both revalidation and invalidation. We examine novel *piggybacking* techniques that reduce the cost of revalidation while decreasing latency to users. We also look at server invalidation techniques whereby servers can provide hints about their resources that have changed.

- **End-to-end information exchange:** The end-to-end information exchange idea capitalizes on the information available at the various components in a Web transfer: clients, proxies, and origin servers. This builds on the piggybacking approach and adds hints from the proxies to help tailor server-based hints. The idea is to construct a signature of a cache's policy as a *filter* and send it to an origin server, which can apply the filter locally to the set of hints.

- **Prefetching:** Prefetching is a general technique to retrieve information before it is needed or requested. The primary motivation is to reduce user-perceived latency. Following the steps of a typical Web transaction, prefetching can be done at the Domain Name System (DNS) layer (looking up names of hosts that are likely to be contacted), TCP layer (prefetching a transport connection), and HTTP layer (prefetching a resource that is likely to be requested).

We explore each research area in detail by looking at its motivation, novelty, and related work.

13.1 Cache Revalidation and Invalidation

The key changes in HTTP/1.1 related to ensuring that cached responses are never accidentally returned as fresh. Cache revalidation involves checking if the origin server would return the same response as the cached entity. Invalidation is notification that could be sent to a cache indicating that a cached response is no longer fresh. Both in Chapter 7 (Section 7.3) and in Chapter 11 we examined the various issues related to Web caching and introduced several cache-related terms such as *expiration* time, *freshness* lifetime, and *age*.

A cache may be forced to return a cached response that is stale. For example, the cache may be disconnected from downstream servers. Most caches try to adhere to the notion of semantic transparency and use a variety of techniques to ensure that the cached response is still fresh before returning it as a valid response to the requesting client. The most common technique is revalidation with the origin server. In both HTTP/1.0 and HTTP/1.1, validation is often accomplished by using the `GET` request with the `If-Modified-Since` request modifier. HTTP/1.1 also provides the `If-None-Match` request modifier to be used with entity tags. Upon receiving such a request, the origin server would either return a `304 Not Modified` response with no entity body, or a `200 OK` response with the full entity body.

The fact that revalidation is performed on a regular basis has been reflected in a variety of studies. Several Web server logs show that at least 10% to 30% of traffic consists of revalidation requests. For example, a workload characterization study [AFJ99] of a proxy in a cable modem environment showed that nearly 16% of all responses were 304 Not Modified. Simply counting the 304 Not Modified responses in a server log yields the *lower* bound on the number of revalidation requests. Some revalidation requests yield 200 OK responses that include an entity body. There are three reasons for a revalidation request to yield a 200 OK response, as follows:

- The resource has actually changed, and the server is sending the new value.
- The server does not know the correct last modification time. For example, the resource is a script whose output might change only occasionally, but the server may not be aware of this. The client might have revalidated with an ETag rather than last modification time.
- The 304 Not Modified response is not a mandatory requirement on servers (it is a SHOULD requirement as per the protocol specification).

In the rest of this section, we examine in detail the costs associated with validation (and invalidation) and three techniques that attempt to reduce the user-perceived latency without increasing the cost. The three techniques are prevalidation, piggybacking, and server-driven invalidation. Prevalidation involves revalidation of cached objects that may have passed their expiration time *before* they are requested by clients. Prevalidating may indicate that the cached response is stale (in which case it can be removed from the cache) or fresh (in which case, its freshness interval can be increased). Piggybacking is a technique first proposed in [KW97] to perform prevalidation at low cost. Server-driven invalidation is a way for an origin server to notify caches that a cached response is no longer fresh. Prevalidation triggers request traffic, whereas server invalidation might require connections back from the server. Piggybacking avoids triggering new request or response traffic.

13.1.1 Costs associated with revalidation

Consider the various costs in the following scenario:

- A client is connected to a single proxy that is capable of sending requests directly to origin servers.
- A client sends a request. The proxy, instead of returning a response directly from its cache, sends a revalidation request to the origin server.
- The revalidation request results in a 304 Not Modified response, and the proxy forwards the cached response to the client.

The average size of an HTTP request with an If-Modified-Since request modifier is around 200 bytes. An HTTP response with a 304 Not Modified response code is less than 200 bytes, and it may be as little as 50 bytes. A revalidation request in HTTP/1.0 requires establishing a connection with the origin server (or a proxy, if one is in the path). Several packets are required for the HTTP setup (TCP's three-way handshake) and teardown (TCP's four packet teardown). A revalidation request is still a regular HTTP request as far as the origin server is concerned; the server must accept a connection, parse the request, send back a response, optionally log the exchange, and close the connection. In other words, the cost to an origin server is similar to that of handling any other request, except for the overhead of obtaining the resource from the disk and writing the response body.

Some of the costs are minimized if the HTTP request is part of a persistent connection. The connection setup and teardown costs are amortized over many other requests and responses. However, if we examine the latency experienced by the client in waiting for the response message, we notice that there has been only a small reduction. The latency in transferring the complete contents of the resource from the origin server to the sender has been reduced because only an HTTP response header is returned, with no accompanying entity body. This is likely to be only a small fraction of the overall cost. If the response had been located in the proxy's cache, the connection between the proxy and origin server itself would have been avoided, as well as the request-response exchange between the proxy and the origin server. The connection of a client to a proxy might be better than a typical proxy's connection to various origin servers, thus reducing the latency to transfer the resource from the proxy to the client. Reducing revalidation can lower user-perceived latency significantly.

13.1.2 Prevalidation

Obtaining information before it is actually used eliminates waiting at the time of request. Prefetching is an old technique that has been used in various areas of computer science. Just as resources can be prefetched before they are requested, information about resources can also be prefetched. *Prevalidation* is the prefetching of validation information.

HTTP's HEAD method permits fetching a resource's metadata without actually transferring the resource. A cache could issue a HEAD request and verify that the cached response is still fresh. If the metadata returned in the response to the HEAD request reveals that the cached response is stale, the cache could send a GET request. However, the HEAD request still requires an HTTP connection and thus all the overhead associated with GET except for the actual transfer of the resource. Thus in cases in which the cached response is stale, two separate requests are needed, resulting in twice the overhead. The cache may use a heuristic to decide if it should send a HEAD or a GET. Prevalidating via HEAD requests has the potential to reduce bandwidth usage but has the same amount of impact on the origin server in terms of number of requests. Note that if a cache uses GET with an If-Modified-Since header, it is not just prevalidation. A server receiving such a request might send a 200 OK response and the contents of the resource.

Pipelining the prevalidation requests is a viable option because it does not suffer from the head of line blocking problem (discussed in Chapter 7, Section 7.5.4), since HEAD requests typically may not require significant work on the part of the origin server. Also, there are no user agents waiting for the prevalidations to complete. Prevalidation will not have any impact on overall latency reduction in transferring the resource to the user, except maybe to increase latency in cases in which the cached response is actually stale. If the prevalidated resource is not requested in the future, the HEAD request has also added needless load on the origin server.

13.1.3 The piggybacking approach

HEAD requests can be used to determine if a cached response is stale without transferring the resource. However, a key component of latency is the connection cost in establishing connections to the origin server. This is partially due to the fact that the actual time spent in transferring a response from an origin server to a proxy is relatively low given that most responses are small. For very large or dynamically generated responses, the amount of time spent in generating the resource could exceed the actual transfer time.

One way to eliminate the connection cost is to avoid the connection setup altogether. HTTP/1.1's persistent connections provide one way to reduce the need for new connections. However, a busy origin server may close persistent connections, as permitted by the protocol. If a connection to an origin server is already open, a proxy could send HEAD requests for revalidation without the overhead of opening connections. However, because most caches have a default time interval during which they assume that a cached response is still fresh, it would not make sense to revalidate before this interval has expired.

Consider the technique, described originally in [KW97], that keeps track of cached resources that have passed their freshness time on a per-origin-server basis. Now suppose a request for a resource triggers a connection to one of these origin servers. The connection to that origin server is going to be made anyway, therefore the set of responses from that origin server that have expired are revalidated. This revalidation is done by *piggybacking* those resources at the end of the regular request. For example, suppose a proxy has a dozen responses belonging to origin server www.a.org and four of them have been in the cache longer than the default freshness assumption. Upon receiving a request for www.a.org/other.html, the proxy generates a GET request on behalf of the client. The proxy appends information about four of the expired resources to the request for www.a.org/other.html. The appended information consists of the name of the resource, its last modification time, and possibly its size. The origin server responds to the request for www.a.org/other.html and could append metadata about the four other resources.

An origin server that sends information about the other responses being revalidated does less work because it is not involved in a full-scale re-
quest/response exchange. Suppose the proxy had piggybacked a list of resources
to be prevalidated along with the proxy's view of their last modification time
(or entity tag, if the ETag information is available). The origin server sends back
a list of URLs of the responses that are no longer fresh along with the response
for www.a.org/other.html. The proxy returns the response for other.html to
the requesting client, after stripping the revalidation information. Separately
the proxy can process the revalidation information by extending the freshness
time of the responses that are still fresh and removing the stale responses from
its cache. The mechanics of whether the additional information is sent as part
of the response for other.html or in separate messages is a matter of implementation, as we discuss later in this section.

Figures 13.1 through 13.4 show the various steps involved in the piggybacking process. A client is communicating via a proxy with three origin servers, A,
B, and C. The proxy has two resources (r2, r3) obtained from origin server B
in its cache. Now suppose that the client sends a request also to origin server
B for resource r1 (Figure 13.1).

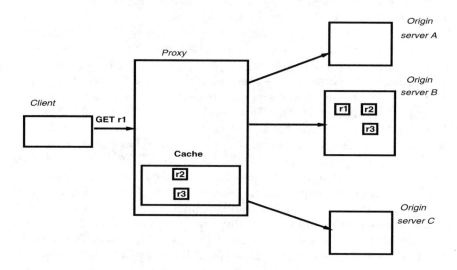

Figure 13.1. Client requesting resource r1 from proxy

At this point, the proxy does not have resource r1 in its cache and must
forward the request to origin server B which has resource r1. Suppose the
two resources in its cache, r2 and r3, must be revalidated per the cache's
revalidation policy. The proxy would now piggyback these two resources, along
with the request for r1, to the origin server B, as shown in Figure 13.2.

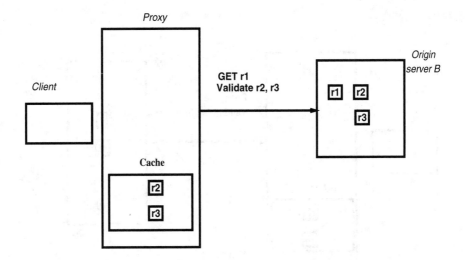

Figure 13.2. Proxy requesting r1 and piggybacking validations

The origin server B returns the resource r1 and the validation information for resources r2 and r3, as shown in Figure 13.3.

The proxy returns the response for the resource r1 to the client and updates its cache with the validation information for the resources r2 and r3. As Figure 13.4 shows, the proxy has removed the resource r3 from the cache, presumably because it was determined to be stale based on the validation information returned from the origin server B.

The advantages of piggybacking are obvious: no new connections are made specifically for prevalidation and no connections are wasted. Only stale responses are revalidated. By revalidating these cached responses, the proxy increases the probability of avoiding future revalidation and reducing the user-perceived latency for such requests.

IMPLEMENTATION CONSIDERATIONS OF PIGGYBACKING

We now examine the ways by which proxies can send prevalidation requests and how origin servers can respond to such requests. From the proxy's perspective, it is simply revalidating a set of responses in its cache that are past their freshness time. Two ways in which the request portion of the prevalidation can be implemented are as follows:

1. The proxy could send a set of HEAD requests to the origin server. The HEAD request would include the If-Modified-Since request modifier, whose

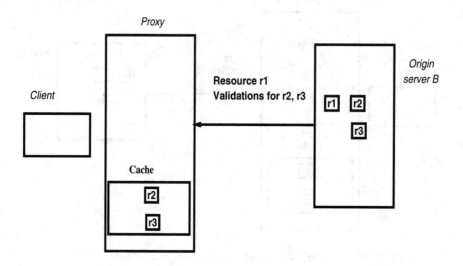

Figure 13.3. Origin server B returning **r1** and validation information

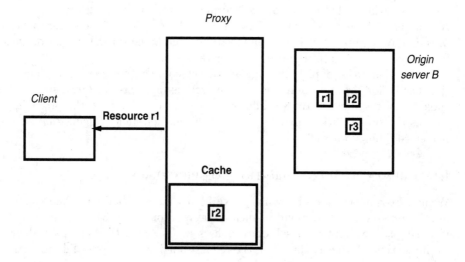

Figure 13.4. Proxy returning **r1** and updating its cache

value is obtained from the `Last-Modified` header in the cached response. Obviously, if the response were dynamic or otherwise did not include `Last-Modified` information, the cache would not include such a response in the prevalidation list. In fact, many caches are not likely to cache dynamically generated responses anyway. If the HTTP connection is already open, this does not introduce any connection overhead. The `HEAD` requests can in fact be pipelined. This implementation technique works within HTTP/1.0 protocol and works better in HTTP/1.1. However, for each additional request, the server must return a revalidation response even if the resource has not changed.

2. The proxy constructs a simple data structure consisting of URLs of the stale responses and the timestamps corresponding to the `Last-Modified` header in the cached response. This data structure would be appended to the regular request, as outlined above. The proxy assumes that the origin server would know to extract the data structure. This can be achieved by servers that know how to react to piggybacked requests. If, on the other hand, HTTP has been modified to handle piggybacking, then proxies can expect compliant servers to act on it.

Upon receiving a prevalidation request, the origin server can act in one of the following two ways:

1. In the first style of revalidation, in which separate `HEAD` requests are sent, the origin server simply returns appropriate responses. No change in its behavior is required.

2. In the second style, in which the prevalidation requests are piggybacked onto a regular request, the origin server must be able to extract the appended data structure. The origin server can revalidate each of the entries in this structure and append the result to the regular response. A smarter origin server could just send back a list of resources that are invalid, with the understanding that the rest of the resources are still fresh. In either case there is a potential increase in latency to the regular response. If the origin server supports HTTP/1.1 and the proxy could handle HTTP/1.1 responses, the origin server can take advantage of the `Trailer` header of HTTP/1.1 and piggyback the additional information onto the response for `other.html`.

As an example, one way in which the second style of piggybacking exchange could proceed is as follows:

A proxy includes a `TE:Trailer` request header, and the server sends the piggybacked information in the trailer of the response. The proxy sends the request

```
GET /other.html HTTP/1.1
Host: www.piggy.com
```

```
TE: trailers

URL1 LMT: ...
URL2 LMT: ...
URL3 LMT: ...
URL4 LMT: ...
CRLF
```

The origin server sends back the response

```
HTTP/1.1 200 OK
Content-Type: text/html
Content-Length: 2100
Transfer-Encoding: chunked
Trailer: Piggy
...
<body of response>
...
Piggy: <piggybacked information here>
```

In Section 13.2.3, we provide an explanation of the syntactic elements of the protocol used in the example above. Technically there would be no need for the proxy to include a TE header or the server to use a trailer to include the piggyback information. The server could simply include the requested prevalidation in a header preceding the entity body. Doing so would imply that no part of the actual entity body of the response is sent until the requested prevalidation is done and marshaled into the appropriate response header. By including the piggyback information in the trailer, the proxy can immediately forward the entity body of the response and avoid latency increase for interactive users. The proxy can handle the trailer after forwarding the entity body.

13.1.4 Server-driven invalidation

The cache has a clear idea of what resources to prevalidate. On the other hand, the origin server is the component with the direct knowledge of when a resource has changed on its site. Thus, instead of the client or proxy revalidating a request, the origin server could notify interested parties of changes to resources. Such a notification is called *server-driven invalidation*. Invalidation is similar to a *push* model, and revalidation is analogous to a *pull* model.

The mechanics of server-driven invalidation require several questions to be answered:

- How does the server send the invalidation information?
- Which clients and proxies are the target of invalidation information?
- What is the frequency with which the invalidations are sent?

The answer to the first question is straightforward: In HTTP, an origin server cannot initiate message transfers. Requests must arrive before a server can respond. This implies that invalidation can only be sent in response to some request. In the research work described in [KW98], which followed up the Piggybacked Cache Validation work described in Section 13.1.3, an approach was explored to piggyback the invalidation information on responses. As in the case of piggybacking validations, this avoids new connections.

The second question concerns state maintenance at the server that sends invalidations. A busy origin server might receive requests from thousands of proxies and clients. To maintain information about all of them in order to be able to send invalidation information would require the origin server to maintain a significant amount of state. In some sense, the origin server must *know* which proxies are likely to benefit from invalidation information. The server could use a lease-based approach (similar to the one described in Chapter 11, Section 11.7), but this still requires state maintenance. Proxies may no longer be interested in invalidation information about certain resources but would continue to receive such information. Useless invalidation information adds to the overhead of servers, as well as proxies that have to process the piggybacked information.

The third question regarding the frequency of sending invalidation requires examining the rate of change of a resource. An origin server might be very interested in ensuring that proxies do not serve stale data. At the risk of having more requests directed to them, origin servers might insist that responses be fresh. If an origin server could be sure that a proxy would honor invalidation information faithfully, it might be willing to set a higher expiration time for the responses and send invalidations as soon as resources change. For frequently changing resources, this can increase traffic significantly.

The lease-based approach described in [LC97] differs from the piggybacked invalidation approach. The lease-based solution requires HTTP connections from the server to the client/proxy when resources of interest change within the lease period. In the piggyback approach, the invalidations are piggybacked on subsequent requests from the client or proxy.

One lesson to draw from server invalidation idea is that the granularity of invalidation information cannot be at the individual resource level. Otherwise, there is a potential for a significant amount of state to be maintained and for a large amount of traffic, piggybacked or otherwise. Another lesson is that origin servers and proxies both have incomplete knowledge. An origin server knows when resources change but does not have a good idea of which clients are interested in the resources. Even if an origin server maintained detailed logs for long periods, it will not know about responses that are returned from caches and thus will never know the actual popularity of a resource on a per-client basis. Proxies, on the other hand, know about interest of clients for resources but have no idea on when or how often resources change. The granularity of information and the bidirectional information exchange required leads us to the next topic: end-to-end information exchange.

13.2 End-to-end Information Exchange

The previous section discussed techniques that provide a proxy with information about the freshness of cached responses in advance of client requests. In this section, we generalize the notion of information exchange between proxies and servers to support a wide range of proxy applications, such as cache coherency, cache replacement, and prefetching. A proxy's effectiveness can be improved by exploiting information about resources that are likely to be requested in the future. However, the origin server has the most complete view of the access patterns for the requested resources across a large collection of clients. Following the approach in the previous section, the server can piggyback *hints* about these resources in a response to a request from the proxy. The server constructs these hints by grouping resources that are likely to be accessed together into *volumes*.

However, some of the resources in a volume may not be relevant to the proxy. The proxy alone knows its caching policies and the resources currently available in the cache. This information can be summarized in a *filter* that is applied at the server to tailor the hints to the requesting proxy. The proxy can piggyback the filter on the request message. Then the server applies the filter to the volume associated with the requested resource to produce the list of hints that are piggybacked on the response message. The bidirectional exchange of information ensures that the proxy receives a small set of useful hints. In this section, we describe a study that proposed this combination of server volumes and proxy filters, including the protocol details for piggybacking filters and hints, as well as the algorithms for volume construction [CKR98, CKR99]. We also describe the study's comparison of volume-construction algorithms based on a collection of server logs.

13.2.1 Server volumes

In the proposed scheme, the hints piggybacked on response messages depend on the resource requested by the proxy. In response to a request for resource r, the server returns hints about resources that are related to r. Previous research on file systems introduced the abstract notion of a *volume* as a group of related resources. Work on Piggybacked Server Invalidation [KW98], a follow-up to the Piggybacked Cache Validation [KW97], applied volumes to server-driven cache invalidation in the Web. Constructing volumes requires the server to have some heuristic for grouping related resources, such as the following:

- Accessed close together in time (temporal access pattern)

- Share a syntactic prefix (in the same directory in the UNIX sense)
- Share resource attributes (similar content types, sizes, etc.)
- Modified together (e.g., resources that changed within the last five minutes)

The server could associate an identifier with each volume, and the proxy could keep track of groups of cached resources by their volume identifiers. For example, suppose a proxy knows which resources belong to volume V1 at a server. In sending hints related to V1, the server could transmit a small amount of information about how the resources in V1 have changed. Upon receiving hints related to V1, the proxy can take collective action on the cached resources belonging to V1.

The appropriate volume-construction heuristic depends on the application. The first heuristic, based on temporal access patterns, is well suited to applications, such as prefetching and cache replacement, that depend on accurate predictions of future client requests. Based on past accesses, the server can identify which resources are requested soon after a request for resource r. If many clients request resource s a short time after requesting resource r, other clients may follow this same pattern. The most obvious scenario occurs when r is an HTML file and s is one of the embedded images. By including s in the volume for r, the server can piggyback information about s in response to a proxy's request for r. While forwarding the response for r to the requesting client, the proxy could prefetch the embedded image or update the metadata about its cached copy of s. In other cases, the resource s may be a particularly popular hypertext link in r or reachable within a few "clicks" of r. We discuss this approach to volume construction in more detail later in Section 13.2.4.

The second volume-construction technique is based on the assumption that the content at a Web site is organized into directories in the server's file system. Related resources may belong to a common directory, allowing the server to group resources by examining the file names up to the directory level. Consider a Web site with three subdirectories *dotty, lefty,* and *neato.* Each of these directories may have several files underneath them. A one-level volume would include just URLs of the form /dotty/index.html, /dotty/src/graph.c, and /dotty/src/Makefile. However, information about the resources /lefty/editor.c and /neato/download.html will not be included in the one-level volume. Directories with a large number of resources would result in very large volumes. To reduce the size, the server could group resources that share several levels of directories. For example, resources in directories starting with /dotty/src/ could be assigned to a single volume.

The third volume-construction technique uses the intuition that resources that have similar physical attributes should be grouped together. A proxy may have policies that restrict the caching to particular content types or resource sizes. For example, a proxy might decide never to cache resources that are of a type expected to change frequently. This technique points out the problem of making decisions purely from the viewpoint of the origin server. If the caching proxy notified the origin server somehow that it did not cache resources of certain content types, the origin server could use that information to tailor the hints, rather than making *a priori* assumptions about the proxy policies. Similar to content types, size constraints of a proxy cache might require it to never cache resources over a certain size. By constructing volumes that are based on sizes, origin servers can decide to include or not to include certain volumes in hints.

The fourth volume-construction technique gathers resources that are modified within a specific interval of time. The intuition behind this heuristic is that the proxies need information about which resources have changed during a period of time. Grouping resources that changed during this period helps the server limit the number of hints. In addition, resources that change at the same time may be related to each other. A request for one of these resources may be followed by a request for other resources in the same volume. By assigning these resources to the same volume, the server can provide the proxy with hints about the resources in advance of these requests.

Constructing volumes introduces computational work at the server. Computing a volume as part of processing each request may delay the transmission of the response message and may incur significant overhead on the server. In practice, the volumes can be precomputed based on previous accesses to the server. For example, a separate program running on a different computer could construct the volumes based on a server log. Volumes computed in one period could be applied by the server for the next period. As an alternative, the server may be able to execute the volume-construction algorithm in the background to update the volumes over time. This would allow the server to provide more up-to-date hints to proxies, at the expense of additional overhead. The exact trade-off depends on the computational overhead of the volume-construction algorithm and the frequency of changes to the volume assignments.

13.2.2 Proxy filters

Volume construction draws on information available at the server. Any particular proxy may not be interested in *all* of the resources in a volume. For example, consider a proxy that serves a collection of users connected to the Internet over low-bandwidth wireless links. This proxy may choose not to cache images or any resources larger than 1 MB. Sending hints about these resources would impose an unnecessary load on the server and the proxy. However, the server is not in a position to know the caching policies of the many proxies that send requests to the Web site. Instead, the proxy could include information about its caching policies in its request messages. The proxy sends a concise filter, and the server applies this filter to select the appropriate hints from the volume. Associating the filter with the request message obviates the need for the server to store the filters for a large collection of proxies across successive requests.

The proxy filter serves several purposes. First, the filter can be used to limit the hints to certain resources of interest, such as resources with particular content types or sizes. Second, the filter can indicate which metadata should be included in each hint. For example, information about the last modification time would enable the proxy to evict stale resources from the cache and revalidate resources that have not changed. On the other hand, a proxy that performs prefetching may want to know the resource sizes and popularity. Third, the filter may be used to control overhead by limiting the number of hints. The filter could include an "on-off" bit to enable or disable hints, allowing the proxy to control whether the server includes hints in the response message. The proxy could keep track of the frequency of hints from the server to decide whether or not to enable hints on a particular request. In addition, the proxy filter can limit the number of hints that are piggybacked on a particular response message. For example, the proxy filter could request that the server send only the top ten hints, where the hints have been sorted in some agreed upon order of importance.

Because request messages can include filters, the origin server does not have to maintain state for the potentially thousands of proxies sending requests. A proxy, on the other hand, can use the same filter across a variety of origin servers. Hence, having the proxy store and transmit the filter when needed is much more efficient than placing this burden on the origin servers. The proxy and the server must agree on the format of the filter, because the two components require a consistent interpretation. In addition, the definition of the filter affects the hint-related data structures at the server. For example, if volumes can be filtered based on resource size, the server may divide the resources in a volume based on their size. With a separate list for each range of resource sizes, the server can quickly apply a filter that restricts the hints to resources less than a particular size. This efficient data structure for storing the volumes eases the burden of applying a filter as part of processing a proxy's request.

13.2.3 Volumes and filters: Practical details

Deploying the combination of server volumes and proxy filters requires a more precise specification of volumes, filters, and piggybacking. A volume consists of a unique identifier and a list of elements, each corresponding to a particular resource at the Web site. Each element includes a URL and a collection of attributes, such as the resource's last modification time, the size, and the content type. The server can store the volume elements in one or more first-in first-out lists, partitioned based on the key resource attributes. For example, the server may have separate lists based on the resource size or content type to reduce

Table 13.1. Range of filter elements

Filter element	Typical values	Implication
Hints	On/Off	Should hints be sent?
RPV	{1, 2, 4}	Server should not send listed volumes
MaxPiggy	5, 10	Maximum # of hints in a message
MinAccess	100	Minimum # of accesses of a resource
MinProb	0.8	Minimum probability of next access
Level	0, 1, 2	Hints share prefixes to specified level
Size	1 MB, 10 KB	Volume elements size limitation
OKType	HTML	Limit hints to specified content types
NotOKType	CGI	Do not send hints about this type
Lastmod	1 min	Minimum time since last modification
HTTP method	PUT	Resources must allow listed method
HTTP header	ETag, Accept	Resource must match header criteria

the overhead of applying proxy filters. In addition to the volume elements, the server sends the volume identifier to the proxy. By maintaining statistics about the Recently Piggybacked Volumes (RPVs), the proxy can instruct the server not to transmit these hints again by including the volume identifiers in the filter piggybacked on subsequent requests. Upon receiving this filter, the server would omit hints associated with these volume identifiers.

Having the proxy piggyback the filter on request messages obviates the need for the server to maintain information about each proxy. Otherwise, the system would not scale to a large number of proxies. The proxy filter includes a variety of fields, as summarized in Table 13.1. The list can be extended to incorporate other filtering parameters. Any additional filtering parameters should satisfy two key design goals. First, the parameter should be useful for customizing the hints to the requesting proxy. Second, the server should be able to apply the filter in an efficient manner. Table 13.1 identifies two sets of filter elements: control parameters and resource attributes. Control parameters allow the proxy to dictate how often the server sends hints, how many hints are piggybacked on a response message, and how useful the hints should be. Resource attributes indicate which kinds of resources should be included in the hints. For example, the proxy may or may not want to receive hints about resources of a certain size, content type, or last modification time. In addition, the proxy may want to tailor the hints based on the presence or absence of a particular HTTP header, such as `Accept-Language`.

Exchanging the filters and hints requires an effective way to piggyback the information on HTTP request and response messages. The filters and hints could be included as additional lines in the HTTP request and response headers.

However, this approach would require the server to generate hints before transmitting the body of the response message. Any delay in applying the proxy's filter would introduce latency in satisfying the client's request. Instead, the hints should be sent at the *end* of the response message. This can be done by exploiting the ability to send metadata in the trailer of an HTTP/1.1 message. Trailers can be included in messages that use chunked transfer-encoding and the `Trailer` header, as discussed earlier in Chapter 7 (Section 7.6). The request message must indicate that the proxy can handle responses with trailers, and the header of the response message must indicate that the message ends with a trailer.

For example, the proxy could send the request

```
GET /random.html HTTP/1.1
Host: smartserver.com
TE: trailers
Piggy-filter: maxpiggy=5; content-type=gif
```

to the server. The `Piggy-filter` header includes the proxy filter, and the `TE: trailers` header indicates that the proxy can handle a response with chunked encoding and a trailer. The filter in this case indicates that the proxy wants at most five hints and it is interested in hints about resources with content type GIF. A server that is not capable of supplying volume hints would ignore the `Piggy-filter` header. A server participating in the scheme could send the following response message:

```
HTTP/1.1 200 OK
Trailer: P-volume
Transfer-encoding: chunked
 < Size-of-chunk >
     <data>
  ...
 0
P-volume: vol=7; pe="/random-img1.gif,895527629,546";
    pe="/random-img3.gif,891527021,192";
    pe="/random-img21.gif,821993421,900"
CRLF
```

The response header has the requisite `Trailer` header with the value `P-volume` indicating that a header with this name appears in the trailer of the message. The response is chunk-encoded, and the trailer appears after the zero-length chunk at the end. The trailer includes a volume identifier (7) and three volume elements, including the name, last modification time, and size of each resource.

The piggybacking mechanism does not require that all proxies and servers recognize the new headers. HTTP components ignore headers that they do not understand. A server that is not capable of sending hints would ignore the unfamiliar `Piggy-filter` header and generate a normal response. A non-participating proxy would generate normal requests that do not include the `Piggy-filter` header. For proxies and servers that participate, the piggybacking scheme introduces a small amount of data to the request and response messages. For example, a hint consists of a name and a few resource attributes. An average URL consists of about 50 1-byte characters (not including the site name), and the last modification time and size attributes consume eight bytes each. Hence, each hint requires about 66 bytes. Sending five hints would add about 300 bytes to the response message. This is small relative to the average size of a Web resource—about 8 KB, as discussed in Chapter 10 (Section 10.4.2). At most, sending a few hints would require the server to transmit one extra TCP packet. In fact, the hints may fit in the same packet as the end of the response body, obviating the need to send an additional packet. The proxy filters are even smaller than the server hints, and the entire request message may fit in a single packet.

13.2.4 Volume-construction algorithms

The benefit of combining server volumes and proxy filters depends on whether the hints sent by the server are useful to the proxy. The value of the hints, in turn, depends on the quality of the volume construction algorithm.

PERFORMANCE METRICS

Designing and evaluating volume-construction algorithms relies on having concrete, measurable performance goals. Ideally, the server should send a small number of hints, with every hint being useful and every client request predicted in advance. This suggests several possible performance metrics, as follows:

- **Hint size:** The average number of hints piggybacked on a response message provides an indication of the overhead imposed on the server, the network, and the proxy. A small hint size results in lower overhead, at the expense of conveying less information to the proxy.
- **Recall:** Recall measures the fraction of client requests to the proxy that are predicted in advance by a hint from the server. A high recall implies that many requests benefited from the server's hints, whereas a low recall suggests that many requests were not predicted in advance.
- **Precision:** Precision measures the fraction of hints from the server that successfully predict a future request. A high precision implies that many of the hints were useful, whereas a low precision implies that the server sent many hints that were not useful to the proxy.
- **Update fraction:** The update fraction captures the likelihood that a client request was predicted in advance *and* accesses a resource that was

requested from the proxy in the past. A high update fraction implies that a hint allows the proxy to update the cached copy of a resource before a future client request.

The recall and precision metrics are used widely in evaluating information retrieval systems, such as search engines, as discussed in Chapter 2 (Section 2.7.3). In the context of volume construction, recall and precision capture the tension between the desire to predict most requests in advance and the need to avoid generating incorrect predictions. For example, achieving high recall may require the server to send a large number of hints, which would result in low precision since many of the hints might not be useful.

The recall, precision, and update fraction metrics attempt to capture the effectiveness of server hints. In practice, the usefulness of a hint may depend on the time that elapses between the delivery of the hint and the time of the predicted request. Predicting a request just moments before it arrives may not give the proxy sufficient time to act on the prediction. For example, the proxy may not have enough time to prefetch the resource from the server before receiving a request for the resource from a client. Likewise, a hint delivered long before the client request may not be very useful. For example, prefetching a resource an hour in advance of a client request may not be very useful. The prefetched resource would consume space in the proxy's cache. In addition, the resource may be modified at the origin server before the client request arrives. When the client request arrives, the proxy would have to revalidate the cached response and, perhaps, receive a new copy of the resource from the origin server.

These timing constraints can be captured by considering a fixed time interval after each hint. Suppose the proxy receives a hint about resource s. If the client requests s less than τ seconds later, the hint is not useful. Similarly, if the client requests s more than T seconds after the hint, where $T > \tau$, the hint is not useful. In other words, a hint benefits only requests that arrive between τ and T seconds after the proxy receives the hint. A volume-construction algorithm generates a volume v_r for each resource r, where v_r is a set of resources sent as hints whenever resource r is requested. Applying these volumes to a sequence of requests results in specific values for hint size, recall, precision, and update fraction. Balancing the trade-offs between the four metrics suggests several approaches to volume construction. An algorithm could attempt to maximize or minimize one metric subject to a bound on another. For example,

- Maximize recall subject to an upper bound on average hint size
- Minimize hint size subject to a lower bound on recall
- Maximize recall subject to a lower bound on precision
- Maximize precision subject to a lower bound on recall

The first formulation starts with a target hint size and attempts to predict as many requests as possible. In contrast, the second formulation starts with a target recall and attempts to send as few hints as possible subject to that constraint. Similarly, the last two formulations address the trade-off between precision and recall. However, none of these optimization problems has an efficient solution [CKR99], motivating the need for effective heuristics.

ALGORITHMS BASED ON TEMPORAL LOCALITY

The first heuristic in Section 13.2.1 suggests a way to group resources that are typically accessed together. The heuristic suggests that volume v_r should include resource s if a request for r is typically followed by request for s by the same client; the request for s should come more than τ seconds and less than T seconds after the request for r. To decide whether or not to include s in v_r, the algorithm counts the number of requests for r that are followed by a request for s. This number is divided by the total number of requests for r to compute a ratio. If the ratio exceeds some threshold, then s is included in v_r; otherwise, it is not. In fact, the algorithm can count the number of requests for each resource and the number of times each pair of resources appear together, while sequencing through a log of the requests to the server. Then, after processing the log, the algorithm computes the ratios to determine which resources to include in each volume. This basic approach has been considered in other studies of Web prefetching [PM96, Bes95, JK98].

Although the algorithm is computationally efficient, there are two main weaknesses to this approach. First, the algorithm must maintain a large number of counters, especially for Web sites that have thousands of unique resources. Storing these counters can consume a large amount of memory. Enhancements to the basic algorithm can reduce the overhead by focusing on the most popular resources and by eliminating counters for pairs of resources that rarely occur together [CKR99]. Second, the algorithm includes some resources in a volume that do not tend to generate new predictions. If the server piggybacks hints on every response message, a proxy may receive multiple hints for the same resource. These additional hints do not provide extra information. Removing the resource from one or more volumes avoids the generation of these extraneous hints. This reduces the hint size and can help increase precision. Removing a resource from a volume increases precision by avoiding situations in which a hint does not successfully predict a future request.

An extension to the original algorithm can remove ineffective hints by *thinning* the volumes. Starting with the volumes created by the initial algorithm, the two-pass algorithm sequences through the log a second time to simulate the generation of hints based on these volumes. Then the thinning algorithm counts how often each member of a volume generates a *new* prediction of a future request. After computing these statistics, the algorithm removes the ineffective members from each volume. The idea of removing ineffective predictors can be generalized to an algorithm that sequences through the log several times.

On the first iteration, this multipass algorithm identifies the predictor that is most effective in predicting a resource. Then, on the next iteration, the greedy algorithm considers the next best predictor for the remaining requests. By repeating this process several times, the greedy algorithm constructs volumes that produce very few redundant predictions.

The original single-pass algorithm has the lowest computational complexity, at the expense of generating redundant hints. The two-pass algorithm removes ineffective hints, at the expense of additional computational overhead. The multipass algorithm carefully constructs a very effective set of hints, at the expense of even higher computational overhead. Balancing these trade-offs requires understanding how much the more complicated algorithms improve performance and increase the time required to construct volumes. In some cases, the extra computation time may not matter. The trade-off depends on the frequency of volume construction, as well as the differences in performance and computational overhead between the three algorithms. In addition, it is important to compare these three algorithms to simpler approaches, such as the heuristic in Section 13.2.1 that groups resources based on the structure of the URLs. These important issues cannot be resolved without evaluating the algorithms on realistic server data.

13.2.5 Evaluation of volume-construction algorithms

The performance and overhead of the algorithms depends on the number of resources at the server, as well as the client access patterns. The experiments described in [CKR98, CKR99] evaluated the algorithms on server logs from a variety of Web sites, as well as proxy logs from large corporations. The duration of the logs varied from one to seven weeks, the number of requests ranged from 180,000 to 13,000,000, with up to 218,000 clients accessing 94 to 30,000 unique resources. In the proxy logs, 16% to 19% of the requests resulted in 304 Not Modified responses. In the server logs, nearly 85% of the requests were for about 10% of the unique resources. These statistics suggest that correctly predicting the requests for these popular resources could improve proxy performance. For example, hints containing the Last-Modified times of resources at the server would enable the proxy to update the freshness time of cached responses that have not been modified or evict responses that have changed.

The experimental evaluation attempted to establish whether it is possible for a server to deliver useful hints to proxies in an efficient manner. The experiments compared the various volume-construction algorithms in terms of the four metrics of hint size, recall, precision, and update fraction. The evaluation focused on a single proxy filter that limited the number of hints piggybacked on each response. In response messages for resource r, the server piggybacked hints for the resources most likely to be requested after a request for r. The number of hints per response message was varied across the experiments. In constructing volumes, the algorithms considered all resources that were accessed at least ten times. This substantially reduced the complexity of the volume-construction algorithms by removing the large number of less popular resources. Constructing volumes for these less popular resources would not result in many useful hints.

The study concluded that each of the volume-construction algorithms can offer high recall and a high update fraction. However, for directory-based volumes, the high recall comes at the cost of an excessive hint size and low precision. The server sent many hints that did not predict any future requests, and many redundant hints were generated. The algorithms based on access patterns resulted in much higher precision and lower hint sizes. In general, sending a larger number of hints resulted in lower precision, with only a marginal increase in recall. By removing ineffective hints, the two-pass and multipass algorithms offered further reductions in hint size and increases in precision. The two-pass algorithm performed almost as well as the more expensive multi-pass algorithm. Across the collection of logs, the two-pass algorithm achieved a recall of 60% to 80% and a precision of 80% to 88% with a hint size of 2 to 10 hints per message. These results held for predictions applied to a range of time intervals, with T varying from 60 seconds to 5 minutes and τ of 0.

Applying the algorithms to large server logs with millions of records was a fairly time-consuming process. The overhead could be reduced by executing the volume-construction algorithm on a smaller version of the log. Creating a smaller log involves sampling the clients at random and focusing on the requests generated by these clients. The study considered smaller logs ranging from 3% to 50% of the requests in the original logs. The experiments showed that constructing volumes based on these smaller logs did not degrade performance. In another set of experiments, the study generated volumes from the requests in one period and applied the volumes to another period from the same log. Using the same volumes from one hour or one day to the next did not degrade the results. However, recomputing volumes periodically is important to adapt to a shift in access patterns, such as weekday versus weekend traffic, or the reorganization of the content at the Web site. These observations suggest that periodic construction of volumes based on samples of the logs may be sufficient for many servers.

The experiments do not suggest one ideal way to balance the trade-off between the various performance metrics. The emphasis on one performance metric over another depends on how the proxy uses the hints from the server. For example, prefetching content based on server hints would introduce substantial overhead if the precision of the hints is low. Low precision implies that the proxy would prefetch many resources that are not requested in the future. On the other hand, the proxy may use the hints to revalidate (or invalidate) cached resources. Low precision may not introduce as much overhead in this context, suggesting that the proxy should tolerate low precision in exchange for higher recall. Different proxies can select different trade-offs based on their filters. A proxy performing prefetching may prefer aggressive filtering, whereas a proxy performing cache validation may use a relatively liberal filter.

13.2.6 End-to-end information exchange summary

This section described an end-to-end approach to improving the performance of Web proxies based on server hints. The server groups related resources into volumes and applies filters to customize hints to the requesting proxies. Experiments with several server logs show that effective volume-construction algorithms can produce a small number of hints that predict a large fraction of future requests. The most promising algorithms compute the likelihood that resources are accessed together and omit hints that generate duplicate predictions. The combination of proxy filters and server hints can be deployed without requiring modifications to HTTP/1.1. The proxy filter can be sent in a new request header, and server hints can be sent in the trailer of the response message. Working within the existing standard significantly lowers the barrier to deploying the scheme in practice. Otherwise, a lengthy standardization process would be required. The expressiveness of HTTP/1.1 facilitates the introduction of new ideas without changing the protocol.

The study introduced the idea of server volumes and proxy filters, and it described and evaluated several volume-construction algorithms. Yet, several open issues remain. Proxies may send a wide variety of filters with different parameters. Finding an efficient way to apply these filters to server volumes introduces interesting algorithmic problems. The study proposed an initial approach of storing the volume elements in separate first-in first-out lists, depending on the attributes of the resources. However, this may not be the most effective way of handling a large number of filtering parameters. In addition, proxy applications differ in the importance they place on recall, precision, and update fraction. Identifying exactly how these metrics affect application performance would be an interesting avenue for future work. The results could guide the development of new techniques for volume-construction and the selection of parameters for the proxy filters.

Another open issue concerns the server's ability to construct volumes that group resources that are accessed together. The server does not necessarily see all of the requests for the resources. First, some requests are satisfied by the proxy without contacting the origin server. This limits the server's ability to discern the client access patterns. To address this problem, the proxy could inform the server about these requests. For example, suppose a client requests resource s after accessing resource r and that the proxy satisfies the request for r but must contact the server regarding resource s. Then the request for s could include information about the previous request for r. This would enable the server to associate requests for resource s with resource r. Similarly, the server does not handle all of the requests that stem from embedded images and hypertext links in its HTML files. Some of these resources reside at other servers. With some cooperation between Web servers, the hints sent to the proxy could include information about resources located at other servers.

13.3 Prefetching

Satisfying a Web request involves several key steps, including the DNS resolution, establishing a TCP connection, and the HTTP request-response exchange. Web clients, such as user agents and proxies, can perform some of these tasks *in advance* of the user's request. This can reduce the delay perceived by the user at the expense of additional load on the network and the server. During the past few years, Web researchers have proposed and evaluated a variety of prefetching techniques. Thus far, deployment of these ideas has been limited because of concerns about the overhead. However, the desire to improve user performance may ultimately outweigh some of these concerns.

13.3.1 DNS prefetching

Before establishing a connection to a Web server, a client must translate the host portion of the requested URL into an IP address. The client invokes a system call, such as *gethostbyname(),* that sends a query to the local DNS server which may, in turn, contact other DNS servers, as discussed earlier, in Chapter 5 (Section 5.3). Waiting for a response from the local DNS server introduces delay in satisfying the user's request. To avoid this delay, the Web client could initiate the name-to-address translation in advance of the user's request. For example, consider a user who visits a Web page that contains several hypertext links that point to other Web servers. The client could determine the IP addresses of these servers while the user is reading the page. If the user clicks on one of these hypertext links, then the client can immediately establish a TCP connection to the Web server. This reduces the latency experienced by the user in downloading the new page.

The reduction in latency depends on the time required to satisfy the DNS query. The DNS query does not introduce much latency if the local DNS server already has a cached copy of the Web server's IP address. However, the delay can be more significant if the local DNS server must contact other DNS servers to satisfy the query. Delays of several seconds for a reasonable fraction of requests are not uncommon [CK00, HW00]. Cache misses are likely for less popular Web sites or for name-to-address mappings with small time-to-live (TTL) values. Small TTL values are relatively common when the responses to DNS queries are used to balance load across the replicas of a Web site. However, small TTLs also limit the benefits of prefetching DNS information far in advance of the user's request. Although prefetching ensures that the Web client and the local DNS server have a copy of the Web server's IP address, the cached information may become out of date before the user requests content from this Web server. The recent popularity of content distribution networks that depend on small TTL values to locate better replicas for a resource complicate the case for DNS prefetching.

Prefetching the Web server's IP address reduces user-perceived latency at the risk of imposing additional load on the network and the DNS servers. The Web client performs the name-to-address translation in the hope that the user eventually visits the Web site. However, the user behavior is not known in advance. If the user never clicks on the hypertext link, then the DNS query was not necessary. The query imposes load on the local DNS server and, perhaps, on other DNS servers as well. Satisfying this query may have delayed these DNS servers in handling other requests, resulting in higher latency for other DNS queries. Additionally, there might be DNS cache contention for server names that are rarely used. If a large proportion of Web clients perform DNS prefetching, this could result in a substantial increase in the number of queries handled by DNS servers in the Internet. These queries would also result in an increase in Internet traffic. The benefits of DNS prefetching need to be weighed against the various costs.

13.3.2 Connection prefetching

As part of handling an HTTP request, the Web client establishes a TCP connection to the Web server or to an intermediary such as a proxy. Opening a TCP connection requires a three-way handshake between the client and the server, as discussed in Chapter 5 (Section 5.2). The latency for this step of the Web transfer depends on the round-trip delay between the two hosts, as well as the queuing delay at the server and additional delay to recover from packet loss. To hide these delays from the user, the Web client could establish a TCP connection to the server in advance of the user's request [CK00]. Then, when the user clicks on a hypertext link, the client can immediately send the HTTP request over the open TCP connection. If the user does not initiate a request, either the client or the server would eventually close the TCP connection.

The delay in satisfying a request for static content is dominated by the overheads introduced by TCP. For the many small response messages, the extra round-trip time for opening the TCP connection is a visible fraction of the total delay. However, successfully hiding this delay from the user depends on two factors. First, to achieve the full performance benefit, the connection establishment must complete before the user clicks on the hypertext link; otherwise, the client must wait before sending the HTTP request. Second, the user request must occur before the client or the server decide to close the connection. Web servers typically impose a time limit on how long a TCP connection can remain idle. A user request invoked after the server has closed the connection, or while the server is in the process of closing the connection, does not enjoy the performance benefit. Existing open idle TCP connections might actually result in new connections being queued for a longer period. Worse yet, the number of open connections can lower the idle timeout value of sessions in progress.

Optimistically opening a TCP connection to the server reduces the user-perceived latency at the expense of overhead on the network, the client, and the server. The three-way handshake introduces three IP packets to the network, not including any retransmitted packets and the additional packets necessary to close the connection. Even if the client closes the TCP connection without sending an HTTP request, the server consumes resources to open and maintain the connection. The Web server creates state for the connection and may assign a process to handle the anticipated HTTP request(s). In fact, the Web server typically must retain state for a period of time after the connection has been closed. Accepting this TCP connection may prevent the server from accepting TCP connections from other clients. In fact, opening and closing a TCP connection without sending an HTTP request could be viewed as a denial of service attack on the Web server. The overheads on the server and the network need to be weighed against the potential performance benefits to the user.

13.3.3 HTTP prefetching

After establishing a TCP connection, a Web client issues an HTTP request to the Web server. Even if the client has a cached copy of the requested resource, the server may have to be contacted to revalidate the cached version. The latency in receiving the HTTP response depends on a variety of factors, including the response generation time at the server, the size of the response message, and the bandwidth available from the server to the client. The client can hide the delay from the user by issuing the HTTP request in advance and caching the response. If a user requests the resource, the client can provide the response directly from its cache. Assuming that the cached response has not become stale, the client can satisfy the user's request without determining the server's IP address, opening a connection to the server, and sending the HTTP request. The user would receive an almost immediate response. In addition, prefetching can make more efficient use of TCP connections than traditional Web transfers that are driven by user actions. The prefetching client could pipeline a series of requests over a single persistent connection, and the back-to-back transfers of the response messages could avoid the overhead of repeating the slow-start phase of congestion control.

Prefetching HTTP responses has been the focus of a number of research studies [Bes95, PM96, JK98, CB98, Duc99]. Despite the potential reduction in user-perceived latency, retrieving Web resources in advance of user requests could introduce a substantial load on the Web server and the network. Prefetching is not useful unless a user requests the resource and the prefetched response is still fresh. In addition, network and server bandwidth devoted to transmitting the response competes with other ongoing transfers. For example, consider a user accessing the Web via a low-bandwidth modem connection [HL96, LB97]. On the one hand, prefetching during periods of inactivity can make more effective use of the limited bandwidth. On the other hand, prefetching when the user is downloading another Web page would result in higher user-perceived latency for the current page. In addition, the prefetched resource may displace other items in the client's cache, resulting in higher latency for responding to other requests in the future.

Rather than prefetching the resource, the server could prefetch the metadata about the resource. For example, the client could send a HEAD request to the server, as discussed earlier in Section 13.1.2. The HTTP response should have the same headers as the response to a GET request. This information is particularly useful if the client already has a cached copy of the resource. Depending on whether or not the resource has changed at the origin server, the client could invalidate the cached resource or update its freshness lifetime. The headers in the response message may be useful even if the client does not have a cached copy of the resource. For example, the client could inspect the headers related to caching, such as Last-Modified, Cache-Control, or Content-Type, to determine whether it is worthwhile to prefetch the entire resource. The client could decide not to prefetch a resource that is not cacheable or changes often. In addition, the client could inspect the Content-Length header to determine the size of the resource. The client may decide to prefetch a resource if the Content-Length header indicates that the size is below some threshold. This would avoid prefetching resources that would introduce a large amount of network traffic.

Rather than issuing a HEAD request to determine the size of the resource, the client could directly control the amount of prefetched data by sending a GET request with the Range header (assuming that the Web server permits Range requests). For example, the client could request the first 1000 bytes of the resource. This would allow the client to fetch a small resource in its entirety, as well as the initial portion of a large resource. In some cases, prefetching the initial bytes, or *prefix,* of the resource may be very useful [Hor98, SRT99]. For example, the first few bytes of a GIF file includes the image size and may have a low-resolution version of the picture. Having the prefix of the image in advance of the user request would allow the browser to start rendering the image. Similarly, the prefix of an audio or video clip may contain enough frames to start playing the stream [SRT99, GRB00]. Once the user requests the resource, the browser can send a second Range request to fetch the remainder of the content. From the user's viewpoint, the content starts to appear immediately, even though the browser has not fetched the entire resource in advance.

13.3.4 Trade-offs in prefetching

Prefetching introduces a tension between reducing user-perceived latency and increasing load on the network and the components of the Web. Several issues play a role in balancing these trade-offs, as follows:

- **Which tasks to perform in advance:** Prefetching can involve performing a DNS query, opening a TCP connection, retrieving metadata, and fetching all or part of a resource. Performing more tasks in advance offers further reductions in user-perceived latency at the expense of extra overhead.
- **Which resources to consider:** Prefetching is most effective when the information is likely to be used and to stay up-to-date. This suggests focusing on the most popular resources and servers and on resources that do not change very often. Otherwise, prefetching may introduce significant overhead without offering significant benefits. The client may have heuristics for identifying these resources or draw on statistics about past access patterns.
- **Which component should do the prefetching:** Any client can perform prefetching. Prefetching by the user agent moves the data close to the user but consumes more network resources, including the user's connection to the Internet. If the user agent communicates via a proxy, the server's response may also be cached at the proxy. As an alternative, the proxy could prefetch resources on its own. This reduces the load on the links between the proxy and the user agent, at the expense of extra delay for the user agent to retrieve the data from the proxy if the user requests the resource.

Letizia [Lie95] was an early HTTP prefetching system that parsed HTML files and prefetched resources based on the hypertext links, as discussed in Chapter 2 (Section 2.8.2). Letizia opened additional windows to display the prefetched content. The system could be configured to follow the links in these documents to prefetch multiple levels of hypertext links. However, prefetching all of the hypertext links on a page may introduce too much overhead. As a heuristic, the client could prefetch the first few links in the page, assuming them to be more popular. Consider a Web page that contains a list of URLs returned by a search engine. The user is likely to consider the items in the list in order because typically some relevancy ranking has already been performed by the search engine. However, in some cases, the popularity of the URLs may not relate to their position on the page.

The user agent may be able to gauge the popularity of the URLs based on previous requests. For example, Letizia kept track of the user's preferences and browsing patterns to decide which resources to prefetch. Compared with user agents, a proxy may be in a better position to judge the popularity of resources by observing requests from a collection of clients. Based on these access patterns, the proxy can determine which hypertext links are most popular. Upon receiving a request for the HTML file, the proxy can also prefetch the popular resources reachable from that page. However, the proxy does not have sufficient data about the access patterns unless several clients have requested the HTML file in the past [JK98]. The server has more complete information about client access patterns. Thus the server could provide hints to the proxy about which resources are likely to be requested in the future, as discussed earlier in Section 13.2.

Rather than sending hints to the proxy, the statistics about resource popularity could be embedded in the HTML file. For example, a hypertext link could include additional information about the likelihood that a user selects this link after reading the containing page. This would require adding a new variable to HTML and updating the statistics for a page periodically. Such techniques are likely to have more impact in specific applications such as search engines rather than for all HTML pages. In some cases, the person who writes the HTML file can have direct control over prefetching. For example, suppose the HTML file `http://www.foo.com/index.html` contains a hypertext link to an HTML `http://www.foo.com/neat.html` that contains an embedded image `http://www.foo.com/pic.jpg`. Referencing `pic.jpg` in `index.html` would ensure that a client fetches the image as part of downloading the initial Web page. Then the image would already reside at the client site when the user requests `neat.html`. To avoid showing the image as part of the first page, the HTML code could specify that the image should be displayed in a very small region of the screen, such as a single pixel.

Most research on prefetching has focused on fetching HTTP responses from the server. The results of these studies are somewhat mixed. User latency can be reduced as long as prefetching does not degrade the performance of other requests. However, fetching resources that are never requested by the user introduces substantial overhead on the network and the server. Prefetching DNS information, TCP connections, and HTTP metadata does not introduce much network traffic. However, prefetching DNS information imparts load on the DNS servers, and prefetching TCP connections and HTTP metadata imparts load on the Web servers. In some cases, prefetching HTTP metadata on an existing TCP connection may actually reduce overhead by avoiding the need for a separate TCP connection in the future.

The deployment of prefetching in the Web depends on whether the performance gains outweigh the costs. Prefetching may become more popular if bandwidth becomes cheaper and more plentiful over time or if users become increasingly intolerant of large delays. Balancing the trade-off between overhead and performance requires a better quantitative understanding of how much prefetching reduces user-perceived latency and how much lower delay enhances the user's experience in browsing the Web, at the expense of increased load on Web servers and the underlying network.

13.4 Summary

In this chapter, we examined three strands of research dealing with Web caching. The first section dealt with cache revalidation, an important factor in providing semantic transparency in caching. The piggybacking technique demonstrated that it is possible to reduce the cost of revalidation while lowering user-perceived latency as a result of advanced validation. The bidirectional approach using filters and volumes makes full use of the information available to both proxies and origin servers. The result is tailored hints to proxies at low cost to the origin server and the network. The class of algorithms involved in constructing volumes is a rich area for further exploration. Exploration of the various performance metrics enables the application of the algorithms in various scenarios. The discussion of prefetching at the DNS, TCP, and HTTP levels covers the various ways in which user-perceived latency can be reduced. Each of the techniques has associated costs that have to be examined under realistic scenarios. In the various studies, we notice the crucial role played by actual data. Although extensive data is generally hard to obtain, recent improvements in construction of data repositories (discussed in Chapter 14) may increase the chances of research ideas being verified against realistic measurement data.

14

Research Perspectives in Measurement

Collecting and analyzing measurement data plays an important role in evaluating Web protocols and software components. Web researchers frequently draw on logs and traces to characterize Web traffic and evaluate new ideas for improving Web performance. This has led to considerable work in the Web research community on effective ways to acquire and process traffic measurements. Conducting research on Web measurement requires an understanding of Hypertext Transfer Protocol (HTTP) and the underlying network protocols, as well as the ability to develop efficient and robust software. Web measurements typically involve a large amount of data. Like other networking protocols, HTTP was not designed with measurement in mind. Despite the importance of collecting measurement data, generating accurate measurement records is not a primary task for most Web proxy and server implementations. Therefore these records can have mistakes and inconsistencies that complicate the analysis of the data. Detecting these errors requires defensive programming that verifies both the syntax and the semantics of the records.

Web performance depends on the interplay between a diverse collection of protocols. User-perceived latency and server throughput for HTTP transfers depends on the underlying transport level. The performance of multimedia applications depends on the complex interaction of several different protocols for transferring control messages, transmitting audio and video data, and exchanging feedback about current network conditions. Characterizing the interaction between the protocols requires detailed traces that capture the activity at each of the layers in the protocol stack. Traditional proxy and server logs do not capture these details. Packet traces offer a possible alternative for studying the impact of the network on application-level performance. However, packet monitors have traditionally collected data at the network level and transport level without providing information about the application-level protocol, such as HTTP headers that may be spread over multiple IP packets. Studying the interplay between the application and transport levels requires more advanced packet monitoring software that extracts information about the application-level messages.

In this chapter, we focus on the following four topics:

- **Packet monitoring of HTTP traffic:** Most research studies of Web traffic measurements have drawn on logs collected from proxies and servers. However, these logs typically do not include low-level information about HTTP request and response messages and the timing of the various stages in Web transactions. Packet traces collected by monitoring a network link can provide much more detail, as discussed in Chapter 9 (Section 9.2.4). In this chapter, we describe the software challenges in capturing IP packets on a network link, reconstructing the stream of bytes for each Transmission Control Protocol (TCP) connection, and reconstructing the HTTP request and response messages.

- **Analyzing Web server logs:** Server logs have been used in a wide variety of research studies. However, analyzing server logs introduces a variety of practical challenges because of the large number of records, the frequency of errors, and the diversity of log formats. Preprocessing the logs can significantly reduce the complexity of the analysis software, as discussed in Chapter 9 (Section 9.4). In this chapter, we describe experiences in developing software for parsing, filtering, transforming, and analyzing a collection of server logs. The discussion identifies several common pitfalls in processing server logs and describes how to exploit existing library routines to develop robust and efficient software.

- **Publicly available logs and traces:** The importance of Web traffic measurements to the research community has led to several efforts to create repositories of publicly available logs and traces. The measurement data are typically available on the Web. We present a brief overview of existing Web sites that provide access to measurement data. Most of these sites provide access to data in a variety of different formats on an "as is" basis. The World Wide Web Consortium (W3C) has developed a formal description of the syntax and semantics of server logs and provides access to clean, certified logs in a uniform format.

- **Measuring multimedia streams:** Although most Web measurement work has focused on HTTP traffic, the emergence of multimedia streaming as an important Web application has spawned several measurement studies of multimedia traffic. Characterization of audio and video streams considers many of the same workload parameters as previous work on HTTP traffic, as well as additional properties unique to multimedia data. Measuring multimedia traffic introduces new challenges because of the diverse collection of protocols for streaming audio and video data, as discussed earlier in Chapter 12 (Section 12.3). We describe four studies based on static analysis of multimedia files on the Web, analysis of multimedia server logs, packet monitoring of audio transfers, and packet monitoring techniques for collecting both control messages and data packets.

Throughout the chapter, we emphasize the important role of software in collecting and analyzing traffic measurements.

14.1 Packet Monitoring of HTTP Traffic

Packet monitoring is an effective way to capture detailed information about Web traffic. The packet monitor is a computer that receives a copy of the packets traveling over one or more network links and runs software that processes the packets to generate a trace. Traces may be stored in memory, disk, or tape at the packet monitor and then copied to another machine for archiving and analyzing the data. In this section, we provide an overview of various stages in collecting packet traces of HTTP traffic:

- Tapping a link carrying IP packets
- Capturing packets from HTTP transfers
- Demultiplexing packets into TCP connections
- Reconstructing the ordered stream of bytes
- Extracting HTTP messages from the byte stream
- Generating a log of the HTTP messages

Measuring HTTP traffic with a packet monitor requires dealing with vagaries at the TCP and HTTP levels. At the TCP level, the monitor must handle missing, out of order, and duplicate IP packets. At the HTTP level, the monitor must allow for persistent connections that transfer multiple HTTP messages and aborted transfers. In addition, the monitor must tolerate HTTP messages sent by Web components that are not compliant with these protocols. An early attempt at online reconstruction of HTTP messages from IP traces is described in [Fel00a].

14.1.1 Tapping a link

Collecting packet traces requires an effective way to tap a link in an operational IP network. The difficulty of tapping a link depends on the underlying technology and network configuration, as follows:

- **Shared media:** Many local area networks consist of shared media, such as an Ethernet, a FDDI ring, or a wireless network. Every machine on the network sees every packet, including packets from and to other hosts. Tapping the shared medium simply requires attaching the packet monitor to the network, as shown in Figure 14.1(a). A normal host on the shared medium only receives a copy of packets directed to it. However, many network interface cards can be configured to run in *promiscuous mode* to make a local copy of every packet. The packets must be copied from the interface card into the monitor quickly enough to ensure that the interface

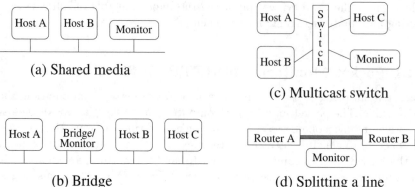

(a) Shared media

(c) Multicast switch

(b) Bridge

(d) Splitting a line

Figure 14.1. Techniques for tapping a link

has enough memory to store subsequent packets as they arrive. This operation is passive and does not affect the other hosts on the network. In fact, the rest of hosts on the network would not be aware that the packet monitor is collecting data.

- **Bridge:** An alternative approach involves monitoring traffic at a bridge that carries traffic between network segments, as shown in Figure 14.1(b). A special-purpose bridge could be configured to acquire a copy of each packet as part of directing packets from one segment to another. By participating in the forwarding of each packet, the bridge can ensure that every packet is captured. Unlike promiscuous monitoring, capturing packets at a bridge may delay the forwarding of traffic on the network. Care must be taken to record the relevant information about each packet quickly to avoid degrading the throughput of the bridge.

- **Multicast switch:** Some networks consist of switches that direct packets from a collection of input links to a collection of output links. Switches typically have higher throughput than shared media because traffic can flow on each link at the same time. Compared with monitoring a shared medium, capturing packet traces at a switch is fairly difficult. No one link sees a copy of every packet. One approach to receiving every packet is to connect a packet monitor to every input link or every output link. However, this may be expensive. Another alternative is to devote one output link on the switch to a packet monitor and to have the switch perform *multicast* forwarding to direct copies of outgoing packets to the monitor, as shown in Figure 14.1(c). The switch would direct the packet to its assigned outgoing link and to the monitor. However, copying every packet from every input link may exceed the capacity of the link to the monitor.

Instead, multicast forwarding is most appropriate for sampling a fraction of the packets traversing a switch.

- **Point-to-point link:** Installing a bridge or a switch with multicast capability is not always possible. An alternative approach to packet monitoring involves splitting a link into two parts, as shown in Figure 14.1(d). The figure shows a bidirectional link that consists of two unidirectional links between two routers. Each unidirectional link is split and fed to the packet monitor. In some cases, a link in an operational network may already be split for testing and diagnostic purposes. Connecting to the split link ensures that the packet monitor receives a copy of any packet transmitted between the two routers. However, splitting a link may weaken the electrical or optical signal traveling between the two routers. In some cases, equipment such as an optical amplifier may be necessary to avoid degradation of the signal received by the routers and the packet monitor.

14.1.2 Capturing packets

In addition to tapping the link, the monitor must have an effective way to identify which IP packets to capture and which packets to discard as they arrive. Application-level protocols typically have a well-known TCP port, such as HTTP's use of port 80. To monitor HTTP traffic, the packet monitor can limit itself to considering TCP traffic traveling to or from port 80. This can be decided on a per-packet basis by inspecting the protocol field of the IP header and the source and destination port numbers of the TCP header. However, isolating all HTTP traffic is difficult. Some Web sites do not use the well-known port, choosing instead to use an unreserved port such as 8000 or 8080. In addition, some applications may communicate via port 80 using a different protocol. Although ports are allocated to particular applications, an application developer or system administrator could disregard these guidelines by using port 80 for an application that uses a different protocol.

In addition, some Web traffic uses HTTPS on port 443. A packet monitor could capture HTTPS traffic by monitoring TCP traffic with source or destination port 443. However, data transferred via HTTPS are encrypted using the Secure Socket Layer (SSL). The monitor cannot identify the HTTP messages transferred over these TCP connections. Still, the monitor could capture the port-443 traffic to compute basic statistics, such as the number of connections and bytes using HTTPS. Other transfers initiated by a Web browser may use other application-layer protocols. In some cases, this traffic can be captured by monitoring the ports allocated to these protocols. However, several applications use protocols that do not use static port numbers for transferring data. For example, a File Transfer Protocol (FTP) client and server may dynamically select the port number for the TCP connection used for data transfer. Similarly, multimedia streaming protocols typically do not use well-known ports for

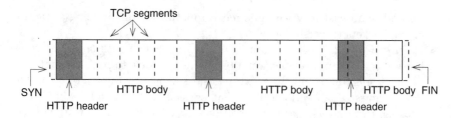

Figure 14.2. HTTP messages consisting of a sequence of TCP segments

transferring audio and video data, as discussed in more detail later, in Section 14.4.4.

Capturing traffic with particular IP and TCP headers requires applying a filter to IP packets as they arrive. Filtering packets as early as possible reduces the overhead incurred in copying and processing packets that are ultimately discarded. The packet monitor may have dedicated hardware that classifies the packets as they are received by the network interface card. When hardware support is unavailable, packets can be filtered in the operating system or at the application level. A wide variety of packet monitoring has been done using the *tcpdump* tool [JLM, Tcp] based on the Berkeley Packet Filter (BPF) [MJ93]. BPF filters packets based on multiple combinations of IP and TCP/UDP header fields and retains a fixed number of bytes for each packet that passes through the filter. For example, BPF could be configured to capture the first 40 bytes of all packets using TCP with source or destination port 80 or using UDP with destination port 23. The BPF software can be installed inside the operating system on many platforms.

For computing basic statistics about Web traffic, retaining the IP and TCP headers may be sufficient. However, inspecting the HTTP messages within the TCP connection requires access to the bytes following the IP and TCP headers. HTTP transfers may be split into IP packets in a variety of ways. Hence, HTTP-level information may occur within any IP packet in the TCP connection, as shown in Figure 14.2. The first HTTP request or response message in a connection starts with the first packet after the three-way handshake establishes communication between the two hosts. However, the HTTP header may span multiple packets. In addition, several HTTP transfers may travel over the same persistent connection. The HTTP headers may occur at any point in the TCP connection. In fact, a header may even start in the middle of an IP packet. Thus capturing each of the HTTP transfers requires inspecting the contents of the IP packets.

Packet monitoring of HTTP traffic involves capturing the full contents of each IP packet that contains a TCP segment with source or destination port 80. Ideally, the monitor captures every such packet. However, the monitor may lose

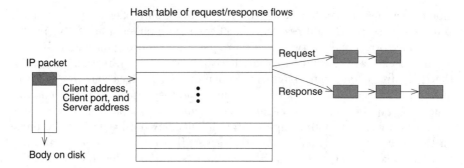

Figure 14.3. Hash table for demultiplexing packets into flows

packets if the network interface card or the operating system cannot keep pace with the high rate of packet arrivals. When capturing and filtering the packets, the monitor can associate each packet with a timestamp that indicates when the packet was received by the monitor. To protect user privacy, the monitor could scramble or encrypt the source and destination IP addresses of the captured packets; however, this does not prevent access to private information in the HTTP headers and message bodies. After passing through the capturing and filtering stages, the packet can be stored in memory or on disk for subsequent processing. As the captured traffic is reconstructed into HTTP messages, the monitor can reclaim the storage space by discarding some of the IP packets. The packet monitor needs to make efficient use of the speed and capacity of the storage subsystem to capture HTTP requests and responses at a high rate.

14.1.3 Demultiplexing packets

Any particular link in the Internet typically carries traffic on behalf of several different TCP connections. The monitor needs an effective way to associate each packet with the appropriate TCP connection. However, the packet monitor is not the source or destination of the TCP connection, and the monitor may not see every packet between the two hosts. Instead, the monitor must *infer* the existence of a TCP connection from the information in the packets' IP and TCP headers. A TCP connection is identified by the source and destination IP addresses and port numbers. The monitor can group packets that have the same source and destination IP addresses and ports numbers. To distinguish this grouping of packets from the associated TCP connection, we refer to the stream of packets as a *flow*. Packets with a destination port of 80 are part of a request flow from a Web client, and packets with a source port of 80 are part of a response flow to a Web client.

To demultiplex the packets, the monitor can maintain a hash table of flows, as shown in Figure 14.3. Assuming that the Web server uses port 80, the monitor can use a key that is the concatenation of three fields—the client IP address, the server IP address, and the client port number. Each entry in the hash table corresponds to two flows—a request flow and response flow. Hence, when a packet arrives, it is associated with a key and a direction, based on the IP addresses and port numbers. Depending on its location, the monitor may not see the packets for both the request and response flow. If the monitor resides directly in front of the client or server machine, all packets between the two hosts traverse the link being monitored. This may not be the case for links on the path between the client and the server. IP routing does not guarantee that all packets between the same source and destination follow the same path, and traffic from the client to the server may not traverse the same links as the path from the server to the client.

Hence, the monitor cannot depend on seeing every packet between the two hosts. In fact, even if every packet traverses the link, the monitor may miss some of these packets during periods of heavy load. Instead, the monitor simply demultiplexes packets into flows. An efficient design of the packet monitor is necessary to avoid losing packets by running out of memory or disk space. To avoid losing packets in this manner, the monitor can give top priority to the capturing and filtering of packets. Other tasks, such as the demultiplexing of packets into flows, can be given lower priority. For example, the monitor can copy packets to memory or disk as they are captured and filtered, and a second, lower-priority process can perform the remaining tasks. To further enhance efficiency, the software that performs these tasks can avoid reading or copying the contents of the IP packets whenever possible. Packet demultiplexing only draws on the IP and TCP headers, not the contents of the packet. Accessing the rest of the packet can be deferred to a later stage or avoided entirely, as discussed below.

14.1.4 Reconstructing the ordered stream

In processing the packets in a flow, the monitor must perform many of the functions of a TCP receiver. In particular, the monitor must handle out-of-order, corrupted, and duplicated packets. IP does not guarantee reliable, ordered delivery of packets; hence, packets may be corrupted or arrive out of order. In addition, a monitor may see duplicate packets as a result of retransmissions by the TCP sender. A TCP sender may mistakenly infer that a packet had been lost and transmit the data again. Alternatively, the original packet may be lost somewhere between the monitored link and the TCP receiver. That is, the monitor may capture a packet that never reaches its intended recipient. In either case, the monitor may receive duplicate data. To further complicate matters, TCP does not guarantee that retransmitted data is packetized in the same way as the original data. Hence, the monitor cannot simply detect and delete duplicate packets. Instead, the monitor must detect duplication of ranges of bytes in the TCP stream.

Like a TCP receiver, the packet monitor can use the information in the TCP header to construct an ordered byte stream from the sequence of packets. Corrupted packets can be detected and deleted based on the checksum field in the TCP header. Out-of-order packets can be reordered based on the sequence number field in the TCP header. Repeated data can be detected based on the sequence numbers and segment lengths. For example, consider two packets with the same source and destination addresses and port numbers, with one packet having sequence number 50 and length 10 and the other packet having sequence number 55 and length 20. The last five bytes of the first packet overlap with the first five bytes of the second packet. In processing the data in this flow, the monitor should consider these five bytes a single time by skipping the last five bytes of the first packet or the first five bytes of the second packet. In other cases, where one packet is completely subsumed by another, the monitor can discard the redundant packet.

At some point, the monitor needs a way to determine that a flow is "done." The possibility of out-of-order and retransmitted packets makes this more complicated. A flow is complete if it has a beginning, an end, and everything in between. That is, the flow should represent a complete TCP connection with a SYN packet, a FIN or RST packet, and the full stream of bytes. The number of bytes expected between the SYN and the FIN/RST can be determined based on the sequence numbers in the SYN and FIN/RST packets. However, a flow may not satisfy these three criteria. The monitor may miss packets, some packets may follow a path that does not traverse the monitored link, or an abort operation may cause a TCP connection to end before all lost packets have been retransmitted. In an extreme case, the TCP sender may crash before the connection completes, resulting in a flow with no FIN or RST packet. In any of these scenarios, the packet monitor may never be able to successfully finish constructing an ordered, reliable byte stream out of the flow.

Flows that do not complete consume resources on the packet monitor. In addition, at some time in the future, a different TCP connection between the same hosts may use the same port numbers. This could cause the monitor to mistakenly associate packets from the new TCP connection with the flow for the old TCP connection. Instead, the monitor should ultimately stop waiting for additional packets to arrive to a flow. The simplest approach is a timeout-based scheme. If a flow has not received any new packet for a period of time, the monitor could assume that the TCP connection has ended. Selecting the appropriate time period is a delicate matter. A large timeout results in higher resource consumption on the packet monitor and increases the likelihood that a new TCP connection collides with the existing flow. However, a small timeout value results in a higher likelihood that a flow is retired when the associated

TCP connection is still active. For example, a persistent connection may be idle for several tens of seconds between successive HTTP requests or responses.

The flow timeout policy should depend on the details of TCP and HTTP implementations. The flow timeout should be larger than any timers used to control the transmission of packets in TCP and the closure of idle TCP connections by HTTP clients and servers. Investigation of measurement data and server software can lend insight into the appropriate timeout values. In practice, the monitor can retire idle flows by periodically inspecting the entries in the hash table. For each entry, the monitor can determine the time that has elapsed since the last packet arrival. The flow is retired if the time exceeds a preconfigured threshold. As with the demultiplexing of packets into flows, reconstructing and retiring the flows does not require reading or accessing the data in the TCP segments.

14.1.5 Extracting HTTP messages

Extracting the HTTP messages from each flow requires the monitor to inspect the byte stream. In discussing the extraction process, we initially assume that the flow has been completely reconstructed. Later, we discuss how to accommodate lost packets and how to overlap the extraction of HTTP messages with the reconstruction of the ordered byte stream. Each HTTP message consists of a header and an optional body, and each flow consists of one or more HTTP messages, as shown earlier, in Figure 14.2. Processing the flow requires identifying the header of one message and locating the beginning of the next message. The flow should start with a valid HTTP header. For example, a request flow should start with a request method, a Request-URI, and a protocol version; a response flow should start with a protocol version and response code. The header should end with a double carriage-return and line-feed (CRLF), followed by the optional body.

Locating the boundary between two consecutive messages depends on the HTTP-level details of the first message. In reconstructing the response messages, the packet monitor must handle the same scenarios as any other HTTP/1.1 component, as follows:

- **Absence of body:** In some situations, the monitor can assume that the message does not include a body and that the next message starts immediately after the double CRLF. For example, GET requests and 304 Not Modified responses should not include a message body.
- **Presence of Content-Length:** Some messages include a Content-Length header that indicates the size of the body. This enables the monitor to identify the point in the byte stream where the next message begins without inspecting the bytes in the body of the first message.
- **Chunk-encoded message:** Some HTTP messages include metadata inside the body. Under chunked encoding, the HTTP entity is divided into

one or more chunks, as discussed earlier, in Chapter 7 (Section 7.6). Each chunk includes a chunk header that indicates its length. Identifying the end of the message requires the monitor to consider each chunk header to locate the beginning of the next chunk. The message ends with a zero-length chunk.

- **Multipart/byteranges:** A response message with the `Content-Type: multipart/byteranges` header has multiple ranges of data in the body, as discussed earlier, in Chapter 7 (Section 7.4.1). The HTTP response header identifies a boundary string that marks the beginning of each byte range in the body. The monitor can locate the beginning of each range and sequence to the beginning of the next range, similar to sequencing through the chunks in a chunk-encoded message.

- **End of TCP connection:** The final way for the monitor to detect the end of a response message is to note that the TCP connection has ended with a FIN or RST packet. This may occur because the server uses the closure of the TCP connection to indicate the end of the response body or because the client or the server has aborted the TCP connection.

The addition of chunked encoding and multipart byteranges to HTTP/1.1 complicates the identification of message boundaries by requiring the packet monitor to inspect the contents of message body. This would not be necessary for HTTP/1.0 traffic. In addition, the boundary between two messages may occur within a single IP packet because of pipelining.

After identifying the end of one message, the monitor can begin extracting the next message. The process repeats until all messages have been extracted from the flow. However, lost packets introduce extra complexity to the extraction process. In fact, in some cases, a lost packet may make it impossible to continue processing a flow. For example, recovering from a missing `Content-Length` header or a missing double CRLF would be difficult, if not impossible, because the monitor would not know how to identify the end of the message body and the beginning of the next message. Similarly, the loss of a chunk header or a multipart/byterange header inside the message body would make it difficult to locate the end of the message. When these kinds of packet loss occur, the monitor can simply record an error message to indicate that the rest of the flow could not be processed. Having a small packet loss rate is extremely important. Otherwise, a high proportion of flows would experience one or more unrecoverable losses. The likelihood of packet loss depends on the speed and traffic load on the link, as well as the efficiency of the hardware and software on the packet monitor.

Although losing a packet from an HTTP header introduces considerable problems, losing a packet in the middle of an entity body does not necessarily disrupt the processing of a flow. Losing a few hundred bytes of a large postscript document does not preclude the monitor from locating the next message in the flow. In fact, processing the entity body may not be necessary at all. If the monitor records the entity body or statistics computed from the entity body, then the packet loss would keep the monitor from logging the information for this request. Still, the monitor could proceed to the next message in the flow without difficulty. If the monitor logs only the HTTP headers, then the entity body does not need to be processed at all. In this scenario, the monitor can avoid the overhead of reading the contents of most of the captured IP packets. A typical HTTP response message consists of around 300 bytes of header and around 10 KB of body. Ignoring the body obviates the need to inspect about 97% of the bytes that have been captured.

14.1.6 Generating HTTP traces

Ultimately, the monitor can record a wide variety of information about the HTTP traffic. The appropriate collection of fields depends on what kinds of analysis may utilize the traces. In contrast to traditional proxy and server logs, the packet trace can include information at several protocol levels (IP, TCP, HTTP), as well as timestamps for the key steps in each HTTP transaction. Sample fields are listed in Table 14.1. No formal or informal standards exist for trace formats for packet-level measurements of Web traffic. Therefore a packet trace could record virtually any information that can be extracted from the raw data. However, extracting, writing, and storing the fields introduces overhead on the packet monitor, potentially interfering with the capture and reconstruction of the HTTP traffic. The exact trade-offs vary depending on the volume of traffic on the link, as well as the speed of the monitoring platform and the efficiency of the reconstruction hardware.

At the IP and TCP level, the monitor could record the client and server IP addresses, as well as the number of bytes and packets transmitted in each direction. The TCP connection starts with a three-way handshake with a client SYN, server SYN-ACK, and client ACK. The timestamps for the two SYN packets mark the beginning of each direction of the TCP connection. Similarly, the timestamps of the FIN or RST packets in each direction mark the end of the connection. Noting whether the connection ended with a FIN or an RST provides a useful way to identify aborted transfers. In addition, the trace could identify whether or not the monitor experienced packet loss for this TCP connection and whether the loss disrupted the reconstruction process. In addition to the fields listed in Table 14.1, the monitor could conceivably record the size and timestamp for each packet on the TCP connection. This information would be useful for some kinds of analysis, at the expense of writing and storing the extra information.

At the HTTP level, the packet monitor could record the HTTP request and response headers. Alternatively, recording a select subset of the headers would reduce the overhead of writing, storing, and analyzing the trace. The choice

Table 14.1. Example fields in an HTTP packet trace

Category	Examples
TCP/IP	Client and server IP addresses
	Number of packets and bytes transmitted
	Timestamp for beginning of TCP connection (SYN)
	Timestamp for ending of TCP connection (FIN/RST)
	Termination method for flow (FIN vs. RST)
	Errors (missing packet within flow)
HTTP	HTTP request header
	HTTP response header
	Timestamp for beginning of HTTP header
	Timestamp for beginning of HTTP body
	Timestamp for ending of HTTP body
	Errors (message with invalid HTTP syntax)
Entity	Checksum of entity body
	Embedded HREFs/IMGREFs

depends on the trade-off between the overhead of collecting the data and the desire to analyze the data in a wide variety of ways. Each HTTP message spans some portion of the byte stream of the underlying TCP connection, as shown earlier, in Figure 14.2. Because a single connection may handle multiple HTTP transfers, knowing the timestamps for the beginning and end of the TCP connection does not necessarily provide a good indication of the time when each HTTP message was sent. The packet monitor can record timestamps for the key parts of the HTTP message—the beginning of the header, the beginning of the body, and the end of the body. To determine these times, the monitoring software would need to consult the timestamps associated with the corresponding IP packets.

Some of the HTTP messages contain an entity body. In theory, the packet monitor could record the body of every HTTP message. However, this would introduce significant overhead for writing and storing the data, because the message body is often much larger than the HTTP header. Still, information about the entity is useful for a variety of analyses. For example, a checksum of the entity could be used to identify whether a Web resource changes from one request to the next. In addition, recording the hypertext links and embedded images in an HTML file would be useful to determine the Web resources that are identified within a Web page. The monitor could selectively record the entity body, or information about the entity body, depending on information in the HTTP header. For example, inspecting the `Content-Type` header would enable the monitor to identify HTML resources that may have hypertext links and embedded resources. In addition, the monitor could employ an HTML parser to extract the URLs and record them in the trace. Alternatively, the monitor could record the entire HTML file and postpone the parsing of the data to a later stage.

14.2 Analyzing Web Server Logs

Manipulating large and diverse collections of measurement data introduces a number of practical challenges, as discussed in Chapter 9 (Section 9.4). This section presents an overview of our experiences in processing Web server logs, with an emphasis on the key software components used in parsing, filtering, transforming, and analyzing the data [KR98].

14.2.1 Parsing and filtering

Evaluating new techniques for improving Web performance requires substantial evaluation of the idea over a collection of different Web workloads. However, Web server logs may have mistakes and inconsistencies that complicate analysis of the data. In addition, the results of analyzing any one server log may not be representative of the expected performance for other servers. Analyzing multiple logs from a diverse set of Web sites helps in separating the general performance trends from the traffic characteristics at a particular site. On the surface, performing the same analysis on multiple server logs does not seem more difficult than analyzing a single log. However, Web servers generate logs in a variety of formats, with differences in the number and type of fields, as discussed in Chapter 9 (Section 9.3). The clocks at the various servers are usually not synchronized with each other, resulting in different notions of time across the various logs. In addition, the syntax of a field may vary from site to site. Converting the server logs to a uniform format is an effective way to hide these details from the software that analyzes the data.

Parsing each log is a critical first step. This requires identifying the format of the records, in terms of the number of fields and their syntax. Based on a control string that specifies the format of the record, the program reads each line of input and assigns each portion of the data to a variable of a particular type. For example, the HTTP response code in a server log could be assigned to an integer variable, whereas the HTTP request method could be assigned to a character string. However, in practice, server logs may include erroneous records that cause the input parsing to fail. A record may not have the correct number of fields, or the fields may not have the correct syntax. Defensive programming is a crucial part of identifying erroneous records in the log. The program can check that the input line had the correct number of fields and that each field had the expected syntax.

Although most fields and records are printed correctly, occasional problems can arise depending on the implementation of the Web server. Some Web servers spawn multiple processes to handle HTTP requests concurrently, as discussed in Chapter 4 (Section 4.4). These processes compete to write records into the server log. If the server does not serialize these operations, some records may be interleaved. Despite the possibility of errors, the server may permit the processes to write independently to avoid the overhead of coordinating these operations. Correct generation of server logs is not necessarily an important part of handling HTTP requests. Even if the server attempts to serialize the logging operations, programming mistakes may result in occasional errors. Similarly, in some cases, the server may not assign values to each of the fields in a record, which may result in erroneous output. As a result, large server logs often have errors. The software for parsing these logs should check for mistakes in the records.

Records that result in parsing errors can be manually inspected, or the program can automatically skip to the next record. In some cases, a closer look at the record may reveal the source of the problem. For example, a URL may contain an embedded newline character (cntl-M) that causes the parser to mistakenly detect the end of a line. The record can be fixed by removing the offending newline character. The length of the URLs introduces another challenge. URLs may be arbitrarily long; therefore any assumption about the maximum length of a URL may be incorrect; URLs that are more than 4000 characters long sometimes arise in practice. In some programming languages, the standard I/O routines assume that the memory for each input variable has been allocated in advance (e.g., the *scanf()* routine in the C programming language). If the URL exceeds the expected length, the parsing routine would write past the end of the allocated memory space and corrupt other memory. These kinds of errors are particularly difficult to detect and fix. To prevent memory problems, the program could allocate the space for each string as part of parsing the record. Alternatively, the program could have a separate routine for processing long URLs when they occur.

Another practical challenge arises from the diversity of timestamp fields across the server logs. Over a collection of real server logs, we have seen at least 14 distinct ways of representing the date and time. Writing software to parse and interpret the various formats is tedious and error-prone. Having a separate library of routines for parsing and converting the timestamp field in server logs is very useful. These routines can be carefully debugged and used repeatedly in a variety of different applications. In addition, the routine can convert the timestamp to a uniform time representation, such as the number of seconds since midnight on January 1, 1970 (UNIX time). This permits the rest of the software to ignore differences in representing time across the various logs. However, this does not address problems caused by differences in clocks between the different Web servers that generated these logs. In practice, it is difficult to correlate the time of requests across different logs. In addition, the meaning of the timestamp in the log may vary across servers, as discussed earlier, in Chapter 9 (Section 9.3.1).

After parsing a record and checking for syntax errors, each field is inspected for semantic errors. Each field should fall within the appropriate range of values. For example, all HTTP response codes should be three-digit integers starting with 1, 2, 3, 4, or 5, and all timestamps should lie within the time interval when the log was collected. Entries with invalid fields can be manually inspected and removed. Ultimately, checking for errors in the records proves very useful. Aggressive error checking also simplifies the process of writing and debugging the software for analyzing the measurement data. In addition, operating on logs in a uniform format allows this software to ignore the differences in the original representation of each server log. For example, analysis could draw on a reduced log format that includes the client name (or IP address), the Request-URI, the response code, and the request time.

14.2.2 Transforming

Removing erroneous records and creating a uniform log format addresses some of the challenges of processing server logs. However, writing analysis software that operates on URL strings is somewhat tedious. URLs have a wide range of acceptable formats, leading to multiple representations for the same resource at a Web site. Consider the resource `foo.html` at the Web site `www.xyz.com`. Log entries for this resource could have a variety of different URLs, including `http://www.xyz.com/foo.html`, `www.xyz.com/foo.html`, `foo.html`, or `www.xyz.com///foo.html`. Converting each URL to a canonical form requires manipulating strings to identify and remove characters. These kinds of operations are usually tedious to program in languages such as C, though they are relatively simple in scripting languages. Having a separate library of routines for parsing and manipulating strings can reduce the burden of writing log-processing software.

The URL can be reduced to a condensed, canonical format by performing a variety of string manipulations that attempt to mimic the transformations applied by the Web server in handling the request. For example,

- Removing the "http://" and host name, when present, is useful. Otherwise, an analysis program might not recognize that `http://www.xyz.com/foo.html` and `foo.html` refer to the same resource. The server name may have an alias, where `http://www.xyz.com/foo.html` and `http://xyz.com/foo.html` refer to the same resource.
- Duplicate "/" characters can be deleted. For example, `/bar//foo.html` could be converted to `/bar/foo.html`.
- Portions of the URL can be extracted. For example, the suffix of the URL often identifies the content type of the resource (e.g., `.html` or `.gif`).

Identifying resources that start with the same path involves removing the resource name at the end of the URL; for example, `/files/bar/foo.html` has path `/files/bar`.

Although many URLs can be resolved, some cases are difficult to handle without additional information about the configuration of the server. For example, `http://www.xyz.com/bar` could refer to a resource `bar` or could actually resolve to `http://www.xyz.com/bar/index.html` if `bar` is a directory. In addition, the server may be configured to treat one URL as an alias for another URL. Recognizing that the two URLs correspond to the same resource would be difficult without extra information about the server configuration. String manipulations are also useful for processing the host name of the requesting client, if available. For example, extracting the last component of the host name is useful for identifying the requests that come from educational institutions (e.g., `.edu` in `users.berkeley.edu`).

For most analysis, having the specific URLs and client names or IP addresses is not necessary. Instead, knowing which records have the same URL or client may be sufficient. To simplify the analysis, the URL and client fields can be converted to integer values. This representation reduces the memory requirements for storing the data and avoids the need to deal with variable-length strings in the remainder of the software. In addition, the integer representation avoids revealing the identity of the requesting user and the Web resources to anyone who analyzes the transformed log. The transformation of strings to integers can be performed in a single pass through the log, in conjunction with canonicalizing each URL to a uniform format. The software associates an integer with each URL, in order of occurrence, by constructing a hash table. A separate hash table can be used to map each client name or IP address to a unique integer.

The hash table stores the integer associated with each canonicalized URL. For each new record, the software checks whether or not the canonicalized URL already exists in the hash table to determine which integer corresponds to this resource. Otherwise, the software associates the new URL with the next integer and inserts the entry in the hash table. Processing logs with a large number of different URLs requires an efficient hash-table implementation. Web server logs with tens of thousands of unique URLs are common, and the number of unique clients may be even larger. The hash tables created by scripting languages, such as Perl and awk, typically consume a large amount of memory. Once the space requirements exceed the available memory on the computer, the operating system continually swaps portions of the hash table to and from the disk. This can result in substantial delay in processing a log. Efficient hash routines for languages such as C or Java typically consume much less memory, resulting in a much faster transformation of the data.

After converting the client identifiers and the URLs to integers, each record consists of a small set of integers. Analyzing the logs involves sequencing through the requests to compute certain metrics or simulate a particular policy or mechanism. In some cases, the analysis treats each client or each resource independently. For example, consider the problem of characterizing the time between successive requests by each client. One natural approach involves sequencing through the log one request at a time, updating the information about the requesting client. However, this requires allocating memory for each client. An alternative approach involves reordering the log to group requests by client. The reordered log would have all of the requests by client 1, followed by all requests by client 2, and so on. Sorting the log by client identifier greatly simplifies the task of computing statistics. Similarly, for other problems, sorting by the resource identifier would be more appropriate.

The sort may need to consider multiple fields in the log. For example, studying client access patterns would require sorting the records by the client identifier, breaking ties based on the time of the request. This would ensure that the resulting log has the requests by each client in order of request time. However, in some cases, multiple records may have the same client identifier and timestamp. For example, a client may issue multiple requests to download an HTML file and embedded images. These requests arrive close together in time, perhaps within the same second. Server logs typically record the request time at the one-second level. In the unsorted log, the records associated with these requests appear in the order they were written by the Web server. The sorted log should preserve this order. Ensuring that the sorting routine performs such a *stable* sort is critical to avoid changing the relative order of these log entries.

Sorting the records in advance facilitates substantial reductions in the complexity of the analysis software and its memory requirements. In addition, the sorted log may be used in a variety of different analysis tasks, thereby amortizing the overhead of performing the initial sorting operation. Because sorting is such a basic task used in a variety of applications, a sorting routine can be highly optimized. In many situations, sorting the data is more efficient than running a complex analysis program that is written from scratch. Perhaps most importantly, presorting the data can reduce the time required to write the analysis software, facilitating a wider range of experimentation in the early stages of analyzing the measurement data.

In summary, analyzing a large and diverse set of server logs requires facing several software challenges. Preprocessing the data to delete malformed records, remove unwanted fields, and convert strings into integers significantly reduces the complexity of the analysis software. In addition, sorting the log based on one or more of these fields can further simplify the analysis. The software for preprocessing and analyzing the data can draw on efficient support for reading and writing files, matching regular expressions, converting time formats, hashing, and sorting. Drawing on existing, efficient implementations of these functions reduces the effort involved in developing, debugging, and optimizing the software. For example, our work on analyzing Web server logs has drawn extensively on the *sfio* (safe/fast I/O) and *libast* libraries [KV91, FKV95], which enabled us to write efficient and robust C programs for preprocessing and analyzing the measurement data.

14.3 Publicly Available Logs and Traces

Many research studies of Web traffic measurement draw on public collections of client, proxy, and server logs and packet traces. The logs and traces tend to become out of date or may no longer be available. Several attempts have been made to provide a central repository of logs and traces. Among them are the Internet Traffic Archive [ITA], the World Wide Web Consortium's Web Characterization Group repository [WCA], the collection at NLANR [IRC], and CAnet Squid Logs [Can].

Logs are typically provided on an "as is" basis—in the form recorded by the proxy or server. In some cases, the logs may be represented in a compressed form to reduce the storage requirements. Some fields such as the name/address of the requesting client may have been removed or transformed to protect privacy. The organization providing the logs may not have much incentive to convert the logs to a standard format or to check for obvious inconsistencies in the measurement records. However, the users of the data have to pay the price for using unsanitized data, with the corresponding problems outlined in Section 14.2. Alternatively, the users must perform various semantic checks as dictated by the particular application of the data. However, the checks performed after a user downloads the log are not useful for anyone else using the same data from the repository.

Ideally, logs would be checked for errors *before* they are made available. In addition to providing access to logs, a repository could include the list of error checks and the software for performing these checks. With a repository of certified logs, applications using the data can be compared in a meaningful manner. The repository could also provide access to the raw logs to allow users to verify the correctness of the software that checks for errors.

The attempt by the Web Characterization Group involved defining a generic format for log entries and then specifying a schema preferably in a language such as the eXtensible Markup Language (XML). A schema is a terse semantic description of how the fields in a record should be interpreted. One reason for using the popular XML language as the description language is that existing tools can be used to validate the XML description of the log entries. Once a log has been represented in the chosen XML format, a generic validation tool can perform various checks, as follows:

- The tool can ensure that each measurement record has the expected number of fields. This makes it easy to write a simple parser for the log without having to worry about pathological conditions.
- The tool can ensure that each field has the expected type and range of values. For example, these checks would detect any response code that does not match one of the set of valid codes.
- The tool can explicitly correct any errors it finds to facilitate the transformation from a raw log into a semantically clean log that has entries in an expected format.

14.4 Measuring Multimedia Streams

Measurement and analysis of Web traffic has played an important role in evaluating Web protocols and software components. However, relatively little work has been done on measurement of multimedia traffic. This section presents an overview of four techniques for collecting measurements of multimedia streams—downloading multimedia resources from Web sites, logging requests to a multimedia server, collecting packet traces in front of a server, and collecting detailed packet traces of control messages and data traffic. We describe how these methodologies have been applied in existing studies.

14.4.1 Static analysis of multimedia resources

Initially, HTTP was the dominant protocol for transferring the audio and video streams available on the Web. One of the first studies of multimedia content on the Web considered the characteristics of video files accessible from Web servers [AS98]. In addition to traditional workload parameters such as resource size, the study considered additional properties of video data, such as the encoding format, the number of frames per second, the dimensions of the picture, and the average bandwidth requirement. Analyzing the video content available on the Web introduced three challenges—locating the video content at various Web sites, acquiring a copy of each file, and computing statistics based on the file contents. In theory, addressing each of these measurement challenges could have required developing new software. Fortunately, existing software could be exploited to simplify the tasks of locating the video files and analyzing their contents.

To search for video files on the Web, the researchers exploited an existing search engine that allows users to search for certain strings within the URLs referenced in a Web page. Searching for a string such as ".mpg" or ".avi" would produce a list of Web pages containing one or more hypertext links with ".mpg" or ".avi" in the URL. The query to the search engine produced a list of URLs for Web pages. Then the researchers wrote a separate program to visit each Web page and extract any hypertext links with the desired file extensions.

Because some video files were referenced in multiple Web pages, the list was preprocessed to remove duplicate URLs.

Based on the list of URLs, a separate program attempted to retrieve the resources by sending an HTTP GET request for each URL. Nearly half of the requests were unsuccessful for one reason or another. Some requests returned a 404 Not Found because the requested resource did not exist at the Web site. In other cases, the Web server returned a 200 OK response. However, this did not necessarily imply that the response contained a valid video file. For example, the file extension of the URL may not correspond to the actual encoding format of the file. In addition, some files may have properties that violate reasonable expectations. For example, some files had a duration of less than half a second or a frame rate of less than four frames/sec. In some cases, attempting to "play" the contents of the file demonstrated that the resource was a static image rather than a video clip. Omitting the invalid URLs and the seemingly erroneous files removed about half of the URLs in the initial list.

Detecting the erroneous files and computing statistics about the valid files required a way to parse the video data. Writing software to decode video data is complicated in practice. Fortunately, public-domain software was available for the most common video formats—MPEG, QuickTime, and AVI. In some cases, the decoding software could not process a given input file, suggesting a problem with the data format. Otherwise, the software reported a variety of statistics, such as the frame rate, the width and height of the picture, and the time duration. These parameters could be combined to compute other statistics, such as the average bandwidth requirement (bits/second) or the aspect ratio (width/height). Files with unusual parameters could be excluded from further study. The analysis considered the values of the various statistics and how they varied with the encoding format. In addition, the analysis considered whether or not the file included both audio and video data.

Although the study provided a broad view of the video content available on the Web, the static analysis had certain limitations. First, any search engine has an incomplete view of the resources available on the Web. Some Web pages with links to video content may not have been indexed. In addition, some URLs for video files may have had file extensions that were not included in the search. Second, and perhaps most importantly, the study could not ascertain the popularity or request patterns for the various video files. Characterizing the popularity of the resources would require a trace or log of clients retrieving video data from a server or the results of a separate study by a rating company. Third, the emergence of new protocols for multimedia streaming limits the effectiveness of the techniques for fetching the video files. Increasingly, video streaming uses protocols such as the Real-time Transport Protocol (RTP) and the Real Time Streaming Protocol (RTSP) instead of HTTP. The hypertext links in Web pages often reference session descriptions, Java scripts, or multimedia presentations that do not reveal that the URL corresponds to multimedia content.

14.4.2 Multimedia server logs

Analyzing the request patterns for multimedia streams requires access to a log or trace. Characterization of logs and traces could consider the wide variety of workload parameters that have been applied to traditional Web content. Properties such as resource size, response size, resource popularity, and temporal locality apply to both multimedia content and traditional Web content. However, analysis of audio and video content can consider additional metrics that are unique to streaming media. While watching a multimedia stream, a user may invoke VCR functions such as play, stop, rewind, fast-forward, and jump. VCR operations have important implications for allocating resources at proxies and servers and in the network. If most users watch streams in their entirety, then the resource requirements are known as soon as the server receives a request. In contrast, frequent VCR functions introduce variability in the bandwidth requirements and also limit the effectiveness of sending a large number of frames to the client ahead of time.

Whereas a Web server records information about each HTTP request, a multimedia server generates a record for each user action, such as VCR operations. Loose standards exist for the format of Web server logs. However, no such guidelines exist for multimedia servers. In addition, multimedia server logs are not widely available. Existing studies of multimedia server logs focus on measurements collected at academic institutions. Many universities have Web sites providing access to educational material, such as course lectures, for online viewing. Logs from these sites provide an opportunity to analyze the request patterns for multimedia streams, albeit for a restricted user community accessing a certain type of content. The wide variety of multimedia applications makes it difficult to establish general results about resource characteristics and access patterns. Still, the methodology for processing the server logs and characterizing the workload of these sites may be applicable to other applications and user communities.

Studies of two distance-learning sites illustrated the challenges of collecting and analyzing logs from multimedia servers [PK99, ASP00]. Despite differences in format, the two logs have the same kind of information. Both logs included a mixture of traditional HTTP requests for HTML and image content, coupled with requests to start and stop a multimedia transmission. For multimedia requests, each log entry corresponded to a single user action, such as starting or stopping the transmission of a multimedia session. Each entry included a timestamp, a client identifier, the requested action, and the name associated with the multimedia content. In one of the studies, the server log was preprocessed to remove requests from a particular client that was used for testing purposes; otherwise, the requests from this client could have skewed the analysis of the access patterns [ASP00]. In addition, redundant log entries, such as repetitive "stop" commands by the same client, were condensed to a single entry.

Traditional workload parameters, such as resource popularity and temporal locality, have characteristics that are similar to prior measurements of HTTP traffic. Both studies found that users rarely watch a stream in its entirety. Some users stop watching a stream after previewing the initial portion, suggesting that caching the first few minutes of a stream at a proxy may be an effective way to reduce load on the server and improve user performance. Other users perform frequent VCR functions, such as jump, rewind, and fast-forward. Some rewind operations move over a small segment of frames. This suggests that retaining a small number of frames in a client buffer would allow the client to handle these operations without retrieving the frames from the server. Small fast-forward operations could be satisfied without delaying the user by playing frames that are already available at the client. However, a small fraction of VCR operations jumped to an arbitrary point in the stream. These requests would typically require loading new data from the origin server, at the expense of additional delay to the user.

14.4.3 Packet monitoring of multimedia streams

Analysis of server logs provides insight into user access patterns. However, server logs do not include sufficient detail to study the transport of multimedia data over the Internet. In traditional Web transfers, the server writes the response message into the socket buffer and depends on the underlying TCP connection for delivery of the data. In contrast, multimedia streaming requires the server to pace the transmission of audio samples and video frames over time, resulting in very different traffic patterns. Characterizing multimedia traffic at the transport level requires collecting and analyzing fine-grain packet measurements. A recent study presented a detailed analysis of the transport of audio streams from a RealAudio server for an online radio station [MH00]. The study consisted of collecting the packet traces, analyzing the properties of the traffic at the packet and stream levels, and developing a model that captures the key workload parameters.

Collecting packet traces requires tapping a link, capturing packets, and generating measurement records. The packet traces for the study were collected from an Ethernet switch by directing copies of the packets traveling to or from the audio server to a link connected to the monitor, following the approach illustrated in Figure 14.1(c). The audio server could stream data to the client using UDP, TCP, or HTTP-over-TCP. Capturing the packets required configuring the packet monitor with a filter that identifies the IP address, protocols, and port numbers of interest, as described earlier, in Section 14.1.2. Although the server always selected port 80 for HTTP-over-TCP transfers, streaming audio over UDP or TCP could use any unreserved port (i.e., port numbers 1024 to 65,535). In practice, the server used a small, fixed set of port numbers that was known to the researchers conducting the study. The packet monitor was configured to capture packets with these port numbers. The monitor recorded the first 96 bytes of each audio packet to ensure that the trace included the IP and TCP/UDP headers, as well as audio data header. This detailed trace permitted the analysis to focus on low-level transport issues related to the timing of packet transmissions from the server to the clients.

The analysis grouped packets that belonged to the same TCP or UDP session; that is, packets with the same source and destination IP addresses and port numbers were considered part of a single audio flow. The transport mechanism for the flow could be classified as UDP, TCP, or HTTP-over-TCP based on the protocol and port numbers. The protocol field indicated whether UDP or TCP was used, and the server's TCP port number distinguished the HTTP traffic (port 80) from other TCP traffic. Most of the traffic consisted of UDP packets. This was significant because applications using UDP do not necessarily adjust the transmission rate in response to network congestion. Instead, the audio server transmitted the audio data in a periodic fashion. To develop a workload model, the analysis focused on typical packet sizes and the time between packets within a flow. In addition, the study determined the time between the beginning of one flow and the start of the next flow, as well as the duration of the flows. The variability of each of these parameters was captured in probability distributions.

Together, the probability distributions derived from the measurement data form a model of audio traffic at the flow and packet levels. This model could drive experiments that evaluate the impact of audio traffic on the server and the network. The values of the parameters depend on the nature of the multimedia application. An online radio station would have different properties than a site that allows users to listen to audio clips. Few clients listened to more than one audio stream, and half of the flows lasted longer than 45 minutes. For the most part, the flows had a few different bit rates, depending on the type of audio content. Stereo-quality music required a higher bit rate than talk shows and sporting events, because speech compresses much better than music. In all three cases, the audio encoding was limited to about 20 Kb/sec to ensure that users connecting to the Internet with 28.8 Kb/sec modems could receive the streams. The server also used specific packet sizes for the UDP transfers. A change in the multimedia content, the user community, or the server implementation could result in different workload characteristics.

14.4.4 Multi-layer packet monitoring

In contrast to traditional HTTP transfers, most multimedia streaming applications use separate sessions for control and data traffic. For example, the client and the server may exchange RTSP messages to coordinate the transfer of one or more RTP streams; each RTP stream may have a corresponding RTP Control Protocol (RTCP) stream for exchanging feedback about the quality of the transmission. A detailed characterization of multimedia traffic could depend on having information from each of these protocols. The requested URLs and the client VCR functions are conveyed in RTSP messages, whereas the actual audio and video data are contained in RTP packets. Measuring both the control and data traffic introduces two challenges. First, the contents of the control messages must be reconstructed from the underlying flow of packets, similar to the problem of reconstructing HTTP messages in Section 14.1. Second, the monitor must identify the data traffic associated with the control messages. This is very challenging in practice, because the data transfers use UDP and TCP port numbers that may not be known in advance. Instead, the port numbers for the data traffic are negotiated via the control messages.

For example, consider a client sending RTSP messages to a multimedia server to establish a session consisting of a single audio stream using RTP for data transfer and RTCP for feedback. After retrieving a description of the session, the client sends an RTSP SETUP message to create the two transport connections. The server's response message includes a Transport header that identifies the protocol (e.g., UDP or TCP) and the port numbers at the client and server, as discussed earlier, in Chapter 12 (Section 12.4.3). A client requesting a session with separate audio and video streams would issue two SETUP requests to create two sets of connections, one for each stream. Each connection is uniquely identified by a set of five numbers—the client and server IP addresses, the client and server port numbers, and the protocol.

Identifying these connections is somewhat complicated. The client and server IP addresses match the addresses used for the RTSP connection, whereas the port numbers and protocol depend on the server's response to the SETUP message. As a simple approach to this problem, the monitor could capture *all* packets on the link or all packets using unreserved port numbers (i.e., 1024 to 65,535). Then a separate program could identify which data transfers are associated with each of the control sessions. However, this could require the monitor to capture and store an extremely large amount of data, especially on high-speed links. For example, the monitor might capture packets from large FTP transfers and IP telephony calls that do not relate to any of the RTSP control sessions.

Instead, the monitor could inspect the control messages as they arrive to learn which port numbers to track. This requires the monitor to perform two main tasks as the packets arrive—parsing the control messages to learn the port numbers and changing the packet filter to capture the data packets using these ports. The *mmdump* tool [vCCS00] performs these tasks. The tool captures the full contents of packets associated with the control protocol, identified by a well-known port (e.g., 554 for RTSP), and reconstructs the control messages. The tool includes software for parsing various multimedia control protocols, such as RTSP and H.323. After extracting the protocol and port numbers for each data stream, *mmdump* updates the packet filter to capture the data packets. The tool may capture the full contents of these packets or be configured to record some smaller number of bytes from the beginning of each data packet.

Monitoring control and data transfers facilitates a wide range of analysis. For example, consider a multimedia presentation that consists of a mixture of images, audio, video, and text. The control messages identify the URLs for the various resources, and the data packets reveal the size or bit rate for each stream. Knowing the URLs also enables analysis of the popularity of various multimedia resources in the Internet. Having both the control messages and data packets is useful for studying the impact of network congestion on multimedia streaming applications. Some control messages include a client request for a change in the transmission rate, which may trigger a change in the bit rate of the data stream. These feedback effects would be very difficult to study without jointly capturing the control and data traffic.

14.5 Summary

Software for measuring and analyzing Web traffic plays an important role in evaluating Web performance. Packet monitoring provides a detailed view of Web transfers at both the HTTP and TCP layers. However, collecting packet traces of Web traffic requires efficient software for reconstructing HTTP messages from a stream of IP packets. Many studies of Web traffic draw on proxy and server logs. Effective software for parsing, filtering, and transforming the logs simplifies the process of analyzing the data. Several repositories of Web traffic measurements provide researchers with access to logs and traces. Checking for errors and converting the data into a common format assists researchers in using the repository for a variety of analysis studies. In comparison to Web traffic studies, the measurement and analysis of multimedia streams is at a very early stage. Multimedia streaming introduces new challenges in measurement because of the use of separate protocols for control messages and data transfer, as well as the diversity of encoding formats. Workload characterization also becomes more complicated as a result of the presence of new parameters related to packet sizes, bit rates, and VCR operations.

15

Research Perspectives in Protocol Issues

Chapters 13 and 14 examine research perspectives in caching- and measurement-related research. In this chapter, we examine some of the protocol research issues associated with the Web—notably with TCP and HTTP. In practice, HTTP is layered on top of TCP for transport; we examine some proposals related to TCP that may have a significant impact on the Web. We also examine a few ideas related to alterations and extensions related to HTTP. Once the Internet became dominated by Web traffic, several attempts were made to improve HTTP. In Chapter 7, we cataloged various attempts to fix the problems in HTTP/1.0 that led to HTTP/1.1. Although the protocol passed through the various stages (draft standard, proposed standard), several issues were unresolved. Among the reasons for standardizing in the face of unresolved issues were the following:

- The omitted issues were not considered serious enough to delay standardizing the protocol.
- The urgency to deploy the improved version of the protocol to alleviate the known problems in HTTP/1.0.
- The proliferation of numerous *so-called* HTTP/1.1 versions of components even before the standardization. Such components claimed to be compliant with an intermediate document, (Request for Comments, RFC 2068 [FGM+97]), which was far from a standard.

Because IETF working groups function on the basis of generating consensus, individual issues did not hold the overall protocol standardization hostage. Several issues were deferred to smaller working groups to see if smaller documents on the unresolved issues could help achieve consensus. Several topics that were under discussion, such as hit metering and transparent content negotiation, did not survive the standardization process and were either dropped from consideration or deferred to a separate standard. In addition, several new issues came to the fore that were not widely discussed during the move from HTTP/1.0 to HTTP/1.1. We examine some of these issues in this chapter. A subset of the issue is going through the standardization process, while others are still being discussed informally. New ideas for improving the protocol can be proposed by anyone, in the form of an Internet Draft. Interested participants can join in the discussion and offer constructive suggestions.

The topics we discuss in this chapter are as follows:

- **Multiplexing HTTP transfers:** The interplay between HTTP and TCP has important implications on Web performance in particular and the efficiency of the Internet in general. A Web client typically establishes multiple TCP connections to the same server to retrieve embedded images in parallel and to reduce user-perceived latency. However, parallel TCP connections introduce fairness problems, in which an aggressive client receives a higher share of the network bandwidth than other clients. In addition, many multimedia applications use UDP and do not react to network congestion in the same way as a typical TCP connection. Addressing these issues requires revisiting how application-level protocols such as HTTP relate to the underlying transport level. We present an overview of three proposals that suggest changes to how HTTP transfers are multiplexed at end hosts—WebMux, TCP Control Block Interdependence, and Integrated Congestion Management.

- **Addition of a differencing mechanism to HTTP/1.1:** Suppose a cache has a copy of an earlier instance of a resource and the new instance of the resource on the origin server differs slightly from the cached version. Rather than sending the new version of the resource in its entirety, the origin server could send the difference against the earlier version, assuming the difference is smaller. The goal of augmenting the protocol to transmit the difference would be to reduce the latency experienced by users and to reduce the number of bytes transmitted over the network. We discuss the motivation for a differencing (or "delta") mechanism, the set of available differencing algorithms, evaluating the algorithms based on responses obtained on the Web, and the various considerations related to deployment of the mechanism in HTTP/1.1.

- **HTTP protocol compliance:** Compliance with a protocol means that the implementations of the components meet the various MUST, SHOULD, and MAY requirements imposed by the specification. Although protocol standardization requires interoperability testing of components for each of the features, there is no overall compliance testing mechanism. Checklists are available for the individual component implementors to agree on the various features. The lack of a reliable, comprehensive, and, most importantly, *required* compliance testing mechanism is a weakness of the standardization process. Noncompliant implementations can cause problems for users, Web site owners, and the network. HTTP is not unique in this regard—most IETF protocols are not tested for compliance in a formal way. We discuss the methodology of an HTTP compliance study (named

PRO-COW) and the results from a longitudinal study that tested servers for a large collection of popular Web sites.

- **End-to-end measurements to study the impact of protocol improvement on Web performance:** Several of the HTTP protocol changes were discussed in the Working Group and deployed without any performance measurements. At a practical level, detailed performance measurements based on deployment would not be possible without changes percolating to the field and the components implemented and available. An end-to-end measurement of Web performance would have to measure end-to-end response for clients in various locations contacting Web servers in several different sites. We present a performance evaluation methodology and results of an experiment that performed active measurements on Web servers from a global collection of client sites. Given the skewed nature of request traffic to Web sites (a few thousand Web sites receive a significant portion of all requests), it is possible to study the impact of the changes to the protocol by examining the behavior of request and response traffic to these sites.

- **Other extensions to HTTP:** Several extensions to HTTP have been proposed that have not been accepted widely. However, some have shown to have more promise than others. We examine three of them in this chapter, beginning with a framework for HTTP extension proposed in RFC 2774. We then examine the current state of Transparent Content Negotiation, which was moved out of HTTP/1.1 during the discussion that led to RFC 2616, the draft standard of HTTP/1.1. Finally, we examine the Distributed Authoring and Versioning (WebDAV) protocol introduced to enable multiple authors to edit resources.

15.1 Multiplexing HTTP Transfers

In downloading Web pages, a Web client typically opens multiple TCP connections to the same server. Parallel connections introduce important performance and fairness issues, as discussed earlier, in Chapter 8 (Section 8.3). In this section, we discuss three proposals for changing how application-level sessions relate to the underlying congestion control mechanisms at the transport level. The WebMux proposal suggests a way to multiplex a collection of HTTP sessions on a single TCP connection. The TCP Control Block Interdependence proposal introduces a tighter coupling between TCP connections to the same remote host. The Integrated Congestion Management proposal focuses on the allocation of bandwidth across a collection of packet flows below the transport level and investigates how to give applications more control over how they adapt to changes in the available bandwidth.

15.1.1 WebMux: An experimental multiplexing protocol

In downloading a Web page, a browser may establish multiple parallel connections to the Web server to start receiving and displaying the embedded images. Parallel connections allow the browser to address a limitation of how HTTP relates to the transport layer. HTTP transmits messages in a serial fashion over an application-level socket, which is directly associated with an underlying TCP connection. Having multiple simultaneous transfers requires the browser to have multiple sockets that, in turn, require multiple TCP connections to the server. One approach to addressing this problem would be to extend HTTP to allow interleaving of multiple messages on the same transport connection. However, this would constitute a substantial modification to the protocol and would require changing the implementation of Web clients, proxies, and servers. The standardization process and the large installed base of Web software components make this an unpalatable solution.

As an alternative, the WebMux proposal advocates breaking the one-to-one association between sockets and TCP connections. WebMux is an experimental multiplexing protocol that does not require changes to HTTP or Web software [GN98]. Instead, WebMux allows multiple application-level sockets to send and receive data over the same underlying transport-level connection. Data written into a socket are divided into one or more fragments. WebMux divides the data from each socket into fragments and transmits the fragments over the TCP connection. Each fragment has a WebMux header with a session identifier that enables the receiving end of the TCP connection to direct the data to the appropriate recipient. The WebMux header also includes various TCP-like flags for opening and closing a session. The underlying TCP connection treats the WebMux fragments as normal data to deliver from one end point to the other.

Multiplexing several sessions on a single TCP connection introduces challenges related to the sharing of bandwidth and memory. Sending a large number of fragments on behalf of one session may starve other sessions. To prevent starvation, the WebMux sender sequences through the sessions in a round-robin fashion to transmit outstanding fragments. Although the WebMux sender determines the transfer order, the underlying TCP connection controls the transmission of data subject to the congestion window and the receiver's offered window. On the receiving end point, the TCP receiver reconstructs the incoming packets into an ordered, reliable stream of bytes. The WebMux receiver extracts each fragment and associates it with the appropriate socket based on the session identifier. However, the WebMux receiver must retain the fragment until the receiving application reads the data from the associated socket. If one session consumes all of the buffer space, the other receiving sockets associated with the same TCP connection must block waiting for data.

To avoid blocking the other sockets, the WebMux receiver allocates a portion of memory to each session. Having separate memory enables the WebMux receiver to read and buffer independently for each session. However, this does not completely solve the problem. The underlying TCP receiver also has limited buffer space that restricts the transmission of data by the TCP sender. A single session could conceivably consume the TCP reception buffer, which would preclude the TCP sender from transmitting data on behalf of other sessions. To address this problem, the WebMux proposal introduces the notion of *credits* associated with each session. Each credit permits the WebMux sender to transmit a certain amount of data on behalf of the session. By limiting the number of outstanding credits, the WebMux receiver ensures that the session cannot consume too much memory. The credit-based flow-control scheme is conceptually similar to the use of acknowledgments and a receiver window in TCP. However, credits are associated with each session, whereas the receiver window is associated with the underlying TCP connection.

The WebMux proposal addresses several of the challenges of associating multiple application-level sessions on a single transport connection. The primary advantage of the approach is that WebMux does not require changes to TCP, HTTP, and Web software components. In addition, support for multiplexing sessions could be useful for other application-level protocols. Although WebMux was motivated by concerns about HTTP, the ideas do not depend on the application-level protocol. However, a complete realization of WebMux would require careful resolution of the challenges to sharing network bandwidth and buffer space across the sessions. If standardized, WebMux would need to be incorporated into the major operating systems and deployed on computers throughout the Internet. The WebMux protocol was submitted as an Internet Draft in the fall of 1998 [GN98] as part of the larger HTTP Next Generation (HTTPng) effort [SJ00]. The HTTPng effort ultimately stalled, and development of the WebMux protocol did not proceed through the rest of the IETF standardization process.

15.1.2 TCP Control Block Interdependence

The WebMux proposal suggests a scheme for multiplexing several application-level sessions on a single TCP connection. An alternative approach could consider the interaction between multiple TCP connections. Traditionally, each TCP connection operates independently, even when there are multiple connections between the same pair of hosts. Each connection performs its own estimation of the round-trip time (RTT) to the remote host and determines the maximum segment size (MSS) for transmitting data. In addition, each connection performs TCP congestion control to select an appropriate transmission rate, without benefiting from the experiences of the other connections. Each connection begins with a small initial window size during the slow-start phase, even if a previous connection had already discovered a reasonable congestion window. In addition, multiple connections acting independently may consume a larger portion of network bandwidth than another client with a single TCP connection.

The TCP Control Block Interdependence proposal [Tou97] revisits the assumption that TCP connections operate independently by suggesting a closer coupling between connections to the same remote host. Each TCP connection at the local host is associated with a control block that stores information about the state of the connection. The control block includes local process state, such as pointers to the send and receive buffers for the application-level socket, as well as connection state, such as port numbers, the send and receive window sizes, and various timers. These portions of the control block cannot be shared across TCP connections. However, other connection state, such as RTT estimates, the MSS, and the size of the congestion window, relate to the pair of communicating hosts. These parameters could be shared between connections. Sharing of information across connections is coordinated by the operating system, without requiring changes to the application-level protocol (e.g., HTTP) or the applications (e.g., Web browser or Web server). The proposal identifies two possible scenarios for interdependence between TCP connections to the same remote host—*ensemble* and *temporal* sharing.

Ensemble sharing occurs when two or more active connections cooperate to share state information. The simplest example is initializing the control block of a new connection with the parameters from an ongoing connection. Afterward, the connections would proceed independently. Starting with an accurate estimate of RTTs would aid the new connection in setting its retransmission timeout (RTO). A more complex example involves continued cooperation to determine the size of each connection's congestion window. For example, the ensemble could be treated as a single TCP connection for the purposes of congestion control. Then the resulting congestion window could be divided evenly between the individual connections. This would ensure that the aggregate traffic behaves as if it were part of a single TCP connection. Such a policy would enable a Web browser to have multiple connections to a Web server without an unfair advantage over other clients in competing for network bandwidth. The Web-Mux proposal addresses the same fairness problem. The key difference is that WebMux multiplexes multiple transfers on a single TCP connection, whereas the TCP Control Block Interdependence proposal coordinates the sharing of bandwidth over an ensemble of separate TCP connections.

Temporal sharing consists of initializing a new connection's control block with parameters from a connection that has already terminated. In closing a TCP connection, the MSS, the congestion window, and the average and variance of the RTT could be saved for future use. For example, consider a Web browser that establishes a TCP connection to a Web server to retrieve an embedded image after downloading the containing HTML file. If the server's TCP implementation supports temporal sharing, the new connection could start with a larger initial congestion window and a more accurate RTT estimation. This would reduce the user-perceived latency in downloading the image. In contrast to ensemble sharing, temporal sharing requires caching state for old connections, on a per-host basis. In addition, the information from the cached control block may be out of date, depending on how long ago the connection terminated. Both of these factors can be reduced by limiting how long the state is cached.

The TCP Control Block Interdependence proposal attempts to optimize the transient behavior of TCP without changing its long-term properties. The proposal is especially relevant to HTTP traffic because of the large number of TCP connections involved in retrieving Web pages. In addition, user-perceived latency for the many short Web transfers is heavily influenced by the transient behavior of TCP. Effective techniques for managing collections of TCP connections may also reduce the need for protocols, such as WebMux, that interleave multiple sessions on a single TCP connection. The Control Block Interdependence proposal draws on previous work that addressed the sharing of RTT and MSS parameters, as well as techniques for reducing the overhead of opening and closing TCP connections [Bra92, Bra94]. Deployment of the ideas requires implementation changes in the operating systems running at end hosts in the Internet and further investigation of policies for sharing control-block parameters such as the congestion window. The TCP Control Block Interdependence proposal was published as an Informational RFC in the IETF in 1997 and did not proceed through the rest of the IETF standardization process.

15.1.3 Integrated Congestion Management

The WebMux and TCP Control Block Interdependence proposals suggest a tighter coupling between application-level sessions that exchange data with the same remote host. However, the success of the Web and the commercialization of the Internet have introduced several additional challenges related to congestion control. Some commercial products enhance communication performance at the expense of other users by disabling or changing TCP's underlying congestion control algorithms. Many audio and video streaming applications use UDP rather than TCP, as discussed in Chapter 12. These applications do not necessarily adapt to congestion in the same way as TCP. The growing amount of traffic that does not adhere to congestion control poses a threat to the stability of the Internet. For example, a Web server could conceivably send data more aggressively than suggested by TCP congestion control to reduce latency for transferring HTTP response messages. These transfers would consume an unfair share of the network bandwidth, at the expense of well-behaved connections, and cause an increase in network congestion. In addition, the conventional socket interfaces do not provide explicit feedback to applications that can adapt the transmission to the available bandwidth. For example, a multimedia application may be able to transmit a lower-quality version of a video stream during periods of low throughput.

The Integrated Congestion Management proposal introduces a framework for addressing these new challenges, as well as the fairness problems caused by parallel TCP connections. In addition to efficient traffic multiplexing, the proposal presents an architecture for congestion control and an interface for applications to react to varying bandwidth [BRS99, BS00]. The Congestion Manager includes several software modules that control the transmission and reception of flows of packets between the end hosts. An implementation of TCP could build on top of these modules. On the sending side, the Congestion Manager determines the bandwidth available for transmitting data to the remote host by applying a congestion control algorithm. This algorithm draws on feedback from past data transmissions and periodic probes between the sender and receiver. The periodic probes ensure that the Congestion Manager has timely information about network congestion, even if the receiving application would not normally provide this feedback. For example, a media player receiving UDP packets might not provide feedback to the media server in a timely manner.

The sender combines the explicit feedback from the receiver and the statistics from the periodic probes to construct an accurate view of the available bandwidth. The congestion control algorithm is conceptually similar to TCP, with some modifications. Like TCP, the Congestion Manager transmits data based on a congestion window, which increases linearly in the absence of packet loss and decreases multiplicatively in response to loss. The window size drops to a small value in response to persistent congestion, analogous to the slow-start phase of TCP. Unlike traditional TCP implementations, the Congestion Manager paces the transmission of packets to avoid introducing a burst of traffic into the network. The Congestion Manager transmits data more slowly in the absence of feedback from the receiver to avoid overloading the network. Hence, the Congestion Manager sends data at a lower rate when accurate information about network congestion is not available.

After determining the available bandwidth to a remote host, the Congestion Manager allocates the resources to the various flows sending data to this remote host, similar to the idea of ensemble sharing in the TCP Control Block Interdependence proposal. This addresses the fairness problem introduced when a Web client and server communicate over multiple TCP connections simultaneously. The simplest allocation policy divides the available bandwidth equally between the competing flows. Then the Congestion Manager notifies the application responsible for each flow of the allocated bandwidth. The application, such as a Web server, decides which data to send based on the bandwidth allocation. Providing explicit feedback to the application about the available resources requires a new application programming interface. The communication model differs from the traditional socket abstraction. The application expresses an interest in transmitting data. After some time, the Congestion

Manager notifies the application that permission to transmit has been granted. Then the application decides which data to send. The Congestion Manager can also notify the application about changes in the underlying transmission rate. This is useful for multimedia servers that can dynamically adapt the quality of the audio or video stream to the available bandwidth.

The Integrated Congestion Management proposal revisits the role the end hosts play in controlling Internet congestion and supporting application requirements. Thus the scope of the proposal is much broader and more ambitious than the work on WebMux and TCP Control Block Interdependence. The proposed approach requires changes in the application programming interface, which makes widespread deployment more difficult. On the other hand, incremental deployment is possible because a sending Congestion Manager can communicate with traditional receivers (i.e., receivers running on hosts that do not have a Congestion Manager). The Congestion Manager was introduced as an Internet Draft in July 2000 [BS00] as part of the IETF Endpoint Congestion Management Working Group. Judging the ultimate outcome of the effort is difficult at this early stage in the standardization process.

15.2 Adding a Differencing Mechanism to HTTP/1.1

For several years, there has been a growing concern about the amount of traffic on the Internet and the need to reduce user-perceived latency in obtaining responses for Web requests. In this section, we discuss the proposed addition of a differencing mechanism to HTTP/1.1 to address this problem. The proposed differencing solution was preceded by two other approaches: compression and selective downloading of response. Reduction of unnecessary bits on the network is an important goal, and the evolution path traced in this section shows the steps taken by the HTTP protocol community. The history of the evolution also sheds light on how certain ideas arise that require changes to the protocol and how a protocol can continue to evolve to accommodate such changes.

A common mechanism that could achieve the twin goals of reducing the number of packets sent on the Internet and reducing user-perceived latency is compression. A response would be compressed by the sender (often the origin server) and decompressed by the receiver. Fewer bytes would be transmitted, and typically it would take less time to transmit these bytes. During the evolution of the HTTP/1.1 protocol, it was noted that many Web resources were transmitted in an uncompressed form. End-to-end compression was available as a feature in HTTP/1.0. Text, which lends itself well to compression, was still a significant part of Web traffic. Text resources are generally smaller than images, and the popular image formats are precompressed (e.g., GIF, JPEG). The ready availability of fast compression and decompression algorithms for text documents made this approach even more attractive. Besides, it is possible to use compression algorithms tailored to the kind of content. For example, special purpose dictionaries that know the distribution of the alphabet of the language can be used. Such dictionaries are constructed to optimize the lookup of commonly used words in the language.

Apart from compression of messages in software, modems may perform their own form of compression. However, given that a Web message traverses multiple links, modems represent only one of the many hops. Because fewer bits can be typically transmitted in less time, there can be a cumulative savings when we consider the multiple hops a response travels between a sender and a receiver. Experiments show that traditional data compression is significantly better than simple modem compression [Nie97].

A specific problem associated with HTTP's use of TCP as transport mechanism is the nonlinear behavior of TCP. The latency cost of the first packet of TCP is higher than the later packets. A container document consisting of text (HTML) and images is transferred by downloading the HTML first and then the images. Compressing the HTML page (often found in the first packet) would imply that subsequent images would come faster. The overall latency of accessing a container document is lowered. A browser can begin to render the document sooner, thereby reducing the perception of latency to the user.

Compression is a general mechanism to reduce the number of bytes transmitted between an HTTP sender and a receiver. Existing mechanisms in HTTP, such as the `Accept-Encoding` and `Content-Encoding` headers, can be used to specify the choices of compression formats. Another way to reduce the number of bytes is conditional requests in HTTP—for example, the `If-Modified-Since` header is used to retrieve a resource only if it has been modified since a particular time specified in the request. This is useful in the presence of caches where previous instances of responses are cached.

The range request mechanism in HTTP/1.1 was a step in this direction and allowed the transmission of the portions of a resource that were of interest. However, the range mechanism is capable of sending only multiple contiguous portions of a resource. Suppose a resource changed in a way that the new parts alone could be requested via a range request. Such a request would result in a minimal number of bytes transmitted. However, resources often change in a way that clients cannot know the location of the changes and thus clients cannot request just those subparts via contiguous byte-ranges.

Taking a broader view of compression and selective retrieval, transmitting just the *necessary* bits for a particular Web transaction would be ideal. This reduces bandwidth usage and the latency perceived by the user. In the presence of cached instances of earlier responses, it is natural to see if just the difference between the cached instance and the current instance can be transmitted. The notion of generating differences between instances is quite old in computer science. Multiple algorithms exist and have been perfected over the years for a wide variety of data formats. Differencing tools for traditional files are quite popular. However, in the case of the Web, a differencing mechanism must meet certain specific constraints that may not apply in the older, traditional file system model.

We begin this section by examining the motivations for adding a differencing mechanism for HTTP messages. Next we evaluate the choices of differencing algorithms by examining a study undertaken for this purpose. This is followed by a look at how a differencing mechanism would be deployed as part of HTTP/1.1. We end with a report on the current status of the proposed addition of a differencing mechanism to HTTP/1.1.

A note on terminology: HTTP/1.1 does not have a term to describe the value that would be returned in response to a GET request at the current time for the selected variant of the specified resource. The term *instance* is introduced for this purpose.

15.2.1 Motivations for a differencing mechanism for HTTP messages

As discussed earlier, in Chapter 10, Section 10.4, resources on the Web change frequently, and these changed resources are often requested again by the same client [DFKM97]. Suppose the difference between the instances of the resources is small when measured in bytes. For example, a response might include the number of times a resource has been requested. If two different instances of this resource differ only in the value of this number, the difference between the instances is tiny compared with the resource. The origin server can either send the full instance or the difference between a cached instance at the receiver and the current instance on the origin server. Sending the difference and quickly re-creating the new instance on the receiving end would benefit various parties involved in the transaction. An origin server might spend less time in constructing and sending the difference than in constructing and sending the full instance. Additionally, an origin server may be able to cache the differences against different versions and amortize the cost of constructing the difference. Network bandwidth is saved because the difference is often much smaller than the full instance. In fact, if the difference was larger, the server could send the full instance instead. The receiving client or proxy must process the response and create the full instance from the cached instance and the difference. If this can be done quickly, the user is not likely to notice any additional latency. Such latency would be seen only by the first user for whom the update is triggered. The modified instance would be cached, and future references to the resource would result in a cache hit. If a proxy is present in the request-response path, the difference would be stored and forwarded, assuming the proxy is participating in the differencing mechanism. A proxy can also apply the delta to its cached entry and use the updated cached response as a complete response for future requests from clients that are not delta-capable. Additionally, future requests from such clients can be converted into a delta request before being forwarded to origin servers.

Periodic changes in resources reflect the need for a low-cost mechanism that can construct the difference between versions and a way to transport the difference within the framework of the HTTP protocol. We next look at the various ways in which differences can be computed.

15.2.2 Evaluation of delta algorithms

Multiple algorithms exist to compute differences between versions of resources. In the traditional world of file systems, a popular UNIX command *diff* is used to generate a textual difference between two files. The difference could be presented to the user in a way that highlighted the difference in terms of additions, deletions, and changes. Using the *-e* option of *diff* generates a script that can be used by the *ed* editor program to automatically apply the changes to one variant to obtain the other. Thus difference could be computed on one end and transmitted to the other end in the form of a script, and the script would be applied to create the modified version. The assumption is that the difference would be much smaller than the new version.

In order to evaluate delta algorithms for resources on the Web, we must keep the following criteria in mind:

- The time for computing the difference between resource variants
- The size of the difference
- The rate of change of the resource

The criteria do not necessarily lead to the same choice of a delta algorithm. For example, an algorithm that can compute differences quickly may yield large differences by sacrificing space for speed. Such an algorithm is less useful for resources that change often. Such considerations have led text-difference algorithms, such as those of Revision Control System (RCS [Tic85]) and Source Code Control System (SCCS [Roc75]), to use *forward differences*. A forward difference accumulates the difference against the most recent version so that the differences are all kept together for rapid application to create the latest version. The second criterion to remember is that although the amount of information may increase slowly, at any stage, the difference between two proximal versions is generally small. The key observation is that depending on the application, the amount of difference between versions, and the size of the difference, a different algorithm might be appropriate. The third factor is that not all content types of resources show a similar rate of change. For example, textual resources change more often than images [DFKM97].

In the rest of this section, we report on a study conducted in 1997 to evaluate the need to augment the protocol with a delta mechanism. We begin with the methodology and details of the experiment, along with the results.

We then discuss different places where deltas can be applied and the general deployment considerations in the HTTP/1.1 protocol framework. We end with a look at the status of the addition of a delta mechanism to the HTTP/1.1 protocol.

METHODOLOGY OF THE STUDY

To evaluate delta algorithms for use in the Web, those conducting a study must keep the following methodological considerations in mind:

- A wide set of resources must be examined to ensure various attributes, such as content type and size, are well represented.
- Differences across the various versions of resources over time have to be computed.
- The experiment should be repeated over a period of time across resource collections selected from a wide variety of places.

Those conducting the study must also take the following criteria of resources into consideration:

- The frequency with which resources change
- The time to compute the difference between versions of resources
- The savings in bytes in transmitting the difference rather than the full response

The outcome of the study should aid in coming up with a mechanism by which all browsers, proxies, and servers can start using differencing. Any protocol changes necessitated as a result of the study must be standardized. Often this step alone requires more time and effort than the rest of the steps combined.

We now present a brief report of a study, first reported in [MDFK97a], with a more detailed report on the experiment available in [MDFK97b]. The study is now a few years old, but the only key factor that would have changed in the meantime is the traffic mix (fewer textual documents, more dynamic responses, and more image formats). No significant change has occurred in the availability of faster differencing or compression algorithms.

A crucial difference between this study and earlier ones (such as [HL96]) was using a reference stream (i.e., actual requests and responses) on the Web as opposed to choosing a collection of documents and examining the feasibility of differencing techniques on them. The study began by examining what resources are fetched by examining proxy logs and packet traces. The study gathered two sets of resources from two different physical locations (sites) consisting of users who were on opposite ends of the U.S. One site used an instrumented proxy in front of a large group of users in a corporation in which all the outgoing requests were tracked. Only two days worth of data were recorded (about 9

RESEARCH PERSPECTIVES IN PROTOCOL ISSUES

Gigabytes consisting of nearly half a million traces from nearly 8000 different client sites). At the second site, a corporate research organization, a packet-level trace was obtained by monitoring all requests and responses. This site recorded 19 Gigabytes of data over a period of 17 days, with about a million usable traces from nearly 7500 client hosts. The packet trace method captured low-level data and reconstructed them into HTTP requests and responses, as described in Chapter 14 (Section 14.1). The set of resources for evaluating differencing was chosen from these two collections.

For measuring usefulness of a delta mechanism, only requests to resources that changed during the duration of the test were of interest. Responses to the same resource that had 200 OK status code with more than one instance were identified, and the value in the Last-Modified response header was used to infer if resources were changed. Once such pairs of instances were identified, a variety of differencing mechanisms were applied to each pair to examine the size of the difference of the second instance against the first. This is the delta encoding that would have been sent by the origin server if a suitable delta mechanism was available. Such pairs of instances were labeled "delta-eligible."

The study examined three different delta-encoding algorithms based on their perceived popularity and availability. The first one was the UNIX command *diff* with the *-e* option to construct a script that could be applied on the other end to the first instance of the resource to recreate the second instance. The second compressed the output of *diff -e* via the *gzip* program to reduce the size of the difference. The third method used a novel differencing algorithm termed *vdelta* (since renamed *vcdiff* [KV00]), which not only computed the difference between instances, but also inherently compressed the difference.

Several resources were excluded from the study because the content types were considered poor candidates for differencing. For example, GIF and JPEG image types that are precompressed do not lend themselves to useful differencing. Likewise, programs such as *diff* are meant strictly for text resources and do not work on binary resources. However, *vcdiff* works on all input formats and was thus used in the study on all resources, including images.

EXPERIMENTAL RESULTS OF THE STUDY

We briefly summarize the results of the study here. The delta-eligibility metric gives a bound on the usefulness of the delta mechanism in general. Around 38% of the resources were delta-eligible in the proxy trace study, whereas only around 10% of the resources were delta-eligible in the packet trace. The primary reason for this difference is that the proxy study excluded a few content types—mostly nontext types such as GIF, JPEG, MPEG, and audio formats. A broader study would not exclude any of the formats and would gather data at a variety of places to ensure that the content types seen on the Web are well represented.

Two sets of global metrics were computed: the number of bytes that would have been saved if only the differences between instances were transmitted and the approximate time savings achieved by not retrieving the complete response. The study excluded the cost of computing the delta encoding (and the decoding) in the savings computation. Because differences are computed only upon changes, the cost for delta encoding and decoding was low when considered on an amortized basis.

The study showed that nearly 30% of all the full-body response bytes would not have been sent if *vcdiff* was used as the delta-encoding mechanism. If the recipient already had a cached copy of the prior instance, 83% of the response-body bytes would not have had to be transmitted. The study also reported on the cost of computing the delta and applying the delta to the previous instance. Also, the study reported that of all the algorithms tested, *vcdiff* gave the best result in a vast majority of the cases.

The bottom-line result was that a library implementation (which is likely to be the way in which differencing is implemented in real-life Web servers) of *vcdiff* operated at a throughput of a T-1 line (193 KB/sec). Thus all users who have connections less than or equal to a T-1 line could benefit from delta encoding and compression. The study confirmed that *vcdiff* was the most time-efficient for delta encoding and for compressing. The study also showed that delta coding and compressing fared favorably against a modern modem's inherent compression ability, especially for large files.

The conclusion of the study was that a widely available delta mechanism could result in significant reductions in the number of bytes transferred on the Web without increasing latency for the differencing and reconstruction of responses. For the proxy trace, the study showed that nearly a third of the response bytes could have been reduced, with almost 40% reduction in the transfer time of the responses that were amenable to differencing. For the packet trace, with its wider mix of content types (nontextual types were not ignored), a very large fraction of bytes (around 85%) could be saved if the response was delta-eligible. However, including all content types reduced overall effectiveness to around 9%. The study effectively concluded that delta-eligible responses should be delta-encoded, and others should be simply compressed to at least save the number of bytes transferred on the network.

OTHER CONSIDERATIONS IN A DELTA MECHANISM

After selecting a delta mechanism, we must choose the place where the delta can be best applied. For a delta to be applied, the earlier version must be available. A natural choice is a proxy that can maintain multiple earlier versions of several resources to maximize the benefit for several clients behind it. However, a browser that has its own cache of earlier versions of a set of large, very frequently requested resources may also be a plausible location for applying the delta. The size of the browser cache may limit the number of different instances that could be stored in a browser, especially if the response is large. A user's slow link to the Internet may be the primary bottleneck, and applying the delta close to the user could considerably reduce latency. As long as the delay in applying a delta is less than the time to fetch the full resource, the user enjoys the benefit of latency reduction. By caching the result of the applied delta, a caching proxy might be able to return the latest full version to subsequent client requests. Of course, if deltas can be applied at both a client and a proxy, a client might request a delta and receive just the delta from the proxy even though the proxy might have the full version of the resource. The consideration in this case is for the delay in transmitting a large resource between two components, a client and a proxy that are close to each other in terms of network latency and the delay in reapplying the delta at the client.

15.2.3 Deployment issues of delta mechanism in HTTP/1.1

Deploying any delta mechanism requires studying the changes required in the HTTP/1.1 protocol. The client or proxy must be able to express its ability to handle the delta mechanism. The server receiving a request must be able to generate deltas against specific versions and identify the deltas as such. An Internet Draft [MKD+01] on this proposal has moved through some of the standardization stages and is currently a proposed standard as this book goes to press. Because the draft has been under discussion for over two years, the basic proposal appears to have matured. Some additions that are not related to the core delta proposal have been separated into a different Internet Draft [MDH].

We next present a brief precis of the proposal in three parts:

1. Major issues in delta deployment
2. An outline of the steps in transforming an HTTP message through the delta encoding process
3. A brief examination of some of the key transformation steps

Deployment considerations   The major issues in deploying the delta mechanism in HTTP/1.1 include the following:

- **Identification of instances:** A client must identify the instance(s) against which it would like the difference. A client that has multiple cached instances may apply a heuristic to determine the instances it plans to include in its request. The cached instance and the associated delta against that instance must be properly identified in order to obtain the latest instance on a server. Not all instances that are cached at the client may still be available at the origin server.
- **Syntax:** The syntax regarding specification of content and transfer codings for the client and server to agree upon a choice of delta encoding/decoding

mechanism must be specified. A client may accept only a subset of delta algorithms and may have an order of preference among them. The client should be able to express the order of preference to maximize its chances of obtaining a delta in a preferred format. The decision to express preferences might depend on the content type and size of the cached response.

- **Realization:** The construction, transfer, application, and caching of the delta are all issues related to the realization of the delta mechanism in practice. The origin server might assign cost to a delta mechanism based on the time required to construct deltas against its collection of instances. If the generated delta is larger than the current instance, the origin server might simply send the instance. A well-behaved server might opt to tailor its choice according to the client's preferences if this does not increase the cost to the origin server. For example, an origin server might find it cheaper to generate delta in a single preferred format over all others. If the origin server had cached deltas against older instances using a particular delta mechanism, it might choose that mechanism even if that particular mechanism was not the first choice of the requesting client. Deciding which deltas to cache and how long to retain the cached values are additional tasks that an origin server must undertake.

Outline of HTTP message transformation   The basic set of steps outlined in [MKD+01] relating to the various transformations that an HTTP message might undergo include the following:

- Identification of the requested resource by the server
- Selection of a variant of the resource
- Generation of an entity tag associated with the *instance* (not the entity) of the resource
- Construction of a delta-encoded entity
- Transfer of the message consisting of the delta-encoded entity

At any of the stages, the server might decide not to generate a delta: the client may not be able to accept deltas, the instance against which the delta could be created may not be available to the client to apply the resultant delta, and so on. The draft goes into depth about dealing with ranges, because ranges are also a form of instance manipulation. The reason this is important is that it is possible for a delta-capable client to request a delta against a range or a range of a delta-encoded instance. The presence of range capability means that the order in which delta encoding is done becomes important and the client must specify the sequence, lest the response be ambiguous. A new request header was introduced to let the client specify the order in which instance manipulations should be performed. A new response header was introduced so that the server can specify the order in which two or more instance manipulations have been performed.

Exploration of key steps in delta process The key steps in the process of a client requesting and handling a delta-encoded response are as follows:

- Client's expression of interest in delta encoding
- Server's computation and transmission of a suitable delta
- Potential interaction of ranges and proxies
- Availability of multiple instances at the client

First, a client expresses both its interest and capability in delta encoding via the `A-IM` (Accept-Instance-Manipulation) header, which specifies the set of acceptable delta encoding algorithms. For example,

```
GET /chap15.html HTTP/1.1
Host: www.vcdiff.com
If-None-Match: "38432-s8-13"
A-IM: vcdiff, diffe, gzip
```

means that the client prefers the *vcdiff* encoding and then the *diffe* encoding for delta and *gzip* as compression format, even if the response were not to be delta encoded. The `If-None-Match` header identifies the instance against which any delta should be applied. As always, the server can return a `304 Not Modified` if the current instance of the resource `chap15.html` is the same as the variant signified by the entity tag "38432-s8-13". If the current resource has a different entity tag, a delta-capable server could compute the delta between the current instance and the instance referred to by the entity tag "38432-s8-13". The client's preference is for the *vcdiff* encoding, and the server should try to use that differencing mechanism if at all possible.

The server might choose not to compute a delta for several reasons. For example, the server may have reason to believe that the response in the delta-encoded format would be larger than the current instance of the resource. The server might use a heuristic based on the size of the current instance or past experience with the encoding mechanism. A server might have cached the delta against this pair of instances if they happened to be frequently requested and could just send the cached value. In any case, the server's response would look something like this:

```
HTTP/1.1 226 IM Used
Date: Sun, 2  Jul 2000 23:35:35 GMT
ETag: "192-qpt-899"
IM: vcdiff

...
```

The server uses the new response code 226 `IM Used` and the response header `IM` indicating the choice of delta encoding. The instance of the resource has a new entity tag (192-qpt-899), which will presumably be stored by the proxy or client for future use.

Suppose the client was interested in only a portion of the difference between two instances. The client could request that the server compute the difference and then extract a portion of the difference:

```
GET /foo.html HTTP/1.1
Host: www.vcdiff.com
If-None-Match: "38432-s8-13"
A-IM: vcdiff, range
Range: bytes=0-200
```

The server might send a response as follows:

```
HTTP/1.1 226 IM Used
Date: Mon, 20 Nov 2000 11:48:45 GMT
ETag: "192-pqr-99"
IM: vcdiff, range

...
```

which implies that the server computed a *vcdiff* delta-encoding of the current instance against a copy of the instance with entity tag "38432-s8-13", then extracted the first 201 bytes of this *vcdiff* encoded instance. Note that the Instance Manipulation (IM) header indicates the order in which instance manipulation was done: delta-encoding followed by range extraction.

The existence of proxies that do not understand delta encoding forced the introduction of a new response code. Because most of the proxies currently do not even run the latest version of HTTP, it is even less likely that, for the foreseeable future, the proxies would understand delta encoding. Most proxies ignore response codes they do not understand and forward such responses without caching them; therefore they can be expected to behave in the same manner for a response with a new code 226 `IM Used`. A proxy that does not understand delta encoding but mistakenly caches a delta-encoded response might return such a response to a client that is not capable of handling delta encoding. With the new 226 `IM Used` response code, a proxy that does not understand the delta mechanism is not likely to cache the response because it does not understand the response code. Thus there is a lower probability that the proxy would return an invalid response to a client requesting the same resource later.

The client might have multiple instances against which it is willing to accept deltas, and the server computing the delta might send deltas against one of those multiple instances. In such cases, the client could simply use the existing `If-None-Match` header to list *all* the instances it has against which deltas are acceptable. A client could send a request as follows:

```
GET /chap15.html HTTP/1.1
Host: www.vcdiff.com
If-None-Match: "38432-s8-13", "97-ru486-v", "2-dumbya-1f"
A-IM: vcdiff, diffe, gzip
```

indicating that it has three base instances against which it is capable of accepting deltas. The server could use a heuristic to decide which of those three it wants to compute the delta against and then indicate the chosen base instance as follows:

```
HTTP/1.1 226 IM Used
Date: Sun, 2  Jul 2000 23:35:35 GMT
ETag: "282-ela-899"
IM: vcdiff
Delta-Base: "97-ru486-v"
...
```

The server chose the instance with the entity tag "97-ru486-v" to compute a delta against the current instance of the response. The chosen instance is indicated in a new header named Delta-Base. The ETag field in the delta response identifies the current instance of the response. The client now knows how to reconstruct the latest version of the resource. If there was no indication of the instance against which the delta was created, the understanding is that the request should be able to uniquely identify the base instance. The server simply returned the delta against that base instance and was not required to provide any additional information.

Figures 15.1 to 15.4 show a simplified version of some of the steps involved in the delta process. A client has in its cache an instance v1 of a resource r with entity tag "xyz" associated with it obtained from origin server A. Now suppose that the client sends a request to the origin server A for the resource and a If-None-Match header indicating the ETag of the instance it has in its cache. (Figure 15.1).

The origin server has a new instance of the resource, namely v2, with the entity tag "abc" associated with it. The origin server A constructs a delta between the instances v1 and v2 and returns it to the client along with the entity tag of the new instance, namely "abc." (Figure 15.2). The client reconstructs the current instance r' from its cached instance v1 and the delta.

Figure 15.3 shows a client requesting the same resource when it has two cached instances, v1 and v2.

The current instance is v3. The origin server computes the delta between the instances v2 and v3 and includes the entity tag of the new instance, namely "pqr." It also includes the Delta-Base header with value "abc" to notify the client that the base instance against which the delta was computed was v2 (Figure 15.4).

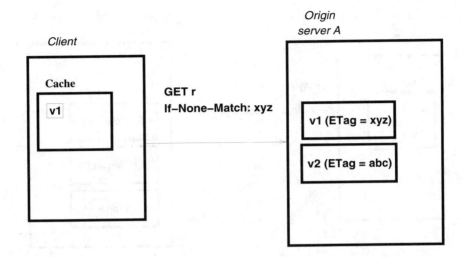

Figure 15.1. Client requesting resource **r** from origin server

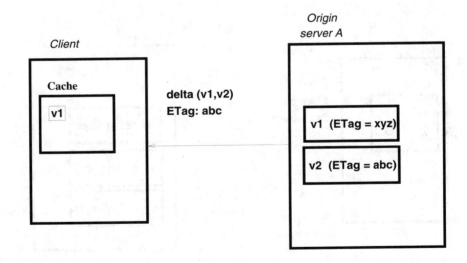

Figure 15.2. Origin server returning delta against instance v1

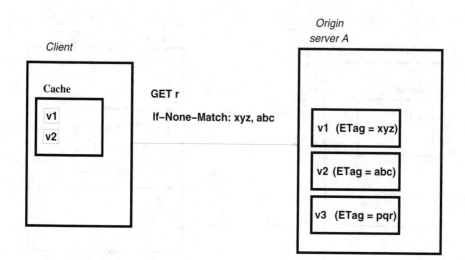

Figure 15.3. Client requesting resource **r** indicating its cached instances

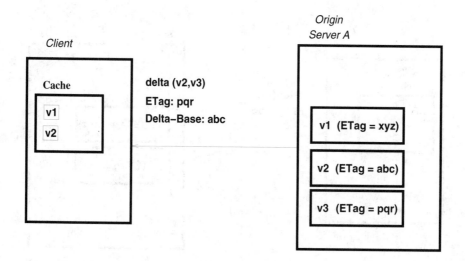

Figure 15.4. Origin server returning delta of current instance against **v2**

A server needs to decide how many of the base instances to retain and for how long. The decision is similar to a cache replacement decision—based on frequency of usage, time of creation, and so on. With each base instance retained by the server and choices expressed by the client, other decisions must be made by the server. For example, the server must decide if it should compute multiple deltas and send the best or just pick one at random. The server also must select a replacement policy for discarding older instances to be replaced by new instances. Such policy issues are viewed as outside the scope of the proposal and not discussed in the delta draft.

15.2.4 Status of adding delta mechanism to HTTP/1.1

The proposed standard version is currently pending at the IETF as this book goes to press. There are at least two known implementations. Interoperable implementations are yet to be created, though there has been indication of work in some universities.

15.3 HTTP/1.1 Protocol Compliance

With the advent of HTTP/1.1, numerous implementations of browsers, proxies, and servers became available. In a fairly short time, the realignment of the software market of Web components has led to a few brands dominating the market. By the fall of 1999, three Web server implementations—Apache, Microsoft/IIS, and Netscape-Enterprise—had over 95% of the market. A year later, in the fall of 2000, there were still only three server implementations, with a slight realignment of market share among them. Among browsers, there were just two popular brands (Netscape and Internet Explorer), and this has remained largely unchanged.

The issues in protocol compliance are straightforward: are the various implementations compliant with the requirements specified in the protocol? In Chapter 6 (Section 6.5) we discussed the various levels of requirement imposed on the software components of a protocol implementation. For a realization to be considered compliant with the protocol specification, the various MUST, SHOULD, and MAY requirements dealing with the syntax and semantics must be met. Any implementation that does not satisfy all of the MUST requirements is considered *not* compliant with the protocol specification. An implementation satisfying all the MUST and SHOULD requirements is *unconditionally* compliant. If not all the SHOULD requirements are satisfied, the implementation is labeled *conditionally* compliant.

Oddly enough, there has been an absence of mechanisms to study whether even the few popular software realizations meet the compliance requirement of the HTTP/1.1 protocol specification. In this section, we examine how to verify which of the various HTTP compliance requirements outlined in RFC 2616 are obeyed by server implementations. We also examine the impact of non-adherence. This section is largely derived from the report [KA01] on the first large-scale longitudinal HTTP compliance study conducted over a 16-month period between June 1999 and September 2000. We look at the testing methodology and then the results of the study. Note that the same sites were not tested in all three studies because the popularity of sites changed over the period of the study. The results, however, were not dissimilar when the testing was confined to the sites that were uniformly popular through the three different study periods.

15.3.1 Motivation for protocol compliance study

Information on compliance allows us to estimate the rate of adoption of the protocol and the usefulness of the new features of the protocol. Measuring the compliance is necessary to estimate the percentage of Web traffic that uses the particular version of the protocol. Site administrators can use information about the penetration rate of a protocol version to decide if they should upgrade to the newer version as well. Compliance studies help protocol designers. Evidence of widespread absence of compliance of a particular feature is potentially useful feedback. Designers can try to understand why some features were adopted quickly and others were not.

Interoperability of different implementations of clients, proxies, and servers relies on the fact that the components are compliant with the protocol. Because the components are built by different groups of people, the only uniting factor that guarantees proper functioning of Web exchanges is the expectation each component has of the other. If a browser cannot expect that a particular request would be honored by a server claiming to be running a particular version of a protocol, it cannot offer a uniform interface to the users behind the browser. The task of a proxy is already complicated given that it must function as a server to clients and as a client to servers. If, in addition, the proxy must adjust to variations in levels of protocol compliance of each of the client and server variants, its complexity would increase significantly. Although compliant implementations may still be vulnerable to denial of service attacks or other security violation attempts, a noncompliant server faces a higher risk.

15.3.2 Testing compliance of clients and proxies

Discussion of server compliance raises the question of compliance of the two other main Web components: client and proxy. Testing of clients is generally easier than testing compliance of servers. Browsers expose some of their options as configuration parameters. For example, IE 5.0 lets the user select which version of the protocol to use (HTTP/1.0 or HTTP/1.1). The choice is not between HTTP/1.0 and all of HTTP/1.1 but a subset of HTTP/1.1 features. More importantly, it is not clear if the available features are implemented in a compliant manner. For example, a browser might claim to implement the Range request feature of HTTP/1.1, yet send requests without proper byte ranges and get the full body of the response instead of just the necessary ranges. However, given that the user has control over the browser, a locally installed packet monitor can display the set of headers included in requests. The set of response headers can be easily gathered. The protocol requirements imposed on the clients are generally less stringent and easier to isolate and test than those on servers.

However, testing proxy compliance is significantly harder. The protocol specification is largely silent on specific rules for proxies except for the generic understanding that because a proxy is both a client and a server, a compliant proxy is both a compliant client and a compliant server. Although this increases the complexity of a proxy, testing its compliance is harder for other reasons. A proxy's compliance with the protocol has to be tested both while it acts as a client and as a server. Permission is needed to direct a request through a proxy on the Internet. Although there are several proxies that are lax enough to let requests travel through them, it could be viewed as improper use of their computing resources. Next, even if we were permitted to test the compliance of a proxy, we would not know the actual contents of the request that the proxy sent to the origin server. Proxies' configurations differ significantly from each other—system administrators modify a proxy's configuration for caching. More importantly, very few of the proxies even claim to run HTTP/1.1. To complicate matters, examination of proxies has shown that there are several HTTP/1.0 proxies implementing some of the HTTP/1.1 features. The HTTP message path between a client and an origin server can go through several proxies, some of which may be HTTP/1.0 proxies, whereas others are HTTP/1.1. Compliant HTTP/1.1 proxies can be detected by the presence of Via headers, but we would not be able to identify the HTTP/1.0 proxies. It would make sense to test proxies for compliance when the end-to-end message path largely consists of HTTP/1.1 components.

The rest of the section focuses only on testing server compliance.

15.3.3 Methodology of testing compliance

The following are the ways to test the compliance with a protocol:

- Implementors of components could consult a table [Fea] generated by the World Wide Web Consortium (W3C) consisting of various features and check off the features implemented. Presumably, they would ensure that the implementation also adhered to the requirements specified in the protocol. However, in reality, this is not always the case.
- The software could be run through a thorough set of regression tests with part of the regression test suite consisting of compliance tests. This also appears not to be very widely practiced. Most regression test suites ensure

that the component would survive a high request rate (for servers) and verifies the ability to render arbitrary responses (for browsers). However, we are not aware of compliance tests being part of regression test suites.

- The running version of different servers could be tested *online* by sending requests from remote clients. This is a reasonable way to test a wide variety of servers. Each Web site could have its Web server tested remotely by a set of clients generating requests and ensuring that the responses are valid.

The last approach is the best way to test compliance, because a test of an installed and operational Web server alone provides a realistic answer to the compliance question. Web servers, as we saw in Chapter 4 (Section 4.6), are configured with many parameters, each with a different value depending on the site. The popular Apache Web server has been known to be run with over 700 combinations of configuration options [KA01]. Thus the approach of running tests locally with all possible combinations of configuration options is not feasible. The reason for configuring sites in different ways may be related to the mix of resources on the site, the typical request arrival rate, and the time to service a request. Separately, some requests have side effects. Many requests alter the contents of a site, and scripts may have to be executed in a particular environment. Thus the notion of trying to recreate all of these conditions across thousands of sites in a local setting is not feasible.

Once we decide to test operational Web servers, we still must choose which servers to test from the millions of available Web sites. The following are some of the different ways of selecting servers:

- **Sampling:** A sampling technique might suggest choosing a random set of servers from the millions. However, we have to choose from different implementations and different configurations of each server type. To exhaustively test one server from every possible configuration is not practical.

- **Functionality:** Earlier, in Chapter 4 (Section 4.1), we saw a variety of ways in which sites could be classified based on functionality. The choice of servers may also be made on the basis of a internal company site, special event site, portal site, search engine site, e-commerce site, etc. The degree of compliance of servers might vary with functionality of the site. More importantly, the failure of a server to comply with certain requirements may matter more on some sites than on others. For example, an e-commerce site might be much more worried about lack of compliance that opens up the possibility of a denial of service attack than an internal corporate site where such attacks are generally rarer. Thus it is hard to make a reasonable selection on the basis of functionality.

- **Popularity:** Another approach is to consider the popular Web *sites* and examine their server implementations and configuration options. The rate of access to the different Web sites on the planet is heavily skewed toward a few thousand sites. Studies of popular sites have reported that a few hundred sites receive nearly half of all requests. Given this heavily skewed access pattern, it might suffice to test compliance of servers in the top several hundred sites. Among the many companies that rate the popularity of Web sites are MediaMetrix [Med], Hot 100 [Hot], Alexa1000 [Ale], and Netcraft [Netc]. Each company uses a different technique to generate popularity figures and update their results periodically.

The study we discuss next chose the popularity technique, although future studies could test sites chosen based on a different methodology. To ensure broader coverage, the study merged the results from the rating sites with sites from two other collections—the Fortune 500 [For99] and Global 200 [Glo98] sets of companies. The merged set of sites in some sense represents a canonical list of popular sites.

15.3.4 PRO-COW: A large-scale compliance study

The methodology of the Protocol Compliance on the Web (PRO-COW) study was to generate a variety of requests covering the various HTTP/1.1 features and check the responses automatically to see if they adhered to the requirements outlined in the specification. For example, if each response was supposed to have a `Date` header, responses from servers that lacked this header were deemed to be noncompliant. A more detailed version of the PRO-COW compliance study is described in [KA01].

The description of the compliance study is divided into four parts, beginning with the various categories of tests. After looking at whether client location for the tests matters, we briefly examine the testing environment and software used to carry out the tests. Finally, we examine the actual tests and their results. Given the nature of flux in Web technology, the durability of the test results is a concern. By conducting three separate measurements over a period of 16 months, this study reduced the risk of transience of results.

CATEGORIZATION OF COMPLIANCE TESTS

Because not all violations of compliance requirements are equally serious, the importance of the various compliance tests must be ranked. Accordingly, the compliance testing is divided into three parts in descending order of importance:

1. **Testing the various MUST compliance conditions:** These requirements are clearly stated, with the expectation that components must adhere to them fully. Any implementation that does not meet *all* the MUST requirements is considered to be noncompliant. The designers of the protocol stress that failure to comply with a MUST requirement of a feature might lead to semantic violations. For example, the HTTP/1.1 draft standard stresses that all messages on a persistent connection MUST have

self-defined length. Suppose a server that maintains a persistent connection sends a message without a clear notion of length. The receiver does not know if it has received the entire message. Given that an additional message might be sent (because the connection is persistent), the receiver has no way of knowing how to separate the two messages. Similarly, a proxy MUST NOT send a message with a protocol version indicator greater than its actual version. The protocol version is an indicator of the capability of the sender. The receiver might mistakenly assume that the sender implements certain features. For example, the receiver might think that the sender is capable of receiving and decoding messages sent using chunked transfer-coding.

2. **Testing the important new features in HTTP/1.1:** There is an inherent ranking of dozens of new features (Chapter 7 covers the various changes between HTTP/1.0 and HTTP/1.1). Some of the features, such as persistent connections, range requests, and Internet address conservation are more important than some of the other changes, such as error notification. However, a full compliance test suite should test all the new features of the new version of the protocol. For example, range request is a new and important addition to HTTP/1.1. However, as discussed in Chapter 7 (Section 7.4.1), acceptance of range requests is not mandatory in HTTP/1.1. Servers are encouraged to accept them because this would reduce the number of packets being transmitted on the network. Likewise, acceptance of persistent connections, while a default, is not a MUST requirement in HTTP/1.1.

3. **Testing a subset of the miscellaneous other changes:** The number of changes in HTTP/1.1, as outlined in Chapter 7, is large. After categorizing the set of changes and ordering them, several miscellaneous features can be tested. For example, several specific warnings have been stated for handling messages of arbitrary lengths. The server may not be able to handle long Request-URIs. Although the protocol specification does not include a specific length limitation, it does introduce a 4xx class error response code (414 Request-URI Too Long). Server implementations would be wise to check for buffer overflow errors when they receive a request message with a very long URI.

Location of testing clients

Once the set of tests is chosen, the location of the testing clients must be identified. Technically, the location of the client issuing the requests should not matter. Web servers that are not basing the response on location and identity of client should respond in the same way, independent of the requests' origin. In a test that sends the requests directly from client to the origin server, this is not an issue. However, if a request flows through one or more proxies, the location of the client is a factor. The location of a client might be a factor in which server replica receives and replies to the request. The study ignored the role of proxies—all requests were sent directly to the origin server. A broader compliance study would test the role of proxies in the compliance—both to see if the proxy is compliant with the protocol and if the proxy affects the compliance test while forwarding the requests to the origin server. If the origin server has a surrogate or has other local servers (e.g., that serve images), they need to be tested as well. These other servers may not run the same version of the server software as the origin server. Surrogate servers may not even run HTTP/1.1 and thus not be required to be compliant with HTTP/1.1. Different client locations were used to test the hypothesis of whether client locations affected the compliance results.

COMPLIANCE TESTING ENVIRONMENT

Once the choice of tests and location has been settled, software for the tests must be identified. It is possible to test basic compliance by contacting a Web server simply via *telnet* (to port 80, say), but it is not suitable for running an extensive series of tests periodically in an automated fashion. The primary software used for generating the set of requests was the *httperf* [MJ98] client tool. *httperf* is a configurable Web performance measurement tool with three primary logical components: an HTTP engine that sends HTTP requests and parses HTTP responses, a workload generator that generates HTTP request streams, and a statistics collector that gathers statistics about the requests made. *httperf* is able to handle HTTP/1.1 and is available in source code form enabling easy modification. The choice of client sites to run the tests is harder. Ideally one would like to select representative client sites similar to how server sites were selected. However, unlike statistics about server popularity, hard data about client locations is not available. As it turned out, the client locations did not matter, and so this was not a problem. However, as we will see in the summary section (Section 15.3.5), future broader studies may not be able to ignore client location. This study ran the tests from the authors' research organizations, as well as a variety of places around the world.

TESTS AND RESULTS OF COMPLIANCE STUDY

The compliance study was carried out on three occasions over a period of 16 months. The three most popular servers[1] during the tests were Apache, Netscape-Enterprise, and Microsoft-IIS. Together, these three servers accounted for 95% of all servers tested. The respective popularity of the servers within the test set is not necessarily representative of the Web at large. For example,

---

[1] We use the term server from now on as shorthand for the version of a running origin server on the tested site.

the Apache Web server has consistently had around 60% of the total market share [Netc], while the tested sample had around 30% of servers running Apache. Different configuration information could be gleaned from the `Server` response header for Apache and Netscape-Enterprise servers. Among the several hundred different configuration options that were gleaned from Apache and Netscape servers are

```
Server: Apache/1.3b3 mod_perl/1.07
Server: Netscape-Communications/1.1+SiteTrack 1.10i26mck
Server: Apache/1.2.5 FrontPage/3.0.3
```

However, Microsoft-IIS servers did not have any configuration options other than the software version number identifiers (e.g., IIS/4.0 and IIS/5.0). The results of the study are on a per-server basis and do not apply to all deployed versions.

The Category One set of tests included testing of the `GET` and `HEAD` methods, as well as testing for proper reaction to the absence of the `Host` request header. Recall that proper handling of the `Host` header (discussed in Chapter 7, Section 7.8) is a MUST-level requirement, and all HTTP/1.1 servers are obligated to return an error if the header is not present in any HTTP/1.1 request. About one third of the servers were found to be noncompliant with respect to handling of the `Host` header.

Conditional compliance results from the absence of `Content-Length` or `Transfer-Encoding: chunked` headers. Over 80% of servers handled the `GET` method properly. Compliance with `GET` requires servers to send the expected status code (200 OK) and for the response to include appropriate headers such as `Date` and either `Content-Length` or `Transfer-Encoding: chunked`. Over 70% of servers were unconditionally compliant in handling the `HEAD` method. This required that the response include the same entity headers seen in the response to the `GET` request, as well as the proper `Date` header.

Apache and Microsoft-IIS servers fared well in the sense that none of them failed all of the tests; nearly 20% of the Netscape-Enterprise servers failed all the tests. Later versions of Netscape-Enterprise servers had more problems than earlier versions. Although the results have been aggregated across servers here, considerable variation occurs within the Apache, Microsoft-IIS, and Netscape-Enterprise server groups. Over one fifth of all servers failed at least one of the three tests. By the time of the last study, in fall 2000, the overall failure rate was still around 20%, although there was a slight decline in the number of servers that failed all three tests.

The Category Two tests involved testing the important new features introduced in HTTP/1.1, such as persistent connections, pipelining, and range requests. As discussed in Chapter 7 (Section 7.5.2), persistent connections are a SHOULD-level requirement. However, because persistent connections were viewed to be beneficial, they were made the default in HTTP/1.1. In other words, a server must be configured explicitly to *disable* persistence. Nearly 70% of servers provided persistence, and nearly as many handled pipelined requests. However, only half of the tested servers were able to handle range requests. Again, handling range requests is a SHOULD-level requirement in the protocol specification. When the Category Two tests were taken as a whole, only 40% of servers tested were found to be fully compliant, and 20% of them failed all the tests. The third study, done in fall 2000, did not show significant improvement over the previous two studies.

Merging both Category One and Two tests, about 30% of servers passed all tests, and 7% failed all tests.

Finally, Category Three tests examined a range of other minor features, such as less frequently used methods (`OPTIONS`, `TRACE`), potentially risky situations (long URIs), and different formats of date specification. Although the tested methods are not yet in wide use now, they could be used more widely in the future. The `OPTIONS` method (described in Chapter 7, Section 7.7.1) can be used to find out about the capabilities of a server. A sender can verify that a server can handle chunked transfer encoding, for example, before sending a request.

The most revealing test was the test for handling of a long Request-URI—a few servers were not checking for buffer overflow that resulted in the server program exiting abnormally. Fortunately, this was fixed shortly after the study authors notified the developers of the particular server software. Given that many e-commerce companies' existence depends on their Web sites remaining accessible, a simple problem such as this should not have gone undetected. One reason might be that developers tended to pay less attention to SHOULD-level compliance requirements, and the check for handling long URIs was a SHOULD-level requirement. Protocol developers might want to decide on compliance-level requirements based on additional criteria, such as potential for catastrophic situations that arise as a result of a particular feature not being tested thoroughly. Not all bugs can be removed simply by stronger mandates. However, the relatively permissive interpretation of a SHOULD-level requirement should be taken into consideration in risky situations. An alternative possibility is to add potentially risky situations to the Security Considerations section of the protocol specification.

15.3.5 Summary of protocol compliance

The studies done over a 16-month period showed that protocol compliance had improved, but the testing process needs to be more rigorous. There have been discussions in various electronic mailing lists on having a set of *silent* tests whose results are not publicized, to avoid embarrassing the implementors. Although this is an interesting idea, a published test with major vendors testing their implementations against a standardized set of compliance tests would be significantly better. Users and server software administrators can see at a glance the levels of compliance of the various Web components. More openness would encourage implementors to make their software more compliant to the protocol specification.

A broader compliance test would choose a larger collection of client sites and ensure that proxies were tested along with origin servers. Toward the end of 2000, HTTP/1.1-compliant proxies were not yet widely available, although this is expected to change soon. Similarly, the technique for choosing server sites to be tested could be based on other criteria such as nature of sites (e.g., event, e-commerce, etc.). Also locally popular sites could be included; that is, if the tests were being run from Italy, the top few sites popular in Italy could be included, even if they did not appear in the globally popular set of sites.

15.4 End-to-end Web Performance Measurements

After examining the compliance to the protocol specification, it is natural to see if the changes to the protocol actually result in improvements in Web performance. Web performance includes several factors, including user-perceived latency in fetching Web resources, load on the network in the form of packets required to transmit responses, and the load on the Web server in handling the requests.

A simple way to test performance is to generate a set of requests to servers running the two different versions of the protocol and compare their performance. A more general approach is to set up a global testbed consisting of client sites that can be used to generate a synthetic workload of requests to a set of representative server sites. A set of representative Web sites is easier to generate given that the list of popular sites is routinely published and vast numbers of requests are being directed to just a few sites. However, identifying a set of representative clients is more difficult.

In this section, we discuss measuring end-to-end response for Web servers as seen from a variety of client sites. We begin by identifying the factors contributing to end-to-end Web performance and focus our attention on protocol-related issues. We then report on one end-to-end study [KW00], briefly recapturing the details and results of that study. A combined study that examines all the factors simultaneously is hard to perform. A large number of variables must be considered, and it is generally impossible to perform controlled studies. However, it is worth examining the *influence* the various factors have on each other, and we will do that in the concluding section. Any study purporting to capture end-to-end performance must clarify the parameters being studied and assumptions made in ignoring the other factors.

15.4.1 Identifying the factors in end-to-end performance

Several factors affect the end-to-end performance of a Web transaction. Among them are the connection speed of the end user, the presence of proxies in the path between the client and the origin servers, congestion and packet loss on the network, and the load on the origin server. Not much data is available about where requests originate or the nature of connections that clients have to the Internet.

Table 15.1 shows some of the contributing components to Web performance. The taxonomy does not show the actual contribution to delay by each of the factors. The two reasons for this are: absence of conclusive large-scale studies and the variability inherent in any large end-to-end performance study. Although conducting a comprehensive study that encompasses all factors is not easy, it is possible to start by examining some of the key factors while bounding the impact of others. Additionally, the table is not comprehensive—not all the factors that are capable of affecting end-to-end delay are listed. For example, ambient temperatures may have adverse impact on conductivity. The table attempts to gather the *most common* sources of delay.

The first column in Table 15.1 shows the various steps of a Web transfer from the user's browser click to the final rendering by the browser of the response. The second column gives examples of potential variability in the transfer that might obviate a step in the first column or complicate the work done in that step. Examples of variability include the bypassing of the Domain Name System (DNS) lookup of the server if the server's IP address is found in the DNS cache. Another example is the parsing of an HTML document resulting in additional requests for embedded images. The third column lists other variables that can affect the end-to-end delay but are generally of a second order compared with the second column.

Consider a typical Web transaction that begins with a user selecting a URL and ends with the browser displaying the response. In Chapter 2 (Section 2.3.1), we discussed a canonical example. We ignored the potential presence of several other components such as interception proxies and other possible actions such as server redirection. We also ignored the connectivity to the user's Internet Service Provider (ISP) and/or to the Internet and the potential delay resulting from congestion in the network. Table 15.1 tries to give the complete picture of the various steps in a Web transaction. The user's browser click results in a check against the browser's cache to see if the resource is available locally. If not, the click is translated into an HTTP request.

Suppose the user is connected to an ISP for Internet access. The connection could be over a slow dial-up connection, a fast cable modem, or a Digital Subscriber Loop (DSL) connection. The ISP itself may be connected to the rest of the Internet via links shared by other ISPs. ISPs may employ one or more proxies for a variety of purposes such as forwarding messages, sharing,

Table 15.1. End-to-end delay components

Web transaction step	Factors affecting delay
Browser click	—
Browser cache lookup	DNS cache hit/miss, client machine speed
HTTP request construction	Protocol version
DNS query for proxy's address	DNS cache hit, contacting root server
Interception proxy	Hardware speed/proxy farm
TCP to proxy	ISP/net connectivity/persistent connection
	Load on proxy/caching
Proxy to hierarchy	UDP/ICP
DNS of upstream server	DNS cache hit
Proxy to next proxy in chain	Protocol versions, network delay
TCP to origin server	Presence of surrogate
Server redirection	Connection to new server
Server parsing HTTP request	Static/dynamic resource, Delay in CGI
Server load	Server side delay
Server writing response	Send socket size
Browser parsing and rendering	Making additional requests

and caching. A proxy could be explicitly configured by modifying the browser used by the ISP's customers.

A proxy in the path between the client and origin server may have been configured at the client directly as an IP address or as a name. If the proxy is configured as a name (e.g., `proxy01.aol.com`), a DNS query is sent to obtain the proxy's IP address. As discussed in Chapter 5 (Section 5.3.3), the string representation of the proxy's hostname is sent to the local DNS server, which may have the answer cached, in which case the delay is minimal. If not, several seconds may elapse before the address is resolved if other DNS servers have to be contacted. In most cases, such a DNS query is likely to be sent only once, because the information will be cached either in the browser or at the local DNS server.

Even if no explicit proxy was configured, the request might still be intercepted by an interception proxy (discussed in Chapter 11, Section 11.10.2). Note that the browser is unaware of such interceptions. If the response came from one of the caching proxies, the overall latency may be low. If however, the response is not found in any of the caching proxies, the request must be forwarded upstream.

Suppose an explicit proxy that is part of a cache hierarchy is contacted. The proxy would query the cache hierarchy when it is unable to locate the resource in its own cache. The cache query is typically a UDP message sent using the Internet Cache Protocol (ICP) to the rest of the caches in the hierarchy. A successful response from one of the caches in the hierarchy will keep the overall delay low. However, if none of the caches in the hierarchy respond successfully, the request still must be sent to upstream servers toward the origin server. The typical delay for checking in a Squid hierarchy is on the order of a few milliseconds, assuming that the UDP messages are not lost.

In both the explicitly configured proxy and the interception proxy case, the load on the proxies is another variable. If the proxies are busy handling other requests, there might be an additional delay.

So far we have discussed the role of browsers and proxies. Now we examine the role played by the HTTP protocol in terms of connections and caching. If the client already has a persistent connection established with the proxy, the new request does not require the DNS lookup of the proxy or the TCP connection setup. Suppose the request has not been satisfied at the browser's cache, in the proxy close to the user, or in any of the proxies in the proxy farm of the ISP. Then the request must be sent to an upstream server. This brings into play the connectivity between the user's ISP network and the Internet. Correspondingly, the delays resulting from congestion and lost packets become an additional factor. Typically network delays are not an issue between the user and the proxy close to the user. If the request is forwarded to another proxy that is farther away from the user, the factors include the DNS lookup of and load on the upstream proxy. The total delay between the edge of the ISP's network and the final proxy (which might be a surrogate in front of the origin server) might be equal to the sum of the various delays between the components. This part of the measurement (from the edge of the ISP's network to the final proxy in front of the origin server) is highly variable and has not been studied widely.

Once the request arrives at the Web server complex where the origin server is located, a surrogate server in front of the origin server might see the request first. The surrogate server can maintain its own cache of resources that are frequently requested. If not, the surrogate redirects the request to an appropriate server based on load balancing policies. The surrogate or the origin server, based on the request, might decide to redirect the request to a different site altogether. Such a redirection might be due to load balancing, the existence of better suited mirror sites, or because the resource has moved.

Assuming the resource has not moved and is available, the response will be generated. The load on the origin server is a significant factor in the delay in generating the response. Independent of the load on the origin server, servicing the request can take considerable time depending on the action that needs to be performed. For example, if the request causes a back-end database to be uploaded, the server must maintain the connection until the database upload is completed. Eventually, the server's response is queued on the outgoing network connection and eventually reaches the browser after traveling through the various intermediaries. The browser can start parsing the response. Parsing and rendering the response is another factor in the overall latency. Rendering a response might require parsing of enclosed Javascript and interacting with local plugins before being finally displayed to the user. If there are embedded resources in the response, the browser must fetch them as well. These embedded resources may actually be present on a machine different from that of the origin server. If we label the origin server the base server for the container document, then the alternate servers could deliver the embedded images or other content associated with the container document, such as advertisements.

The growing popularity of origin servers distributing their content from other machines must be considered in any end-to-end performance study. Two reasons for such alternate server content delivery are the lowered load on the origin server and the potential of alternate machines serving the rest of the content more effectively. Along with lowered load, the origin server maintains control and serves more users overall. From the user's perspective, the original request was made to the origin server and all the content was delivered from the origin server. Content distribution networks (discussed in Chapter 11, Section 11.13) play an increasingly important role on the Web.

The impact of packet loss on the network can have varying degrees of impact on the end-to-end delay. If the DNS query is lost, retransmission of such a request may add considerable latency. Likewise, the loss of a SYN packet during setting up of the TCP connection may add substantial delay, as discussed in Chapter 8 (Section 8.1.1). Other kinds of losses are not as important.

15.4.2 Report on an end-to-end performance study

Starting in late 1999 and into the year 2000, a study [KW00] was conducted to examine some of the factors that affected the end-to-end performance of the Web. The infrastructure and methodology for this study was based on the earlier protocol compliance study reported in Section 15.3.4. The set of Web sites was enlarged to include popular sites that run HTTP/1.0.

In this section, we briefly report on the study, beginning with its methodology, the experimental details, and the results of the study. Although the numbers reported in [KW00] may have changed, the primary reason to report on this study is to focus on the steps of the experiment. Along the way, we stress what aspects of the study were generic and what could be done in future broader studies. A more detailed report on the study is available in [KW00].

METHODOLOGY OF END-TO-END STUDY

The end-to-end study was an active measurement study—requests were generated and sent to many sites. A set of client sites was chosen around the world, primarily based on access to the authors of the study rather than geographical distribution and client representativeness. In an ideal setting, the set of client sites would be chosen such that they are representative of the various kinds of clients on the Web. For example, the nature of the browser (version, capability, different cache settings, etc.), the connectivity to the Internet (different speeds), and the presence of proxies in the local area network would have to be considered to ensure client representativeness. For a truly global testbed, various time zones and some understanding of typical network activity of other clients in the proximity are other important factors.

The end-to-end performance study ignored any role a proxy might play. Instead, the client sites generated request traffic directly to servers using the *httperf* [MJ98] tool. The goal of *httperf*, as described in Section 15.3.4, was to enable generation of HTTP request traffic, set up the connection, send the request, and obtain timing information. There are several gaps in the tool to act as a full-fledged client for a true end-to-end performance study. The tool sends a request from a client directly to the origin server and does not have any provision for one or more proxies to be in the path. Although several aspects of *httperf*, such as its ability to maintain persistent connections and report timing information on the different steps in the process, make it attractive as a client tool, it is not a complete HTTP/1.1 client. For example, it does not perform the role of a browser in rendering the response and consequently underestimates the overall end-to-end delay. A representative client would either be a complete HTTP/1.1 client that is also capable of being giving timing information or a compliant browser that has been modified to report the necessary statistics.

Once client sites were identified, the next step was to identify the set of servers. Small studies tend to examine local area Web servers or a collection of servers in a campus environment. Broader studies try to gather data from a wider set of servers, often based on popularity of sites. A truly representative study would take into account a variety of factors related to the Web site:

- **Popularity:** The overall popularity of the site is a measure of how accurately a user's experience is reflected in the study. The study should not focus on a few obscure Web sites that are rarely visited but should focus largely on highly popular sites that receive a significant fraction of the request traffic.
- **Representativeness:** The collection of sites studied must include event sites (Web events such as Olympics or a major news event) or a portal site (one that receives tens of millions requests daily from hundreds of thousands of different clients). An e-commerce site would include a multiplicity of forms, with a single Web session requiring several pages to be seen in sequence, with a high probability of cookies being exchanged.
- **Version and option configuration:** The protocol versions of the server might vary (e.g., HTTP/1.0 or HTTP/1.1). For a particular version of the protocol, there are many implementations, such as Apache or Netscape. Within a software implementation, there are many different ways to con-

figure a runtime version, such as enabling or disabling handling Secure
Socket Layer (SSL).

- **Site configuration:** Sites are configured in different ways—multiple sites
  on a single machine, single site spread over multiple machines, mirrored
  sites, multiple servers behind a surrogate server, and so on.
- **Server architecture:** Different server architectures, such as event-driven,
  single server process, multithreaded, pool of processes and so on (as outlined in Chapter 4, Section 4.4) have to be taken into consideration.
- **Server content:** There is significant variance in the nature of content on
  Web sites—some sites are laden with images, some have largely textual
  resources, and others have a preponderance of dynamically generated resources. Other resource attributes include cacheability and rate of change.
- **Content Distribution Network's (CDN) role:** Some sites have a significant portion of their resources delivered by a content distribution service. Including such sites is important to ensure that the role of content
  distribution networks is not ignored.

The above is not meant to be an exhaustive enumeration of factors related to
Web sites. However, the list should be taken into account for any meaningful
end-to-end performance study. The range and complexity of the factors points
out the difficulty of a truly representative study.

Once the client and server sites are chosen and a piece of client software
has been identified, the next step is to design the actual set of tests. Typical goals of an end-to-end study involve measuring latency as perceived by the
user, the amount of bytes transferred and the delay on a per-byte basis, connection alternatives (e.g., a single persistent connection for downloading multiple
resources), impact of features of the protocol, time of day effects, role that content distribution networks play, and so on. The study considered a subset of
these issues and focused on protocol features, time of day analysis, and the role
of content distribution sites. The two parts of the study consisted of a set of
requests from many client sites to many server sites, followed by a more focused
study across different times of the day.

END-TO-END STUDY: EXPERIMENT DETAILS

In this section, we examine the details of the experiment carried out to study
end-to-end Web performance. Eleven client sites around the world were chosen
to send a variety of requests. The set of server sites was chosen based on just
two of the criteria listed above: popularity and protocol version. The focus
of the study was performance improvement based on protocol version, and
inclusion of popular sites ensured that at least a reasonable cross section of
sites accessed by typical users would be covered. The set of servers and clients
used in the end-to-end study built upon the earlier PRO-COW study [KA01]

discussed earlier in Section 15.3.4. In fact, some of the choices made for the end-to-end study were driven by the earlier choices of the PRO-COW study. The advantages were the reuse of software and a reasonable infrastructure and methodology to build on. The *httperf* software used in PRO-COW was modified in the end-to-end performance study to gather additional information. The set of server sites tested was augmented by including HTTP/1.0 sites, because they were not considered in the earlier PRO-COW study (which examined HTTP/1.1 compliance). In all, 711 server sites were tested. However, there were some drawbacks in reusing the PRO-COW infrastructure and methodology. The choice of sites to be tested might have been different if the protocol and popularity had not been the only considerations. For example, other server implementation versions not found among the popular sites might have been included.

The end-to-end performance study focused primarily on four factors:

- **Protocol options:** The study examined the difference between HTTP/1.0 and HTTP/1.1, from the point of view of a connection persisting beyond a single request-response. The study did not examine the subset of HTTP/1.0 servers supporting persistent connections via the Keep-Alive header.
- **Caching:** The variance in cache effectiveness as a result of using different protocol options used was studied.
- **Range requests:** The latency difference in obtaining only a portion of the resource instead of the full resource was examined.
- **Content distribution:** The response time difference in fetching the embedded resources when the resources in a container document were not all returned from the base server was studied.

Several other factors could be studied in a broader end-to-end performance study, including the effect of DNS delays, requests that are redirected to other servers at the HTTP level, presence of proxies surrogate servers, and chunk encoding for dynamically generated responses.

The choice of URIs was limited to just the "home page" of each site chosen. Again, this may not be an ideal choice because the home page may not be representative of the popular page on all sites. Fetching a resource that was several links away from the home page might be a common occurrence. In other words, although the site www.vpopular.com may be very popular, the resource http://www.vpopular.com/topten.html may be responsible for the popularity of the site. The time to fetch the home page http://www.vpopular.com/ may differ from that needed to fetch http://www.vpopular.com/topten.html.

The study used *httperf* to obtain the base URI and extracted any embedded resources. For the servers that had embedded resources, the same set of documents were requested using four different connection mechanisms.

1. Serial: The first method made four separate connections to retrieve the container document and its embedded resources serially using the HTTP/1.0 protocol.
2. Burst mode: The first method was modified so that up to four connections are made in parallel.
3. Persistent: The third method involved using an HTTP/1.1 persistent connection *without* pipelining the requests.
4. Persistent and pipelined: The fourth method involved using an HTTP/1.1 persistent connection with the requests being pipelined on that connection.

A narrower set of server sites was chosen to examine the variance in the results resulting from time of day effect. The study was repeated at different times of the day (four times a day at six-hour intervals) to examine any such variance.

The caching part of the study posited a client-side cache and assumed that an absence of change in the resource size across successive responses indicated that the resource was not modified. The use of size change is a simple heuristic—response headers such as `ETag` or `Last-Modified` could also be considered. In a broader test, it would be more realistic to use a checksum to ensure that the resource had indeed changed. This is to ensure coverage of the cases in which a resource changes without a change in its content length. Along with a simple cache effectiveness study, the cost of revalidating and the return of 304 `Not Modified` was studied.

RESULTS OF END-TO-END STUDY

The end-to-end performance study was conducted from 11 client sites to the 711 server sites. We present a brief summary of the results of the study.

Not all servers responded successfully to the requests, and the ones that did respond did not always return all of the embedded resources. Some resources were not found (the response included a code 404 `Not Found`) or were redirected (with 302 `Found`). One of the more surprising results was that when a set of resources was requested in a pipelined fashion on a persistent connection, not all resources were returned. Server implementations have different heuristics for deciding when to close a persistent connection. In Chapter 7 (Section 7.5.5) we examined the various reasons for a server to close an existing persistent connection. Server implementations close connections for a variety of reasons. They include duration of the idle period (when no requests are made on an existing persistent connection), the load on the server, the number of requests made on a connection, an inter-request timeout, and the response status requiring a close.

In the study, because all the requests on a persistent connection were made one after another and the connection was closed thereafter, connections were not idle for any length of time. In the study, the closing of persistent connections appeared to be driven by the number of responses served on a single connection. The study labeled a connection as a *perfect* persistent connection if all the requested objects were obtained over a single connection. Servers tended to exhibit perfect persistence only up to a certain number of resources requested. The study found that whereas two-thirds of servers exhibit some form of persistence, only around a quarter of servers tested exhibited perfect persistence. A quarter of servers did not indicate why they were not handling persistent connections; that is, they did not explicitly send a `Connection: close` response header but closed the connection. The performance in terms of overall user-perceived latency appears to be the best when servers exhibit perfect persistence. Part of the reason for the poorer performance of servers not exhibiting perfect persistence is the overhead of establishing a new connection. In contrast, if the burst HTTP/1.0 connection technique (multiple parallel connections) was used, they tend to perform better than servers exhibiting imperfect persistence. The main reason appears to be that the reconnection costs for dropped or lost connections overshadowed the performance improvement obtained by persistence.

Relative performance of the protocols did not vary significantly with the time of day. Part of the reason is that the set of servers was chosen based on popularity rather than geographical location. Almost all of the popular servers are in North America. The only visible distinction coincided with the busy time periods in North America. A client that had better connectivity to the Internet had better overall performance at all time periods, and the differences for a client across the time periods were only marginally visible. The study examined only a subset of server sites from only a subset of client sites. If other parts of the world were represented in the set of sites tested, it would have been possible to see if the effect of the busy time period was seen everywhere. A broader test would include servers based on a per-country or per-region popularity and test those sites from clients in different parts of the world. A broader study would also include several more client sites.

The cache study was not truly representative because most of the resources were static and the duration of the test was just one week. The study assumed zero time for a cache hit and showed that reusing a cached response can significantly lower response time. Caching showed the maximal benefit when resources were requested serially over an HTTP/1.0 connection that had the highest latency among the four connection techniques. Caching lowers cost primarily by retrieving fewer objects. Correspondingly, the connection technique that had the highest overhead for retrieving objects gains the most. In examining the impact of revalidation cost (when a `GET If-Modified-Since` request is issued), the study showed that for the serial HTTP/1.0 connections, overall time to retrieve a resource was much higher. The revalidation results were cross-tested by including an `If-None-Match: *` header (discussed in Chapter 7, Section 7.3.3) in the `GET` requests to obtain a `304 Not Modified` response. There was an improvement in the relative performance of the serial HTTP/1.1 compared with other options when cache revalidation was accounted. Overall, caching study showed that there is less difference between the various protocol options when fewer objects are retrieved.

A broader study should repeat the retrieval over a longer period of time and have a better mix of resources—static and dynamic. It should also examine the cost reduction due to revalidation requests resulting from the same persistent connection, similar to the piggybacking technique described earlier.

In terms of multiserver content, the study examined the set of alternate servers responsible for parts of the content. The study labeled the origin server as the base server for the content and divided alternate servers into the following four categories:

- **Helper servers:** Servers typically colocated with the base server. If the alternate server and the base server had the same suffix (e.g., `images.cnn.com` and `www.cnn.com` have the same suffix, `cnn.com`), the servers were considered to be colocated.
- **Ad servers:** Servers used to serve advertisements (these typically began with the string `ad`).
- **Content distribution network servers:** Servers used to serve specific content (such as images) from mirror sites closer to the user. However, relatively few origin servers in the study employed content distribution servers.
- **Miscellaneous:** Other servers that did not fall in any of the earlier three categories.

Although the categorization might be reasonable, accurate mapping of each server to the proper category might not always be possible. For example, an advertisement server could be recognized by some well-known names or prefixes such as `ad.` in the server name. Similarly, content distribution servers could be recognized by well-known prefixes such as `akamai` in the server part of the embedded resource's URI. However, not all URIs that include `ad.` could be viewed as advertisement sites, and several resources served by content distribution sites do not include the name of the CDN.

The study showed that among the popular server sites, about 13.5% of the sites served some part of their content outside of the base servers. Among these sites, a higher percentage of objects rather than bytes were being served by the alternate servers. The difference between object and byte percentage is significant. If only a small fraction of the embedded objects were to be served by the base servers, the overall number of HTTP requests that the base server had to handle would be lowered. Accepting an HTTP request, parsing it, and writing back the response is a significant part of the overall work that origin servers do. Thus reducing the number of objects served from a base server is helpful in reducing the load on an origin server.

CDNs (discussed in depth earlier in Chapter 11, Section 11.13) operate on the principle of locating the mirror server closer to the user in the network sense, if not necessarily geographically. Overall, studies [JCDK00] have shown they do a reasonable job of locating proximal servers. This end-to-end study also showed that data rates of delivering content were much higher when the resources were obtained from content distribution servers compared with the base servers, although the location of the client mattered. The most common CDN found in the end-to-end study was Akamai [Aka]. Akamai's customers rewrite the URI of the embedded resource into one that identifies an Akamai site by including the string `akamai` in it. This ensures that Akamai's mirrors deliver the resource rather than the base server. For example, `http://www.cnn.com/foo.gif` would be rewritten as `http://a138g.akamaitech.net/0923/sdh2/www.cnn.com/foo.gif`. The study fetched the embedded resource from both the CDN mirror server and the base server to compare the data rate.

15.4.3 Summary of end-to-end performance study

Overall the end-to-end study confirmed that persistent connections with pipelining improves performance. However, servers serving a small number of objects may not see any significant performance improvement. Servers exhibiting perfect persistence, whereby all the pipelined requests received responses on the same TCP connection, had the best performance. Content distribution demonstrated significantly improved performance, though not many sites in the study used remote content distribution servers. There has been appreciable growth in this area recently.

However, the study did not include a detailed end-to-end comparison between obtaining resources from base servers and alternate servers. For this, the study would have had to compare the cost of establishing connections to the alternate servers and evaluate the policies of servers with respect to closing persistent connections (with and without pipelining). A browser that uses multiple parallel connections to the base or auxiliary servers might notice an overall reduction in latency at the expense of higher network costs. The study laid the foundation for a broader end-to-end study that could take additional factors into account.

The end-to-end study we examined is just an initial step in a larger end-to-end study that examines all the parameters identified in Table 15.1. A broad end-to-end study would examine different kinds of clients (e.g., their connectivity to the Internet and the client's compliance to the protocol) and choice of server sites along the variety of axes discussed in Chapter 4 (Section 4.1), among other things. For example, some of the steps identified in Table 15.1 may have to be decomposed and analyzed in greater detail. For example, evaluating the load on the proxy would require examining the impact of imperfect persistent connections maintained between the client and proxy, as well as between the proxy and the upstream server. The latter connection may or may not be a persistent connection. Likewise, in the context of alternate server content, the cost of establishing connections to the auxiliary servers must be studied as well.

15.5 Other Extensions to HTTP

Five years were spent in discussing the migration from HTTP/1.0 to HTTP/1.1. At the same time, there were other attempts to extend HTTP in other directions. Because the process of protocol extension works on the basis of consensus, several proposals to amend HTTP did not survive the decision-making process of the HTTP Working Group. Some suggestions came too late, other suggestions did not meet the approval of the Working Group, and some proposed amendments would have required significant alterations to the HTTP protocol. However, several suggestions were made in the form of Internet Drafts, and some of the proposals went through a few iterations before being dropped from consideration for incorporation into the final version of HTTP/1.1. For example, Transparent Content Negotiation [HM98] which described an extensible negotiation mechanism for selecting the most suitable version of a URI that was available in multiple versions, was originally suggested to be part of HTTP/1.1. Similarly, an HTTP Extension Framework [NLL00], an attempt to coordinate the various extensions proposed to HTTP, did not become part of the proposed HTTP/1.1 standard. The attempt to deal with shared updating of Web resources and dealing with the resulting versioning problem led to a separate effort called WebDAV—Web Distributed Authoring and Versioning [GWF+99].

15.5.1 Transparent Content Negotiation

The idea of Transparent Content Negotiation (TCN) [HM98] arose in the context of discussion of content negotiation in the HTTP Working Group. Content negotiation was discussed in depth in Chapter 7 (Section 7.9). It is a way for a client to indicate its preference to choose among variants of a resource available at an origin server. The expression of preference could be made for a choice of languages or character sets, for example.

The basic process of content negotiation is straightforward: a client expresses a preference, and, if the preference is acceptable to the origin server, the resource is returned in that format. During the discussions for extending HTTP/1.0 to HTTP/1.1, the negotiation capabilities of HTTP/1.0 were significantly expanded. The HTTP/1.0 protocol support for negotiation required clients to state acceptable languages, character sets, and so on, and the server would pick the best possible variant of the resource. Given the potential range of preference values for a client, such a mechanism simply would not scale. As we discussed earlier, in Chapter 7, HTTP/1.1 introduced two forms of negotiation: agent-driven and server-driven. TCN is a combination of agent- and server-driven negotiation created mainly to take advantage of caches in the path between the client and the origin server. Cache-friendliness is an important addition in HTTP/1.1 provided by headers such as `Vary` and `If-None-Match`. TCN capitalizes on the added support for caching in HTTP/1.1 for negotiation based on the user agent. A typical way to provide a choice between variants was to ask the users to select from a set of choices—an explicit selection mechanism.

The basic header used in TCN is the `Alternates` response header, which conveys a list of variants associated with a resource on which negotiation is possible. For example, a copy of this book may be available in multiple formats under the URI `http://www.research.att.com/~bala/books/kandr`. One version of the book may be in the form of a single PostScript file, another in a large HTML container document, and yet another translated into Sanskrit and available in Devanagari Script as a Portable Document Format (PDF) document. Because the response is available in different formats, a response code of `300 Multiple Choices` is used. If a request for the book resource is made, the origin server could include an `Alternates` response header in its response, as follows:

```
HTTP/1.1 300 Multiple Choices
Date: Sun, 2 Jul  2000 17:45:43 GMT
Alternates: {"book.html" 1.0 {type text/html} {language en}},
   {"book_ss.pdf 1.0 {type application/pdf} {language ss}},
   {"book.ps" 0.9 {type application/postscript} {language en}},
   {"book.doc" 0.5 {type application/word} {language en}}
Vary: negotiate, accept-language
ETag: "krbk2921103-2311-dtee"
Content-Type: text/html
Content-Length: 212

<h2>Multiple Choices:</h2>
<ul>
<li><a href=book.ps>Postscript, English version</a>
<li><a href=book.html>HTML, English version</a>
<li><a href=book_ss.pdf>PDF, Spoken Sanskrit version</a>
</ul>
```

The source quality specified in the `Alternates` header is the quality value or *qvalue* (discussed in Chapter 7, Section 7.9), indicating the quality of the alternate representation. In the above example, the Word version of the book is considered to have a quality value less than 1 (0.5), indicating that it is lower than the HTML, PostScript, and PDF representations.

The `Vary` header (discussed in Chapter 7, Section 7.3.3), is used to indicate that the choice of a cached resource is subject to the list of headers. The field value following *negotiate* indicates which attribute is to be used by proxies for content negotiation. In the example, the value is `accept-language`, indicating that servers would use the language attribute. Other choices for attributes include the type of a resource, its character set, and a set of features that affect the quality of the variant such as color-depth, screen-width, or the length of the paper.

An HTTP/1.1 user agent that does not support TCN can display the entity body. If the above response had included a `Location` header, the user agent could have optionally redirected the user to the specified location. An HTTP/1.1 user agent that does support TCN must be able to automatically retrieve and display an acceptable variant after choosing one. If none of the specified variants are acceptable, the user agent can display an error message.

Although there are a few server-side implementations [Hol], there have not been any on the client side to report on the overall penetration of TCN. The IETF has formed a Content Negotiation Working Group for examining content negotiation issues both inside and outside of HTTP.

15.5.2 WebDAV—Web Distributed Authoring and Versioning

Initially, Web content largely flowed from origin servers to clients. The Web could easily be a medium by which content is shared and updated from different places. WebDAV [Weba] is an extension to the HTTP/1.1 protocol for handling distributed authoring and versioning. The WebDAV protocol is specified in RFC 2518 [GWF+99]. Unlike the earlier two extensions to HTTP, WebDAV is quite popular and is available in products such as Microsoft's Internet Information Services (IIS) 5.0 Web server, Office 2000 Web Folders, and Exchange 2000 Web Storage System. WebDAV has made good use of the Extensible Markup Language (XML) to emerge as a key extension to HTTP/1.1. The full details of WebDAV operations are beyond the scope of this book, and we provide a brief overview with help from the Frequently Asked Questions list of WebDAV [Webb].

The stated goal of the WebDAV Working Group per its charter is to

Define the HTTP extensions necessary to enable distributed Web authoring tools to be broadly interoperable, while supporting user needs.

In this respect, DAV aims to complete the original vision of the Web as a writable, collaborative medium rather than a largely one-way, one-user-at-a-time medium. Beyond simple Web page authoring, DAV can be viewed as a network file system capable of dealing with several files at a time with good performance in high-latency environments. DAV is a protocol for manipulating the contents of a document management system via the Web.

The goals of DAV include the following:

- Serve as the primary protocol supporting a wide range of collaborative applications

- Support remote software development teams
- Leverage the success of HTTP in being a standard access layer for a wide range of storage repositories, by extending HTTP's read access to write access beyond PUT
- Supporting virtual enterprises

To support collaborative content updating, the set of authors who have access to the content, last modification time of the content, and other such attributes must be located. Content is not just a single resource but a collection of resources that are organized in some meaningful hierarchy. Collections can be created, deleted, or copied together. Aggregate information about a set of resources may be of interest. When multiple authors seek to view and possibly alter a document, there must be a revision and access control mechanism, such as the ability to lock resources and merge changes. Accordingly, several new methods, request and response headers, and entity body formats have been introduced in WebDAV. New response codes have been added to present multiple status responses (because WebDAV methods can operate on more than one resource) and to better categorize error codes. The set of properties of a resource is extensible.

15.5.3 An HTTP extension framework

During the evolution of the protocol from HTTP/1.0 to HTTP/1.1, several different extensions were proposed. In an effort to coordinate the various proposals, a unified extension mechanism was postulated. The range of extensions proposed include collaborative development (discussed under WebDAV in Section 15.5.2), remote procedure call mechanisms, and printing on the Internet. A proposed extension to a protocol might require a change in one or more Web components. The HTTP Extension Framework offers a simple way for enabling the exchange of information between the extension proposers and those interested in using the extension. The designers of the extension would make all information associated with the extension available via a globally unique URI. Anyone using the extension would indicate that they were using an extension by including a header in the HTTP message with the URI of the extension.

The notion behind the extension framework was to include a pointer to the description of the extension that could be selectively used. The framework provided a way to negotiate syntax and semantics and was flexible enough to separate mandatory extension rules from optional ones. Extension definitions include documentation, a machine-readable specification that defines the semantics of the extension, and code that implements the semantics of the particular extension. The extensions could be done by two interested parties that are just one HTTP hop away from each other (known as hop-by-hop extension) or could be end-to-end. A new response code 510 Not Extended was proposed so that a party could signify that it did not support an extension.

Although the HTTP extension framework did not become part of the HTTP/1.1 standard because of lack of consensus in the community, it was released as part of the experimental RFC track as RFC 2774 [NLL00].

15.6 Summary

The HTTP protocol has been around for a decade and is currently responsible for a large fraction of the traffic on the Internet. Thus it is not surprising that research attempts to improve HTTP and the underlying transport-layer protocol TCP are ongoing. In this chapter, we have examined a few strands of research ranging from multiplexing HTTP transfers by examining the TCP layer to extensions at the HTTP layer itself for improving negotiation between Web components. Improving an existing protocol with a significant deployed base requires close attention to backward compatibility, as we saw in the addition of the delta mechanism to HTTP/1.1. The discussion of the delta mechanism also showed the amount of experimentation required to ensure that protocol enhancements will indeed result in improvements to user-perceived latency and load on the network without significant overhead to the origin server. The compliance study demonstrates the need for examination of the state of the deployed Web components for proper adherence to the protocol specification. A protocol's usefulness is reflected in the correctness of the popular implementations. Most of the users of the Web are unlikely to take advantage of the features of the protocol if the compliance requirements are not met. If a set of MUST conditions are not met in the popular realizations of a protocol specification, applications built on top of HTTP cannot be expected to behave properly. The end-to-end study explored the various factors responsible for Web performance. Although at a preliminary stage, this study pinpointed some of the reasons for delays that are seen in the Web. We also examined some other ongoing projects related to content negotiation and a framework for HTTP extension. The distributed authoring and versioning system, WebDAV, shows promise in moving to the next stage in Web interaction—multiple users accessing and potentially modifying resources instead of simply downloading them.

Bibliography

[AAL⁺92]   Bob Alberti, Farhad Anklesaria, Paul Lindner, Mark McCahill,
           and Daniel Torrey. The Internet Gopher protocol: A distributed
           document search and retrieval protocol, Spring 1991; Revised
           Spring 1992.
           `http://boombox.micro.umn.edu/pub/gopher/`
                `gopher_protocol/protocol.txt`.

[Abb99]   Janet Abbate. *Inventing the Internet.* The MIT Press, June 1999.
           ISBN 0262011727.

[ABCdO96] V. Almeida, A. Bestavros, M. Crovella, and A. de Oliveira. Char-
           acterizing Reference Locality in the WWW. In *Proc. Parallel and
           Distributed Information Systems*, December 1996.
           `http://www.cs.bu.edu/techreports/`
                `1996-011-www-reference-locality.ps.Z`.

[AC98]   J. Almeida and P. Cao. Measuring Proxy Performance with the
           Wisconsin Proxy Benchmark. *Computer Networks and ISDN Sys-
           tems*, 30(22–23):2179–2192, November 1998.
           `http://www.cs.wisc.edu/~cao/papers/cao-wpb/index.html`.

[AD99]   Mohit Aron and Peter Druschel. TCP Implementation Enhance-
           ments for Improving Web Server Performance. Technical Report
           99-335, Department of Computer Science, Rice University, 1999.
           `http://www.cs.rice.edu/~aron/papers/rice-TR99-335.ps.gz`.

[Ade]   Adero. `http://www.adero.com`.

[Adi94]   C. Adie. A Status Report on Networked Information Retrieval:
           Tools and Groups. RFC 1689, IETF, August 1994.
           `http://www.rfc-editor.org/rfc/rfc1689.txt`.

[AFJ99]   Martin Arlitt, Rich Friedrich, and Tai Jin. Workload Character-
           ization of a Web Proxy in a Cable Modem Environment. *ACM
           Performance Evaluation Review*, 27(2):25–36, August 1999. Also
           available as HPL Technical Report HPL-1999-48.
           `http://www.hpl.hp.com/techreports/1999/HPL-1999-48.html`.

[AFP98]   M. Allman, S. Floyd, and C. Partridge. Increasing TCP's Initial
             Window. RFC 2414, IETF, September 1998.
             http://www.rfc-editor.org/rfc/rfc2414.txt.

[AJ00]   M. Arlitt and T. Jin. Workload Characterization of the 1998 World
             Cup Web Site. *IEEE Network Magazine*, 14(3):30–37, May/June
             2000. Also available as HPL Technical Report HPL-1999-35.
             http://www.hpl.hp.com/techreports/1999/
                 HPL-1999-35R1.html.

[Aka]   Akamai. http://www.akamai.com.

[AKMS95]   K. Andrews, F. Kappe, H. Maurer, and K. Schmaranz. On sec-
             ond generation hypermedia systems. In *Proc. ED-MEDIA 95,
             World Conference on Educational Multimedia and Hypermedia*,
             June 1995.

[Ale]   Alexa. http://www.alexa.com.

[Alt]   AltaVista. http://www.altavista.com.

[Ami99]   Amit Gupta and Geoffrey Baehr. Ad insertion at proxies to im-
             prove cache hit rate. In *Proc. 4th International Web Caching
             Workshop*, March/April 1999.
             http://www.ircache.net/Cache/Workshop99/Papers/
                 gupta-final.ps.gz.

[AML+93]   F. Anklesaria, M. McCahill, P. Lindner, D. Johnson, D. Torrey,
             and B. Alberti. The Internet Gopher Protocol. RFC 1436, IETF,
             March 1993.
             http://www.rfc-editor.org/rfc/rfc1436.txt.

[Apa]   Apache Software Foundation. http://www.apache.org.

[APS99]   M. Allman, V. Paxson, and W. Stevens. TCP Congestion Control.
             RFC 2581, IETF, April 1999.
             http://www.rfc-editor.org/rfc/rfc2581.txt.

[AS98]   Soam Acharya and Brian Smith. An Experiment to Characterize
             Videos on the World Wide Web. In *Proc. Multimedia Communi-
             cation and Networking*, January 1998.
             http://www.cs.cornell.edu/zeno/Papers/webvideo/Paper.pdf.

[ASA+95]   Marc Abrams, Charles R. Standridge, Ghaleb Abdulla, Stephen
             Williams, and Edward A. Fox. Caching Proxies: Limitations and
             Potentials. In *Proc. World Wide Web Conference*, December
             1995.
             http://www.w3.org/pub/Conferences/WWW4/Papers/155/.

[ASP00]   Soam Acharya, Brian Smith, and Peter Parnes. Characterizing
             User Access to Videos on the World Wide Web. In *Proc. Multi-
             media Communication and Networking*, January 2000.
             http://www.cs.cornell.edu/home/soam/papers/drafts/
                 videoaccess.pdf.

[AW97]   Martin F. Arlitt and Carey L. Williamson.   Internet Web
            Servers: Workload Characterization and Performance Implica-
            tions. *IEEE/ACM Transactions on Networking*, 5(5):631–645, Oc-
            tober 1997.
            http://www.cs.usask.ca/faculty/carey/papers/ton97.ps.

[BBBC99]   Paul Barford, Azer Bestavros, Adam Bradley, and Mark Crov-
            ella. Changes in Web Client Access Patterns: Characteristics and
            Caching Implications. *WWW Journal*, 2(1/2):15–28, June 1999.
            http://cs-www.bu.edu/faculty/crovella/paper-archive/
                traces98.ps.

[BC94]   H. Braun and K. Claffy. Web Traffic Characterization: An As-
            sessment of the Impact of Caching Documents from NCSA's Web
            Server. In *Proc. World Wide Web Conference*, October 1994.
            ftp://oceana.nlanr.net/papers/2iwwwc.cache.ps.gz.

[BC98]   Paul Barford and Mark Crovella. Generating Representative Web
            Workloads for Network and Server Performance Evaluation. In
            Proc. ACM SIGMETRICS, June 1998.
            http://cs-www.bu.edu/faculty/crovella/paper-archive/
                sigm98-surge.ps.

[BC99]   Paul Barford and Mark Crovella. Measuring Web Performance
            in the Wide Area. In *Proc. ACM SIGMETRICS Performance
            Evaluation Review*, August 1999.
            http://www.cs.bu.edu/techreports/
                1999-004-wide-area-web-measurement.ps.Z.

[BCF+99]   Lee Breslau, Pei Cao, Li Fan, Graham Phillips, and Scott Shenker.
            Web Caching and Zipf-Like Distributions: Evidence and Implica-
            tions. In *Proc. IEEE INFOCOM*, March 1999.
            http://www.ieee-infocom.org/1999/papers/01d_03.pdf.

[BD99]   G. Banga and P. Druschel. Measuring the capacity of a Web server.
            WWW Journal, 2(1–2):69–83, June 1999.
            http://www.cs.rice.edu/~druschel/wwwjsi99.ps.gz.

[BDH+94]   C. Mic Bowman, Peter B. Danzig, Darren R. Hardy, Udi Manber,
            and Michael F. Schwartz. The Harvest Information Discovery and
            Access System. In *Proc. Second International World Wide Web
            Conference*, pages 763–771, October 1994.

[Bes95]   Azer Bestavros. Using Speculation to Reduce Server Load and
            Service Time on the WWW. In *Proc. ACM International Con-
            ference on Information and Knowledge Management*, November
            1995.
            http://www.cs.bu.edu/faculty/best/res/papers/cikm95.ps.

[BL]   Tim Berners-Lee. Web Architecture from 50,000 feet.
            http://www.w3.org/DesignIssues/Architecture.html.

[BL90]   Tim Berners-Lee. Information Management: A Proposal, May
            1990.
            http://www.w3.org/History/1989/proposal.html.

[BL92a]   Tim Berners-Lee. Is there a paper which describes the www pro-
            tocol, January 9 1992. WWW-talk mailing list.
            http://lists.w3.org/Archives/Public/www-talk/
              1992JanFeb/0000.html.

[BL92b]   Tim Berners-Lee. MIME, SGML, UDIs, HTML and W3, June
            1992. WWW-talk mailing list.
            http://lists.w3.org/Archives/Public/www-talk/
              1992MayJun/0038.html.

[BL92c]   Tim Berners-Lee. WorldWideWeb news: New software includes
            Gopher, News, Telnet access, January 24 1992. WWW-talk mail-
            ing list.
            http://lists.w3.org/Archives/Public/www-talk/
              1992JanFeb/0001.html.

[BL93a]   Tim Berners-Lee. Hypertext Transfer Protocol (HTTP): A State-
            less Search, Retrieve and Manipulation Protocol, November 1993.
            http://ftp.std.com/obi/Networking/WWW/
              draft-ietf-iiir-http-00.txt.

[BL93b]   Tim Berners-Lee. Uniform Resource Locators (URL): A Unifying
            Syntax for the Expression of Names and addresses of Objects on
            the Network, October 1993. Expired Internet Draft.
            http://ftp.std.com/obi/Networking/WWW/url-spec.txt.

[BL94]   Tim Berners-Lee. Universal Resource Identifiers in WWW, March
            1994.
            http://www.w3.org/Addressing/URL/uri-spec.html.

[BLC93]   Tim Berners-Lee and Dan Connolly. Hypertext Markup Language
            (HTML): A Representation of Textual Information and MetaIn-
            formation for Retrieval and Interchange, June 1993.
            http://www.w3.org/MarkUp/draft-ietf-iiir-html-01.

[BLCGP92]   Tim Berners-Lee, Robert Caillau, Jean-Francois Groff, and Bernd
            Pollerman. World Wide Web: The Information Universe. *Elec-
            tronic Networking: Research, Applications, and Policy*, 1(1),
            Spring 1992.
            http://www.w3.org/History/1992/ENRAP/Article_9202.ps.

[BLFF96]   T. Berners-Lee, R. Fielding, and H. Frystyk. Hypertext Transfer
            Protocol — HTTP/1.0. RFC 1945, IETF, May 1996. Defines
            current usage of HTTP/1.0.
            http://www.rfc-editor.org/rfc/rfc1945.txt.

[BLFM98]   T. Berners-Lee, R. Fielding, and L. Masinter. Uniform Resource
            Identifiers (URI): Generic Syntax. RFC 2396, IETF, August 1998.
            http://www.rfc-editor.org/rfc/rfc2396.txt.

[BLFN95]   Tim Berners-Lee, R. T. Fielding, and H. Frystyk Nielsen. Hyper-
            text Transfer Protocol—HTTP/1.0, March 1995. Expired Internet
            Draft.
            `ftp://www.ics.uci.edu/pub/ietf/http/history/`
                `draft-ietf-http-v10-spec-00.txt.`

[BLMM94]   T. Berners-Lee, L. Masinter, and M. McCahill. Uniform Resource
            Locators (URL). RFC 1738, IETF, December 1994.
            `http://www.rfc-editor.org/rfc/rfc1738.txt.`

[BM98]   G. Banga and J. Mogul. Scalable Kernel Performance for Internet
            Servers Under Realistic Loads. In *Proc. USENIX*, June 1998.
            `http://www.cs.rice.edu/~gaurav/papers/usenix98.ps.`

[BPS+98]   H. Balakrishnan, V. Padmanabhan, S. Seshan, M. Stemm, and
            R. Katz. TCP Behavior of a Busy Internet Server: Analysis and
            Improvements. In *Proc. IEEE INFOCOM*, March 1998.
            `http://www.ieee-infocom.org/1998/papers/02d_3.pdf.`

[Bra92]   R. Braden. Extending TCP for Transactions—Concepts. RFC
            1379, IETF, November 1992.
            `http://www.rfc-editor.org/rfc/rfc1379.txt.`

[Bra94]   R. Braden. Extending TCP for Transactions—Functional Specifi-
            cation. RFC 1644, IETF, July 1994.
            `http://www.rfc-editor.org/rfc/rfc1644.txt.`

[Bra96a]   S. Bradner. Key words for use in RFCs to Indicate Requirement
            Levels. RFC 2119, IETF, November 1996.
            `http://www.rfc-editor.org/rfc/rfc2119.txt.`

[Bra96b]   S. Bradner. The Internet Standards Process—Revision 3. RFC
            2026, IETF, October 1996.
            `http://www.rfc-editor.org/rfc/rfc2026.txt.`

[BRS99]   H. Balakrishnan, H. Rahul, and S. Seshan. An Integrated Conges-
            tion Management Architecture for Internet Hosts. In *Proc. ACM
            SIGCOMM*, September 1999.
            `http://www.acm.org/sigcomm/sigcomm99/papers/`
                `session5-2.html.`

[BS00]   Hari Balakrishnan and Srinivasan Seshan. The Congestion Man-
            ager, November 2000. Expired Internet Draft.
            `http://www.ietf.org/internet-drafts/`
                `draft-ietf-ecm-cm-03.txt.`

[Bus45]   Vannevar Bush. As We May Think. *Atlantic Monthly*, July 1945.
            `http://www.theatlantic.com/unbound/flashbks/computer/`
                `bushf.htm.`

[Can]   CA*net II Caching Hierarchy Project.
            `http://ardnoc41.canet2.net/cache/.`

[CAR]   Cache array routing protocol and MS proxy server version 2.0.
            `http://www.microsoft.com/technet/Proxy/technote/`

              `prxcarp.asp`.

[Cat92]   V. Cate. Alex—A Global Filesystem. In *Proc. USENIX File System Workshop*, pages 1–12. USENIX Association, May 1992.

[CB95]   William R. Cheswick and Steven M. Bellovin. *Firewalls and Internet Security*. Addison-Wesley, 1995. ISBN 0201633574.

[CB97]   Mark E. Crovella and Azer Bestavros. Self-Similarity in World Wide Web Traffic: Evidence and Possible Causes. *IEEE/ACM Transactions on Networking*, 5(6):835–846, December 1997.
           `http://www.cs.bu.edu/fac/crovella/paper-archive/`
           `self-sim/journal-version.ps`.

[CB98]   Mark Crovella and Paul Barford. The Network Effects of Prefetching. In *Proc. IEEE INFOCOM*, April 1998.
           `http://www.ieee-infocom.org/1998/papers/10a_4.pdf`.

[CBC95]   Carlos R. Cunha, Azer Bestavros, and Mark E. Crovella. Characteristics of WWW Client-based Traces. Technical Report BU-CS-95-010, Computer Science Department, Boston University, 1995.
           `http://www.cs.bu.edu/techreports/`
           `1995-010-www-client-traces.ps.Z`.

[CGC$^+$00] I. Cooper, P. Gauthier, J. Cohen, M. Dunsmuir, and C. Perkins. The Web Proxy Auto-Discovery Protocol, November 2000. Expired Internet Draft.
           `http://www.wrec.org/Drafts/`
           `draft-cooper-webi-wpad-00.txt`.

[CHW99]   Jon Crowcroft, Mark Handley, and Ian Wakeman. *Internetworking Multimedia*. Morgan Kaufmann, October 1999. ISBN 1558605843.

[CI97]   Pei Cao and Sandy Irani. Cost-Aware WWW Proxy Caching Algorithms. In *Proc. USENIX Symposium on Internet Technologies and Systems*. USENIX Association, December 1997.
           `http://www.usenix.org/publications/library/proceedings/`
           `usits97/full_papers/cao/cao_html/cao.html`.

[Cis]   Cisco Content Delivery Networks.
           `http://www.cisco.com/go/cdn`.

[CK00]   Edith Cohen and Haim Kaplan. Prefetching the Means for Document Transfer: A New Approach for Reducing Web Latency. In *Proc. IEEE INFOCOM*, March 2000.
           `http://www.ieee-infocom.org/2000/papers/438.ps`.

[CKR98]   Edith Cohen, Balachander Krishnamurthy, and Jennifer Rexford. Improving End-to-End Performance of the Web Using Server Volumes and Proxy Filters. In *Proc. ACM SIGCOMM*, September 1998.
           `http://www.acm.org/sigcomm/sigcomm98/tp/abs_20.html`.

[CKR99]   Edith Cohen, Balachander Krishnamurthy, and Jennifer Rexford. Efficient Algorithms for Predicting Requests to Web Servers. In

Proc. IEEE INFOCOM, March 1999.
`http://www.research.att.com/~bala/papers/`
`  infocom99.ps.gz.`

[Cla88]   David D. Clark. The Design Philosophy of the DARPA Internet Protocols. In *Proc. ACM SIGCOMM*, pages 106–114, August 1988.
`http://www.acm.org/sigs/sigcomm/ccr/archive/1995/`
`  jan95/ccr-9501-clark.html.`

[Cle]   Clever. `http://www.almaden.ibm.com/cs/k53/clever.html.`

[CMT98]   K Claffy, Greg Miller, and Kevin Thompson. The Nature of the Beast: Recent Traffic Measurements from an Internet Backbone. In *Proc. INET*, July 1998.
`http://www.caida.org/outreach/papers/Inet98/.`

[Con92]   Dan Connolly. MIME for global hypertext, June 1992. WWW-talk mailing list.
`http://lists.w3.org/Archives/Public/www-talk/`
`  1992MayJun/0029.html.`

[Coo]   Cookie Central. `http://www.cookiecentral.com.`

[CP95]   L. D. Catledge and J. E. Pitkow. Characterizing browsing strategies in the World Wide Web. *Computer Networks and ISDN Systems*, 26(6):1065–1073, 1995.
`ftp://ftp.cc.gatech.edu/pub/gvu/tr/1995/95-13.ps.Z.`

[Cro82]   David H. Crocker. Standard for the Format of ARPA Internet Text Messages. RFC 822, IETF, August 1982.
`http://www.rfc-editor.org/rfc/rfc822.txt.`

[CSSa]   World Wide Web Consortium, Cascading Style Sheets.
`http://www.w3.org/Style.`

[CSSb]   Cascading Style Sheets.
`http://www.htmlhelp.com/reference/css/properties.html.`

[DA98]   T. Dierks and C. Allen. The TLS Protocol, Version 1.0. RFC 2246, IETF, January 1998.
`http://www.rfc-editor.org/rfc/rfc2246.txt.`

[Dav99]   Brian Davison. Web Traffic Logs: An Imperfect Resource for Evaluation. In *Proc. INET*, June 1999.
`http://www.cs.rutgers.edu/~davison/pubs/inet99/`
`  imperfect.html.`

[DFKM97]   Fred Douglis, Anja Feldmann, Balachander Krishnamurthy, and Jeffrey Mogul. Rate of Change and other Metrics: A Live Study of the World Wide Web. In *Proc. USENIX Symposium on Internet Technologies and Systems*, pages 147–158, December 1997.
`http://www.research.att.com/~bala/papers/roc-usits97.ps.gz.`

[DH98]   S. Deering and R. Hinden. Internet Protocol, Version 6 (IPv6). RFC 2460, IETF, December 1998.

> `http://www.rfc-editor.org/rfc/rfc2460.txt`.

[Dig] Digital Island. `http://www.digitalisland.net`.

[Din95] Adam Dingle. HTTP should be able to transfer part of a document, March 1995. HTTP-WG Mailing List Archives.
> `http://www.ics.uci.edu/pub/ietf/http/hypermail/1995q1/`
> `0105.html`.

[DMF97] Bradley Duska, David Marwood, and Michael Feeley. The Measured Access Characteristics of World-Wide-Web Proxy Caches. In *Proc. USENIX Symposium on Internet Technologies and Systems*, December 1997.
> `http://www.usenix.org/publications/library/proceedings/`
> `usits97/full_papers/duska/duska_html/`.

[DOK92] Peter B. Danzig, Katia Obraczka, and Anant Kumar. An Analysis of Wide-Area Name Server Traffic. In *Proc. ACM SIGCOMM*, pages 281–292, August 1992.
> `http://www.acm.org/pubs/articles/proceedings/comm/`
> `144179/p281-danzig/p281-danzig.pdf`.

[Dor95] Tim Dorcey. CU-SeeMe Desktop VideoConferencing Software. *Connexions*, 9(3), March 1995.
> `http://www.cu-seeme.net/squeek/tech/`
> `DorceyConnexions.html`.

[Dro97] Ralph Droms. Dynamic Host Configuration Protocol. RFC 2131, IETF, March 1997.
> `http://www.rfc-editor.org/rfc/rfc2131.txt`.

[DS86] R. B. D'Agostino and M. A. Stephens, editors. *Goodness-of-Fit Techniques*. Marcel Dekker, Inc., June 1986. ISBN 0824774876.

[Duc99] Dan Duchamp. Prefetching Hyperlinks. In *Proc. USENIX Symposium on Internet Technologies and Systems*, October 1999.
> `http://www.usenix.org/publications/library/proceedings/`
> `usits99/duchamp.html`.

[ED92] A. Emtage and P. Deutsch. Archie—An Electronic Directory Service for the Internet. In *Proc. Winter USENIX Conference Proceedings*, pages 93–110, January 1992.

[EE68] Douglas C. Engelbart and William K. English. A Research Center for Augmenting Human Intellect. In *AFIPS Conference, Proc. of the 1968 Fall Joint Computer Conference*, pages 395–410, December 1968.
> `http://sloan.stanford.edu/mousesite/Archive/`
> `ResearchCenter1968/ResearchCenter1968.html`.

[Eri94] Hans Eriksson. MBone: The Multicast Backbone. *Communications of the ACM*, 37(8):54–60, August 1994.

[Exo] Exodus. `http://www.exodus.net`.

[FB96a]   N. Freed and N. Borenstein. Multipurpose Internet Mail Exten-
            sions (MIME) Part One: Format of Internet Message Bodies. RFC
            2045, IETF, November 1996. Defines format of MIME message
            bodies.
            `http://www.rfc-editor.org/rfc/rfc2045.txt`.

[FB96b]   N. Freed and N. Borenstein. Multipurpose Internet Mail Exten-
            sions (MIME) Part Two: Media Types. RFC 2046, IETF, Novem-
            ber 1996. Defines MIME multipart types.
            `http://www.rfc-editor.org/rfc/rfc2046.txt`.

[FCAB98]   Li Fan, Pei Cao, Jussara Almeida, and Andrei Broder. Summary
            Cache: A Scalable Wide-Area Web Cache Sharing Protocol. In
            Proc. ACM SIGCOMM, pages 254–265, September 1998.
            `http://www.acm.org/sigcomm/sigcomm98/tp/abs_21.html`.

[Fcg]   FastCGI. `http://www.fastcgi.com/`.

[Fea]   HTTP/1.1 Feature List Report Summary.
            `http://www.w3.org/Protocols/HTTP/Forum/Reports`.

[Fel00a]   Anja Feldmann. BLT: Bi-Layer Tracing of HTTP and TCP/IP.
            In *Proc. World Wide Web Conference*, pages 321–335, May 2000.
            `http://www.cs.uni-sb.de/~anja/feldmann/papers/`
                `blt_httptrace.ps`.

[Fel00b]   Anja Feldmann. Characteristics of TCP Connection Arrivals. In
            K. Park and W. Willinger, editors, *Self-Similar Network Traffic
            and Performance Evaluation*. John Wiley, 2000.

[FF96]   K. Fall and S. Floyd. Simulation-based comparisons of Tahoe,
            Reno, and SACK TCP. *ACM Computer Communication Review*,
            26(3):5–21, July 1996.
            `http://www.acm.org/sigs/sigcomm/ccr/archive/1996/`
                `jul96/ccr-9607-fall.html`.

[FF99]   S. Floyd and K. Fall. Promoting the Use of End-to-End Congestion
            Control in the Internet. *IEEE/ACM Transactions on Networking*,
            7(4):458–472, August 1999.
            `http://www.aciri.org/floyd/papers/collapse.may99.ps`.

[FFBL95]   R. Fielding, H. Frystyk, and T. Berners-Lee. Hypertext Transfer
            Protocol—HTTP/1.1, November 1995. Expired Internet Draft.
            `http://www.w3.org/Protocols/HTTP/1.1/`
                `draft-ietf-http-v11-spec-00.txt`.

[FGM+97]   Roy T. Fielding, Jim Gettys, Jeffrey C. Mogul, Henrik Frystyk
            Nielsen, and Tim Berners-Lee. Hypertext Transfer Protocol—
            HTTP/1.1. RFC 2068, IETF, January 1997. Proposed Standard
            of HTTP/1.1.
            `http://www.rfc-editor.org/rfc/rfc2068.txt`.

[FGM+99]   R. Fielding, J. Gettys, J. C. Mogul, H. Frystyk, L. Masinter,
            P. Leach, and T. Berners-Lee. Hypertext Transfer Protocol —

HTTP/1.1. RFC 2616, IETF, June 1999. Draft Standard of HTTP/1.1.
http://www.rfc-editor.org/rfc/rfc2616.txt.

[FHBH+99] J. Franks, P. Hallam-Baker, J. Hostetler, S. Lawrence, P. Leach, A. Luotonen, E. Sink, and L. Stewart. HTTP Authentication: Basic and Digest Access Authentication. RFC 2617, IETF, June 1999.
http://www.rfc-editor.org/rfc/rfc2617.txt.

[Fie94] R. T. Fielding. Maintaining Distributed Hypertext Infostructures: Welcome to MOMspider's Web. *Computer Networks and ISDN Systems*, 27(2):193–204, November 1994.
http://www.ics.uci.edu/pub/websoft/MOMspider/
    docs/www94_paper.ps.

[Fie95] Roy Fielding. Relative Uniform Resource Locators. RFC 1808, IETF, June 1995.
http://www.rfc-editor.org/rfc/rfc1808.txt.

[Fie97] Roy Fielding. Content encoding problem, February 1997. HTTP-WG Mailing List Archives.
http://www.ics.uci.edu/pub/ietf/http/hypermail/1997q1/
    0151.html.

[FKV95] Glenn Fowler, David Korn, and Kiem-Phong Vo. Libraries and file system architecture. In Balachander Krishnamurthy, editor, *Practical Reusable UNIX Software*, chapter 2. John Wiley, New York, NY, 1995.
http://www.research.att.com/library/books/reuse.

[FL95] John Franks and Ari Luotonen. Byte ranges—formal spec proposal, May 1995. HTTP-WG Mailing List Archives.
http://www.ics.uci.edu/pub/ietf/http/hypermail/
    1995q2/0122.html.

[Flo94] Sally Floyd. TCP and Explicit Congestion Notification. *ACM Computer Communication Review*, 24(5):10–23, October 1994.
http://www.aciri.org/floyd/papers/tcp_ecn.4.pdf.

[Flo00] Sally Floyd. Congestion Control Principles. RFC 2914, IETF, September 2000.
http://www.rfc-editor.org/rfc/rfc2914.txt.

[FLYV93] V. Fuller, T. Li, J. Y. Yu, and K. Varadhan. Classless Inter-Domain Routing (CIDR): An Address Assignment and Aggregation Strategy. RFC 1519, IETF, September 1993.
http://www.rfc-editor.org/rfc/rfc1519.txt.

[For99] Fortune 500 Companies, 1999.
http://www.fortune.com/fortune/fortune500/.

[Fou] Foundry Networks. http://www.foundrynet.com.

[Fra94a]   John Franks. An MGET proposal for HTTP, October 1994.
            WWW-talk mailing list.
            `http://www.webhistory.org/www.lists/`
            `    www-talk.1994q4/0479.html.`

[Fra94b]   John Franks. Proposal for an HTTP MGET Method, December
            1994. HTTP-WG Mailing List Archives.
            `http://www.ics.uci.edu/pub/ietf/http/hypermail/`
            `    1994q4/0260.html.`

[Fra95]   John Franks. Re: HTTP should be able to transfer part of a
            document, March 1995. HTTP-WG Mailing List Archives.
            `http://www.ics.uci.edu/pub/ietf/http/hypermail/`
            `    1995q1/0107.html.`

[FRB93]   P. S. Ford, Y. Rekhter, and H-W. Braun. Improving the Routing
            and Addressing of IP. *IEEE Network Magazine*, 7(3):10–15, May
            1993.

[FTY99]   Theodore Faber, Joe Touch, and Wei Yue. The TIME-WAIT state
            in TCP and Its Effect on Busy Servers. In *Proc. IEEE INFOCOM*,
            pages 1573–1583, March 1999.
            `http://www.isi.edu/~touch/pubs/infocomm99/.`

[Get97]   Jim Gettys. HTTP Connection Management, March 1997. HTTP-
            WG Mailing List Archives.
            `http://www.ics.uci.edu/pub/ietf/http/hypermail/`
            `    1997q1/0656.html.`

[Glo98]   Global 500 Companies, 1998.
            `http://www.fortune.com/fortune/global500/.`

[GN98]   J. Gettys and H. F. Nielsen. The WebMUX protocol, August 1998.
            Expired Internet Draft.
            `http://www.w3.org/Protocols/MUX/WD-mux-980722.html.`

[Goo]   Google. `http://www.google.com.`

[GRB00]   Stephane Gruber, Jennifer Rexford, and Andrea Basso. Pro-
            tocol Considerations for a Prefix-Caching Proxy for Multimedia
            Streams. In *Proc. World Wide Web Conference*, pages 657–668,
            May 2000.
            `http://www.research.att.com/~jrex/papers/www00.ps.`

[Gun96]   Shishir Gundavaram. *CGI Programming on the World Wide Web*.
            O'Reilly, March 1996.
            `http://www.oreilly.com/openbook/cgi.`

[GWF+99]   Y. Goland, E. Whitehead, A. Faizi, S. Carter, and D. Jensen.
            HTTP Extensions for Distributed Authoring—WEBDAV. RFC
            2518, IETF, February 1999.
            `http://www.rfc-editor.org/rfc/rfc2518.txt.`

[HBD97]   Mor Harchol-Balter and Allen Downey. Exploiting Process Life-
            time Distributions for Dynamic Load Balancing. *ACM Transac-*

tions on Computer Systems, 15(3):253–285, August 1997.
`http://www.cs.cmu.edu/~harchol/Papers/TOCS.ps`.

[HBMT99] R. Herriot, S. Butler, P. Moore, and R. Turner. Internet Printing Protocol/1.0: Encoding and Transport. RFC 2565, IETF, April 1999.
`http://www.rfc-editor.org/rfc/rfc2565.txt`.

[Hei97]   J. Heidemann. Performance Interactions Between P-HTTP and TCP Implementations. *ACM Computer Communication Review*, 27(2):65–73, April 1997.
`http://www.acm.org/sigs/sigcomm/ccr/archive/1997/`
`   apr97/ccr-9704-heidemann.html`.

[HJ98]   M. Handley and V. Jacobson. SDP: Session Description Protocol. RFC 2327, IETF, April 1998.
`http://www.rfc-editor.org/rfc/rfc2327.txt`.

[HL96]   Barron C. Housel and David B. Lindquist. WebExpress: A System for Optimizing Web Browsing in a Wireless Environment. In *Proc. ACM/IEEE MOBICOM*, pages 419–431, October 1996.
`http://www.baltzer.nl/monet/articlesfree/1998/3-4/`
`   mnt078.pdf`.

[HM98]   K. Holtman and A. Mutz. Transparent Content Negotiation in HTTP. RFC 2295, IETF, March 1998.
`http://www.rfc-editor.org/rfc/rfc2295.txt`.

[HM00]   Sam Halabi and Daniel McPherson. *Internet Routing Architectures*. Cisco Press, second edition, 2000. ISBN 157870233X.

[HN99]   Allan Heydon and Marc Najork. Mercator: A scalable, extensible Web crawler. *World Wide Web*, 2(4), 1999.
`http://www.research.compaq.com/SRC/mercator/`
`   papers/www/paper.pdf`.

[Hol]   Koen Holtman. Transparent Content Negotiation in HTTP.
`http://gewis.win.tue.nl/~koen/conneg/`.

[Hor83]   Mark R. Horton. Standard for Interchange of USENET Messages. RFC 850, IETF, June 1983.
`http://www.rfc-editor.org/rfc/rfc850.txt`.

[Hor98]   Eric Horvitz. Continual Computation Policies for Utility-Directed Prefetching. In *Proc. ACM Conference on Information and Knowledge Management*, pages 175–184, November 1998.
`http://www.research.microsoft.com/~horvitz/ccfetch.htm`.

[Hos00]   P. Hoschka. The application/smil Media Type, October 2000. Expired Internet Draft.
`http://www.ietf.org/internet-drafts/`
`   draft-hoschka-smil-media-type-06.txt`.

[Hot]   100hot Web Rankings. `http://100hot.com`.

[HPW00]   M. Handley, C. Perkins, and E. Whelan. Session Announcement
            Protocol. RFC 2974, IETF, October 2000.
            `http://www.rfc-editor.org/rfc/rfc2974.txt`.

[HRW98]   Martin Hamilton, Alex Rousskov, and Duane Wessels. Cache Di-
            gest, December 1998.
            `http://www.squid-cache.org/CacheDigest`.

[HTT94]   Minutes of the HyperText Transfer Protocol Working Group, De-
            cember 1994. 31st IETF Meeting.
            `ftp://ftp.ietf.cnri.reston.va.us/ietf-online-proceedings/`
            `94dec/area.and.wg.reports/app/http/http-minutes-94dec.txt`.

[Hui98]   Christian Huitema. *IPv6: The New Internet Protocol.* Prentice
            Hall, second edition, January 1998. ISBN 0138505055.

[Hui00]   Christian Huitema. *Routing in the Internet.* Prentice Hall, second
            edition, January 2000. ISBN 0130226475.

[HW00]   Christian Huitema and Sam Weerahandi. Internet Measurements:
            The Rising Tide and the DNS Snag. In *Proc. ITC Seminar on
            IP Traffic Measurement, Modeling, and Management,* September
            2000.

[ICA]   The Internet Corporation for Assigned Names and Numbers.
            `http://www.icann.org`.

[ICA01]   ICAP Protocol Group. ICAP: The Internet Content Adaptation
            Protocol, February 2001. Work in progress.
            `http://www.i-cap.org/icap/media/`
                `draft-elson-opes-icap-01.txt`.

[IMA]   The IMAP Connection. `http://www.imap.org`.

[Ink]   Inktomi Search. `http://www.inktomi.com`.

[IRC]   A Distributed Testbed for National Information Provisioning.
            `http://ircache.nlanr.net/Cache/`.

[ISO]   Internet Histories. `http://www.isoc.org/internet-history`.

[ITA]   Internet Traffic Archive. `http://www.acm.org/sigcomm/ita/`.

[J. 81]   J. Postel, Editor. Transmission Control Protocol. RFC 793, IETF,
            September 1981.
            `http://www.rfc-editor.org/rfc/rfc793.txt`.

[Jac]   Van Jacobson. Traceroute.
            `ftp://ftp.ee.lbl.gov/traceroute.tar.gz`.

[Jac88]   Van Jacobson. Congestion Avoidance and Control. In *Proc. ACM
            SIGCOMM,* pages 314–329, August 1988.
            `http://www.acm.org/sigcomm/ccr/archive/1995/jan95/`
                `ccr-9501-jacobson.html`.

[JCDK00]   Kirk L. Johnson, John F. Carr, Mark S. Day, and M. Frans
            Kaashoek. The Measured Performance of Content Distribution
            Networks. In *Proc. Fifth Web Caching Workshop,* May 2000.
            `http://www.terena.nl/conf/wcw/Proceedings/S4/S4-1.pdf`.

[JK98]   Zhimei Jiang and Leonard Kleinrock. An adaptive prefetching
            scheme. *IEEE Journal on Selected Areas in Communications*,
            16(3):358–368, April 1998.
            http://www.research.att.com/~jiang/Research/
               Publication/prefetch_jsac98.pdf.

[JLM]   Van Jacobson, C. Leres, and S. McCanne. Tcpdump.
            ftp://ftp.ee.lbl.gov/tcpdump.tar.Z.

[Joh99]   John Dilley. The Effect of Consistency on Cache Response Time.
            Technical Report HPL-1999-107, Hewlett Packard Laboratories,
            September 1999.
            http://www.hpl.hp.com/techreports/1999/HPL-1999-107.html.

[Joh00]   Kevin Johnson. *Internet Email Protocols: A Developer's Guide.*
            Addison-Wesley, January 2000. ISBN 0201432889.

[Jon81]   Jon Postel, Editor. Internet Protocol. RFC 791, IETF, September
            1981.
            http://www.rfc-editor.org/rfc/rfc791.txt.

[Jun]   Junkbusters. http://www.junkbusters.com.

[KA01]   Balachander Krishnamurthy and Martin Arlitt. PRO-COW:
            Protocol Compliance on the Web—A Longitudinal Study. In
            Proc. USENIX Symposium on Internet Technologies and Systems,
            March 2001.
            http://www.research.att.com/~bala/papers/usits01.ps.gz.

[KBM94]   Eric Dean Katz, Michelle Butler, and Robert McGrath. A Scalable
            HTTP Server: The NCSA Prototype. In *Proc. World Wide Web
            Conference*, May 1994.
            http://www.ncsa.uiuc.edu/InformationServers/
               Conferences/CERNwww94/www94.ncsa.html.

[Kes97]   Srinivsan Keshav. *An Engineering Approach to Computer Net-
            working: ATM Networks, the Internet, and the Telephone Net-
            work.* Addison-Wesley, January 1997. ISBN 0201634422.

[Key]   Keynote Systems. http://www.keynote.com.

[KL86]   Brian Kantor and Phil Lapsley. Network News Transfer Protocol.
            RFC 977, IETF, February 1986.
            http://www.rfc-editor.org/rfc/rfc977.txt.

[KL00]   R. Khare and S. Lawrence. Upgrading to TLS Within HTTP/1.1.
            RFC 2817, IETF, May 2000.
            http://www.rfc-editor.org/rfc/rfc2817.txt.

[Kle75]   Leonard Kleinrock. *Queueing Systems, Volume I: Theory.* John
            Wiley, January 1975. ISBN 0471491101.

[KM87]   C. A. Kent and J. C. Mogul. Fragmentation Considered Harmful.
            In *Proc. ACM SIGCOMM*, pages 390–401, August 1987.
            http://www.acm.org/sigs/sigcomm/ccr/archive/1995/jan95/
               ccr-9501-mogulf1.html.

[KM91]   B. Kahle and A. Medlar. An Information System for Cor-
          porate Users: Wide Area Information Servers, November 1991.
          Connexions—The Interoperability Report, 5(11).

[KM00]   David Kristol and Lou Montulli. HTTP State Management Mech-
          anism. RFC 2965, IETF, October 2000.
          http://www.rfc-editor.org/rfc/rfc2965.txt.

[KMK99]   Balachander Krishnamurthy, Jeffrey C. Mogul, and David M. Kris-
          tol. Key Differences between HTTP/1.0 and HTTP/1.1. In *Proc.
          Eighth International World Wide Web Conference*, May 1999.
          http://www.research.att.com/~bala/papers/h0vh1.html.

[KMR95]   T. Kwan, R. McGrath, and D. Reed. NCSA's World Wide Web
          Server: Design and Performance. *IEEE Computer Magazine*,
          28(11):68–74, November 1995.

[KR98]   Balachander Krishnamurthy and Jennifer Rexford. Software Issues
          in Characterizing Web Server Logs. In *W3C Web Characterization
          Group Workshop*, November 1998.
          http://www.research.att.com/~bala/papers/ew3c.html.

[KR00]   James F. Kurose and Keith W. Ross. *Computer Networking: A
          Top-Down Approach Featuring the Internet*. Addison-Wesley, July
          2000. ISBN 0201477114.

[KV91]   David Korn and Kiem-Phong Vo. SFIO: Safe/Fast String/File
          I/O. In *Proc. Summer USENIX Conference*, pages 235–256, 1991.

[KV00]   David G. Korn and Kiem-Phong Vo. The VCDIFF Generic Differ-
          encing and Compression Data Format, November 2000. Expired
          Internet Draft.
          ftp://ftp.ietf.org/internet-drafts/
             draft-korn-vcdiff-02.txt.

[KW97]   Balachander Krishnamurthy and Craig Wills. Study of Piggyback
          Cache Validation for Proxy Caches in the World Wide Web. In
          Proc. USENIX Symposium on Internet Technologies and Systems,
          pages 1–12, December 1997.
          http://www.research.att.com/~bala/papers/
             pcv-usits97.ps.gz.

[KW98]   Balachander Krishnamurthy and Craig E. Wills. Piggyback Server
          Invalidation for Proxy Cache Coherency. In *Proc. World Wide
          Web Conference*, April 1998.
          http://www.research.att.com/~bala/papers/psi-www7.ps.gz.

[KW00]   Balachander Krishnamurthy and Craig E. Wills. Analyzing Fac-
          tors that influence end-to-end Web performance. In *Proc. World
          Wide Web Conference*, pages 17–32, May 2000.
          http://www.research.att.com/~bala/papers/www9.html.

[LA94]   Ari Luotonen and Kevin Altis. World-Wide Web Proxies. In *Proc.
          First International Conference on the World-Wide Web, WWW*

'94, May 1994.
`http://www.cern.ch/PapersWWW94/luotonen.ps`.

[LB97]   Tong Sau Loon and Vaduvur Bharghavan. Alleviating the La-
            tency and Bandwidth Problems in WWW Browsing. In *Proc.
            USENIX Symposium on Internet Technologies and Systems*, De-
            cember 1997.
            `http://www.usenix.org/publications/library/proceedings/`
                `usits97/tong.html`.

[LC97]   Chengjie Liu and Pei Cao. Maintaining Strong Cache Consistency
            in the World-Wide Web. In *Proc. International Conference on
            Distributed Computing Systems*, pages 326–334, May 1997.
            `http://www.cs.wisc.edu/~cao/papers/icache.html`.

[LCC$^+$97] Barry M. Leiner, Vinton G. Cerf, David D. Clark, Robert E. Kahn,
            Leonard Kleinrock, Daniel C. Lynch, Jon Postel, Lawrence G.
            Roberts, and Stephen S. Wolff. The Past and Future History of the
            Internet. *Communications of the ACM*, 40(2):102–108, February
            1997.

[LDV99]   Henry Lieberman, Neil Van Dyke, and Adriana Vivacqua. Let's
            Browse: A Collaborative Browsing Agent. In *Proc. International
            Conference on Intelligent User Interfaces*, January 1999.
            `http://lieber.www.media.mit.edu/people/lieber/`
                `Lieberary/Lets-Browse/Lets-Browse.html`.

[LG99]   Steve Lawrence and C. Lee Giles. Accessibility of Information on
            the Web. *Nature*, 400(6740):107–109, 1999.
            `http://www.neci.nj.nec.com/homepages/lawrence/`.

[Lie95]   H. Lieberman. Letizia: An Agent That Assists Web Browsing.
            In *Proc. International Joint Conference on Artificial Intelligence*,
            August 1995.
            `http://lieber.www.media.mit.edu/people/lieber/`
                `Lieberary/Letizia/Letizia-AAAI/Letizia.html`.

[LK99]   Averill Law and David Kelton. *Simulation, Modeling, and Analy-
            sis*. McGraw Hill, third edition, December 1999. ISBN 0070592926.

[LL99]   Ben Laurie and Peter Laurie. *Apache: The Definitive Guide*.
            O'Reilly, February 1999. ISBN 1565925289.

[LNJV99]   Z. Liu, N. Niclausse, and C. Jalpa-Villanueva. Web Traffic
            Modeling and Performance Comparison Between HTTP1.0 and
            HTTP1.1. In Erol Gelenbe, editor, *System Performance Evalua-
            tion: Methodologies and Applications*. CRC Press, August 1999.
            `http://www-sop.inria.fr/mistral/personnel/Zhen.Liu/`
                `Papers/wagon_perf99.ps.gz`.

[LTWW94]   Will E. Leland, Murad S. Taqqu, Walter Willinger, and Daniel V.
            Wilson. On the Self-Similar Nature of Ethernet Traffic (Extended
            Version). *IEEE/ACM Transactions on Networking*, 2(1):1–15,

February 1994.

[Luo97]   Ari M. Luotonen. *Web Proxy Servers*. Prentice Hall, 1997. ISBN 0-13680-612-0.

[Mah97]   Bruce Mah. An Empirical Model of HTTP Network Traffic. In *Proc. IEEE INFOCOM*, April 1997.
             http://www.ieee-infocom.org/1997/papers/bmah.pdf.

[MCS98]   S. Manley, M. Courage, and M. Seltzer. A Self-Scaling and Self-Configuring Benchmark for Web Servers. In *Proc. ACM SIGMET-RICS*, pages 270–271, June 1998.
             http://www.eecs.harvard.edu/~margo/papers/hbench-web.ps.

[MD90]   J. Mogul and S. Deering. Path MTU Discovery. RFC 1191, IETF, November 1990.
             http://www.rfc-editor.org/rfc/rfc1191.txt.

[MDFK97a]   Jeffrey C. Mogul, Fred Douglis, Anja Feldmann, and Balachander Krishnamurthy. Potential benefits of delta encoding and data compression for HTTP. In *Proc. ACM SIGCOMM*, pages 181–194, August 1997.
             http://www.acm.org/sigcomm/sigcomm97/papers/p156.html.

[MDFK97b]   Jeffrey C. Mogul, Fred Douglis, Anja Feldmann, and Balachander Krishnamurthy. Potential benefits of delta encoding and data compression for HTTP. Technical Report 97/4, DEC, July 1997.
             http://gatekeeper.dec.com/pub/Digital/WRL/
             research-reports/WRL-TR-97.4.pdf.

[MDH]   Jeffrey Mogul, Fred Douglis, and Daniel Hellerstein. HTTP Delta Clusters and Templates. Work in progress.
             http://www.ietf.org/internet-drafts/
             draft-mogul-http-dcluster-00.txt.

[Med]   Media Metrix. http://www.mediametrix.com.

[MF00]   Keith Moore and Ned Freed. Use of HTTP State Management. RFC 2964, IETF, October 2000.
             http://www.rfc-editor.org/rfc/rfc2964.txt.

[MFGF97]   J. Mogul, R. Fielding, J. Gettys, and H. Frystyk. Use and Interpretation of HTTP Version Numbers. RFC 2145, IETF, May 1997.
             http://www.rfc-editor.org/rfc/rfc2145.txt.

[MFH00]   A. Mockus, R. F. Fielding, and J. Herbsleb. A Case Study of Open Source Development: The Apache Server. In *Proc. International Conference on Software Engineering*, pages 263–272, June 2000.
             http://dev.acm.org/pubs/citations/proceedings/soft/
             337180/p263-mockus/.

[MH00]   Art Mena and John Heidemann. An Empirical Study of Real Audio Traffic. In *Proc. IEEE INFOCOM*, March 2000.
             http://www.isi.edu/~johnh/PAPERS/Mena00a.html.

[Mil92]   David L. Mills. Network Time Protocol (Version 3): Specification, Implementation and Analysis. RFC 1305, IETF, March 1992. `http://www.rfc-editor.org/rfc/rfc1305.txt`.

[Mir]   Mirror Image. `http://www.mirror-image.com`.

[MJ93]   Steve McCanne and Van Jacobson. The BSD Packet Filter: A New Architecture for User-Level Packet Capture. In *Proc. Winter USENIX Technical Conference*, January 1993. `ftp://ftp.ee.lbl.gov/papers/bpf-usenix93.ps.Z`.

[MJ98]   D. Mosberger and T. Jin. httperf—A Tool for Measuring Web Server Performance. In *Proc. Workshop on Internet Server Performance*, pages 59–67, June 1998. `http://www.hpl.hp.com/personal/David_Mosberger/httperf`.

[MKD+01]   Jeffrey Mogul, Balachander Krishnamurthy, Fred Douglis, Anja Feldmann, Yaron Goland, Arthur van Hoff, and Daniel Hellerstein. Delta encoding in HTTP, March 2001. Work in progress. `http://www.ietf.org/internet-drafts/draft-mogul-http-delta-08.txt`.

[ML97]   J. Mogul and P. Leach. Simple Hit-Metering and Usage-Limiting for HTTP. RFC 2227, IETF, October 1997. `http://www.rfc-editor.org/rfc/rfc2227.txt`.

[MMFR96]   M. Mathis, J. Mahdavi, S. Floyd, and A. Romanow. TCP Selective Acknowledgment Options. RFC 2018, IETF, April 1996. `http://www.rfc-editor.org/rfc/rfc2018.txt`.

[Moc87a]   P. Mockapetris. Domain Names—Concepts and Facilities. RFC 1034, IETF, November 1987. `http://www.rfc-editor.org/rfc/rfc1034.txt`.

[Moc87b]   P. Mockapetris. Domain Names—Implementation and Specification. RFC 1035, IETF, November 1987. `http://www.rfc-editor.org/rfc/rfc1035.txt`.

[Mog95]   Jeffrey Mogul. A modest proposal, August 1995. HTTP-WG Mailing List Archives. `http://www.ics.uci.edu/pub/ietf/http/hypermail/1995q3/0360.html`.

[Mos]   NCSA Mosaic. A WWW Browser. `http://www.ncsa.uiuc.edu/SDG/Software/Mosaic/Docs/help-about.html`.

[MR95]   J. Myers and M. Rose. The Content-MD5 Header Field. RFC 1864, IETF, October 1995. `http://www.rfc-editor.org/rfc/rfc1864.txt`.

[MSMV99]   G. Minshall, Y. Saito, J. Mogul, and B. Verghese. Application Performance Pitfalls and TCP's Nagle Algorithm. In *Proc. Workshop on Internet Server Performance*, May 1999. `http://www.cc.gatech.edu/fac/Ellen.Zegura/wisp99/`

           `papers/minshall.ps`.

[Muf]   Muffin: World Wide Web Filtering System.
           `http://muffin.doit.org`.

[NA93]   B. Clifford Neuman and Steven Seger Augart. Prospero: A Base for Building Information Infrastructure. In *Proc. INET*, August 1993.
           `http://www.isi.edu/people/bcn/papers/pdf/`
              `9308_prospero-bii.pdf`.

[Nag84] John Nagle. Congestion Control in IP/TCP Internetworks. RFC 896, IETF, January 1984.
           `http://www.rfc-editor.org/rfc/rfc896.txt`.

[NBK99] E. Nahum, T. Barzilai, and D. Kandlur. Performance issues in WWW servers. Technical report, IBM Research, February 1999.
           `ftp://gaia.cs.umass.edu/pub/nahum/Nahu99:Performance.ps`.

[Nel67]   T. H. Nelson. Getting It Out of Our System. In G. Schechter, editor, *Critique of Information Retrieval*, pages 191–210. Thompson Books, 1967.

[Neta]   Network Appliance. `http://www.netapp.com`.

[Netb]   Netcaching. `http://www.netcaching.com`.

[Netc]   The Netcraft Web Server Survey.
           `http://netcraft.co.uk/survey`.

[Netd]   Persistent client state HTTP cookies.
           `http://www.netscape.com/newsref/std/cookie_spec.html`.

[Nie97]   Henrik Frystyk Nielsen. Pipelining and compression effect on HTTP/1.1 proxies, April 1997. HTTP-WG Mailing List Archives.
           `http://www.ics.uci.edu/pub/ietf/http/hypermail/`
              `1997q2/0165.html`.

[NLL00] H. Nielsen, P. Leach, and S. Lawrence. An HTTP Extension Framework. RFC 2774, IETF, February 2000.
           `http://www.rfc-editor.org/rfc/rfc2774.txt`.

[Nov]   Novell. `http://www.novell.com`.

[P3P]   World Wide Web Consortium, Platform for Privacy Preferences (P3P) Project.
           `http://www.w3.org/P3P/`.

[PA00]   V. Paxson and M. Allman. Computing TCP's Retransmission Timer. RFC 2988, IETF, November 2000.
           `http://www.rfc-editor.org/rfc/rfc2988.txt`.

[Pad95] V. N. Padmanabhan. Improving World Wide Web Latency. Technical Report UCB/CSD-95-875, University of California, Berkeley, May 1995.
           `http://www.research.microsoft.com/~padmanab/papers/`
              `masters-tr.ps`.

[Pax97a]   Vern Paxson. Automated Packet Trace Analysis of TCP Imple-
           mentations. In *Proc. ACM SIGCOMM*, September 1997.
           `ftp://ftp.ee.lbl.gov/papers/vp-tcpanaly-sigcomm97.ps.Z`.

[Pax97b]   Vern Paxson. End-to-End Routing Behavior in the Internet.
           IEEE/ACM Transactions on Networking, 5(5):601–615, October
           1997.
           `ftp://ftp.ee.lbl.gov/papers/vp-routing-TON.ps.Z`.

[Pax99]   Vern Paxson. End-to-End Internet Packet Dynamics. *IEEE/ACM
           Transactions on Networking*, 7(3):277–292, June 1999.
           `ftp://ftp.ee.lbl.gov/papers/vp-pkt-dyn-ton99.ps.gz`.

[PDZ99]   Vivek S. Pai, Peter Druschel, and Willy Zwaenepoel. Flash: An
           efficient and portable Web server. In *Proc. USENIX*, June 1999.
           `http://www.cs.princeton.edu/~vivek/flash99/flash.ps.gz`.

[Pea97]   Oskar Pearson. Squid users guide, September 1997.
           `http://www.squid-cache.org/Doc/Users-Guide/Welcome.html`.

[Pel91]   Nicola Pellow. linemode, June 1991.
           `http://www.w3.org/Talks/Seminar_LM.html`.

[PFG+94]   M. St. Pierre, J. Fullton, K. Gamiel, J. Goldman, B. Kahle,
           J. Kunze, H. Morris, and F. Schiettecatte. WAIS over Z39.50-
           1988. RFC 1625, IETF, June 1994.
           `http://www.rfc-editor.org/rfc/rfc1625.txt`.

[PH97]   J. Palme and A. Hopmann. MIME E-mail Encapsulation of Ag-
           gregate Documents, such as HTML (MHTML). RFC 2110, IETF,
           March 1997.
           `http://www.rfc-editor.org/rfc/rfc2110.txt`.

[PH99]   J. Palme and A. Hopmann. MIME E-mail Encapsulation of Ag-
           gregate Documents, such as HTML (MHTML). RFC 2557, IETF,
           March 1999. Obsoletes RFC 2110.
           `http://www.rfc-editor.org/rfc/rfc2557.txt`.

[Pit99]   James E. Pitkow. Summary of WWW characterizations. *WWW
           Journal*, 2:3–13, 1999.
           `http://www.baltzer.nl/www/contents/1999/2-1,2/www024.pdf`.

[PK99]   J. Padhye and J. Kurose. An Empirical Study of Client Interac-
           tions with a Continuous-Media Courseware Server. *IEEE Internet
           Computing*, April 1999.
           `ftp://gaia.cs.umass.edu/pub/Padh97:Empirical.ps.gz`.

[PM95]   Venkata N. Padmanabhan and Jeffrey C. Mogul. Improving HTTP
           Latency. *Computer Networks and ISDN Systems*, 28(1/2):25–35,
           December 1995.
           `http://www.research.microsoft.com/~padmanab/papers/`
               `www-fall94.ps`.

[PM96]   Venkata N. Padmanabhan and Jeffrey C. Mogul. Using Predictive
           Prefetching to Improve World Wide Web Latency. *ACM Com-*

                puter Communication Review, 26(3):22–36, July 1996.
                `http://www.acm.org/sigs/sigcomm/ccr/archive/1996/`
                    `jul96/ccr-9607-pad.html`.

[Pol]   Web Polygraph: Proxy performance benchmark.
                `http://polygraph.ircache.net/`.

[Pos81]   J. Postel. Internet Control Message Protocol. RFC 792, IETF, September 1981.
                `http://www.rfc-editor.org/rfc/rfc792.txt`.

[Pos82]   Jonathan B. Postel. Simple Mail Transfer Protocol. RFC 821, IETF, August 1982.
                `http://www.rfc-editor.org/rfc/rfc821.txt`.

[Pos94]   J. Postel. Domain Name System Structure and Delegation. RFC 1591, IETF, March 1994.
                `http://www.rfc-editor.org/rfc/rfc1591.txt`.

[PQ00]   Venkata Padmanabhan and Lili Qiu. The Content and Access Dynamics of a Busy Web Site: Findings and Implications. In *Proc. ACM SIGCOMM*, August/September 2000.
                `http://www.acm.org/sigcomm/sigcomm2000/conf/paper/`
                    `sigcomm2000-3-3.ps.gz`.

[PR85]   Jon Postel and Joyce Reynolds. File Transfer Protocol. RFC 959, IETF, October 1985.
                `http://www.rfc-editor.org/rfc/rfc959.txt`.

[PR93]   J. Postel and J. Reynolds. Telnet Protocol Specification. RFC 854, IETF, May 1993.
                `http://www.rfc-editor.org/rfc/rfc854.txt`.

[Rag]   Raging Search. `http://www.raging.com`.

[RES]   A Standard for Robot Exclusion.
                `http://info.webcrawler.com/mak/projects/robots/`
                    `norobots.html`.

[RF99]   K. K. Ramakrishnan and S. Floyd. A Proposal to Add Explicit Congestion Notification (ECN) to IP. RFC 2481, IETF, January 1999.
                `http://www.rfc-editor.org/rfc/rfc2481.txt`.

[RGR97]   Aviel Rubin, Daniel Geer, and Marcus Ranum. *Web Security Sourcebook*. John Wiley, 1997. ISBN 047118148X.

[Riv92]   Ronald Rivest. The MD5 Message-Digest Algorithm. RFC 1321, IETF, April 1992.
                `http://www.rfc-editor.org/rfc/rfc1321.txt`.

[RL93]   Yakov Rekhter and Tony Li. An Architecture for IP Address Allocation with CIDR. RFC 1518, IETF, September 1993.
                `http://www.rfc-editor.org/rfc/rfc1518.txt`.

[RL95]   Y. Rekhter and T. Li. A Border Gateway Protocol 4 (BGP-4). RFC 1771, IETF, March 1995.

`http://www.rfc-editor.org/rfc/rfc1771.txt`.

[Roc75]   M. Rochkind. The Source Code Control System (SCCS). *IEEE Transactions on Software Engineering*, 1(4):364–370, December 1975.

[RSA]   RSA Security. `http://www.rsa.com`.

[Sal95]   Peter H. Salus. *Casting the Net: From ARPANET to INTERNET and Beyond*. Addison-Wesley, March 1995. ISBN 0201876744.

[SCFJ96]   H. Schulzrinne, S. Casner, R. Frederick, and V. Jacobson. RTP: A Transport Protocol for Real-Time Applications. RFC 1889, IETF, January 1996.
`http://www.rfc-editor.org/rfc/rfc1889.txt`.

[Sch96]   H. Schulzrinne. RTP Profile for Audio and Video Conferences with Minimal Control. RFC 1890, IETF, January 1996.
`http://www.rfc-editor.org/rfc/rfc1890.txt`.

[Sec95]   IESG Secretary. WG Action: HyperText Transfer Protocol (http), January 27, 1995.
`http://www.ics.uci.edu/pub/ietf/http/hypermail/1995q1/0050.html`.

[Sha86]   M. Shapiro. Structure and encapsulation in distributed systems: The proxy principle. In *Proc. 6th International Conference on Distributed Computer Systems*, pages 198–204, 1986.

[Sin95]   Erik Sink. HTTP/1.2 stuff: try it out!, August 1995. HTTP-WG Mailing List Archives.
`http://www.ics.uci.edu/pub/ietf/http/hypermail/1995q3/0405.html`.

[SJ00]   Mike Spreitzer and Bill Janssen. HTTP Next Generation. In *Proc. World Wide Web Conference*, May 2000.
`http://www9.org/w9cdrom/60/60.html`.

[SM94]   K. Sollins and L. Masinter. Functional Requirements for Uniform Resource Names. RFC 1737, IETF, December 1994.
`http://www.rfc-editor.org/rfc/rfc1737.txt`.

[Smi]   World Wide Web Consortium, Synchronized Multimedia.
`http://www.w3.org/AudioVideo/`.

[Sol]   Solidspeed. `http://www.solidspeed.com`.

[Spea]   SPECweb99 Benchmark. `http://www.spec.org/osg/web99/`.

[Speb]   Speedera. `http://www.speedera.com`.

[Spi]   The search engine watch SpiderSpotting chart.
`http://www.searchenginewatch.com/webmasters/spiderchart.html`.

[SR99]   Henning Schulzrinne and Jonathan Rosenberg. The IETF Internet Telephony Architecture and Protocols. *IEEE Network Magazine*, 13(3):18–23, May/June 1999.

[SR00]   M.-T. Sun and A. R. Reibman, editors. *Compressed Video Over Networks*. Marcel Dekker, September 2000. ISBN 0824794230.

[SRL98]   H. Schulzrinne, A. Rao, and R. Lanphier. Real Time Streaming Protocol (RTSP). RFC 2326, IETF, April 1998.
http://www.rfc-editor.org/rfc/rfc2326.txt.

[SRT99]   Subhabrata Sen, Jennifer Rexford, and Don Towsley. Proxy Prefix Caching for Multimedia Streams. In *Proc. IEEE INFOCOM*, pages 1310–1319, April 1999.
http://www.ieee-infocom.org/1999/papers/09d_04.pdf.

[SSL]   Netscape Secure Sockets Layer (SSL) Version 3.0.
http://home.netscape.com/eng/ssl3/.

[SSL95]   Netscape Secure Sockets Layer (SSL) Documentation, 1995.
http://home.netscape.com/security/techbriefs/ssl.html.

[SSR99]   H. Schulzrinne, E. Schooler, and J. Rosenberg. SIP: Session Initiation Protocol. RFC 2543, IETF, March 1999.
http://www.rfc-editor.org/rfc/rfc2543.txt.

[SSV97]   Peter Scheuermann, Junho Shim, and Radek Vingralek. A Case for Delay-Conscious Caching of Web Documents. In *Proc. World Wide Web Conference*, April 1997.
http://www.bell-labs.com/user/rvingral/www97.html.

[St.93]   M. St. Johns. Identification Protocol. RFC 1413, IETF, February 1993.
http://www.rfc-editor.org/rfc/rfc1413.txt.

[Ste94]   W. Richard Stevens. *TCP/IP Illustrated, Volume 1: The Protocols*. Addison-Wesley, January 1994. ISBN 0201633469.

[Ste98a] Lincoln D. Stein. *Web Security: A Step-by-Step Reference Guide*. Addison-Wesley, October 1998. ISBN 0-201-63489-9.

[Ste98b] W. Richard Stevens. *UNIX Network Programming, Volume 1: Networking APIs—Sockets and XTI*. Prentice Hall, 1998. ISBN 013490012X.

[Ste99]   John W. Stewart. *BGP4: Inter-Domain Routing in the Internet*. Addison-Wesley, January 1999. ISBN 0201379511.

[Syn98]   Synchronized Multimedia Working Group. Synchronized Multimedia Integration Language (SMIL) 1.0. Technical Report Recommendation REC-smil-19980615, World Wide Web Consortium, July 1998.
http://www.w3.org/TR/1998/REC-smil/.

[Tcp]   Tcpdump public repository. http://www.tcpdump.org.

[Tha96]   Robert Thau. Design Considerations for the Apache Server API. In *Proc. World Wide Web Conference*, May 1996.
http://www5conf.inria.fr/fich_html/papers/P20/
     Overview.html.

[Tho96]   Stephen A. Thomas. RTP for Real Time Applications. In *IPng and the TCP/IP Protocols*, chapter 11, pages 351–374. John Wiley, January 1996. ISBN 0471130885.

[Tic85]   Walter F. Tichy. RCS—A System for version control. *Software: Practice and Experience*, 15(7):637–654, July 1985.

[Tou97]   J. Touch. TCP Control Block Interdependence. RFC 2140, IETF, April 1997.
           http://www.rfc-editor.org/rfc/rfc2140.txt.

[TS95]   G. Trent and M. Sake. WebStone: The First Generation in HTTP Server Benchmarking, February 1995.
           http://www.mindcraft.com/webstone/paper.html.

[Uni]   Unitech Networks Ltd—IntelliDNS.
           http://www.unitechnetworks.com.

[vCCS00]   J. van der Merwe, R. Caceres, Y. Chu, and C. J. Sreenan. mm-dump: A Tool for Monitoring Internet Multimedia Traffic. *ACM Computer Communication Review*, 30(5):48–59, October 2000.
           http://www.acm.org/sigcomm/ccr/archive/2000/oct00/
             ccr_200010-merwe.html.

[WAS+96]   Stephen Williams, Marc Abrams, Charles R. Standridge, Ghaleb Abdulla, and Edward A. Fox. Removal Policies in Network Caches for World-Wide Web Documents. In *Proc. ACM SIGCOMM*, pages 293–305, August 1996.
           http://www.acm.org/sigcomm/sigcomm96/papers/
             williams.html.

[Wbe]   Webbench.
           http://www.zdnet.com/etestinglabs/stories/
             benchmarks/0,8829,2326243,00.html.

[WC97a]   D. Wessels and K. Claffy. Application of Internet Cache Protocol (ICP), Version 2. RFC 2187, IETF, September 1997.
           http://www.rfc-editor.org/rfc/rfc2187.txt.

[WC97b]   D. Wessels and K. Claffy. Internet Cache Protocol (ICP), Version 2. RFC 2186, IETF, September 1997.
           http://www.rfc-editor.org/rfc/rfc2186.txt.

[WC98]   Duane Wessels and K Claffy. ICP and the Squid Web Cache. *IEEE Journal on Selected Areas in Communications*, 16(3):345–357, April 1998.
           http://www.caida.org/outreach/papers/pdf/icp-sq.pdf.

[WCA]   Web Characterization Repository.
           http://www.purl.org/net/repository/.

[WCC99]   Web Cache Coordination Protocol, June 1999.
           http://www.cisco.com/univercd/cc/td/doc/product/
             software/ios111/ca111/wccp.htm.

[Weba]   Welcome to WebDAV Resources. http://www.webdav.org/.

[Webb]   DAV Frequently Asked Questions.
            http://www.webdav.org/other/faq.html.

[Webc]   Web History. http://www.webhistory.org.

[WG-99]   HTTP-WG Mailing list archives, 1994-1999.
            http://www.ics.uci.edu/pub/ietf/http/hypermail/.

[WM99]   Craig E. Wills and Mikhail Mikhailkov. Towards a Better Un-
            derstanding of Web Resources and Server Responses for Improved
            Caching. In *Proc. World Wide Web Conference*, May 1999.
            http://www.cs.wpi.edu/~cew/papers/www8.ps.gz.

[WMB99]   Ian H. Witten, Alistair Moffat, and Timothy C. Bell. *Managing
            Gigabytes*. Morgan Kaufmann, second edition, May 1999. ISBN
            1-55860-570-3.

[WTSW97]   Walter Willinger, Murad S. Taqqu, Robert Sherman, and
            Daniel W. Wilson. Self-Similarity Through High Variability: Sta-
            tistical Analysis of Ethernet LAN Traffic at the Source Level.
            IEEE/ACM Transactions on Networking, 5(1), February 1997.
            http://www.acm.org/pubs/articles/journals/ton/
                1997-5-1/p71-willinger/p71-willinger.pdf.

[You94]   N. Young. The k-server dual and loose competitiveness for paging.
            Algorithmica, 11(6):525–541, June 1994.

[Zip49]   G. K. Zipf. *Human Behavior and the Principle of Least-Effort*.
            Addison-Wesley, 1949.

Index

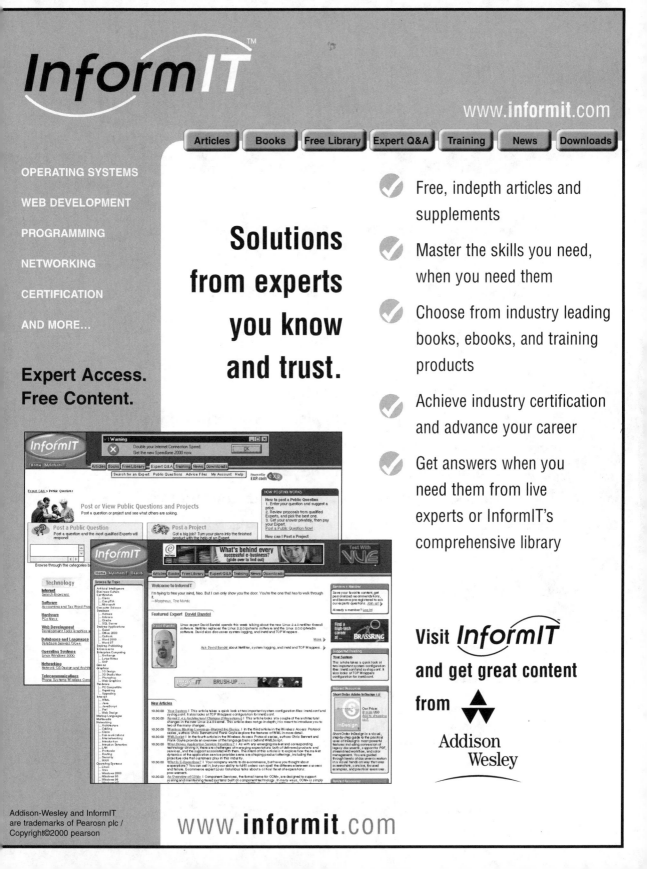

Register
Your Book

at www.aw.com/cseng/register

You may be eligible to receive:

- Advance notice of forthcoming editions of the book
- Related book recommendations
- Chapter excerpts and supplements of forthcoming titles
- Information about special contests and promotions throughout the year
- Notices and reminders about author appearances, tradeshows, and online chats with special guests

Contact us

If you are interested in writing a book or reviewing manuscripts prior to publication, please write to us at:

Editorial Department
Addison-Wesley Professional
75 Arlington Street, Suite 300
Boston, MA 02116 USA
Email: AWPro@aw.com

Addison-Wesley

Visit us on the Web: http://www.aw.com/cseng